# SPAIN IN THE LATER SEVENTEENTH CENTURY
## 1665–1700

432832

# Spain

in the Later Seventeenth Century, 1665–1700

HENRY KAMEN

LONGMAN
London and New York

**Longman Group Limited** London

*Associated companies, branches and representatives
throughout the world*

*Published in the United States of America
by Longman Inc., New York*

*First published 1980*

**British Library Cataloguing in Publication Data**

Kamen, Henry
Spain in the later 17th century.
1. Spain – History – Charles II, 1665–1700
I. Title
946'.053    DP186    79-42884

ISBN 0–582–49036–7

Printed in Great Britain by
Richard Clay (The Chaucer Press) Ltd.,
Bungay, Suffolk

# Contents

# List of maps and diagrams

# Preface

Our knowledge of European history in the seventeenth century has been consistently frustrated by the disappearance from all our books at about the year 1650 of the world's greatest power, Spain. We know almost nothing of its society, its politics, its economy. Historians have assumed that it plunged into an absolute decline from which it emerged only at the end of the eighteenth century. Notable studies, like that of the Chaunus on Seville, stop at 1650. Our only guide to what may have been happening is the uncompleted work of the duke of Maura, essentially a court history centred on Madrid.

Though detailed studies of the economy have begun to penetrate the darkness, the broad outlines remain hazy and indistinct. The present modest study, the first total history of the Spain of Charles II, is an attempt to establish a general context for further work on early modern Spain. In foregoing the *longue durée* and dwelling instead on the traditional and shorter time-span of a reign, I have not forgotten the broader dimensions of my subject.

The later seventeenth century has been considered the classic period of the 'decline of Spain'. A different picture is presented in this book. The decay in population and in agrarian production dating from about 1580, trade difficulties, inflation and war debt, were problems that began to resolve themselves after mid-century. Disintegration of the empire helped to conserve resources. Monetary inflation ended in the 1680s. Already from the 1660s population and with it agrarian production began to stabilise and to expand. Spain did not of course begin to flourish, and contemporaries were too concerned with their problems to think otherwise; but in perspective it was the opening of a new era. The Inquisition decayed, new ideas penetrated the country. Feliu de la Peña evoked for Catalonia the image of a phoenix rising from its ashes; for us, though with some reserve, the image applies to all Spain.

How does this view fit into the schema, proposed by economic historians, of a European depression extending from the late seventeenth to the late eighteenth century? There can be no doubt that for Spain it was in general a period of recuperation. Its development complemented but was not identical to that of other nations. At the periphery of the European system, it benefited from the crises in the core states and attempted to win back some measure of independence.

The story told here is full of gaps and deficiencies. Until recently, few scholars were attracted by a period notorious for its alleged decadence. I have little need, then, to apologise for the areas that I have been unable to cover. Lack of space has compressed much of my discussion, principally on art and culture. A brief chapter on the Church has been omitted, and will be found in the Spanish edition.

This book is the result of a prolonged encounter with Spain. I have laboured to recreate a past epoch, but my perception of it has always been predetermined by my experience of Spain today.

My research was generously and almost exclusively funded by two sources: the British Academy and the Leverhulme Trust. I am extremely grateful to them both. A grant from the Social Science Research Council helped me to investigate material that I had not previously used.

This book has succeeded in taking shape only through the kindness of many people through the years. Karen typed it impeccably. A brief stay as guest of the History Department at the State University of New York, Binghamton, allowed me time for reflection. Michael Sissons, who has been godfather to all my books, helped this one also into existence. The constant advice of Antonio Domínguez Ortiz, doyen of seventeenth-century studies, has helped to orientate me. I must particularly thank Pedro Marset, José María López Piñero, Sebastián García Martínez, Angel Gari and Ricardo García Cárcel for various kindnesses. Pablo Fernández Albaladejo has contributed more than he may realise to helping my final ideas fall into place. Lorna Gladstone and Pierre Ponsot generously let me use some of their unpublished research.

The very many who have helped me, most of all in the archives of Spain; the students and colleagues in Spain and America who have clarified my ideas by criticism; will I hope forgive me for not being able to thank them all by name.

For a particular reason, this book commemorates the shrine of the Santo Niño Jesús in Prague, erected in the seventeenth century by an exile from her native Spain.

Sections of the text were read and helpfully criticised by Henry Cohn, John Lynch and David Ringrose. The hospitality of the History Department at the University of California, San Diego, and the love and tolerance of Karen, Nicholas, Jeffrey, Melanie and Heloise, made it possible for me to complete the proofs and index during a halcyon spring on the Pacific shores of southern California.

*La Jolla*     *H.K.*
*California*

# Abbreviations

References to archival material are abbreviated as follows:

## SPAIN

ACA . . . . . . . . . Archivo de la Corona de Aragón, Barcelona
ACA:CA . . . . . . . Ibid., section Consejo de Aragón
ACA:CR . . . . . . . Ibid., section Cancillería Real
ACS:AC . . . . . . . Archivo de la Catedral de Sevilla, Actos Capitulares
ADZ . . . . . . . . . Archivo de la Diputación, Zaragoza
AGI . . . . . . . . . Archivo General de Indias, Seville
AGPB . . . . . . . . Archivo General de Protocolos, Barcelona
AGS . . . . . . . . . Archivo General de Simancas
AGS:CJH . . . . . . Ibid., section Consejo y Juntas de Hacienda
AGS:DGT . . . . . Ibid., section Dirección General del Tesoro
AHN . . . . . . . . . Archivo Histórico Nacional, Madrid
AHN Inq . . . . . . Ibid., section Inquisición
AHPM . . . . . . . . Archivo Histórico de Protocolos, Madrid
AMC . . . . . . . . . Archivo Municipal de Cartagena
AMM:AC . . . . . . Archivo Municipal de Murcia, Actas Capitulares
AMS:AC . . . . . . . Archivo Municipal de Sevilla, Actas Capitulares
AMV . . . . . . . . . Archivo Municipal de Valencia
AMZ . . . . . . . . . Archivo Municipal de Zaragoza
APV . . . . . . . . . Archivo de Protocolos, Colegio del Patriarca, Valencia
ARV . . . . . . . . . Archivo del Reino de Valencia
ARV:RC . . . . . . . Ibid., section Real Cancillería
BCB . . . . . . . . . Biblioteca de Catalunya, Barcelona
BMV . . . . . . . . . Biblioteca Municipal de Valencia
BRAH . . . . . . . . Biblioteca de la Real Academia de la Historia
BUV . . . . . . . . . Biblioteca de la Universidad de Valencia
BN . . . . . . . . . . Biblioteca Nacional, Madrid, section of manuscripts
RCPV . . . . . . . . Archivo del Real Convento de Predicadores, Valencia

## PARIS

AE:CP(Esp). . . . . Ministère des Affaires Etrangères, Paris, section Correspondance Politique (Espagne)

AN:AE, B$^I$. . . . . Archives Nationales, Paris, section Affaires Etrangères, fonds consulaire B$^I$

Guerre A$^1$. . . . . . Dépôt Général de la Guerre, Vincennes, section A$^1$

## GREAT BRITAIN

Astorga        Astorga Collection, National Library of Scotland

BL        British Library, Department of Manuscripts

PRO:SP        Public Record Office: State Papers

Archival references are prefaced by the appropriate abbreviation and followed by the name of the section used. Terms such as *legajo* (bundle), volume, page and folio have normally been suppressed, and are used only where needed to avoid confusion.

A three-number reference consists of (1) the bundle, volume or *legajo* (2) the document, folder or *expediente* (3) the folio or page; e.g. ACA:CA 580/34/2 and PRO:SP 94/60/227. A two-number reference normally consists of the (1) volume or bundle (2) folio or page; e.g. AE:CP(Esp)114/25.

This study has been written primarily from manuscript sources. It is fully referenced and I have not thought it necessary to give a lengthy list of the thousands of documents consulted.

# Glossary

Books cited are listed in full in the bibliography. In general, specialised words are italicised when first used, but not thereafter. Where relevant, the Catalan form of words is given in parentheses after the Castilian.

*Arbitristas*: name, often used pejoratively at the time, given to writers who drew up *arbitrios* or proposals for economic and political reform.

*Arroba*: a common liquid measure, varying in value according to region and liquid. The *arroba* was also a commercial dry weight, used, e.g. for wool and tobacco. Dillon (*Travels*, I, p. 66) states that 'an *arroba* is 25 lb Spanish weight; 100 lb Spanish equal to 97 lb English'.

*Asiento*: a contract, e.g. the contract to supply slaves to America. Here normally used for contracts by bankers (*asentistas*) to supply money to the Crown.

*Brazo* (*braç*): parliamentary Estate of the realm (sometimes called *estamento*).

*Caballero* (*cavaller*): a knight or gentleman, member of the lower nobility. Aragon was the only realm in which the gentry (called *Caballeros* or *Infanzones*) had an Estate in the Cortes. The rank of *caballero* or *cavaller* was inferior to that of *noble*, which alone gave full nobility.

*Cahiz*: a grain measure, equivalent in Castile to 12 *fanegas* (q.v.), but of differing value elsewhere.

*Censos* (*censals*): annuities drawn (by *censalistas*) from loans made to individuals or public bodies. In the Crown of Aragon the word *censal* sometimes also meant a ground-rent.

*Ciudadano honrado* (*ciutadà honrat*): a 'distinguished citizen', the highest civic rank granted by major towns in the Crown of Aragon, especially Barcelona, Saragossa and Valencia. The rank was deemed equivalent to the bottom rung of the ladder of nobility.

*Cortes* (*Corts*): the parliament of each realm, normally consisting of three Estates, except for Aragon which had four. In Castile by the seventeenth century the

Cortes consisted in practice of only one Estate, that of the towns.

*Diputación (Diputació)*: standing committee of the Cortes, consisting in Catalonia and Valencia of six members or *Diputats* (q.v.), elected for three years. In Aragon there were eight *Diputados*, two from each Estate, elected annually.

*Diputados (Diputats)*: the members of the *Diputación*, they were the highest representatives of the realm and oversaw its government when the *Cortes* was not in session. They had a smaller political role in Valencia than in Aragon and Catalonia.

*Ducat (ducado)* and *escudo*: 'The ducat was a unit of account equivalent to 11 *reales*. The *escudo* was originally a gold coin equivalent to 10 *reales* or 340 *maravedis*. The former was used only in payments inside Castile, to calculate *vellón*, which had no currency outside Castile. Payments in silver were virtually all made outside Castile and were reckoned in *escudos*, which were theoretically worth fewer *maravedis* than the ducat but which in practice came to about the same value, so that estimates in *asientos* use both ducats and *escudos*' (Domínguez Ortiz, *Política y Hacienda*, p. xii).

*Estamento (estament)*: parliamentary Estate of the realm (also called *brazo*).

*Fanega*: '*Fanega* is a corn measure in Spain, five of which make an English quarter of eight bushels' (Dillon, *Travels*, I, p. 66). The *fanega* was also a surface measure, equivalent to about 1.6 acres.

*Fueros (furs)*: local laws and privileges; the term is applied especially to the body of laws of the non-Castilian provinces of Spain.

*Gavacho (gavatx)*: abusive term applied in Spain to Frenchmen.

*Hábito*: a knighthood in one of the military Orders in Spain (those of Alcántara, Calatrava, Santiago, Montesa and St John).

*Junta*: committee, applied here specially to committees of the royal councils.

*Jurado (jurat)*: in some areas, a town councillor. The capitalised form (*Jurat*) is here used only for the city councillors of Valencia. The city councillors of Barcelona were known as *Consellers*.

*Juros*: annuities paid out of state income for loans to the Crown. Holders of *juros* were *juristas*.

*Libra (lliura)*: Catalan and Valencian coinage was reckoned in pounds (*lliures*) shillings (*sous*) and pence (*diners*). In Aragon the currency was also in pounds (*libras, sueldos, dineros*). Currency changes make it very difficult to suggest equivalents, but in general a pound might be equivalent very roughly to one ducat of Castile.

*Maravedi*: 'The maravedi, originally a large Moorish coin, was the smallest unit of account in the Castilian monetary system. A *real*, for example, contained 34 maravedis and a ducat 375 maravedis' (Hamilton, *War and Prices*, p. 38 n.7).

*Media anata*: an irregular tax, first imposed in 1631, which took half a year's income from grants, offices and annuities.

*Mercedes*: grants (e.g. titles, pensions) conceded by the king.

*Millones*: Castilian tax dating from 1590, levied mainly on food (wine, oil and meat) and subject to periodic renewal by the Cortes.

*Pagès*: strictly, in Catalonia, 'peasant', but used here of the wealthy peasantry, the *pagesia*.

*Peso*: treasure from America was reckoned in *pesos*, where each *peso* was equivalent to over 42 grams of pure silver.

*Pueblo*: a village or town.

*Quintal*: the equivalent of 4 *arrobas* (q.v.) dry weight.

*Tercio*: an infantry regiment.

*Tonelada*: 'The Castilian ton or tonelada was equal in weight to twenty quintals or hundredweight, and in Spanish vessels . . . was estimated to represent a space of something over 56 cubic feet' (Haring, *Trade and Navigation*, p. 284). There are several modern calculations of the value of the *tonelada*.

*Valido*: chief minister, sometimes referred to as a favourite, chosen by the king. The period of his authority is referred to as a *valimiento*.

*Vecino*: term used by officials in censuses to denote a household or family, but always used very imprecisely. A census was a *vecindario*.

*Vellón*: 'Vellon was originally a mixture of silver and copper used for fractional coins. Through debasement the silver content was reduced and finally eliminated' (Hamilton, *War and Prices*, p. 38 n.7).

# CHAPTER ONE

# A Spain We Do Not Know

The windmills of La Mancha that startled Don Quixote, were new to Castile. Introduced from the Netherlands towards the middle of the reign of Philip II,[1] they were part of the foreign influence that entered Spain with the House of Austria. A century later they had virtually disappeared: a traveller from France reported in 1672 that 'there are no windmills to be seen in Spain'.[2] Few remain today, yet their image dominates the popular picture of what rural Castile might have looked like. A similar mixture of legend and reality typifies the blurred view that we still have of Spain's history.

Because so much remains of the past in the seemingly unchanging Spanish countryside, we are tempted to think that we can reach out to it from the present. Customs, ideas and people were in fact continually changing: some have eluded our grasp forever. Take for example the 'king of the Patones'. Patones was a little village in the sierra de Guadarrama, in the province of Guadalajara. In the seventeenth century it consisted of a small group of families, ruled not by a village council but by a 'king' elected from among the elders. It is said that even in the eighteenth century when the king in Madrid sent out orders to his administrators he sent one in particular to the 'king' of the Patones. Don Baltasar de Moscoso y Sandoval, cardinal archbishop of Toledo under Charles II, used to visit the village 'since it was a great solace to him to have in his archbishopric such practice of religion in its old simplicity'.[3] By the end of the eighteenth century the community of Patones had vanished, and the last 'king' drifted to Madrid in search of a living.

What survives has not always come down to us in forms that the seventeenth century would recognise. Popular dances and regional costumes have been adapted and formalised over the intervening two centuries. The great vogue for authentic native dress, reflected in Goya's paintings, is a product of the late eighteenth century. 'Flamenco' music and art forms had not yet been stylised. A practice which seems most typical of all – the *corrida* or bullfight – was still infrequent, unformalised and consistently criticised by churchmen.[4] Modern culture has been heavily influenced by the cities, but in the seventeenth century there were few major cities in Spain. Madrid, the largest, was technically only a town (*villa*), without its own bishop.

1

We are separated from the seventeenth century principally by the industrial revolution of the nineteenth. Changes in land use and ownership, new forms of labour, the building of roads and railways, the introduction of medicine, have all created serious barriers to our understanding by their disruption of traditional society. There have also been changes whose impact is not so obvious. Alterations in public law over the last century have obscured the great variety of legal systems governing contracts, marriage and property rights.[5] Only renewed attention to these old laws can help to resurrect the nature of elementary relationships between people in early modern times. The modern advance of the Castilian language has likewise created discontinuity with the past. Navarre has always been racially Basque, and spoke Basque in the seventeenth century. Today central Navarre speaks Castilian, a change that must have profoundly altered the life style of its people.[6] In the same way the moving frontier of language reflects cultural and social change over substantial areas of Valencia.[7]

Complexity, as much as change, has made it difficult to measure the past. More a subcontinent than a country, Spain is a land of extremes, frustrating efforts to solve its problems. The immense contrasts have given scholars an opportunity to consider Spain as a permanent duality: in its land, between the tiny landholdings of the north and the great estates of the south; in its climate, between 'dry Spain', the semi-arid areas of the central meseta and the south, and 'wet Spain', the rainy northern coast and the irrigated Mediterranean littoral; in culture, between the old Christian, feudal north, and the Islamic south of Al-Andalus. These views are analyses but not explanations. The explanation remains to be done.

Of all aspects of the past the one that has most survived into the present is the small rural town or *pueblo*. Its perception of time in the 1970s differs little from that of the seventeenth century. 'The rhythm of life is determined by a relatively fixed yearly cycle of productive activities that is still measured largely by reference to the religious calendar. Villagers know that potato planting should be completed by the day of St Mark (April 25), and that community-controlled irrigation commences on the day of St John the Baptist (June 24).'[8] In this village – Becedas, near Avila – the continuity of life style with the overwhelmingly agrarian society of the seventeenth century, offers a way for us to understand the Spain that we do not know. Traditional society at its most fundamental level must be studied through the *pueblo*.[9] The Spaniard of the seventeenth century was above all a native of his pueblo, which was for him his country (*país*). This was true whether we look at the small closely-knit Basque village with its independent smallholders and nuclear families living in the traditional houses or *caseríos*, or at the depressed Andalucian village with few landholders and with the whole population living in the territory of a great lord. The peasant in his pueblo, in an environment which seemed to offer few opportunities for change, came to represent many of the permanent values of the Spanish people.[10]

Although the pueblo was a small unit with a restricted range of social classes, it may be misleading to call it only a 'part-society'.[11] In the range of its activities and the nature of its links with the outside world, it represented virtually all aspects of social existence. Even in a village that appeared democratic, since there were no nobles in it, such as Belmonte de los Caballeros (Aragon) in the seventeenth century, the ritual of death pointed clearly to social stratification based on wealth. 'Burial in the common grave, in the cemetery, and in the church corresponded to three categories of people, depending on their respective economic standing.'[12] The value in choosing the pueblo as a sort of microcosm of Spain, does not rely wholly on social structure but far more on the types of relationships that went to make up the village or town.

Spain in many respects gave the appearance of being little more than a heterogeneous collection of town units. Very small units, as in Galicia,[13] were content to associate with other adjacent villages in order to constitute a viable society. More often, villages remained bitterly independent, scorning not only the big city but also all neighbouring towns.[14] Antipathy between towns and regions took the form of colourful refrains and enduring prejudice. 'I have found', reported Swinburne in 1775, 'the virtue one province prides itself in as being the specific mark of its inhabitants, not only refused them by a neighbouring country but the very opposite vice imposed upon them as their characteristic.'[15] Intense rivalry and antagonism could be found between adjacent streets in the same town, between adjacent towns in the same region. Many have with good reason seen in this sociocentrism the origin of much of the fratricidal violence in Spanish history.[16] Lengthy and acrimonious disputes between towns and provinces are commonplace throughout Spain's history. In 1689 the province of Guipúzcoa went so far as to threaten war against Vizcaya in an argument over iron ore.[17]

Fragmentation meant a lack of feeling for the larger unit of 'nation'. As elsewhere in Europe, loyalties remained so regional that the feeling of patriotism was virtually non-existent. A Spaniard might fight for his family, his home-town (his *país* or *patria*), his religion or his race, his lord or his king: he seldom fought for 'Spain'.[18] Intense localism, made worse by geographical isolation, led in certain communities to endogamy and exclusion from social commerce with other communities. The result was a number of *races maudites*, the *agotes* of Navarre, the *pasiegos* of the Montaña of Santander, the *vaqueiros* of Asturias, the *maragatos* of León.[19]

What were the solidarities and loyalties of Spaniards? Activities in the pueblo suggest a remarkable degree of communal democracy. In a great number of towns important decisions were always made not by the council but by a public assembly of all the citizens.[20] The pueblo remained the primary source of identity for its inhabitants.[21] The most famous example of this in Andalucia was the historic case of 1476, dramatised by Lope de Vega, when the villagers of Fuenteovejuna, accused of the murder of their lord, claimed that 'Fuenteovejuna', and not any of them in particular, had done it. The incident was far from being unusual.[22] Communal solidarity, it can be argued, also existed in the economic sphere. Joaquín Costa was struck by the degree of agrarian cooperation in some areas of northern Spain in the late nineteenth century. In Cabrera (León), for example, the community ploughed in common, sowed in common, reaped in common, extracted and gleaned the grain in common.[23]

Much if not all of this potential communism was illusory. Although collective action was common, it was not part of a communalist ethic. The sociocentrism of

3

pueblos was paralleled within the pueblo by the firm individualism of families and of each villager.[24] Close cooperation with fellow villagers was, however, made necessary by the type of work involved.[25] Harvest, irrigation, use of pasture and roads, were areas that tended to involve all other producers and workers. On the social and non-economic level, there was likewise an accepted balance between individual and communal roles. A villager's relationship with others was determined by certain types of conduct closely related to his social and moral standing – that is, his *honor* – in the community. His honor was wholly personal, but obtained its sanction from the approval of the community.

Traditional society was not wholly male-dominated. Apparent equality between the sexes in Spain existed principally in the Basque country, where the laws granted women equal property rights with their husbands.[26] This, however, created an equal rather than a communalist society. Communalism existed in some parts of Spain to the extent that women shared the labour with men. In Galicia, Asturias, the Montaña of Santander, parts of northern León and Zamora, women shared in and often did the greater part of agricultural work throughout the year.[27] In Galicia, and to a less extent in the other regions, this was because the men went away to find work during the spring and only came back for the harvest. In south and central Spain, women took no significant part in agriculture apart from the peak harvest period.

The participation of women in agrarian labour helped to give stability to pueblos where the low level of income forced men to look for outside work. This helped to fortify the individualism of women and to give them a practical leadership in the family, and in the village, that the laws usually did not recognise.[28] Solidarity within the pueblo had no weak links: both men and women were equally committed to the daily struggle for existence.

Sociocentrism was reinforced by religion. Devotion to the Catholic faith was universal and profound, but the practical form it took was devotion to the local parish and its patron saint. All the *rites de passage* of a believer, from birth to death, took place in his local church. Multiple loyalties within the parish were catered for by the creation of guilds and confraternities. Belmonte de los Caballeros, with 241 adults in the late seventeenth century, had four: two of Our Lady, one of the Infant Jesus, one of Santa Engracia. Processions involving all the confraternities took place on feast days, and they sometimes went in procession to neighbouring pueblos to share in their feast days.[29] Rival parishes often came to blows over the merits of their respective saints and guilds. In 1673 Francisco Millán of Alcázar de San Juan (Toledo) found himself before the Inquisition for rash words uttered in a dispute of this type.[30] Religion failed to transcend the persistent localism of loyalties. The immense strength of the Church in Spain arose not from a fanatical adherence to the tenets of the faith, so much as from the deep local roots of religion, whose living representative was the *párroco*, the parish priest.

All authority other than the priest was deemed to be from outside, and invited hostility. In the first decade of the century Lope de Vega's *Fuenteovejuna* reminded audiences in the capital of the hostility of villagers to their lords.[31] The Cortes in Madrid in 1618 heard how in many pueblos the permanent majority of

4

commoners was using its votes to elect weakling officials to power so as to be able to frustrate noble administration.[32] Contemporary *comedias* may have exaggerated some aspects of village hostility in order to achieve dramatic effect. But the reality of the hostility is incontestable. The principal motive, and indeed the motive for requests to transfer to royal jurisdiction, was one of taxation. The consequence was that although the nobles and gentry in Spain seem to have had extensive authority over towns and villages, their powers always clashed with stubborn local individualism. Some of the great lords still behaved as, and were treated like, kings in their own regions. But they failed to develop or maintain a system of feudal dependents, like the *fidélités* of France, that could draw on regional loyalty and so pose a threat to the Crown.[33] It was common, as with Valencia in the 1690s and during the War of Succession, to find towns anxious to rebel against their lords in an attempt to gain liberty from taxes.

For all its importance, the town was only a microcosm of a broader identity. The modes of action that men adopted outside the pueblo, show that the larger universe within which they thought and lived was the *comarca*, or canton within the province.[34] Collective action seldom if ever exceeded the limits of the comarcas, which were traditionally differentiated by name: the Tierra de Campos, the Montaña (of Santander), the Campo de Calatrava, the Huerta de Gandía, the Plana de Vic and so on. Fundamentally, each comarca was a geographic zone with compatible patterns of production and social activity. Within the comarca, people grew the same crops, experienced the same environment of soil and weather, did the same types of labour, dressed similarly and spoke the same language. The size of the comarca made it possible to marry outside the pueblo without having to move into a different cultural area. Solidarity of interest therefore existed within the comarca, of a type and degree unattainable in large and more complex areas such as the province. It is not surprising to find that all the rural revolts of the period can be identified with specific comarcas, that of 1688 with the Plain of Vic in Catalonia, that of 1693 with the Marina of Valencia. Rebellions became fragmented and atomised. The biggest uprising of Habsburg Spain, the revolt of the Comuneros in 1520, was not only deeply fragmented; it thrived in complete indifference to the existence of a parallel uprising in Valencia, that of the Germanías.[35] Bandits similarly used specific regions, such as the Huerta of Valencia or the Sierra Morena in Andalucia, as their base.

Unity of interest within each comarca has helped to give the impression, to which we have already referred in the case of pueblos, of a communalist ethic. The apparent communism of rural society was, however, forced on Spaniards by their environment and conflicted sharply with their sociocentrism.[36] Communal exploitation of arable and of limited pasture resources, was essential in order to preserve peace among the pueblos. Common use of land and pasture – 'agrarian collectivism' as Joaquín Costa termed it – was regularly practised in the Montaña of Santander, Pyrenean Navarre, Upper Aragon, the Tierra de Sayago in Zamora, the Montes of Toledo, the Sierra Nevada, and many other regions. An interesting example of collectivism on the borders of Aragon and Valencia may be seen in the agreement made in August 1676 by twenty-eight farmers and two widows of the town of Abejuela (Aragon), for exploitation of lands in the vicinity of La Yesa (Valencia).[37] Realising that communal use of plough-teams was the only practical way to till their holdings, they merged them all into a single large unit:

> To avoid any discord among us, we the above-named make and draw up in friendship the present union, brotherhood and agreement and give each other permission and authority so that at any time of day or night any animals, whether ploughing or otherwise, whether our own or hired, may use, pasture and go freely upon any of the lands freely as often as is wished, and at any task such as tilling, fallowing, ploughing, sowing, weeding, reaping, transporting. . . . And if any of the lands is alienated, the new owner shall be always included in and subject to the above Brotherhood, Union and Agreement.

The origins of many other cases of collectivism remain unknown. We know nothing of the reasons for the practice called *fetosín* in Segovia, used in different parts of the province. The land was partitioned by lot, but because it belonged to the community could not be transmitted by inheritance. Perhaps the best surviving example of an imposed communal discipline concerns the use of water. The old Tribunal of the Waters, composed of village elders, still sits once a week in the Puerta de los Apostoles of Valencia cathedral to give summary and unrecorded judgment on disputes arising among peasants in the Huerta.

Cantonalism in Spain was in some measure enhanced by the multiplicity of seigneurial jurisdictions. In cases such as the Huerta of Gandía in Valencia or the area of Cardona in Catalonia, belonging respectively to the duke of Gandía and the duke of Cardona, there was an almost exact coincidence between the comarca and the feudal lordship. For all practical purposes this completed the identity of those within the comarca: above the duke there was only the king. In most of Spain, however, there was no such coincidence. Rather there was a basic tension between the solidarity of the comarca on one hand, and the demands of many different external seigneurs on the other.

Beyond the canton, loyalties and identities remained imprecise. External symbols began to impose their presence: appeals to language, local rights (the *fueros*), and piety (the Pilar in Saragossa, for example), were among the most persuasive. A major factor in change, the growth of a central city market at the expense of periodic local markets, has never been studied. The cantonalism of the seventeenth century began to fade as other identities, notably the emphasis on 'provinces', took priority.

'Provinces', or 'kingdoms' (to use the more historic Spanish term), were political units normally lacking any homogeneity or cultural unity.[38] A small realm such as the principality of the Asturias had no obvious unity of economy, culture or language. It was even more obvious that a large realm like Andalucia lacked any distinctive character or sense of identity. Studying the past in terms of frontiers created accidentally for political or fiscal reasons, is unlikely to provide the answers we need. Not a single social movement in early modern Spain was based on the 'province'. The response of the Crown of Aragon to the War of Succession, for example, is unintelligible if we fail to realise that Spaniards took sides according to the comarca, not according to the province, in which they lived.[39] The development of a provincial identity came only with the nineteenth century. Few events helped more than the War of Independence against the French, to give the 'provinces' and their *juntas* the definitive leadership in political life. Cantonalism nevertheless remains a living force, as the political movements of 1977–79 have clearly shown.

If Spaniards then lacked a firm sense of provincial loyalty, what were their feelings about the larger unit called 'Spain'? It is difficult to avoid the conclusion that 'Spain' was for them an ideal rather than a fact. Ortega y Gasset has expressed this concisely: 'Spain was not something real, it was a schema of something realisable.'[40] 'Of all parts of the world the best is undoubtedly Europe', claimed a writer in the early century, 'and of Europe the best province is Spain.'[41] True to this extravagant idealisation, every historian praised the country's natural and inexhaustible riches, the fertility of its soil. Contemporary literature appeared to define as Spain the whole geopolitical unit known to ancient writers as Iberia or Hispania. Medieval sources had used the terms 'nation of Spain' and 'kingdom of Spain', but without defining what a 'nation' signified.[42] Imprecision of terms was perhaps a reflection of the lack of unity in the country. Gracián in the early century emphasised that other states might possess unity, but not Spain. 'In the Spanish monarchy, where the provinces are many, the nations different, the languages various, the temperaments at variance, the climates conflicting, great care is required both to preserve and to unite.'[43] Because of this remarkable diversity within the peninsula, 'Spain' was an indefinite word used in varying contexts, much like the word 'Germany'.

There were two principal meanings. Firstly, Spain was the area bounded roughly by the Pyrenees in the north and by the sea on all other sides. Quevedo in mid-century observed that 'properly speaking, Spain is divided into three realms: Castile, Aragon and Portugal'.[44] This was written at a time when Portugal was part of the Crown, but does not do violence to contemporary usage. 'I am a Portuguese Spaniard', claims a character in a seventeenth-century play.[45] It followed that all the peoples in the peninsula could accept participation in Spain without prejudice. To call oneself a Spaniard was a rough-and-ready method of identification, but little more than that. The identification was used exclusively to foreigners, so that effectively the peoples of the peninsula felt themselves to be Spaniards not among themselves so much as over against other peoples.

Spain was, secondly, the physical area falling under the political authority of the government of Castile. This usage could not fail to be controversial. Though seventeenth-century state documents refer regularly to 'Spain', the word in its political sense appears rarely before the sixteenth century. Ferdinand and Isabella, whose realms were united only by the persons of the sovereigns, took great care to spell out the names of the constituent parts of the monarchy rather than submerge them under a common name. Even when Diego de Valera in 1481 produced a *Crónica de España*, he modified this usage by informing Isabella that 'Our Lord has given you the monarchy of all the Spains'.[46] Under the Habsburgs a more centralising policy substituted for these many Spains a broader political unit focused on Madrid. The trend, accelerated in the seventeenth century, caused major stresses that led to the Catalan and Portuguese rebellions of 1640.

When applied to language the term 'Spanish' was equally imprecise.

Portuguese, Basque and Galician were all 'Spanish' languages, as Arabic and Hebrew had been in the Middle Ages. Under Philip II writers produced work in both Portuguese and Castilian. The lingua franca of the peninsula was Castilian, which consequently came to be considered 'Spanish' pure and simple.[47] All official state correspondence was conducted in Castilian, but the Church could not always afford to be so singleminded. In the early seventeenth century the bishop of Calahorra insisted that all sermons in the Basque country be in Basque, since the people understood no other language. A similar use of Catalan was ordered, under threat of excommunication, by the bishop of Solsona for his Catalan parishioners. In Navarre in 1676 a priest applying for the parish of Ujue was required to know Basque, which was 'common and general throughout that village, and many understood no other'.[48] Throughout the peninsula there was a genial coexistence of many tongues. Aggressive linguistic regionalism is a product of the nineteenth century and did not exist in the seventeenth. In Valencian and Catalan documents of the time we can find a frequent and friendly confusion of both Catalan and Castilian words. Civic pride and historic privilege, however, made the cities of Barcelona and Valencia insist on using Catalan in their official letters to Madrid. This was normal practice. But Barcelona's habit of addressing lengthy documents to Madrid in a language that Castilians did not understand, caused intense irritation at court. In spite of this, language was seldom a source of friction, nor did it encourage any cultural separatism.

The real contradictions in the use of the terms 'Spain' and 'Spanish' are associated with the rise of Castilian hegemony. In contrast to the policy of Ferdinand and Isabella, the Habsburgs from Charles V onwards gave Castilians precedence in the monarchy. This was the result not of a deliberate decision but of the rapid growth of a central court-capital, located eventually in Madrid. The élite inevitably gravitated to the court, and by the seventeenth century all the leading aristocrats of the Crown of Aragon had become thoroughly Castilianised. Foreigners and non-Castilians felt that Madrid, and with it Castile, was becoming more and more selfcentred. A traveller in mid-century felt that 'some Spaniards are so ignorant that they believe not there is any other country than Spain, other City than Madrid, or King than their own . . . I mean those mere Castillians who never having quitted their Threshold, know not whether Amsterdam be in Europe or the Indies.'[49] The insularity of Castilians was also commented upon in the 1660s by the Englishman Willughby: 'They are most impertinently inquisitive: whence you come? whither you go? what business you have etc. . . . uncivil to strangers, asking them, What do you come into our Countrey for? we do not go into yours. (This is to be understood of the middle and inferiour sort of people, many of the gentry being very civil and well-bred.)[50]

A Frenchman in Madrid in 1666 commented on Castilian pride in 'the Spanish world, which in their imagination is something apart, all other nations being created only to serve them'.[51] From one point of view this was simply a case of the profound regional pride which characterised all Spaniards.[52] But there were important political implications. A Catalan writer of the sixteenth century accused Castilians of giving 'the impression that they alone are descended from heaven, and the rest of mankind are mud . . . Almost all Castilian historians fall into the same error of writing Castile when they mean all Spain.'[53] Castilian control of the political machine perpetuated the identification of Spain with Castile alone, and agravated relationships with other peoples in the peninsula, who regarded Castilian pretensions as chauvinistic arrogance. A revealing example occurred in 1692. When the Basques refused to accept Madrid's nominee to the temporary governorship of Bilbao, one member of the Council of State angrily called for the 'exclusion' of Vizcaya from Spain.[54]

Portugal finally established its claim to be a sovereign state outside Spain by peace treaty in 1668. Although the Catalans never broke free, they continued to be troubled by the nature of their relationship to the rest of the peninsula. Their position is worth considering in detail.

In medieval Catalan chronicles the word *Espanya* had been used to describe the land from which Catalans came.[55] By the mid-seventeenth century, however, it is difficult to find any firm admission by Catalans that they were indeed part of Spain. It has been suggested that Catalans in the late century were so far reconciled to unity that they claimed in 1674 that 'Catalonia is Spain'.[56] The circumstances were more ambivalent than this quotation infers. In that year the merchants of the Llotja of Barcelona protested vigorously to Madrid on behalf of their compatriots in Cadiz who had been allotted a 'consul', that is, an official to represent their interests in official negotiations. The Catalans in Cadiz were furious partly because the allotted consul was a Fleming, partly because as consul he had a right to draw a fixed tax from Catalan shipments. The protest from Barcelona adopted the argument that consuls were normally appointed only for foreign nations, not for citizens of the same nation:

To have a Consul is for nations that are truly nations, not for those who are direct subjects of a Crown, as Catalans are of Your Majesty's royal Crown. They are, and are called, Spaniards, there being no doubt that Catalonia is Spain . . . Spain includes everything between the Pyrenees and the oceans. It follows that Catalonia is Spain, and that Catalans are Spaniards.[57]

These remarkable affirmations must clearly not be taken out of context. There is no doubt that Catalans were faithful subjects of the Crown, but all the available evidence shows that they used the word 'Spain' quite differently from the way it was used by the merchants of the Llotja. When Gerona was liberated from its French occupiers in 1698, the relieved Catalan population greeted the Castilian troops as they marched in, with cries of 'Long live Spain!' (*Visca Espanya!*). Throughout the war the people distinguished firmly between 'the Catalans' on one hand and 'the Spanish troops' on the other.[58] In the same way during the Catalan peasant rebellion of 1688–89 the insurgents identified their Castilian enemies as *españoles*, and looked on themselves as *catalanes*.[59]

On 17 March 1666 a Catalan officer, Miquel Rius, was about to be executed in the Plaza del Rey in Barcelona for murder and theft. He leapt off the stand and tried to escape but was recaptured. Fearing attempts to help him, a troop of soldiers and cavalry rushed into the little square and through the side-streets, using their pistols and swords to clear the astonished crowds. 'The soldiers cried out in disordered voices "Long live Spain!" ', the city councillors of Barcelona reported to the Queen Regent, 'when nobody had given any cause for such behaviour.'[60] About a dozen people died as a result of the incident. The soldiers' cry was in effect one of Castilians against Catalans, and an alarmed Council of Aragon noted a month later that 'the rumour throughout Catalonia is that it was a clash between Castilians and Catalans, which is clearly an invention of ill-intentioned people trying to arouse old memories . . . '.[61]

Despite their goodwill towards Castile, Catalans never failed to give the impression that they were a distinct nation. Swinburne in 1775 observed that 'here it is not uncommon to hear them talk of a journey into Spain, as they would of one into France'.[62] The fragility of a common identity, however, must not lead us to assume that Catalans also felt politically apart. Regional feeling existed in the late seventeenth century, but it was in some measure a reaction against the failure of 1640 and was neither widespread nor deeprooted. It took a pro-French form in the 1688 disturbances, but never aspired to political independence or separatism. In view of the profound dislike of the French in both Catalonia and Aragon, plots such as the bizarre plan in 1648 to make the duke of Hijar ruler of Aragon with French aid,[63] were bound to fail for lack of popular support. The troubles of the 1640s, which also involved a plot to make Andalucia independent, seem to have purged all remaining separatist tendencies. There were no serious centrifugal movements in the late century, and Spain emerged even from the devastating experience of the War of Succession (1702–13) as a united monarchy. That unity was, except in Catalonia, far less authoritarian than has been supposed. The provinces of the peninsula were content to accept 'Spain' so long as they retained some degree of autonomy. The Bourbon regime did not attempt, and would have failed had it tried, to disturb the regional and cantonal loyalties of Spaniards. Throughout the *ancien régime*, fragmentation of authority gave the country a balanced society: Spain remained stable because atomised. Only the coming of the industrial revolution initiated major changes in economy and society, and gave force to the fissiparous 'nationalisms' of the modern era.

## NOTES AND REFERENCES

1. **Caro Baroja, J.**, *Los pueblos* (Barcelona 1946), p. 373.
2. **Jouvin, A.**, *Le voyageur* (Paris 1672–76), II, 147.
3. Caro Baroja, *op. cit.* p. 377.
4. For the attempt of Cardinal Portocarrero in 1680 to prohibit corridas throughout the monarchy, see **Maura**, *Vida y reinado* (Madrid 1954), II, 146–7.
5. **Moret y Prendesgast, S.**, *Familia foral* (Madrid 1863).
6. Caro Baroja, *op. cit.* p. 264.
7. By the mid-seventeenth century in the Valencian noble Estates, 'things have changed to such an extent that Castilian is used at almost every meeting'. Cited in **Casey, J.**, *The Kingdom of Valencia* (Cambridge 1979). p. 247.
8. **Brandes, S.**, *Migration, Kinship* (London 1975), p. 64.
9. 'The *pueblo* furnishes a completeness of human relations which makes it the prime concept of all social thought': **Pitt-Rivers, J.**, *People of the Sierra* (Chicago 1971), p. 31.

10. Extensive treatment of this theme is given by **Salomon, N.**, *Recherches* (Bordeaux 1965).
11. *Cf.* Brandes, *op. cit.* p. 3, following other sociologists.
12. **Lisón Tolosana, C.**, *Belmonte* (Oxford 1966), p. 56–7.
13. **Lisón Tolosana**, *Antropología* (Madrid 1971), pp. 249, 253–5, emphasises that Galician villages achieved an identity only in the larger grouping of 'parish', which embraced several villages.
14. Pitt-Rivers, *op. cit.* pp. 9–12, dealing with Andalucian villages.
15. **Swinburne, H.**, *Travels* (London 1787), II, 188.
16. **Caro Baroja**, 'El sociocentrismo de los pueblos españoles', in *Razas, pueblos* (Madrid 1957), pp. 263–92.
17. See below, p. 75.
18. *Cf.* the observation of the French general Tessé in 1705: 'I would not trust a Spaniard, however brave, with the defence of a steeple. They fight duels; but as a body, and for their country, is an idea which never enters their heads.' Quoted in **Coxe**, *Memoirs* (London 1815), I, 343.
19. For a short sympathetic study see **Miner Otamendi, J.**, *Los Pueblos Malditos* (Madrid 1978). Like others writers, he includes the Chuetas of Mallorca among his *races maudites*. He observes (p. 120) that among the *maragatos* the woman never chooses her husband; he is instead chosen by her family, a natural result of the restricted choice available.
20. See the discussion below, p. 195. In Grazalema (Andalucia) 'when there is an assembly all the *pueblo* are there by right': Pitt-Rivers, *op. cit.* p. 77.
21. Brandes, *op. cit.* p. 58.
22. For a case in the mid-seventeenth century, see below, p. 179. Pitt-Rivers, *op cit.* p. 12., mentions a similar case in Grazalema in the present century.
23. **Costa, J.**, *Colectivismo agrario* (Madrid 1898), pp. 341–60.
24. Lisón Tolosana, *Belmonte*, p. 351; Brandes, *op. cit.* p. 100; **Pérez Díaz, V.**, *Estructura social* (Madrid 1966), p. 146.
25. 'Cooperation is viewed as a compromise necessitated by economic circumstances': **Freeman, S.**, *Neighbors* (Chicago 1970), p. 199.
26. Moret y Prendesgast, *op. cit.* pp. 83–5.
27. Caro Baroja, *Los pueblos*, pp. 305, 311, 318–19, 333; **Townsend, J.**, *A Journey* (London 1791), II, 67; *cf.* Brandes, *op. cit.* p. 80 and Lisón Tolosana, *Belmonte*, p. 149.
28. On the social leadership of women in popular movements, see **Kamen, H.** *Iron Century* (London 1972), Ch. 10.
29. Lisón Tolosana, *Belmonte* p. 279.
30. AHN Inq. 41/21.
31. See the discussion in Salomon, *op. cit.* pp. 853–62.
32. Cited in *ibid.* p. 845.
33. In the case of great lords, this was because they were regularly absent in the capital and did not often reside locally like the more rural nobility of France. For noble authority in general, see below, Ch. Eight.
34. A basic essay is that by **Lisón Tolosana**, 'On cultural areas in Spain', in his *Ensayos* (Madrid 1973), pp. 40–107. See also Freeman, *Neighbors*, p.xiv: 'when I say that Valdemorans are part of a universe larger than their own village . . . I am saying that their values, cognitive categories, and general style are shared with neighboring settlements, and may be studied in a community of any size throughout the region.'
35. **Pérez, J.**, *La Révolution des "Comunidades"* (Bordeaux 1970), p. 58.

36. Lisón Tolosana, *Ensayos,* pp. 80–1.
37. ARV Manaments y Empares, año 1677, libro 1: mano 5, f. 17.
38. *Cf.* Lisón Tolosana, *Ensayos,* pp. 49–51, discussing the Asturias.
39. There was likewise no 'national' Catalan revolt in 1705. These views call for a revision of the exposition in **Kamen, H.**, *War of Succession* (London and Bloomington 1965).
40. **Ortega y Gasset, J.**, *España Invertebrada* (Austral, Madrid 1964), p. 50.
41. **Herrero García, M.**, *Ideas de los Españoles* (Madrid 1928), p. 63.
42. **Maravall, J. A.**, *Concepto de España* (Madrid 1954).
43. Quoted in **Maravall, J. A.**, *Estado Moderno* (Madrid 1972), I, 128–9.
44. Cited by Pérez, *op. cit.* p. 56.
45. Quoted in Herrero García, *op. cit.* p. 133.
46. **Menéndez Pidal,** cited in **Highfield, R.**, ed., *Spain in the Fifteenth Century* (London 1972), p. 389.
47. The 1978 Spanish Constitution tactfully calls the official language 'Castilian', not 'Spanish'.
48. All these examples are from **Domínguez Ortiz, A.**, *Sociedad Española* (Madrid 1970), II, 173.
49. **Brunel, A.**, *A Journey into Spain* (London 1670), p. 21–2.
50. **Willughby, F.**, *A Relation of a Voyage* (London 1673), p. 493.
51. **Muret, J.**, *Lettres* (Paris 1879), p. 75.
52. Brunel, *op. cit.* p. 211, observed that Aragonese 'are no less proud than the Castilians, and value themselves above them and all others of Spain'.
53. Quoted in **Elliott, J. H.**, *Revolt of the Catalans* (Cambridge 1963), pp. 13, 15.
54. **Labayru y Goicoechea, E. J.**, *Señorío de Bizcaya* (Bilbao–Madrid 1895–1901), V, 561.
55. Maravall, *Concepto de España.*
56. **Vilar, P.**, *Catalunya dins l'Espanya* (Barcelona 1964), I, 414.
57. BCB, Follets Bonsoms 2752.
58. **Vicens Vives, J.**, 'Gerona después de la paz de Ryswick' *Anales Inst. Estud. Gerund,* (1947).
59. The rebellion is discussed below, Ch. Seven.
60. *Consellers* to Queen, 20 Mar. 1666, ACA:CA 319. There are full reports also in *Dietari* (Barcelona 1922), XVII, 419–20, 787–9. Rius was executed the following day. Some standard Catalan textbooks give an absurd figure of 500 deaths.
61. Consulta of 15 Apr. 1666, ACA:CA 319.
62. Swinburne, *op. cit.* I, 106.
63. **Ezquerra, R.**, *Conspiración* (Madrid 1934), pp. 240–3.

# CHAPTER TWO

# How Spain was Governed

No reign in all Spanish history has been castigated so thoroughly as that of Charles II. 'Castile was dying, both economically and politically'; the government was in a state of 'administrative and political stagnation'; the ruling class suffered from 'unmitigated mediocrity . . . moral and intellectual bankruptcy'; in letters and science 'the spirit of inquiry was almost dead'.[1] There is no denying that these views, common to most modern historians, were also held by all foreign commentators of the time. 'The ancient valour of Spaniards has perished', reported the Venetian ambassador in 1678. 'Consumed by idleness, they live as they please.'[2] All the reports of the Venetian envoys during the reign are equally damning, their apparently well-informed judgments constituting a solemn dirge over the Spanish monarchy. 'There are no navies at sea, no armies on land, the fortresses dismantled and unprotected: everything exposed, nothing protected. It is incomprehensible how this monarchy survives.' 'The whole of the present reign has been an uninterrupted series of calamities.'[3] The chorus was joined by the ambassadors of France. In 1689 ambassador Rébenac informed his king that 'if one examines the government of this monarchy at close quarters, one will find it in an excessive state of disorder . . . Enlightened people agree that the government of the House of Austria is leading them inevitably to total ruin.'[4] Like the Venetians, every French ambassador was convinced that Spain was in a state of total political collapse.

The consistent prejudices of foreigners scarcely require explanation. Italian envoys and travellers since the Renaissance had always viewed Spain with contempt.[5] The French ambassadors under Charles II were concerned above all to exaggerate Spanish decadence and to propose France as Spain's saviour. The pessimistic views of some Spaniards may be explained in the same way. The memoirs drawn up by the marquis of Villena in 1700 and by Cardinal Portocarrero in 1703, were both concerned to overstate Spain's problems in order to invite speedy action by the new Bourbon government. Villena spoke of 'justice abandoned, policy neglected, resources sold, religion distorted, the nobility demoralised, the people oppressed, power decayed, and love and respect for the Crown lost'. Portocarrero spoke of 'repeated ill successes, squandering of the treasury, and the ruin of the state'.[6] The marquis of San Felipe, anxious to praise

Philip V, painted a picture in which there was not a word of truth: 'From Rosas to Cadiz there was not a castle or fort which had a garrison . . . The same negligence was to be seen in the ports of Vizcaya and Galicia. The magazines lacked munitions, the arsenals and workshops were empty. The art of constructing ships had been forgotten.'[7]

Peninsular Spain, the object of all these adverse and uncompromising assessments, consisted broadly of two units, the Crown of Castile and the Crown of Aragon. The Crown of Castile consisted outside the peninsula of the Atlantic islands, the north African forts, and America. Within the peninsula – to which this study is restricted – it consisted of the Basque provinces and Navarre in the north, and ranged from the ancient kingdoms of Asturias and León through Old and New Castile to the realms of Andalucia.

Navarre had been incorporated into the Crown of Castile by Ferdinand the Catholic in 1512. Like other realms, it retained the title of 'kingdom'. Originally a large state bestriding the Pyrenees, it had since the sixteenth century shrunk into a French and a Spanish section. Because of its frontier position Navarre was vital to the military security of Spain, and usually had large military garrisons, particularly in the capital Pamplona. The king was represented by a viceroy, but Navarre retained its own laws, Cortes, coinage and customs posts. It had its own civil and criminal administration, and only Navarrese could hold public office. Taxes were voted by the Cortes. Trade across Navarre's Spanish frontiers (with Castile and Aragon) was subject to internal customs, but across the frontiers with France and the Basque provinces it was virtually free. In effect, Navarre was almost wholly independent of the rest of Spain.[8]

The three Basque provinces of Vizcaya, Guipúzcoa and Alava were allied historically and ethnically with Navarre. The ancient Basque language, Euzkadi, was spoken throughout all four realms. The Basque provinces had a curious constitutional character. Each was given the status of an independent republic, with the title of *Señorío* (lordship). Each was ruled by a special representative assembly, the Junta General, which was the equivalent of a Cortes. In Alava and Guipúzcoa the deputies to the Juntas were elected by the towns, but in Vizcaya they were chosen partly by the big towns and partly by the rural districts called *anteiglesias*, so named because the local assemblies in each district met before the parish church.

In Vizcaya after 1500 a royal governor (*corregidor*), with his seat in Bilbao and aided by two deputies of the Junta, was the effective government, operating as the *Diputación* or standing committee of the Junta General when the latter was not in session. The Junta met regularly every two years in July, 'under the tree at Guernica' (this was the historic formula with which records of its deliberations began). Judicial matters were dealt with by a judge for Vizcaya sitting in the court of Chancery (*Chancillería*) at Valladolid. In all other matters the province was independent. It had its own civil, criminal and commercial laws, and voted its own taxes. The king was accepted simply as a feudal seigneur ('king in so far as he is lord of the land', as the Fuero of Vizcaya put it), and had to uncover his head when negotiating with a representative of the province. In 1644 a royal document recognised that Vizcaya 'is held to be a province separate from the kingdom' of

Castile. Its status could not have been better described.

Guipúzcoa's Junta General met twice a year, and its corregidor sat in San Sebastián. In other matters it was as independent as Vizcaya. Alava was the freest of the three provinces. Its Junta met annually on St Martin's Day (11 November). The function of corregidor was carried out not by a royal nominee but by a Diputado General appointed for three years by the Junta, with his seat in the capital Vitoria. No government measures were valid without his approval, and he was simultaneously civil, political and military head of the province. Alava may consequently be considered a full-blooded republic within Spain.

The privileges of the northern realms owed their survival to a strongly independent communal structure in both town and country. The structure can be seen at work also in the principality of the Asturias. Here the *concejos*, or districts, elected fifty-one deputies to a Junta General which met every three years on 1 May, for a period of up to two months. Meetings were held in the chapter house of the cathedral of Oviedo. In between meetings of the Junta, normal business was delegated to a Diputación consisting of six deputies.[9] Similar regional bodies also existed in Galicia.[10]

The localism and constitutionalism of the Cantabrian provinces appear at first sight to be exceptional in the history of the Crown of Castile. The reality is that the fragmentation of authority in Castile, which had no permanent capital city until well into the sixteenth century, encouraged aspirations to autonomy. The period of the Comunero revolt in 1520 saw many of these hopes emerge as part of a serious political programme. Some rebels thought the Swiss cantons an ideal model for localising government, others thought the Italian city states a better alternative.[11] The Comuneros were not inventing or importing new concepts, for cantonalism was already present within the structure of Castile but had never succeeded in becoming institutionalised.

Castile proper may be looked upon as a state which superficially overcame cantonal and feudal tendencies in its provinces, and proceeded to establish an efficient centralised apparatus of government. There was a uniform tax structure throughout all the provinces, internal customs posts were abolished and left only at the international frontiers, civil and military administration in all the provinces was identical, everywhere the official language was Castilian. The whole structure, both of the empire and of Castile, was directed from Madrid.

The Castilian achievement, which we shall consider in detail below, has frequently been described as 'absolutist'. Had this ever been true, we would be justified in thinking of the developments of the seventeenth century as a breakdown of authority. The great success of Ferdinand and Isabella and subsequent rulers was not, in fact, the imposition of authoritarian rule but the ability to persuade the different peoples of the peninsula to live together under conditions of gross inequality. The superficial unity imposed by Madrid was counterbalanced by profound disunity at all levels. The constitutional liberties (*fueros*) enjoyed by one half of Spain, withered away in Castile. By contrast, Castile alone was given the formal right to enrich itself from the Indies. The price Castile had to pay for this enjoyment of an overseas empire was a level of taxation higher than that of the rest of Spain. Wide variations in climate and geography created several economic units in the country rather than one. Differences in agricultural output between the parched interior and the richer coastlands led to serious deficiencies in the food supply. The proliferation of internal customs barriers, which discriminated for example against Castilians and in favour of the Basques, was a major hindrance to unifying commercial exchange within the country. Some impression of the customs network may be gained from Figure 2.1.

The inequalities and disunity in Spain were substantially similar to conditions in other western European states. It is timely to emphasise them in order to disavow the image of Spain as a strong monarchy. Unlike the French, who developed intendants after the early seventeenth century, and the English, who had a good system of local government through justices of the peace, the Spanish Habsburgs never had centralised officials to help them in administration. What government there was, took the form of a bureaucracy located in Madrid. Foreign observers were always impressed by the enormous number of ministers, officials and other personnel busying themselves in the capital. They concluded that Spain was being strongly governed. A lack of firm direction in the capital led them consequently to conclude that Spain was suffering weak government. Had they bothered to examine the nature of authority in the countryside, they would have found that the idea of a 'strong' or 'weak' government in Madrid was largely

Fig. 2.1  Principal Spanish customs posts in the seventeenth century.

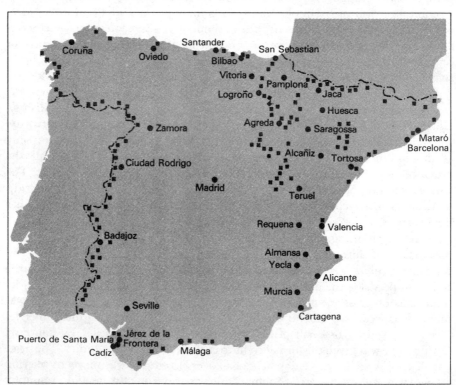

irrelevant to law and order in the regions. Spain under Charles II continued to be governed as it had been under Philip II, by a kind of consensus between various local interests of which the nobles, the Church, the urban oligarchies and the local tax-farmers were the most important. Habsburg Spain was stable because it was largely self-governing, not because it was governed by an absolute monarchy.

The extent of independence from control by Madrid, may be seen most clearly in the Crown of Aragon, which consisted of the three mainland realms of Aragon, Catalonia and Valencia, together with the Balearic Islands. Though associated with Castile since the late fifteenth century, through the marriage of Ferdinand and Isabella, the Crown of Aragon had always retained complete autonomy. The unhappy experience of 1591, when Philip II sent in an army to crush a revolt in Saragossa, had left no mark. Even the great Catalan revolt of 1640–52 had few major repercussions. Each new king was obliged to swear to maintain the laws (fueros), in person and before the Estates assembled in a Cortes, before he could be formally recognised as monarch. Since Charles II during his reign visited only the realm of Aragon, but not those of Catalonia and Valencia, he had to take the oath by proxy in the last two. The king's direct representative was the viceroy, who in turn had to swear to preserve the laws before being invested.

Tenure of office by viceroys was generally for three years at a time. In theory a viceroy exercised all the powers of the Crown, but in practice he was restricted by the fueros. Viceroys fiercely resented this. In Valencia in 1680 a viceroy was recalled for allegedly infringing the fueros, in Barcelona in 1697 the Catalans refused to accept a viceroy because he had not taken the oath in the city.[12] Because the Crown of Aragon was wholly separate from that of Castile, Charles II could not exercise in the former the almost unlimited powers that he enjoyed in the latter. The chief barrier to royal pretensions in Aragon was the Cortes of each realm, which jealously examined every attempt by the king to interfere in the laws, increase taxes or raise troops beyond the legal obligations of the realm. Despite such restrictions, the king held considerable powers. The Cortes, for example, could not meet or be dissolved without his permission. He moreover appointed all the principal officials of each realm. It was in the interest of the ruling classes of the Crown of Aragon to remain on good terms with the king in Madrid.

In the realm of Aragon administration was centred in the capital, Saragossa.[13] Directly subordinate to the viceroy came the *Audiencia* of Saragossa, the chief court of royal justice in Aragon. One historic peculiarity of Aragon was the justiciar's court, which coexisted with the jurisdiction of the Audiencia. It had authority throughout the realm, and was headed by a *justicia* and five other judges known as 'lieutenants'. The justiciar was appointed by the king, the lieutenants were elected by lot in the Cortes; all held their posts for life, and could not be removed by the king. The Aragonese were rightly proud of this court, which offered them justice wholly free of royal interference.

The city of Saragossa was governed by a *consistorio* of five councillors (*jurados*) with extensive powers. The jurados were a committee of the full city council of thirty-five members, elected by lot every year. Annual election was also the rule for the Diputados, or members of the Diputación, the standing committee of the

Cortes of Aragon. The Diputación consisted of eight deputies, two from each of the four Estates (*brazos*) of the Cortes. It was elected by lot every year on 3 May, and its main duty was to oversee the laws of the realm. Aragon was the only part of the Crown to retain four Estates in its Cortes: the others had three.

The Diputación was also responsible for the administration of the customs revenues and other local taxes. The king's feudal revenues in Aragon were administered by a committee consisting of the viceroy, the regent of the Audiencia, and the chief royal tax officials, headed by a bailiff, and a treasurer. In general, revenue from taxes in Aragon was wholly consumed within the realm, mainly on administrative costs, and virtually no money reached the exchequer in Madrid.

Government in the rest of the Crown of Aragon was on similar lines. In Valencia justice was also dispensed through an Audiencia: this consisted of fifteen judges. The city of Valencia[14] was governed by a council (*Consell General*) made up in the late century of 132 members representing various interests. By 1700, according to a contemporary, the membership was down to 112. Majority representation (some 66 in 1677) on the Consell was held by the guilds, who each sent two members. The city parishes also sent two deputies each. Six nobles, four distinguished citizens (*ciutadans*), and four jurists shared the right to membership. Effective government of the city was, as in Saragossa, carried out by a committee of this council, consisting of six *jurats*, two from the nobility, four from the ciutadans, who were elected annually by lot and served without salary. Election by lot, or *insaculació*, was introduced into all the realms of Aragon by Ferdinand the Catholic in the late fifteenth century. Names of eligible candidates were put into a bag or bowl and picked out by a child. The first two persons so elected in Valencia were known as *jurats en cap*.

The Cortes of Valencia had three Estates (*estaments*), but had not met since the year 1645. The standing committee of the Cortes was the Diputació de la Generalitat, made up of six members, two from each Estate. When there was no Cortes the Estates could also meet as independent assemblies. For this purpose special permanent delegates were elected. During the reign of Charles II, as we shall see below, the Estates played an unusually important part in public affairs, even though no assembly of the full Cortes was summoned. As in Aragon, royal finance was supervised by a bailiff, a treasurer, and other officials.

The government of Catalonia[15] resembled that of Valencia. Both realms were allied by history and language. The viceroyalty of Catalonia was the most senior one in the peninsula. Because of the great strategic importance of the principality the viceroy usually also acted as Captain General or military head. The viceroy's deputy, known as the Governor of Catalonia, took care of ordinary details of administration. The Audiencia of Barcelona, like that of Valencia, was divided into three chambers. It normally had seventeen judges, of whom two, the Regent and the Chancellor,[16] were presidents of court. Over and beyond its judicial functions, the Audiencia came to play an active role in public policy. It was 'the most effective organ of royal government in the principality'.[17] The administration of Barcelona was in the hands of the Council of a Hundred (*Consell de Cent*), which consisted in fact of 144 members, of whom 68 represented professions and guilds, 32 represented the merchants of the Llotja, and 48 represented the ciutadans and nobles. The executive committee of this council was made up of five *consellers*, led by the *conseller en cap*. Half of the Consell de Cent was elected every year, and Consellers were elected annually on St Andrew's Day: both elections were by lot.

The turbulent history of the Cortes of Catalonia was succeeded in the reign of Charles II by silence. The responsibilities of the Cortes continued, however, to be managed by the Diputació de la Generalitat. This had six members, two from each of the three estates (*braços*). Three of the members (one from each braç) were known as *diputats*, the other three as *oidors*; they held office for three years. As in the rest of the Crown of Aragon, royal finances were administered by a bailiff and treasurer.

The clear constitutional contrast between neo-absolutist Castile and libertarian Aragon has always fascinated historians. Down to modern times there has been a recurrent suspicion that Castile has attempted to take full control of the destinies of the peninsula, and has thereby harmed the interests of other parts of Spain. The relationship between the two Crowns has accordingly been presented in strictly political terms as a battle to preserve a balance between centralism and federalism.

To some extent the presentation is correct. From Charles V onwards the Habsburgs gave Castile a privileged place in the monarchy. The policies of Olivares were the climax to a long history of Castilian decision-making and impatience with the autonomous realms. The primacy of Castile was logical – it was the largest realm, the most populated, with the greatest foreign obligations in America and Flanders, and the most heavily taxed – but other Spaniards resented the gravitation of political power to the centre. The equanimity with which Castilianisation was accepted may be explained in part by the ambiguous position of the ruling classes. It is significant that the duke of Lerma, who ordered the expulsion of the Moriscos, a measure that hurt Valencia badly, was a Valencian grandee, but a Castilianised one. By mid-century most of the great nobles of the fuero realms were heavily Castilianised. They sat on the councils in Madrid but had often lost touch with regional feeling.

The struggle of the provinces against this trend to centralism can be seen in the many recorded complaints that arose in the Aragonese revolt of 1591 and the Catalan revolt of 1640. Taken at face value, the complaints seem to demand liberty from Castilian neglect and arbitrary rule. Looked at more closely, the complaints essentially express concern for the privileges of the ruling classes of the Crown of Aragon. The defence of 'autonomy' and federalism was in effect a defence of lower taxation and higher political privileges for the élite. The true contrast between Castile and Aragon, it has been observed,[18] was between a Castile that had 'good government, but little defence against the arbitrary fiscal demands of the Crown, and a Crown of Aragon well protected against arbitrary taxation and royal absolutism, but possessed of a constitution easily abused by an irresponsible aristocracy'.

The undoubted political importance of the tension between Castile and Aragon has usually received excessive emphasis, to the detriment of factors such as the social role of the aristocracy, and other aspects of the internal government of the fuero provinces. It is possible that too much attention to Castilian–Aragonese conflict has indeed distorted our view of how the Crown of Aragon functioned. Catalonia always provoked problems because of its special strategic position. But in the day-to-day government of Aragon and Valencia there was very little friction with Castile. In the reign of Charles II even Catalonia was fully reconciled and at peace with Castile. It is clear from the events of the late seventeenth century that there was more friction within each of the fuero provinces than there was in their external relations. The themes of centralism and federalism were basically irrelevant to the real issues in the peripheral states of Spain, where problems of internal social order and economic retrenchment were by far the most crucial.

We need, in brief, to escape from the view that the fuero provinces were cohesive political units where every development was somehow a reaction against Castile. The fictions that Barcelona represented Catalonia, that Saragossa represented Aragon, that Bilbao represented the Basques, were fully exposed by developments in the late century. Cohesion within the provinces depended on an uneasy relationship between cantons, between sections of the ruling class, and between the capital city and the country. It followed that a decision by an urban oligarchy to adopt a cause – as happened with Barcelona in 1705 – did not necessarily represent the views of the majority in the province and was not always in their interests. Other decisions, such as the temporary limitation of imports from Castile into Aragon in this period, were made for reasons of economic policy and not because of friction with Castile.

## THE KING IN GOVERNMENT

The death of Philip IV in 1665 left an infant as prospective king of Spain. It was the first time since the birth of a united Spain under Ferdinand and Isabella, that a child had succeeded to the throne. The Queen Mother became Regent and controlled government for over a decade. But nothing could compensate for the lack of a firm hand at the helm. As in the France of Cardinal Mazarin, a royal minority allowed scope to the ambitions of the ruling élite.

Philip's first son and intended heir, Baltasar Carlos, died prematurely in 1646. Charles II, born on 6 November 1661 in the old Alcázar of Madrid, was the fruit of an incestuous union. Baltasar Carlos had been destined to marry the daughter of Philip's sister the Empress Maria, wife of Ferdinand III. After the prince's inopportune death, Philip himself in 1649 married the girl, his niece Mariana of Austria. This attempt to secure a healthy succession to the throne through marriage between a forty-four year-old king and a fourteen-year-old girl seemed doomed to failure. Mariana gave birth to five children in succession, but the only survivor was a girl, Margarita. Then in 1661 Don Carlos was born. The *Gaceta de Madrid* announced him to be 'very handsome in appearance, with a large head, dark skin and somewhat thick-set'.

Intermarriage within the Habsburg royal line had bred some medical deficiencies in the past. The best known example was that of Philip II's son Don Carlos. Charles II from earliest infancy showed signs of being sickly and retarded.[19] He had to be breast-fed for close on four years, by a total of over fourteen wet-nurses, and the treatment was discontinued in 1665 only out of respect for his ascent to the throne. He was unable to walk until over four years old, because his legs were too weak to support him. At that age 'the crown was firmer on his head than the ground was beneath his feet'.[20] Early signs of rickets were already visible. At the age of nine he could neither read nor write, despite the worthy efforts of his two tutors, the one a royal confessor and the other an ex-professor of Salamanca. His education took place in the palace, where he had no other children to play with. We can imagine the strain put on his delicate constitution by the syllabus, which required that he learn Christian doctrine, Latin, French, Italian, geography, astronomy, history, riding, dancing, fencing, tilting and playing *pelota*. In April 1670, at the age of eight and a half, he went on his first hunt, but on foot. Not until 17 May 1671 did he first ride a horse.

The poor health of the king preoccupied his mother, the public and all Europe. Prognostications current as far afield as Paris and Vienna foretold his death in spring 1670, and when he fell victim of a gastric fever in May that year it seemed the end had come. But this was only the first of several such accidents. There was a limit to precautions that could be imposed on a king. Traditional ceremonial demanded, for example, that mammoth meals (lunch normally consisted of three first courses, three second and a sweet) be placed before him, with no restrictions on what he might eat. It was therefore very difficult to regulate his diet. Nor were restrictions placed on his movements or public appearances. Charles's mother erred if anything on the side of indulgence, in allowing her unfortunate son to take part in as many normal activities as he wished.

The portrait of him at the age of fourteen, by Carreño, presents Charles clearly as a retarded child. At the age of twenty-five he had improved little. The description then made by the papal nuncio is striking:

The king is short rather than tall; frail, not badly formed; his face on the whole is ugly; he has a long neck, a broad face and chin, with the typical Habsburg lower lip, not very large eyes of turquoise blue and a fine and declicate complexion. He has a melancholic and faintly surprised look. His hair is long and fair and combed back so as to bare the ears. He cannot stand upright except when walking, unless he leans against a wall, a table or somebody else. He is as weak in body as in mind. Now and then he gives signs of intelligence, memory and a certain liveliness, but not at present; usually he shows himself slow and indifferent, torpid and indolent, and seems to be stupefied. One can do with him what one wishes because he lacks his own will.[21]

Three grave consequences followed from the king's condition: he was unable to rule personally; he failed to arouse respect from those in closest contact with him, mainly Castilians; and his inability to produce an heir created wideranging international disputes over the succession.

The king's poor health made it impossible for him to travel. He made only three long journeys in his life, one to open the Cortes in Saragossa and two to meet

21

his foreign brides. For the rest of his days he remained confined to the small area bounded by the royal palaces in the heart of Castile. As the least-travelled monarch in Spanish history, he was forced to rely on others for information and advice. His mother Queen Mariana was thereby placed in a very difficult position. Deeply protective of her son, and obviously aware of his inability to rule, she fought bitterly against attempts to free him from her control. Charles in his turn alternated between total dependence on his mother and a profound desire to escape from her tutelage. Aged only thirty-one in the year that her infant son succeeded Philip IV, Mariana had the energy to exercise an active Regency under her official title of Queen Governor, but lacked the expertise to make it successful.

Charles II occasionally showed considerable independence and initiative, but he never ruled in any real sense. For most of his reign he did not attend council meetings, did not confer with ministers, and did not countersign council deliberations, which were usually approved by a minister. Official documents invariably bore facsimiles rather than his real signature. It is possible that he did not make a single major decision throughout his reign. The government lacked an effective head. This did not mean that the monarchy collapsed into disorder. Other means of exercising authority were available, as we shall see. In any case, the Spanish empire was not so highly centralised as to be unhinged by the sudden accession of an incompetent king. A weak king, on the other hand, was an open invitation to factional disputes and rivalry for power among ministers.

Because of his poor health Charles II undoubtedly won a great deal of public sympathy. But as the reign went on his inadequacy and his impotence gave rise to undisguised public scorn, particularly in Madrid. Politically conscious Castilians, anxious to find a more competent ruler, moved irresistibly to support for a successor from Europe's most powerful nation, France. The succession question, which will be discussed in its proper place, arose directly out of two unfruitful marriages. Charles had no desire to marry, and would have apparently preferred a life of pious celibacy. Only the need for an heir, and the undoubted charms of his first wife, Marie Louise of Orleans, won him over. The king's impotence, we gather from the direct testimony of both his wives, was not physical: he was capable of coition, but was not able to generate.

In a state such as the Spanish monarchy, where decision-making had for generations been the prerogative of the king, the lack of a firm royal hand was bound to lead to some political instability. The condition of Charles II was consequently at all times a negative factor. The ultimate effect of this has however been consistently exaggerated. It may even be possible to argue that the weakening of royal control allowed the development, for the first time in Habsburg Spain, of political trends that had for a long time been struggling, validly but vainly, for expression.

## CONCILIAR GOVERNMENT

The Spanish empire was a union of autonomous states, in each of which the king was sovereign and had to rule according to local laws. Since the monarch could not be present in all his dominions, their interests were served by representation on councils sitting in Madrid.[22]

Foremost of the councils was the council of State, which dealt with international issues such as foreign policy and war and peace. Normally presided over by the king, it had two secretaries, one for the 'north' (i.e. northern Europe, particularly Flanders) and one for the 'south' (southern Europe, particularly Italy). It was the chief organ of government in the monarchy, and could determine or reverse the deliberations of other councils. Next in overall competence came the council of War, whose authority was usually restricted to peninsular Spain and adjacent territories. The military affairs of Italy and America, for example, were dealt with largely by officials in those regions, or by the relevant council. All the councillors of State were *ex officio* members of the council of War, which had two secretaries, one for land and one for sea.

There were seven superior or supreme councils which functioned independently of each other and could be overseen only by the council of State. In order of precedence (an important issue at official gatherings) these were the councils of Castile, Indies, Aragon, Inquisition, Italy, Flanders and Portugal. The council of Aragon was the highest governing body, under the Crown, of the realms of the Crown of Aragon. Formed in 1494, it provided the model for government of territories which the king in Castile could not administer personally. It acted as a liaison between the Crown and the various viceroys, received all correspondence on matters of public policy, and despatched orders to the provinces. It was normally presided over by a vice-chancellor (*Vicecanciller*) and all its members, with the exception of the treasurer, had to be natives of the Crown of Aragon. In 1555 the Italian states, which had till then been represented on the council of Aragon, were allotted a separate council of Italy. This followed the important transference (in 1540) of the key territory of Milan from Imperial to Spanish control. The council of Portugal was founded in 1582 after the conquest of the country; that of Flanders was set up in 1588 to help govern the Netherlands. The council of the Inquisition, established in 1483, gave the Crown direct control over the Holy Office.

The most significant council was that of Castile. Though not the highest organ of government, a position occupied by the council of State, it was without doubt the most important. It was headed by a 'governor' or 'president', who enjoyed the highest authority in Spain after the king.[23] The council was entrusted with the administrative and judicial government of the Crown of Castile alone, but since Castile in all its aspects dominated the public business of the monarchy, the council had accumulated enormous responsibilities. By 1700 it had a membership of twenty councillors and was divided into four departments or chambers.

The council of the Indies, with a president and two secretaries, administered the vast possessions in the New World and also oversaw trade between Spain and America. All the other bodies not so far named, were in some measure responsible to the council of Castile. The most important of them was the council of Finance (or *Hacienda*), which in effect dealt with the finances of the whole monarchy. The

23

council of Orders administered the three chivalric orders of Santiago, Calatrava and Alcántara in Castile, and that of Montesa in Aragon. The council of the Crusade (*Cruzada*) was concerned exclusively with a very lucrative tax, the *cruzada*, originally granted by the papacy to finance the fight against the Moors.

Government was conducted from the royal palace in Madrid. 'All councils meet in the palace, and the king by private galleries can go to any of the rooms where they sit. There is a great concourse, and no less noise, when any of them are assembled.'[24] Each council met on a specified day of the week, amid great ceremonial. Business to be transacted was always voluminous, but little of it reached the full council. By the late sixteenth century a number of committees (*juntas*) and sub-committees had been created to determine specific matters. In the case of the council of Castile, administrative correspondence was sent to permanent departments. The Chamber (*Cámara*) of Castile, one of these, dealt with Church affairs and official appointments and grants of privileges. Routine matters were handled by the administrative staff and secretaries. Where discussion was required, business was referred to the plenary meetings of the council, at which opinions (*votos*) were expressed and minuted, and a full report or *consulta* sent to the Crown. The consulta was examined either by the king or his minister, and referred back to the council for action.

Conciliar government had not apparently changed in character for over a century. Its weaknesses were many, particularly where the interests of non-Castilian territories were concerned. In Castile the councils suffered in efficiency mainly from the fact that they governed indirectly rather than directly: they had no officials of their own, no administrative bureaucracy to carry out orders and implement laws. The council of Finance, for example, had to rely for tax-collecting on tax-farmers and local officials rather than on its own personnel. A fundamental criticism made both by foreign and by native commentators was that the class which monopolised power, the upper aristocracy, was unfit to govern. The archbishop of Toledo, Cardinal Portocarrero, in a letter to the French foreign secretary in 1703, shared this view:[25]

In the last few years of the reign of the King our lord Charles the Second, the nobility were brought up and educated without any application, in pure idleness, accustomed to the fact that with the aid of the Palace and with bargaining tricks they could obtain the principal employments in military and political government, without knowledge or experience or any merit of their own, exercising these appointments thereafter with ambition, pride and self-interest, so that the natural results of this unhappy procedure were repeated ill successes, squandering of the treasury, and the ruin of the state.

This was a typical overstatement of what may have been a genuine problem. Few gifted politicians arose in Spain after the fall of Olivares. Membership of the councils was the prerogative of a narrow élite which showed little talent or enthusiasm for public affairs. Attendance at meetings was notoriously poor. In 1691 the king warned councillors that

in view of the many serious matters outstanding in the council of State, and the little business transacted in each meeting, I am charging members to be punctual in arriving at the correct time, four o'clock, and to observe what I have ordered in several decrees, not to deliver lengthy and repetitive opinions; and it will also be to my service that no member leave the meeting before it is finished, without urgent cause.[26]

A quotation like this tends to suggest that councillors were lazy and incompetent. Let us, however, try to look at their point of view. They were well aware that attendance was not after all so crucial, since many if not most major decisions were made elsewhere, often against the wishes of the councils. The fact is that three quite independent developments were tending to subvert the authority of the councils. Firstly, a small core of people, not necessarily members of the councils of State or Castile, saw fit to give advice to the king outside the normal conciliar machinery. This was inevitable during a royal minority. Secondly, the king frequently chose a single person, a *valido*, to act as prime minister and guide his counsels. Finally, the increasing importance of the cabinet office, or *despacho universal*, offered the king a way of transmitting orders without having to go through the councils. We shall consider these developments presently.

Councils under Charles II were not always as supreme as they felt they should be. They were advisory bodies but their advice was frequently spurned. It is astonishing how often their views on, for example, the appointment of viceroys, were ignored. In March 1678 the council of Aragon, discussing candidates for the viceroyalty of Aragon, put forward a long list led by the count of Oropesa. The Crown ignored all the candidates on the list, and nominated the count of Humanes. When Humanes was unable to take up the post, the Crown asked the council to suggest further names. In December they put forward a new list, still headed by Oropesa. The Crown ignored all the named candidates, and instead appointed the duke of Veraguas.[27] In 1684 the council informed the king that the best man for the viceroyalty of Catalonia was the current viceroy, Bournonville; the Crown thereupon nominated the marquis of Leganés.[28] In 1693 it warned the king not to reappoint the marquis of Castelrodrigo as viceroy of Valencia; by return the councillors heard that he had already been reappointed.[29] A careful search would no doubt unearth many such cases. To take a different example: in 1697 the council unanimously opposed the revocation of the banishment imposed upon the chief inquisitor of Barcelona; the Crown nevertheless revoked it.[30]

The frequency of such cases is a reminder that councils were only deliberative and not decision-making bodies. This continued to be true in the reign of Charles II, where one might have assumed that a weak king would have lost his power to the councils. The fact is that even on major questions the king's advisers felt free to make decisions contrary to conciliar advice. In 1680 the council of Finance, with only three dissentients, expressed its opposition to changing the method of tax-collection in Castile. The Crown overruled it and instituted the proposed change.[31]

The government might ignore the councils on specific issues, but could never afford to ignore the political élite represented on them. Not even the strongest valido (Olivares is a case in point) could survive the combined hostility of the councils. In the reign of Charles II they were perhaps at their most powerful under

25

the Regency. They bullied Queen Mariana and rebelled against Valenzuela. After the death of Don Juan in 1679, their initiative was reduced by the several validos who wielded power. Since the councils were monopolised by the grandee class, however, their real strength, both political and social, remained undimmed. In 1705 the councillors of State informed the new king that 'the tribunals are the depositaries of wise counsel, of the oath taken by the king of Spain, and of that which he has received from his subjects . . . they should have cognisance of everything'.[32]

The size and functions of councils remained generally unchanged in the late seventeenth century. This was despite several attempts at reform.[33] On 6 July 1677 a royal decree ordered a reduction in the size of councils, 'to obviate the great delay in the efficient despatch of business caused by the increased number of ministers, as well as the rising cost of salaries'. The council of the Indies, for example, was to be reduced to eight councillors. The measure seems to have failed. On 31 January 1687 another decree ordered the suppression of all superfluous offices in the councils. It is very unlikely that this worked either. An official survey of the council of Aragon in December 1690 showed that it had thirty councillors and over one hundred salaried employees on its books.[34] Three of these were supernumerary, or temporary posts created to reward distinguished councillors for their past services; and a further three were honorary, granted *ex officio* to royal administrators in the Crown of Aragon. At least three of the thirty had an element of venality. The annual salary bill for all thirty (the honorary members drew no salary) came to 517,800 silver reales. Since this situation of expensive over-staffing existed in all councils, a decree of 17 July 1691 ordered that membership be radically reduced. The council of the Indies, for example, was reduced to one president, ten councillors, and a fiscal; the council of Aragon was reduced to one president or vice-chancellor, six councillors (known as regents in this body), and a fiscal. It was an ambitious attempt to streamline the council structure, but the evidence suggests that it succeeded only in part. By 1693 there were twelve members in the council of Aragon, by 1700 there were nineteen in the council of the Indies.

The only council to experience any significant change under Charles II was that of Finance. The perpetual need to find money and get out of debt, encouraged the government to make several changes in financial structure. These and other changes are discussed in Chapter Fourteen below.

## MINISTERS AND VALIDOS

Philip II was the only Habsburg king of Spain to exercise a direct personal rule that came close to absolutism. From Philip III onwards, affairs of state tended to come under the direction of a single nobleman in whom the king put his trust, known as the *valido*.[35] The rise of the valido meant a corresponding decline in the office of secretary of State, which had been filled under Philip II by distinguished and able men. It also meant greater dependence of the Crown on the grandees, since a valido could not survive without substantial support among the aristocrats who sat on the councils. Validos needed to build up a system of patronage in order to keep a firm hold on power. In this way factions and parties took form at the court in Madrid.

The valido was not simply a royal favourite. His position was a formal one, recognised as such by king and councils. In 1612 when Philip III ordered the councils 'to comply with whatever the duke [Lerma] instructs or orders . . . and also to furnish him with any information he requires',[36] he was constitutionally delegating his authority. Subsequent validos usually received an instrument of power from the king. Councils were naturally always reluctant to accept the legitimacy of the *valimiento*. There is no doubt, however, that the office proved to be a very valuable one in the absence of a strong king.

The great defect of government in the early years of Charles II was that no single person such as a valido was allowed to exercise power. Philip IV, for reasons that remain unclear, excluded his natural son Don Juan José from any position of authority. During the Regency, from 1665 to 1675, decisions were made principally by Queen Mariana, but she was closely supervised by the Committee of Government. It is common practice to describe her as weak, but this seems unfair to a young foreign princess who, thrust unexpectedly into the role of the first woman Regent in Spanish history, showed considerable ability in fighting to maintain her position. She was a lone woman in a world of experienced politicians, who accorded her respect only because she happened to be the king's mother. Her heavy reliance on Father Nithard and on Valenzuela was both political and strongly emotional, and an obvious effort to find a strong man to support her. The conflicts which this provoked with the ruling élite caused considerable indecision at court. An English diplomat reported in April 1666 that 'the want of a Minister of State in this government, and the referring all things to the Council of State, where the power is equal and the animosities very high, breeds infinite delays and irresolution in all affaires'.[37]

From 1665 up to Don Juan's death in 1679 no minister of the Crown can properly be called a valido. Nithard and Valenzuela, despite their formal positions on public bodies, were fundamentally palace advisers and never operated as true ministers. Neither belonged to the grandee class or relied on the support of a group of the upper aristocracy. Don Juan, by contrast, was in a unique category. Although formally a valido, he was very much more, being both a prince of the blood and the monarchy's chief general.

The years 1665 to 1675 were those of the royal minority. Mariana declared in 1665 that 'she would never have a valido, for so the late king had ordered'.[38] The Queen Mother deliberately chose her advisers, Nithard and Valenzuela, from those who had no links with the Spanish ruling élite. Ironically, the drift to valimientos was begun by the boy king who, as soon as he attained his majority in 1675, summoned Don Juan to his side. From this time onwards the validos were also known as 'prime ministers'.

The last quarter of the seventeenth century was one of almost continuous valido rule. The exact role of the first minister was not always clear. The two notable validos of the period were the duke of Medinaceli, who was appointed on 22

27

February 1680 and stayed in power till 1685; and the duke of Oropesa, who served from 1685 to 1691 and then again from 1698 to April 1699. One of our best. though by no means unbiased, guides to these ministers is a secretary in the conciliar administration who has left us an absorbing account.[39] He maintains, for instance, that both Medinaceli and Oropesa had domineering wives who ruled their husband's counsels. The main weakness of all the first ministers, however, was that with a weak king in control they had to depend for power principally on the support of their noble faction. They consequently seldom achieved the consensus needed to make conciliar government succeed.

Under Charles II the valido always held the post of president of Castile. This meant that the status of first minister was associated with a recognised post. The rule was not invariable. Oropesa during his first ministry moved from the presidency of Castile to that of Italy, without relinquishing his functions as head of the government. The change made it possible for him to claim, when he was dismissed by the king in June 1691, that he was not a valido and that 'he held no greater part in the monarchy than any other minister'.[40]

As mentioned above, the various developments in government under Charles II tended to subvert the conciliar system, and the grandees were bound to oppose them all in order to defend their political privileges. The resort by the Crown to unofficial advisers, such as Valenzuela, who was called the *duende* or 'familiar ghost' because of his secret comings and goings in the palace, disrupted the process of decision-making but brought about no enduring change in the style of government. The valimiento, on the other hand, was a move towards a system already practised in other countries, and despite their strong opposition the grandees seemed to tolerate it to some extent, since it gave direction to the government when there was a weak executive. The most significant of the developments was the growth in functions of the secretary of the Despacho Universal.

The secretaryship of the king's private office or Despacho was created in 1621.[41] The holder was usually also a secretary of the council of State, and his function was to 'despatch' orders issued by the king or his chief minister. The growth of the office in the late seventeenth century was explained as follows by a French commentator in 1704:

Previous kings of Spain . . . would usually leave the administration of all the business of the monarchy to their prime minister, and it was from him that the secretary of the Despacho Universal would receive and then transmit orders. After the disgrace of the count of Oropesa, the late King Charles II had no prime minister. He himself gave his orders to Don Antonio de Ubilla. It was not judged appropriate to let Ubilla be the only one to bring affairs of state before a young king, inexperienced in matters on which the accomplished secretary of the Despacho might speak to him. It was this reason that led to the institution of this new council.[42]

'This new council' was, in 1704, the cabinet council that had grown out of the Despacho. The secretary had by then evolved into a minister of importance. The trend was foreshadowed under Charles II. It was felt that the secretary, 'if a man of parts, is capable of being, when there is no valido, the salvation of the kingdom'.[43] Among the men who held this crucial post in the last decades of the reign were José de Veitia Linaje (1682–85), Manuel Francisco de Lira (1685–91), Juan de Angulo (1691–94), Alonso Carnero (1694–95), Juan Larrea (1695–97), Juan Antonio López de Zarate (1697–98), and Antonio de Ubilla. The French statement of 1704 seems to suggest that Ubilla was the first powerful secretary of the Despacho. In fact, Charles II began to take over the direction of affairs from as early as 1691, after Oropesa's first ministry,[44] so that the reference of business to the Despacho rather than to ministers dates from then at the very latest. Earlier secretaries also seem to have enjoyed some initiative: Manuel de Lira, for example, was criticised for 'the liberties he took in the Despacho Universal . . . finding himself at the King's side, he would brook no other in a higher position of favour'.[45] The growth in the role of the Despacho strengthened the executive, took business away from the councils, and helped the emergence of cabinet government. From the late 1690s and into the early years of the reign of Philip V, the assistance of one or two other ministers in the Despacho created a strong focus of power in the state.

## THE GOVERNMENT OF CASTILE

Of all the realms of Spain the king exercised most authority in Castile. The largest and most populated of all the provinces, Castile had a unified system of laws, taxes, coinage and language. Constitutional government in Castile was in decay, and there had been no serious opposition since the revolt of the Comuneros in 1520.

The apparently strong position of the Crown in Castile was in practice weakened by feudal geography and a lack of bureaucracy. Innumerable areas of the country were in private hands, out of royal control. The French foreign minister Torcy was advised in 1710 by his ambassador in Spain that the king had jurisdiction over only about two hundred of the seven hundred towns in Castile.[46] An analysis of the province of Salamanca in the eighteenth century has shown that only about a third of the population and territory was under royal jurisdiction.[47] The number of towns under independent seigneurial control – *villas de señorío* – was a hindrance to effective financial and bureaucratic government, but a more profound hindrance was the absence of a body of central state officials. Ferdinand and Isabella had in 1480 appointed corregidores (civil governors), with administrative and judicial duties, to all the main towns of Castile. The measure had given the Crown a powerful initiative in local affairs. But by the sixteenth century most *corregimientos* had become monopolised by local oligarchies, and in effect passed out of royal control.

The corregidor was the highest judicial officer in his region, and represented the Crown's great success in maintaining peace and justice in Castile. Although some seigneurial justice was still permitted, all judicial decisions were subject to the realm's highest courts, the Chanceries (*Chancillerías*) of Valladolid and Granada, and their subsidiary courts (*Audiencias*) in La Coruña and Seville. These

29

four courts were delegations of royal authority, were subordinate to the council of Castile, and acted as courts of justice as well as of appeal.

Perhaps the most notable aspect of Habsburg rule in Castile was the decay of representative institutions during the seventeenth century. The decline had in reality begun much earlier. The Cortes of Castile had for some time been little more than an empty conference of eighteen cities, with the right to assent to taxation but with no power to make laws. Towards the end of the reign of Philip IV representation had been increased to twenty-one cities.[48] This failed to revive the Cortes, which did not meet at all during the reign of Charles II. Its decay was unlamented: the few cities represented were unfitted to speak for the whole of Castile, and the only people to benefit from its sessions were the deputies (procuradores), who drew large salaries during the sittings.

The suspension of the Cortes meant neither a victory for centralist absolutism nor the collapse of Habsburg government. On the contrary, a very efficient system of consultation continued to exist. As in other parts of Spain, the Cortes had its own standing committee or Diputación, which consisted of some procuradores and sat permanently in Madrid. When the government wished to renew the grants of taxes, it appointed a special committee called the Junta de Asistentes en Cortes, consisting of the governor of the council of Castile and the secretary and three members of the Chamber of Castile,[49] to consult with the Diputación. The council of Finance regularly consulted the Diputación on tax proposals. In 1680, for instance, a memorandum of the Diputación was discussed by the council; and in the same year a procurador of the Cortes, the count of Guaro, was a member of one of the council's tax committees.[50]

The basic policy of the Crown under Charles II was to consult each city with a vote in the Cortes and obtain the direct approval of its town council (cabildo), so obviating the need for either procuradores or Cortes.[51] We can see how this worked in July 1667, when the government wrote to all cities with a vote, saying that the millones taxes were due to expire in 1668 and asking for an extension for a further six-year period. At the same time letters were sent to the relevant corregidores, ordering them to obtain this approval and to suspend a cabildo if it showed signs of voting against the tax. Stubborn city councillors (regidores) should be approached one by one. The policy was as successful as could be expected. In August the corregidor of Palencia reported that his city would oppose the tax, but the government wrote back saying that 'other cities have given their agreement and since they are a majority your efforts are not now necessary'. On 1 November 1667 a cédula was issued stating that most of the cities in the Cortes had consented to the tax, which was thereupon renewed for a six-year term. Exactly the same procedure was followed in 1673, when again the government claimed it had the approval of 'most' of the Cortes. Castile continued to function quite happily without a joint meeting of the cities in a Cortes. The only casualties were the procuradores, now left in a clearly anomalous position. Cities saw no point in electing new procuradores, with the result that existing deputies enjoyed virtual perpetuity in their posts, to the great annoyance of other contenders for this purely honorific rank.[52]

It was not the intention of the government to ignore public opinion. Lack of a proper state bureaucracy and of regular contacts through the Cortes, obliged Madrid to improve the flow of information. Several surveys of the kingdom were commissioned, but none appears to have been completed. In March 1669 a detailed questionnaire was sent to all cities with a vote in the Cortes. They were asked 'to suggest measures which would most inexpensively and most suitably serve His Majesty and relieve tax-payers'. We have the replies from Granada, Jaén, Murcia and Cáceres.[53] The government no doubt paid attention to their complaints, but implementing their proposals would have been a different matter. Most surveys were carried out through the corregidores, who were the only practical link between central and regional government. The regime of Don Juan on 15 January 1678 ordered corregidores to make a survey of the commerce of the realm, and on 14 June the same year ordered them to report on cases of depopulation.[54] Their reports, if made, have not survived. Special commissions were sometimes issued, to government officials rather than to corregidores. Such were, for example, the immensely valuable survey conducted by the council of Finance in 1683, and the regional survey of Andalucia conducted by the same body in 1693. If the ministers of Charles II are to be criticised, it is not for a lack of effort to find out the state of the realm and its most pressing needs.

In other parts of Spain representative government continued as normal. Navarre celebrated Cortes during the reign in 1665, 1666, 1675, 1677, 1678, 1680, 1684, 1686, 1688, 1691, 1692 and 1695.[55] The Cortes of Aragon met in two sessions in 1677 and 1684. Valencia had had no Cortes since 1645, but its constitutional life was not thereby cut off. The three estaments of the Cortes of Valencia each elected permanent delegates who met in regular session during the late seventeenth century.[56] The delegates of the third Estate consisted in effect of the non-noble Jurats of Valencia city, which enhanced the already commanding role of the capital in Valencian politics.

## BUREAUCRACY AND THE SALE OF OFFICE

All contemporary critics claimed that there were too many officials in Spain's government. The Venetian ambassador in 1686 reported that there were over 40,000 employed in financial administration; the Imperial envoy in 1687 gave a figure of 50,000 for employees of the councils.[57] Every commentator had his own figures. So expert a person as the financier Francisco Centani, who was subsequently to become one of the Crown's richest bankers, claimed in 1667 that in Castile alone there were 207,000 persons employed in tax administration and that their wages consumed some 37,500,000 ducats.[58] The council of Finance found no difficulty in rebutting these fantastic figures. There was in reality no way of arriving at even an approximate figure for the size of the administrative class, since there was no regular state bureaucracy and most people were in the pay of a wide variety of employers, including the Church.

Criticisms of excessive bureaucracy were invariably directed at the highest level, against the councils. We have seen that constant attempts were made to

31

reduce their size. How was the administrative class recruited? In Castile the upper bureaucracy[59] could be divided into two wings: the *letrado* hierarchy, composed of university-trained jurists, and the more numerous *capa y espada* (cloak and sword) hierarchy. Capa y espada posts were, as the name suggests, occupied by men who were usually of noble status and with a military background. The positions they filled in local government, as corregidores, *alcaldes* and similar officials, had to do with administration and peace-keeping. On the councils they dominated those of War, State and Finance, which required members with long practical experience in war, government and diplomacy. Capa y espada offices required no legal or professional training, were vastly more numerous, and were the most easily subject to bureaucratic abuse. From the time of Ferdinand and Isabella, the Spanish state, like other European monarchies, began to give posts by preference to those who had legal qualifications. The university became the springboard for the letrados, who tended to monopolise all legal posts, not only the Audiencias and Chanceries but also an increasing proportion of places on senior administrative bodies such as the councils. By the seventeenth century most corregidores were letrados.

Aspirants to office wished to participate in administration for the power they would wield, the status they would enjoy, and the salaries they could draw. As in the modern state, bureaucratic growth was inevitable. The demand for office created a certain rivalry between aspirants. A writer of 1679 put the issue forcibly when he claimed that the higher nobility, because of their great debts, 'recognise they cannot live without recourse to employment in the army or politics or the royal household',[60] and were consequently occupying the chief administrative posts, to the detriment of the gentry. In fact the gentry, through their education as letrados, were in Spain as in other countries becoming well entrenched in the state bureaucracy, and their power was increasing.[61] Careers were also open to them in the Church and the Inquisition. A successful career as a jurist led frequently to a noble title, so that Castile, like France, may be said to have developed an aristocracy 'of the robe'.[62]

Since capa y espada posts required no formal qualification, as letrado posts did, they became more vulnerable to purchase and multiplication. Demand for office led in Spain, as it had done in other countries, to the sale of office. At this point a superfluous bureaucracy began to come into existence. The problem was an old one, whose beginnings in Spain have been traced back to the fourteenth century. From about 1540 regular sales of office, tolerated by an impoverished Crown, were begun.[63] So extensive did the confusion and scandal created by venality become, that the Genoese ambassador in 1688 put reform of the system of offices at the top of his list of required changes.[64] The high tide of sales was in the early seventeenth century, but the phenomenon continued into the early nineteenth. The first and most numerous category of sales was in municipal offices, from the very highest (corregimientos and alcaldías) to the lowest. By 1600 alienated municipal offices accounted for three-fourths of the total value of all alienations.[65] In the next major category were administrative and legal offices (*escribanías*) of various sorts. Finally came a broad range of posts and honours, including membership of the councils, which made up in rank and value for their limited number.

Venality was so serious a matter that several honest efforts were made to reduce it. A royal order of 29 May 1669[66] ordered the phasing out of municipal offices with a vote, that had been alienated since 1630. The big cities were excepted from this. Ten years later, in 1679, the council of Castile admitted that though the order had been despatched to the corregidores, 'it is certain that through the failure of the corregidores or the efforts of interested persons, the measure has not been carried out in a great part of the realm'.[67] In any case the council did not have the money to indemnify office holders, and soon the need for more money obliged the government to have further recourse to sales. There was no effective diminution in venality under Charles II.

For an impoverished treasury the granting of honours for cash was one of the few remaining ways of gratifying supplicants or rewarding public service. Consider the case of Don Lorenzo Fernández de Brizuela, who in 1675 asked that his twenty years' service to the Crown be rewarded by a place in the Contaduría Mayor de Cuentas, the important accounting department of the council of Finance. Brizuela had been a personal treasurer to the king and his claim was strong. The council of Finance felt however that the concession would contravene recent orders for reform in the system:

According to the reform ordered in this tribunal [the Contaduria], the places in it should be four, of whom two must by the same reform always be persons who have served in the departments of this council, leaving only two places for others. But so many concessions have been made since the reform was decreed, that the places now exceed twenty-two, of which thirteen or fourteen are currently active. It will thus be many years before the tribunal is reduced to what the reform stipulates.[68]

Here then was a major government department with over five times as many officials as it should have had. The petition by Brizuela was rejected, as we might expect it to have been. A suggestion that he be granted an honorary post, without salary, was also rejected. What is incredible is that only a few months later, in September 1675, an unpaid post on the very same tribunal was granted to the Italian financier Gianbattista Crotta, in return for payment of 16,000 pesos.

Virtually every rank or post in the monarchy was purchasable. Grandeeships, viceroyalties, councillorships, judgeships, were all obtainable for cash. A college in Navarre purchased the privilege of granting degrees in Medicine, even though it had no faculty of medicine.[69] In June 1683 the marquis of Yscar was granted a capa y espada seat on the council of the Indies, in return for 60,000 pesos. In 1687 the government took the seat back, compensating him with some of the cash from another sale (the command of the New Spain *flota*, sold for 100,000 pesos) and with an *encomienda* of Indians in America.[70] These cases — a seat on a council, a naval command — show venality at its highest level. Tenure was brief, and few difficulties arose. The government always took care to sell such posts to persons who were fully qualified.

The real problem caused by venality was its hereditary nature. The overwhelming mass of offices were bought outright by their purchasers, with a view to succession in the family. But purchase of a post in perpetuity, though it seemed to secure hereditary tenure, did not dispose of all obstacles.[71] The holder was allowed to renounce his tenure of the post and pass it to another, but there was a rule that he must survive for twenty days after the renunciation, otherwise the title would lapse. The successor to the post also had to pay charges for the succession, as well as the first half-year's income for the *media anata* tax. Gerónimo Pérez Angulo bought in 1658 the office of *alguacil mayor de alcabalas*, a supervisory tax position, in Medina del Campo. The post carried a salary of 60,000 maravedis a year, and to purchase it in perpetuity Gerónimo paid 750 ducats. When in 1689 his son Joseph wished to succeed, he had to pay the purchase price of 750 ducats for the privilege, and also 25,000 maravedis, representing the *media anata*.

It was common for the twenty-day rule to be specifically set aside in the title to a sale, thus creating undisturbed hereditary tenure. The fortunate holders of such posts might be able to keep an office in their family forever. In July 1687 Jaime Moranzo, a notary and official of the Audiencia of Valencia, applied for permission to renounce his post in favour of his son-in-law. He had served for twenty-six years, and his father and grandfather had held it before him: over a century of service, as the viceroy commented favourably.[72] Ginés Gonzálbez, a royal official in Alicante, reported in 1694 that his post had been in his family since 1589.[73] Don Joseph Orti, a famous and distinguished gentleman who in 1696 was secretary to the estaments of Valencia, claimed that his family had held the post of secretary to the noble estament for over two centuries; in that year he asked to be allowed to pass the post to his nephew.[74] The requests show that alienated offices still had to go through certain procedures when they were passed on. Without such checks, the Crown would have had no control over the suitability of successive holders of important offices.

There was frequently no suitable successor to an alienated office. Provision was made for this. When an office was sold the purchaser could also buy a privilege to have a substitute serve in the actual post (*facultad para nombrar teniente*). The privilege meant, for example, that a rich widow could buy an administrative post without having to serve in it. It opened the way to multiple office-holding. In the 1680s the fee for this privilege was fifty ducats.[75] A similar difficulty arose when the successor to an office was not yet of the legal age. In 1671 Don Manuel de Oms, owner of an hereditary captaincy in a Catalan regiment, died and was succeeded by his twelve-year-old son Antonio. Since he was clearly too young to serve, temporary tenure of the post was granted to a real serving officer.[76] When the age gap was not too great, one could purchase a facultad to increase the candidate's age. This happened, for instance, with Nicolás de Herrera Baca, whose father was a city councillor (*regidor perpetuo*) of Toledo and died in January 1684. Nicolas was unfortunately only sixteen years old and could not succeed to the hereditary post. For a price of eighty ducats his age was increased to the legal minimum of eighteen, which enabled him to succeed without interruption.[77]

The constant demand for offices was met by creating superfluous posts, most of them salaried. Many offices were desired, however, for their status rather than their income: in such cases it was possible to create honorary posts without function or salary. Among the most notorious honorary posts was that of 'secretary of His Majesty'. If we look at the one hundred or so employees, most of them venal, of the council of Aragon in 1690,[78] we find that they included nineteen titular secretaries, not one of whom was a working secretary attached to the council. The practice of appointing these officials dated from the first decade of the century.[79] The title was 'ad honorem and without salary . . . so that from now and for your whole life you may be my secretary', enjoying in theory full power to seal royal documents and with full rights to all the privileges of a royal secretary.[80] Some secretaries were non-functional but with a salary: their number grew so quickly that in 1622 Philip IV decreed that they be restricted to twelve only.

The extent of sale of office in Spain should not be exaggerated. At no time did venality approach the scale on which it was practised abroad, particularly in France. When François Bertaut visited Spain in mid-century he got the impression that sale of office was the exception rather than the rule; and that the few venal offices that existed, in municipal government, were filled by the most worthy men.[81] Sales were more extensive in Castile, where the government had vast patronage; but in the fuero provinces there were far fewer offices within its gift. At a national level venality made no serious impact at all. There was no flourishing market in offices, no complaint of inefficiency and corruption on a wide scale, no fear of a subversion of the social and political order by the accession of the lower classes to posts of distinction. A few such complaints were voiced, but they were exceptional, and based in any case on random examples.

The most significant impact of sale of office was in municipal politics.[82] Venality enabled the most influential posts in local government to fall into the hands of a small local oligarchy, and at the same time enabled the municipalities to remain independent of control from Madrid. In a few towns this certainly led to corruption. In others it reinforced the dedication of the local élite to their town, and strengthened their traditions of public service. An entrenched oligarchy became determined to prevent further proliferation of offices: the city of Granada, replying to the Crown in 1669, advised 'that ministers of councils, Chanceries and Audiencias be reduced to the necessary number and that supernumerary places and duplication of salaries be allowed to die out'; the city of Jaén advised 'reform of excessive public offices, because of the harm suffered by royal finances since holders of office cease to contribute to taxes'.[83] They were not simply the voices of towns with a vote in the Cortes: they represented regional élites that helped to keep government functioning at a time when weak policies at the centre threatened to undermine confidence.

## NOTES

1. Elliott, J. H., *Imperial Spain* (Harmondsworth 1970), pp. 361–7.
2. Ambassador Girolamo Zeno, 1673–8, in **Barozzi, N.**, and **Berchet, G.**, *Relazioni* (Venice 1860), II, 433.
3. Reports of Giovanni Cornaro in 1682 and Carlo Ruzzini in 1695, in *ibid.* pp. 489, 557.

4. Dispatch of 20 May 1689 to Louis XIV, cited in **Weiss, C.**, *L'Espagne depuis le règne de Philippe II* (Paris 1844), II, 371, n.1.
5. See, e.g. **Arnoldsson, S.**, *Leyenda Negra* (Goteborg 1960).
6. Both cited in Kamen, *War of Succession,* pp. 25, 83–4.
7. **Bacallar y Sanna, V.**, marquis of San Felipe, *Comentarios* (Madrid 1957), p. 25.
8. For Navarre and the Basque provinces see **Desdevises du Dézert, G.**, *L'Espagne de l'Ancien Régime* (Paris 1897–1904), I, 18–25, and sources there cited; also **Valdeavellano, L.**, *Instituciones Españolas* (Madrid 1968), pp. 511–13.
9. **Fugier, A.**, *La Junte Supérieure des Asturies* (Paris 1930), pp. 10–11; **Beneyto Pérez, J.**, *Historia de la Administración* (Madrid 1958), pp. 371–2.
10. **Fernández Villamil, E.**, *Juntas del Reino de Galicia* (Madrid 1962).
11. Beneyto Pérez, *op. cit.* p. 373; Pérez, *La Révolution des "Comunidades",* p. 524.
12. For 1680, see below, p. 210. In 1697 the viceroy, Corzana, could not swear in the city because it was in French hands; his nomination was withdrawn and he was replaced in February 1698 by Darmstadt. See **Feliu de la Peña, N.**, *Anales* (Barcelona 1709), III, 452–3.
13. The brief account that follows is based principally on Kamen, *War of Succession,* pp. 242–5, 270–1.
14. For what follows see **García Martínez, S.**, *Els fonaments* (Valencia 1968), Ch. 3; **Lapeyre, H.**, 'L'organisation municipale', *Annales Faculté Lettres de Nice,* 9–10 (1969), 127–37; and **Macanaz, M.**, 'Informe dado al Rey sobre el gobierno antiguo de Aragón, Valencia y Cataluna', in *Regalías* (Madrid 1879), pp. 4 ff.
15. The best survey of the government of Catalonia in the seventeenth century is in Elliott, *Revolt of the Catalans,* Chs. IV–VI.
16. The Chancellor was 'the most important royal official in Catalonia after the viceroy': *ibid.* p. 85.
17. *Ibid.* p. 87.
18. *Ibid.* p. 16.
19. Most of what follows is drawn from the basic but difficult work of **Maura**, *Vida y Reinado de Carlos II* (Madrid 1954). A thinly researched medical view is given by **García Argüelles**, 'Figura de Carlos II' *Actas II Cong. Hist. Med.* (Salamanca 1965), II, 199–232.
20. Maura, *op. cit.* I, 21.
21. **Pfandl, L.**, *Carlos II* (Madrid 1947), p. 386.
22. The standard contemporary source is **Núñez de Castro**, *Sólo Madrid es Corte,* published in three editions in 1658, 1669 and 1675. The 1675 edition was reissued in 1698. My account is drawn from my *War of Succession,* pp. 35–7, and the source there cited.
23. Beneyto Pérez, *op. cit.* p. 355.
24. Brunel, *Journey into Spain,* p. 18.
25. Portocarrero to Torcy, AE:CP (Esp) 114/25.
26. Order of 14 Mar. 1691, AGS Estado 4139.
27. Consultas of 20 Mar. and 15 Dec. 1678, in ACA:CA 923.
28. Consulta of 2 Sept. 1684, in *ibid.* 336.
29. Consulta of 16 Nov. 1693, in *ibid.* 932.
30. Consulta of 15 Feb. 1697, in *ibid.* 340.
31. Consulta of 9 Nov. 1680, AGS:CJH 1028.
32. Consulta of State, 9 Nov. 1705, AE:CP (Esp) 149/134.
33. **Lynch, J.**, *Spain* (Oxford 1969), II, p. 271–2; **Schäfer, E.**, *Consejo real* (Seville 1935–47), I, pp. 275–85.

34. 'Relacion de los ministros que componen el Consejo de Aragon', enclosed in consulta of 7 Dec. 1690, ACA:CA 147.
35. On the *valido* see **Tomás Valiente, F.**, *Los validos* (Madrid 1963), and Lynch, *op. cit.* II, 23–30.
36. Tomás Valiente, *op. cit.* p. 9; Lynch, *op. cit.* II, 28.
37. From Robert Southwell in Madrid, 22 Apr. 1666, PRO:SP 94/50/164.
38. Archbishop of Embrun, the French ambassador, to Louis XIV, 9 Oct. 1665, AE:CP (Esp) 51/320.
39. *Memorias Históricas*, in **Valladares, A.**, *Semanario Erudito*, XIX (Madrid 1788), 3–155.
40. *Ibid.* p. 70.
41. **Escudero, J. A.**, *Los secretarios de Estado* (Madrid 1969), I, 253.
42. *Recueil des Instructions*, ed. **Morel-Fatio** and **Léonardon**, XII, *Espagne* (Paris 1898), 94.
43. *Memorias Históricas*, p. 111.
44. *Ibid.* p. 86.
45. *Ibid.* p. 60.
46. AE:CP (Esp) 203/141.
47. **Mateos, M. D.**, *Salamanca*, in the series *Antiguo Régimen* (Salamanca 1966).
48. **Domínguez Ortiz, A.**, 'Concesiones de votes', in *Crisis y Decadencia* (Madrid 1969), pp. 97–111. For the Cortes in general, see Lynch, *Spain*, II, 86–93.
49. **Danvila, M.**, *Poder civil* (Madrid 1887), VI, 448–55.
50. Consulta of Finance, 9 Nov. 1680, AGS:CJH 1028; Guaro as member of the Sala de Cobranzas in 1680: *ibid*. 1040.
51. What follows is based on Danvila, cited above.
52. See the printed protest by 'Las Ciudades de Voto en Cortes', of 1691, in AHN Consejos 7204/57.
53. Documentation in AGS:CJH 1912. The replies are discussed below, p. 68.
54. Danvila, *op. cit.* (Madrid 1885), III, 238.
55. *Ibid.* p. 232.
56. García Martínez, *Fonaments*, p. 91–2. The deliberations of the *estaments* are well documented in ARV:RC, section Estamentos.
57. Ambassador Foscarini in Barozzi and Berchet, *Relazioni*, II, 530; ambassador Lancier in **Maura**, *Documentos inéditos* (Madrid 1927–31), I, 19.
58. Consulta of Finance, 14 Mar. 1667, AGS:CJH 885.
59. The ablest summary of the subject is Kagan, 'Education and the State', Cambridge 1968, Ph.D. thesis.
60. 'Menor edad de Carlos II', CODOIN 67 (Madrid 1877), 61.
61. **Kagan, R.**, *Students and Society* (Baltimore 1974), Ch. 5 on 'The Letrado Hierarchy'.
62. *Ibid.* p. 86.
63. **Domínguez Ortiz**, 'La venta de cargos' *Anuario Hist. Econ. y Soc.*, 3 (1970), 105–37, is the only available study of Spanish venality. For venality in America, see **Parry, J.**, *Sale of Office* (Berkeley 1953).
64. Ambassador Spinola, in **Ciasca, R.**, *Istruzioni*, V, 174.
65. Domínguez Ortiz, *op. cit.* p. 131.
66. Danvila, *op. cit.* III, 237 gives the date 9 May 1669.
67. Domínguez Ortiz, *op. cit.* p. 125.
68. Consulta of Finance, 22 Jan. 1675, AGS:CJH 979.
69. Domínguez Ortiz, *op. cit.* p. 127.
70. *Ibid.* p. 126.

71. The discussion that follows is based on material in AGS Registro General del Sello, bundle for December 1689.
72. Consulta of Aragon, 2 July 1687, ACA:CA 925.
73. Petition from Gonzálbez, Aug. 1694, *ibid.* 933.
74. Petition from Orti, Jan. 1696, *ibid.* 934.
75. The price is cited in documentation in AGS Cámara de Castilla 1489.
76. Consulta of Aragon, 7 Feb. 1671, ACA:CA 325.
77. Documentation of Mar. 1684 in AGS Cámara de Castilla 1489.
78. See above, p. 26, and n. 34.
79. 'A mas de 80 años que hazen estas mercedes': 'Relacion de los ministros', ACA:CA 147.
80. From the title granted in 1689 to D. Mathias de Nava, AGS Registro General del Sello, Dec. 1689.
81. 'En Espagne les gouvernemens, les charges de judicature, et les militaires ne se vendent point. . . . Il y en a quelques-unes qui se vendent comme les nostres, et ce sont celles qui sont remplies des plus honnestes gens, et du gouvernement desquels on se plaint le moins . . . Toutes les autres Charges ne se vendent point': **Bertaut, F.**, *Relation d'un voyage* (Paris 1664), pp. 128–33.
82. Domínguez Ortiz, *op. cit.* p. 134.
83. Letters in AGS:CJH 1912.

CHAPTER THREE

# Patterns of Life and Death

The great Spanish epidemic of 1596–1602 confirmed the end of demographic growth in the peninsula and began a century of population disaster. The plague cost over half a million lives.[1] A decade later the expulsion of the Moriscos was under way: some 300,000 Spaniards were driven out of the country.[2] Just over a generation later another onslaught of the plague occurred in 1647–52, this time throughout the Crowns of Aragon and Castile: more than half a million people perished.[3]

The long chain of catastrophe has helped to confirm the impression that Spain in the late seventeenth century was plunging to extinction. Not a single *arbitrista* failed to discuss the population problem in gloomy terms. Writers in the late century repeated the complaints of a previous generation – about loss of manpower to the Netherlands, emigration to America, clerical celibacy, the expulsion of the Moriscos – as though they were still active causes of decay. Fascinated by their own misfortunes, they surrendered to a degree of fatalism that hindered them from entertaining hope. Many of the standard explanations for depopulation were now in fact not valid. Though the Netherlands, for example, was still a major item in the budget, the military establishment there had sharply declined.[4] Commentators who clung to the old attitudes probably felt they were doing so with good reason, since no legislative steps had been taken to cure such problems as emigration and clerical growth. But the most convincing reason for pessimism in the late century was the ten-year outbreak of epidemics from 1676 to 1685, when up to one quarter of a million Spaniards may have died.

The timing of the 1676–85 outbreak is deceptive. It occurred in fact during a period of undoubted demographic recovery. The fatal signs of decay were reversed, population began to rise. The reign of Charles II experienced, for the first time since the great epidemic of 1596–1602, a renewal of hope.

## POPULATION STRUCTURES

Because we know virtually nothing about the Spanish family or its place in society

39

at this period, it is difficult to understand the way of life of ordinary Spaniards. The basic domestic unit, called a *vecino* by census makers at the time, was almost certainly an extended rather than a nuclear family. The number of persons represented by a vecino tended to vary according to each census. In 1741 an Aragonese official reported that 'those of us who are experts in *vecindarios* agree that each vecino must represent if not five persons then at least four, including servants and children'.[5] The equivalent of a vecino half a century earlier was probably just over four persons, as in the Basque census of 1704 which gave 4.1 persons per household.[6] The actual number of persons in the household was certainly over five, since censuses ignored young children and infants. We cannot deduce much from such indications, since a vecino was little more than an *average* demographic unit useful to demographers and tax-collectors, and did not pretend to reflect the real size of Spanish households.

Some foreign visitors thought that Spaniards had small families. Bertaut in mid-century reported that 'children are not very numerous there'; Lady Ann Fanshawe, in Madrid in 1665, said that Spaniards 'seldom have many children'.[7] They were not wholly mistaken. The general pattern of Spanish families probably differed little from that of France and England.[8] In late sixteenth-century Valladolid young people had tended to marry early, girls at about twenty, men at about twenty-five. In the mid-seventeenth century isolated samples from Valencia and Saragossa show that girls were still marrying fairly young.[9] But by the late century in rural Galicia the marriage age was higher, girls marrying at twenty-four to twenty-seven, men at twenty-three to twenty-six, a reversal of the normal pattern for men to be older.[10] In the Galician parish of Hio a look at over 200 marriages in the period 1690–1789 shows that the average length of a marriage was over twenty-nine years. Even so, over 47 per cent of marriages were interrupted by death before the family had been 'completed', that is, before the end of the wife's fecund period. To preserve the unity of the family, remarriage was normal. Most widowers who remarried did so within two years, as they also did in Pedralba in Valencia; of 118 marriages contracted here between 1623 and 1675 one in three was a remarriage.

Wives in Galicia completed their family and had their last child at about forty-one years. A completed family managed to have, on average, 5.7 children. If uncompleted families are put into the picture, the average number of children per family falls to just over 4.5. Only about 4 per cent of completed families had ten or more children. As a rule, then, families were not large. A survey of the city of Córdoba in 1683 showed that nearly 58 per cent of families had no more than two children, an additional 32 per cent no more than four.[11] In the same period in Talavera de la Reina the number of legitimate live births per married couple was 2.8.[12] In Pedralba the average family had 4.2 children.

The marriage cycle everywhere followed the agricultural seasons. Early winter, from November to February, was a favourite choice: it coincided with the end of the harvest season and went up to the beginning of Lent, when marriages could not be solemnised. Early spring, depending on the work commitments of the population, was another favourable time. In Talavera in the late century most children were born in January and February; in the area of Xallas in Galicia the peak of births was in March. Wives tended to conceive immediately after marriage. Pedralba, where the marriage age was younger, is an exception: there the first child came after about twenty months. In Xallas there was an interval of 26.4 months before the second child was born; in Pedralba it was thirty-two months.

Survival was the first great human trial in pre-industrial Europe. Lorenzo Sánchez de Paramo, a farmer by profession but also an official of the local Inquisition, was born and raised in the village of Fuensalida (Toledo). At the age of twenty-four, in 1648, he married a local girl and had eleven children. Six of these died before they were three years old.[13] Juana Vázquez, of Barcelona, was born in 1642: 'she had ten brothers and sisters and all died in infancy.'[14] Esteban Núñez lived in Málaga, where in 1632 he married his first wife: she bore him nine children, and all died before they were two months old.[15]

In Galicia the life expectancy of a child at birth was about thirty-five years. If the child was lucky enough to survive the first year, expectancy rose to above forty. Highest child mortality was in the first five years of life. About 40 per cent of children died before the age of ten; over 54 per cent died before they were twenty. In Pedralba the loss was slightly lower: two out of every five children could expect to die before the age of twenty. These appalling figures were normal. They are similar to data for Valladolid and Palencia in the late sixteenth century. They make it possible to say, for Spain as for Beauvais in France in the same period, that two live births were necessary to produce one adult life.

The birth rate varied according to area and period, but was generally positive in the late seventeenth century. In one parish of Granada the annual rate from 1669 to 1677 was 48.9 per thousand, from 1692 to 1701 it was 37.7 per thousand.[16] These rates may reflect the residual Morisco component in the population of Granada, but are not seriously at variance with the known expansion of the period, touched on below. In Xallas, for instance, the population increase from 1598 to 1651 was 25.7 per cent, but from 1651 to 1708 was as high as 60.6 per cent.

In Catholic Spain, as elsewhere in Europe, many young couples did not wait for marriage before going to bed together. In the village of Abanqueiro, in Galicia, 7.5 per cent of children were born within seven months of the wedding. In another nearby village, Entrecruces, the rate was 3.8 per cent. Illegitimacy in this area in the late century was about 4.1 per cent. The level was the same in other parts of Galicia, but remained fairly high for Spain. In Talavera, by contrast, the illegitimacy rate between 1660 and 1700 was seldom above 2.5 per cent, and in the epidemic years of the 1680s was as low as one per cent. We know from the example of Belmonte in Aragon that it was common for marriages to be consummated before the ceremony in church. On the basis of his pastoral visit to the town in April 1690 the archbishop denounced 'abuses by which those who are engaged to be married enter the houses of the fiancees before contracting marriage, with frequency and familiarity, sometimes under the eyes of the parents, other times without their noticing, whereof ensue many offences against God under the cloak and pretext of future marriage, thus beginning the married state in a manner deeply offensive to Our Lord God and exposing the fiancees to the danger of the loss of *honra* should their fiances fail them, leave the pueblo, or change their minds'.[17]

In the present state of our knowledge it is unwise to assume that any of the regional evidence we have cited is typical of Spain as a whole. Unusual local factors, such as the high level of emigration (in Galicia) or the presence of a population of Moorish origin, complicate the situation. Whatever variations may have existed, there can be little doubt that Spain was biologically a European country: its patterns of birth, marriage and death did not differ significantly from those of France and England.

## THE REVERSAL OF THE DEMOGRAPHIC TREND

'Under Charles II the Spanish people enjoyed a relative rest that would have allowed them to make good their losses', had other disasters not befallen. 'Despite everything, it is possible that the population of Castile in 1700 was somewhat higher than it was a half century earlier.'[18] With these words a distinguished Spanish historian in 1963 ventured a conclusion for which at the time little real evidence existed. Later work has made it clear that the slow recuperation of Spain's population did indeed begin in the reign of the last Habsburg. 'From the 1680s', it has been claimed, 'demographic growth was common throughout Spain.'[19] It would be more correct to push this date back by twenty years, into the 1660s. A rough indication of the trend in the late century may be seen in the towns of Old Castile, where population decline was notorious. Figures supplied by the nineteenth-century archivist Tomás González give us the picture shown in Table 3.1 (in vecinos). The figures justify the standard image of

Table 3.1

|  | 1591 | 1693 | % loss |
|---|---|---|---|
| Valladolid | 8,112 | 3,637 | − 55.2 |
| Medina del Campo | 2,760 | 942 | − 65.8 |
| Medina de Rioseco | 2,006 | 1,330 | − 33.7 |
| Avila | 2,826 | 965 | − 65.8 |
| Peñaranda | 815 | 690 | − 15.3 |

a catastrophic decline in Castilian population, with the reign of Charles II at the bottom of the trough. Let us, however, produce a different range of figures (Table 3.2), giving data for the years 1683 and 1693 as percentages of data for the year 1646.[20] Except for Avila, which continued to shrink, the figures suggest that after mid-century the towns began to expand, with a check to expansion only after 1683, caused by the epidemic of that period. Though the population of the towns in 1693 was well below its level of 1591, a half century of recovery had been taking place.

Table 3.2

|  | 1646 | 1683 % | 1693 % |
|---|---|---|---|
| Valladolid | 3,000 | + 33 | + 21 |
| Medina del Campo | 650 | + 52 | + 45 |
| Medina de Rioseco | 1,100 | – | + 21 |
| Avila | 1,123 | + 5 | – 14 |
| Peñaranda | 449 | + 66 | + 54 |
| Arévalo | 254 | + 48 | + 32 |

The pattern indicated is confirmed by evidence for every other part of Spain. Few areas were as fortunate as the Xallas region of Galicia, where growth between 1651 and 1708 was, as we have seen, as high as 60.6 per cent. In general the expansion was very slow, and frequently interrupted by demographic crises. A typical area in this respect was the province of Segovia, where recovery after mid-century took place 'very slowly and with frequent reverses'.[21] Data for twenty-seven towns and villages in the province show a steady increase in the number of baptisms from a ten-year index of 67 in 1650–59 to one of 78 in 1700–09.[22] These moderate figures mask considerable growth in some towns: in seventeen of the towns the general increase in baptisms over the same period was from an index of 54.6 to one of 81.4.

In Fuensaldaña (Valladolid), a village which in 1683 had only about 395 people and was described as being 'in a poor state, both in circumstances and population',[23] the registers show a steady rise in births from about 1665, interrupted only by the epidemic of 1683.[24] The seven settlements in the comarca of Valldigna (Valencia) had a total of 725 vecinos in 1609, just prior to the expulsion of the Moriscos. By 1646 the impact of the expulsion was such that only three towns remained, with a total of 235 vecinos, a fall of 67.6 per cent. But after this there was a decisive recovery: by 1692 the population had increased by 50 per cent.[25] In the parish of El Salvador in Orihuela city, a birth-rate index of 100 for the five years 1625–29 fell to 67 in 1650–54, thanks to the great epidemic of 1648, but rose to 100 by 1685–89 and to 109 by 1695–99.[26] In Catalonia the evolution was similar. In the three major cities of Barcelona, Gerona and Lérida the birth-rate between 1656 and 1700 improved by between 20 and 30 per cent.[27]

These examples come from both urban and rural areas. They are evidence that demographic decay was no longer a blight on the countryside. The pattern that emerges is one of population expansion throughout Spain until the end of the sixteenth century, then a decline in the first half of the seventeenth century, reaching its lowest point in the mid-century plagues. Thereafter a slow recovery took place in the late seventeenth century, as a preparation for the more rapid advances of the eighteenth. The demographic crisis in Spain had various causes, but can be identified most closely with the two great epidemics located in the period 1596 to 1652.

The development of the birth rate in Spain is charted for a number of towns in Figure 3.1. The towns are located in the general map, Figure 3.2.

43

Fig. 3.1  Growth in the birth-rate in late seventeenth-century Spain

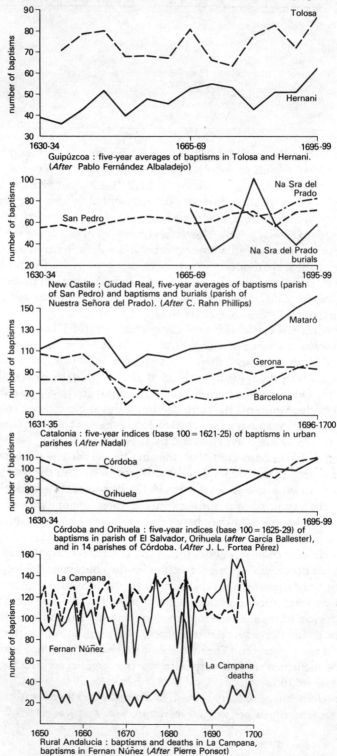

Guipúzcoa : five-year averages of baptisms in Tolosa and Hernani.
(*After* Pablo Fernández Albaladejo)

New Castile : Ciudad Real, five-year averages of baptisms (parish
of San Pedro) and baptisms and burials (parish of
Nuestra Señora del Prado). (*After* C. Rahn Phillips)

Catalonia : five-year indices (base 100 = 1621-25) of baptisms in urban
parishes (*After* Nadal)

Córdoba and Orihuela : five-year indices (base 100 = 1625-29) of
baptisms in parish of El Salvador, Orihuela (*after* García Ballester),
and in 14 parishes of Córdoba. (*After* J. L. Fortea Pérez)

Rural Andalucia : baptisms and deaths in La Campana,
baptisms in Fernan Núñez (*After* Pierre Ponsot)

Fig. 3.2  Epidemics of the late seventeenth century in Spain.

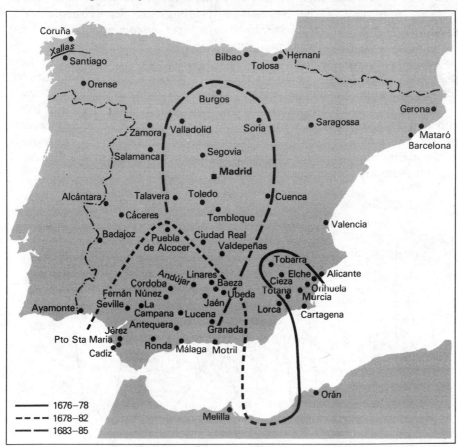

The fact that a reversal of the population trend took place at the very same time as the major epidemics of 1676–85 is testimony to the health of the Spanish people. Negative factors which historians have emphasised in the case of other countries, were notably absent in Spain. Birth control and abortion were practised, but on a negligible scale, and seem not to have made any impact on population figures.[28] Exposure of infants, most of whom were taken into hospitals, was a horrifyingly successful form of population control, since most of them died.[29] It is possible that most exposed children were illegitimate. The impact of their death on population trends was negligible. Public sanitation in Spain was sharply criticised by foreign travellers, but the population, particularly in Madrid,[30] had become accustomed to it.

Short-term crises were a regular feature of the pre-industrial economy and possibly the principal brake on growth. Even in good years Spaniards relied on internal trade to bring an adequate food supply. Bad years were like a surgical operation, cruel but quick. One local subsistence crisis occurred in Galicia in 1693. The city council of Santiago reported on 'the great lack of food and

45

supplies . . . reaching such an extremity that most of the people have died of hunger, and most of the houses and dwellings are depopulated'.[31] The exaggerations reflected a real crisis. In Xallas most of the conceptions of 1693–94 were wiped out in the infant mortality of 1694–95. There were thirty-eight marriages in the parishes in 1691, and only twelve in 1695. The combined effects of war and of famine can be seen in the repeated disasters suffered by the Catalan fortress of Gerona in the late century. Figure 3.3 shows how the nationwide famines of 1678 and 1684, aggravated by the siege of 1684 and the war in 1696, threatened the birth rate. A subsistence crisis that remains to be studied was that of 1699, when most of central Castile suffered severe famine: there were uprisings in the major cities, including Madrid. In Talavera de la Reina, it was the year of highest mortality in the whole seventeenth century.[32]

Fig. 3.3 Subsistence crises in Gerona (Catalonia), 1670–1700. (After Nadal.)

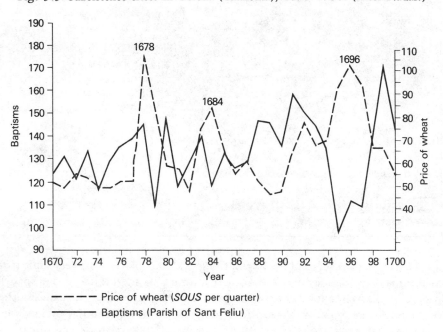

---- Price of wheat (*SOUS* per quarter)
—— Baptisms (Parish of Sant Feliu)

## THE EPIDEMICS OF THE LATE CENTURY

I have not offered in these pages any estimate of the total Spanish population, for the simple reason that all existing estimates have an unacceptable range of error. The global figures used by historians suggest a total Spanish population of 8.1 million in 1591 and 7.5 million in 1717.[33] Both figures are inspired guesses. The situation is even worse for the seventeenth century. The three great plague epidemics of 1596, 1647 and 1676 created such havoc as to make all global population estimates useless and out of date. The problems this posed for the government can be imagined. In 1678, according to an arbitrista, 'the council of

Castile says that there are in these realms of Castile and Leon 5,333,000 persons',[34] but the figures cited were for 1630. It would seem that the government was forced to work with data that ignored the impact of the mid-century epidemics. Tax assessments, unless revised, were therefore continually out of date and unfair. In such a situation, the historian can only resign himself to ignorance.

Of the three plague epidemics the last was the least severe. It was preceded in the reign of Charles II by other less extensive illnesses. In the early autumn of 1672 a fever spread through the regions of Castellón, Valencia, Alicante and Orihuela. The incidence was serious: doctors reported the case of a town of eighty households which had 480 patients, or virtually the entire population. But the authorities were not alarmed, since few died. In the town of Nules the mortality rate among patients was 5 per cent; in general it was more like 4 per cent.[35] Other evidence of illness in these years is vague and undocumented.[36] In the Málaga area in 1674 there was an outbreak of *catarro*, probably influenza, in which some eight thousand are supposed to have died.[37]

In mid-June 1676 the authorities in Cartagena reported a growing number of patients with suspected signs of the plague. In the council of Castile it was suggested that the illness was 'possibly caused by the bad diet that the poor have had this year, or by some clothing brought in by some English ships, or that brought from Algeria by captives'.[38] There were few deaths, so the doctors were unable to confirm whether the outbreak was contagious, though one of them described the symptoms as 'fever . . . with tumours behind the ears and on the finger-tips'. The outbreak died away during the winter, with no cases in December or January. Officials from the city of Murcia visited Cartagena late in January, agreed that the outbreak was over and allowed trade to resume in mid-February. On 11 April 1677 a report from the village of Fuente Alamo, near Lorca, stated that a resident had brought back clothing from Cartagena and had died of a boil within twenty-four hours. On the 20th a letter from Cartagena's alcalde mayor arrived in Murcia, reporting that the contagion had returned and that twenty-nine people had died of it in the preceding week. The city immediately ordered all its gates closed, forbade all further entry, and ordered out everybody who had entered from Cartagena in the preceding forty days.[39]

The sequence of events took on a fatal inevitability. The city of Cartagena had deliberately minimised the extent of the contagion in order to preserve its trade with the world outside.[40] Murcia followed the same path. The municipal minutes for 26 May record the receipt of a letter from neighbouring Orihuela, which sent a doctor and surgeon 'to look into the sicknesses which our residents are said to be suffering'. Murcia agreed 'to welcome the said gentleman, and to satisfy the city of Orihuela about the health of the citizens of this city'. The real situation behind this pretence put on by the city council, may be seen from the report of two doctors from Alicante who inspected Murcia that very week. In one hospital, they reported,[41]

we found two who had died, with boils and carbuncles. In the afternoon we visited the sick from the parishes of San Pedro, San Antolin and San Andrés and saw over thirty sick

47

with boils, inflammations and carbuncles (and this at a time when they told us there were barely six patients). Not to mention four others whom we found dead, whom their doctors thought were still alive. . . . It is claimed that since the outbreak began, which was on Palm Sunday, until now, the dead amount to thirty. We have found the numbers much higher, because the night before we arrived ten died (a pharmacist told us this); and seven on the day we arrived, as the city doctors admit; and four the next day, all from the illness, without counting those already mentioned and excluding cases we don't know of. All are buried at night: the sacraments are carried in silence and no bell is tolled when anyone dies, so that nobody may know. What is certain is that the deaths are very rapid: many died on the second day, others on the third, the longest was till the seventh; some with boils, others with carbuncles and black spots, others with boils and two or three carbuncles, others with inflammations, and finally others with none of these. It is certain that it is contagious.

The first admission of 'contagious illness' in the municipal minutes was on Tuesday 1 June 1677, when there was a proposal to postpone the public celebration of the feast of Corpus Christi. After this, action was rapid. Patients were gathered at the Hospital General of Nuestra Señora de Gracia; entry into the city was controlled, infected clothing destroyed, and food supplies gathered in for what could be a state of siege. A report from the city to the council of Castile stated that 'in the week from the 15th to 22nd June there died 87 persons, leaving in the hospital 56 still sick and 29 convalescing; in the next week there were 120 deaths, with 48 sick and 60 convalescing'. The epidemic drifted into adjacent country areas, notably to the town of Totana. By November it had died away. On Saturday 13 November the city council ordered its doctors to proclaim a state of good health.[42]

In spring 1678 the infection spread northwards and into the kingdom of Valencia. It had not, however, ceased in Murcia. Throughout the spring there were scattered cases, and as late as Tuesday 9 August there is this entry in the municipal minutes: 'It is agreed that there is a recovery in health from the contagious infection, for since the 25th July, when the doctor who came from Madrid to help cure the sick in the hospital died, there have been no illnesses or deaths.'[43] By this time the chief concern was Orihuela. On 27 April that city had written to Murcia to deny rumours of infection, saying that 'they enjoy perfect health and that the rumours are spread by towns ill-affected to Orihuela'. The facts were, of course, quite otherwise. From mid-April citizens had been emigrating from Orihuela. On 13 May Murcia published an order expelling from its confines anyone who had come from Orihuela within the preceding week. At the same time they sent a team of doctors to Orihuela to make a report on victims of the illness. Their exhaustive examination of thirty-nine cases was put before the city council on 20 May. Some of the evidence was as follows:

We visited a child, son of a mace-bearer, aged ten, in the third day of his illness. He had a boil under his right arm as large as two hazel-nuts, and an outbreak all over his body of black spots like pennies. He was delirious and had a carbuncle on his left arm. He died later.

In the suburbs, Diego Rodríguez, aged thirty, had continuous fever; a carbuncle on his right buttock, and a pustule; difficulty in urinating and great loss of strength, in the third day of his illness.

In the house of Francisco Navarro, girdle-maker, he said his three sons had died within six hours, with an outbreak of spots.

A youth of eighteen, in his fourth day, with continuous fever, great loss of strength, vomiting of a green colour, and a boil on his left groin. He died later.

The wife of Francisco Navarro, aged thirty-six. With continuous fever, vomiting of a green colour, great loss of strength, in a coma and with a boil on her right groin, in the first day of her illness.

Within the last month over 120 persons have died of the same symptoms and the same illness, all in the third or fourth day of their sickness, without more than about ten persons recovering from it since it began.

Faced with this evidence, Murcia declared a state of infection to exist in Orihuela. The latter in the same month declared itself infected, and continued to suffer the epidemic until September.[44] Not until 28 January 1679, however, did Murcia resume trade with it. Fortunately for other towns in Valencia, the infection did not spread north. But the toll it left behind was considerable. A survey made of Murcia in August 1678 showed that in its eleven parishes a total of 1,098 had died and 286 had recovered. The biggest toll had been in the parish of Santa María, where 226 had died and only fifty had recovered. In the parish of San Antolin 185 died and forty-seven recovered. The overall figures show that 80 per cent of all patients died. But if we assume the total numbers in the city to have been about 25,000, the mortality rate per head of population was only just over 4 per cent. The range of the epidemic of 1677–78 had been limited to the towns within the area enclosed by Cartagena, Murcia, Orihuela, Elche, Tobarra, Cieza, Mula and Totana.

In the summer of 1678 there was a new outbreak, to the west, in Andalucia. It was not, as has been supposed,[45] a direct continuation of the previous one. On the other hand, it may have been substantially the same infection, transmitted not through Spain but from Africa.[46] On 28 May 1678 a ship put into Málaga from Orán (where there had been a plague infection until 14 August 1677, when good health was declared). Some sailors lodged in the city; two days later a boy died in the same house. Soon there were five other victims: their symptoms were malignant pustules, boils on the groin and under the arm, and fever. Three eminent doctors certified that the symptoms were the same as those of the great plague of 1649. But a heated controversy ensued, because two university professors of Granada denied that the infection was plague. Eventually the gravity of the situation was recognised and the council of Castile sent a doctor to supervise arrangements. The impact of the outbreak is not clear. In one of the hospitals, the Caridad, there were in all 1,213 patients, of whom 896 died.[47] Several other hospitals also had many patients. In one mid-December week the city had 296 cases on its hands, but most were recovering and there had been only thirteen deaths that week.

The problem was to contain the infection. An elaborate double cordon was thrown round Málaga. It was manned by three hundred guards on horseback, and five hundred on foot, with specially pitched quarters, at a cost of over 29,000 escudos. The council of Castile also gave grants to other towns to maintain their own cordons. The precautions did not stop the plague spreading rapidly. By

49

December it was in Vélez and Ríogordo. In the latter, a town of about 2,000 people, 103 had died by the 20th.[48]

For the next few years the epidemic was destined to come in waves, large ones that engulfed entire populations, but also small ones that attacked one year, withdrew for a while, then returned a subsequent year with renewed force. In Málaga, for example, in the third week of December 1678, 'this city appears in the opinion of doctors to be healthy: the patients in hospital, who are less than ten, are being treated with viper's grass water and bezoar stone, and the illness is being sweated out'. In the second week of January 1679 there were ten deaths. On 5 July it was reported that 'today, the day of our great protector and apostle Santiago, it has pleased God that the hospital be closed, for there are no sick in the city'.[49] By April 1680, however, the plague was back again.[50] These irregular attacks confused the authorities, aggravated the situation, and gave the epidemic an appearance of immense duration. In the next few pages we shall consider first the chronology of the outbreaks, then their social impact, and finally the consequences for demographic growth.

In spring 1679 the plague was active in most of the bigger cities of eastern Andalucia, such as Málaga and Ronda. In June it finally hit Granada despite a cordon round the city. I have been unable to look into its impact on the city, but there is no doubt that the effect on the area was very serious. The village of Cañar claimed to have had 100 households before the epidemic; it lost 117 dead, or two-fifths of its population, and that year there was nobody to reap the harvest.[51] The town of Padul had had 110 households: it lost 204 dead.[52] In the area of Pinos del Valle out of sixty households a total of 191 people, or nearly two-thirds of the population, died.[53] Albuñuelas claimed to have had 200 households in 1679 and to have suffered 260 deaths, a loss of well over one-fourth. To the town 'it seemed as though the end of the world had come'.[54]

A contemporary writing in October from Lucena, to his brother, has left us a graphic if not wholly reliable impression of the impact of the epidemic:[55]

The plague went to Málaga and made off with two thousand people and was very mild; it went down to Antequera and made off with twenty-four thousand people, and then it came to Lucena, where its harvest has been very light, up to about three hundred people. Yesterday, Monday, the hospital in this city was closed, but the city is not completely free of it. It has pleased God that neither in Málaga nor in Lucena has anyone of quality been taken. Today we are all full of thanks to God. There have been many other adversities that I shall not bore you with. We do not yet have trade with any other city. Granada and the towns in its region have been hit; they say that in Granada over twenty-six thousand persons have died, and very few cities and towns in Andalucia have escaped suffering this epidemic. Countless are said to have died in Seville, among them eleven doctors. In Antequera many religious and nuns died.

The rumour of 'countless' deaths in Seville was certainly false. No extraordinary measures were taken by the city council, apart from the very strict cordon around the city.[56] The impression that Seville had a lucky escape is confirmed by the chapter of Seville cathedral. In July 1680 the chapter ordered daily prayers 'for God to preserve us from the threat of the plague'. On Sunday 22 February 1682 public thanks were given in the cathedral for 'the goodness and singular mercy of

God our Lord to this city in preserving it from the contagious epidemic that has been raging all round it for over six years'.[57]

By the end of October 1679 the contagion had died away. Granada declared itself healthy on 6 October; the last plague death in Motril was on 1 October, in Antequera on 27 August, in Ronda on 10 December. Málaga in August celebrated the end of the onslaught: 'In the fourteen months of suffering, during ten of which there was open hospital, the deaths both inside and outside the city were less than 2,000, and of these up to 25 July only 1,253 died in the hospital.'[58] Trade resumed. In Madrid the extensive cordon that had been set up in July was lifted in November, though guards remained posted round the city. That winter, once again, the plague followed its custom of hibernating.[59]

In spring 1680 the infection returned to the very same regions, but in a milder form. Málaga continued to get cases, but at the rate of only eight or nine a day, 'which', reported the council of Castile, 'is a small number for so crowded a town'. A great many smaller towns were affected, which continued to give cause for alarm. Among those infected this summer were (near Lucena) Benamexi, Cabra, Doña Mencia, Rute, Puente de Don Gonzalo, Priego and Aguilar de la Frontera; (around Málaga) Ronda, Marbella, Istan, Alora, Cartama, Casarabonela and Torrox. There were also dangerous signs of the epidemic extending beyond the main Málaga region, since Marchena, to the west near Seville, and Andújar, to the north beyond Jaén, were both invaded by the contagion this year. The town of Madrid set up its cordon again in June. By November 1680 the menace had again retreated. Lucena, which had prematurely declared itself healthy in March, continued to get cases up to August, but none thereafter. Andújar had no cases after 28 July.

The plague, which had hovered over this part of Andalucia for two whole years, now began to move away. But it had left enormous scars. The city of Antequera later claimed to have suffered 30,000 dead in 1679 and 1680 alone.[60] This was certainly an exaggeration, since the city's whole population was barely 30,000; but the figure may possibly have included its rural areas. Towards the north of the epidemic zone the village of Lupión, near Baeza, had sixty-two households at the beginning of 1680, consisting of 327 persons. Of these, 180 persons (55 per cent) died in the outbreak.[61] The fate of Motril is outlined in a consulta of the council of Finance of October 1680:[62]

Of 1,715 households that it has, the contagion affected 1,436, the remaining 279 being spared because they abandoned their homes. Since the declaration of health only 619 have been resettled, the others being left deserted and ruined. . . . And of ten thousand *marjales* of land only four hundred have been tilled this year. . . . The two hospitals were open for almost six months, with a constant attendance of one thousand patients, and there died over nine thousand persons, whose medical costs came to 343,147 reales.

If these figures seem excessive, so too may seem the claim of Granada to have lost 40,000 people in the epidemic.[63] But it is unlikely that the truth was stretched too far in documents that had to face close scrutiny by government officials. Losses were undoubtedly extensive. Casarabonela (Málaga) lost 250 persons within forty days in 1680,[64] a major shock by any standards.

51

To the sufferings of the year 1680 must be added at least one further natural disaster. On Wednesday 9 October 1680 a major earth tremor shook Andalucia. The epicentre seems to have been near Málaga, but it was also bad in Jaén, Seville and Córdoba; and strong enough to be felt in Madrid. Warnings of such an event had already occurred in 1679: the Savoyard merchant Lantéry in Cadiz, for example, reported a tremor lasting two days.[65] The impact on Málaga, already hard pressed by the plague, was catastrophic.[66] The four parishes of the city had a total of 4,296 houses: 852 were demolished, 1,259 rendered uninhabitable, and many others left unsafe. In brief, half the city was wrecked, and at least thirty-five people were killed. Another casualty nearby was the town of Cartama, which had also suffered the plague. Of its 277 houses 145 collapsed in the tremor and a further 120 had to be rebuilt: a casualty rate of over 95 per cent.[67]

The plague broadened its appetite in 1680 and reached the Atlantic. 'In this year at the beginning of July', Lantéry wrote in his memoirs, 'the plague was discovered in Puerto de Santa María, although the inhabitants continued to deny it, and attempted to stone Dr da Costa, the Portuguese doctor of the dukes [of Medina Sidonia] and the best known physician in Andalucia, because he declared that it was the plague they were suffering.'[68] The infection was raging at the same time in Melilla, the Spanish fortress on the coast of north Africa, where some 200 people died in the summer of 1680. In Puerto de Santa María it was particularly virulent. The only details I have found, for the week 30 November to 7 December, show that 269 more people contracted the plague in that time, 201 died of it, the hospital had 209 patients, and 154 were recovering.[69] Early in 1681 the infection reached Cadiz. Thankfully, reports Lantéry, 'it pleased His Divine Majesty that it did not touch any merchant house. . . . The day of the Magdalen, 22 July, it ceased completely.'[70]

By early 1681 the plague had established itself over the greater part of Andalucia, within all the territory ranging from the Sierra Morena to the Atlantic. The main towns affected were Cadiz, Jérez and Puerto de Santa María in lower Andalucia, and Jaén, Ubeda and Baeza in upper Andalucia; but incidental outbreaks continued throughout the south. Illora (Granada) lost 771 dead out of 500 households, a fall of some 31 per cent.[71] The fate of the town of Jódar (Jaén) was expressed as follows in a memorial it sent to the council of Finance:[72]

From 20 January 1681, when God our Lord permitted its citizens to suffer the contagion, up to 10 September, the illnesses were so rigorous and fierce that they spared no house, whether poor or rich, in the population, and all were totally ruined and destroyed. When this illness began a census was made of all persons, large and small, female and male, and there were 2,135 persons. When the contagion was seen to have ceased another was made, and it was found that 1,055 had died. Those who were left were wholly destroyed and ruined. No way is left for them to maintain themselves, because most of them were touched by the infection, and in order to cleanse themselves and escape with their lives they not only burned all the clothes they were wearing but also all the furniture in their houses, and went out as fugitives into the countryside for their period of quarantine, with no help or succour but the little they could find from the livestock they came across, and cutting down olive branches to build shelters. Many of them were in such a needy state that after the quarantine they stayed out in the fields so that their clothes should not be burnt, since they had nothing else to wear. Those who entered the town had their clothes burnt, and had to wait for charity. And since this town consists of poor farmers, whose income was in the sown fields, they could not harvest it, and so the whole harvest was lost.

After the winter of 1681–82 the infection seemed to have died away. The cordon was removed from around Madrid and public thanks were given. But in April there was a further outbreak, principally in the province of Córdoba, affecting the city itself and also the towns of Montilla, Castro del Río, La Rambla, Espejo and Alcaudete.[73] By June there were cases noted in Puebla de Alcocer,[74] causing great concern in Madrid. But this was the farthest north that the plague ever reached. No serious cases were reported after the end of 1682 and no further areas were invaded. It was the end of a mortal onslaught that had devastated most of Andalucia for four years. It was also the last great epidemic of bubonic plague ever to afflict Spain.

Although the plague disappeared in 1682 it was followed almost immediately by another virulent epidemic. This lasted from 1683 to 1685 and penetrated not only into Andalucia but into Old and New Castile as well. Referred to in documents as the *epidemia general de enfermedades* (general sickness), the evidence suggests that it was typhus. All the major cities of central Spain, from Segovia down to Ciudad Real, and not excepting Madrid, were hit. The general zone of the epidemic extended from Burgos and León as far as Andalucia: the most severe impact seems to have been in the Toledo region. An explicit reference to the nature of the illness can be found in a report on Jódar, in which the 'general sickness of fevers and typhus' is described as 'among the worst experienced in that realm' of Jaén. The causes are not clear. The town of Morón de Almazán (Soria) blamed the outbreak on 'the lack of food'.[75] This is confirmed by the food crisis of these years. A long and persistent drought throughout 1682 and 1683 was broken only in spring 1684, when heavy and torrential rain fell. A further drought followed in 1684 and 1685. Poor food and dry, unhealthy conditions were the ideal setting for illness. There were scattered cases in 1683, reported for instance in Borox (Madrid) and Valencia de Don Juan (León). The latter lost 242 dead between January 1683 and May 1685.[76]

The full fury of the new disease commenced in spring 1684. The two earliest casualties were the towns of Villacañas and Los Yebenes, both in Toledo province. Each dated its casualties from 1 May 1684. For the next twelve months a catastrophe of major dimensions overtook those towns that had been spared the agony of the plague. Some towns, like Linares in Jaén and Albuñuelas in Granada, suffered both plague and typhus: the former complained that 'the general epidemic is no less destructive than the plague'.[77] In the parish of Santa María in Los Yebenes, the annual mortality in the period 1669 to 1677 was between thirty and thirty-eight: in 1684 it was officially 205. In nearby Sonseca a priest wrote: 'During this epidemic, from the first of May 1684 until today the tenth of November, fifty dead infants whose parents remain unknown have been left at the doors of the church.'[78] In Talavera de la Reina, with a population of about 7,500, the recorded deaths in 1684 were over 400.[79] In Segovia the epidemic came in the summer and autumn and severely hit the city's industries.[80]

From Madrid an English diplomat wrote: 'We have had some young persons of quality dye of late, and generally our Court is full of catharrs, tabardillos, feavers and some other diseases, much beyond any other former years.'[81]

By its nature the epidemic of 1683–85 was not as terrifying as the plague. It succeeded nevertheless in causing extensive mortality in some areas, especially to the south of Madrid. The toll may be judged by the examples given in Table 3.3.

Table 3.3

| Town | Province | Year before | Year after | % loss |
|---|---|---|---|---|
| | | (in vecinos) | | |
| Astudillo | Burgos | 1680: 559 | 1687: 248[82] | 56 |
| Morón de Almazán | Soria | 1683: 150 | 1685: 71[83] | 53 |
| Castromocho | Valladolid | 1683: 376 | 1692: 271[84] | 28 |
| Padilla de Duero | Valladolid | 1680: 90 | 1692: 35 | 61 |
| Villardefrades | Valladolid | 1683: 200 | 1692: 124 | 38 |
| Melgar | Valladolid | 1676: 263 | 1686: 78[85] | 70 |
| Alcova | Toledo | 1684: 50 | 1687: 12[86] | 76 |
| Gálvez | Toledo | 1683: 153 | 1685: 121[87] | 21 |
| Lillo | Toledo | 1683: 714 | 1686: 385[88] | 46 |
| Tembleque | Toledo | 1684: 1,219 | 1685: 75[89] | 94 |
| El Toboso | Toledo | 1683: 752 | 1685: 403[90] | 46 |
| Villacañas | Toledo | 1683: 589 | 1684: 150[91] | 75 |
| Villanueva de Alcardete | Toledo | 1681: 450 | 1685: 150[92] | 67 |
| Villarrubia de Santiago | Toledo | 1624: 720 | 1686: 277[93] | (62) |
| Carrascosa del Campo | Cuenca | 1677: 528 | 1685: 294[94] | 44 |
| Bolaños | Ciudad Real | 1679: 221 | 1687: 181[95] | (18) |
| Valdepeñas | Ciudad Real | 1683: 1,140 | 1687: 708[96] | 38 |
| Linares | Jaén | 1679: 1,007 | 1687: 636[97] | 37 |

Many other cases are mentioned in the documents. The town of Madridejos (Toledo) claimed that 'in the epidemic of 1684 it was reduced to less than half its population'.[98] Consuegra (Toledo), which in 1685 had about 600 vecinos, lost 2,063 dead in the epidemic the previous year.[99] The city of Ciudad Real, which by its own reckoning had 800 vecinos in 1681, had 1,198 fatalities from 1 May 1684 to 16 January 1685, and the epidemic was still raging.[100] It may have lost nearly half its population.

From 1685 till the end of the reign no major epidemics occurred in Spain. As far as is known, the plague disappeared completely from the country.


## THE IMPACT OF EPIDEMIC

It is a common fallacy that the medical knowledge of this time was so primitive that most epidemics were attributed to plague. The Spanish records make it plain that plague was never declared by mistake: the symptoms were too well known, the consequences of an erroneous declaration too costly. It was more common for everybody to maintain that the infection was not 'plague', a word which was never used in the early stages, if at all. Throughout the years 1677–78 the municipal council of Murcia never once employed the word in its minutes. Doctors, with their reputation at stake, proclaimed the truth as soon as they were certain; but such a declaration was a very serious step, and was always unpopular. In Cartagena in 1677, according to a contemporary report, 'there were many disturbances in the city between the doctors and the people. The latter did not wish an epidemic declared, for in the previous year they had suffered much hunger through the refusal of ships to call; while the former insisted on declaring it.'[101]

There was particular opposition to the declaration of an epidemic as 'contagious'. A town infected with a contagious disease was immediately isolated from its neighbours and denied all commerce with the outside world. It remained in a state of total siege until the emergency had passed. The sudden interruption of normal trade led to severe hardship, not merely for townsmen denied access to places outside, but more specially for the peasantry, who could not sell their produce in the city markets and were forced to watch their crops rot. The natural reluctance of towns to admit a state of plague is illustrated by the city of Baeza, from which a council of Finance official reported in July 1681: 'Today we are in a worse state than ever in this city, which has turned into a hospital. . . . Since I entered it everything has been one long disaster, for the city has kept maintaining that there is no plague, which has never been true, my estimate being that three thousand people have died so far.'[102]

The precautions taken by Madrid in July 1679 to protect itself against the infection then raging in Andalucia, show how a typical cordon operated.[103] Two major cordons of guards were set up to stop all egress northwards from the infected area. The first line was set at various crucial points well south of the river Guadalquivir, the second just south of the city of Ciudad Real. In Madrid all entrances to the city save five were sealed, and day and night patrols were posted. All crossings of the river Tagus (south of Madrid) between Talavera and Toledo were suspended, and others strictly controlled. A well-maintained cordon often guaranteed immunity. Despite its notorious lack of hygiene, Madrid was never infected. Seville escaped similarly in 1681. Thanks to its efficient measures, Archidona, despite being next to afflicted Antequera, remained untouched in the epidemic of 1678–82.[104] Since exit from an infected area was difficult, it followed that few cared to enter one. The problem of food supplies became in these circumstances a major priority. In Murcia in 1677 the chief preoccupation of the authorities was that 'because of the contagion suffered by this city, all the cities, towns and villages of these realms have cut off commerce with it, without allowing us to bring in any supplies and especially wheat, which is what is most needed'.[105] Grain within city limits was sequestrated, but prices soared; the situation was made worse by the very poor harvests of the late 1670s.

Hygiene precautions were exacting, and ruinous. Clothing was commonly singled out as the carrier of infection, and the garments of all recent arrivals in a city were accordingly burnt. In the village of Cañar (Granada) in 1679 all the clothing in the village, which had 100 families, was burnt in an effort to remove the infection. With the additional loss of the harvest, their main source of capital, the villagers could not hope to reclothe themselves without a grant, which the government usually gave in such cases. The purification procedure in an infected house, as laid down by a professor of medicine in Orihuela in 1678, was as follows:[106] clean the patient's bed and burn all his used clothes; other clothing, if silk, to be fumigated in a mixture of pine-resin, incense, colophony and juniper in a coal fire, or if other cloth to be boiled and then aired for nine days; metals to be sponged with vinegar; pictures to be fumigated and aired for six days; books touched by the patient to have their bindings burnt and contents fumigated, all other papers and books to be aired for eight days; all wood touched to be burnt, other wood to be washed with lye mixed with incense and colophony otherwise washed down with lime or vinegar; all walls to be washed down with lime. Towns had purification procedures at every gate, and letters were wiped with vinegar. In Murcia all those having business outside the city in the fields were obliged to carry passes; the wearing of coats or cloaks, which might hide signs of illness, was forbidden; and those in whose house there was infection were to carry a cane-stick to help identification.

The first reaction to a feared or real outbreak was panic. Towns and cities became deserted. In Murcia in 1677 'the greater part of the population fled out into the fields and farms when the plague began, leaving in the city the poorest people and those who by reason of their official duties could not absent themselves'.[107] We have Lantéry's report on Cadiz: 'Every day the fear grew greater, but I was never afraid because I never failed to go out into the streets every day to find out what was going on. There were very few people to be seen. Cadiz seemed deserted.'[108] The flight of the richer and more prominent citizens to the more salubrious countryside helps in part to explain the low fatality rate among them. 'No one of consideration', wrote Lantéry, 'died in the plague.' Many public officials deserted their posts, but the heroism of those who remained stood out the more clearly. In Cartagena in 1676 all the public notaries fled save for one, who was promptly appointed to the highest post in his profession.[109] In Murcia the city council (from which several were absent) publicly thanked its corregidor for his services throughout the epidemic, and proposed that a canon of the cathedral be put forward for a bishopric as a reward; black slaves who had worked in the hospitals were given their freedom.[110] Religious orders were always the most prominent in their devotion to the suffering. Many medical men, like Dr José de Herrera in Cadiz in 1681, worked tirelessly among the sick, in the certain knowledge that their lives too would be forfeit: 'he ate and joked among the sick-beds, and within a few days the infection took him and all his jests to the next world.'[111] Dr Juan de Garivay came from Madrid to help the city of Murcia in its fight and died there in July 1678, the last recorded victim of the plague.

In spite of the emergency and the obvious danger of looting and other crimes against property, there is little evidence of public disorder in the infected towns. The lack of food probably caused the greatest tension. In November 1677, when Murcia sent a supply of wheat to Totana, the shipment was seized by local bandits led by the Menarques brothers.[112]

# THE PORTUGUESE WARS

Epidemics were not the only check to population growth in the late century. A catastrophe with graver and more enduring consequences was brought about by the war with rebel Portugal. No other single event in Castilian history of the early modern period, excepting only epidemics, did more to destroy the country from within. For over a quarter of a century, from the Portuguese revolt in 1640 to the conclusion of peace in 1668, the western half of Castile was ceaselessly subjected to all the rigours of a prolonged military confrontation. At its most intense the conflict involved movement of big armies across the frontier areas. But the long years of low-level conflict were the most ruinous. The impact fell most heavily on the parched, infertile plains of Extremadura.

Every suitable town near the border was turned into a fortress with a small garrison. When not exposed to the demands of their own troops, the towns were subjected to enemy raids. A typical casualty was Ceclavín, near Alcántara and close to the frontier. From 1640 it became a garrison town with a permanent detachment of troops. Almost every other year the Portuguese raided it: in 1665, for example, they made off with 7,000 head of sheep. In 1640 the town had 1,000 households, by 1660 this had fallen to 850, in 1666 it was only 430.[113] The documentation for every town and village near the frontier is similar. In 1674 Burguillos del Cerro, near Jérez de los Caballeros, blamed its decline on the Portuguese 'carrying away cattle and killing and capturing many men; nearly half the houses have collapsed, so that entire streets and quarters are in ruins; and none of this is reflected in the tax-census'.[114] Examples from other places repeat the picture. Casar, near Cáceres, had 900 households in mid-century and only 460 in 1666.[115] Gata, near Alcántara, had 600 households in 1640 and 374 in 1682.[116] Valencia de las Torres, near Llerena, had 600 households in 1640 and 50 in 1667.[117] Valverde del Fresno, just south-west of Ciudad Rogrigo, had 600 households in 1640 and less than 200 in 1667.[118] Garrovillas, near Cáceres, had 1,350 households in 1626 and 758 in 1687.[119] Jaraicejo, near Trujillo, had 584 households in 1628 and 776 houses; in 1687 it had 168 households and of its houses 607 were uninhabited, 'a very considerable decay in a town that was one of the best in its district, all this because of what it suffered during the war with Portugal'.[120] Assuming these estimates to be roughly correct, the rate of population decline in Ceclavín was 57 per cent, in Gata 38 per cent, in Valencia de las Torres 92 per cent, in Valverde 33 per cent, in Garrovillas 44 per cent and in Jaraicejo 71 per cent.

It may be thought that these figures are not representative, since they apply to the smaller towns, which were obviously more vulnerable. Yet the situation was exactly the same in the biggest towns and cities. Brozas, near Alcántara, had over 1,415 households in 1592 and 1,300 in 1644; after the war, in 1692, it had 551, a decline since 1644 of some 57 per cent.[121] The city of Cáceres had 1,428 households in 1594 and 1,053 in 1685, by which date it had 276 ruined dwellings, allegedly as a result of the wars.[122] Of the city of Ayamonte, in the extreme south, it was claimed that 'before the uprising in Portugal it was very prosperous and rich and had over 1,700 households'. In 1676 it had only 600, a decline of nearly 64 per cent.[123] Badajoz, provincial capital and heart of the military effort in Extremadura, had 3,000 households in 1640 and 1,700 in 1691, a fall of 43 per cent.[124] Jérez de los Caballeros, in 1640 a rich and populous city of some 2,000 households, shrank by 1653 to only 700, a diminution of 65 per cent. In 1692 it still had only 835 households.[125]

It would be difficult to exaggerate the ruin caused by this frequently forgotten war. In 1667 when the citizens of the province of Galicia were asked to contribute to a theoretically voluntary *donativo*, the city of Orense, in the name of the towns in its region (*partido*), refused to pay. It alleged its state of poverty, 'all caused by the proximity of the rebel of Portugal eighteen leagues away'. The city and province had therefore 'arrived at the painful position of not being able to serve Your Majesty with anything but their lives'.[126] In the same way the city and province of Zamora in 1680 claimed that their poverty 'arises from the region being poor and unfruitful, and from the wars which lasted so long with Portugal'.[127] The Crown had no option but to accept these excuses. The evidence was so irrefutable that in 1661 the government decreed that all places within five leagues of the Portuguese border should pay no further taxes for the duration of the war.[128] The concession in practice lasted only two years, and taxation resumed in 1663.[129] Lack of money made it necessary to do this. But severe ruin in the frontier areas made it equally necessary to remit tax debts for many years to come.

The impact of the war was not limited only to the provinces near Portugal. The council of Finance issued a gloomy report on the situation in 1664.[130]

The council has discussed it [the state of Extremadura] at great length, and has recognised with great feeling the state of affairs in those realms, and the depopulation and misery occasioned there by the conquest of Portugal; and although it realises that war brings with it so many ills that it is not possible to heal them all, it remains the duty of the council and of Your Majesty's ministers and subjects, to see what can be done by the royal treasury and by the taxpayers.

The billeting of soldiers in Extremadura consumes the entire income from taxes. The lord Don Juan says moreover that there has been continuous quartering of troops, lasting for four and a half months every year, which has eaten up both past and current revenue and drawn on much future revenue, putting a burden even on private resources. . . . And this does not affect the towns of Extremadura alone, for the soldiers are also billeted in a great part of the towns of La Mancha and New Castile where they will also consume all the revenues.

Our desire to find a remedy for such grave disorder makes it necessary for us to represent to Your Majesty that it is not good for things to go on as they have done till now, nor should it happen that the soldiery cause such excessive costs in billeting.

The burden of their own soldiery, if we may believe the towns of Castile, caused as much ruin as the attacks of the Portuguese rebels. A lengthy complaint in 1661 from the towns and villages around the city of Salamanca, which was certainly not close to the war zone, spoke of a loss of half their population within the preceding eight years. The causes, they said, were having to supply men for the campaign; having to pay extra taxes as a substitute for billeting; and having nevertheless to billet cavalry.[131] The consequences of this war, from Galicia which probably suffered most from recruitment of troops, to southernmost

Extremadura, were simple and far-reaching. There was extensive and enduring depopulation. Extremadura lost between one-third and one-half of its population, and remained into modern times one of the most depressed provinces of the peninsula. Poor at the outset, it did not have the natural resources which made it possible for other parts of the peninsula to recover from a demographic crisis. The twenty-five towns and villages in the jurisdiction of the city of Trujillo complained in 1690 that 'since the beginning of the wars with Portugal they have declined to less than half their population and resources'.[132] Apart from human numbers the most striking decline was in the major capital resource of the area, livestock. Navalvillar de Ibor, for example, had 212 plough teams and 18,430 sheep in 1639; in 1690 it had 46 teams and 575 sheep. In Extremadura, then, we are faced not merely by a problem of population decline but by a major disaster to every aspect of the natural and animal environment.

## POPULATION MOVEMENTS

Foreign travellers in Spain always complained of the parochialism of the Spanish and their limited knowledge of the world. In fact, Spaniards were among the best travelled of all European peoples, thanks to their empire. Castilian soldiers served everywhere. 'Has Flanders not been the honoured graveyard of Spaniards?' asked a writer of this time. 'Is Germany not defended and succoured by them? Is not the richest and most populous part of Italy governed by Spaniards?'[133] The same writer suggested that there were more Spaniards living outside Spain than within it. The exaggeration was symptomatic of the general conviction that Spain was being bled to death by emigration. Contemporaries still spoke, for instance, of ruinous emigration to the New World; when in reality there was a perfectly acceptable level of departures to America.[134]

The constant movement of Spaniards within the empire did not occur to the same extent within the peninsula. As in other traditional societies, Spaniards were tied by economic and family interests to the village or comarca in which they grew up. However, rural Spain was probably not as immobile as Pierre Goubert suggests ancien regime France may have been. A crucial distinction must here be made between the experience of the Crown of Castile and that of Aragon. Because of its predominant role in the empire, Castile supplied the overwhelming majority of soldiers for the European army and emigrants for the Indies. The tens of thousands of ordinary people who left in the sixteenth and seventeenth centuries, many of them never to return, came from Castilian villages. By contrast the Crown of Aragon contributed very little to this great outflow of population. The military and settler needs of the empire were therefore the first significant cause of the unusual demographic mobility in Spain. The second major stimulus to movement came from official policy to the Moriscos. The 117,000 Moriscos expelled from Valencia in the early century, for example, were replaced by 22,000 Old Christians from Valencia itself and from other parts of Spain.

The third major reason for mobility, and the one which most concerns us, was economic disequilibrium between the regions. In the seventeenth century this did not take the form, as has sometimes been suggested, of a movement of people from the north to the south or from the centre of the peninsula to the periphery. There is no evidence of any significant redistribution of this sort.[135] Mobility was of two kinds: out of the inhospitable countryside into the towns,[136] a movement which tended to be definitive; and seasonal migration in search of labour. Given the great differences in wealth between the regions, it was inevitable that people should move, if only temporarily, from poorer into richer areas. When the migration assumed large proportions it contributed to the problem of vagabondage.[137]

As far as we know, the two areas with the most substantial rate of emigration were the northern Cantabrian provinces, the most densely populated in the peninsula, and Andalucia, where rural poverty encouraged escape. Many Andalucians no doubt used Cadiz as a means of fleeing to America. Others thronged to the towns: a survey of 14,534 people married in four parishes of Granada in the period 1665–1700 shows that 40.4 per cent of them originated from outside the city.[138] In terms of distance migration was always limited. As a general rule Spaniards did not go farther than the next province. Most of the immigrants to Granada were from Andalucia and Castile. The distances travelled by 122 emigrants from the Basque port of Lequeitio who died away from home in the period 1680–1729, are an interesting testimony to the extraordinary mobility of Basques.[139] Thirteen died elsewhere in Vizcaya, twelve in Guipúzcoa, six in other Cantabrian provinces, five in Cadiz or Seville, two on the Mediterranean coast, eight in the interior of Spain, one in Portugal, twelve in France, three in English prisons, twenty-eight in America, thirty in the Newfoundland fisheries, and two in other places. The figures confirm the outstanding role that Basques were continuing to play in the development of America. Immigration to the area is of less interest. Of seventy immigrants who died in Labastida (Alava) in 1700–09, thirteen were from Alava, seventeen from Vizcaya, three from Guipúzcoa, three from Santander, one from Asturias and Navarre respectively, seven from Burgos, three from Logroño, four from France, twelve from Galicia and six of uncertain origin.[140]

Galician migration is the best known aspect of demographic movement within Spain. With its flourishing population and inadequate small farms, the province continued throughout modern Spanish history to export its labour reserves. It was the preferred recruiting-ground for soldiers: some 68,000 Galicians were estimated to have fought abroad for Philip IV between 1621 and 1659.[141] In the first decade of the twentieth century Galicians flocked in overcrowded ships to South America; as late as the 1930s they thronged the trains southwards to Castile in search of work. In the seventeenth and eighteenth centuries they supplied the seasonal labour needs of rural landowners in Castile.[142] In the late century most seasonal emigrants from the Xallas region went to Portugal (86 per cent) rather than to Castile (14 per cent).[143] Galicians were nonetheless in Castile the biggest single group after local migrants. In Talavera de la Reina, for example, out of 563 known immigrants in the years 1680–1700, over 56 per cent were from Galicia.[144] The Galician workers tended to leave their homes in May and to return in the early autumn with their savings. In their absence their womenfolk had to maintain the farms.

## THE NEW PATTERN OF GROWTH

The universal recovery and stabilisation of the birth rate in Spain after mid-century, must now be considered in the light of the many negative factors we have described. Epidemics and emigration failed to check growth. Galicia suffered no epidemic, but had to endure subsistence crises, maldistribution of land, military levies, seasonal emigration and a ruinous war with Portugal. Its population by 1700 had nevertheless recovered the high levels of the late sixteenth century. In Xallas the population doubled in the course of the seventeenth century.[145] In the province of Valladolid the epidemics of 1684 did no more than slow down the rate of growth: they did not arrest it. In the kingdom of Granada, which suffered grievously from epidemics in both 1679 and 1684, population totals by 1700 exceeded those of the late sixteenth century.[146]

Within this picture of Spain's new ability to resist mortality there were several important divergences. The population reverses of the late seventeenth century in fact confirmed the long-term economic trends. All the affected areas shown in Fig. 3.2 – Extremadura with its wars, Andalucia and the two Castiles with their epidemics – were pushed into a backward role from which they have still not fully emerged. By contrast, the Cantabrian and the northern Mediterranean regions were totally unaffected by these disasters, and were able to seize an initiative which they have maintained into our own day. If we draw a line from Alicante through Madrid and towards Galicia, and exclude from our northern sector the epidemic areas, we obtain a rough-and-ready division into Poor Spain to the south-west and Rich Spain in the north-east. To some extent this division can be identified with the now commonly accepted one between a Wet and a Dry Spain, based on rainfall.[147] In proposing the concept of a Rich Spain, I intend to emphasise the escape of the northern and eastern periphery from the crises of Castile; and their seizing of this advantage to prepare new bases for later expansion.

Though Poor Spain was able to maintain a healthy birth rate despite demographic reverses, the long period of crisis left it seriously weakened. The industry of Granada suffered a blow that the city regarded as fatal. Crippling tax debts mounted up in towns that had, albeit temporarily, lost a population capable of paying. Though the crisis was Castile's last,[148] it was also its most definitive, and left a permanent imbalance in the country's development.

The evidence of Fig. 3.1, and of the other cases already cited, establishes firmly that demographically the 'crisis of the seventeenth century' took place within the first half of the century only. The decline of the birth rate from the 1590s to the 1650s, was arrested. After an interval brought about by the plague of 1647–52, population levels began to stabilise and increase from the 1660s. Recovery was slowed down by the epidemics of 1676–85 and by subsistence crises. The War of Succession created a further delay, but thereafter the birth rate rapidly overtook the high levels of the late sixteenth century.

## NOTES

1. **Bennassar, B.**, *Recherches* (Paris 1969); Domínguez Ortiz, *Sociedad española*, I, p. 81. See also **Vincent B.**, 'Peste atlántica', *Asclepio*, **28** (1976), 5–25.
2. Domínguez Ortiz, *op. cit.* pp. 81–6; **Lapeyre, H.**, *Géographie* (Paris 1959).
3. Domínguez Ortiz, *op. cit.* Ch 2–3.
4. In 1661 the Spanish contingent there was only 5,481 men: see **Parker, G.**, *Army of Flanders* (Cambridge 1972), pp. 28, 272.
5. Official named Colomo to D. José Campillo, 12 Aug. 1741, AGS Secretaría de Hacienda 537.
6. **Fernández de Pinedo, E.**, *Crecimiento económico* (Madrid 1974), p. 209.
7. Bertaut, *Relation d'un voyage*, p. 36; **Fanshawe, A.**, *Memoirs* (London 1907), p. 168.
8. In addition to sources cited below, I have used the very informative article by **Vincent, B.**, 'Récents travaux' *Annales Demog. Hist.* (1977), 463–91.
9. **Bennassar, B.**, *Valladolid* (Paris 1967), p. 197; Casey, *Kingdom of Valencia*, p. 17.
10. All data quoted for Galicia are generalised conclusions from the following studies: **Barreiro, B.**, *La Jurisdicción de Xallas* (Santiago 1973); *idem*, 'Dos muestras', in *Las Fuentes y los Métodos* (Santiago 1977); **Rodríguez Ferreiro, H.**, 'Demografía de Hio', in *ibid*. References to Pedralba in Valencia come from Casey, *op. cit.* Ch. I.
11. Cited in Domínguez Ortiz, *op. cit.* p. 64.
12. **González Muñoz, M. C.**, *Talavera* (Toledo 1974), p. 207.
13. AHN Inq. 209/25.
14. *Ibid.* 735/277.
15. *Ibid.* 73/52.
16. Vincent, 'Récents travaux', p. 479.
17. Lisón Tolosana, *Belmonte*, p. 264.
18. Domínguez Ortiz, *op. cit.* p. 113.
19. Vincent, *op. cit.* p. 479.
20. 1646 figures are from **González, T.**, *Censo* (Madrid 1829); 1683 figures, drawn from the official estimates of Pedro de Oreytia in AGS:CJH 1066 and of Núñez de Prado in *ibid*. 1960, are: Valladolid 4,000, Medina del Campo 990, Medina de Rioseco 1,372, Avila 1,179, Peñaranda 745, Arévalo 376.
21. **García Sanz, A.**, *Segovia* (Madrid 1977), p. 75.
22. *Ibid.* p. 53. The base index 100 is from the years 1720–49.
23. Pedro de Oreytia to council of Finance, 17 Mar. 1683, AGS:CJH 1066.
24. **Anés, G.**, *Crisis agrarias* (Madrid 1970), graph 6, p. 461.
25. **Brines Blasco, J.**, 'Comarca de Valldigna' *III Cong. Hist. Med.* (Valencia 1969), II, 219–34.
26. **García Ballester, L.**, and **Mayer, J. M.**, 'Peste de Orihuela' *Medicina Española*, 65 (1971), 317–31. The indices for the reign of Charles II were 1660–64: 71, 1665–69: 82, 1670–74: 71, 1675–79: 80, 1680–84: 90, 1685–89: 100, 1690–94: 98, 1695–99: 109.

27. Nadal, J., and Giralt, E., *Immigració francesa* (Mataró 1966), p. 26.
28. See the discussion below, p. 297.
29. See the discussion below, p. 281.
30. See the discussion below, p. 167.
31. Barreiro, *La Jurisdicción de Xallas*, pp. 225–30.
32. González Muñoz, *Talavera*, p. 262.
33. See the discussion in Vincent, 'Rećents travaux', p. 473.
34. Díaz de Noreña, 'Respuesta', BN MS. 4466.
35. Reports dated Oct. 1672, in AHN Consejos 7236.
36. Villalba, J., *Epidemiología* (Madrid 1802), II, 113–14, mentions an epidemic throughout Spain in 1666, but I have found no proof of it.
37. Díaz de Escobar, N., *Epidemias de Málaga* (Málaga 1903), p. 43.
38. Consulta of 23 June 1676, in AHN Consejos 7236, from which source some of the information in this chapter will be drawn, without further reference.
39. These and subsequent details on Murcia come from the municipal records: AMM:AC 1676–78.
40. Soler Cantó, J., *Epidemias en Cartagena* (Cartagena 1967), basing himself on records of the monastery of San Diego, reports (p. 19) that the populace was strongly opposed to a declaration of epidemic, because of the economic repercussions.
41. Copy of report, dated Saturday 29 May, ACA:CA 595/3/62.
42. Villalba, *op. cit.* p. 124, mentions a work by Dr Blas Martínez Nieto, *Discurso sobre la naturaleza . . . y curación para el contagio de peste que hoy padecen las ciudades de Cartagena, Murcia y Totana* (Madrid 1677), that I have been unable to locate.
43. AMM:AC 1678.
44. I have not been able to locate the contemporary study by Juan Bautista Orivay y Monreal, *Teatro de la verdad, y claro manifiesto del conocimiento de las enfermedades de la ciudad de Orihuela del año 1678* (Saragossa 1679).
45. By me, in 'The decline of Castile', p. 73; and by Domínguez Ortiz, *Sociedad española*, I, 76, where he assumes that it travelled along the coast, when in fact there are no cases recorded for the very large area between Murcia and Málaga.
46. Villalba, *op. cit.* II, 125–35; Díaz de Escobar, *op. cit.* pp. 44–8.
47. Figures of Díaz de Escobar, *op. cit.* p. 47.
48. Details from AHN Consejos 7236.
49. All reports from *La Gazeta Ordinaria* of Madrid, in Astorga, G.25 f.4.
50. I have not seen the report of the doctor sent to Málaga by the council of Castile: Diego Blanco Salgado, *Tratado de la epidemia pestilente que padeció la ciudad de Málaga el año 1678 y 1679* (Málaga 1679).
51. Petition of 1681 from Cañar, AGS:CJH 1038.
52. Consulta of Finance, 30 Sept. 1682, *ibid.* 1049.
53. Report of 1681 in *ibid.* 1030.
54. Printed memorial of 1682, *ibid.* 1058.
55. D. Fernando Muñoz to D. Francisco de Zamora 'mi hermano y senor', 3 Oct. 1679 from Lucena, in BL Sloane MS. 1087/115–6.
56. Municipal measures may be seen in AMS:AC 1678–1681.
57. ACS:AC 81/42 and 82/14.
58. *Gazeta Ordinaria* of 22 Aug. 1679, in Astorga, G. 25 f.4.
59. An epidemic unconnected with the plague occurred in Burgos province in 1678–79. In Melgar de Fernamental 116 vecinos (or over 500 people) were reported to have died: see AGS:CJH 1044.
60. Memorial of 1683 in *ibid.* 1059.

61. Report of 1682 in *ibid.* 1047.
62. Consulta of 14 Oct. 1680, *ibid.* 1029.
63. Printed memorial of 1682, *ibid.* 1049.
64. Consulta of committee of Finance, 14 May 1682, *ibid.*
65. **Lantéry, R.**, *Memorias* (Cadiz 1949), p. 100.
66. Statement of 15 Oct. 1680, in AHN Consejos 7190.
67. Consulta of committee of Finance, 5 July 1681, AGS:CJH 1033.
68. Lantéry, *op. cit.* p. 116.
69. 'Relacion del estado de la salud de Andalucia', 17 Dec. 1680, ACA:CA 572/86.
70. Lantéry, *op cit.* p. 127.
71. Printed memorial of June 1682 in AGS:CJH 1054.
72. Memorial of 31 May 1682, *ibid.* 1052. In another memorial in 1685, the town claimed to have lost 1,600 dead between January and October: *ibid.* 1105.
73. For the crisis of 1682 in Córdoba see **Fortea Pérez, J. I.**, 'Córdoba', *Actas I Cong. Hist. And.* 1 (Córdoba 1978), 393. The epidemic in the city lasted from May to July.
74. The epidemic in Puebla de Alcocer lasted for eight months but cost only 126 lives: AGS:CJH 1063.
75. 1685 petition, in *ibid.*
76. Petition of 7 May 1685, in *ibid.* The figures are only for epidemic deaths.
77. Report of 5 Aug. 1687, *ibid.* 1107.
78. Yebenes and Sonseca cited in **Weisser, M.**, *Montes* (Chicago 1976), pp. 70–1.
79. González Muñoz, *Talavera,* p. 262.
80. **Larruga, E.**, *Memorias* (Madrid 1787–1800), XIII, 187.
81. Letter of 13 July 1684, PRO: SP 101/92/160. 'Tabardillos' were fevers or typhus.
82. AGS:CJH 1111.
83. About 54 vecinos perished; the rest fled: *ibid.* 1089. The real death rate was therefore 36 per cent.
84. This and the next two towns feature in a consulta of Finance, 30 July 1692, *ibid.* 1174.
85. From 21 Feb. 1684 to 4 May 1685 the town lost 101 dead: *ibid.* 1963.
86. *Ibid.* 1106.
87. The dead were estimated at 48 vecinos, or 31 per cent of the 1683 population: consulta of Finance, 3 Oct. 1686, *ibid.* 1100.
88. The town is reputed to have lost 3,000 dead in 1684, which would have meant an outright loss of about 600 vecinos. This is hard to reconcile with the figures above: *ibid.* 1106.
89. Tembleque had 4,253 recorded deaths between June 1684 and June 1685, an average of about twelve a day: *ibid.* 1100. This corrects my footnote in 'The decline of Castile', p. 74 n.3. The town was soon repopulated. In 1697 it had 730 vecinos: *ibid.* 1226.
90. These figures are for *vecinos contribuyentes,* i.e. taxpayers. The full population in 1683 would have been over 800 households. In 1684 there were 440 deaths in the town: report of 27 Aug. 1685: *ibid.* 1086.
91. 'Every day twenty or thirty people died.' The count from 1 May 1684 to 7 Nov 1684 was 3,150 dead: *ibid.* 1090.
92. Report of 9 May 1685 in *ibid.* 1089.
93. From 7 Feb. 1684 to 27 Dec. 1685, 282 persons died. This represents a loss of about 60 vecinos, making the real mortality between 1684 and 1686 about 18 per cent: *ibid.* 1095.
94. *Ibid.* 1088.

95. Memorial of 30 Sept. 1687: 'the mortality was so great in 1683 and 84 that there died and were buried 143 vecinos and 72 children': *ibid.* 1105. The real rate in 1684 was probably therefore over 40 per cent.

96. Consulta of 12 June 1687, *ibid.* 1111.

97. The losses in Linares cover both the plague (in 1681) and the epidemic of 1684: report of 5 Aug. 1687 in *ibid.* 1107.

98. Consulta of Finance, 30 Oct. 1691, *ibid.* 1161.

99. *Ibid.* 1088. This suggests a mortality rate of 40 per cent in 1684.

100. Report of 16 Jan. 1685, *ibid.* 1090.

101. Soler Cantó, *Cartagena,* p. 19.

102. D. Miguel de la Moneda to D. Ignacio Baptista de Ribas, 22 July 1681, AGS:CJH 1031.

103. 'Para la Guarda del Contagio de las Ciudades de Granada, Motril, Antequera', etc., AHN Consejos 7236.

104. **Conejo R.**, 'Sanidad en Archidona', *Actas II Cong. Hist. Med.*, II, 113–23.

105. AMM:AC 1677, minute of Tues. 26 Oct. 1677.

106. Instructions by Dr Francisco Moratón, AHN Consejos 7189. The list of medicaments used during the outbreak in Murcia is listed in AMM 2760, dated Aug. 1678.

107. The city to council of Castile, 8 July 1677, AHN Consejos 7236.

108. Lantéry, *op. cit.* pp. 125–9.

109. AMC Libros de Cabildos, volume for 1671–76.

110. Details in AMM:AC 1676. The corregidor was D. Juan de Henao, the canon Dr Diego Reynoso.

111. Lantéry, *op. cit.* p. 125.

112. AMM:AC 1677, date 13 Nov. 1677.

113. AGS:CJH 883.

114. *Ibid.* 977.

115. Consulta of council of Finance, 17 Apr. 1666, *ibid.* 885.

116. Consulta of 4 July 1682, *ibid.* 1050.

117. *Ibid.* 890.

118. The town claimed it had only 140 households: consulta of 22 Jan. 1667, *ibid.* 894.

119. *Ibid.* 1106. There were more empty than inhabited houses in the town in 1687.

120. Report of 11 Jan. 1687, *ibid.* 1110. In fact, some of the decay was also caused by natural disasters in 1682–4.

121. *Ibid.* 1170.

122. Consulta of council of Finance, 22 Sept. 1685, *ibid.* 1090.

123. *Ibid.* 986.

124. Report by Francisco de Ozio Salazar, 5 Jan. 1691, *ibid.* 1158.

125. Domínguez Ortiz, *Sociedad española,* I, 123.

126. Petition from Orense in AGS:CJH 894.

127. *Ibid.* 1029.

128. Decree of 19 Aug. 1661, copy in *ibid.* 883.

129. Consulta of council of Finance, 3 July 1667, *ibid.* 891.

130. Consulta of 15 Mar. 1664, *ibid.* 1078.

131. Domínguez Ortiz, *op. cit.* p. 122.

132. Memorial of 26 Oct. 1690, AGS:CJH 1158.

133. **Friar Benito Peñalosa**, *Libro de las cinco excelencias del español que despueblan a España* (Pamplona 1679), cited in Domínguez Ortiz, *op. cit.* p. 91.

134. See the discussion in Domínguez Ortiz, *op. cit.* pp. 89–90.

135. See *ibid.* p. 111.
136. See below, pp. 98–9.
137. See below, pp. 279–80.
138. Cited in Vincent, 'Récents travaux', p. 485, p. 62.
139. Fernández de Pinedo, *Crecimiento económico*, p. 142.
140. *Ibid.* p. 144.
141. Domínguez Ortiz, *op. cit.* p. 95 n.90.
142. **Meijide Pardo, A.**, 'Emigración gallega', *Estud. Hist. Soc. Esp.* 4, ii (1960), 461–606.
143. Barreiro, *Xallas*, pp. 249–55.
144. González Muñoz, *Talavera*, p. 260.
145. Domínguez Ortiz, *op. cit.*, notes that the population levels in 1591 and 1714 were both around 120,000 vecinos; for Xallas, see Barreiro, *op. cit.* p. 88.
146. An increase of about 72,000 to 79,000 vecinos: Domínguez Ortiz, *op. cit.* p. 110.
147. Domínguez Ortiz, *op. cit.* p. 110, also adopts this distinction when discussing population patterns.
148. Kamen, 'The decline of Castile: the last crisis', cited above in n.44.

# CHAPTER FOUR

# The Recovery of the Economy

Spain was one of the most backward industrial countries in western Europe. The clear contradiction between this fact and the reality of Spain's immense imperial power, troubled generations of thinkers. There was no doubt that Spain had some potential: large supplies of wool and silk were available for the factories; metals (iron, mercury), wine, oil and other goods could be exported; markets existed not only inside the peninsula but in the whole overseas empire; and bullion from America supplied investment funds. But by the mid-sixteenth century there were two undeniable trends that threatened any possibility of economic growth. The bullion did not materialise where it was most needed, and Spanish markets began to be flooded with foreign manufactures. Modern historians have usually presented this as the beginning of the 'decline of Spain'.

The concept of 'decline' has always been ambiguous and has never helped us to understand what really happened in Spain.[1] All standard accounts, without exception, have considered the seventeenth century to be one of accelerating decay, with the reign of Charles II as the period of most extreme depression. It is true that the empire abroad was crumbling, but it was precisely in the late century that Spain's internal economy showed signs of recovery from the crisis of the early century. For many historians, that crisis and indeed the whole 'decline' was to be blamed in some measure on the inability of Spaniards to think like capitalists. 'It seems to have been an attitude of mind which stood in the way of economic advance', we are told.[2] Though the *hidalgo* mentality was often responsible for traditionalist attitudes, we can no longer accept this idealist explanation for Spanish backwardness.

The material facts are evidence enough of Spain's difficulties. Since the Middle Ages Castile and Aragon had relied for wealth principally on exports of wool. The legitimate interests of wool producers, the Mesta and the government, made them support wool exports to the detriment of domestic industry. Bullion imports into Spain created spiralling inflation, and aggravated the price differential between it and other industrial nations. Cheaper foreign imports undercut native textiles, and consolidated the state of dependence into which Spain had fallen respective to foreign manufacturers. As an exporter of raw materials and an importer of manufactured goods, the country was forced into a situation from which it could escape only by raising production and substituting for imports. The discovery of America offered no solutions: the manufactured goods it required could not be supplied by Spain and had to come from other European countries on whose trade Spain was already dependent.

Spain's predicament was no different from that of many developing nations in the modern world. To blame its difficulties on an aristocratic attitude of mind, or on inadequate government policy, is to ignore the radical problem of economic dependence. Spaniards who tried to invest in industry rather than in government bonds (*juros*), or governments that tried to discriminate in favour of native enterprise, found equally that the options available to them were very limited, because of the country's weak position relative to foreign interests.


## THE CONTRIBUTIONS OF ARBITRISTAS

*Arbitristas* (proposers of *arbítrios* or expedients) of the seventeenth century were seldom taken seriously by contemporaries. They were written off as men who lived by memories of a glorious past and dreams of a spurious future. Most of them felt that there was one single cure (*único remedio*) for the problems of the monarchy.[3] Sancho de Moncada in 1619 singled out foreign capitalists as the chief blight on the economy. 'The ills of Spain rise from the new trade of foreigners. . . . The radical cure is to prohibit foreign manufactures. . . . Spain's remedy is in producing its own goods.'[4] The same point was pursued at greater length by Francisco Martínez de Mata, who produced his best work in the last years of the reign of Philip IV.[5] He insisted that all Spain's problems arose from allowing imports of foreign manufactures, and that if existing laws on trading were properly observed then the country would return to its former prosperity.

Since no Cortes met in Castile under Charles II, we have no systematic record of popular grievances; unlike the sixteenth century, when the Cortes acted as a voice for public opinion. Our most valuable guide to economic problems in the seventeenth century is the large body of writings produced by the arbitristas, who usually proposed impracticable remedies but whose analyses were invariably perceptive. The arbitrista best known to us from the late century is Miguel Alvarez Osorio y Redín. In his *Universal Discourse* of 1686,[6] written in times of inflation and military defeat, he complained of an excessive number of administrators, profiteering in grain, frauds in the tax system, and an incompetent noble élite. In *The Watchman*,[7] written the following year, he discussed problems of agrarian and industrial production, and obstacles such as noble prejudice, backward universities and superfluous clergy.

Though the full Cortes of Castile did not meet, the government kept in touch with opinion in the cities. In March 1669 all the cities with a vote in Cortes were asked to suggest proposals that might help the treasury but also bring relief to taxpayers. Their replies did not differ in substance from the ideas that had long been discussed by arbitristas. The city of Jaén suggested that the taxes normally administered by tax-farmers be put into the hands of the local authorities and that paid officials be appointed to collect them; that common lands, alienated royal lands, and forest land, be restored to their old use and made available for pasture; that the tax on salt be lowered; that the great number of venal public offices be reduced, since their owners were enjoying exemption from taxes; that towns sold by the Crown be bought back; that interest rates be reduced; and that the state debt to juros be cut back by renouncing certain classes of juros. The city of Murcia proposed two revolutionary measures: 'abolish all juros so that nobody draws from the treasury any income other than his wages or salary . . . abolish the *millones* tax, the main source of the ruin of this monarchy.'[8]

The volume and complexity of complaints reaching the government, make it difficult to assess the relative importance of grievances. Ministers must often have been baffled by the extravagant proposals of arbitristas. Osorio y Redín, for example, esteemed himself as a mathematician, and marred at least one of his works, the *Extensión Política y Económica* of 1686,[9] with improbable and specious calculations. It would be wrong to think that the government therefore ignored arbitristas: it has been suggested that there was 'utter disregard by statesmen of sound advice'.[10] The facts show that advice was listened to, but that practical action was not easy to take. However, Pedro Fernández de Navarrete's *Conservation of Monarchies* (1626) was in its day the basis for considerable legislation.[11] His writings were quoted in a meeting of the council of Castile on 30 July 1699; and a suggestion that small peasants selling their own grain should not have to pay any sales tax, was adopted.[12] Martínez de Mata found rather less favour with the authorities. He wandered round Andalucia dressed in the brown robe of the Franciscan Order, calling himself 'servant of the afflicted poor', and publicising radical solutions to the problems of the time. Shortly after 1660 he was condemned to serve four years in a fortress for forging an official decree. This did not stop his output. In August 1666 he presented a memorial to the council of Castile, asking for the establishment of a central credit bank (*monte de piedad*). The councillors took pains to read it 'despite', as they reported, 'the discredit of this subject, who occupies himself in impractical proposals of this type, and is at present in prison here in Madrid'.[13]

In addition to the systematic works of the arbitristas, there was a large body of tracts produced by occasional writers. The most stimulating and informative of these to be found in the seventeenth century, emerged during the historic Cortes of Aragon in 1677. Because the pamphlets were addressed to the Cortes they were bound together with the official record of proceedings, and were fortunate enough to survive. The practice of giving advice to the government through tracts was widely accepted in Spain. In 1694, for example, the Catalan bishop of Solsona addressed to the Crown a memorial[14] outstanding for its temerity, since it compared the regime of Charles II unfavourably with that of Louis XIV. More in the traditional style was the tract prepared by the veteran captain Antonio de Somoza in 1680. His *Sole Truth and Perfect Remedy*[15] advised the king that 'the general shortage of necessities, notable bankruptcy of our textiles and trade, excess of taxes and high cost of collecting them, multitude of officials who administer and spend them, inobservance of the laws, growing depopulation of these realms, weakness of our armed forces, and depressed price of gold and silver: are the eight mortal ills that this Catholic kingdom is suffering'.

For all the weaknesses in their arguments, and the frequent attacks on them by contemporaries (the historiographer royal, Alonso Núñez de Castro, made a bitter attack on them in his best-selling *Sólo Madrid es Corte*, in 1658[16]), the arbitristas were singularly important. Outside the Church, they were possibly the only group of writers with almost unlimited licence to criticise the defects of the economic system under which Spaniards lived. Their data are almost always suspect, since they exaggerated shamelessly in order to prove an argument. But much of their information continues to be useful, and the rich variety of their views is our best guide to the state of informed opinion in Spain.

## PROBLEMS OF INDUSTRY

The main difficulty in trying to assess industry in the seventeenth century is that we know almost nothing about it. The first adequate survey of resources in Castile did not take place till the mid-eighteenth century, with the Catastro of the marquis of Ensenada. Fortunately, few major changes occurred in the general structure of the economy during this period, so that a look at the position of industry in the late eighteenth century should give a reasonable picture of the situation in earlier years. According to the national census ordered in 1797, in the province of Salamanca the agrarian sector (crops and animals) accounted for nearly 90 per cent of output by value. In the four provinces of Old Castile (Burgos, Soria, Avila, Segovia) it constituted over 91 per cent.[17] The figures emphasise the overwhelmingly non-industrial character of the Spanish economy at this time. On the other hand, a proportionately larger number of persons was employed in the secondary, industrial, sector: in Salamanca over 17 per cent of the active labour force, as against 70 per cent in the primary, agrarian, sector; in Segovia, one of the biggest centres of textile production, over 24 per cent. Though industry was still a tiny portion of the economy, then, its importance was enhanced by the considerable number of people who depended on it for a living.

### Woollens

Wool was by far the most important industry in seventeenth-century Spain, with production centres situated close to the areas where sheep grazed. In Castile the sheepowners who belonged to the Mesta continued to enjoy extensive privileges of pasture. Their joint flocks, some two million sheep in the late century,[18] were migratory (*transhumantes*), moving southwards in late September in search of pasture and northwards again in April to the hills of Old Castile. If we follow the reckoning of the writer Miguel Caxa de Leruela that the non-migratory flocks (*estantes*) were normally four times as great as those of the Mesta,[19] the total number of sheep in Castile was probably close to ten million. Foreign demand continued to be the principal stimulus to wool production. A valuable report of

1667, by the English envoy Sir William Godolphin, summarised Spanish wools as follows.[20]

The Woolls of Spain are commonly known by the Names of Segovia, Soria and Andalusia; Segovia is the finest, and is sold at 70 Reales Vellon the Arroba, an Arroba is 25 lb weight; Soria Woolls are next in fineness. . . . Andalusia Woolls are the worst and coursest, and are in like manner sold at 20 Reales the Arroba.

It is calculated that there is Yearly exported out of Spain, from 36,000 to 40,000 Bags of all sorts of Wooll; and that usually from the port of Bilbao are Shipped of 20,000 Bags of Wooll in a Year.

It is judged that these Woolls are taken off in this manner, viz.

| | |
|---|---:|
| Holland, Hamburgh, and the Adjacent Countries | 22,000 |
| England, from 2,000 to | 7,000 |
| France, from 6,000 to | 7,000 |
| Venice, and the Ports of Italy | 3,000 |
| Africa, viz. Tunis, Algiers, and Sancta Cruz | 1,000 |

This Exportation is of all sorts of Wooll, and of this perhaps 27,000 Bags may be Segovia and Soria Woolls; what are spent in Spain are usually of the third sort of Soria and Segovia Woolls.

Since the early sixteenth century, if not earlier, the question of wool exports had aroused bitter controversy. Manufacturers, and towns that relied on textiles for employment, blamed industrial decline on the export of raw materials. In practice, though the finer wools were preferred for export, manufacturers never lacked adequate supplies. The profits made from trade were indeed responsible for the new investments that helped industry in Segovia survive in the late sixteenth century.[21]

From mid-century Segovia's woollen industry began to expand. Throughout the province demographic growth was accompanied by a rise in grain and wool production.[22] The increase in the volume of wool produced by non-migratory flocks was phenomenal. In the area of Carbonero el Mayor, production rose from an index of 25 in 1640 to 75 in 1695, in Pradena from one of 20 in 1645 to 65 in 1700.[23] It is not clear what effect this had on textile production. Certainly in Segovia, both city and province, the woollen industry escaped from the decay of which other towns complained. The royal factory in Segovia, with about 300 looms in the 1640s, suffered only temporary setbacks thereafter. Up to 1680 there were about 100 looms, in 1682 only fifty. During the last decade of the century there was a steady improvement: 170 working looms in 1691, 252 in 1697. In 1699 the factory, apparently stimulated by the gesture which Charles II made in 1694, of dressing himself in Segovia textiles, thereby obliging the nobility to follow his example, was producing an annual 2,976 pieces of cloth. In 1700 it produced 3,078 pieces. Output thereafter remained well above this level.[24]

Royal interest in Segovia, and the favourable conjuncture of the late seventeenth century, assured the survival of its industry. It was a similar story in Palencia, which in 1674 had 246 looms producing baize and quilts. The number remained at about this level for the rest of the century. In 1691 it was estimated that 3,500 persons were employed in the industry.[25] Against these successes we must set Avila, which declined in both population and industry, until in 1692 it allegedly had only fourteen looms;[26] Córdoba, which claimed to have had 200 looms in 1677, before the epidemics, and only five in 1687;[27] and numerous other towns both large and small which claimed comparable decay in their industry.

Complaints of decay were also commonplace in Aragon. In the 1680s there were probably some 1,400,000 head of sheep in the kingdom, a calculation based on the estimates of Ignacio de Asso.[28] In 1676 there were 124 looms working in Saragossa,[29] a figure that compares favourably with many Castilian cities, but tells only part of the story. For though the capital was the biggest industrial city in Aragon – the textile output of Teruel in 1677 was by value only 29 per cent that of Saragossa, that of Albarracín was only 24 per cent – it was not the chief consumer of wool. The Diputados of Aragon in 1677 estimated that the towns of Rubielos de la Cérida (north of Teruel) and Illueca (near Saragossa) each used more wool for textiles than Saragossa did.[30] Aragon went through some hard times in the century, but it is difficult to believe the contemporary claim that the number of looms in the kingdom had fallen by nine-tenths between 1626 and 1678.[31]

The differences in conditions between distinct parts of Spain make it impossible to suggest a common cause for industrial problems. The decline in factory looms, for example, may have signified little more than a move to the 'putting-out' system. In Palencia between 1692 and 1701 several looms were put out into neighbouring villages, where labour was presumably cheaper.[32] It is undeniable, however, that there were profound obstacles facing Spanish manufacturers. Moncada, Martínez de Mata and other writers had proposed strict protectionism as the only way to help native textiles compete with foreign imports. Why did foreign textiles enjoy the upper hand? They benefited, most obviously, from the price difference between inflationary Spain and their own country. They were also not usually bound by the guild system of manufacturing in Spain; nor by the rules, which the Spanish government enforced for tax purposes, about the quality and dimensions of each piece of cloth. A major complaint was that foreign imported cloth did not observe regulations on size and quality, and consequently enjoyed an unfair advantage in the market-place; in addition to which, imports had a finish and sheen not usually available in Spanish cloths. Foreigners, above all, had an excellent system of marketing and distribution, using native retailers as their agents.

A typical casualty was the town of Calcena (Aragon), which in 1667 reported as follows to the Diputados in Saragossa:[33]

This town, with a population of four hundred vecinos, has since 1640 up to now lost two hundred families,[34] and this ruin has been caused by the lack of sales for the fabric manufactured here. The French, with their industry, have introduced merchandise, and the common people have clothed themselves in it, because of the novelty and the low price, without attention to its poor durability, so that there is no way of selling even a yard of our cloth. . . . Driven by their poverty and wishing to find sustenance for their children, in this year alone fifty families have left, and most of them are in Saragossa, where they are finding the same difficulty in selling their cloth.

Calcena is an example of the economic dependence of Spain, whose internal markets were swamped in the seventeenth century by the commercially advantaged producers of other western European nations. Both in Spain and in America, consumers developed a taste for imported goods, which in the long run proved to be more powerful than simple considerations of price or quality. Feliu de la Peña, who later played an important role in the Committee for Trade, criticised the public for 'importing and buying foreign clothing, not because it is good, not because it is cheap, but because whether expensive or cheap it is preferable because foreign: this is the vanity to which we Spaniards are all given'.[35] Preference for foreign textiles is amply documented at all social levels, from the court downwards. So unexciting a cloth as black for mourning, widely used among Spaniards, was also purchased from abroad. In 1715 the English merchants in Seville complained that the laws of Charles II restricting mourning had led to a sharp fall in the consumption of black Colchester baize.[36]

The ineptitude of Spaniards for capitalist enterprise was never a serious issue. In order to recapture their own markets Spanish manufacturers probably required two primary things: a reorganisation of production methods, which in most cases meant circumventing guild regulations; and heavy investment to overcome high costs and low profit margins. In the early seventeenth century, potential investors probably got higher returns from putting their money in government and municipal bonds (juros and censos); and the insecurity of the money market may therefore be partly blamed for the failure to invest in industry. Some contemporaries blamed their wealthy élite, the aristocracy, for the lack of industrial cash.[37] Modern experience has shown that heavier investment alone would not have been sufficient. When the Committee for Trade was set up in 1679, it put in hand instead a deliberate policy of import substitution, by encouraging manufacturers to produce within Spain the goods that would normally have been sent in by foreign traders.

### Silks

The second largest textile industry in Spain, silks were produced principally in the south east, in Toledo, Granada, Seville and Valencia. Silk production was heavily localised: in Granada practically all the neighbouring towns and villages cultivated silkworms in order to supply the city's looms. Silk output declined in volume during the century, partly because it was a luxury product in a time of steep inflation, but principally because of competition from foreign imports. Toledo and its area had 9,561 looms in 1663, only 2,530 in 1690 and no more than 622 in 1695.[38] The great majority of these looms were located not in the city but in outlying villages, if we may credit a report by an official who estimated that Toledo itself had about 500 silk looms in 1691 and only 285 in 1692.[39] Decrease in production at Granada was continuous, and made worse by the epidemic of 1679. Production fell from 130,000 pounds of silk in 1678 to only about 5,000 in 1684, a decline of 96 per cent.[40] The epidemics also harmed Toledo, which apparently lost over two-thirds of its looms in 1684–85.[41] Of Córdoba it was reported in 1687 that in mid-century the city had two thousand silk looms, 'and now there are only twenty looms on which taffetas, mantles and crapes are spun; and twenty-five looms, established three years ago, of the fabrics accompanying this report. There also used to be over a hundred spinning-wheels for ribbons and silks but now there are only six working'.[42]

Figures for output in Aragon vary widely. The Diputados estimated that the kingdom was producing 188,150 pounds of raw silk in the year 1672.[43] Ignacio de Asso, however, suggests that production in about 1680 was no more than 40,000 pounds, of which three-fourths was consumed on the looms of Saragossa.[44] The first figure is certainly more correct and represents normal output. By 1680, on the other hand, the new policies of the Cortes of 1677 had disrupted industry.[45] In Valencia there was a sadder story to be told. The guild of silk manufacturers, the Colegio de Terciopeleros, informed the authorities that

around 1600 it was so opulent that it had over four thousand looms, and there was one merchant who alone had three hundred. But there was a decline from the 1660s to 1672, because the French extracted raw silk from the realm, transported it to France, and brought it back again, as satins and tabbys, to the realms of Castile and Aragon. The city was left with only thirty looms, not all fully working, which led to the ruin of over 800 master-workers and with them over 3,000 employees and apprentices, and over 5,000 women.[46]

Allowing for all exaggerations, the fate of the Spanish silk industry was obviously grimmer than that of woollens. The disruption caused by the epidemics of the late century was such that it took over half a century for production to resume old levels. The social consequences were serious. Granada at this time was the biggest industrial city in Spain, with a population of about 100,000, of whom over a fifth were dependent on silks for employment.[47] In the Córdoba industry they 'employed a great many people in combing and spinning',[48] as they did also in other towns. In 1699, a year of subsistence crisis, the silk guilds in Toledo claimed that there were over 3,000 silkworkers unemployed, thanks largely to the high price of raw silk from Valencia, where French bulk purchases had driven up the cost.[49] The difficulties of the silk industry must be looked at not only in economic terms, but also as a serious threat to social order in southern Spain.

Because of the lack of any studies of silk, we can only guess at some of the internal problems of the industry. The tax burden may have been a hindrance: in Granada in 1686, on an average low price of 22 reales a pound, a total of 502 maravedis or 67 per cent made up the tax element.[50] The city, however, put the blame for its troubles less on the tax system than on speculation by middlemen who bought up the crop, raised prices artificially, and in default of purchasers in Granada sold the raw silk to manufacturers in Córdoba, Jaén and the town of Priego.

## Mining

The two most significant extractive industries in Spain were mercury and iron-ore mining. Both metals were exported in quantity. The richest veins of iron-ore were in the Basque provinces, but the early history of this major industry remains unwritten.[51] Substantial quantities of ore were exported, in the mid-sixteenth century at least one-third. By the 1680s production of ore from the ironworks of Vizcaya and Guipúzcoa probably totalled some 250,000 *quintales* a year. By contrast, output of ore for cannon slumped under Charles II, because of diminishing imperial commitments. In the ironworks at Liérganes (Santander), production between 1650 and 1700 averaged only 4,000 quintales a year, compared with 24,000 quintales in 1639 and 20,000 in 1703.[52]

As in other aspects of their economy, Vizcaya and Guipúzcoa were competitors rather than partners. From the early century there were disputes over the export to Guipúzcoa of the high quality ore at Somorrostro in Vizcaya.[53] The quarrel developed into the most serious inter-provincial dispute of the century. In October 1686 the Junta General of Vizcaya resolved 'that iron-ore not be exported to any realm, particularly not to the Orozco valley', which was in Guipúzcoa.[54] To justify its decision, the Señorío claimed that its purpose was to limit output as a precaution against over-production; and that the restrictions on Guipúzcoa were because that province was actually exporting ore to France. A ferocious argument ensued. Guipúzcoa had its own iron mines, but they were less in number than its neighbour's, and Guipúzcoa said that it relied heavily on imports from Vizcaya. Vizcaya in 1689 had 147 active ironworks and 128 exhausted sites,[55] but in its turn relied on Guipúzcoa for coal supplies in the factories.

Vizcaya's move was part of a campaign against outside interests. Between 1688 and 1707 it directed several petitions to the government in support of a ban on all imports of iron into Spain or America from Belgium, Germany and France. Supplies to Guipúzcoa from Somorrostro were cut off indefinitely from October 1686. With no solution in sight, Guipúzcoa in July 1688 sent four Diputados to Madrid, not to seek a compromise but with the extraordinary ultimatum that if its demands were not met it would invade Vizcaya with force. Orders for mobilisation went out in Guipúzcoa. Eventually the council of Castile arrived at a compromise, which in substance was favourable to Vizcaya. A royal decree of 4 May 1689[56] ordered that for a period of twelve years in the first instance Vizcaya should allow the export to Guipúzcoa of an annual 400,000 quintales of ore from the veins at Somorrostro. Since exports had previously been unrestricted, Guipúzcoa continued to protest but without success.

## THE ESTABLISHMENT OF THE COMMITTEE FOR TRADE

The Real y General Junta de Comercio, to give it its full name, was created by a royal decree of 29 January 1679. Larruga, the historian of the Junta, says that the idea for its formation came from the duke of Medinaceli.[57] This is almost certainly wrong. The chief minister in power at the time was Don Juan José of Austria, who made all major decisions, and who had already, in Aragon in 1674, established a similar committee for trade. We can therefore state categorically that the Committee for Trade was a creation of Don Juan.

It was made up of four ministers, one each from the councils of Castile, War,

Finance and the Indies. They were, respectively, Carlos Herrera, Ramírez de Arellano, Francisco Centani, and José de Beytia.[58] Despite its title, the Committee was concerned not with trade but with fostering industry. Only once before, with the founding in 1625 of the Junta de Población, Agricultura y Comercio, had a Spanish government attempted to set up such a body, and on that occasion it had achieved nothing. Precedent was respected by the use of a similar title for the new Committee.

The primary purpose of the 1679 body seems to have been fiscal, to promote an economy that would pay adequate taxes. This was the common policy of governments of the time, including that of Colbert. The long-term aim of the Committee, however, was nothing less than the rejuvenation of the country. Its instructions directed it to find a remedy for the depopulation of Spain, and one solution proposed was 'the foundation of montes de piedad to help the needy, in order to re-establish production, trade and shipping'.[59] We cannot discount the possibility that the influence of Martínez de Mata, who in 1666 had put before the council of Finance his proposals for founding montes de piedad throughout the realm, had some part to play in the suggested policy.[60] It is significant that in his *Eighth Discourse* he had presented the montes as 'the only way to restore trade and population'.

The Committee encountered unexpected difficulties. Its first meeting was on 3 February 1679. Subsequently it was decided that the Committee should meet in the residence of the governor of the council of Castile. This seems to have restricted its authority to Castile in the first instance, though by the end of the year it was given jurisdiction throughout all the territories of the monarchy. Then in April 1680 it was indefinitely suspended. It would be wrong to attribute this to 'administrative lethargy and indifference'.[61] The deepening crisis of the late 1670s, culminating in the devaluation of February 1680, caused widespread chaos in Castile and made the work of the Committee impossible. The suspension was carried out by the new prime minister, Medinaceli.

On Christmas Day 1682, when Medinaceli was still chief minister, a decree reconstituted the Committee. It now consisted of Carlos Villamayor (council of Castile), Luis Cerdeño[62] (Indies), Luis de Hoyo (Finance), Francisco Soto Guzmán (War), Andrés Martínez Navarrete the regidor of Madrid, and a secretary in the person of Sebastián del Castillo. In March 1683 a royal order made the Committee independent of the jurisdiction of all other councils. To broaden its terms of reference, in 1684 the president of the council of Aragon was made a member, and so too were the corregidor of Madrid and one alcalde of the city. A special link with Catalonia was promoted by appointing in Barcelona a direct agent of the Committee, the lawyer Narciso Feliu de la Peña, whose work will concern us presently.

The Committee of 1682 was no half-hearted effort. We must remember that it was operating in the shadow of the chaos caused by the monetary decrees of 1682 and 1686, and extensive epidemics in the south of the country. Even in these adverse circumstances, 'subsidies were granted to enterprising manufacturers, measures were taken to restore Spain's depleted merchant shipping, and plans were drawn up for the improvement of navigation on internal waterways'.[63]

The achievements of the late 1680s are discussed below. They were by no means negligible. In practice most of the work was being done in Castile rather than throughout Spain, so it became advisable to change the Committee's structure in order to devote more attention to non-Castilian regions. In June 1691 the existing Committee was dissolved, and a new one set up in November, with an emphasis on the needs of Castile and Madrid. The president was the count of Monterey, the members were Diego Flores (council of Castile), Felix Marimón (Aragon), Agustín Espinola (Finance), Joaquín Aguirre (alcalde of Madrid), Andrés Martínez Navarrete (regidor of Madrid), and Francisco Ronquillo (corregidor of Madrid). At the same time the other regions of Spain with important industries were given local Committees of Trade (*Juntas Particulares*).

The first local body was set up as early as 1684. On 16 December 1683 the king approved the establishment of a Committee in Granada, to oversee the needs of the silk industry. On 17 March 1684 its members were nominated. They were the count of Torrepalma, corregidor of Granada; Fernando Iravedra de Paz, judge of the Chancery; Alvaro Matías de Rueda, *veinticuatro* (alderman) of the city; and Andrés Domínguez, *jurado* (councillor).[64] In 1687 a Committee was also set up in Seville, but I have found no details of its composition or work. One consequence of the founding of the June 1691 body in Madrid was a need for attention to the industries of the Crown of Aragon. This led to the birth of the Committees in Valencia and Barcelona. From 1693, however, there were growing conflicts of jurisdiction between the main Committee in Madrid and other government agencies. By the end of the reign the whole experiment was in decline. The Committees in Madrid and Granada continued their fitful existence into the reign of Philip V, when they were re-established on a new footing.

The order to form a Committee in Valencia was despatched to the viceroy, marquis of Castelrodrigo, on 26 February 1692. The intention was 'to remedy the damage suffered by trade through the introduction into Castile of silks of inferior quality'. It was proposed 'to form a Committee for Trade like those of Seville and Granada, and through it to publicise the regulations as to weight, quality, threads and brand for fabrics in this realm'.[65] It would seem from this statement that a fairly restricted programme was planned for the Committees, and that the main concern was to be little more than regulation of the silk industry. There was, however, an inexplicable delay. Ten months later the Valencian Committee had still not been constituted. Eventually, in response to an urgent letter from the secretary of the council of Aragon, the viceroy reported on 17 December that he had 'nominated D. Juan de la Torre, D. Manuel Mercader, Don Lorenzo Matheu and Dr Vicente Pasqual, who have seemed to me the most experienced, and there is no president because I myself will attend, as with other committees'.[66]

The Committee at Madrid had meanwhile been pushing ahead with its programme. Its achievements, though limited, were in no sense a failure. It encouraged native manufacturers by granting tax-exemption and monopoly privileges; invited several foreign manufacturers into Spain; attempted to enforce standards of quality and size; and promoted investment in industry. Every major industry of Castile was examined. A few examples will illustrate its work.[67]

In 1685 the Committee encouraged the plans of Melchor Lorenz and Sebastián Hernández, residents respectively of Cebolla and Noves (Toledo), to manufacture baize, with a ten-year exemption from taxes. By 1689 they and their colleagues claimed to be employing some five hundred people. Many similar enterprises by native manufacturers are on record, though there is no indication of how successful they were. The papers of the Committee give many cases of the establishment of new manufactures in Burgos, Segovia, Siguenza, Plasencia and other centres both large and small. What remains beyond doubt is that new industry was stimulated. Noves in 1692 had only nineteen looms, but it employed 89 artisans, 789 female workers and 19 apprentices, and produced an annual 636 pieces of woollen baize.[68] This was a tiny output, but Noves flourished: in 1721 there were thirty-eight looms.

The native manufacturers seem to have been active mainly after 1686; in, that is, the period of greater price stability and recuperation after the great epidemics. The new Spanish entrepreneurs included Juan de Brizuela, of Palencia, who in 1686 established four looms in Palencia and two in Burgos for baize-cloths; Gregorio Esteban, native of Segovia, who in 1688 obtained an eight-year tax exemption on his cloths; Juan Antonio Collarte and friends, all natives of Burgos, who in 1691 undertook to establish twenty-four looms in the city; Francisco Sierra, a Galician, and José Agustín of Madrid, who in 1691 proposed the manufacture of Holland cloths; Alonso de San Pedro, native of Prado (?Seville), who established five looms for woollens in the town in 1692; Francisco Muñoz and his five colleagues who in 1691 formed a company in Plasencia to promote the production and sale of woollens; Alonso de la Cuesta and his five colleagues who in 1692 proposed to set up twenty-two looms for woollens in Seville; and Miguel Manuel de Enguera and Francisco Morato, who in about 1693 established a manufacture of oil-cloths in Madrid and received appropriate exemptions from taxes. Their enterprises may have been pious hopes: we have no information on whether they were successful. But no one can doubt that throughout Castile there were numbers of native capitalists who were willing to commit themselves to manufacture if they could obtain government support.

Active help from the authorities was decisive in at least two cities, Palencia and Córdoba; and in both a key role was played by the distinguished administrator Don Francisco Ronquillo. We have touched above on the relative success of industry in Palencia, where efforts were made to restore manufactures by Ronquillo and by Pedro Núñez de Prado respectively, when they each held the post of corregidor.

A full report on Córdoba and its industry was made by Ronquillo when he was corregidor of the city in 1687.[69] The principal industry of the city and its region was agriculture, but there was also considerable silk and woollen production. By the 1680s there was a heavy fall in the output of textiles. The epidemics and monetary adjustments of the period must have been a major cause. But the basic reason given was 'the introduction of foreign cloths of smaller size and less durability but with a better finish'. Foreign traders also bought up the best wool, leaving little for domestic industry. The first observation of the city of Córdoba was that this led to heavy unemployment, since both males and females were normally employed in the factories from the age of ten. The second result was a consequential fall in the purchasing power of the public, with bad effects on retailers and on tax revenues.

In 1684 some efforts were made to establish industry in Córdoba, but with little success. By the end of 1686 there was a little improvement: the city then had fifteen new looms for silks, ten for cloth of silver, five for broad baize, and seven for serge and camlets. To encourage production of raw silk, all taxes on it in the area were removed. By April 1687 the number of new looms had risen from the thirty-seven in January to a total of thirty-nine in silks alone and twenty-two in woollens, with the promise of many more. Since we have no exact figures of the number of looms already in existence, it is not possible to assess what increase was represented by these sixty-one looms.

The improvement was clearly not enough, for Ronquillo now adopted a plan to which there seems to have been no other parallel in this period. He wrote to the English ambassador in Madrid, asking for English artisans to be brought to Córdoba. The ambassador agreed, presumably because only French exports would suffer from this. The council of Castile was also agreeable, on the sole condition that the English must be good Catholics. The merchant body of Córdoba agreed to cooperate fully with this programme, and steps were taken to send a representative to Flanders to attract workers; a search was also made in Málaga and Seville for French workers. Many other concessions were made to the manufacturers about conditions of trade. Tax-free allowances of food (ten *arrobas* of oil and twenty of wine per year, plus a daily two pounds of meat for every two full-time looms) were given to the loom workers.

It was in the attraction of foreign artisans that the Committee for Trade was perhaps most successful. All such efforts appear to date only from 1683, when an expert in making fans was brought from Rome to work in Madrid. His manufactory continued production, but with some difficulty, up to 1700. In the same year the Fleming Dionis Bertet, then resident in Valencia, was brought to Madrid in March, to teach Castilian workers how to improve the sheen on their textiles. He spent a year and a half in Castile, and visited the factories in Toledo, Seville and Granada.[70] A glass and crystal works was founded by the Fleming Dieudonné Lambot in the town of San Martín de Valdeiglesias (between Madrid and Avila). His contract with the government obliged him to bring into Spain twenty-five foreign artisans, 'there being no Spanish experts'. Lambot later went into partnership with a Spaniard, Antonio de Ovando, who took over the crystal monopoly in return for half the profits.[71]

In October 1684 the Crown gave its approval to a proposal by the city of Valencia for Joseph Seguers, a Flemish silversmith resident in the city, to invite his brothers from Brussels to establish woollen manufactures in Valencia. One brother and two artisans came in the first instance, and produced satisfactory samples. By September 1687 there were fourteen Flemish artisans at work in the city. For reasons which remain obscure the experiment failed and all the artisans returned in a short while to Flanders.[72]

The silk artisan Jacques Contegius was brought from Flanders to Madrid in 1684, but seems to have achieved little.[73] In 1686 the Flemish paper manufacturer Nicholas Gregeois set up a mill in Segovia, with exemption from taxes for ten years. His compatriots Adrian Roo, consul in Galicia, and Balthasar Kiel, contracted in spring 1686 to introduce linen production into Galicia. A significant contribution to industry in Cuenca was made by Hubert Maréchal of Hainault, who arrived in 1686 and set up woollen manufactures, with the active help of the Committee for Trade.[74] In 1691 he had ten looms, by 1700 there were twenty-two. In 1727 the concern was still flourishing, with sixty-six looms. The rate of production in 1703 was estimated at about three yards (*varas*) per loom per day. The total of working looms in Cuenca in 1700 was put at fifty-one, of which, as we have seen, twenty-two were under Maréchal.

In 1687 Pedro García de Heredía established a baize factory in the city of Sigüenza, but imported artisans from French Navarre to work it. The enterprise was put under the direction of the Navarrese Jean de Cauhape Infante. In 1688 Heredía brought twenty-two more workers from France to help. Active support for the scheme was given by the bishop of Sigüenza, who strongly recommended Cauhape to the Committee for Trade, in the hope that employment would thereby be found for the poor of his diocese. In 1690 Cauhape invited to Spain his compatriot Jean Baptiste Turon, who came and helped set up a factory not only in Sigüenza but also in Cifuentes, further south. Cauhape's enterprise in Sigüenza had ten operative looms in 1692, and in the same year Bernard and Pierre Solance put forward to the Committee proposals to establish fifteen more looms for woollens. The later history of these schemes is not clear: Larruga reports that most of them had collapsed by 1695. The city of Sigüenza, however, still had a total of thirty-six looms in 1732.[75]

In 1689 in Valencia Benito Bertet proposed that the Seguers failure be remedied by yet another attempt to bring workers from Flanders.[76] In 1690 the Flemings Michel Raiballart and Henri Leconte were supported by the Committee in their plans to set up woollen manufactures in Toledo. Similar support was given in 1696 to two other Flemings, Jacques van der Hagen and Theodore Pelichy, who wished to do the same in Alcalá de Guadaira (Seville). Many other names appear in the papers of the Committee, but little is known of their activities.

Though some of the workers brought into Spain were French, the great majority came from the southern Netherlands. As natives of the country with the greatest industrial expertise in Europe, they were obviously very welcome.[77] But it was also most convenient that they were both Catholics and subjects of the Spanish Crown. The importance of Belgian aid was clearly the main reason why, when the Committee was reconstituted in 1682, a member of the council of Flanders, Louis Scockaert count of Tirimont, was coopted on to it.

Inevitably there were difficulties with some Spanish manufacturers. Few of the foreign artisans could have established themselves in Spain without the protecting hand of the Committee. On the other hand, it was precisely this protecting hand, and the numerous privileges that went with it, that must have aroused the hostility of some Spanish traders. The guilds would have been the first to be offended. Consider the terms under which Benito Bertet in 1689 proposed to establish his new factory in Valencia.[78] The workers were to be independent of all existing guilds; members of other guilds could not work in the factory: Bertet was to have sole control for ten years, with monopoly rights, and could deal with any other guilds of his choice. The very important issue of training apprentices was thereby removed from the jurisdiction of the normal guilds. This, of course, was the classic way in which foreign technical expertise had been introduced into many western countries. The Committee was more concerned with this diffusion of skills than with protecting the guild privileges of Spanish towns. Nor did it wish the new expertise to remain the preserve of the few. When Dieudonné Lambot in 1683 agreed to pass on to Antonio de Ovando his formula for glassmaking at San Martín de Valdeiglesias, the authorities were concerned that not only Ovando but all the artisans under him should have full knowledge of the technique, so that the country as a whole could benefit.

There were serious difficulties to be overcome even if production went ahead. The new cloths made by both Spanish and immigrant manufacturers were not welcomed by established merchants. Commenting on a report of the Committee, the council of Castile in October 1688 reported that 'the traders do not wish to buy material from the new factories to supply to their shops, for reasons of their own; and this can be verified because it is a fact that if one looks for anything from the new factories in the shops in Madrid, nothing can be found'.[79] On this occasion the council gave permission to a manufacturer (it was Hubert Maréchal) to open his own retail shops. The problem was general, and potentially damaging to the new industries. Melchor Lorenz in 1689 had to institute a costly lawsuit to force the guild in Madrid to recognise his privileges and to sell his cloths. The problem of marketing was virtually insuperable, for the majority of retailers had a vested interest in selling foreign cloths, when they were not committed to selling fabrics produced by the established guilds. It is more than likely that the real reason for the failure of many of the new entrepreneurs was not incompetence in production but quite simply an inability to break into a market firmly controlled by distributors of foreign textiles.

At the time, many of the Committee's efforts may have seemed unproductive. In retrospect we should instead see in its activities a sign of the rebirth of Spanish industry. Though Spaniards were obviously not as advanced as other nations in technique, they were, as the papers of the Committee prove amply, willing to invest their cash and energy in capitalist manufactures. It is highly significant that the Bourbons took over and adapted its structure. The Committee represented the first serious effort at state direction of industrial enterprise in Spain, and heralded the successes of the economy in the late eighteenth century. In this, as in other respects, the reign of Charles II marks the inauguration of a new era.

## THE CATALAN COMMITTEE FOR TRADE AND NARCISO FELIU DE LA PEÑA

In 1692, as we have seen, a Junta Particular de Comercio was set up in Barcelona.

It was to have a difficult but long history, and contributed substantially to the economic resurgence of Catalonia.[80] But already before that, in 1684, the Committee at Madrid had coopted the services of a Catalan, the Barcelona lawyer Narciso Feliu de la Peña. The career of this very remarkable man is crucial to the history not only of the Catalan Committee but of Catalonia itself.

Our rediscovery of the importance of Feliu de la Peña is due in some measure to Jaime Carrera Pujal,[81] but principally to Pierre Vilar. In his fundamental works of 1962 and 1963,[82] Vilar presented Feliu as a symbol of the new Catalonia that was shaking off the burden of Castilian decadence. Feliu himself has been best known through his own published works, the *Político Discurso* (1681), the *Fénix de Cataluña* (1683), and the magisterial three-volume history taken down to his own day, the *Anales de Cataluña* (1709). His family came from the bustling seaport of Mataró, but his parents were settled in Barcelona, where Feliu and his only brother Salvador were born. The father, Narciso Feliu de la Peña, was a wealthy merchant who in 1637 was admitted into the exclusive merchant corps of Barcelona. His sister-in-law married another wealthy merchant, Juan Llinás. The close relationship between the two families was to be of inestimable advantage to the younger Narciso in his later work.

Neither Narciso nor Salvador followed the father's profession. Narciso studied law and gained a doctorate at the university of Barcelona. Salvador entered the Church. As the eldest, Narciso inherited his father's fortune. Despite his legal career, he continued to maintain close links with the merchant body and to pursue a deep interest in the economic problems of Catalonia. He put both his money and his learning at the service of the merchant community.

In 1680 there was an unusual number of bankruptcies among the traders of Barcelona, as Feliu informed the president of the council of Aragon:

The merchants and officials asked me to write a paper on the present situation and on the harm done by the excessive import and use of foreign cloths. The proposal seemed important and I carried it out, writing and publishing a *Political Discourse* which I put before the city of Barcelona and sent to Madrid for the attention of the councils of Aragon and Castile, and I sent a good number to most of the capital cities of Spain and the chief bodies in this principality, all at my own expense.[83]

In the *Discurso*, Feliu blamed Spanish problems on excessive dependence on foreign manufactures.

Why do foreigners come, to enrich themselves, or us? To make themselves rich to our benefit, that I doubt. To make themselves rich at our expense, that I believe. This is the ill suffered by our principality, and its total ruin, leaving its people without money, and manufactures and trades destroyed.

His solutions were the standard ones: prohibit imports, stop the export of raw materials. But the principal remedy was to boost native manufactures, 'so that the trade of Catalonia may rise again, like a phoenix from its ashes'.[84]

From this point onwards Feliu dedicated all his energies to the promotion of industry in Catalonia, a fact well appreciated both in the principality and in Madrid. His undeniable importance in public life makes it all the more curious that he never aspired to civic eminence, and unlike his closest colleagues he never took political office nor did he seek the honours of noble rank.[85] When the War of Succession broke, Feliu and his friends were openly pro-Habsburg and anti-French. Their whole economic programme had, after all, been against French commercial domination. He died during the siege of Barcelona by the Bourbon forces, on 14 February 1712. Because he had never married, the usufruct of his estate was willed to his brother.[86]

Feliu's efforts to promote manufactures in Catalonia occupied the whole period 1680 to 1697. The policy he adopted was that Spaniards must imitate foreigners, and produce textiles identical in quality to theirs. His aim therefore was threefold: to introduce into Catalonia foreign workers, foreign machinery and foreign techniques. These aims could only be achieved under conditions of absolute secrecy. He chose a group of six experienced artisans and sent them abroad at his own expense, to Flanders, France and Germany, to learn foreign techniques. They returned home after eighteen months, with their newly-acquired knowledge. The six were Antonio Burgada, weaver in linen and wool, who went to Flanders and Nimes to learn to work twills and camlets; José Gou, wool-dresser, who went to France to study serges and coloured worsteds; Francisco Cortines, silk-weaver, who went abroad to learn how to give sheen to satins and how to dye silks and camlets; Jacinto Cantarell, dyer, who went to France to learn how to dye stockings; José Prats, wool-dresser; and Mariano Julián. On their return, they were all helped by Feliu to set up in production.

One of the six had a special task to perform. This was Mariano Julián, a merchant of Barcelona, who went to France not to learn but to bring back secretly with him French artisans and looms, a task he completed 'with great trouble and risk',[87] for there was apparently a death penalty in France for industrial espionage. Féliu's own contribution was to compile a book in Catalan on production techniques in Belgium, France and England. At the request of the Committee for Trade in Madrid, he sent them a Castilian translation.

All this activity, from 1680 to 1682, must have consumed a great deal of Feliu's capital. There were some constructive results. The city of Barcelona granted to Burgada the use as a factory, for eight years, of a section of the Hospital de la Misericordia. Feliu estimated that in 1683 some two thousand workers in various places were contributing to Burgada's production. A major setback occurred when Juan Bautista Vivers, a silk merchant of Barcelona, in October 1682 obtained from the Crown a ten-year monopoly to manufacture silk stockings on looms introduced from France. The privilege would have undone all the efforts of Julián and Feliu, who both made strenuous efforts to have it revoked.

The Audiencia of Barcelona gave its judgment on the Vivers case on 26 May 1685.[88] Both Vivers and Julian claimed to be responsible for having introduced the looms from France, consequently each claimed the right to a monopoly. The Audiencia found that Julián had indeed been to France and had brought back four iron looms on a ship in March 1682, but that the cost of the whole enterprise had been borne by Vivers, who was consequently justified in retaining his privilege.

Meanwhile Feliu had been busy writing a little book which he finished in January 1683. The inspiration behind the book was the merchant Martín Piles, who in February 1683 wrote to the council of Aragon for permission to publish, saying that

he and other individuals intend to set up a big company to restore in that principality the decayed trade and navigation which formerly rendered such lustre and service to the Crown. To this end they have composed and put together a discourse and model to stimulate the restoration of shipping in that principality to what it used to be in past times, and to introduce new factories. Its title is *Phoenix of Catalonia*. Being a matter of such consequence he entreats Your Majesty to permit its publication in the said city of Barcelona.[89]

The *Fénix de Cataluña*, published in 1683, was undoubtedly the most significant work to emerge in Catalonia in the late seventeenth century. Though Feliu claimed to be its author, the facts are a bit more complex. He certainly wrote it, and the style and composition are his. But the originator of a scheme for a trading company was Piles who, as the penultimate sentence of the *Fénix* put it, 'thought of this way to resuscitate the poor health of this province'. The *Fénix* therefore carried Piles's name on its title-page, while that of Feliu was left to the last page of the book. Nor were Piles and Feliu the only ones in the project. With them was a small group of prominent Catalans, not only traders but also nobles and men in political life, who were determined to bring new life to their country.

On 2 January 1684 the king wrote to the council of Aragon to say that since 'the Committee for Trade has represented that it would be desirable not only to maintain the factories for different kinds of textiles of silk and wool that Dr Narciso Feliu has set up in the principality of Catalonia, but also to further them', the royal thanks should be sent to Feliu. One result of all this was that Feliu was made an associate of the Committee in Madrid. This was opportune, since he needed help for his schemes. The council reported on 24 October that 'Dr Narciso Feliu has written to the president on the 7th, giving an account of the opposition he is experiencing from those who, helped by some powerful people in Catalonia, have recourse to trade with foreigners; and in order to succeed in forming a Company and introducing new textile factories in that principality, he asks that an order be sent to the new viceroy, marquis of Leganés, to favour him with his protection'.[90] Instructions to this effect were sent to the viceroy.

In his *Anales*, Feliu expresses his bitter disappointment with the period of his collaboration with the Committee: 'events up to 1697 were very unfavourable to our efforts and labour'.[91] A detailed and useful account of his difficulties may be found in a letter from him which was discussed in the council on 16 December 1687.[92] In addition to opposition from certain quarters, he blamed the popular insurrections that began in 1687. The position by the end of that year was as follows. Burgada's tenancy in the Misericordia was abruptly terminated. Prats was opposed by several manufacturers and had to leave Barcelona. Piles failed after several fruitless months to receive permission to set up a factory in Barcelona. Julián had trained several artisans in the preceding three years and some of them had now gone to Valencia. Julián himself was in Saragossa, setting up a new factory; but in his absence from Barcelona his looms, which were located in Feliu's own house near the Hospital, were removed by officials. In response to this letter the council of Aragon wrote at once to the viceroy with instructions to help Feliu. It was not, however, a propitious time. Catalonia was convulsed by insurrections in 1688, and in 1689 war with France broke out again. The only successful step taken was the foundation in 1690 of the long mooted company, now named the Company of Santa Cruz, and dedicated to the production of textiles. Feliu, Llinás and Piles were among the directors, and the nobleman Bernardo Aymerich became its spokesman.

When in 1692 it was decided to create a Junta de Comercio in Barcelona along the lines of the one in Valencia, the viceroy, duke of Medina Sidonia, was asked to submit a list of suggested members. The eventual Committee, which had its first session on 30 December 1692, was made up of: Don Manuel de Llupiá the military governor of Catalonia as president; Don Josep Galcerán de Cartellá y Sabastida, marquis of Cartellá; Dr Narciso Feliu; Agustín Martínez; and Magín Mercader.[93] In his report the viceroy had said in recommending Feliu that 'without him little or nothing will be done; to his diligence, application and money are due all the factories that are now advancing in Barcelona'; Martínez he described as 'passionately concerned to make trade in Catalonia grow, independently of foreign nations'; and Mercader was said to 'have great intelligence, and he is maintaining some factories of serges and camlets'.[94] Unlike the Valencia Committee, that of Barcelona had two active merchants as members, and another (Feliu) whose work fell into the same category. This professional composition should have augured well.

Unfortunately we have to agree with Feliu's view that there is no evidence of any substantial achievement. The Barcelona Committee continued in existence for five years. There is some documentation of its activities. In 1695 the council sent it a report on a proposal from the merchant Raimundo Verdeny.[95] In 1696 the Committee opposed the concession of a patent to Burgada and Prats, the former colleagues of Feliu, who with Lorenzo Llaseras were seeking a ten-year monopoly to manufacture twills and coarse cloths. The Committee's view, written in his own hand by Feliu, was that 'the best patent is where everyone works with full application, and it is from this that one will derive benefit'.[96] This decision against monopoly may well have been one of the last acts of the Committee, which ceased operating in 1697. It was the year of the fall of Barcelona to the French.

The Catalan Committee was a disappointment to Feliu, but we should not therefore conclude that everything had failed in Catalonia. The activities of **Martín Piles** are proof that some of the new manufacturers were continuing their work. In 1682 he had invented a new milling process. In 1688 he obtained a patent for twelve years to use a new production method, which seems to have been a type of multiple loom. In 1690 he and the sail-maker Francisco Clavaria obtained a twenty-five year patent to set up a factory connected with the Company of Santa Cruz. By the 1690s his son Juan Pablo Piles had joined him as a partner.[97] Other manufacturers attempted, like Piles, to establish a market in domestic textiles. There is some evidence, as we shall see, that economic activity had increased. The countervailing factors typical of a dependent economy were however still dominant: 'the opposition of many traders dealing in foreign cloths'

(Feliu's words), the open preference of the Catalan upper classes for foreign luxury goods, the lack of investment and (in the words of Feliu's friend, the geographer José Aparici) 'the greatest fault of this our land, that the nobility do not wish to patronise public trading'.[98] The greatest direct blows to resurgence were delivered by the events of the years 1687–89, 1697 and 1705–14. In these difficult circumstances, the regeneration of Catalonia was postponed to the eighteenth century.

## THE RURAL ECONOMY

In 1797 the overwhelming majority of the Spanish people lived outside the cities, and nearly 71 per cent were engaged in agricultural production. The proportion of people in the agrarian economy may be assumed to have been much higher in the seventeenth century. Unfortunately our information on the period is virtually non-existent. Some two hundred years separate the ambitious survey ordered by Philip II in 1575[99] and the reports presented to the council of Castile under the ministry of Jovellanos.[100] The period in between is liberally scattered with the complaints and solutions of arbitristas. In those two centuries the nature of the problem remained basically unchanged. The invaluable reports of the intendants of Castile, collected in 1784 on the orders of Campomanes,[101] serve as a grim reminder that the same 'obstacles (estorbos) to prosperity', as Jovellanos put it, were still operative.

The estorbos that Jovellanos discussed in 1795 fell into three main categories. There were, firstly, political and legal obstacles. These included the privileges enjoyed by pasture, in common lands and in the sheep-walks of the Mesta. They also included the enormous tracts of fertile land owned by the Church in mortmain (amortización) and by the aristocracy in entails (mayorazgos). The great estates, or latifundia, were common in the centre and south of the peninsula, and were seen as a major cause of inadequate agricultural production and of rural unemployment. The second category of estorbos arose out of human ignorance: farmers and labourers needed to be taught how best to exploit their limited resources, and the government needed to extend help to rural producers. Natural and physical estorbos were the third and arguably the most serious.

Spain's geography and weather were unfavourable to a flourishing agriculture.[102] The climate is one of extremes. Forty per cent of Spain is over 500 metres above sea level, making it the most elevated country in Europe after Switzerland. Agriculture at this altitude, particularly in the central Meseta, has to cope with unusual difficulties and a wide range of temperatures. In some regions subtropical and mountainous climates coexist side by side. Droughts are common: over 36 per cent of the peninsula, precipitation is less than an average of 500 mm (20 inches) a year. When the rain comes it is in short periods during the winter and spring, and the concentration helps contribute to soil erosion. In very dry regions, where the baked earth will not accept the rain, it leads to regular floods. With good reason, Jovellanos emphasised insufficient rainfall and irrigation as the major natural obstacles.[103] The rivers, of which the Ebro is the most important, provide little help, since they shrink precisely when most needed, in the summer.

The richest agricultural soil was in the well-watered north (Galicia, Asturias, the Basque provinces) and the coastal plains of Catalonia and Valencia. The amount of land available for cereals was however never adequate. The hilly terrain in Asturias and the Basque lands diverted wealth into livestock rather than agriculture, so that as Bowles observed in the eighteenth century, 'they are forced to get corn from Castile'.[104] Valencia, despite the remarkable output from its *huerta*, had to resort regularly to imports of grain. By contrast, some arid areas were capable of high production. In Córdoba in the 1680s grain output was so high that one good year could carry the region through four lean years.[105] Part of the problem for Spaniards was that the land had to produce cash crops as well as crops for subsistence. The fruits of the soil accounted for a high proportion of Spanish exports. Indeed Spain in the 1660s was very much like Spain in the 1960s, an exporter not of industrial goods but of agricultural produce, fruits and wine. These were 'products that in the great majority of cases could be qualified as luxuries in the importing countries'.[106] The quotation, very apt for the seventeenth century, is in fact from a report of the Spanish Ministry of Agriculture in 1964.

The immense diversity of Spanish agriculture baffled foreign visitors. Some saw only barren landscapes and empty distances; others, like Lorenzo Magalotti, journeying through the peninsula with prince Cosmo de Medicis of Tuscany in 1669, were favourably impressed by Spanish farming.[107] Willughby in 1664 praised the huertas of Valencia and Gandía, where 'the earth is always wrought, and never lies fallow or idle'; but he also had praise for the region 'by Osuna, La Puebla and El Arahal . . . this Countrey was the best we saw since we came into Spain, the land being for the most part well planted and cultivated'. He judged the land 'between Carmona and Ecija . . . a very good Countrey, abundance of corn and olive trees', and felt that 'between Toledo and Madrid the Countrey is very populous and the soil very good'.[108] The proximity of rich soil to barren scrub and arid wastes created a major problem not simply of production but of disproportionate food supply between the regions. Osorio y Redín was aware of the issue, which he discussed in his *Extensión Política y Económica* (1686). 'Ignorant people', he wrote, 'say that there is no need to sow two million *fanegas* of land, since there is a surplus of wheat and barley in many places. They are unaware that over half the population is out of work and only a third of these have food, many having to live off wild plants and fruits'.[109]

The land did not produce enough food for the people. The agrarian problem has been blamed on low yields, unfair land distribution, inadequate investment and innovation, and depopulation. Low yields were a symptom and not a cause of crisis. There is no doubt that harvests in the seventeenth century were some 50 per cent less by volume than in the late eighteenth century, and also considerably smaller than in the sixteenth.[110] This agrarian depression of the seventeenth century is simply explained. The cause was the demographic crisis: low yield was a result of population loss, as we shall see from the cases cited below. A truer picture of output should be obtainable not from total production figures but from yield ratios, or proportion of seed sown to grain reaped. The data are unfortunately fragmentary. It has been suggested that villages in New Castile in the late sixteenth century had yield ratios of 1:8 in wheat.[111] This seems high, but the level is close to that attained at the end of the eighteenth century. In the seventeenth century, on the other hand, the level was apparently low. In the country around Segovia the ratios in wheat did not rise much above 1:4.[112] This level of output resembled eastern Europe more than the intensive farming methods of the west.

Commentators varied in their explanations. Foreigners such as Townsend in the eighteenth century were critical of the archaic tools used in agriculture. Superficial tillage was also criticised. Though many villages used only cows for ploughing (as in Extremadura in this period), the majority used mules. Mule-teams were cheaper, more mobile and adaptable, and a larger area could be sown more rapidly.[113] Unfortunately, they ploughed at a shallower depth and so exhausted the topsoil more rapidly.[114] In Aragon and especially in the territories of Barbastro and Benabarre where mules were used almost exclusively, Ignacio de Asso observed in the eighteenth century that 'with such poor tools it is impossible to plough well, and ploughing does not reach the necessary depth'.[115] Rotation methods left land untilled for lengthy periods. Over most of Spain the most common system was *año y vez*, or one year in use and one fallow. But there were also variations from Avila province and Zamora, with a three-year cycle, to Jérez de los Caballeros with a four-field system.[116] The recourse to three-, four-, and even five-year cycles was not caused exclusively by the poverty of the soil. The first of the fallow years was, on the contrary, necessary in order to find fodder for the herds. Only in the second, fallow, year was the ground prepared for further sowing.[117]

Land distribution was, as it has remained down to modern times, a major obstacle to efficient production. Holdings varied from the latifundia of south and central Spain to the minifundia of Galicia from which tenants escaped to Castile in search of an extra seasonal wage. The status of the peasantry decreased from north to south. There was a preponderance of smallholders in the northern provinces, with tenants as a majority in the central areas, and landless labourers in the south. Comparison of those engaged in agriculture in the provinces of Burgos to the North and Avila towards the centre, shows the following percentages in 1797:[118]

Table 4.1

|        | Proprietors | Tenants | Labourers |
|--------|-------------|---------|-----------|
| Burgos | 36          | 35      | 29        |
| Avila  | 10          | 41.4    | 48.6      |

There were two main classes of peasant proprietor: the whole community as a corporate body, owning lands and agrarian rights in common;[119] and the smallholders, sometimes called *labradores*, who ranged from the pitifully poor to the comfortably off with tenants of their own.[120] The overwhelming mass of the peasantry in Spain was, as elsewhere in western Europe, landless. These day-labourers (*jornaleros*) were inevitably in the worst economic condition of all. In Andalucia in 1797 they made up over three-fourths of the population engaged in agriculture. The contrast between large underexploited private holdings on one hand, and a huge army of rural unemployed on the other, was a problem to which no hopeful solution was offered in the seventeenth century.

Improvements to Spanish agriculture did not make an appearance before the late eighteenth century. This was in line with a general lack of agricultural development in Europe during the seventeenth century.[121] The early sixteenth century in Spain had been a time of progress. The bestseller among improvement manuals was Gabriel Alonso de Herrera's *Agricultura General*, first published in 1513 and issued repeatedly thereafter. In the half-century 1600–50 only one significant new work on agriculture, and that by a Catalan, was published.[122] From 1650 to 1700 not a single original contribution to improvement was published in Spain, and only one reprint of Herrera was issued, in 1677. Jovellanos was later to claim that nothing of value on agriculture had been written since Herrera.[123] Bowles' comments on farming in the Madrid region in the 1750s suggest considerable need for innovations in technique:[124]

Near the town they chiefly sow barley, and here and there have some trifling vineyards. Their tillage is much the same as in Old Castile, that is, just to scratch up the earth and scatter the seed at random, then to cover it over with a similar indifference, and wait for the coming of the poor labourers from Galicia, to get in their harvest. The farmers pretend that if they were to make use of a stronger plough, they should have less corn.

In northern Europe innovation was often brought about by gentry who had travelled abroad. Spanish gentry did not go abroad except on diplomatic or military missions, and apart from Italy had little in common with the culture of other European nations. They showed limited interest in estate management, which was invariably done through agents or bailiffs. Rural investment was not one of the issues with which the Committee for Trade was concerned, and despite the movement of large sums of cash through the rural economy in the form of censos (discussed in Chapter Seven), agricultural improvement did not materialise.

In the teeth of these and other drawbacks that we have yet to discuss, production levels in grain rose dramatically in the late seventeenth century. The coincidence between production levels and population increase is striking. A study by Pierre Ponsot of yields on five farms (*cortijos*) belonging to the cathedral chapter of Córdoba, in the area around the city, shows that the yield of wheat per hectare between 1650 and 1710 rose by over 50 per cent; in barley the increase was over 200 per cent.[125] Evidence confirming this trend is plotted in Figure 4.1, which illustrates the quantity of tithes in wheat and other grain collected from twenty-two villages by the cathedral chapter of Segovia.[126] Tithes were a constant proportion of the harvest (though not necessarily a strict tenth) and give a reliable reflection of total production. The increase in tithes between the 1630s and

1710s was of the order of 48 per cent in wheat and 127 per cent in other grain. A more modest but still unmistakable increase in tithe returns has been documented by Pierre Ponsot for four towns in the vicinity of the gulf of Cadiz; it was a similar story in both Valencia and Catalonia.[127] The apparently gloomy reign of Charles II was precisely the one when agricultural output expanded throughout Spain and began to recover the levels it had reached in the late sixteenth century. In general the increase in grain probably came from putting more land under the plough. At best, a combination of fair weather and more intensive labour may also help to explain the higher output noted by Ponsot in Córdoba and by Casey in the region of Morella in Valencia. The most significant development in both Córdoba and Segovia was the very large increase in production of non-wheat cereals, which may in part have been required to feed growing numbers of livestock.

Fig. 4.1  Grain output in Segovia.

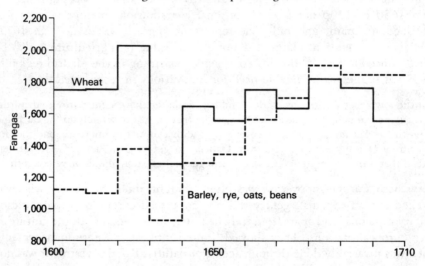

The increase in yields: ten-year averages of tithes received by Segovia cathedral. (After Angel García Sanz)

# THE WEATHER 1665–1700

In an overwhelmingly agrarian economy the life of towns depended heavily on the weather. Two or more bad years in succession could be crippling. The village of Sotos Cuevas (Burgos) had 126 households in 1659, 'but since then because of the bad weather the harvests have been so small that they did not suffice to pay the rent to the landlords from whom the land was held, and they fell into such poverty that they were forced to seek land elsewhere, so that now [1666] only eighty-seven households are left, and all poor'.[128] When a resident from the next village explained to an official in 1674 why the town of Fuente el Viejo (Guadalajara) had all but disappeared from the map, his only explanation was the weather. In 1624 there had been 250 families, now in 1674 there were only twenty-seven, 'and not more than four or six with a mule team, and most are poor labourers, for which reason most of its lands are untilled and many overgrown'.[129]

Continuous details for weather are scanty. The year 1666 was one of extensive drought in Old Castile. The towns of Palencia province, demanding relief in 1667 from taxes, claimed to have lost their crops in the drought, and their cattle in the freezing winter of 1666–67.[130] Unfavourable weather may well have been the reason why prices leapt in the period 1664–69. Taking the year 1662 as a base of 100, wheat prices in Toledo in 1664 stood at an index of 200, in 1667 at 126.5, and in 1668 at 227.[131] In 1668 there was drought in Valencia. 'There was great scarcity of water because not a drop had rained all winter, and the wheat was drying up. They made rogations and public penances and on Ash Wednesday there was a procession of flagellants and all the images of devotion were taken out, and before it finished there was a little rain, and the next day it poured.'[132] In 1670 there was drought in Catalonia and the export of grain was forbidden.[133] In that same dry summer, locusts were blamed for destruction of crops in the kingdom of Granada.[134]

The year 1671 again brought dry weather through most of Spain, and a harvest failure in Valencia. In Murcia, on the other hand, there were heavy rains for part of the year. On Sunday 15 March 1671 a violent whirlwind struck Cadiz at 4 a.m. and left a trail of damage.[135] The winter of 1671–72 brought widespread floods. 'It rained four months and it was so humid that much sickness ensued, and particularly fever, of which many died. The river overflowed several times and finally rose so high that it threatened the city.'[136] So runs a diary entry for Valencia. Another Valencian diarist recorded that

from Wednesday 11 November, St Martin's day, it began to rain and it rained until 10 February 1672, without there being more than twelve fair days. . . . All the corn in the fields was flooded. . . . Throughout the kingdom all the rivers and streams overflowed, causing great damage in the fields and villages. . . . The poor farmers were dying of starvation. . . . Many poor had no food for their wives and children, and they all perished from hunger.[137]

In the spring of 1672 there were also extremely heavy rains in Catalonia, until early April.[138] In most of Castile the year was dry and sterile. On 28 August there was a moderate earth tremor in Murcia.

The region of Huete suffered from locust swarms in 1674, 1675 and 1676, bringing ruin in particular to the town of Leganiel.[139] On 9 August 1674 at 11 p.m. a slight earth tremor shook the city of Lorca in Andalucia. There were more tremors in the next few days, and finally on 28 August at 9.30 a.m. a major earthquake destroyed half the city and killed thirty people.[140]

From 1676 to 1686 Castile, and with it other parts of the peninsula, suffered a prolonged crisis in which the weather played an important part. There was a poor harvest in Castile in 1676; the same thing happened in Catalonia, where grain had to be imported from Aragon.[141] On the other hand the Cadiz area had a good harvest and exported grain to the Canaries.[142] There were winter and spring floods in 1677, and 'the grain harvest throughout Andalucia was lost'.[143] Shortage was nationwide in 1677, and grain had to be specially imported from France. In Madrid the council of Castile reported bread shortages from May, and began to purchase grain for the municipal granary (*pósito*). When the city of Granada began to stock up in this way, prices there leapt from 12 to 110 reales a fanega.[144] The steep rises are not reflected in Hamilton's price series. If we take 1674 as a base year for grain prices in Toledo, his data give an index of 132.4 for 1675, 112 for 1676, 169 for 1677, 212.2 for 1678 and 144.3 for 1679.[145] These unrealistic figures, due no doubt to the fact that hospitals (on which Hamilton relied for his series) had privileged sources of grain, do not reflect the genuine market prices, which were catastrophic.

The disaster of 1677 led inevitably to a climax in 1678, which was the year of the highest grain prices experienced in the whole reign, not only in Castile but also in Andalucia and Catalonia.[146] Dry conditions continued throughout 1678. In the market in Valencia a fanega was priced at 68.5 reales, in Córdoba at 110 reales.[147] In the early hours of 21 May this year a moderate earth tremor was felt in Barcelona.[148] The dry summer was followed by a freezing winter. 'On all sides', wrote a correspondent from Saragossa in February 1679, 'there are complaints of the rigours of the winter, but from here we can report that the ice and snow is greater and sharper than the oldest men can recall. . . . For some time the farmers have been unable to cultivate the earth.'[149] The year 1679 continued to be 'fatal not only for Córdoba', as the city annalist recorded, 'but for all Andalucia',[150] because of the drought. There was a poor harvest in Castile. Lantéry this year noted two small earth tremors in Cadiz. Alhaurin el Grande, between Málaga and Marbella, reported a tremor on 9 October, in which it claimed that nearly half the 280 buildings in the town were levelled.[151]

The year 1680 was from every point of view the grand climacteric of the reign of Charles II. After three years of bad harvests, accompanied in the south by plague, the population had reason to hope for better times. They were to be bitterly disappointed. In February came the big monetary devaluation, which caused havoc for several months. Then, after three years of dearth, the heavens opened in early autumn. From the first week in September torrential rain and hail began to fall, bringing wholesale destruction to the countryside. Reports from all the provinces in Old and New Castile speak of floods and the destruction of crops. A succinct account is available in the 1680 *Second Relation of all that occurred in the memorable and disastrous month of September of the present year*,[152] which is a narrative of 'the many misfortunes suffered by some cities and towns of Castile, Andalucia and La Mancha'. In Valladolid the Pisuerga overflowed, 'obliging the inhabitants to move about in the Venetian style, with boats everywhere'. The same happened with the river Tormes at Salamanca. In Alcalá a dyke had to be built against the flooded river. In Talancon and Yepes twenty-three houses were washed away and over fifty people drowned. In several other places bridges were carried off, mills destroyed, cattle and people drowned, and crops ruined.[153] At Toledo the La Rosa changed its course and swept away both crops and cattle in its path. In Zafra (Extremadura) inhabitants climbed on their roofs to escape the waters. In Osuna

(Andalucia) on 6 September a violent hailstorm lasted from 2.30 to 3 p.m., with stones as large as eggs; it injured over a thousand people and damaged every roof in the area. In a rainstorm that followed, seventeen people died. In Madrid, which suffered storms and flooding from 26 to 28 September, the Manzanares overflowed and the Toledo bridge was dislodged.[154] On 9 October came the big earthquake, whose impact on Málaga and Cartama has already been mentioned. An English correspondent in Madrid reported that 'on 9 October, about 7 o'clock in the morning wee had an earthquake here, which shook all the town in general. It lasted about eight minutes, and did no other harm that I can hear of besides the frightening many of the people and makeing them run out of their warm beds into the cold streets'.[155] Since the epicentre was in the south, the damage in Madrid was minimal. The biggest impact of the earthquake was psychological. The French ambassador, marquis de Villars, commented that

this misfortune had been preceded by great floods which for more than a month had ravaged several towns, already laid waste by the plague. For two years these visitations, added to the poverty and disorder in government and business, had filled Spain with sombre thoughts of the present and new fears of the evils to come.[156]

The year, which was also that of the great *auto de fe* in Madrid, ended with an ominous and epoch-making sign in the heavens. 'This year 1680 on 22 December we saw a very large, brilliant comet, golden in colour, which continued for five weeks in the west',[157] noted the Valencian diarist Ignacio Benavent. In Barcelona it appeared as 'a large comet which slowly mounted in our sky, broad and large with a tail like an arrow'.[158] This was the second appearance of the comet, which had first been sighted in European skies at the end of November. Considerable speculation was aroused throughout the continent over its possible significance, but discussion in Spain was restrained. The *Discurso del Cometa del año de 1680*,[159] for instance, was written mainly to reassure the public that there was no threat to the king's life.

In 1681 there were continuous heavy rains in all parts of the country. From provinces as far apart as Navarre, Burgos and Cuenca there were reports of hail and floods in the summer months. In Melgar de Fernamental (Burgos), for example, 'there was no harvest in 1680 and 1681 because of the hail and freezing weather'.[160] In Póbeda de la Sierra (Cuenca) a flood on 15 June swept away all its mills and bridges.[161] There was a return to drought conditions in 1682 and 1683, throughout Spain from the Basque provinces to Extremadura.[162] Seville subsequently complained of 'the fatal year 1683, when drought made the fields sterile and there was no harvest, and desperate need drove people into extreme misery, so that men sought wild plants to sustain their bodies and in the parched fields there was no grass or water to support the herds'.[163] A resident of Seville, Francisco Godoy, reported that 'in all 1683, up to the end of November, no rain fell. The earth of almost all Andalucia dried up'.[164] In the north of Spain, there was some rain late in the spring. But the south had to wait till the end of the year. When the rain came, it was torrential. Rivers overflowed, crops were ruined, cattle were drowned. A member of the council of Finance, speaking gloomily in March 1684 of the previous year's harvest failure, referred to the present 'three months and more of continuous rains which have caused floods and very considerable losses'.[165]

Famine conditions prevailed over most of Castile, Murcia and Andalucia in 1684. In April the council of State refused permission to Cadiz to import 100,000 fanegas of wheat from France in French ships, and directed the city to look to Sicily.[166] That same month the famine in Murcia led to the proclamation of street curfews to prevent looting of food.[167] In Andalucia, if we may follow Hamilton's data, the price of grain reached a level it was not to surpass for another hundred years.[168] From 1684 to 1687, dry conditions alternated with periodic flooding. The province of Burgos suffered drought during these years. In 1685 there were reports of famine in Murcia, and severe drought in Galicia, where the rivers dried up.[169] On Wednesday 12 July 1684 a total eclipse of the sun occurred. 'Yesterday at three here was seen in our horizon an eclipse of ye Sunn', wrote an English correspondent from Madrid. A Barcelona annalist recorded that 'we could see an eclipse of the sun which began slowly to be covered. . . . It lasted about two hours and many stars were visible.'[170]

The depressing reality of these long years of bad weather is reflected in the long statement sent back to the council of Finance in 1683 by Don Julián de Cañas, a councillor engaged in readjusting the tax levy on Seville and its region:[171]

During my visit I have looked at the best towns that Your Majesty has in the kingdom of Seville, without being able to stop to look at more than was necessary, travelling by day and by night, which at my age no one else would do. . . . These realms which used to be the opulent granaries of Spain and the best stores of oil and the most plentiful in cattle, are now without fruit of any kind, the inhabitants fleeing and lost in the countryside with no work to do, the best of them eating grass and others robbing farms and stealing cattle. . . . And the greatest threat to this kingdom [of Seville] in view of past years is that no grain is expected in the coming one, and this is not only for lack of seed but of draught-animals, some of which have died of hunger while others have been taken to the slaughter-house. . . . I came to the richest land in Spain and it has been the poorest and most sterile of all the twenty-one provinces.

In Valencia the year 1686 was one of grain shortage. There were bread riots which the nobility had to appease.[172] The winter was cold. The duke of Montalto wrote from Madrid to Don Pedro Ronquillo on 31 January 1687 that 'for five days it has done nothing but snow, though this is more tolerable than the continuous and severe freezing weather that we have had since the winter began'. In 1687, dry through most of Spain, the most notable event was the arrival of the locust swarm in Catalonia. Since 1684 there had been early signs of the menace, but the brood was at its fullest size in 1687. A contemporary chronicler has left us his impression:

This year [1687] they passed from Cervera up to Ampurdán, a distance of twenty-five leagues. In the region of Urgell and most of Segarra they left neither green nor grain, and it was the same from Cervera to Gerona. . . . I saw them pass, and stop for entire days, like swarms of bees so that there seemed to be a fog across the sun. Sometimes they blotted out the sun, and it was necessary to carry a branch to brush them off the roads. . . . People were stunned: it was as though the end of the world had come throughout Catalonia.[173]

In July the council of Aragon was informed that 'there remains only a tiny part of the province that has not suffered this epidemic' of locusts.[174] Fortunately the winter of 1687–88 was bitterly cold in Catalonia. This, and the subsequent floods in spring 1688, finished off the brood. But the disaster was to have profound consequences for the principality.

Heavy spring rains were also recorded in Madrid, where the Manzanares overflowed in March.[175] For the next few years there was a distinct improvement in climatic conditions. In 1688 in Valencia 'wheat was at such a low price that good quality sold at four lliures a *cahiz* [17 reales a fanega] and the best at five and a half '; in Toledo the price was even lower, at 14 reales a fanega.[176] The harvest was poor in Valencia in 1689, but in Castile despite some regional reverses, such as the nation-wide hailstorms of 15 and 16 July,[177] the price of corn stayed low. In December 1689 a comet was seen in the southern sky, as reported from Valencia.[178] The weather in 1690 was unremarkable. Winter in 1691–92 was, however, unpleasant; the spring and summer of 1691 were extremely dry, followed at the end of the year by heavy rains.[179] In December there were 'great storms and floods that did extensive damage throughout Valencia'.[180] Alexander Stanhope reported from Madrid in February 1692 that 'we have had as bad a winter as ever I have seen in England for rain, snow and cold'.[181] The spring of 1692 was, on the other hand, extremely dry in Catalonia, Valencia and Murcia. Both in Valencia and in Castile the harvest this year was very small: Hamilton's data show that prices of wheat in Toledo were at their highest for six years. In Aragon the winter that followed these dry conditions was bitterly cold, and large losses of cattle were reported.

In some areas the dryness continued into 1693. In Galicia, as we have already seen, it was a year of famine.[182] Alicante informed the council in November 1693 that 'this year the wheat harvest in its region has been little or nothing, since it has not rained for over fourteen months', and claimed that famine conditions existed throughout Valencia.[183] Permission was given to import wheat from Castile, where the harvest was better. Late December 1693 and early January 1694 were days of the great freeze. Stanhope complained of 'our weather, which has been for twenty days past as cold as ever I felt in England, the king having been every day, with vast multitudes of people, to see sliding on skates, in the great ponds of the Retiro'.[184] Benavent in Valencia noted in his diary that 'on 7 January it snowed a great deal, and there followed such a great cold and freeze that very old men said they had seen nothing like it since the river Ebro froze over'.[185]

That spring of 1694 it did not rain in Castile. Stanhope in May wrote that it had not rained for four months, that the price of food had risen and famine was feared; at the same time, locusts appeared in Andalucia and Extremadura.[186] Conditions improved later in the year. The winter of 1694–95 was one of 'great snows and rains', according to Stanhope. The year 1695 seems to have been normal, but winter 1695–96 was wet. Reports from Valencia speak of heavy rains from October through January. Benavent in Valencia city described the storms and rains of November as 'so copious that it seemed a second deluge . . . the whole huerta looked like a sea'. Supplies of basic materials such as salt and wood fuel were exhausted.[187] Murcia suffered floods at the same time. The result in

1696 was a shortage of grain in the Levant provinces. Madrid in 1696 had a very hot summer, 'the hottest in my life', according to Stanhope.[188]

No information on the weather of 1697 is available apart from Benavent's account in Valencia of the memorable fourth of February when 'the air was so cold that within doors the jugs of water froze and at night the fountain in the market froze so that all of it looked like one block of ice, and plants and trees froze and many old people died'. From him we also learn of the strange spring weather, with snows and rain in January and February, followed by a hot March, and then a cold late spring, with snowfalls in mid-May.[189] The chief event of 1698 was the failure of the wheat harvest in Castile, with political repercussions that we shall touch on later.

The impact of natural reverses should not be underestimated. The town of Uceda (Guadalajara), which suffered badly in the 1683 drought, is a typical example:

Its population is reduced to eighty-five families who live in the outskirts, since in the spot where the town used to be there have remained only five rickety houses, and those in the outskirts are almost in ruins, and the inhabitants all poor without any income from trade or commerce. The damage done by the hail in 1680 to the vines and fields which they own, was so considerable that in subsequent years they have reaped no crops and this year the wheat has failed so that they have stopped sowing most of their holdings.[190]

This description was drawn up not by a representative of the town but by an official of the council of Finance, whose task was to assess the town's ability to pay taxes rather than to exaggerate its difficulties. A similar report, again by a Finance official, is available for the town of Leganiel (Cuenca), which

from 1636 to 1640 had about three hundred households, and these had eighty mule teams; at present [1677] it has 147 households and 25 mule teams. There are 150 ruined houses, and this ruin and depopulation arise from the bad harvests caused by bad weather and the number of locusts in that area in the years 1674–76.[191]

The impact of hail, a regular weather hazard, on the province of Logroño in July 1681 gives a striking insight into the degree of damage that could be caused. In the town of San Asensio the harvest of all grain in 1680 was 13,500 fanegas, in 1681 it was 2,500; in Hormilla in 1680 it was 7,100 fanegas, in 1681 it was only 830. The evolution of the total grain and wine harvest in the little town of Cervatos de la Cueza (near Carrión de los Condes, in Old Castile) over the six crisis

Table 4.2

| Year | Grain | Wine |
|------|-------|------|
| 1676 | 100 | 100 |
| 1677 | 57.2 | 82.8 |
| 1678 | 66 | 90.4 |
| 1679 | 10.4 | 4.6 |
| 1680 | 18.6 | 1.7 |
| 1681 | 12.3 | 10.7 |

years 1676–81 (Table 4.2), shows how the terrible decade 1676–86 must have affected some towns. The year 1676 is taken as a base index of 100.[192]

The figures are fluent testimony to disaster. In most years grain reaped would barely have sufficed for the next year's sowing. The harvest, moreover, represented more than food. It was also the fund from which rents and taxes were paid. By themselves low grain returns might not always spell ruin; but if the town had no other resources to fall back on, such as industry or livestock, then a series of disaster years such as these could put it into an economic situation from which it might never escape.

## THE RURAL ECONOMY AND DEPOPULATION

The low agricultural yields of the seventeenth century were primarily the result of a fall in population. Farmers tilled the fields most accessible to them and left the distant areas for pasture. Willughby in 1664 observed that 'within a quarter of a league of a town you begin to see ground ploughed, else all a wild countrey, and nothing but rosemary, cistus, juniper, lavender, broom, lenticus, etc. growing in the fields and on the hills'.[193] How much then did the average household produce in rural Spain? Let us take the example of Torrejoncillo, near Huete, with a population in 1654 of 544 households.[194] In 1631 its annual production of wheat (measured over the five years 1630–34) was 18,900 fanegas; in 1641 it was 20,750 fanegas. At a rough estimate, we can say this represents an output per household of 33 fanegas. By 1684 the population was only 304 households, and the harvest return in wheat that year was 9,040 fanegas.[195] The decline in output between 1630 and 1684 was well over 50 per cent. The output per household, however, remained much the same, about 30 fanegas. It was almost as though the town, which presumably still possessed the same extent of land, had voluntarily restricted its output while attempting to maintain the same subsistence level per household.

Wheat production at Torrejoncillo was probably close to the national average. It has been suggested that in the late sixteenth century a harvest of 28 fanegas was the essential minimum for a household of four.[196] Osorio y Redín in 1686 produced a comparable estimate. 'Each fanega', he wrote, 'makes over seventy pounds of bread. Allowing one and a half pounds of bread a day, each person requires in the year about eight fanegas.'[197] For a household of four this meant annual consumption of thirty-two fanegas of wheat as a minimum. Since 1684 was a bad year throughout Spain, Torrejoncillo was obviously fortunate in being able to produce enough for its basic needs. Other towns were not so lucky. Los Santos de la Humosa, near Toledo, had 200 households in 1580, 100 in 1680. In 1679 its harvest produced sixteen fanegas wheat per household, which by our estimate was only half its minimum needs.[198] Not far away was the town of Villatobas. In 1641 it had 763 households, in 1674 only 372. In 1671 it harvested a total of only four fanegas of wheat, in 1673 only three. A local priest testified that 'we sowed 34 fanegas and reaped three'.[199]

Towns in these difficult circumstances invariably experienced a loss of population. Eighteenth-century demographic sources give various figures for the number of depopulated villages. In Old Castile the number by the 1790s has been put as high as 7 per cent of all towns.[200] Absence of detailed information renders this figure valueless, and indeed the extent of permanent depopulation has sometimes been exaggerated. Sharp falls in population were very common, permanent desertion of a site much rarer. Four main causes of depopulation stand out: mortality, weather, taxes and alienation of land. All the first three factors were reversible: high mortality could recede in the face of a healthy birth rate, weather could improve, taxes could be remitted. So long as the lands were not alienated to outside interests, peasants would return. There are numerous cases of villages that remained uninhabited for a period, then returned to life. Quintana de Bureba (Burgos) suffered a sudden fall in population between 1679 and 1687, from fifty to thirteen households.[201] The cause had been a series of bad harvests. The trend would have been to extinction: in fact the town flourishes today. In an analysis made in 1687 by the council of Finance, among the thirty-eight towns around Valladolid owing most taxes to the treasury, four — Villanueva de los Infantes, Castrobol, Arroyo and Eban — were noted as being wholly depopulated.[202] The report said that in Villanueva, 'depopulated without a single household, the land is suitable for grazing and cultivation, and some living nearby wish to go and resettle it'. The town, like Arroyo, flourishes today.

The shrinkage in certain provinces was undeniable. Apart from Extremadura all the most notorious cases appear to have occurred in the early years of the century. Official reports usually fail to give precise dates. The council of Finance stated in 1682 that the region of Arévalo used to have eighty-three towns, presumably in the late sixteenth century, and now had only fifty-three; but none of this depopulation was claimed to be recent.[203] On the other hand, a clear trend was shown by figures the council offered for Medina del Campo and its region. In 1591 the area (excluding the city) had 3,435 tax-paying households, in 1639 it had only 921, but by 1659 the figure had risen to 1,050. The last figure represented the population in twenty out of thirty-nine towns in the region, the other nineteen being 'depopulated'.[204] Of the nineteen, fourteen had been depopulated before 1641. The big collapse around Medina had therefore come between 1591 and 1640, when the tax-paying population had fallen by 73 per cent. By 1659 there had been a recovery of 14 per cent, initiating the growth of the late century.[205]

Depopulation of the countryside did not necessarily mean demographic catastrophe. 'Depopulation' was a product of fluctuations in the rural economy, rather than a sign of permanent decay. Village sites became deserted, but only because the villagers had moved a short distance away to escape demands from landlords and tax-collectors. In the comarca of Armuña in Salamanca province, the village sites at Cañada, Hortelanos, Sordos, El Hoyo and Velasco Muñoz became wholly deserted between the sixteenth century and the eighteenth. The lands of these 'depopulated' villages continued, however, to be actively cultivated from nearby towns. Some of the villages contained houses that were inhabited for part of the year, and woods continued to disappear despite the apparent lack of villagers.[206]

The continuing crisis in the countryside encouraged some emigration, but it is not clear how serious this was. There is no evidence of substantial permanent movement after the mid-century, nor did people drift very far away. Movement was localised, and rarely beyond the immediate area. As in the early years of the century, the trend was for labourers to leave for the towns. From Villatobas (near Madrid), which had declined by 30 per cent from 763 households in 1641 to 536 in 1670, it was reported that 'over 150 households have left this town to go and live in the town of Ocaña, and others have gone to Madrid'.[207] From Haro (near Miranda del Ebro), which in 1667 had only 234 households, a fall of one-third in twenty years, the emigrants 'went to live in Alava, Guipúzcoa and Vizcaya, which are exempt from the taxes here'.[208] In a petition of 1667 the residents of villages in the region of Palencia claimed to have lost nine-tenths of their population in the preceding forty years, 'households and residents moving to the large towns such as Valladolid, Rioseco, Palencia and other nearby cities, deserting their houses and property through lack of capital'.[209]

The loss of people from the countryside, added to deficient production, were serious problems that seem to have begun to improve during the late century. Little attention, however, is usually given to another form of population loss, that of the animal population. Very few towns relied only on the soil (that is, on grain, wine and oil) for income. It was more normal to have *labranza y crianza*, both tillage and animal husbandry. Mules and cows were necessary for ploughing. Any village with a fall in its number of plough teams was bound to suffer in agricultural production. The seizure of mules for military use was thus one of the most cruel acts that the soldiery inflicted on the civilian population. When the province of Orense (Galicia) refused to pay a tax levy in 1667, the seizure of draught animals was one of the grievances it listed.[210] In bad years a plough team remained the peasant's sole remaining capital, which he might eventually be forced to sell, bringing irreversible ruin on himself and the land. The quantity of draught animals in a town was for this reason a sure guide to its wealth. We have already cited the town of Leganiel, which between 1640 and 1677 saw the number of its plough teams diminish from eighty to twenty-four.[211] In the same area the town of Carrascosa (Cuenca) had 700 households and 170 mule teams in 1630; in 1689 it had 294 households and thirty-five pairs of mules.[212] In most cases the decline in draught animals was a result rather than a cause of distress. The major exception to this was where, as in Extremadura during the Portuguese wars, mules were stolen by soldiers; a situation that contributed to the widespread use here of cows for ploughing.

Richer towns owned livestock over and above their plough teams. Goats, pigs and above all sheep provided a major source of income independent of harvest fluctuations as well as supplying material for rural industry. The herds, like other sectors of the rural population, shrank in the seventeenth century. Aldeanueva de Figueroa (near Salamanca) in mid-century had some 3,000 sheep and 300 cows in its confines; by 1686 it had only 500 sheep and no cows.[213] Campo (near Trujillo) in 1674 had a herd of over 11,000 sheep; by 1690 this had shrunk to 400.[214] Both towns are extreme examples, being casualties of the Portuguese war.

Historical literature has unfortunately been indifferent to the fate of livestock.

The influential historian Julius Klein has argued that 'probably the chief cause of agricultural decline' was the persistence of towns in maintaining their pasture lands for livestock.[215] This is not a convincing view. Arable supplied basic needs, but very seldom produced a sufficient marketable surplus; livestock, on the other hand, was readily marketable[216] and supplied the capital urgently needed for economic stability and expansion. Livestock and pasture were essential to a viable rural economy; indeed, when their best arable had been alienated to absentee landholders, villagers might have nothing else to cling to but their precious flocks. It is difficult not to agree with the contemporary expert Caxa de Leruela (to whom Klein gives short shrift) that 'pastoral farming is the readiest benefit given by nature to prosper human life. In comparison to it, and without its support, tillage is unbearable, inadequate, and bitter toil'.[217]

The search for grazing rights was a crucial problem. Some villages were fortunate to have pasture close at hand; others had to rent land or even send the herds some distance to be fed. No single issue was so ready a ground for quarrel. This often became only an academic question, as villages lost control over their pastures and saw their herds vanish. The disappearance of livestock prejudiced the last hope of raising capital among a peasantry who did not own the land they worked. The fate of sheep in Castile was symptomatic. By the seventeenth century it was proving difficult to obtain pasture for the flocks, which consequently shrank. In the 1680s the account books of the Mesta show regular bankruptcy.[218] The attempt to give new life to the sheep guilds, particularly with Olivares's charter of 1633 and its renewal in 1680, must therefore be seen as a progressive attempt to support a bulwark of the Castilian economy. Without exception, however, historians have followed Klein in denouncing all support for the Mesta and the pastoral industry as unenlightened. This view is superficial. The fate of the pastoral industry involved not only the Mesta but also the non-migratory flocks whose numbers were, as we have seen, estimated by Caxa de Leruela as being 'four times greater than those of the Mesta'.[219] As a former official of the Mesta, Caxa de Leruela favoured a policy of more protection and privileges for the smaller non-migratory flocks, which he saw as the mainstay of the rural economy. He singled out as a threat three classes of person: the big flock owners (including the Mesta), for their reluctance to share pasture; the landlords, for raising rents of pasture or converting to arable; the growers of vines, for ploughing up pasture land. It was a legitimate and powerful case, but no firm policy was ever adopted by the government apart from attempts to aid the ailing Mesta. By mid-century agrarian difficulties were forcing many communities to fall back on pasture and sheep-rearing. It is however absurd to suggest, as Klein does, that under Charles II 'the wool growing industry was allowed to run riot and to annihilate almost the last vestiges of agriculture'.[220]

## PRICES AND WAGES

The great nightmare was inflation. It devoured the incomes of both rich and

Fig. 4.2 Prices in Spain, 1651–1700. Base 100=1671–80. (After Hamilton and Vilar.)

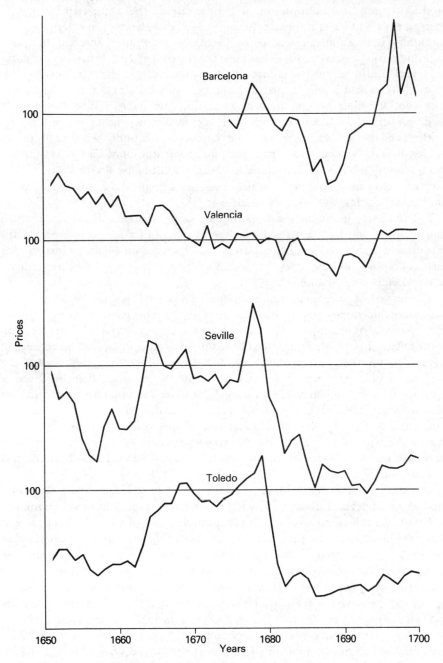

poor, depressed industrial growth and left the home market exposed to foreign goods. Spain continued to suffer inflation long after other west European countries had brought theirs under control. To a large extent inflation was aggravated by low production levels and high demand. Price levels in basic products (wheat, for example) tended to be among the highest in Europe.[221] Foreign envoys in Madrid constantly complained that their salaries were not high enough for the cost of living in Spain. There was also a purely internal monetary inflation caused by successive debasement of the copper-based currency, leading to lack of confidence in the coinage and to pressure from foreign money.[222]

We have looked briefly at prices in the light of weather conditions and must now consider their general movement during the reign. There was a wide variation between different regions of the peninsula, depending on geography, markets and distinctive currencies. The most accessible published data for prices in Castile and Valencia come from the pioneering studies of Earl J. Hamilton. More recently a series for Barcelona has been published by Pierre Vilar.[223] The data are used in Figure 4.2, which presents a general impression of price movements during the reign of Charles II.[224]

Though price levels on the Levant coast were substantially higher than in Castile, there was far more stability. Fluctuations in Castile were greater than Hamilton's data show, since his sources were the account-books of institutions such as hospitals and convents. These did not necessarily buy their commodities at the normal market rate.

The impact of price levels on the Spanish people will not be known until we have more information about incomes. Among the most common complaints of the time was that of a chronic shortage of money, or 'lack of specie'. This seems to point to two things: the widespread hoarding of good coin, and a real absence of enough cash for everyday transactions. The disappearance of good coin and the dominance of copper was notorious. In 1659 the traveller François Bertaut commented that 'one can scarcely find gold or silver and must use copper money even in large cities'.[225] The government itself was driven to pay all its debts in this small change. Unrestricted resort to a copper coinage began after 1598, during the reign of Philip III. By the mid-seventeenth century the astonishing state was reached where Spain, the world's biggest importer of bullion, had almost no gold or silver in public circulation.

The most common coin in use was the vellón real. *Vellón* was originally a mixture of copper and silver, but by the seventeenth century most vellón minted in Castile contained no silver. The comparative price of silver and copper was therefore one of the most practical ways of measuring the value of currency that had little intrinsic value. The higher the price of silver in terms of vellón, the greater was the effective inflation of the currency. As measured methodically by Hamilton, the premium of vellón on silver (that is, the extra quantity of vellón money required to make it equal silver coin of the same face value) in New Castile increased from 50 per cent in 1652 to 150 per cent in 1664, and then after that year's devaluation from a level of 50 per cent to 275 per cent in February 1680.[226] This reflected a crippling fall in the worth of the official vellón coinage, which came to be exchanged by weight rather than by value. Irrespective of the exact number of coins in it, a six-pound bag of vellón was at one time the current price in Seville for ten pounds of cheese.[227]

Because good coin vanished from circulation and copper coin was being used in greater quantities there was a need for more cash. Philip IV recognised the problem and from 1660 onwards issued large quantities of milled vellón (called *moneda de molino*), which had a silver content. The face value put on the coins was, however, higher than the intrinsic value of its silver content, so that the government was making a profit out of what was effectively false money. Between 1660 and 1668 some 16 million ducats of this coin was issued, with a corresponding profit to the government of 9,417,890 ducats.[228]

Monetary disorder was rampant in the early years of the reign. It was aggravated by counterfeit money, speculation and a number of other factors. The government found itself in a financial crisis to which it could suggest no solutions. Unacceptable price levels in Castile, and the enormous increase in the premium of vellón on silver, finally forced a decision. A move to reform vellón had already been taken under Philip IV by a pragmatic of 14 December 1664, which had halved the value of a mark of vellón from 24 to 12 reales. The move had brought temporary confidence, and the premium on silver had for a few months fallen by two-thirds to 50 per cent. Now on 10 February 1680 a long and careful decree repeated the devaluation, but with interesting and significant differences.

The reform was part of the bold programme of improvement planned by Don Juan José of Austria. In 1679 his ministers began to consider ways of providing the country with a stable coinage. Long discussions culminated in a decision to devalue, made by the *Junta de Moneda* on 13 August 1679, when Don Juan was on his sick-bed. The final decree, issued two weeks before the duke of Medinaceli came to power as prime minister, was thus the undoubted legacy of Don Juan.[229]

The February decree[230] devalued the mark of milled vellón by 75 per cent from its current value of twelve reales, to three reales. All other pure copper vellon was likewise reduced to one-fourth its current value. At the same time the extraordinary step was taken of legalising all false and imported vellón at one-eighth of its nominal value. This decision must have been reluctantly made, but showed clearly that the quantities of illegal money in Castile were so great that it would have been impracticable to drive it out of circulation. No other single measure was more indicative of the monetary disorder in the country, and the weak position of the government. The premium on silver was simultaneously reduced from 275 to 50 per cent.

There were three important concessions in the decree. At the new rate a mark of vellón was worth only 102 maravedis (i.e. three reales), but owners of genuine moneda de molino who went to a mint or agency within sixty days could exchange it at a premium of 50 per cent and thus receive 247.5 maravedis (the silver content of 165 maravedis in the old mark, plus the premium). Secondly, all past debts on the royal taxes up to the end of 1673 were wiped out, a loss estimated at over 12 million ducats. Finally, those wishing to pay debts for the three years 1674 to 1677 inclusive were allowed to do so in moneda de molino at the old rate, providing this was done within sixty days.

This drastic measure was rounded off on 22 May by a decree abolishing the legal tender of all the old coinage. Owners could thereafter exchange it only at current equivalents. It is impossible not to be impressed by these decrees, which were among the most ruthless ever issued in Spanish history, and attempted to cut through the Gordian knot of monetary inflation at a single stroke. The result throughout most of Spain was catastrophic.[231] The business world suspended operations for several weeks while financiers registered their specie holdings with the authorities. There was panic and dismay everywhere. Because the old coinage could not be used until restamped, whole communities suddenly found themselves without cash. Barter became common. Thousands lost their savings. Since, as Hamilton observes, 'Castilian coins constituted the bulk of the circulating medium in Aragon, Catalonia, Navarre and Valencia in the second half of the seventeenth century', it was the whole of Spain and not Castile alone that experienced the crisis.[232]

The decree of 10 February should be viewed not as the last desperate act of a bankrupt government, but as a courageous move to break out of an uncontrollable inflationary spiral. Though the new coin and price values remained stable for several years, the decree was not entirely successful. The precious metals still stayed out of circulation. Accordingly on 14 October 1686 the silver coinage of Castile was devalued by about one-fifth. At the same time the relative values of gold and silver (the bimetallic ratio) were adjusted.[233] Foreign traders, whose cash transactions were in silver rather than vellón, suffered considerably from having to accept devalued coin. But the government kept firm on both its 1680 and its 1686 measures. The result was an unprecedented restoration of stability to the monetary system of Castile. The devaluations created conditions in which economic recovery could take effect. To keep costs in line with new coinage values, regular lists of official prices were published.

Nothing so clearly illustrates the favourable conjuncture in Castile's economy, as the movement of prices in the last two decades of the century.[234] Agricultural prices fluctuated according to the weather. Non-agricultural prices, on the other hand, experienced a moderate and steady rise from the 1680s up to the end of the War of Succession over thirty years later. Manufacturers were able to make reasonable profits without having to cope with inflationary costs.[235] A basic precondition for economic recovery had been achieved.

The relation of wages to prices is difficult to determine for this period. Very often wages in kind, such as tools or food, made up part of the full wage, so that

Table 4.3   Prices and wages in Valencia, 1656–1705

| Years | Real wages | Grain prices |
|-------|-----------|--------------|
| | (five-year period, base 1726–50 = 100) | |
| 1656–60 | 88.2 | 103.5 |
| 1661–65 | 91.8 | 95.8 |
| 1666–70 | 101.7 | 91.2 |
| 1671–75 | 106.2 | 82.9 |
| 1676–80 | 109.1 | 102.3 |
| 1681–85 | 110.6 | 85.9 |
| 1686–90 | 115.1 | 78.9 |
| 1691–95 | 121.3 | 82.7 |
| 1696–1700 | 99.0 | 93.3 |
| 1701–05 | 106.3 | 89.0 |

wage figures in isolation became meaningless. Hamilton encountered great problems in trying to construct wage series for the late century. The fragmentary details he has published relate only to Valencia. They are set out in Table 4.3, against the corresponding grain prices.[236]

These figures suggest that the reign of Charles II was not as disastrous for wage-earners in Valencia as might have been supposed. The monetary reforms of 1680 and 1686 in particular created a strikingly favourable situation that increased the earning power of workingmen in the province.

## THE RECOVERY OF THE ECONOMY

The bleakness of much of the reign of Charles II is apparent and needs no emphasis. The ritual complaints and patent exaggerations, however, were a reflection less of contemporary conditions than of the depression of the early and mid-seventeenth century. The experience of that depression was felt both in central Castile and in provincial Catalonia, and provoked the tensions that split the peninsula apart in 1640.[237]

From mid-century recovery in Spain took place in two distinct stages. The Crown of Castile, covering the centre and south of the peninsula, was held back by two major obstacles: the epidemics of the decade 1676 to 1685, and the disastrous monetary inflation down to 1680–86. Despite these drawbacks, there is indisputable evidence that population growth and a rise in agrarian production were already from mid-century laying the foundations for the stability and modest expansion that characterised Castile after the 1680s.

The Cantabrian and Mediterranean provinces were not seriously affected by either the epidemics or the monetary chaos, and initiated their recovery a full generation before Castile. Both Basques and Catalans committed themselves to a programme of commercial and industrial expansion that quickly gave them superiority in the peninsula.[238] In Catalonia stable agricultural prices, a rise in rural production and an increase in population created a firm basis for 'a long period of prosperity and creation' that Vilar suggests began in the 1670s[239] but which may have begun even earlier.

## NOTES

1. See **Kamen, H.**, 'The decline of Spain: a historical myth?', *Past and Present*, **81** (1978), 24–50.
2. Elliott, *Imperial Spain*, p. 297.
3. **Vilar, J.**, *Literatura y Economía* (Madrid 1973), p. 141.
4. **Moncada, S.**, *Restauración* (Madrid 1619), pp. 4, 7, 13.
5. The useful modern edition by **Anés, G.**, *Memoriales y Discursos* (Madrid 1971), includes all his known writings. For an unpublished work not included in the Anés edition, see n.60 below.

6. *Discurso Universal de las causas que ofenden esta monarquía,* printed in **Campomanes**, *Apéndice* (Madrid 1775–77), I, 311–432.
7. *El Zelador General para el bien común de todos*, in *ibid.* pp. 207–310.
8. Replies from the cities of Jaén, Granada, Murcia and Cáceres, dated Apr. to May 1669, in AGS:CJH 1912. The significance of *juros* and of the *millones* is explained in Ch. Fourteen below.
9. Printed in Campomanes, *op. cit.* I, 7–206.
10. Hamilton, E. J., 'Decline of Spain'.
11. See the note to one of Martínez de Mata's Discourses, by José Canga Argüelles, reprinted in Anés, ed., *Memoriales y Discursos*, p. 610 n.3.
12. BL Add. MS. 20.977/221.
13. Consulta of 17 Aug. 1666, AHN Consejos 7176/60.
14. The memorial, dated 18 June 1694, is printed in Valladares, *Semanario Erudito*, XXX, 256–78, and attributed to Solsona. A version of it in BL Eg. MS. 330/21–33, is attributed to the bishop of Vic.
15. Somoza, *Unico Desengaño*, printed in *ibid.* XI, pp. 225–56.
16. Núñez de Castro issued his book in two editions, in 1658 and 1675, in Madrid. The edition published in Barcelona in 1698 is a reissue of that of 1675.
17. Data summarised in the excellent series edited from Salamanca University under the general title *La España del Antiguo Régimen*. My details come from **Mateos, M. D.**, *Salamanca* (1966) and **Calonge, P.**, *et al.*, *Castilla la Vieja* (1967).
18. **Klein, J.**, *The Mesta* (Cambridge, Mass. 1920), p. 342.
19. **Caxa de Leruela**, *Restauración de la Antigua Abundancia de España* (Naples 1631), pp. 49, 95.
20. 'A discourse by Sir William Godolphin touching the wools in Spain' (1667), in **Godolphin**, *Hispania Illustrata* (London 1703), pp. 106–9.
21. **Ruiz Martín, F.**, 'La empresa capitalista', *Third Int. Conf. Econ. Hist.* (Paris 1974), V, 270.
22. García Sanz, *Segovia*, p. 124.
23. *Ibid.* p. 123, graph 20. In both cases the index base 100 is from the years 1745–54.
24. Larruga, E., *Memorias*, XI, 262–348.
25. *Ibid.*, XXXIII, 38–47.
26. *Ibid.*, XX, 56.
27. 'Relacion de las fabricas, tegidos y tratos que havia en Cordoba', 2 Jan. 1687, AHN Consejos 7199/1.
28. **Asso, I.**, *Economía Política* (Saragossa 1798), pp. 114, 117.
29. *Ibid.* p. 135.
30. Memoir on wool presented to the Cortes of 1677, ACA:CA 1370.
31. ADZ 577/175 vo.
32. Larruga, *op. cit.*, XXXIII, 45.
33. Calcena to Diputados, 5 Oct. 1667, ADZ 523/417.
34. This demographic information is misleading. In 1650 Calcena had in excess of 1,000 inhabitants, of whom nearly 40 per cent died in the plague of 1653. See **Maiso, J.**, 'Peste de Calcena', *Estudios* (Saragossa) (1977), pp. 85–92. The figure of 400 vecinos probably refers to the late sixteenth century.
35. **Feliu de la Peña, N.**, *Político Discurso* (Barcelona 1681). I have consulted the copy in BCB, Follets Bonsoms 2799.
36. Memorial of 14 July 1715 in PRO:SP 94/212.
37. Although the élite did invest in industry: see Ch. Nine below.
38. Larruga, *op. cit.* VII, 210, 220, 232.

39. Report in 1692 by the corregidor of Toledo, ACA:CA 588/5/6. He complained of competition from Valencian silks.
40. Report of 1686 in AHN Consejos 7223.
41. Larruga, *op. cit.* VII, p. 220.
42. 'Relaçion de las fabricas', AHN Consejos 7199/1.
43. Memoir of 1677, ACA:CA 1370.
44. Asso, *op. cit.* pp. 117, 137. Contrast this estimate with the report of the Diputados in 1677, noted above.
45. See below, Ch. Thirteen.
46. Memorial of Apr. 1692, ACA:CA 931.
47. 'Over 20,000 persons are dependent on the wage they earn daily on the looms': city of Granada to council of Castile, 31 July 1679, AHN Consejos 7236. This probably accounted for half the active labour force.
48. 'Relacion', AHN Consejos 7199/1.
49. Memorial of 14 July 1699, AHN Consejos 7225.
50. Report of 1686 in *ibid.* 7223.
51. The best summary available is in **Fernández Albaladejo, P.**, *Guipúzcoa* (Madrid 1975), pp. 52–65. See also Fernández de Pinedo, *Crecimiento económico*, pp. 30–3.
52. 'A quintal of ore will produce about thirty-five pounds of good iron, and the residue about thirty pounds of slag': **Dillon, J. T.**, *Travels* (Dublin 1781), p. 200. This work is basically an edition of the mid-eighteenth century letters of D. Guillermo Bowles. For Liérganes, see **Alcalá-Zamora, J.**, *Los altos hornos* (Santander 1974), pp. 21, 94, 238.
53. Fernández Albaladejo, *op. cit.* pp. 61–5.
54. Labayru y Goicoechea, *Señorío de Bizcaya*, V, 532.
55. The figures, and most of the details in this section, are from the papers in AHN Consejos 12.434.
56. The text of the decree bears the date 4 May; but standard works (e.g. Labayru, *op. cit.* V, 749) all give the date 2 May.
57. Larruga, *op. cit.* IV, 229: 'At the instance of the duke of Medinaceli, Charles II ordered a Junta to be formed'.
58. Centani's career is discussed below in Ch. Fourteen.
59. Larruga, 'Historia de la Junta' (in MS., Madrid 1789), I, 8. Much of the information in what follows is taken from this source without further reference.
60. Martínez de Mata's text, a variation of his *Eighth Discourse*, remains unpublished. The original is in AGS:CJH 1895, *Medio con el qual se veran los vassallos libres de todo genero de tributos, por medio de un Monte de Piedad.* For a summary of the history of *montes* since 1576, see Anés, ed., *Memoriales*, pp. 75–82. The montes or *montepíos* are defined by W. Callahan as 'mutualist associations of artisans and small manufacturers created with royal approval to provide necessary capital to their members': see **Callahan**, 'A note on the Junta', *Econ. H. R.* 21 (1968), 520 n.4. Martínez de Mata, however, also had in mind associations to help find capital for peasants.
61. Callahan, 'A note', p. 520.
62. Luis Cerdeño y Monzón was the author of a proposal to establish a trading company: see **Colmeiro, M.**, *Biblioteca de los Economistas* (Madrid 1900), n. 152.
63. Callahan, *op. cit.* p. 521.
64. All details on the Granada Committee are from **Garzón Pareja, M.**, *Industria Sedera* (Granada 1972), pp. 267–319.
65. Castelrodrigo to king, 30 Dec. 1692, ARV: RC 594/160–61.

66. *Ibid.* to D. Joseph de Haro, 17 Dec. 1692, *ibid.* 594/160. Torre was regent (or councillor) for Valencia on the council of Aragon, Mercader and Pascual were judges of the Audiencia. Lorenzo Matheu y Sanz was one of the most distinguished jurists of Valencia, a former regent, and author of the standard (1677) study of the government of Valencia. For the later history of the Committee, which expired in 1700 and was reconstituted under Philip V, see **Molas, P.**, 'Valencia i la Junta', *Estudis*, 3 (1974), 55–111.

67. Unless otherwise indicated, the information that follows is from AHN Consejos 7223, a bundle of the 'Junta de Comercio 1689–1725'.

68. Larruga, *Memorias*, IX, 88. Larruga dates the commencement of the Noves manufactures to 1682.

69. What follows is based on the already cited 'Relacion de las fabricas' of 2 Jan. 1687 in AHN Consejos 7199/1; and on the 'Relacion de lo que Don Francisco Ronquillo correxidor de la Ciudad de Cordova ha executado', in AHN Consejos 7223, dated 30 Apr. 1687.

70. Larruga, *Memorias*, III, 128, 155.

71. Consulta of council of Castile, 27 Sept. 1683, AHN Consejos 7223.

72. Details in memorial of 16 Nov. 1686 by Jurats of Valencia, ACA:CA 926; and in their letters of 23 Sept. 1687 and 22 Nov. 1689 to the king, in AMV Lletres Misives, books 61 and 62 respectively.

73. Larruga, *Memorias*, II, 19–20.

74. *Ibid.* XIX, 1–23.

75. For all this, *ibid.* XVI, 180–96; and documentation in AHN Consejos 7223.

76. Jurats to king, 22 Nov. 1689, AMV Lletres Misives, book 62.

77. For the role of Belgian expertise in the dissemination of capitalist methods, see **Kamen, H.**, *Iron Century* (London and New York 1971) Ch. 3, and bibliography there cited.

78. 'Capitols que proposa Benito Bertet pera la nova Fabrica dels teixits', ARV:RC (libros registros) 593/104–5.

79. Consulta of 24 Oct. 1688, AHN Consejos 7223.

80. What follows is a condensed version of the material in **Kamen, H.**, 'El Fénix catalan', *Estudis*, 1 (1973), 185–203; and in my introduction to Feliu de la Peña, *Fénix* (Barcelona 1975 edn). In both these, fuller quotations and references are given. The later history of the Catalan Committee is studied by **Molas, P.**, 'La Junta de Comercio de Barcelona', *Anuario Hist. Econ. y Soc.*, 3 (1970, publ. 1974), 235–79. There are additional details on Feliu de la Peña in **Molas, P.**, *Comerç i Estructura* (Barcelona 1977), pp. 70–120.

81. **Carrera Pujal**, *Historia política y económica de Cataluña* (Barcelona 1946–7).

82. **Vilar**, *La Catalogne* (Paris 1962), published in Catalan as *Catalunya* (Barcelona 1964–68); and *Le Manual de la Companya Nova* (Paris 1963).

83. Feliu to D. Pedro de Aragon, 11 Dec. 1683, ACA:CA 336.

84. I have consulted the copy of the *Discurso* in BCB Follets Bonsoms 2799.

85. He accepted a knighthood in the Order of Santiago only towards the end of his life, from the Archduke Charles of Habsburg.

86. The full text of his will, an interesting and very important document, is printed in my introduction to the 1975 edition of his *Fenix*. The original is in AGPB, notary Tomás Simón, 'Tercius liber testamentorum 1676–1726', no. 30.

87. 1683 letter of Julián to council of Aragon, unsigned, in ACA:CA 535.

88. The text of the judgment is in *ibid.* 451.

89. Piles to the council, *ibid.* 535.

90. The foregoing correspondence is in *ibid*. 336.
91. Feliu de la Peña, *Anales* (Barcelona 1709), III, 381.
92. ACA:CA 540.
93. Letter from Committee in *ibid*. 338.
94. Medina Sidonia to D. José de Haro, secretary of the council, 25 Oct. 1692, *ibid*. 338.
95. Letter from council, 11 Aug. 1695, *ibid*. 544.
96. Report of Committee to viceroy, 20 Nov. 1696, *ibid*. 469.
97. For all this, see Kamen, 'El Fénix catalán', pp. 30–1.
98. Aparici, a Barcelona merchant and Conseller, is one of the key figures of the period. His manuscript work, cited here from BCB MS. Arch. 516, has been printed by **Llobet, S.**, 'Descripción geográfica', *Hispania* (Madrid), 6 (1946), 632–69.
99. The Relaciones of 1575 are best approached through **Salomon, N.**, *La Campagne* (Paris 1964).
100. **Jovellanos, G.**, *Ley Agraria* (Madrid 1795).
101. *Memorial ajustado sobre Decadencia de la Agricultura* (1784). I have consulted the selection by **Antonio Elorza** in *Revista de Trabajo*, 17 (1967), 138–310.
102. **Flores, X.**, *Estructura* (Madrid 1969), p. 69. See also the excellent short sketch in Carr, *Spain*, Ch. I.
103. *Ley Agraria*, art. 368, pp. 211–12.
104. Dillon, *Travels*, p. 170.
105. 'Relacion', of the corregidor Ronquillo, 30 Apr. 1687, in AHN Consejos 7223.
106. Quoted in Flores, *op. cit.* p. 40.
107. **Magalotti**, in **Sánchez Rivero** ed., *Viaje* (Madrid n.d.), I, p. xxiii.
108. Willughby, *A Relation*, pp. 479, 483, 486–8.
109. *Extensión Política*, p. 16, in Campomanes, *Apéndice*, I, 7–206.
110. See the graphs of production in **Anés, G.**, *Crisis agrarias* (Madrid 1970), especially graphs 15 and 18.
111. Salomon, *La Campagne*, p. 243.
112. García Sanz, *Segovia*, p. 156.
113. Salomon, *op. cit.* p. 95 n.2, emphasises the benefits of mules to the peasant producer in the sixteenth century.
114. Anés, *op. cit.*
115. Asso, *Economía Política*, p. 119.
116. **Costa, J.**, *Colectivismo agrario* (Madrid 1898), pp. 341, 359.
117. **García Fernández, J.**, 'Champs ouverts', *Annales* (1965), p. 695.
118. **Calonge, M. P.** *et al.*, *Castilla la Vieja* (Salamanca 1967), p. 34.
119. Cf. Salomon, *op. cit.* pp. 134–56.
120. See the sketch of 1732 by Zabala y Auñón, reprinted in **Domínguez Ortiz, A.**, *Sociedad española siglo XVIII* (Madrid 1955), p. 280.
121. Slicher van Bath, B. H., *Agrarian History* (London 1963), pp. 218–20.
122. **Miguel Agustín**, *Llibre dels secrets de Agricultura* (Barcelona 1617). See **Tolsada Picazo, F.**, *Bibliografía* (Madrid 1953).
123. *Ley Agraria*, art. 342, pp. 195–6.
124. Dillon, *op. cit.* p. 75.
125. From 'Rendements et production des céréales en Basse Andalousie 1610–1840', information and data kindly communicated by Pierre Ponsot.
126. García Sanz, *Segovia*, p. 105, table 13.
127. Ponsot, P., 'En Andalousie occidentale', *Etudes rurales*, 34 (1969), 97–112; Casey, *Kingdom of Valencia*, pp. 75–6; **Serra i Puig, E.**, 'Consideracions', *Estud. d'Hist. Agr.*, 1 (1978), 120–53.

128. Consulta of Finance, 27 Mar. 1666, AGS:CJH 885.
129. Report in *ibid*. 978.
130. Consulta of Finance, 2 Mar. 1667, *ibid*. 886.
131. **Hamilton, E. J.**, *War and Prices* (Cambridge, Mass. 1947), pp. 238–9.
132. **Benavent, I.**, 'Cosas mas notables', RCPV, MS. 41 f.4, cited hereafter as Benavent.
133. *Dietari*, XVII (Barcelona 1965), 219.
134. Granada to council of Finance, 8 Mar. 1683, AGS:CJH 1069.
135. *Relacion verdadera de los daños que en la ciudad de Cadiz . . . causo el huracan*, BUV MS. 700/28 bis.
136. Benavent f.5.
137. **Agramunt, J.**, 'Casos sucedidos', RCPV, MS. 49/369.
138. 'Anales de la ciudad', BCB, MS. 1479.
139. Report of 2 Nov. 1677 in AGS:CJH 1941.
140. City of Lorca to Queen Regent, 3 Sept. 1674, AHN Consejos 7184/11.
141. See the introduction by J. Sobrequés Callicó to *Dietari*, XIX.
142. Lantéry, *Memorias*, p. 47.
143. *Ibid*. p. 66.
144. **Various Reports in AHN Consejos 7225.**
145. Hamilton, *War and Prices*, pp. 239–40.
146. The only exception was Valencia: see *ibid*. p. 119.
147. Benavent f.7; Ramirez de las Casas Deza, *Anales*, cited in Domínguez Ortiz, 'La crisis de Castilla', p. 8, n.8.
148. 'Anales de la ciudad', BCB, MS. 1479.
149. Letter of 28 Feb. 1679 in *La Gazeta Ordinaria* of 7 Mar., in Astorga G. 25 f.4.
150. Las Casas Deza, as cited above.
151. AGS:CJH 1054. The date 1679 is specifically given in the letter from the town, but the coincidence in dates between this and the tremor of 1680 is worth noting.
152. Astorga G. 18 b 1 no. 56; also in BUV, MS. 700/29.
153. In Valdepeñas (Ciudad Real) the Veguilla overflowed and washed away eighty-seven houses and quantities of crops: consulta of 12 June 1687, AGS:CJH 1111.
154. 'Relacion verdadera en que se refieren las rezias tempestades y avenidas que han sucedido en Madrid', BL Eg. MS. 360/70.
155. Letter of 17 Oct. 1680, PRO:SP 101/92/137.
156. Villars, *Mémoires* (Paris 1893), p. 219.
157. Benavent, f.8 vo.
158. 'Anales de la ciudad', BCB, MS. 1479.
159. Astorga G. 18 b 1 no. 54.
160. AGS:CJH 1044.
161. Letter of 3 Mar. 1682, AGS:CJH 1043.
162. Labayru, *Señorío de Bizcaya*, V, 517; report of 11 Jan. 1687 on Jaraicejo, AGS:CJH 1110.
163. City of Seville to king, 17 May 1684, AHN Consejos 7196/49.
164. Cited in Domínguez Ortiz, 'La Crisis', p. 10, n.14.
165. D. Ignacio Baptista Ribas, in consulta of 10 Mar. 1684, AGS:CJH 1079.
166. Consulta of State, 6 Apr. 1684, AGS Estado 4133.
167. **Blanco, R.**, *Murcia* (Murcia n.d.).
168. *War and Prices*, p. 183. The five-year index for 1681–85 was exceeded only in 1781–85.

169. Domínguez Ortiz, 'La Crisis', p. 9 n.10.
170. Report from Madrid, 13 July 1684, PRO:SP 101/92/160. For Barcelona, 'Anales', BCB, MS. 1479. A Valencian account is in BUV, MS. 700/79: *Juizio del eclipse celebrado en el presente año 1684 en 12 de Julio a las 3 horas del día.*
171. Cañas to Finance, 29 June 1683, AGS:CJH 1069.
172. **Perales, J.**, *Décadas* (Valencia 1880), III, 811.
173. 'Sucessos de Cataluña', BCB, MS. 504/11 vo.
174. D. Pedro Montaner to D. José de Haro, 19 July 1687, ACA:CA 456.
175. Duke of Montalto to D. Pedro Ronquillo, 11 Mar. 1688, CODOIN, 79 (Madrid 1882), p. 430.
176. Benavent, f.13; *War and Prices*, p. 240.
177. AGS:CJH 1128.
178. **Benavent, f. 14 vo.**
179. 'Sucessos de Cataluña', f.102.
180. Benavent, f. 17 vo.
181. **Stanhope,** *Spain under Charles* (London 1844), p. 28.
182. Barreiro, *Xallas*, p. 226.
183. Consulta of council of Aragon, 12 Nov. 1693, ACA:CA 600/87/9.
184. To Secretary Vernon, 13 Jan. 1694, in Stanhope, *op. cit.* p. 58.
185. Benavent, f. 21.
186. To Earl of Galway, 6 May 1694, in Stanhope, *op. cit.* p. 59–60.
187. Benavent, f. 25.
188. Stanhope, *op. cit.* p. 98.
189. Benavent, ff. 28, 30 vo.
190. Report of D. Miguel Crespo, 19 Nov. 1683, AGS:CJH 1078. Contrast the town in 1575 when, with 500 households, it produced 'much grain and wine in great abundance . . . some oil . . . all kinds of cattle': Salomon, *La Campagne*, p. 71.
191. Report of 2 Nov. 1677, AGS:CJH 1941.
192. For Logroño, the report by D. Pedro Veluti, 21 Oct. 1681; for Cervatos, memorial of 1681: both in *ibid.* 1030.
193. *Relation*, p. 493.
194. Report of 21 Nov. 1686, AGS:CJH 1102.
195. Though 1684 was a poor year, 1683 was worse, with a harvest of 4,430 fanegas.
196. **Da Silva, J. G.**, *En Espagne* (Paris 1965), p. 86.
197. Osorio, *Extensión Política*, in Campomanes, *Apéndice*, I, 20.
198. 1680 petition in AGS: CJH 1029.
199. *Ibid.* 977.
200. Calonge, *Castilla la Vieja*, p. 12.
201. Consulta of 28 Apr. 1687 in AGS:CJH 1111.
202. 'Minuta de la planta de las villas y lugares de la provincia de Valladolid mas adeudados', in *ibid.* 1029.
203. Consulta of 27 Oct. 1682, *ibid.* 1052.
204. Order of council, 24 Jan. 1667, *ibid.* 886.
205. Petition of 1680 by towns in the region, *ibid.* 1952; **Marcos Martín, A.**, *Medina del Campo* (Valladolid 1978), pp. 251, 258, dates the population recovery from the 1660s and says (p. 252) that 'the period 1590–1634 is, demographically speaking, the most disastrous suffered by the town in the sixteenth and seventeenth centuries'.
206. **Cabo Alonso, A.**, 'La Armuña', *Estud, Geog.*, 58 (Feb. 1955), pp. 92, 105–9.
207. Memorial of 1672, AGS:CJH 977.
208. *Ibid.* 892.

209. Consulta of 2 Mar. 1667, *ibid.* 886.
210. Petition of 1667 in *ibid.* 894.
211. *Ibid.* 1941.
212. *Ibid.* 1088.
213. *Ibid.* 1963.
214. *Ibid.* 1158.
215. Klein, *The Mesta*, p. 337.
216. Pigs were reared for meat, sheep for wool.
217. Caxa de Leruela, *Restauración* (Naples 1631), p. 6.
218. Klein, *op. cit.* p. 342.
219. Caxa de Leruela, *op. cit.* pp. 49, 95.
220. Klein, *op. cit.* p. 343. This fine book is seriously marred by a tendency to blame all the ills of agriculture on sheep-farming and the Mesta. Cf. Phillips, *Ciudad Real*, p. 48: 'It is not accurate to blame the Mesta for agricultural stagnation in Ciudad Real.'
221. Cf. the graph by Braudel and Spooner in *The Cambridge Economic History of Europe*, IV (Cambridge 1967), 471, giving prices in silver.
222. The standing of the Castilian copper maravedi against other currencies is illustrated in *ibid.* p. 458.
223. Hamilton, *War and Prices*; Vilar, *Catalunya*, I, 376–9.
224. Regional names supplied by Hamilton have been replaced by town names, in part for accuracy, in part to emphasise that the prices might not always be representative of the region. Thus I put Toledo for New Castile, Valladolid for Old Castile and Seville for Andalucia.
225. Hamilton, *op. cit.* p. 10, n.4.
226. *Ibid.* pp. 28–9.
227. *Ibid.* p. 33.
228. Domínguez Ortiz, 'La crisis de Castilla', p. 13. Full details of the coinages are in Hamilton, *op. cit.* pp. 16–21.
229. I owe the firm identification of the 1680 decree with Don Juan, to the thesis of Mario L. Sańchez, 'Attempts at Reform', unpublished Ph.D. thesis (Notre Dame 1976), p. 128.
230. AGS Contadurías Generales 1792. See also Hamilton, *op. cit.* pp. 20–1, 126–9.
231. See below, Ch. Fifteen.
232. Hamilton, *op. cit.* p. 10, n.3.
233. Full details in *ibid.* pp. 22–6. For the effect of the 1686 legislation on Valencia, where the new 1686 coins were known as *marías*, see **Mateu y Llopis, F.**, *Historia Monetaria de Valencia* (Valencia 1955), pp. 40–4.
234. Details from Hamilton, *op. cit.* pp. 172–3.
235. For example, Larruga, *Memorias*, VII, 220: 'In 1686 there was a monetary reform and Toledo considered that this offered it the chance to expand its industry.'
236. Wage data from Hamilton, *op. cit.* pp. 208–15. I have used only the indices for grain (*ibid.* p. 183), since this was a basic commodity. Hamilton's full price data include up to thirty items.
237. Vilar, *Catalunya*, I, 316–17: 'tant a Catalunya com a Espanya, la fuga de la moneda, la crisi no tant del comerç com de la balança comercial, l'angoixós triomf econòmic dels estrangers'.
238. On the Basques, see **Bilbao, L. M.**, 'Crisis y reconstrucción', *Saioak*, 1 (1977), 157–80.
239. **Vilar, P.**, *Le 'Manual'* (Paris 1962), p. 80.

# CHAPTER FIVE

# The Commercial System

From the beginning of its rise to world power status, Spain was burdened by the fact that its weak industrial capacity prevented it becoming a commercial power. This lay at the root of many of its economic problems. The commercial difficulties of the late seventeenth century, though aggravated by the depression of the preceding fifty years, were in substance similar to those prevailing in the early years of the empire of Charles V. In the sixteenth century Spain's manufacturing industries had been directed almost exclusively to the domestic market. External trade consisted largely in the export of raw materials, of which wool was the most important. As population expanded, the smallness of domestic industry led to a growing reliance on the import of manufactured goods. The gap between expanding imports and shrinking exports had to be made up with bullion. This was already a serious problem by the mid-sixteenth century, when Luis Ortiz presented (in 1558) his famous memorial against the export of precious metals.[1] A further consideration made the problem graver. Imports from America were rising: what could be sent back in exchange? At first there was a flourishing trade, from Andalucia and through Seville, of raw materials and basic manufactures. But very soon foreign manufactures took the initiative. At no time had Spain been capable of meeting the challenge of the markets offered through empire.

There was, of course, no reason why economic weakness should have led to economic dependence. Spaniards had constantly before their eyes the example of Holland, a nation with little in the way of industry or natural wealth, which had in a short time become a leading economic power. Why then was Spain not as rich as Holland? Let us consider what Sancho de Moncada was saying in 1619. 'The poverty of Spain', he wrote, 'has resulted from the discovery of America.'[2] The greed of Europeans for American bullion had made them unload their produce on Spain in order to get silver in return. Moncada claimed that 'the root remedy for Spain is to forbid entry to foreign manufactured goods'.[3] At the same time foreigners must be excluded from any part in the finances or industry, and the nation's remedy would be to produce its own goods. From Luis Ortiz onwards, the majority of Spanish writers shared these and similar views, which historians have called 'mercantilist'[4] though a simpler term would be 'protectionist'.

Contemporary obsession with America obscured the fact that the problem antedated America. The location of the wool staple in Flanders at the end of the fifteenth century made it inevitable that international finance would shape the future ·of the wool trade. Foreign finance was subsequently given further advantages by the enormous scale of royal debts caused by imperial commitments. The riches to be gained from the wool trade were no more than a stepping stone to the riches to be coaxed out of the commerce of the New World.

Writers such as Moncada and Martínez de Mata have frequently been criticised for their singleminded view that exclusion of foreign goods and encouragement of native industry were the principal solutions to the trade crisis.[5] But a fair consideration of their arguments, and of the later course of Spanish history, suggests that much of what they argued was reasonable. The Spaniards of the late seventeenth century were anxious to prove that, given the opportunity, they were capable of shaping their own commercial fortunes. The most common solution they proposed was the establishment of trading companies.

In 1668 a Dominican preacher, Fray Juan de Castro, presented to the Queen Regent an ambitious plan to set up a trading company, with armed as well as commercial ships of its own, to monopolise trade to America. Castro was not content to let the company operate within the existing system. He proposed, in effect, that the monopoly be abolished, that all American ports be free to take part in trade, and, most radical of all, that all Spaniards should participate: 'If we extend this facility to Valencia, Aragon and Catalonia, since they are subjects and Spaniards, and if they are included in the Indies trade, royal revenue will increase and the strength of the kingdom will be unified.'[6] The government was so far converted to the plan that enquiries were made in 1668 and 1669 among all the kingdoms to explore the possibilities. The Basques signified their interest in August 1668.[7] In a communication to Valencia in January 1669 the government enclosed its final proposals, 'that this Company, which Her Majesty has resolved to set up in Spain, is to consist not of a few persons, as all others hitherto have been, but is to be a General Association in which all the realms and provinces may take part, and all subjects with some capital who wish to place their surplus in a Common Fund'. Moreover, a share in this company could be held 'not only by native born Spaniards but also by foreigners who are or wish to be domiciled in these realms'. The company was to be managed not by Castilians alone but by a board of directors drawing its membership from each realm.[8] This astonishing but over-ambitious project seems to have expired by the end of 1669.

The notion of a 'company' modelled on those currently being operated by the English and Dutch, came perilously close to being the *único remedio* for Spain's arbitristas in the late century. Proposals for companies invariably aimed to exclude foreigners from the trade of the peninsula, and usually involved some modification of the Sevillian monopoly. Among the numerous plans known to have been suggested in this period was one in 1669 by Eugenio Carnero, one by Martínez de Mata, and one by Juan Cano.[9] Luis Cerdeño y Monzón, a member of the Committee for Trade, in 1685 drew up a proposal for 'a company for the kingdoms of Castile under whose direction will run the commerce of America'.[10] The capital value of each share was to be 500 pesos. The plan seems to have been approved by a committee in the same year. The kingdom of Aragon pressed for its own national company in the 1680s. Manuel de Lira proposed a trading company, to be financed partly by Jewish merchants. Osorio y Redín in his *Extensión Política* (1686) called for a commercial company to be set up.[11] The activities of Feliu de la Peña in the late century culminated, under Philip V, in the establishment of the New Gibraltar Company, studied by Pierre Vilar.

This widespread demand for trading companies pointed, if to nothing else, to a general awareness that Spain's commercial backwardness was the direct result of foreign economic dominance. Every proposal for a company that may have interfered with the Seville monopoly, however, was doomed to be shipwrecked by vested interests within the country. It was not that Spain lacked the naval expertise. The absurd claim by a contemporary nobleman that 'the art of constructing ships had been forgotten',[12] was typical of the gross untruths tossed around by contemporaries and accepted uncritically by later historians. In fact coastal trade and the fishing fleets continued to flourish. Construction of ocean-going vessels was still in evidence, despite the conclusion of the leading modern authority that 'owing to the absolute lack of resources shipbuilding in Spain slowly disappeared' under Charles II.[13] It is true that considerable shipbuilding was carried on by preference in Havana and other American yards, where timber was plentiful and labour cheap; on the other hand, construction materials there were more expensive. When merchants wished to construct large, professionally built vessels, they did so in Spain. The Basque yards were still capable of building ships of up to 500 toneladas without difficulty,[14] and on occasion, as with a government contract placed in 1697, they built ships of over 1,200 toneladas.[15] A typical official contract of 1673 to build five vessels for the Atlantic armada, resulted in three ships of 420, 822 and 934 toneladas being constructed in Guipúzcoa, and two of 664 and 623 in the Asturias.[16] Analysis of 239 vessels employed in the fleet voyages to and from America between 1669 and 1700 shows that only 90 (37% of the sample) were foreign built, while 47 (20%) were constructed in American yards and 102 (43%) in Spain itself. Of the Spanish vessels, 66 were Basque-built, and most of the rest were built in the Seville area. The largest ships used on the crossing were all Basque.[17] The evidence for the first decade of the eighteenth century confirms these conclusions. Of 97 vessels whose origin is known, 48 were built abroad, 18 in America and 31 in Spain. Of these last, 5 were constructed in Seville and Cadiz, the rest in Basque shipyards. The Andalucian vessels did not exceed 113 toneladas, and the American ships seldom exceeded 400; the Basques, on the other hand, produced for the fleets that sailed in 1706 from Cadiz galleons of 728, 797, 807 and 934 toneladas.[18] These impressive figures speak for themselves.

The irony was that though Spaniards had ships and expertise, both were employed in the interests of foreign merchants whose goods constituted the bulk of Spain's trade. The picture was even clearer in the Mediterranean ports, where virtually all deep-sea vessels were foreign for the simple reason that foreigners controlled all sectors of the market: traffic, destination and finance. There was thus no need for Spanish shipping. The relative lack of a mercantile marine in Spain was the result not of 'decline' or of incompetence, but of the unfavourable balance of trade. A policy of protectionism, as advocated by Martínez de Mata, was never seriously considered by the Madrid government. This seems inexplicable when we recall that it was precisely in the late seventeenth century that Colbert began to protect French manufactures and the English imposed protective tariffs.[19]

## MARITIME TRADE

Even in the difficult days of the mid-century, Spain remained one of the biggest world centres of trade. It continued to have a modest trade with Italy and a more substantial one with northern Europe and the Netherlands; the largest volume of trade was still that to America.

### Andalucia

Andalucia was by far the most important commercial area in the peninsula. On its great estates, dominated by big landlords, it produced Spain's largest quantities of grain and foodstuffs. The textile industry in Seville and Granada still employed thousands of workers. But the early promise held out for Andalucian development by the riches of America was not sustained. By the reign of Charles II Andalucia was consuming all its own grain, and its exports consisted principally of olive oil, olives, raisins and wine, most of which went to the Indies. The volume of these items that went to northern Europe did not in the 1660s exceed the cargo of six vessels of 300 toneladas each. Most of the textiles of Andalucia were consumed locally; what was exported went mainly to America.[20] The real importance of Andalucia lay not in its limited exports but in its massive imports. Our attention must be focused principally on the trading complex that comprised the four ports of Seville, Cadiz, Puerto de Santa María and San Lucar de Barrameda.

Though primarily engaged in the trade to America, these four ports were the obvious channel for commerce into and out of Castile. After mid-century the relative decay of Seville — a result of epidemics, taxes, and silting of the river — meant that the outports normally used by ships were Cadiz and Puerto de Santa María, though the whole machinery of customs control remained in Seville. The existence of significant trade at other Andalucian ports may be judged by the presence in 1659 of French consuls at the additional ports of Gibraltar, Málaga and Motril. The English, on the other hand, had consuls in this period only in Seville, Cadiz and Málaga. The whole length of the Andalucian coastline, from San Lucar through Málaga to Cartagena, became a focus of smuggling, with adverse effects on local markets and royal revenues. The administration of customs dues was consequently unified under one person to ensure better management. For most of the reign, this lucrative tax-farm was controlled by Francisco Báez Eminente, perhaps the wealthiest financier of his time.[21]

The external trade of Andalucia with Europe was almost wholly in the hands of foreigners. The total value of foreign trade passing through Andalucia in 1670 was estimated by the French consul in Cadiz, Pierre Catalan, at some thirteen million pesos. Of this total only 1.5 million, or 11.5 per cent, remained in Spain; the other 88.5 per cent went to the Indies.[22] Figure 5.1 illustrates the origin of foreign goods, as detailed by Catalan. The nature of the goods represented in Figure 5.1 is shown in Table 5.1.

Fig. 5.1   Foreign trade to Andalucia, 1670.

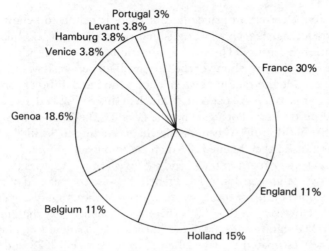

Table 5.1

|         |                                                              | %             |
|---------|--------------------------------------------------------------|---------------|
| France  | textiles (discussed below)                                   | 30            |
| England | draperies, serge, baize, camlets, silk stockings, lead and tin | 11         |
| Holland | wax, draperies, serge, linens, spices                        | 15            |
| Belgium | lace, silk, Cambrai and Brabant cloths, camlets, fustians    | 11            |
| Genoa   | silks, satins, damask, velvets, ribbons, lace, brocade       | 18.6          |
| Venice  | crystal, glass, mirrors, silks                               | 3.8           |
| Hamburg | wax, linens, copper                                          | 3.8           |
| Levant  | musk, camlets                                                | 3.8           |
| Portugal| black slaves, sugar, Brazil tobacco                         | 3             |
|         |                                                              | 13,400,000 pesos |

Though there was a high level of economic activity in Andalucia, most of it was geared to the American trade. It is consequently very difficult to study Andalucian commerce in isolation from American. The proportions of goods given in Figure 5.1 for instance, are (as Catalan intended them to be) an exact reflection of the goods traded to America through Cadiz by those countries.

No modern studies have been dedicated to the foreign trade of Spain, so that it is impossible to measure the degree of change during the century.[23] The domination of commerce by foreigners was an accepted fact. Godolphin reported from Madrid in 1675 on

the wonted opinion here that all other Nations live and grow rich by their Commerce with the Dominions of this Crown, which though true to a great measure, yet is not to the extravagance the Spaniards flatter themselves. Tis certain that of all others the French are the greatest gainers by the Spanish Trade, especially thro their Manufacture of Linnen.[24]

This was no doubt correct in principle, but there is reason to believe that the Andalucian trade, and French and English participation in it, declined during the late seventeenth century. There is no indication of this from the trade figures for London, which after the slump of the Cromwellian period show an increase in imports from the Mediterranean between about 1665 and 1700 of some 27 per cent, and in exports to it of 32 per cent.[25] Much of this probably derived from the newly expanding trades to Portugal and the Levant. The English in Spain were conscious rather of a decline. When the merchants trading to Seville looked back in 1715 at its causes, they blamed the increase in output of French goods, the excessive tax levies on American trade, and the legislation of Charles II restricting consumption of foreign textiles.[27] The French likewise complained of a decline. This was occasioned quite obviously by the continuous wars against Spain waged by Louis XIV. However, in the 1680s there was evidence that the English and Belgians had taken significant areas of the textile trade to Andalucia, of which the French share was estimated to have fallen sharply between 1628 and 1686.

Despite its common land frontier with Spain, France exported most of its goods for the Castilian market by sea through Cadiz. Textiles, which constituted over 98 per cent of French exports to Castile, were manufactured principally in the northern provinces and in Brittany, making the sea route the cheapest and quickest mode of transport. A virtual monopoly of the textile trade to Cadiz was held by the flourishing Breton port of St Malo. The main reason, however, for concentrating French trade on Cadiz was quite simply because most of the commodities were intended for re-export to America. Our most useful guide to French exports to Andalucia is the memoir drawn up in 1686 by the French intendant Patoulet. Albert Girard's analysis of this memoir[28] makes it possible to give a composite profile of French exports to Cadiz in about 1686 (Table 5.2).

Apart from the produce of Lyon and Marseille, which used the port of Marseille to leave France, most of these items came through St Malo. By the 1680s competition from the Dutch and Belgians, added to German (Hamburg) exports, led to the relative decline we have noted. Patoulet gives no general indication of what proportion of these goods remained in Spain. My estimate is that under 10 per cent of silks were for the Castilian market, about 7 per cent of hats, and under 13 per cent of lace. One might suggest a conservative estimate of about 12 per cent for the volume of French textiles that stayed in Andalucia instead of going to America. This coincides well with the figure given by Catalan for 1670.

There was of course considerable competition from other nations. Patoulet's memoir fortunately gives an idea of the quantities involved. Belgian lace coming

Table 5.2

| Material | Place of origin | Annual value (livres) | % |
|---|---|---|---|
| Linens | 36.3% Rouen, 4.1% Cambrai, 59.6% Brittany | under 6 million | 66 |
| Woollens | Lille | 1 million | 11 |
| Silks | 65% Tours, 35% Lyon | under 1 million | 10.7 |
| Lace | Le Puy, Burgundy, Paris | 800,000 | 8.8 |
| Hats | Paris and Marseille | 225,000 | 2.5 |
| Haberdashery | Rouen | 50,000 | 0.6 |
| Stockings | Paris, Flanders | 40,000 | 0.4 |

through Cadiz in 1686 was destined 58.5 per cent for south America, 29.3 for Mexico and 12.2 for Spain; English silk stockings were 55.6, 33.3 and 11.1 respectively; English woollen stockings were 51.8, 39 and 9.2 per cent respectively. The figures give a consistent portrait of Cadiz as primarily an American port, with Andalucian trade playing only a small part in its economic life.

English trade to Andalucia was modest in comparison with that of France, but Spain was still England's fourth most important European market. Judging from Whitworth's trade statistics,[29] from 1697 to 1700 Spain was the third biggest recipient in Europe of English goods, and had the biggest balance in favour of England. A passage in Cary's *Discourse on Trade* (1745)[30] summarises Anglo-Spanish commerce in the late seventeenth century:

To begin with Spain, by which I mean that part from the Bay of Cadiz inclusive eastwards into the Straits of Gibraltar, as far as Catalonia: whither we send all sorts of woollen manufactures, lead, fish, silk and worsted stockings, butter, tobacco, ginger, leather, beeswax and sundry other things. And in return we have thence things fit only for consumption, such as fruit and wine; other things for our manufactures such as oil, cochineal, indigo, anata, barilla and some salt,[31] with a great part of gold and silver wherewith they are supplied from their large Empires on the mainland of America, whither they export much of the goods we carry to them.

Thanks to the recent researches of Everaert, it is possible also to consider aspects of Belgium's trade with Spain. The activities of the Antwerp firm of Jean Boussemart in the years 1670–77 confirm the outline for 1670 given by Catalan. About one-third of Boussemart's textile imports into Cadiz were destined for the Andalucian market; the remaining two-thirds were sold to shippers who dispatched the goods to America.[32] Over the same period the commodities sent back from Cadiz to Belgium by Boussemart consisted 69.1 per cent of colonial goods, mainly dyes; 19.9 per cent silver bullion; and 11 per cent Spanish produce (6 per cent wool, 2 per cent wine, 2 per cent oil and 1 per cent fruits).[33]

## Valencia

The region of Valencia came second only to Andalucia in the variety of its trade,

119

but the total volume of commerce was considerably smaller. Cartagena, Murcia's port and Spain's biggest naval base, was situated at the southern extremity of the trading area and Valencia at its northern: between them lay Alicante, which outdid them both in trade and was by far the largest and most active port in Spain outside the Seville–Cadiz complex.

Alicante's excellent harbour and favourable situation athwart the sea routes, attracted a large foreign merchant community. Low import duties were a major advantage. By 1659 the French consuls in the area were stationed at Almeria, Cartagena, Denia, Valencia and Alicante. The English, significantly, had no consul in Valencia city but one in Alicante. Our best information on maritime trade in the region comes from the French consul Robert Prégent, who was in Alicante from September 1664 and in 1669 drew up a long report which runs substantially as follows.[34]

The manufactures of this region consist only of some silk which is produced in Valencia and Murcia, and transported to Granada, Madrid and other places in Spain; the rest is used in the province.

The inhabitants of these three provinces [the Crown of Aragon] are not very industrious, either through poverty or through lack of knowledge. They are content merely to receive on commission goods which come from Genoa and Holland, and to freight for Venice some Segovia wool, brought by road because there is no navigable river here and very little water for irrigation. Every year there are three convoys of five to six ships which unload here a quantity of paper and different Italian silks for Madrid, and then go on with their main cargo to Málaga and Cadiz, from where they bring back silver.

From Holland three times a year there comes a convoy of fifteen to twenty ships normally, with two warships. They stop off first at Cadiz and Málaga, and then here, where they stop four to five days to unload spices valued at about 70,000 livres, and manufactures of Holland and Flanders, Norwegian timber, and Swedish iron, valued from seventy to eighty thousand livres. After that some go to Marseille, others to Genoa, Livorno and Smyrna.

Apart from the English ships already mentioned,[35] there arrive some 120 others which unload here various spices, draperies, Swedish iron, and lead, to the value of 200,000 livres. They go on with the remainder of their cargo to Italy and other parts of the Levant. There is no money market here but only in Madrid, with a loss of 6 to 7 per cent against the drawer.

Every year to this city of Alicante come six to eight ships from St Malo, bringing eighteen to twenty thousand *quintaux* (hundredweight) of dried cod caught off the north of Newfoundland. The same amount is brought by the English in fifteen to twenty of their small ships, from catches off the south of Newfoundland.

From Brittany in five or six ships come 2,500 to 3,000 barrels of sardine caught off the same coast; from Ireland and England a further three thousand. A third of all the above fish is consumed locally: mostly in Alicante, and the rest in Valencia and the coast of Catalonia.

In Alicante, Murcia and Cartagena they purchase about 40,000 livres of Brittany linens. The above-mentioned French ships make their return journey to St Malo and Havre de Grace with from 2,500 to 3,000 quintaux of soap, which is manufactured three leagues from here, and 20 to 25,000 quintaux of soda from Alicante and Cartagena. The rest of the cargo is various oils, loaded in Mallorca. The English make their return journey with oil, almonds and aniseed.

The shipments from Provence, made up of ships and settees,[36] bring to Barcelona, Valencia, Alicante and Cartagena every year about 2,500 bales of Lyon linen, mostly manufactured in Germany, worth about a hundred livres each.

The same shipments also bring some hardware of little value, as well as manufactures from the Levant, mainly blue cloths for cushions, and about thirty to forty bales of linen.

Whenever there is a need for corn in Spain, there come a number of French and other vessels which load up at Tunis, Sardinia, Sicily and Tabarca, and unload from Catalonia to Cadiz. Their return cargo consists of silver bullion, 12 to 15,000 bales of wool and 18 to 20,000 quintaux of soda, according to the demand in Provence.

In addition every year there come fifteen to twenty large and small settees to load coir for the Provence coast. Throughout the coast of Catalonia, Valencia and Murcia there are no more than twenty to twenty-five large and small settees trading.

This invaluable memoir gives us a clearer guide to the trade of Alicante than we have for any Spanish port outside Seville and Cadiz. There was an overwhelming preponderance of imports over exports, and almost all the ships participating in the trade were foreign. Exports from Alicante were either extremely bulky (soda and soap) or of limited value (almonds, aniseed). Imports on the other hand, were of considerable value. Faced by an obvious imbalance in trade, how did the Alicante merchants cope? Some bullion was exported but it must have been minimal, since unlike Cadiz the port had no easy access to silver. The answer lay in a very effective business organisation, which we shall consider in its proper place.

The general origin of imports into Alicante for the three years 1667–69 is shown in Figure 5.2. The merchandise in this trade was made up as shown in Table 5.3.[37]

Fig. 5.2  The import trade of Alicante, 1667–69.

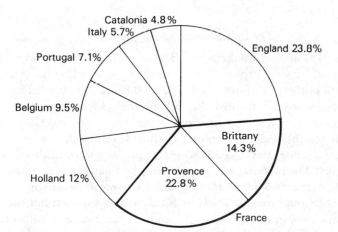

In addition to these items, which were mostly destined for the local market, there was an annual import from Italy of some 250,000 livres worth of goods which went directly to Madrid without tarrying in Alicante. If Prégent's assessment is correct, annual imports to Alicante were in the region of 950,000

Table 5.3

| | | % |
|---|---|---|
| England | fish (cod and sardines), Virginia tobacco, lead, baize, worsteds, grogram, serge, twills, silk and woollen stockings | 23.8 |
| Brittany | cod and sardines, linens, brittanys | 14.3 |
| Provence | various linens, hardware, German re-exports, cottons, drugs, paper and Levantine goods | 22.8 |
| Holland | pepper, cloves, cinnamon, sugar, dyes, wood, butter and cheese | 12 |
| Belgium | textiles (cotton, camlets, serge, twill, etc.) | 9.5 |
| Portugal | sugar, Brazil tobacco, tuna | 7.1 |
| Italy | paper, steel, linens, silks, Levantine goods | 5.7 |
| Catalonia | baize, oil, cheese and pork | 4.8 |

Total: 2,100,000 livres

livres, or only 2.4 per cent of the imports of Cadiz in the same period. This enormous disparity in the trade activity of the two ports is clear evidence of the unusual concentration of commercial interests on the Indies trade at Cadiz.

The trade of Marseille with Spain's eastern ports was substantial. The bulk of it seems to have been with Alicante, to which the largest French vessels were directed for soda. The French ambassador Villars reported of Murcia and Valencia in 1680 that French settlers exported wool and bullion out of the area.

These realms are full of foreigners and do a good trade. Considerable silk is grown and then sent as manufactures to Castile and America, bringing in a great deal of silver. There are many good sea-ports, particularly Alicante through which a lot of French merchandise enters Castile. Soda is exported from Alicante to make soap and glass in France, while France every year sends over 1,500 colts or mules.[38]

## The Cantabrian and Basque Coasts

The overseas trade of the Cantabrian and Basque coast had for nearly two centuries been dominated by wool exports, still imperfectly studied by historians. In the early sixteenth century two ports, Santander and Bilbao, contended for control of the trade; the quarrel continued throughout the seventeenth century. In the mid-sixteenth century wool exports from Santander, which was closely linked to Burgos, were roughly twice the volume of those from the Basque ports. Despite its subsequent decline, Burgos in 1686 entered a claim to be made sole outlet for Castilian wools. The proposal was accompanied by financial offers from traders in Burgos and in the two ports that would have most benefited, Laredo and Santander. The Committee of Trade in 1688 gave its support; but the claims of Bilbao eventually won recognition. Through its river valleys Bilbao had easier communication with Vitoria and the interior of Castile, and its relative size (5,000 people to some 1,300 for Santander) testified to growth.[39]

The presence of consuls was the outstanding indication of its importance. The only English consul in the entire north was stationed at Bilbao. Cary's comments on the 'Biscay trade' are as follows:

By Biscay I mean all that part under the Spanish Government that lies in the Bay of Biscay or adjoining it. The commodities we send thither are generally the same as we do to Spain [i.e. Andalucia], and in return we have wool, iron and some bullion, whereof the first is the best and most profitable commodity, which could we secure wholly to ourselves 'twould be a great advantage to the nation, but both the Dutch and the French come in for a share.[40]

The comments of Villars in 1680 relate to French settlers:[41]

In Galicia and Asturias there are a few French traders, because of the seaports to which Spaniards import 150,000 fanegas of salt from La Rochelle and Nantes. In Cantabria the chief commerce of the French, who are in Bilbao and San Sebastian, is in cod from the Newfoundland fisheries, French produce, and some manufactures.

The most important development of the period was the rise to predominance of the port of Bilbao.[42] One of the principal advantages enjoyed by Basque ports was the relative freedom from customs dues. Standard port dues were low, though the taxes on wool and iron were higher.[43] In the sixteenth century Vizcaya exported iron but imported nothing of consequence. The region served only as an entrepot for Castilian wool and foreign manufactures. Traders in iron made profits, but few other Basques benefited from a commerce that was almost wholly in foreign hands. In 1566, for example, Bilbao merchants controlled directly less than three per cent of the town's wool exports. It followed that fluctuations in foreign demand dictated the state of the Basque economy. When, as in the late sixteenth century, import substitution by foreign powers and simultaneous war at sea helped to dislocate trade, the whole economy suffered. Conversely, international events in the early seventeenth century helped to stimulate Bilbao's trade.[44] The outbreak of war with France drove traffic away from San Sebastian to Bilbao: the non-belligerent English cut their trade to the former by two-thirds, and doubled their exports to the latter. Acting as neutral carriers, the English also restored to Bilbao the major part of the wool trade with Flanders. The partial withdrawal of the English as a result of their Civil War in 1642 encouraged Flemish and Bilbao merchants to play a greater part in the trade of the port.

By the late seventeenth century Bilbao found itself in a completely new and favourable position. The nominal annual income of the merchant guild (*consulado*) from the *avería* or port duty increased by 250 per cent between 1650 and 1700.[45] The town controlled 70 per cent of all wool exported from Castilian ports and the totality of all wool from the Cantabrian coast. Attempts of other ports to break into the monopoly were bitterly contested. In 1678 the Cantabrian port of Castro Urdiales petitioned the king to be integrated into the Basque provinces. Bilbao was horrified at the proposal. 'If Castro succeeds', wrote the Basque representative from Madrid, 'we can say Goodbye Vizcaya.' The city voted the Crown a special grant of 30,000 ducats, and the Council of State then rejected Castro's pretension.[46] By 1696 native merchants of Bilbao dominated the wool trade, to the exclusion of foreigners. Out of a list of the twenty-two richest merchants in Bilbao in 1718,[47] only two (both Flemings) appear to have been foreigners by origin. The city expanded in size. By the end of the seventeenth century it was so rich, according to a contemporary report, 'that the city is

123

bursting and there is so much building that the city is almost twice as big as it used to be, with people so rich that they build houses for 40 to 50,000 ducats'.[48]

The rise of Bilbao was greeted with hostility by the other Basque capitals, Vitoria and San Sebastian, which stood to lose by the diversion of trade and hence of customs revenue through Vizcaya. In 1699 Bilbao confirmed its strength by passing new town Ordinances that prohibited non-domiciled foreigners from taking part in the wool trade. Santander promptly in September 1700 signed an agreement for English traders to move their business to that town and to divert Castilian exports to the Burgos-Santander outlet. Unfortunately for Santander, the English were to be Spain's enemies in the subsequent War of Succession. Bilbao's privileges were ratified by the new French dynasty.

## Catalonia

In volume and importance the smallest of all the Spanish trades we have discussed was that of Catalonia. Both the English and French had consuls in Barcelona, and their interest in trade undoubtedly also extended to Catalan politics. Because of Catalonia's common frontier with France, some trade was by land and hence not reflected in details of maritime commerce. A report for 1686 by the French consul Laurent Soleil, whose jurisdiction included the whole coastline from Cadaqués to Tortosa, goes as follows:[49]

In this country within the last eight or ten years industry has begun to thrive, through the large number of workmen who pass thither and settle, and this has greatly harmed French manufactures. Besides this, the English carry there all kinds of drapery and fish; and the Dutch all kinds of spice, linens, metals and anascotes, which are serges from Bruges, worn by everybody here in Catalonia. As for silk cloth, it is cheaper here than in France, because of the abundance of silk. . . .

Mataró does the most trade, Sant Feliu deals in salt fish, and a great quantity of wine is shipped for Cadiz, Orán, Cartagena and Barbary. The same at Salou. . . . A great quantity of brandy is made for the Canaries, England, Holland and Orán, which the English ship from Salou. This year the oil, corn and vegetables are abundant, but when there is a lack and when export from France is allowed, corn for here is loaded at Narbonne or else in Sardinia, Naples, Sicily or Barbary.

The manufactures that come from France and are most in vogue are Rouens, both white and plain. Silk stockings are currently being made in Barcelona. . . . The English have most of the trade in it, bringing manufactures from Holland and England. To this port every year come 200 tartanes, of which at the most 100 unload and load; the rest take refuge in Salou, Barcelona, Palamos or Cadaqués to shelter from the bad season.

This interesting account can be compared with what we know about the trade of Barcelona at this time. Figure 5.3 gives a visual impression of the trade by value at two different periods.[50] Table 5.4 presents each item expressed as a proportion of the year's trade. The total value is given in Catalan pounds (lliures).

The trade of Barcelona expanded significantly in the late century. The customs duty called the periatge, which was levied on both imports and exports, has been used by historians as a basis for calculating overall trade. It would appear that in the course of the century there was an expansion as shown in Table 5.5.

Fig. 5.3   The trade of Barcelona in the late seventeenth century.

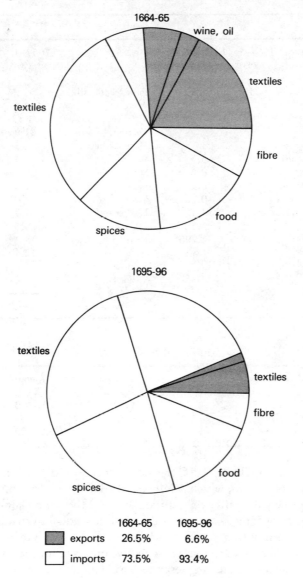

|  | 1664-65 | 1695-96 |
|---|---|---|
| exports | 26.5% | 6.6% |
| imports | 73.5% | 93.4% |

These figures suggest an increase in the annual value of trade by 1699 of 60 per cent since 1654 and of 25 per cent since 1679. It would be rash to conclude that Barcelona and Catalonia were therefore resurgent. Figure 5.3 brings out clearly the enormous adverse balance of trade, the apparent decline of exports, and the heavy reliance of Catalonia on imports of textiles, spices and fish. The increase in trade over the century may reflect not so much the rise of Catalonia's economy[52] as its greater subjection to foreign interests.

Ambiguity in the trade figures, however, cannot contradict the reality of

Table 5.4

| Exports | | | Imports | | |
|---|---|---|---|---|---|
| | 1664–5 (%) | 1695–6 (%) | | 1664–5 (%) | 1695–6 (%) |
| Textiles | 65.0 | 80.4 | Fibre (wool, silk, etc.) | 10.6 | 6.1 |
| Wool | 0.6 | | | | |
| | | | Textiles | 41.0 | 29.1 |
| Spices, etc. | 1.9 | 3.7 | Haberdashery | 4.3 | 5.8 |
| Food (wine, oil) | 11.3 | 5.5 | Paper | 1.4 | 1.4 |
| Leather | 8.1 | 0.2 | Spices | 15.6 | 24.2 |
| Metal (iron) | 1.9 | 0.9 | Wax | 1.4 | 3.0 |
| Millstones | 1.9 | 0.7 | Metal (iron) | 2.0 | 5.8 |
| Books | | 3.1 | Leather | 4.5 | 1.8 |
| Various | 9.3 | 5.5 | Esparto | 0.6 | 0.9 |
| | 160,000 | 54,700 | Food (fish, cheese, etc.) | 17.4 | 15.9 |
| | | | Soap | | 0.8 |
| | | | Various | 1.2 | 5.2 |
| | | | | 443,000 | 774,000 |

Table 5.5

| Period | Annual traffic (in lliures) |
|---|---|
| 1654–7 | 768,300 |
| 1679–80 | 978,500 |
| 1698–99 | 1,223,100 |

Catalan revival under Charles II. Our evidence comes less from Barcelona than from the seaport of Mataró, which Soleil described in 1686 as the biggest trading centre in the principality after the capital. By 1702 the town claimed to have 'a commerce which for some years now has been almost equal to that of Barcelona, so that vessels laden with goods from various realms which previously received instructions to unload in Barcelona, now receive orders to unload in Barcelona or in Mataró'.[53] The most interesting testimony to Mataró's commercial importance comes from the contemporary economist José Aparici, who in 1708 conjured up the vision of a prosperous and booming seaport, thriving on the export of textiles, its citizens flourishing since at least 1670:[54]

I have seen Mataró, a small and very ordinary town, abolish its duties. Within my lifetime they have all taken to trading by sea. The wives risked their handiwork of hosiery and lace which they entrusted to their relatives who were ships' masters. These traded it for other merchandise, and the women thereby made profits for their houses and families. Within forty years the people have become rich, they have built many opulent houses. . . . Now it has become a city, its population double what it was, its people well off. . .

Mataro's success was due in great measure to its lower customs duties. In 1684 Barcelona's silk merchants claimed that 'their trade and commerce had passed to the town of Mataró because the duties there are lower than in this city'. In 1700 the exchange brokers (*corredors d'orella*) of Barcelona claimed that 'because of the freedom from customs in the town of Mataró far fewer goods enter this city than formerly'.[55] Mataró's new importance earned for it the title of 'city' under Philip V in 1702. Soleil's picture of a thriving Catalonia was fully justified. In 1680 the French ambassador Villars explained the small number of French in the principality by the fact that the Catalans were very industrious and there was little scope for foreigners.

## Other coastal trade

The smaller coastal traffic of Spain was in Spanish hands. Along the Levant coast, as we know from Prégent's report of 1669, there were about two dozen small vessels which specialised in local trade. Until the late eighteenth century, when a programme of roadbuilding was carried out, sea traffic still offered the most economic method of carriage. The whole economy of Galicia, for example, would have collapsed but for the regular trade in small vessels between its ports. When in times of poor harvest wheat had to be brought from Castile it came along the Cantabrian coast from Santander to Vivero and other ports in the far north-west.[56] Long-distance coastal traffic was more likely to be in foreign hands. English carriers supplied the Basque ports with Andalucian produce, and transported grain or wine around the peninsula.[57]

## OVERLAND TRADE

Water transport was the most efficient and cheapest method of moving goods in Spain. Unfortunately the rivers were unsuited to any but minor traffic. The greater Spanish rivers, the Ebro and Duero, were only partly navigable; and the move of ocean traffic from Seville to Cadiz was in part caused by the difficulty in negotiating the Guadalquivir. The ambitious project to make the entire Ebro navigable in this period came to nothing. In spite of the inadequate roads in Spain, traders seem to have tolerated the difficulties and no significant improvements were made to the road system till the late eighteenth century.

This situation makes it the more surprising that the Spanish postal system, a state monopoly and since the sixteenth century operated by Italians, should have been so efficient. Godolphin's despatches to London give us a good view of the postal service in 1671:[58]

The Correo Mayor of Spain hath in Madrid three Offices kept in distinct places: the first for extraordinary Expresses, and the other two for ordinary Posts, and Communications abroad.

Of these latter, the one is employed in sending and receiving Couriers to and from Italy and Flanders, as also to and from the farthermost parts of Catalonia and some parts of Valencia. The Flanders Courier . . . during the Summer usually arrives every other Friday, in 15 Days from Brussels; but in the Winter tarrying 2 or 3 Days longer . . .

The other Office manageth the conveyance of all Letters between this Town and Navarre, Biscay, Galicia, Portugal, Andalucia and the adjoyning parts of Valencia, which pass to and fro in four different Master Roads, and are carried by distinct Couriers that come in and go out every Week upon several but set Days . . .

The Spanish Port of Letters is very small, in respect of the English or French, since a Packet of 3 or 4 sheets of Paper pays no more than a single Letter; and from any of the furthermost parts of Spain, as Cadiz, Alicant, Barcelona &c. pays here only a half Real Vellon, which corresponds to about 3 Farthings English . . .

According to a recent study of Castilian transport in the eighteenth century, 'a sizable proportion of all commodities transported anywhere in Castile ended up on the Madrid market'.[59] Madrid's domination of the Castilian commercial system in modern times should not blind us to the fundamental fragmentation and localisation of Spain's markets. Figure 5.1 above emphasises how customs barriers broke up the country's unity. Within provinces, restricted market structures created big variations in prices. The range can be illustrated by considering wheat prices in a normal year in central Castile. If for the year 1719 we use the price of wheat in Toledo (at 13 reales a fanega) as an index of 100, the percentage price levels throughout Spain range as follows: Avila 61%, Barcelona 230%, Burgos 85%, La Coruña 108%, Ciudad Real 92%, Cuenca 115%, Requena 200%, Granada 115%, Guadalajara 108%, León 70%, Málaga 115%, Badajoz 70%, Murcia 208%, Palencia 77%, Segovia 70%, Seville 100%, Valladolid 61%, Zamora 61%, Saragossa 169%, Jaca 154%.[60] Apart from the case of Barcelona, then subject to virtual wartime conditions, the price variations emphasise the dangers of considering Spain as in any way a single integrated market.

There were two major land frontiers for external trade, with Portugal and France. Trade with Portugal was conducted by sea from the Andalucian ports. 'From Málaga are exported great quantities of wine, raisins and oil for London; and Granada, although far from the seaports, has traffic with Lisbon for the sale of its silks.'[61] In turn the Portuguese sent their colonial produce to Spain. But an unmeasured quantity of trade made its way by the land route. The principal commodity was sugar from Brazil. Smuggling over the frontier, in an area so close to the trade centres of Cadiz and Seville, was frequent. In 1681 the council of State complained that bullion was being extracted from Spain by this route, and 'in the recent past more than two million [pesos?] have entered Portugal from Castile'.[62] Strict control was attempted over the Extremadura customs posts, but smuggling of sugar to Spain and of bullion to Portugal was never effectively checked.

The only landlocked realm of Spain was Aragon, which conducted most of its external commerce by road. Because it was deprived of access to the sea, Aragon had strong views about participating in overseas trade. The province's aspirations to a seaport are discussed below in Chapter Fourteen.

Aragon seems to have maintained good levels of wheat production for its population, and exports to France, Catalonia and other areas were common. Wool, as in the sixteenth century, was the single largest item. Wine was also sent out, particularly to France and Castile, but attempts to export to the Basque country in this reign met with bitter opposition from the Rioja growers.[63] Olive oil was the fourth substantial export. Few manufactured goods left the realm in any quantity. Salt for Catalonia and France, and manganese (from Crivillén), were significant.

The bulk of Aragon's foreign trade was with France. Textiles and other goods were imported from the other Spanish realms, but they were small in value and not very popular. Figures for the year 1675, which were cited as representative by deputies to the Aragonese Cortes of 1677, show that the authorities received 42,075 libras in the year from duties (*generalidades*) levied on goods entering from France.[64] In the same year, the duty on Aragonese goods going to France was only 9,372 libras. A further quantity of French goods entered under disguise through Navarre. Taking these also into account, we can say that Aragon imported from France about five times by value what it exported there. Exports and imports in 1675 are detailed by percentage in Tables 5.6 and 5.7, illustrated in Figure 5.4.

Table 5.6   Exports to France from Aragon, 1675, by value

|  | % |
|---|---|
| Washed and unwashed wool | 78.0 |
| Olive oil | 16.3 |
| Corn (wheat, barley, oats) | 2.2 |
| Wine and salt | 3.5 |

Table 5.7   Imports from France into Aragon, 1675, by value (per cent)

| | | |
|---|---|---|
| Textiles: | | |
| Woollen cloth, ribbons, stockings | 22.6 | |
| Gold and silver cloth and lace | 0.4 | |
| Black and white lace | 1.4 | |
| Silks | 3.3 | |
| Hollands | 2.0 | 51.6 |
| Linens: of Cambrai, Brittany, Rouen, Paris | 6.2 | |
| Linens from Gascony | 7.1 | |
| Other linens | 8.6 | |
| Spices (pepper, sugar, cloves, cinnamon, etc.) | | 21.4 |
| Mules | | 5.7 |
| Horses and ponies | | 3.0 |
| Fish, entering through Navarre and from France | | 6.7 |
| Cattle and pigs | | 3.2 |
| Iron manufactures and iron | | 1.4 |
| Other items | | 7.0 |

Fig. 5.4   Aragon and France: imports and exports by value, 1675.

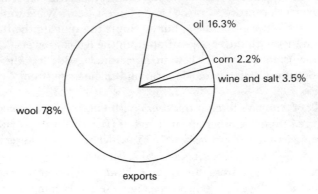

exports

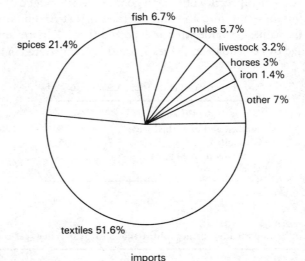

imports

Figure 5.4 reveals the extremely vulnerable state of the Aragonese economy, which was involved more closely with France than with Spain. The position of textiles tells the full story. In 1675 the total value of textile imports from all other parts of Spain was only 5.7 per cent of the value of textiles brought from France. The figures confirm the subordination of Spain to foreign manufactures.

Aragon's unfavourable trade situation led in the seventeenth century to numerous attempts to ban or restrict the entry of French goods. The most important was the decision of the Cortes at Barbastro in 1626 to stop the import of all woollens, silks and luxury textiles.[65] The prohibitionists were led by the city of Saragossa, which contained the chief manufacturers of the realm. In 1651 and again in 1675 the capital issued statutes banning imports, but with little success because of opposition to the moves. One of the most beneficial consequences of the government of Don Juan of Austria in Aragon was the open debate on foreign trade. In 1674 Don Juan instituted sessions of a Great Committee (*Junta Grande*), which 'put forward various suggestions about improving the general welfare of the realm, and gave rise to the publication of several writings on the economy'.[66] So great was the prohibitionist tide that when the Cortes of Aragon met in 1678, it swamped all other opinion. 'The Cortes of that year, overwhelmed by the authority of the said writers and by the repeated demands of manufacturers enclosed in a petition issued in the name of the forty-two guilds of Saragossa, finally decreed a ban on textiles.'[67] The decision was unfortunate. A victory literally of force over reason, it led to bitter disputes and was never properly put into effect.[68]

## THE INDIES TRADE

The reign of Charles II is the least studied but most crucial period in the history of American commerce. In 1672 a leading official of the House of Trade (*Casa de la Contratación*) at Seville published the first systematic study of the Atlantic crossings. This was José de Veitia Linaje, later (in 1682) to become secretary of the king's Despacho, whose *Norte de la Contratación de las Indias* (*The Pole Star of American Trade*) remains a primary source for historians. In 1681 the government published in four volumes the first compendium of American laws, the *Recopilación de leyes de los reynos de las Indias*. Despite these contemporary works no historian has ventured to study the late seventeenth century, apart from Clarence Haring in his authoritative survey of the Atlantic system.[69] Hamilton's work on bullion imports stops short at 1650, as does the monumental analysis of Seville's trade by the Chaunus:[70] a recent study of Cadiz by Antonio García Baquero only begins in 1717.[71]

Universal neglect of the late seventeenth century has been influenced by the conviction that it was a period of complete decadence in the Indies trade. Had this been true it would not have been possible for France's consul, Catalan, to write to Colbert in 1670 that 'the trade in this port of Cadiz is the greatest and most flourishing in Europe'.[72]

All commercial links between Spain and America had in general been restricted to the area of Seville and its adjacent ports. The council of the Indies in Madrid and the two major bodies in Seville – the House of Trade (founded in 1503) and the Consulado (1543), which grouped the merchants trading to America – together administered the monopoly. Though the system remained in force for over two centuries and most trading vessels were obliged to cross the bar at San Lucar and unload their cargo twenty leagues up the Guadalquivir at Seville, concessions were made early on for ships to call instead at Cadiz. The jurisdiction over cargoes (*juzgado de Indias*) granted in 1535 to Cadiz, which had a large natural harbour and which ships of heavy tonnage found preferable to having to negotiate the Guadalquivir, rapidly undermined Seville's monopoly. Protests by the House of Trade forced the government to defend Seville's claims in 1664, and from 1666 to 1679 the American traders were obliged to load and unload only at Seville.[73] By this time, however, the greater accessibility of Cadiz had attracted most of the merchants as well as the business involved in the trade. The Consulado itself, formerly a bastion of Andalucian traders, found itself invaded by Basque merchants.[74] Finally in 1680 the government recognised realities and made Cadiz the obligatory port for loading and unloading. The administrative machinery of the House of Trade remained in Seville but was officially transferred to Cadiz in 1717.

The rise of Cadiz was notoriously a consequence of foreign control over the Indies trade, and brought the whole concept of a monopoly into disrepute. The seventeenth century witnessed numerous proposals either for strengthening the monopoly or, more commonly, for breaking it altogether. In 1628 the government was considering ways of establishing multiple trading companies as an alternative to the existing system.[75] All the other proposals we have mentioned, notably that of Juan de Castro, began from the premise that the monopoly must be modified or abandoned. In 1667 Málaga attempted to revive an old claim to be allowed to take part in American trade.[76] The Aragonese, when pressing for a seaport in the 1670s, assumed that this might eventually allow them to participate. The Catalans, who already operated on a limited scale from Cadiz, nursed ambitions that bore fruit briefly in the War of Succession.[77]

The organisation of the fleets to America on the *carrera de Indias* had changed very little since the early sixteenth century.[78] Two distinct fleets were involved: the *galeones*, which sailed to central America, stopping principally at Cartagena on the mainland of South America (called Tierra Firme), and at Portobelo on the isthmus of Panama; and the *flota*, which sailed to Vera Cruz in New Spain. The galeones consisted of about a dozen warships (the flagship was called the *capitana* and that of the rear-admiral the *almiranta*), ranging from 500 to 800 tons, all heavily armed; and about fifteen merchantmen ranging from 400 to 800 tons each. They left Cadiz at no fixed period, and in normal times returned in about thirteen months; emergencies could delay the return by as much as three years. The flota consisted of two galleons (the capitana and almiranta) and an escort ship, with about fifteen armed merchantmen of about 500 tons each. Flotas had to leave Cadiz in June or July in order to arrive before the fifteenth of September, when the stormy season began in the Gulf of Mexico; they normally returned within fourteen months.

Several other vessels made the crossing independently. *Navíos de aviso* or advice ships carried despatches. *Navíos de registro* or register ships helped to supply parts of America not serviced by the fleets. They were private vessels under special licence, with a registered cargo of goods for regions such as Honduras or Buenos Aires. The *navíos de azogues* or mercury ships were two war vessels that transported the produce of the quicksilver mines at Almadén in Spain for use in the silver mining industry of Mexico. These and indeed all vessels on the Atlantic crossing tended to smuggle goods without registering them.

Thanks in part to the dispute between Seville and Cadiz during the period that the *juzgado* was located in Cadiz, official registers of sailings are defective. From 1680 the register book of sailings appears to be complete. Figure 5.5 charts the known total of departures and arrivals at Cadiz in the years 1669 to 1700. The departures and returns of the galeones and flotas are listed in Table 5.8.[79]

Table 5.8

| Year | Galeones | | Flota | |
|------|----------|--------|-------|--------|
| | Depart | Return | Depart | Return |
| 1669 | 10 June, | June 1670 | – | |
| 1670 | – | | 10 July, | 23 Aug. 1671 |
| 1671 | – | | 15 July, | Sept. 1672 |
| 1672 | 1 Mar., | 19 Mar. 1673 | – | |
| 1673 | – | | 13 July, | 30 Oct. 1674 |
| 1674 | – | | – | |
| 1675 | 14 Feb., | 17 Mar. 1676 | 11 July, | Nov. 1676 |
| 1676 | – | | – | |
| 1677 | – | | – | |
| 1678 | 14 July, | 20 Aug. 1679 | 14 July, | 24 Sept. 1679 |
| 1679 | – | | – | |
| 1680 | – | | 4 July, | 6 Nov. 1681 |
| 1681 | 28 Jan., | 1 Sept. 1682 | – | |
| 1682 | – | | – | |
| 1683 | – | | 4 Mar., | 14 Dec. |
| 1684 | 25 Sept., | 13 Sept. 1686 | – | |
| 1685 | – | | – | |
| 1686 | – | | – | |
| 1687 | – | | 30 June, | 9 Nov. 1688 |
| 1688 | – | | – | |
| 1689 | – | | 14 July, | 19 Nov. 1690 |
| 1690 | 14 Mar., | 1–5 Nov. 1691 | – | |
| 1691 | – | | – | |
| 1692 | – | | 18 July, | Nov.–Dec. 1693 |
| 1693 | – | | – | |
| 1694 | – | | – | |
| 1695 | 25 Sept., | 4 June 1698 | 9 July, | Mar. 1697 |
| 1696 | – | | 28 July, | 20 Sept. 1698 |
| 1697 | – | | – | |
| 1698 | – | | 23 July | |
| 1699 | – | | 19 July | |
| 1700 | – | | – | |

Our study of the reign of Charles II has argued for a revival in the nation's economy. No such argument can be applied to the Indies trade as measured by the number or tonnage of vessels clearing Cadiz. The decay is indisputable. It is true that the number of vessels alone is not a clear pointer to decay, since their average tonnage had increased substantially. A law of 1628 decreed that no ships in the carrera should exceed 550 toneladas,[80] but by the end of the century this limit was regularly exceeded. Even taking heavier tonnage into consideration, however, figures were a fraction of what they used to be. The peak year for the late century was 1695, with fifty-seven sailings out of and into Cadiz; the total tonnage involved was well below 20,000 toneladas, the figure that Juan de Castro had adopted in 1669 as the normal capacity of the galeones and flota combined.[81] Compared with the shipping and tonnage figures of the early century, those for

Fig. 5.5   Cadiz and America: registered departures and arrivals, 1669–1700.

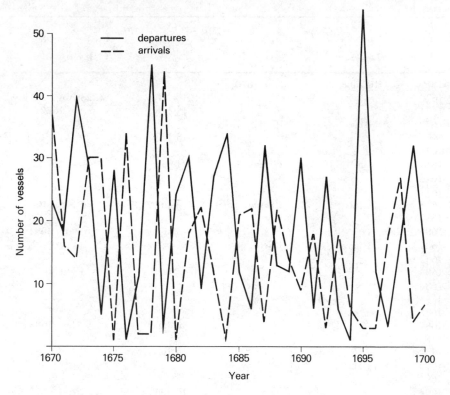

the reign of Charles II are catastrophic, well below even the worst levels of the 1630s and 1640s.[82]

The disaster was paralleled by events in the New World. Under attack from foreign interlopers, both the trade and the security of the Indies were in a parlous state.

Between 1655 and 1671 alone, the corsairs had plundered eighteen cities, four towns and more than thirty-five villages – Cumana once, Cumanagote twice, Maracaibo and Gibraltar twice, Río de la Hacha five times, Santa Marta three times, Tolu eight times, Portobelo once, Chagres twice, Panama once, Santa Catalina twice, Trujillo once, Campeche three times, Santiago de Cuba once. . . . The marquis of Varinas in 1685 estimated the losses of the Spaniards at the hands of the buccaneers since the accession of Charles II to be sixty million crowns, without including the loss of merchant ships and frigates.[83]

This long dirge is nevertheless not an essential part of our story. Because the bulk of the Indies trade was, as we shall see, in foreign hands, the trade was in no way a reflection of Spain's economy. The decay of American commerce was even to be welcomed, in so far as it weakened the hold of foreign finance on Cadiz.

The available figures suggest an absolute decline in shipping from Cadiz, but it does not follow that the volume of wealth from America also declined absolutely. Smuggling was so extensive that the amount of goods registered from the Indies was invariably only a proportion of the real amounts; as little as a half, according to a source of 1691.[84] The problem of contraband has regularly confused the study of bullion imports. As the commodity most likely to be smuggled, bullion would rarely have been registered in the correct quantity. Yet the official returns, as used by Earl J. Hamilton, have been generally accepted as a rough indication of the trend of imports.

Hamilton's tables, in five-year totals, suggest that bullion entering Spain from America attained a peak of 35.1 million pesos in 1591–95 and dropped to 17.1 million in 1631–35, declining rapidly thereafter. In Lynch's words, 'after this the fall was irretrievable', with a total of only 3.5 million in 1656–60.[85] The clear implication is that, as in everything else, the reign of Charles II was in an even worse state, with negligible bullion receipts.

The true situation is suggested in Figure 5.6. Official Spanish documentation would have been most unlikely to record true bullion figures. Foreign consular reports, on the other hand, had no reason to hide the truth and are probably more reliable. This is particularly true of the French, who owned the major part of most shipments and were concerned to get accurate statistics. Hamilton's bullion figures are drawn from official accounts and, at least for the period after 1630,[86]

Fig. 5.6   Imports of American bullion to Spain, 1501–1700.

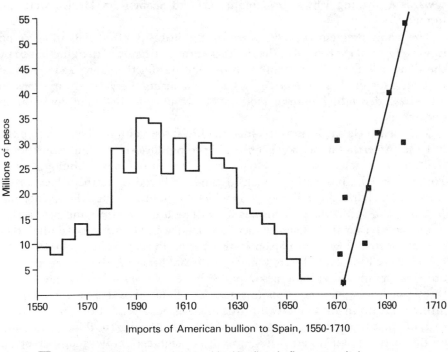

Imports of American bullion to Spain, 1550-1710

⌐L  Registered imports as measured by Hamilton in five-year periods

■  Total imports in specific years in the late century

╱   General volume of bullion imports 1670-1700

are so seriously deficient as to be unusable. Use of unofficial sources makes it clear that bullion imports in the late century, far from plunging towards extinction, reached new heights. Everaert concludes that

there were record years at the end of the century, notably over 40 million pesos on the galleons of 1691 and 30 million on the flota of 1697. Over the period 1671–1700 the five-year totals, though based on incomplete data, range from 35 to 66 million pesos, thereby exceeding the peak of 1591–1600 indicated by Hamilton.[87]

The difficulties in arriving at reliable figures for bullion are almost insuperable. It was notorious that great quantities of unregistered bullion came to Spain. The sums normally registered for 'the king' and for '*particulares*' were at all times only minimal figures. Smuggling even in Cadiz was often easy. A French memorandum of 1691 observed that 'in the customs they only open cases of linen and silk, but never those containing other merchandise'.[88] No guidance at all as to bullion shipments can be obtained from the sums registered in America. In 1682, for example, the treasury in Peru sent a net total of 1,837,106 pesos registered for the king, to be carried in the returning galeones. As much as 1,494,194 pesos of this, however, was spent in Panama on the expenses of the galleons and on costs of military fortification in America, leaving only a tiny sum for shipment.[89] 'The rising cost of defence', it has been pointed out, 'goes far towards explaining why Crown remittances to Spain from Mexico were not higher.'[90]

The whole problem is made worse by the inability of officials to agree on figures. In 1670 the council of the Indies disagreed strongly with figures given by the Consulado for bullion brought on the galleons for the Crown, and claimed that an error of over 100 per cent had been made. Very large variations in estimates, depending on the method of accounting used, are common in documents.

The apparently small sums recorded in official sources should not obscure the fact that American mines were continuing to produce substantial quantities of bullion. In minor areas, as in Honduras, silver output was declining; but at Potosí in Bolivia production remained good; at Parral in northern New Spain there was 'thriving mineral production which continued through the seventeenth century'; and at Zacatecas there was a 'swift resurgence of mining production from 1665 onwards'.[91] These indications lend weight to the possibility that precious metals flowed into Spain in this period in some volume. In 1670 the French consul in Cadiz, Pierre Catalan, estimated that on average the galleons brought up to 24 million pesos per shipment, one-quarter in goods and three-fourths in silver and precious stone. The flota, he said, brought about 10 million, a third in goods and two-thirds in gold and silver.[92] In the period 1670 to 1700 there were eight arrivals of galeones and fourteen of the flota. Assuming, on the basis of Catalan's estimates, a return of eighteen millions for each of the galeones and seven millions for each flota, we arrive at an overall total of 242 million, or five-year averages of about forty million pesos, well above the highest totals recorded by Hamilton.

A detailed look at the available figures shows that there is nothing improbable

Table 5.9

| Arrival | | King | Particulares | Total bullion |
|---|---|---|---|---|
| 1666 | flota[93] | 613,700 | | |
| 1667 | flota[94] | 366,355 | | |
| 1667–8 | galeones[95] | 1,911,007 | | |
| 1670 | flota[96] | 389,974 | | 8,500,000 |
| 1670 | galeones[97] | 2,000,000 | | 22,000,000 |
| 1671 | flota[98] | 1,400,000 | | 7,800,000 |
| 1672 | flota[99] | 900,000 | | 2,000,000 |
| 1673 | galeones[100] | | | 19,000,000 |
| 1674 | flota | | | |
| 1676 | galeones | | | |
| 1676 | flota[101] | 1,748,808 | 3,583,269 | 5,332,077 |
| 1679 | galeones[102] | | 20,000,000 | 21,583,202 |
| 1679 | flota[103] | 719,599 | 323,173 | |
| 1681 | flota[104] | 1,037,791 | | 10,000,000 |
| 1682 | galeones[105] | 848,558 | 20,000,000 | 20,866,977 |
| 1683 | flota[106] | 683,548 | | |
| 1686 | galeones[107] | 1,232,086 | 30,000,000 | 32,000,000 |
| 1688 | flota[108] | | | 24,000,000 |
| 1690 | flota | | | |
| 1691 | galeones[109] | | | 40,000,000 |
| 1693 | flota | | | |
| 1697 | flota[109] | | | 30,000,000 |
| 1698 | galeones[110] | | | 36,000,000 |
| 1698 | flota[110] | | | 18,000,000 |

in this conclusion. Table 5.9 lists registered arrivals of bullion for the king and for particulares, together with total bullion figures (in pesos) drawn mainly from consular sources. Spaces are left blank where I have no documented information.

This fragmentary evidence, as presented in Figure 5.6, leaves no doubt that the government and merchants under Charles II continued to draw on the riches of America. The late seventeenth century was far from being a period of decline in bullion imports.

The bulk of the Indies trade was, as we have seen, in foreign hands. A French memoir of 1691 claimed that of the goods shipped from Cadiz only 5 per cent were Spanish. French exports to Cadiz apparently came to 10 million pesos-worth a year, of which two-thirds were re-exported to America. The profit for French goods in Spain was 12 to 15 per cent, whereas the profit in America was from 40 to 50 per cent.[111] Evidence for the massive export of European textiles to America is unquestionable. In 1686 the French intendant Patoulet drew up detailed memoranda[112] showing that the textiles exported from Cadiz on the galeones were twice the volume of shipments on the flotas. Yet the official Spanish records of cargoes say not a word about foreign items. The register of goods on the flota that left for New Spain in 1668, suggests that nothing but Spanish produce was carried on the entire fleet.[113] Wine, olive oil, hardware, wax and paper allegedly made up most of the shipment. The nature of imports from America at this time can be illustrated (Table 5.10) by the cargo of the two fleet arrivals in February (flota) and June (galeones) 1670:[114]

Table 5.10

| Flota | Galeones |
|---|---|
| 6.5 million pesos coin | 22 million pesos bullion |
| 1 million pesos silver | 150,000 pesos uncut emeralds |
| 1 million pesos gold | 150,000 pesos pearls (Panama) |
| 2,000 cases cochineal | 50,000 pesos pearls (La Margarita) |
| 6,500 cases indigo | 5,500 cases indigo |
| 35,000 quintales campeche | 3,000 quintales campeche |
| 50,000 raw hides | 40,000 raw hides |
| Sugar | 4,000 tanned hides |
| Cacao | 200,000 pounds Havana tobacco |
| | 600 chests tobacco |
| | 100,000 pounds vicuna wool |
| | 6,000 fanegas cacao |
| | 200 cases cochineal |
| | 600 cases ($\times$ 400 lb) Cuban sugar |
| | 7,500 cases ($\times$ 250 lb) Havana sugar |

The long list of goods in the galleons should not mislead us. The most valuable cargo was always bullion. The galleons that returned to Cadiz on 20 August 1679 were assessed at over 24.5 million pesos, of which only 12 per cent by value consisted of merchandise. The arrival of 13 September 1686 was valued at 34.8 million, of which goods represented only 7 per cent.

As Girard has pointed out in some revealing pages,[115] the greater part of all bullion never entered Spain. It was transported from the galleons directly to foreign vessels waiting in the bay of Cadiz. Girard estimates that about three million pesos went directly to France from each fleet that arrived. The French consular papers illustrate the process. The flota of 1670 arrived in February. Between 2 March and 14 April the consul recorded transports of bullion from Cadiz in foreign ships, as shown in Table 5.11.[116]

Table 5.11

| | |
|---|---|
| On 2 March to Genoa in English ships | 1,500,000 pesos |
| On 9 March in ships from St Malo | 1,000,000 |
| A ship to Marseille | 70,000 |
| On 30 March in ships to Hamburg | 500,000 |
| Ibid. in Dutch ships | 700,000 |
| Ibid. in English ships | 300,000 |
| On 14 April a ship to St Malo | 80,000 |
| | 4,150,000 pesos |

These figures mean that nearly half (49 per cent) of the bullion in the flota had gone directly to non-Spanish destinations within a month of the fleet's arrival. In

August 1671 the next flota arrived, with an estimated total of 7,800,000 pesos on board. Between 18 October and 5 March the consul recorded the departure of twenty-four French vessels from Cadiz, loaded with bullion whose value he put at 3,826,000 pesos, or 49 per cent of the total on the fleet.[117] Amounts taken to other countries must have spoken for most of what remained. A final example will suffice. On 1 September 1682 the galleons put into Cadiz, after a voyage full of mishaps, with a bullion cargo of 20,866,977 pesos. Within six weeks the following sums had been transported from the same harbour:[118]

Table 5.12

| | |
|---|---|
| To France | 2.5 million |
| To England | 2.5 |
| To Holland | 3.5 |
| To Genoa | 4.5 |
| | 13 million pesos |

This sum represented 62 per cent of all the bullion on the galleons. With arrival after arrival the story was the same. Foreign vessels had the right to remove treasure since it legally belonged to them despite the regulations of the monopoly.

The evidence shows conclusively that most of the bullion from America did not come to Spain and played no part in its economy. The rich mines of the Indies were robbed in Cadiz harbour. But the loss of bullion did not stop or even begin there. Let us take the personal testimony of a leading Aragonese official, Pedro Borruel, in a thirty-one page printed memorial addressed to the Cortes of Aragon in 1677:[119]

Early in December in the year 1648 I was in Marseille and I saw one morning a large ship unloading several cases of coin. As soon as I saw them I said: These cases come from the Indies. Later I had occasion to look at the coins, which were inferior Peruvian money. I asked if they had come from the port of Cadiz or from another port at which the flota had arrived. I was told that the money had not come from any Spanish port, and had been taken elsewhere off the vessels in the flota. Later on I learnt when the flota had arrived in Spain, and I compared that with the day I had seen the cases unloaded: the ship had arrived in Marseille even before the flota had arrived in Spain.

There was then a heavy loss of bullion at three points: in America itself, during the crossing to Europe, and in Cadiz harbour. Spanish commentators questioned whether America brought any wealth to them at all. 'The trade still remaining to Spain in America is negligible', Martínez de Mata claimed in mid-century in his *Sixth Discourse*. 'What use is it to bring over so many millions worth of merchandise, silver and gold in the galleons, at so much cost and risk, if it comes only for the French and Genoese?'[120]

The question was a serious one and it is worth trying to answer it. The American trade consolidated a system of dependence whereby Spain's weak economy became subject to foreign interests. Within this system, however,

America brought certain advantages. The Crown benefited: it drew emergency income from the fleets and was in a position to levy *indultos* (fines) on unregistered cargo. Spanish merchants in Cadiz and Seville could normally expect a profit. Finally, the commercial exchange between Spain and America, though it brought little material wealth to the mother country, helped to stimulate a certain level of economic activity in the south of the peninsula. Without it, and without the foreign goods that flowed through Andalucia, Spain may well have remained the quiet backwater it was before the discovery of the Indies.

## A SPANISH MERCHANT UNDER CHARLES II: FELIPE DE MOSCOSO

Little is known of the Spanish merchant community in the seventeenth century. Fortunately, documentation survives on the career of a merchant trading from a town, Alicante, that was at the focus of international commerce in the Mediterranean. Felipe de Moscoso was born in 1635, in Orán, of Jewish parents. His father was Jacob Saportas, *xeque* or secular head of the Orán Jewish community, who was banished in 1657 to Italy for a reason that remains unclear. At some time in his early life Felipe became a convert to Christianity and settled in Castile. His uncle Samuel and cousin Solomon Saportas lived as traders in Orán; from 1660 Jacob was resident in Genoa.[121] From 1660 into the 1680s Felipe lived and traded in Alicante as a leading member of the merchant body. Our knowledge of his affairs comes from an invaluable letter-book now deposited in the Archive of the Realm of Valencia.[122] Neither Felipe nor his younger brother Manuel (who later inherited his estate) seems to have suffered harm from having immediate members of the family as practising Jews.[123]

By 1661 Moscoso was 'now a citizen' of Alicante, 'in possession of freedom from paying the customs duty on goods on my account, namely two per cent less than the six that all pay: a concession that foreigners cannot enjoy, but only Castilians'. At the same time he felt that 'it was divine and not human disposition that introduced my presence to this city'.[124] He was destined to prosper, along with the trade of Alicante. From November 1660, when he seems to have first established himself in the city, Moscoso traded principally in hemp: 'The merchandise in which I deal primarily is blue hemp, which is the most easily sold of goods that come to this city, its intrinsic value being always four pesos and its sale value a bit higher. . . . I deal in other goods only incidentally.'[125] In fact he also spent considerable time in importing wheat and tobacco, and exporting esparto grass. By the end of 1660 he had established regular commercial correspondence with colleagues in Orán (Samuel Saportas), Livorno (Giacomo Barla, the Borges, Duarte and Luis de Silva), Valencia (Christófol del Mor), Cartagena (Antonio de Montoya) and Barcelona (Onofre Argemir).[126] In Alicante his affairs during occasional absences were handled by Gaspar and Francisco Moxica.

Through Moscoso's correspondence it is possible to learn a great deal about the trade of Alicante in the seventeenth century. According to him the bases of

Alicante's wealth were fishing and the trade with England. 'En la pesca se pesca mucho dinero', he wrote to one correspondent in February 1661: in fishing there is a lot of money to be fished. 'It is very well known in this city to be the best trade, in absolute terms, to have; and through it alone many have become rich within a few years.' 'Fishing' did not refer to the local industry so much as to the large import trade from England, possibly the biggest single business in Alicante. In return, 'the principal products remitted from this city to England are olive oil, soap, raisins, almonds and other items'. Moscoso's praise of fishing must be balanced against his likewise optimistic view of the soap trade. 'Soap', he informed the Borges in June 1661, 'is the best commodity of all that are loaded in this port, and the principal foundation of the biggest business. It promises outstanding profits and never a loss.' There was no contradiction: Moscoso was pointing to fish as the richest import and soap as the richest export.[127]

Though a newcomer Moscoso very soon got his credit accepted. By March 1661 he was trading 'wholly on credit, and very little or nothing in cash; and with very reliable persons who cause me no concern or worry'. The bulk of his dealings in this early period were (despite his praise for the English trade) with Italy, to which he made payments in bills of exchange, sent always by ship and never by other postal means, drawn either upon bankers in Italy or sometimes upon the captain of the ship. The normal interest rate for bills of exchange in 1661 was 12 per cent. Since Moscoso had no ships of his own, all his trade was done on English or Dutch carriers. Without the help of these Protestant seamen the effective trade of Alicante would have been negligible.

By the end of 1661 Moscoso had established good links with the traders Jorge and Domingo Rodríguez Francia, both then in London. In this year he began to send large quantities of soap to London (148 quintales on one English ship in June, at 96 lliures a quintal, with a promise of 300 quintales in the next shipment), and to receive in exchange lead, pepper and Irish linen, 'which are merchandise that will sell very well',[128] in addition to fish. By April 1662, when Moscoso began dealings with Diego and Bernardo Monson of Livorno, his activities had considerably expanded.

Every year in this port many ships take on crude esparto for Lisbon, this being a commodity that promises a good profit. . . . Saffron is also a very good commodity for Lisbon. On this coast there is a good trade for fish and for the produce we send in return, which is chiefly soap in bars, glass-wort, raisins, wine and almonds; and most of these are shipped to St Malo, Rouen, Amsterdam and London.[129]

At this date his correspondents included agents in Barcelona (Raymond Roman, the French consul), Málaga (Sebastián de Argüello, administrator of tobacco) and Venice.

Moscoso is an example of a Spanish merchant with a full and active dedication to trade. He never married, and kept his money invested only in his business. His great conscientiousness is illustrated by his care always to duplicate his letters and send them by different channels (to London, for example, via Pamplona or Madrid), a practice he urged upon all his correspondents. He never took an interest in the Indies trade. When a friend asked him to recommend agents in

141

Cadiz he replied, 'When the Indies fleets get lost or delayed even the wealthiest merchants go bankrupt, so I don't dare to recommend anybody. I correspond with the Tamaninos of Cadiz, but though I have friends in Seville we do no business in that place.'[130] His annual turnover was modest: Moscoso was well aware that Alicante was a small port with a limited outlet, and consequently advised a correspondent in Genoa to send goods in small quantities to make sure of quicker dispatch. He seems to have been a merchant with a cautious and careful eye to the market. There is no doubt that Jewish and converso connections were a conspicuous help to him, whether in Lisbon, Orán or Italy. But none of this would have been of use had he not been a conscientious businessman within his own, Spanish, environment.

Figure 5.7 gives a summary view of the extremely wide range of activities of this remarkable and hitherto unknown Spanish merchant. In the 1670s he began

Fig. 5.7   Trade links of an Alicante merchant: Felipe de Moscoso 1661–81.

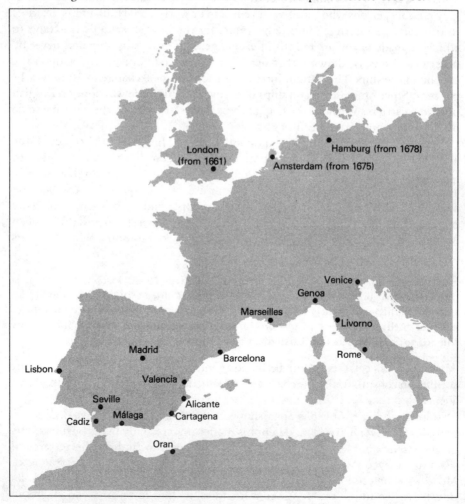

to employ French vessels for his dealings in Marseille and in Portugal. In Lisbon his agent, with whom in 1673–74 he had serious disagreements, was Francisco González Enríquez. The range of goods in which he traded was now also vast, including items such as Brazilian tobacco and sugar, and Segovian textiles. For trade within the peninsula his correspondents included Rafael de Silveyra in Madrid and Antonio Gómez de Silveyra in Granada. He was on good terms with the marquis of Leganés, viceroy of Catalonia, and with his secretary, 'my intimate friend', Don Francisco Hoz. In June 1675 for the first time he opened a correspondence with Amsterdam (letters normally took 27 days) through Duarte de Silva, now resident there. 'I have not had any business there and have a mind to establish it through you, particularly in soap, which I shall send in reasonable quantity every year'.[131] A summary of his outlook at this date, with some comment on the northern trades, can be found in his letter to de Silva that July:[132]

Struggling against adverse fortune in the course of the fifteen years that I have been here, I find myself at the age of forty so tired and worn out that I am resolved to work with all my strength for some four or five years more, at the most, before resting. Every year I shall ship a considerable quantity of fruits in the way that I can be absolutely assured is the most profitable, trading in English goods which promise a forty or fifty per cent profit. All the English who deal in them have become and continue to become very rich in a few years. Joseph Erne came to Alicante with nothing but his contacts, and returned four years ago to London with over 100,000 pesos; Benjamin Newland with over 20,000 and so on.[133]

I propose to place in your hand, in London and Hamburg, merchandise to the value of 10,000 pesos, so that you may on your own account as well as mine be able to spend 20,000 pesos on the supply of cloth from England. . . . For Hamburg I shall send a good quantity of almonds, for London aniseed and soap, and for Amsterdam whatever you advise. . . . If 20,000 pesos seems too large a sum to lay out as a start, reduce it by ten or twelve thousand, as you see fit.

De Silva was not a fortunate correspondent to have, for his business failed two years later and in January 1677 he was paying off his debts at a rate of 24 per cent of what he owed.[134] Moscoso subsequently worked with other Amsterdam correspondents, with Jacques Sena and Louis Vandenboos. To the former in 1678 he reported a typical case of trading expertise by himself:

I have loaded on the *Catherine*, captain William Burret, Englishman, twenty-six pipes and a barrel, making 1,153 cantaros of wine, though in the advice I put only 1,052; one quarter-cask with 17 cantaros of syrup, though I put 15; twenty-four sacks of wool with 310 arrobas, though I put 254; and eight barrels of aniseed with 137 arrobas, though I put only 117.[135]

Assuming that his bill of lading was accepted as written out, Moscoso had understated the cargo by up to 15 per cent and made a corresponding saving on customs duties.

At the end of 1678 he began direct correspondence with Hamburg through Jacques Raphael. He was encouraged to do this by the growing difficulties in Alicante of the Solicofres, the only major trading firm to specialise in imports from Hamburg.[136] Moscoso was now fully committed to the northern trades in addition to his other business. The risky long-distance ventures from the north were all covered by special insurance in Amsterdam.[137] In spite of the distances and the difficulties of carriage (in 1675 he had had to wait six months, from June till December, before he could find a ship empty enough to carry a cargo of soap to Amsterdam), he preferred the north. Only occasionally did he continue his Mediterranean trade. In 1679 he explained to a new correspondent in Livorno:[138]

I would like to get to know you to see what business can be arranged, for I have none in Livorno, but only in Amsterdam, Hamburg, London and other parts in the west. I am very little inclined to trade in the Levant [i.e. east from Spain], because the profit is smaller.

By May that year he was negotiating to sell raw wool to Italy, and in the same month he began dealing with imports of tobacco and sugar from Lisbon through a new correspondent there, Antonio Vega de Lemos. The north remained his chief commitment. In July he used Dutch ships to send 3,000 arrobas of unwashed wool to his Amsterdam correspondent Rafael de Arredondo; and was arranging with Jacques Raphael to import Swedish iron from Hamburg. Moscoso's trade with the north was so substantial that when in 1681 Arredondo (who already had his own vessel, the *Angel Raphael*) suggested having a ship built for their trade, he replied that 'having to make two voyages a year from here to there, it would be very well for us to have one built on our account, and I confirm that I am interested in the expenses and the cargo for one fourth'.[139] There is no evidence of the ship having been built.

The letter-book ends in 1681. Moscoso continued trading in Alicante till his death in 1686. He was not one of the great and wealthy merchants of his time, but an ordinary, active trader whose devotion to commerce can therefore be seen as a typical and normal commitment. In just over one quarter of a century the scale of his operations, and presumably also his working capital, expanded visibly. He was not a sedentary merchant: he travelled frequently to Madrid, and family connections obliged him to visit Orán and Genoa. His career is a living refutation of the belief that Spaniards had no serious interest in commerce.

## THE MERCHANT COMMUNITY IN SPAIN

Because commercial activity required extensive use of money and credit, it stimulated finance and banking. This could happen, however, only in the international trade centres. In Spain there were substantial money markets only in Madrid and Cadiz. The limited amount of trade at other centres did not generate enough business to attract financiers. Barcelona had no effective bank or credit facilities: traders usually drew their funds from Madrid. Alicante, despite its commerce, was in the same position: the French consul in 1669 reported that 'there is no bank here but only in Madrid, with a loss of 6 to 7 per cent against the drawer'.[140] 'The kingdom of Aragon', a French intendant reported in 1706, 'is without any facilities . . . Banking is almost unknown there, and at most there are two or three merchants who conduct a few transactions in bills of exchange between Saragossa and Madrid.'[141]

Spain's trade relationship with other states was, as we have seen, characterised by overwhelming foreign control of the market. A direct consequence was that foreign traders preferred to carry their own produce to Spain. Spanish merchants did not need to buy their own ships, and relied for transport on the English, French and Dutch. A visitor to the harbours at Cadiz or Alicante, thronged with foreign vessels, would thereby gain the impression that Spaniards were not interested in trade. When the ambassador of Morocco visited Spain in 1691 he reported of his hosts that 'pomp and luxury have prevailed over them, and none of their race can be found who carries on commerce, or travels to other countries for that purpose, as is the custom of other Christian nations'.[142]

The limited evidence that we have on banking and shipping confirms the subordinate role playing by Spaniards in the commerce of their own country. From Moscoso's evidence we know that in Alicante 'there are at present six English firms with big interests taking very great care not to allow anyone not of their nation to take part in the trade' to northern Europe: this was in 1675.[143] The soap trade to France was likewise cornered by 'a rich French trader of this city, who every year sends a shipload of soap to Rouen via Le Havre';[144] indeed in 1679 the Frenchman had bought up all the soap in the market and Moscoso had to find alternative goods for his shipment. In conditions like this it is not very surprising that Spanish traders found it almost impossible to compete.

The principal trade centres of Spain could usually be identifed by the presence of a foreign consul. In the reign of Charles II the English had consuls in La Coruña, Bilbao, Barcelona, Alicante, Málaga, Seville and Cadiz; the French had them additionally in San Sebastián, San Lucar, Gibraltar, Cartagena, Valencia and other locations.[145]

The biggest and most important community remained that in the Seville–Cadiz complex.[146] Cadiz contained the biggest group. The Savoyard merchant Raymond Lantéry singled out 87 leading firms in the 1670s, made up as follows: 12 Spanish (i.e. under 14 per cent), 27 Genoese, 11 French, 10 British, 7 Hanseatic and 20 Flemish or Dutch.[147] The real number of active firms was much higher. In 1670, that is at about the same date as Lantéry's observations, there were twenty-one French merchants in residence in Cadiz.[148] The foreign population of the city in 1709 was around 10 per cent, and we may presume this to be roughly true of the late seventeenth century.

The quality of commercial life in the Cadiz of Charles II is best examined through the memoirs of Raymond Lantéry, who began writing his observations in 1696 and covered the whole period 1673 to 1700.[149] The fragility of fortunes in the Indies trade struck also at Lantéry, who in 1685, twelve years after first settling in Cadiz, suffered a major disaster as a result of losses among the galleons. 'I lost everything, by my account nearly 13,000 pesos of principal, which together with other accidents came to over 20,000 pesos that I lost. At which I reckoned it better to return to my own country.'[150] He put his entire family on board ship for Nice, where they stayed for five years, returning in 1690 when his fortunes improved.

Investment in Cadiz was affected by political and business factors just as much as by the movement of the Indies trade. When the Dutch firm of van Herten and

Meyer, which Lantéry described as 'the biggest and most opulent in Cadiz', went bankrupt in 1688, their ruin was attributed mainly to internal quarrels. French activity was restricted by the hazards of war, and repeated expulsions and sequestrations kept the number of permanent residents down: only in the eighteenth century did they expand without interruption.

Despite the immense importance of the American trade in Spain's economic life, it was clearly a parasitic growth and contributed little to economic development. Lantéry, in so far as he considered himself a citizen of Spain and therefore did not remit any of his profits back home to Savoy, was typical of the Cadiz merchant class in his outlay of cash. His priorities were a large mansion in the principal street, the *calle Nueva*; half a dozen black slaves; and an expensive education for his sons. He improved his life style rather than his business commitments. Society in Cadiz became aristocratic in outlook rather than entrepreneurial. This situation was paralleled nowhere else in the peninsula.

It is not easy to trace the merchant class in other cities. The twenty-two rich merchants listed in official documentation for Bilbao in 1718,[151] refer to a period when the Consulado of the city had excluded non-domiciled foreigners from participation in the wool trade. In Alicante in 1683 there were 78 names listed among 'all the merchants and traders of the present city'; in 1686 there were 96.[152] Of the traders in 1683, whose names are heavily disguised by being written in a Spanish form, we might estimate that about 21 were French, 23 English, 4 Flemish, 11 Italian and 19 (or 24 per cent) Spanish. The biggest firms were all foreign. Between 1683 and 1687 the merchants with the largest turnover, measured by their customs returns, were Anthony Basset, Samuel Wates and Thomas Jeffreys, all English. Anthony Basset, the most flourishing merchant in Alicante, was typical of the city's traders in having close social links with the merchant class of Valencia.

North from Alicante the role of international trading was so small that there was no need for a resident community of foreign traders. No foreign merchant of any repute was based there. The English, French and Dutch monopolised seagoing transport in the area, but few of their nationals found it necessary to live in Catalonia. Catalans were therefore in the wholly unique position of being able to reclaim control over their own commerce without facing opposition from resident foreign interests. Mataró committed itself to the programme by launching a range of small vessels into the coastal trade.[153] Some of the ships traded internationally: the *saetía* named *Santiago* took on tobacco in Lisbon in 1700 and discharged its cargo at Cadiz, Gibraltar, Málaga, Cartagena and Salou.[154] Collaboration between merchants of Mataró and Barcelona, notably in the company formed by the traders Feu and Feliu de la Peña,[155] was particularly fruitful. In 1684 a vessel captained by Pere Exides and chartered by the merchants Ramon Alamany and Salvador Feliu, was trading directly to Genoa. Its cargo was wine taken on at Mataró and textiles taken on at Barcelona. On its return voyage from Genoa in December 1684 it was captured by the French.[156] Despite many similar reverses suffered by the enterprising merchants of the Catalan ports, they began successfully to recover control of their own fortunes and of the economic life of the principality. The capital enemy, as we have seen from the programme of Narciso Feliu de la Peña, was France. It followed that the merchant oligarchy of Catalonia dedicated itself to undermining French control over the principality's economy. The first municipality to adhere to the pretender in the War of Succession was, not surprisingly, Mataró. The oligarchy in Barcelona did the same. 'The war of 1705 was', as Vilar has pointed out, 'part of the dream of the Catalan mercantile bourgeoisie of becoming, through a policy of Free Trade, another Holland.'[157]

The extremely unfavourable trade position of Spain produced, precisely in the late seventeenth century, developments of major significance in the country's modern history: the emergence of Bilbao and Barcelona under the leadership of a native oligarchy determined to win control of their own commerce. It was a small beginning, but it heralded a new era.

## NOTES

1. **Carande, R.**, *Carlos V* (Madrid 1965–67), I, 211–14.
2. Moncada, *Restauración*, p. 22.
3. *Ibid*. p. 7.
4. **Hamilton, E. J.**, 'Spanish merchantilism', *Facts and Factors* (Cambridge, Mass. 1932), pp. 214–39; **Larraz, J.**, *Epoca del mercantilismo* (Madrid 1944).
5. Cf. Lynch, *Spain*, II, 153.
6. BN MS. 10921/51. See also BL Eg. MS. 339/350–413.
7. Letter from Queen to Vizcaya, 25 Aug. 1668, in Labayru, *Señorío de Bizcaya*, V, 730.
8. 'Advertencias importantes a la total comprehension de la Real voluntad en la formacion de la Compañia Española para el Comercio Armado', Valencia 15 Jan. 1669, BMV, Reales Pragmáticas, Ch. 1636–105/10.
9. References to these in **Carrera Pujal, J.**, *Economía Española* (Barcelona 1943–47), II, 30–4. For proposals in the early century, see **García Baquero, A.**, *Cádiz* (Seville 1976), I, 134.
10. Cited in Sánchez, M. L., 'Attempts at Reform', p. 92.
11. *Extensión Política*, p. 139.
12. The marquis of San Felipe. See note 7, Chapter Two above.
13. **Haring, C. H.**, *Trade and Navigation* (Cambridge, Mass. 1918), p. 271.
14. Labayru, *Señorío de Bizcaya*, V, 444.
15. AGS Contadurías Generales 189.
16. *Ibid*. 1719.
17. Details from AGI Contratación libro 2900 no. 2.
18. Details from *ibid*. libro 2901.
19. For England see **Davis, R.**, 'Protection in England, 1689–1786', *Econ. H. R.*, (Aug. 1966), p. 306.
20. Memoir of 19 May 1669 by Jean de Montaut, deputy French consul at Cadiz, AN:AE, B¹ 211/12.
21. For his career, see below, Chapter Fourteen.
22. AN:AE, B¹ 211/53. Catalan's *écus* are given by me as pesos: in livres the figure is 39 million. It is interesting to note that this memoir is completely misread by **Girard, A.**, *Commerce français* (Paris 1932), p. 446, to represent shipments *from* America.

The breakdown given by Catalan should be compared with that of 1691 reproduced in **Everaert, J.**, *De internationale* (Bruges 1973), p. 278, where French goods come to 38.4 per cent, English to 18.5 per cent, Belgian to 6 per cent.

23. Valuable indications of trade in the early century are given by **Taylor, H.**, 'English Road', *Econ. H. R.*, **25** (May 1972), 236–60.

24. Godolphin to Arlington, 20 June 1675, *Hispania Illustrata*, p. 237.

25. **Davis, R.**, 'English foreign trade', *Econ. H. R.*, **7** (1954), ii.

26. Memorandum of 14 July 1715, 'We the consul and merchants of Sevilla', PRO:SP 94/212.

27. This 'Memoire sur le commerce de Cadiz et des Indes', of which there is a copy in AE:CP (Esp) 70/183–218, is used extensively by Girard, *Commerce français*, and is there cited at p. 166 n. 70.

28. *Op. cit.* Ch. VIII, summary on p. 411.

29. As published by **McLachlan, J.**, 'Documents', *Camb. Hist. Jl.*, 4 (1934), 298–311.

30. *Ibid.* p. 309.

31. Cochineal and indigo came from America, barilla and salt from the Levant area (see below).

32. Everaert, *De internationale*, pp. 284–94,. 325.

33. *Ibid.* p. 459.

34. Memoir of 20 May 1669, in AN:AE, B$^1$ 146.

35. No such ships are explicitly mentioned. The reference is presumably to the 'convoys of five to six ships' from Genoa.

36. Settees (*saéties* in French, *saetías* in Spanish) were small ships used in the Mediterranean. The word is used interchangeably with tartans (*tartanes*, in French), fishing or trading ships with a twenty-ton capacity. In 1680–82 the vessel departures from Marseille to Spain were 157, 153 and 165 vessels respectively, almost all tartanes. See **Rambert, G.**, 'Ports espagnols 1660 à 1789', in **Mollat, M.**, ed., *Le Navire* (Paris 1958), p. 27.

37. 'Memoire de l'estimation des marchandises qui sont entree en cette ville d'Alicant en les annees 1667, 68 et 69', AN:AE, B$^1$ 146.

38. AE:CP (Esp) 64/273.

39. **Palacio Atard, V.**, *Comercio de Castilla* (Madrid 1960), pp. 48, 181–3.

40. Cary, *Discourse*, in McLachlan, 'Documents', p. 309.

41. AE:CP (Esp) 64/273.

42. See **Bilbao, L. M.**, 'Crisis y reconstrucción', *Saioak*, 1 (1977), 157–80; and **Laborda Martín, J. J.**, 'Recuperación comercial', *Saioak*, 2 (1978), 136–79. I am grateful to Sr Laborda Martín for sending me an offprint of his article.

43. 'By 1667 the royal duties on wool exports [through Bilbao] consisted of the following tariffs: (1) two *ad valorem* duties amounting to $11\frac{1}{2}$ per cent; (2) three tariffs totalling six reales silver per *arroba*; and (3) a tariff of four ducats per ten *arrobas*': **Smith, R. S.**, *Spanish Guild Merchant* (Duke U. P., 1940), p. 74.

44. Taylor, H., 'English Road', pp. 256–9.

45. On the *avería* see **Guiard y Larrauri, T.**, *Consulado* (Bilbao 1913), I, 338; Smith, *Spanish Guild Merchant*, p. 89.

46. Bilbao had been prepared to offer up to 160,000 ducats. See Guiard y Larrauri, *Consulado*, I, 301.

47. List drawn up by the Secretary of War, see Laborda Martín, *op. cit.* p. 157.

48. Quoted in **Guiard, T.**, *La industria naval* (Bilbao 1917), p. 102.

49. Soleil to M. Delagny, director general of trade, 26 May 1686, AN:AE, B$^1$ 178/89.

50. The diagrams and the tables are based on **Fontana Lázaro, J.**, 'Comercio exterior',

*Estud. Hist. Mod.*, 5 (1955), 199–219. Some of his data do not tally and I have made adjustments.

51. Data derived from Smith, R. S., *Guild Merchant*, p. 140; Vilar, *Catalunya*, I, 384. See also Fontana Lázaro, *op. cit.* p. 219. There are some errors in the calculations in Vilar's table. Annual traffic figures are calculated on the basis of the *periatge*, which was levied at about 0.8 per cent *ad valorem*.

52. **Vicens Vives** argued in his *Historia Económica* (Barcelona 1959), p. 423, that the figures show an increase in Catalonia's potential as contrasted with a decline in Castile, reflected in the trade of Seville.

53. Cited in **Llovet, J.**, *Mataró* (Mataró 1966), p. 54.

54. 'Descripcion y planta del Principado de Cataluña', BCB MS. Arch. 516.

55. Cited in Llovet, *op. cit.* pp. 30, 31–2.

56. **Meijide Pardo, A.**, *Economía marítima* (Valladolid 1971), p. 187.

57. Harland Taylor, 'English Road', *loc. cit.* p. 255.

58. Godolphin to Mr. Ellis, 31 Mar. 1671 Old Style, in *Original Letters* (London 1724), p. 120.

59. **Ringrose, D. R.**, *Transportation* (Durham, N. C. 1970), p. 23.

60. Toledo price from Hamilton, *War and Prices*, p. 247; other price levels from Kamen, *War of Succession*, pp. 413–14.

61. Uztáriz, G. de, *Theórica* (Madrid 1742), Ch. 107, p. 405.

62. Consulta of 23 June 1681, AGS Estado 4130.

63. Asso, *Economía política de Aragón*, p. 227.

64. The details that follow are from ADZ 734, 'Registro del Brazo de Cavalleros Hijosdalgo en las Cortes de los años 1677 y 1678', folios 276–406. Total values are calculated on the basis of tax returns. This is possible because the *generalidades* were levied *ad valorem* at an unvarying rate on all goods.

65. Asso, *op. cit.* p. 236.

66. *Ibid.* p. 237.

67. *Ibid.* p. 238.

68. The proceedings of the Cortes are considered in detail below in Chapter Thirteen.

69. **Haring, C. H.**, *Trade and Navigation* (Harvard 1918).

70. **Chaunu, H.** and **Chaunu, P.**, *Séville et l'Atlantique* (Paris 1955–59).

71. García Baquero, *op. cit.*

72. Cited in Everaert, *De internationale*, p. 37.

73. Haring, *op. cit.* p. 14.

74. Everaert, *op. cit.* p. 190.

75. García Baquero, *op. cit.* I, 134.

76. Haring, *op. cit.* p. 17.

77. I have been unable to consult the unpublished thesis of **C. Martínez Shaw**, 'El comercio entre Cataluña y America (1680–1756)', Barcelona 1973.

78. For the sixteenth century see Haring, *op. cit.* pp. 201–30. What follows here is based largely on Everaert, *op. cit.* pp. 194–208, 884–6; and other sources.

79. All information on Cadiz sailings is from AGI Contratación libro 2900 no. 2. There is a good summary of the same information in Everaert, *op. cit.* pp. 190–222. My list excludes some major sailings not classified as galeones or flotas.

80. Haring, *op. cit.* p. 213.

81. BL Eg. MS. 339/359.

82. See Chaunu's figures, as cited by Lynch, *Habsburgs*, II, 189–91.

83. Haring, *op. cit.* pp. 249–50.

84. On contraband see Haring, *op. cit.* pp. 62–7, 111–15; **Dahlgren, E. W.**, *Les*

*relations commerciales* (Paris 1909), Ch. 2. My reference is to Dahlgren, p. 42.

85. Hamilton, *American Treasure* (Cambridge, Mass. 1934), pp. 34–6; Lynch, *Habsburgs*, II, 186.

86. Cf. Everaert, *op. cit.* p. 902.

87. *Ibid.* p. 902.

88. 'Memoire touchant le commerce des Indes occidentales par Cadix', 1691, from AE:CP (Esp) 80/22–393, printed in **Sée, H.**, *Documents* (Paris 1927), p. 31.

89. Details in consulta of council of Indies, 8 Oct. 1682, AGI Contaduria 571.

90. **Bakewell, P. J.**, *Silver Mining* (Cambridge 1971), p. 233.

91. On Honduras, **MacLeod, M.**, *Spanish Central America* (Berkeley 1973), p. 149, fig. 13; on Parral, **West, R. C.** *The Mining Community* (Berkeley 1949), p. 13; on Zacatecas, Bakewell, *op. cit.* p. 220, and graph I.

92. Report of 1670 in AN:AE, B¹ 211/53.

93. Income to Crown in AGS:CJH 1895. See also AGI Contratación 4926.

94. Crown's income in AGS:CJH 1898.

95. Crown's income in report of D. Lope de los Rios, 27 Jan. 1668, AGS:CHJ 906: 'Resumen general ultimo de lo que importan los efectos de Su Magd y Rl Hazda.'

96. This sum for the Crown is described in an order of 28 Feb. 1670 as 'el caudal que hia traydo por quenta de la Rl Hazda . . . la flota': AGI Contaduria 570. The total for bullion (6.5 million in pesos, 1 million in silver, 1 million in gold) is the consular estimate in AN:AE, B¹ 211/29: 'Memoire de ce que contient la flotte'. The consul estimated the full value of the flota at 13 million.

97. Estimates from 'Memoire de la charge qu'ont apporté', in *ibid.* 211/60. The galleons alone brought 413,458 pesos for the king, but the council contested this, claiming the total should have been 850,218 pesos: AGI Contaduría 586.

98. Consular estimates, AN:AE, B¹ 211/109. The amount for the Crown is confirmed by the accounts of Veitia Linaje, then treasurer of the Contratación showing total receipts from the fleet of 1,247,233 pesos: AGI Contratación 4598.

99. *Ibid.* 211/131. The total value of the fleet was put at 4.4 million pesos.

100. The 1673 total is cited in Girard, *Commerce français*, p. 447 n. 73.

101. The 1676 flota returns are from PRO:SP 101/92/104: 'An accompt of ye treasure'. The fleet was valued at a total 6,132,077 pesos.

102. AN:AE, B¹ 211/256. A further 3 million pesos worth of goods made up the total value of the fleet.

103. 'Sumario General', AGI Contratación 4926. The amounts registered were brought both in the flota and in the returning navíos de azogues.

104. The 1681 figures for the king come from a memorandum of 31 Dec. 1683, AGI Contaduria 571. The total is cited in Girard, *op. cit.* p. 449.

105. 'Relacion del tesoro de quenta de Su Magd y de particulares que viene en los Galeones', AGI Contratación 4926. A consular report giving exactly the same information is in AN:AE, B¹ 212/64–7, with a version in Italian following. This type of coincidence between Spanish and foreign reports helps to confirm the reliability of consular information.

106. 'Ajustamiento universal del thesoro traido en la flotta', 23 Sept. 1684, AGI Contaduría 571. But cf. the different figures, of 226, 489 for the king and 306,757 for particulars, in the 'Sumario General' of 24 Jan. 1684 in *ibid.* Contratación 4926.

107. Figures from 'Memoire du Sr Catalan', AN:AE, B¹ 212/408–9. The sum for the king, however, is from the 'Relacion Sumaria' in AGI Contratación 4926. Catalan says only 400,000 came for the king. The total value of the fleet was estimated at 34,800,000 pesos.

108. These figures are cited in Girard, *op. cit.* p. 452.

109. The totals for 1691 and 1697 are cited by Everaert, *op. cit.* p. 395. In each case his source is Belgian documentation. For alternative estimates covering this period see **Morineau, M.**, 'D'Amsterdam à Seville', *Annales*, 23 (1968), p. 196. Everaert's total estimates compared with those of Morineau are in *op. cit.* p. 396. For the king's share in 1697, see Stanhope, *Spain under Charles*, p. 111: 'Yesterday (28 May 1697) came to town from Cadiz sixty mules laden with silver on the king's account.'

110. The totals for the 1698 arrivals are cited by Girard, *op. cit.* p. 452.

111. 'Memoire touchant le commerce', in Sée, *Documents*, pp. 31–2, 46–7.

112. There are analyses of his memoranda in Girard, *Commerce français,* esp. Ch. 8; and Everaert, *op. cit.* pp. 375–93

113. 'Relacion de los frutos y mercaderias', AGI Contratación 4926.

114. Details from AN:AE, B$^I$ 211/29, 60.

115. Girard, *op. cit.* pp. 444–55.

116. 'Extrait de ce que les nations ont remis apres l'arrivee de la flote 1670', AN:AE, B$^I$ 211/39.

117. 'Memoire des navires marchands françois sortis', *ibid.* 211/118–19. Girard, *op. cit.* pp. 446–7, has figures which are wrong.

118. AN:AE, B$^I$ 212/92–3: 'Memoire de l'argent embarqué'.

119. ACA:CA 1370; the quotation is at p. 20.

120. *Memoriales*, ed. Anés, pp. 149–50.

121. Further details on Saportas are given below, p. 306.

122. 'Registro de las cartas de un comerciante de Alicante 1660–1681', libro 74 in the section Varia of ARV. The volume is unfolioed.

123. Manuel's will, dated 1698, is in ARV Manaments y Empares 1699, libro 3, mano 36, f.22. Manuel was a 'captain', presumably in the army.

124. Letter of 29 June 1661 to Giacomo Vicenzio Barla in Genoa.

125. To Fabio and Camilo Borge in Livorno, 3 Dec. 1660.

126. Del Mor was a ciutadà of Valencia and one of the principal merchants of that city. Argemir, a leading merchant of Barcelona, became a ciutadà in 1670, when it was claimed that 'his income is 1,500 libras in rentals': consulta of council of Aragon, 23 Aug. 1670, ACA:CA 241/17.

127. Quotations in this paragraph are from letters to the Borges, dated 19 Feb. and 29 June 1661.

128. To the Francias in London, 19 July 1661.

129. To the Monsons in Livorno, 19 Apr. 1662.

130. To the Cardonas in Livorno, 23 Apr. 1663.

131. To Duarte de Silva in Amsterdam, 24 June 1675.

132. To *idem*, 8 July 1675.

133. The Alicante merchant body in 1683 included a 'Jorge Nolin y Erne', presumably George Nolan with Erne as an absent associate. In the same year a 'Juan Risbel y Neulant' appears. See ARV Maestre Racional 516/10396.

134. To D. Jaime Gavalla in Cadiz, 1 Feb. 1677.

135. To Jacques Sena in Amsterdam, 3 Jan. 1678.

136. On the Solicofres, see e.g. **Rambert, G.** ed., *Commerce de Marseille* (Paris 1949–59), IV (1599–1789), *passim*.

137. 'En Amsterdam se me hazen los seguros de lo que va y viene por mi quenta': 27 Feb. 1679, to Raphael in Hamburg.

138. To Ruy López Núñez in Livorno, 26 May 1679.

139. To Arredondo in Amsterdam, 24 Feb. 1681.

140. Memoir of 20 May 1669 by Prégent, AN:AE, B¹ 146.

141. Cited in Kamen, *War of Succession*, p. 71 no. 50.

142. Stanley, H. E. J., ed., *Account of an embassy*, (n.p., n.d.), p. 9.

143. 8 July 1675, to Duarte de Silva in Amsterdam.

144. 5 June 1679, to Raphael in Hamburg.

145. For the French, see the list in Girard, *op. cit.* p. 134 n.1.

146. My brief treatment should be supplemented by Girard, *op. cit.* Ch. 2–7; and Driesch, W. von den, *Die ausländischen Kaufleute* (Cologne 1972), part B. The important articles by Domínguez Ortiz and Sancho de Sopranis are cited in my bibliography.

147. As cited in von den Driesch, p. 246.

148. Names in Girard, *op. cit.* p. 549 n.22.

149. Lantéry, *Memorias*. See also the comment by Ponsot, P., 'Chronique gaditane', *Mélanges Braudel*, pp. 471–86.

150. *Memorias*, p. 179.

151. Laborda Martín, 'Recuperación comercial', *loc. cit.*

152. ARV Maestre Racional 516/10396, 10398.

153. See the appendices to Llovet, *Mataró*.

154. *Ibid.* p. 39.

155. See Molas, P., 'La Companiya Feu-Feliu', *Cuad. Hist. Econ. Cat.*, 12 (1974).

156. AN:AE, B¹ 178/63. Other merchants contributing to the cargo were Pau Feu, with textiles from Barcelona; and Francisco Feliu de la Peña, with wine from Mataró.

157. Vilar, *Catalunya*, I, 416.

# CHAPTER SIX

# The Urban Environment

Spaniards of the seventeenth century took a great pride in their towns. Strong regional loyalties tied them to their birthplace and their sense of history was expressed most vividly when they wrote of their native soil. The best historical writing of the time took the form of urban histories, such as Vicente Mares's magnificent *La Feñix Troyana* (1681), a study of his native Chelva; or Gerónimo de la Concepción's ambitious history of Cadiz, *Emporio de el Orbe* (1690). The most famous, and in many ways still useful, study was *Sólo Madrid es Corte*, an extravagant but meticulous work produced by the historiographer royal Alonso Núñez de Castro. First published in 1658, it was revised for the edition of 1675. Most of these were pious works, in which the felicities of local soil and climate vied with those of the garden of Eden.

Contemporaries looked back beyond present difficulties to a time when their towns once flourished. The late sixteenth century was commonly accepted as being the era of largest population. Epidemics, inflation, economic crisis and population displacement had since then aggravated the crisis in urban centres. By the late seventeenth century, however, the crisis was being succeeded by stability. A leading authority has referred to 'the collapse of the towns of Castile after 1640', and has argued that 'in the second half of the seventeenth century Spanish towns had not only fallen in size but were no longer capable of attracting immigrants'.[1] We have already seen that Medina del Campo was an exception to this. What we know of other towns in the late century tends to confirm the impression that, far from suffering collapse and decay, towns under Charles II benefited from demographic recovery and could look forward to a century of expansion.

Table 6.1, based on various sources, gives a rough idea of the population of some Spanish towns at three distinct epochs.[2]

Stability and modest growth were the characteristics of urban population in the late seventeenth century. Except in very large centres such as Madrid there was no clear distinction between town and countryside, and it would be wrong to distinguish urban from rural development. A high proportion of all town-dwellers in fact worked in agriculture, and the fields produced the food that helped towns survive.

Table 6.1

| Town | c. 1591 | c. 1646–50 | c. 1700 |
|---|---|---|---|
| Avila | 12,700 | 5,050 | 4,340 |
| Barcelona | 32,000 | 64,000 | 50,000 |
| Burgos | 20,000 (1560) | 3,000 | 8,500 |
| Cadiz | | 6,700 | 40,000 |
| Córdoba | 28,200 | 36,000 | 31,100 |
| Cuenca | 25,000 | 3,600 | 6,500 |
| Ecija | 23,000 | 22,500 | 11,100 |
| Jaén | 25,200 | 17,000 | 18,000 |
| León | 4,700 | 4,800 | 3,000 |
| Madrid | 60,000 | 127,000 | 150,000 |
| Málaga | 10,700 | | 30,000 |
| Medina del Campo | 12,400 | 2,930 | 4,240 |
| Murcia | | 19,800 | 25,770 |
| Saragossa | 25,000 | 30,000 | 30,000 |
| Seville | 122,000 | 65,000 | 72,400 |
| Segovia | 25,000 | | 7,300 |
| Toledo | 50,000 | 22,500 | 22,500 |
| Tudela | 9,000 | 7,350 | 8,000 |
| Valencia | 65,000 | 50,000 | 50,000 |
| Valladolid | 36,500 | 13,500 | 16,400 |

The epidemic reverses of the century meant that this was not an age when towns greatly increased their size. The obvious exception is Madrid, where the significant changes seem nevertheless to have taken the form of rebuilding rather than of an extension into the rural areas. Adopted as Spain's capital by Philip II in 1560, Madrid flourished in the seventeenth century, thanks in part to the money poured by the aristocracy into its development.[3] By 1669, according to Núñez de Castro, fifty dukes, nine princes, twenty marquises and fourteen counts had palaces in the capital. The destruction of the Plaza Mayor by fire in 1631 led to a major reconstruction which continued into the reign of Charles II. There was, unfortunately, another serious fire in 1672.[4] Don Fernando de Valenzuela during his period of influence in the 1670s embarked on an ambitious programme of public works with which he hoped to impress the populace. Wealthy merchants and gentry also contributed to the embellishment of the capital under Charles II. In a list of the richest residents in the year 1689, we find Simon Ruiz de Pessoa in the Calle San Luis, Domingo Grillo in the Calle de Alcalá, Francisco Báez Eminente in the Calle de San Bernardo, Francisco Centani in the Calle de Atocha; and so on.[5] Possession of a stately mansion in Madrid was a confirmation of worldly success. When Willughby visited the city in 1664 he was particularly impressed by the use of glass: 'Madrid is very populous, well built with good brick houses, many having glass windows, which is worth the noting because you shall scarce see any in all Spain besides.'[6]

Other provincial capitals did not normally benefit from rebuilding in the seventeenth century. The higher nobility directed their interests either to their country seats or to Madrid. The austere noble class of Catalonia had never been dedicated to palace building and Barcelona saw little of them. We know the Valencia of this time very well from the remarkable town plan by Father Tosca at the end of the century: noble houses were few and the dominant structures were religious houses. Lack of investment thus depressed urban growth. Population, however, continued to increase, creating problems both of accommodation and of social welfare. In this sense the figures given above for Barcelona and Saragossa, to choose only two cities, are deceptive. The identical figures given for Saragossa in 1650 and 1700 mask the grim mortality of 1652, when about one-fifth of the inhabitants perished,[7] so that the later figure represents a degree of recovery. In Barcelona the obstacles to growth were the epidemic of 1651, the siege of 1652, postwar difficulties and the further siege of 1697. Alone of the big cities, Madrid remained inexplicably free of all scourges, and blossomed tranquilly in both size and fortune.

No satisfactory censuses of Spanish towns were made before the eighteenth century. To obtain a profile of a Spanish city, I shall refer to surveys made shortly after the reign of Charles II. The census returns for Barcelona in 1717[8] give a basic population total of 33,010 persons. The figure is a gross underestimate: only 203 of the total, for example, are classified as clergy, and soldiers, vagabonds and the poor are not accounted for. Two aspects of the census can be made to yield acceptable information: there are details of the age structure in one district of the city, and of the professions followed in the whole city by adult heads of families. The data are presented in Figure 6.1.

Fig. 6.1   Age and profession in Barcelona, 1717.

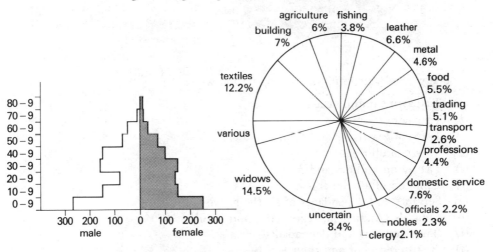

The limited information given in this figure is consistent with what we know of the society of this time. Over 45 per cent of the population sample was aged under twenty years, a common feature of preindustrial societies. Just over 5 per cent was aged over sixty.

Saragossa underwent no major upheavals in this period, and it is likely that the report on its population drawn up by the intendant in 1723[9] was an accurate reflection of the city's structure in the last years of Charles II. The census showed that the larger buildings in the city consisted of 17 parish churches; 42 convents and monasteries; 7 religious hospices; 4 hospitals; 2,645 houses (and 126 uninhabited) owned by clergy and occupied or leased by them; and 1,628 houses (and 92 uninhabited) owned by laymen. Since the total of houses in the city and its suburbs was put at 4,892, it followed that the enormous proportion of 54 per cent of all houses belonged to the Church. The total residential population of the city, estimated plausibly as 30,039 persons in 1723, can be divided into the categories shown in Figure 6.2.

Fig. 6.2   The population of Saragossa, 1723.

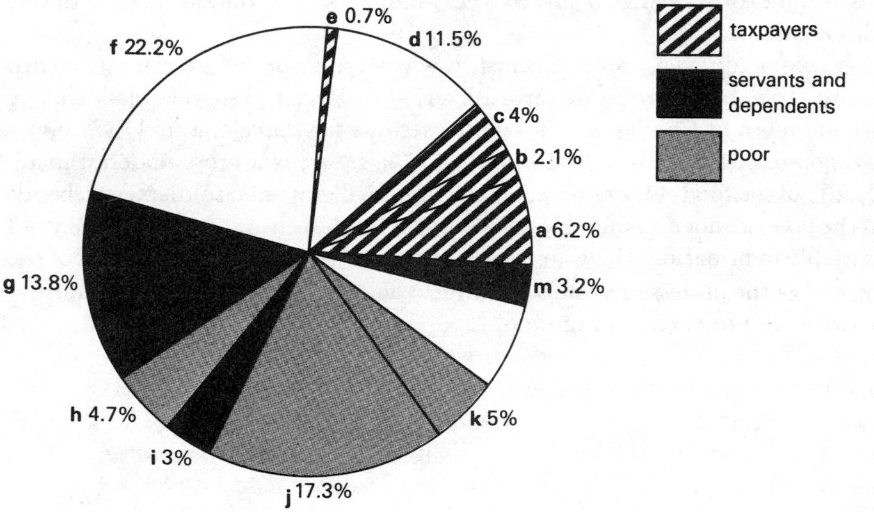

The general categories of the population were:

(a)  Taxpaying middle class
(b)  Taxpaying farmers
(c)  Taxpaying artisans and farm labourers
(d)  Wives of above
(e)  Taxpaying widows and minors
(f)  Children of all the above
(g)  Servants and dependants of all the above
(h)  Officials (Audiencia, taxes, etc.) and families
(i)  Their servants and dependants
(j)  Registered poor and their families
(k)  Poor in hospitals
(l)  Clergy male and female
(m)  Servants of clergy

The difference from Barcelona is obvious. Where less than 8 per cent of Barcelona workers appear to have been in domestic service, in Saragossa the proportion was

156

extremely high at about 20 per cent. This dissimilarity is consistent with the nature of the two cities: Barcelona a centre of industry even in times of crisis, Saragossa a quiet backwater with little productivity. The number of registered (that is, exempt from taxation) poor in Saragossa was high at 22.3 per cent. Adding vagabonds and the taxpaying poor, the proportion of people living in conditions of dire poverty must have been about one-third of the city. In other ways, too, the Aragonese capital showed every sign of being a city in decay. The number of nobles living within its precincts was so small as to be negligible, and though there were 8.5 taxpaying citizens for every citizen exempt from taxes, the latter category consisted almost wholly of public officials. Those described as children in the census come to 9,661 persons, or 32 per cent of the total. If we add infants, and children among the servants, to this figure, the proportion of young persons must have exceeded 40 per cent of the population. There were at least 14,000 females – roughly half the people in Saragossa.

In pre-industrial Europe only a small minority of the population had regular employment. The predominance of agriculture meant that short-term labour was the rule. Only a few skilled workers (artisans, leatherworkers, etc.) were required to serve the needs of the community. Unemployment was normal, and even those with professions were only partly employed. Analysis of urban professions should not therefore be taken to mean that there was a firm division of labour in the community. Many artisans were also cultivators of their own plot of land. We know very little about the type of work townspeople did. In the Crown of Aragon, for which evidence is limited,[10] we have the case of the Catalan city of Tarragona.[11] In the late seventeenth century, artisans here seem to have been the biggest group of those paying taxes (35 per cent), followed by farmers (about 28 per cent), fishermen (20 per cent), traders (under 8 per cent) and the liberal professions (6 per cent).

For Castile we must be content with random examples. In Talavera de la Reina in 1632,[12] of 1,512 households a total of 43.2 per cent (10 per cent were nobles and 4.4 in the Church) had no identifiable occupation; a further 15 per cent were labourers in casual employment, more usually in none. This left only 42 per cent of the people with a recognised calling. Of these the biggest categories were: 7.7 per cent in textiles, 4.9 in agriculture, 4.5 in leatherwork, 3.4 in food, 3.4 in liberal professions, 3.3 in retail trade and 4.2 in metals and ceramics. Talavera was not a flourishing town, but its division of occupations was healthier than that of the decaying towns of Avila and Arévalo.[13] In 1683, when Avila was credited with 1,179 households, some 8.1 per cent of its population were clergy, 16.4 registered beggars, and 55.2 with no identifiable profession. In Arévalo out of 376 households, 4 per cent were clergy, 12.5 registered poor, and 60.4 with no recognised occupation.

The general impression from these three Castilian towns is that those in active employment seldom exceeded one-fifth of the population. Casual labourers (jornaleros) and non-productive groups such as widows and the poor, generally made up between half and two-thirds of residents: in Avila they were 80 per cent of the population, in Arévalo 77 per cent. Towns, it would seem, consisted principally of a vast pool of unemployed. By contrast, the countryside population was more productive. Figures for the administrative regions of Avila and Arévalo in 1683, taking both town and country together, show that no less than one-third of the vecinos were engaged either in agriculture or in industry, with one person in industry for every five in agriculture.[14]

Avila and Arévalo are admittedly extreme examples, but there were many others like them. Ciudad Rodrigo in 1682 included in its population of 1,159 households an active sector of 173 in trades and 137 in agriculture, or some 26 per cent altogether.[15] This meant a non-productive sector of nearly three-fourths of the population. The city of Calahorra, with 1,088 households in 1683, consisted in the main of three groups: an active agrarian sector (16 per cent); the poor, widows and clergy (30 per cent); and casual labourers (41 per cent).[16]

Most Spanish towns were on this evidence made up of a wealth-creating sector that seldom exceeded one-fifth of the population. The labouring poor might constitute a further two-fifths; and the rest of the citizens lived off the resources created by these others. Apart from the large numbers recognised as poor, and officially so declared (*pobres de solemnidad*), the two biggest classes of dependants were widows (in Calahorra in 1683 they constituted 13 per cent) and clergy. Perhaps the most conspicuous example of a Castilian city suffering from a non-productive population was Valladolid, the former and now half-ruined capital of Spain, in which (it was said in 1683) 'what collapses is not rebuilt, nor because of the excess of old buildings are there any new ones'. 'It seems', said the same source, a government minister, 'that this city is made up principally of consumers only.'[17]

Because most Castilian and Aragonese towns were situated in a vulnerable agrarian environment, they failed to develop a big industrial population. The towns of the periphery, on the other hand, made up for a possible absence of industry by active dedication to the sea. Tarragona has already been cited. Another Catalan example is Mataró, with a population at the end of the century of over 1,000 families. Within the active labour force of this town rural labourers accounted for 25.4 per cent, artisans for 48 per cent, and seamen for as much as 26.6 per cent.[18] The fishing industry continued to give economic life to the towns of the seaboard in a way that other local enterprises could not always do.

Spanish towns did not have a specifically urban class. They tended to contain a complete cross-section of society. Noblemen, who might have been expected to live on their rural estates, shunned the countryside and preferred the towns. To this extent they were unlike the nobility of France and England. 'The upper crust of the privileged classes of nobility and clergy was largely urban. So too were the most economically enterprising sectors of the Third Estate.'[19] The Spanish town contained within itself the extremes of both rich and poor, and so presented a clear microcosm of Spanish society.

## GOVERNMENT OF THE TOWNS

It is common to hear of the political decline of Spanish towns under the

Habsburgs. This was true largely of the Crown of Castile, in the sense that the towns in the Cortes had no real constitutional power and no effective voice in the government of the country. But it was certainly not true of the Crown of Aragon, where towns continued to play a major part in constitutional assemblies. In Castile towns compensated for a lack of influence at the centre by remaining strongly independent and autonomous in the provinces. The concept of Habsburg 'absolutism', sometimes suggested by historians, must have appeared incomprehensible to urban oligarchies. 'Absolutism' suggests a strong central government pitted against weak municipalities. The reverse was probably true. Habsburg government was secure only because stability was created by autonomous political control in the townships. When social tension arose it fragmented itself in a decentralised urban environment, rather than building up into unified pressure against the central government in Madrid.

We do not know whether Castilian towns sought a bigger role for the Cortes. They do not seem to have demanded it. A few towns took steps to purchase seats in the Cortes, but their aim was status rather than power.[20] The Crown in any case continued, as we have seen, to consult the towns regularly on the matters that most affected them, particularly taxation. No major decisions on internal policy were taken or could be taken without reference to the provincial towns. The absence of a Cortes did not as a consequence strengthen central government: on the contrary, it weakened it by forcing ministers in Madrid to maintain a constant contact with provincial opinion. When considering the internal ordering of Spain in the Habsburg era we are faced not by the steady erosion of absolutist central power but by the virtual absence of such power. In the seventeenth century the lineaments of power were to be found in the municipalities, not in Madrid.

Political loyalties were fiercely regional, enhanced in some areas by local kinship patterns. In the towns the three great strengths of political regionalism were aristocratic influence, hereditary tenure of office, and local autonomy in finance.

The most outstanding example of urban aristocracy was probably the great Mendoza family at Guadalajara. A quick comparison of towns over which the Crown and the nobles had jurisdiction, suggests that the king was not wholly master in his own kingdom. Figures for the eighteenth century show that in Old Castile, and particularly in Burgos province, the duke of Frias for example owned 258 towns and villages.[21] Such towns were not always tiny units. In the province of Avila in 1797 the average population of a seigneurial town was over 700 households. If even half this level is allowed for 1697 the figures are still impressive. In the four Old Castilian provinces of Burgos, Soria, Segovia and Avila, some 43 per cent of the towns were owned by the nobles;[22] in the province of Salamanca 60 per cent of the larger towns were in the same category.[23] A report of 1710 made a rough estimate that in the whole of Castile the nobles controlled 500 of the 700 largest towns and cities.[24] By the end of the eighteenth century an official census reported that aristocratic jurisdiction throughout Spain extended to 15 cities, 2,286 towns and 6,000 villages.[25] It is certain that the Crown controlled less than half the centres of population in the peninsula. In the kingdom of Valencia, according to Melchor de Macanaz, 'the king has only 73 large and small towns, and over 300 are seigneurial'; in Aragon the Crown had jurisdiction over only one-fifth of towns.[26]

Erosion of royal rights in the towns continued to occur with the active collaboration of the Crown itself, through outright sale. The procedure was referred to as a 'sale of vassals'. In effect the government was alienating for cash the tax liability of its subjects. Sales had been common in the early century, but had taken place on such a scale that a limit was finally adopted.[27] Since the sixteenth century sale of villages belonging to the Church had been common: in the seventeenth the Crown followed suit, with sales reaching their peak under Philip IV. The purchasers were invariably members of the rising nobility. The first known permission for sales granted by the realm in Cortes was in 1625 when the Crown was authorised to sell towns to a total of 20,000 vassals. Sales included rights both to taxation and to justice, including sometimes the right to appoint officials. Individual sales by the Crown in fact preceded this date, though we do not know on what scale they occurred.[28]

The price for each sale was arrived at as a multiple of the taxable citizens in a town. In 1605 a normative price was adopted of 14,000 silver maravedis for each vecino: the level was much the same under Charles II. Permissions for sale granted by the Cortes in 1626, 1630 and 1639 added up to a total of 40,000 vassals, but according to a check made by the ministry of Finance in 1670 the total number alienated up to that date was 53,089 vassals or vecinos.[29] This figure, at 4.5 persons a household, added up to 239,000 people transferred out of royal jurisdiction. The total of towns alienated was in the region of 300.[30]

Sales were not necessarily harmful to the interests of the town. About 38 per cent of the vassals represented towns that purchased their own jurisdiction from the Crown. One such was Castillo de las Guardas (Seville) which in 1667 paid 4,775,000 maravedis to obtain its independence from royal control. Although only 17 per cent of vassals were sold to nobles, they were the cases that probably caused most argument. There is no record of how many towns were alienated after 1670, but they were probably few.

In 1668 the village of Aguaio (Burgos), with all its jurisdiction and lordship (señorío), was sold to its parish priest at a price of 15,000 silver maravedis for each of its ninety-two vecinos. This meant that the whole village now passed out of the ownership of the king into that of Don Martín de la Llana, the priest; and the Chancery at Valladolid was appointed to intervene in any disputes between Aguaio and its new lord. A similar sale was that of the village of Olmos (Valladolid), with all its jurisdiction and señorío, to a knight of Calatrava, Don Andres de Sarria, living in Madrid. The year was 1666, the price 21,875 silver maravedis per vecino. On this occasion the city of Valladolid began a lawsuit contesting the sale and in 1669 successfully obtained the return of the village to its own jurisdiction. The city of Avila was less fortunate when in 1668 it protested against the sale of the nearby village of Los Patos to Don Luis de Peralta, a prominent member of the council of Finance. The corregidor and other officials of Avila were arrested and a fine imposed on the city. 'Sale of vassals' aroused strong opposition from cities which considered that it freed the towns from contributing to the common tax burden. Many alienated towns, on the other hand, stood to be more heavily taxed under a seigneur, and opposed sales for this reason.[31]

Despite sales of small towns, the Crown could take comfort in the fact that virtually all big cities remained in royal jurisdiction (*realengo*). In theory the king might there appoint most officials, collect all taxes and dispense all justice. But the system of tenure of offices intervened to block this control. In the major cities of the Crown of Aragon elections were by lot, in which the king could not intervene except to disqualify candidates. The municipal independence of Barcelona, Saragossa and Valencia was therefore complete. When the Crown wished to interfere it had to do so either through the viceroy or, more normally, through the Audiencia, which dispensed justice. In Castilian cities there was the same weakness of royal authority, but for different reasons. The regidores and alcaldes who held civic office did so either thanks to the patronage of a powerful person or through hereditary tenure of office. Noble authority and venality of office combined to frustrate the effective exercise of royal authority. The biggest Castilian cities were in this way controlled by an élite whose primary interest was the maintenance of order in the provinces. The quietness that descends on the cities of Spain in the centuries after the Comunidades of 1520–21, is due in great measure to the strength of municipal oligarchies rather than to the efficacy of absolutism.

In some towns nobles were by tradition excluded from office, in others they could hold no more than half the offices. Aristocratic influence increased all the same. In 1638 Philip IV decreed that regidores of Madrid must be drawn only from the blood nobility, on the same terms as practised in Seville, Córdoba and Toledo.[32] According to Domínguez Ortiz, these city councils as well as those of Plasencia, Trujillo, Ciudad Real, Avila, Soria, Ubeda, Santa Cruz de Tenerife and many others, were wholly aristocratic in composition. The urban oligarchies were sometimes narrow to a degree that seems incredible. In Cáceres the twenty-four regidores were nominated half by the Carvajal family, half by the Ovando family; in actual practice the two families acted as focal points for alliances among the oligarchy as a whole.

Elections to town councils were so fiercely contested that the Crown in the seventeenth century tended to prefer a system of *mitad de oficios*, whereby nobles and commoners shared power equally. This was the most common system in Castile. But many towns kept the nobles out and protected their autonomy. In Castile the old commercial centres of Medina de Rioseco and Medina del Campo successfully excluded the aristocracy in the interests of the urban gentry.[33] In the kingdom of Aragon in 1718 over 30 per cent of towns remained under independent, non-seigneurial, control.[34]

The problem of jurisdiction went further than issues of power and finance: it involved economic stability in the town. Nobles seldom served personally in the civic posts they controlled; they were moreover exempt from taxes and seldom contributed to wealth in the town. In Oviedo, the capital of Asturias, a city in 1683 of 1,500 households, the city council consisted of sixty regidores, all local gentry. They lived in their country villas and never took part personally in municipal government.[35] In the city of Guadix (Andalucia) in 1693, with a population of 1,500 households, 'the persons preeminent in quality are the marquis of Diezma and the marquis of Corres; but there is none preeminent in wealth, the reason being that all the possessions and lands of the city are in entail, and all the owners – and there are many of them – who can manage to live elsewhere off the rents from their entails, do not live in the city'.[36] In both cities noble control was parasitic.

The third important aspect of provincial power was autonomy in finance. Central government would have been more vigorous in Spain but for a weak fiscal system. The towns also had problems. Although their difficulties were usually serious, and the situation of smaller towns was normally worse than that of large cities, in general the municipalities of Spain possessed an economic equilibrium that the state could never hope to achieve.

In the reign of Charles II the cities continued to enjoy two main sources of revenue, one municipal (the excise taxes on consumption) and one private (rents and annuities), which together helped to give them some degree of financial independence. They also had two major liabilities: government taxation, and municipal debt in the form of censos. Two examples from the kingdom of Valencia will allow us to look more closely at both income and expenditure.

The city of Elche was owned by the dukes of Arcos and in 1690 had a population of 1,500 households. Between 1675 and 1680 its average annual municipal income was 4,340 lliures, and its average outgoings 3,231 lliures, leaving a small margin for extraordinary expenditure.[37] At this period the chief produce of the region was olive oil, which explains the high income from mills. The main sources of Elche's revenue in 1682 were:

|  |  |
|---|---|
| Excise (sisa) | 20.8% |
| Contracted supplies | 18.4 |
| Meat sales | 17.7 |
| Mills | 15 |
| Bread sales | 12.3 |
| Wine | 5.7 |
| Other | 10.1 |

Obligations in 1682 were in three main categories:

| | | | | |
|---|---|---|---|---|
| Censals and debts in Valencia | (a) Church 13.8% | (b) lay | 14.4 |
| Censals and debts in Elche | (a) Church 13.4 | (b) lay | 29 |
| Wages to various officials | | 29.4% | |

The balance in favour of Elche was about 1,109 lliures a year, but from this the town had to meet royal taxes, running expenses, and the costs of a lawsuit it was then conducting to be removed from the jurisdiction of the duke of Arcos and Maqueda. A favourable balance was not common in municipal budgets.

In the prosperous city of Alicante the financial situation was even more cheerful.[38] In 1664 its municipal income totalled 32,744 lliures and its basic obligations 20,100 lliures. The income consisted of:

| | |
|---|---|
| Taxes on fishing and trade | 63.7% |
| Excise on oil and meat | 3.8 |
| Taxes on salted goods and tobacco | 13.5 |
| Contracted supplies | 8 |
| Wharfage | 1.2 |
| Taxes on bread and meat | 4.8 |
| Other | 5 |

The two main obligations were censals totalling over 10,799 lliures and an administrative bill of 9,301 lliures. The chief holders of censals against Alicante were:

| | |
|---|---|
| Ecclesiastical | 2.5% |
| Escorsia family | 28.9 |
| Bojoni family | 12 |
| Roca family | 10.5 |
| Moxica family | 5.8 |

Unlike Elche, and indeed unlike the vast majority of Spanish towns, the censals of Alicante were in the hands not of the clergy but of the city's own commercial bourgeoisie. This gave its finances a stability that may well have contributed to its commercial success. The items that made up administrative costs are expressed below as a percentage of the sum of 9,301 lliures:

| | |
|---|---|
| Public feast days | 11.4% |
| Street cleaning | 1.7 |
| Church charities | 10.6 |
| Jurats | 4.3 |
| Medical and hospital | 5.3 |
| Officials (less doctors and jurats) | 22.0 |
| Orphanage and wet-nurses | 21.5 |
| Cathedral | 10.7 |
| Musicians | 6.7 |
| Other | 5.8 |

As with Elche, these obligations did not include irregular expenditure on such items as lawsuits, water and road works, harbour repairs and so on. Since over a third of Alicante's annual income remained uncommitted, it is unlikely that the city faced severe problems at this period.

Why then did so many towns in Spain have money problems? The simplest answer is a combination of bad management and lack of resources. The second was by far the most serious, for the tax-exemption of clergy and nobility, together with other factors, made it difficult to raise cash in order to pay off emergency loans. Accumulated debt in the form of censos (which will be considered in the next chapter) could choke a town's finances. The city of Tarragona in 1682, for example, had an income of 6,824 lliures but annual obligations of nearly 9,000 lliures. In 1671 it had been forced to take on a *concordia* (agreement to pay) with its creditors, but by 1682 its accumulated debt, of which 85 per cent was for censals, still stood at 140,171 lliures.[39] In Barcelona the Diputació was in an even worse state. In 1670 it was forced into a concordia with its numerous creditors.

Its accumulated debt, calculated from the year 1652, exceeded 900,000 lliures.[40] The city of Saragossa, despite an apparently healthy budget, in fact had numerous unpaid censos which forced it into a concordia with its censalistas in 1686.[41] Our last example is a small town: Jijona, in Valencia. In 1695 its annual income (from land-rents, mills and taxes on trade and food) totalled 2,371 lliures, but its annual commitments came to 3,418 lliures, of which 49 per cent was for censals.[42] For many towns, large and small, censals continued to be 'the plague and ruin of Spain', as Cellorigo had phrased it in 1600.

From the other main type of investment, juros, towns could sometimes actually profit. Bennassar has indicated the case of Valladolid, where in 1597 the 232 holders of juros drew as much income from the *alcabala* tax as the whole city paid in duties for the same tax.[43] The *juristas* emerge as a parasitic class, but one which in this case was clawing back money paid out to the government in Madrid. The case of Ciudad Rodrigo is even more striking. In 1667 the taxes paid by the city for its alcabalas came to 3,000,000 maravedis and 675 fanegas of wheat. The sum received by residents of Ciudad Rodrigo with annuities on the alcabala amounted to 7,800,000 maravedis and 786 fanegas, or roughly twice the value of taxes paid by the whole city.[44] About one-fourth of those holding juros were ecclesiastics.

Municipal finance suffered greatly from the conversion of property into mortmain or into entail: both had the effect of reducing a town's taxable income. The problem was referred to in a petition of 1681 from Ciudad Real, one of Castile's few shrinking cities at this period.[45] Between 1610 and 1680, the city claimed, about 800,000 ducats worth of property had been lost to the city by donations. Three new convents had been founded, at a total cost of 300,000; then in 1673 one gentleman had left his entire fortune of 126,000 ducats to a local church. The passing of such large sums into Church hands took them forever out of reach of the civil authorities.

We have so far touched on some financial problems in towns. But it must be remembered that though municipal finance was often shaky, the bulk of the wealth in towns was solid and secure. Unpaid censals are no real guide to the economic condition of a town. In the unequal struggle between town and country – a struggle largely for control of the land and its resources – it was the towns that had the unmistakable advantage. The seventeenth century in Spain was an era when the urban economy devoured the rural. Both land and possessions passed out of the hands of the rural classes into those of urban proprietors.

A leading citizen of Valencia, writing about his home city in the 1680s, described it thus: 'Within its walls are 8,000 houses, and 3,400 in the suburbs, and for two miles around there are over 800 country houses, which make up the property of the gentry and citizens of Valencia, who are occupied in cultivating silk.'[46] But the investment of the richer people of Valencia, as indeed of all leading Spanish towns, extended to more than the immediate environs. Over the years they bought up lands, villages, censals, drawing wealth increasingly from the countryside and contributing ever more to the concentration of wealth in urban centres. In Ciudad Real, for example, city people controlled all the surrounding land.[47] When the village of Valparaiso de Arriba, with forty households in the year 1681, looked for capital to finance the next year's harvest, it went searching among moneyed men in the nearby cities of Cuenca and Huete, and likewise sought relief there from its debts to its principal landowners, residents of those selfsame two cities.[48]

## FOOD AND SANITATION

The provisioning of towns was a problem made worse as population grew in the late century. Because poor harvests were a constant threat, towns had a traditional practice of keeping stores of grain (*pósitos*) for use in emergencies. Scarcity brought a rise in prices, but it was usual to sell the reserves at normal rates. Pósitos were also used as banks from which grain could be loaned for sowing. They thereby performed a vital dual function, helping both consumer and producer.

Natural conditions (climate, soil) and distance were the most formidable of obstacles to good supplies of food. Compare Guadix with neighbouring Almería.[49] Guadix had local supplies of wheat, barley, wine, hemp, flax and silk, much of which was sold profitably to other regions; only olive oil had to be imported. Almería by contrast had to import to supplement all its food needs, so that the price of wheat there was 100 per cent more than in Guadix, barley and wine 40 per cent more. This startling difference between towns so close to each other, emphasises the significance of inadequate supplies and transport costs. Poor transport contributed a great deal to economic difficulties in Spain.[50] Until well into the eighteenth century the lack of communications split the country up into an endless number of small marketing areas having little contact with each other.

Diet in the towns was broader and more balanced than rural diets. Travelling with a friend from Gibraltar to Chiclana in 1677, Lantéry was offered food which his companion refused to touch. It was *gazpacho*, 'a thing', Lantéry explains, 'for shepherds and peasants who have nothing else to eat, being made of garlics, vinegar, bread and water'.[51] Meat was generally absent from rural meals. Bertaut in mid-century observed that in the rural areas of Castile 'you will find hardly any butcher's meat, though along the roads they make use of partridge and hares'.[52] Osorio in 1686 claimed that 'most rural labourers in Spain live off barley bread, as may be seen today in Andalucia and other parts'.[53] A century later, in 1775, Swinburne recorded that 'the peasantry seem very poor, and frugal in their diet: bread steeped in oil, and occasionally seasoned with vinegar, is the common food of the country people from Barcelona to Málaga; a bunch of grapes or a slice of melon serves as a dessert'.[54] In the Cantabrian provinces, and particularly in Galicia, maize rather than barley was the basic grain of the poor peasantry.[55]

In towns, on the other hand, meat was a central component of diet. A writer of the early seventeenth century, Alvarez de Toledo, estimated the daily expenditure of a typical poor consumer to be 30 maravedis, of which the meat took up five.[56] His estimate, converted into percentages, is presented as an annual outlay in Table 6.2, where it is compared with the estimate made by an Aragonese official, Pedro Borruel, of annual living expenses in 1677.[57]

Table 6.2

| Alvarez de Toledo | (%) | Pedro Borruel | (%) |
|---|---|---|---|
| Meat | 16.7 | Food (1s 4d daily) | 48 |
| Wine | 13.3 | Trousers, doublet etc. | 18 |
| Olive oil | 3.3 | Two pairs shoes | 2 |
| Fruit | 3.3 | Two pairs stockings | 1.2 |
| Vinegar | 1.7 | Two shirts | 3.2 |
| Vegetables | 1.7 | Linen, silk etc. | 5 |
| Bread (1½ lbs a day) | 13.3 | Two collars | 1.2 |
| Clothing, shoes | 35 | One hat | 1.4 |
| Heat and light | 6.7 | House expenses | 10 |
| Soap | 3.3 | Medical | 5 |
| | | Other | 5 |

Alvarez de Toledo's list includes details of clothing, such as an annual three pairs of footwear and three shirts. Borruel's list unfortunately gives no breakdown for food. Writing in 1686, Osorio y Redín confirmed that the average individual consumption of bread was 'a pound and a half daily'.[58] Discussing the daily consumption of the average citizen of Madrid, Osorio estimated it to be, in addition, 'one pound of meat, one litre of wine; necessities such as bacon, oil and coal; vegetables, spices and soap for the clothes'.[59]

An estimate of 1657 assessing the consumption of the clergy in Toledo makes it possible to arrive at an alternative picture.[60] It is difficult to give a precise value to the measure used, but the average consumption of a priest in some items appears to have been as follows:

|  |  |
|---|---|
| wine | 1.8 litres a week |
| vinegar | 0.28 litres a week |
| oil | 0.65 litres a week |
| meat | 8 oz a day |
| soap | 4 oz a day |

The meat figure differs from the others in that it applies to only two-thirds of the days in the year, excluding Lent and days of abstinence. Taken together with a pound and a half of bread, this was probably the basic structure of an ecclesiastical diet in mid-century. Real consumption would of course vary considerably. The figures for Gandía in 1721 show that consumption of olive oil in a labouring household varied from one to two litres a week, and of wine from three to six litres.

Bread supply was a major concern of municipal authorities. In Madrid it was a constant worry.[61] Food contractors became the key to social stability, and popular discontent was sometimes directed against them as profiteers. In Madrid the contractors were known as *obligados*, while contractors who sold meat in the Rastro market were called *rastreros*. All these suppliers operated under a system of fixed prices agreed with the town. People of independent means, such as clergy and gentry with their own sources of supply, were granted *despensas* which freed them of the need to buy only through contractors.

Sanitation was one of the few public concerns of a municipality. Seventeenth-century travellers have left few indications of the state of Spanish towns, but were unanimous that Madrid was probably the dirtiest capital in Europe. An Italian nobleman in 1668 described Alcalá's streets as 'intolerable for their filth', while Willughby in 1664 categorised those of Madrid as 'very foul and nasty'.[62] The notorious lack of hygiene in the capital was oddly enough tolerated by public opinion. It was felt that though the excrement offended the eye and nose it was soon absorbed into the air and helped to protect the city from major epidemics.

Madrid in fact suffered badly in the epidemic of 1599.[63] Though little is known of its demographic history in the seventeenth century, there was certainly high mortality. The council of State in 1671 declared that 'in Madrid in these last years there have been some harsh epidemics, and the council is convinced that one of the causes might be the lack of cleanliness in the streets'.[64] Five months later the council complained that nothing had yet been done to remedy the situation. A century later the government was still concerned about the problems, but its proposals to improve hygiene were opposed by medical men who clung to the attitude we have noted. The best contemporary refutation of this opinion came from the distinguished doctor Juan Bautista Juanini, whose *Discurso físico y político* appeared in 1679.[65] He argued that the filth in the streets was a direct cause of the noxious fumes in the city, of the many fevers and diseases that afflicted its inhabitants, and of the short life-span of madrileños.

## PUBLIC ORDER AND CRIME

By modern standards Spanish towns in the seventeenth century were under-policed. One law officer (*alguacil*) was normal for a town. Large cities still had few officials, but there were various jurisdictions — royal, municipal, Inquisition — that could cooperate to keep order. Madrid was unique in having a large and well-organised police system.[66] Judicial control of the city was exercised by the Sala de Alcaldes, a committee of the council of Castile. The Sala, numbering about sixteen people, was divided into criminal and civil sections. The Sala for crime had final jurisdiction over all crime in and within five leagues of the capital; it could impose any punishment save death, on which the king had to be personally consulted.

Crime levels in Spain were indubitably low. Moral imperatives, religion, and community solidarity all acted as restraints. Thanks to its size and cosmopolitan character, Madrid was the great exception. The reports of contemporary diarists, particularly Pellicer and Barrionuevo under Philip IV, depict a capital in which murder was common and crime frequent among all social classes.[67] These writers may no doubt be trustworthy, but their evidence has never been checked against the records: though violence was common, it is likely that they overstate its incidence.

The records of the Sala de Alcaldes are the basis for the statistics of crime in Madrid shown in Table 6.3. The table must be read with the following reservations: it is incomplete, not only because of undoubted omissions (e.g. in 1665 and 1666) but particularly because it lists *detected* rather than undetected offences; it gives the number of offences but not the number of people involved (e.g. the eighteen people arrested in 1699 for the Oropesa riots appear as a single offence); and it divides offences into distinct categories that are arbitrary and

Table 6.3

| | a | b | c | d | e | f | g | h | | |
|---|---|---|---|---|---|---|---|---|---|---|
| Year | Assault | Rape | Brawls | Theft | Murder | Sex | Fraud | Marital | Other | Total |
| 1665 | 6 | 2 | 3 | 6 | 6 | 5 | 2 | | 10 | 40 |
| 6 | 14 | 3 | | 9 | 8 | 7 | 3 | 2 | 9 | 55 |
| 7 | 16 | 10 | 12 | 18 | 25 | 9 | 3 | 5 | 12 | 110 |
| 8 | 21 | 5 | 11 | 17 | 17 | 7 | 6 | 6 | 13 | 103 |
| 9 | 26 | 5 | 7 | 11 | 18 | 5 | 3 | 2 | 10 | 87 |
| 1670 | 13 | 2 | 15 | 13 | 20 | 4 | 2 | 3 | 5 | 77 |
| 1 | 19 | 3 | 13 | 14 | 25 | 9 | 5 | 2 | 9 | 99 |
| 2 | 26 | 6 | 19 | 21 | 37 | 4 | 6 | 8 | 17 | 160 |
| 3 | 41 | 8 | 34 | 20 | 36 | 11 | 6 | 12 | 21 | 189 |
| 4 | 21 | 6 | 14 | 11 | 19 | 3 | 4 | 4 | 14 | 96 |
| 5 | 14 | 3 | 15 | 8 | 11 | 4 | 4 | 2 | 7 | 75 |
| 6 | 11 | 1 | 4 | 6 | 9 | 3 | 1 | 1 | 7 | 43 |
| 7 | 19 | 3 | 14 | 11 | 14 | 9 | 5 | 2 | 13 | 90 |
| 8 | 29 | 8 | 20 | 20 | 17 | 15 | 4 | 9 | 21 | 143 |
| 9 | 26 | 2 | 10 | 20 | 21 | 12 | 1 | 1 | 11 | 104 |
| 1680 | 14 | 4 | 12 | 19 | 25 | 3 | 5 | | 3 | 85 |
| 1 | 14 | 3 | 9 | 15 | 7 | | 2 | 1 | 14 | 65 |
| 2 | 21 | 2 | 8 | 6 | 23 | 6 | 1 | 3 | 7 | 77 |
| 3 | 31 | 5 | 7 | 11 | 15 | 9 | 1 | 1 | 5 | 85 |
| 4 | 20 | 2 | 15 | 9 | 20 | 1 | 2 | 2 | 6 | 77 |
| 5 | 15 | 2 | 7 | 14 | 18 | 4 | 2 | 7 | 4 | 73 |
| 6 | 23 | 6 | 14 | 12 | 15 | 11 | 3 | 3 | 8 | 95 |
| 7 | 25 | 4 | 14 | 20 | 27 | 4 | 2 | 5 | 4 | 105 |
| 8 | 24 | 8 | 18 | 18 | 26 | 5 | 6 | 4 | 11 | 120 |
| 9 | 39 | 6 | 16 | 19 | 20 | 5 | 5 | 6 | 10 | 142 |
| 1690 | 38 | 9 | 18 | 21 | 20 | 13 | 5 | 6 | 7 | 144 |
| 1 | 21 | 8 | 12 | 32 | 20 | 14 | 3 | 7 | 18 | 135 |
| 2 | 29 | 18 | 13 | 47 | 29 | 15 | 7 | 5 | 20 | 183 |
| 3 | 73 | 14 | 29 | 36 | 37 | 29 | 6 | 4 | 19 | 247 |
| 4 | 30 | 9 | 20 | 20 | 26 | 16 | 6 | 12 | 15 | 154 |
| 5 | 39 | 6 | 19 | 27 | 29 | 15 | 6 | 9 | 10 | 160 |
| 6 | 40 | 18 | 26 | 37 | 24 | 34 | 7 | 11 | 12 | 209 |
| 7 | 25 | 8 | 14 | 24 | 25 | 15 | 8 | 7 | 5 | 131 |
| 8 | 27 | 6 | 26 | 40 | 19 | 18 | 2 | 12 | 15 | 165 |
| 9 | 26 | 13 | 27 | 42 | 15 | 34 | 5 | 8 | 21 | 191 |
| 1700 | 75 | 23 | 8 | 59 | 33 | 39 | 25 | 11 | 47 | 320 |

often misleading (e.g. the two marital offences in 1677 both involved murder). With these important cautions in mind, the table can be read as a fairly reliable survey of crime in a preindustrial capital of about 150,000 people.[68] The information from Table 6.3 is represented in Figure 6.3 under the three major headings of violence, theft and sexual crime.[69]

Fig. 6.3   The incidence and prosecution of crime in Madrid, 1665–1700.

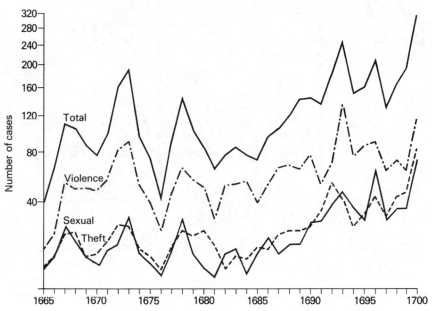

The incidence and prosecution of crime in Madrid, 1665 – 1700 (logarithmic scale)

This revealing though incomplete statement of offences punished by the alcaldes of Madrid can be compared with the types of common crime punished by the judicial officers of the city of Valencia within the same period. Table 6.4, again no doubt incomplete, is based on the fiscal accounts of the criminal justice officers of Valencia for the years 1665 to 1693.[70]

The very different pattern of prosecuted crime reflects the contrast between a large urban society and a smaller traditional community. Violence, with or without weapons, was by far the gravest threat to public order. The 102 recorded assaults and brawls in Madrid in 1693 represented a peak of violence that in that year involved the arrest of over 300 persons. In the opinion of the authorities, public disorder tended to originate in three main places: bars, gaming houses and brothels. At the same time there were two classes of people for whom the alcaldes were on the lookout: soldiers off duty, and strangers to the city. All these were taken into account during the lightning sweep that the alcaldes made of Madrid in March 1665, when they arrested scores of people, principally on immorality charges, and drew up detailed lists of all lodging-houses and resident outsiders

Table 6.4

| Year | Arms | Murder | Sex | Theft | Violence | Other | Totals |
|---|---|---|---|---|---|---|---|
| 1665 | 3 | 4 | 2 | | 2 | | 11 |
| 6 | 7 | 1 | 21 | | 2 | 6 | 37 |
| 7 | 8 | | 17 | | 2 | 1 | 28 |
| 8 | 2 | 1 | 49 | | | 2 | 54 |
| 9 | 5 | 1 | 39 | | 1 | 3 | 49 |
| 1670 | 8 | 3 | 11 | | | | 22 |
| 1 | 17 | 11 | 3 | | 4 | 1 | 36 |
| 1675 | 10 | 10 | 6 | | 3 | 2 | 31 |
| 6 | 5 | 9 | 21 | 1 | 7 | | 43 |
| 7 | 2 | 8 | 9 | 1 | 8 | | 28 |
| 8 | 8 | 5 | 28 | | 6 | | 47 |
| 9 | 7 | 12 | 10 | 2 | 17 | 1 | 49 |
| 1680 | 11 | 2 | 27 | 1 | 8 | 1 | 50 |
| 1 | 5 | 2 | 1 | 1 | 3 | | 12 |
| 2 | 6 | 1 | 4 | | 1 | 2 | 12 |
| 3 | 8 | 5 | 22 | 4 | 3 | 1 | 43 |
| 4 | 9 | 10 | 23 | | 8 | 2 | 52 |
| 5 | 1 | 18 | 8 | | 5 | | 32 |
| 6 | 11 | 3 | 9 | | 2 | | 25 |
| 7 | 2 | 3 | 7 | | 2 | 1 | 15 |
| 8 | | 2 | 11 | | 1 | | 14 |
| 9 | 5 | 2 | 9 | | | | 16 |
| 1690 | 3 | 3 | 3 | | | 1 | 9 |
| 1 | 13 | 5 | 5 | 2 | 2 | 2 | 29 |
| 2 | 10 | 13 | 5 | | 1 | 1 | 30 |
| 3 | 3 | 5 | 3 | | 1 | 1 | 13 |

and vagabonds.[71] In October 1665 the Sala de Alcaldes commenced a campaign against

the gaming houses in this city, all frequented by soldiers of the guards, over whom the Sala has no control. . . . Although these houses are always a source of grave concern the situation is worse as winter approaches, since the long nights and harsh weather cause to gather in them all the vagabonds and working people who play away by night what they earn by day and so fail to maintain their families.[72]

With their report the Sala enclosed a list of fifty gaming houses in Madrid. The violence in Valencia was on an altogether smaller scale, involving neither gaming houses nor soldiery.

The culpability of soldiers, particularly during the long years of war with Portugal, cannot be denied. In 1665, after the murder of the corregidor of Jaén, the councillors of Castile informed the Queen Regent that 'the present state of things is occasioned by the great number of soldiers billeted in these realms, which cannot fail to provoke disorder and crimes'.[73] In 1669 the council complained that 'no day or night goes by in this capital without crimes, murders, robberies and complaints caused by the soldiers'.[74] In 1671, commenting on the behaviour of cavalry in Segovia, the council said that 'the excesses of the soldiers are such that no woman is secure in her honour, and there is no robbery which they will not attempt'.[75] In Almería in 1672 we find a complaint to the council by 'the bishop and mayor, of the continuous and repeated outrages, attacks and robberies committed in that city, with no possibility of punishment, since the culprits are soldiers and claim that their crimes are subject to military and not to civil justice'.[76]

Law authorities were frequently ineffective against serious violence. In 1665 the council of Castile confessed itself unable to deal with the mayor of the town of Castellar (La Mancha), 'who committed many crimes, but no one dared to arrest him'. In such cases the nearest corregidor was usually entrusted with the task, but when the corregidor of Alcaraz was sent to seize him the mayor promptly turned highwayman, robbed him *en route* of his money and papers, and continued to exercise his functions undisturbed. The town of Ontecilla presented similar problems of law enforcement:[77]

Atrocious crimes were committed by several citizens of the town, and Don Gerónimo de Alzate was sent to enquire and punish. He issued condemnations against many without actually punishing anyone there. Later a judge was sent to carry out the sentences and collect the fines, but when he arrived he found awaiting him fifty or sixty men with arquebuses, who told him to his face to go back or they would kill him.

A substantial proportion of crimes and violence was perpetrated by the upper classes. Of the cases prosecuted in Madrid in 1693, nobles were implicated in incidents of assault, rape, brawls, theft, wife-beating and murder. One brawl that year involved eleven gentlemen; another group of five was connected with a gang of thieves; and the murder, of the marquis of Vaides, was committed by his wife. *Desafíos* or duels were among the most frequent occasions for violence, death and consequently vengeance. Castilian codes of honour, both real and exaggerated, required men to fight upon the least slight to their integrity. Rules of precedence assumed a major role, for instance when noblemen had to give way to each other's coaches in a narrow street. A grievance nurtured by a noble might be shared by his whole household, so that pitched street battles between retainers was a regular hazard. In an effort to stop duels the council of Castile in 1684 proposed full enforcement of the law against challenges, with a firm use of the penalties of confiscation of goods, and death in the case of a fatal duel. The council of State overruled this, on the grounds that in living memory the full rigor of the law had never been applied. It proposed instead ten years' service in Africa for nobility and gentry, and twenty years for commoners.[78]

Notorious crimes by nobles were always punished, but not always severely. In 1683 the count of Molina quarrelled with a poor peasant trying to sell him wood, and stabbed him to death though he begged for mercy on his knees. The Sala de Alcaldes promptly condemned him to an identical death and fined him 6,000 ducats, but the count escaped.[79] He seems to have remained a fugitive, for the king confirmed the verdict. Murders of this type occurred regularly, but we know little of their outcome. In 1682 Don Francisco de Alarcón was murdered in broad daylight by the marquis of Valero, brother of the duke of Béjar. Valero was later taken into custody, while his victim's mother, the marquesa de Palacios, quickly disavowed any revenge on the killer so as not to precipitate an inter-family bloodbath.[80] In Madrid at least there was a strong group of alcaldes unafraid to act against nobility. The records show that in 1693 their arrests included one count, two marquises and a regidor of Madrid.

In provincial towns it was less easy to act against the privileged. In Burgos in 1668 it was the sons of the nobility who terrorised the townspeople and committed various robberies. 'Being related to the nobility here, they think no one will dare go against them, and so the justices overlook these excesses so as not to enter into a matter which will bring ill-repute on noble blood.'[81] When conflicts occurred between nobles and commoners, as in Esquivias in 1683,[82] it was the commoners who were singled out for exemplary punishment.

A high proportion of the cases analysed in my tables, concerned sex. In Valencia the justices gave considerable attention to adulterous affairs. In 1668, of forty-nine cases listed seventeen were for illicit affairs, seventeen for adultery and fifteen for making advances to convent nuns or to ladies in church. In 1680 out of twenty-seven cases prosecuted, eight were against women for sexual relations with a priest. In the comparatively small Valencian community the predominant sexual offences were simple ones against morality and did not involve violence. By contrast the sexual cases in Madrid were steeped in violence. In 1693, the year I have chosen at random, sexual cases accounted for 19 per cent of all prosecutions, while rape represented 5.7 per cent of all cases. Rape in Madrid does not make pleasant reading. The victims were usually young, sometimes raped by more than one person, and occasionally killed. In 1693 two brothers from Valdeolivas raped, murdered and buried a twelve-year-old girl.

It is difficult to imagine why thefts featured so little in the duties of the Valencian justices, though there is the unlikely possibility that no culprits were caught in the years 1665 to 1671. The Madrid figures show that thieving was an active profession. Gangs of urban and suburban robbers operated over so broad an area that the alcaldes must be given great credit for bringing them to justice. In 1680, for instance, a gang of twelve men, including four gentlemen, was prosecuted for housebreaking; in 1683 a gang of fourteen men and one woman was found guilty of highway robbery and murder. These cases confirm the evidence of Barrionuevo's *Avisos* on the regularity of violence and theft even in broad daylight.

The punishment of crime was an expensive and unprofitable business.[83] Fines were normally exacted, even where the sentence was death. But criminal administration always ran at a loss. An official in mid-century in Valencia explained why this was so.

Three-fourths of those condemned are in fact absentees. Most of them are wretches from whom you neither ask nor expect to get any payment. For those few who have some money, the court seizes their goods, which are always realty such as houses or land. These are assessed and put up for sale, but very rarely are any offers made, because nobody wishes or dares to fall foul of the owners, and so it is necessary to put the property under the administration of the local justices.[84]

Any dependants of the accused also had to be supported out of the revenue. The

172

efficacy of justice was thus affected both by the flight of accused and by a chronic shortage of money.

The problem of flight also faced the justices in Madrid. Sending in a report from the Sala de Alcaldes for the year 1693, the council of Castile reported that of 382 criminal prosecutions completed that year, 212 (or 55.5 per cent) involved absentees. No details were given of the types of punishment imposed on the remaining 170, apart from saying that four were hanged, sixty-six sent to garrison service (in the *presidios*), seven to the galleys and two to the mines of Almadén.[85] There are few more revealing aspects of a society than the way in which it punishes its criminals. In seventeenth-century Spanish society the punishments for crime were not consistent and consequently not easy to categorise; different regional practices as well as competing jurisdictions all helped to make the rules for justice extremely variable.

Since most crime was urban, and certainly came under urban jurisdiction, we are justified in looking at the question in a discussion of towns. The only major form of rural crime was banditry, which will be considered in the next chapter. In towns the chief problem was vagabondage.[86] Vagabonds were not only the unemployed poor. They included all the drifting rural population with no fixed urban residence. A report of 1675 on Madrid vagabonds by officials of a poor hospital said that 'many have come recently from the kingdom of Galicia, fleeing from the levies being made in that realm'.[87] The normal fate of vagabonds was that specified for instance in 1694: 'All those proved to be vagabonds be taken to the garrisons in Africa . . . Others taken in vicious living, idleness and bad ways to be detained in prison until there is a sufficient number to send to the army.'[88] The great majority of culprits were sent to garrisons, which was the most economic and useful way to deal with them. In Valencia the viceroy described the practice regarding garrisons as follows:

Subjects of this realm condemned to garrisons are mostly of the worst type, disturbers of the public peace, who are most conveniently placed somewhere secure where they will stay for the period of their sentence. This consideration, and the well-known experience of flights by criminals condemned to the garrison of Orán, have made me send them instead to the garrisons of Tuscany, Mahon and the Peñón.[89]

In practice the seizure of victims for the garrisons was made more with an eye to military need than as a punishment for crime. In 1692 the corregidor of Toledo, Don Francisco de Vargas, protested to the council against indiscriminate seizure for garrisons:

I cannot fail to state that I find many of the justices in the villages venting their hatred against these poor people, sending subjects who should be sent to hospital rather than to serve the king. I have found that among those brought from Olmedo some were boys who should have gone to school rather than a garrison, and others were so old and feeble it would have been a miracle had they reached the port.[90]

The previous week a transport of 132 men had been sent from Toledo, the local collection point, to Cartagena: 121 had been condemned to garrisons, eleven to the galleys. The rounding up of vagabonds in these months in response to council requests, was so efficient that in May 1692 alone the Toledo region produced 200 men.

What crimes had been committed by these unfortunates? Fragmentary evidence is available for those condemned by the Sala de Alcaldes between 1672 and 1675. In December 1672 a total of thirty-five prisoners was sent from Madrid to the prison at Toledo to await transportation southwards: twenty-seven of them were going to garrisons, five to the galleys, three to the mines at Almadén. Of the three for Almadén, two were guilty of murder and one of assault; at least two going to the galleys were there for murder; the garrison prisoners included two for murder, two for armed robbery, and at least one for riot. Of thirty-eight prisoners sent to Toledo in February 1673, twenty-four were for garrisons, seven for galleys and seven for Almadén. The garrison men included three for murder, and others for theft, housebreaking and riot. A further detachment of prisoners sent from Madrid to Toledo in September 1673 included thirty-nine for garrisons, two for galleys and two for Almadén. The prisoners for Almadén merit some attention. Of the seven sent in February 1673, six were blacks and of these five were sentenced for life, one of them merely for resisting arrest. There is no doubt that the alcaldes had strong prejudices against people like blacks and gipsies, both deemed to be of *mala raza* (bad race). The transport of eight prisoners to Almadén in November 1672 consisted of only blacks and gipsies, most of them sentenced for theft.[91]

The two most severe punishments were undoubtedly the galleys and Almadén. When Francisco del Río and Joseph Rodrigo Fernández were sentenced in 1675 for stealing from a church and eating the sacred hosts, their penalty was ten years in the galleys. This was in effect the maximum sentence possible; a condemnation for 'life' was in practice restricted to ten years. The council of War stated this clearly in 1690 when it objected to Spaniards in Italy being sentenced to the galleys for 'life' literally. No sentence in Spain, the council ruled, could ever be for more than ten years.[92] Only Almadén was deemed to be worse than the galleys. When the Sala in 1691 diverted some prisoners from the galleys to Almadén, they ordered 'that a year be cut off the sentence, since the punishment is worse'.[93]

Torture was an essential part of the judicial process in Spain.[94] Occasionally its use had to be restricted, as in 1679 in Valencia when the *estaments* declared the current use of the rack in the province to be unconstitutional and illegal.[95] Modern horror at its use must be tempered by the consideration that contemporaries were relatively tolerant of physical punishment. For them, as in any traditional society, the worst punishment was that of public infamy. As with the penalties imposed by the Inquisition, the secular penalty of *vergüenza* (shame) reflected not only on the accused but on all his kinfolk. The most common type of shame was a public whipping, applied in cases of adultery, prostitution and similar offences. The seriousness of a vergüenza judgment can be illustrated by the turmoil caused in Valencia in 1691 when the criminal magistrate of the city, Carlos Sobregondi, on his own authority and without a trial ordered two carpenters who had been caught stealing a pot, to be stood at the court entrance for two hours with a pot each hung round the neck, exposed to public humiliation. The viceroy explained to the king how serious the consequences might be:[96]

In this realm, my lord, the punishment of exposure to shame is held in common opinion to be graver than the gallows or the galleys, and it brings even greater dishonour on the relatives of the punished man. It is deeply felt when the sentence is imposed and even more when it is carried out. Resistance to the punishment is permitted and unrest is inevitable if the practice is not restricted. If there has been no trouble in this case it is because everyone believed that the accused had first been tried.

Unfortunately for any study of crime and punishment in seventeenth-century Madrid, the vital *libros de acuerdos*, recording the judgments of the alcaldes, are missing. We can, however, place some confidence in a libro de acuerdos available for the year 1751; this is because as late as 1745 an official of the Sala could accept as a correct guide to current practice a text which has been dated to 1670.[97] The only significant difference between practice in 1670 and 1751 was the disuse of galleys, which were suppressed as a punishment in 1748. Some of the crimes and corresponding sentences laid down in 1751 were as follows: for vagabondage, six years in a regiment; for theft and outrages, six years in the garrisons; for illtreating his wife, four years in a regiment in Orán; for attempted sodomy, ten years in the mines; for murder, ten years in the mines; for dangerous coach-driving, six years in the garrisons; for robbery and murder, hanging commuted to garrotting; for prostitution, six years garrison for pimps, six years in the house of correction (*galera*) for the women; for rape, four years' garrison and a payment of 150 ducats to the girl, or alternatively freedom if there was an undertaking to marry the girl and to pay prosecution costs.[98] These are random examples: the variation in sentences makes it impossible to say that there were standardised punishments.

## URBAN DISORDER AND RIOTS

Town authorities lived in regular fear of riots. In the Sala de Alcaldes the opinion was that 'the reasons for which the populace are most easily stirred up, tend to be lack of bread and other supplies, heavy taxes, rising prices and changes in coinage'.[99] Spain had recently passed through an era of urban disorder,[100] and the authorities were aware of the problems involved. Then in October 1664, in the penultimate year of the old king, changes in the coinage led to serious disturbances in Madrid and threats to the king's life. '*Si el Rey no muere, el Reino muere!*' (Unless the king dies, the kingdom dies!) went one chant. The refrain '*Levántate Sevilla, te seguirá Castilla!*' (Arise Seville, Castille will follow!) was heard in the streets.

The apparently somnolent reign of Charles II was no stranger to urban disorder and sedition. One conclusion of the present study has been an emphasis on the great fragmentation of mentality in Spain. We can see this very clearly in the way in which public disorder was invariably contained within the limits of the town.

Tensions and social conflict remained inwardly directed, towards the immediate community, and appealed only to local ideals. When towns revolted, they did so against themselves rather than against the upper classes or the state. They seldom if ever combined themselves into a confederacy, for they did not share common problems or aspirations.

The revolts of 1647–52 in Andalucia had been virtually unprecedented. No similar cluster of urban revolts occurred in the rest of the century, but agitation remained a regular phenomenon. The few examples to be found in government reports suggest that troubles were caused by fairly normal conditions. Conflict was usually endemic in the structure of the urban community. The events in Calahorra in 1665 demonstrate this.[101] In a memorandum to the council of Castile, the chapter of Calahorra cathedral denounced the *regidores perpetuos* (regidores who held their posts permanently through sale of office) for corruption in exempting the rich from taxes and burdening the poor. The cathedral chapter donated 10,000 ducats to the municipality to buy back the posts of regidores. This seemed to promise well, but then it was discovered that the new regidores were still only nominees of the oligarchy, and the posts 'remained in the hands of the same families and houses'. A report went around that the families planned to buy back their offices. 'The result was that on the evenings of the 12th and 13th January this year (1665) a large crowd gathered to put fear into those attempting to buy the regimientos.' A minor incident at the Feast of the Purification (2 February) led to an arrest, and the alcalde mayor and some richer citizens and regidores patrolled the streets. In the Plaza de Santiago they encountered some peasants. Words led to the regidores crying, 'Kill these rabble', and they set about the peasants with their swords. Immediately the report shot through the city that peasants were being killed. After some clashes the peasants chased out the alcalde mayor and appointed their own. They also changed the tax system so that the rich paid out on those taxes they were deemed to owe.

Calahorra was a city of some 5,000 people, but in all these disturbances not a single person was killed. For almost three months the common people, supported by peasants, clergy, guilds and some members of the upper classes, ran the administration. They elected their own corregidor and alcalde mayor and other public officials. Early in February, when they first took over, armed bands roamed the city at night, firing at doors and windows; but this conduct did not last. Virtually all the rich fled the city, but their houses remained untouched. In the second week of April 1665 the Council sent Don Alonso de Llano y Valdés, regent of Navarre, to take over. He entered the city with an armed troop, met no resistance whatever, and issued a pardon to all the rebels save their six principal leaders.[102]

Similar internal conflicts arose in the town of Ubeda, north of Granada, in 1677. In a petition to the king, the wives of two accused blamed 'the tyranny and violence of the nobles (*poderosos*), who are those who have reduced that city to its deplorable state'.[103] As a result of the pacification measures some sixty of the poor were imprisoned and another hundred fled the city. The same situation could be seen in the Catalan town of Sitges in 1676.[104] The town had been in dispute with its seigneur, the cathedral chapter of Barcelona, for a considerable time: in 1664 it petitioned the king to buy back the jurisdiction. The regent of the Audiencia in Barcelona, D. Lorenzo Matheu y Sanz, reported in November 1677 that the quarrel had arisen over rights in the land, and that a riot on St Bartholomew's Day in 1676 had cost four deaths. He advised that the Crown resume jurisdiction over the town. The council however thought this would prejudice the position of other seigneurs, and disagreed. Not until 1679 was a compromise arrived at: the chapter kept its jurisdiction, and a general pardon was issued to the town.

Occasionally a town might rebel against outside authorities. The best example to hand is that of Santiago de Compostela, scene of one of the most successful tax revolts of the century. In May 1683 tax commissioners visited the city to carry out an assessment then being made all over Castile. The commissioner, Don Juan de Feloaga Ponce de León, became the centre of a riot involving clergy and students.[105] On 7 May just after midnight some shots and stones were fired against his house. The guards went out and arrested a student with a pistol. The next day, when the commissioner began examining the student, a large number of people including clergy and armed students surrounded his dwelling, and refused to leave until the prisoner was handed over to the city alcalde. That afternoon, Friday 8 May, a crowd yelling 'Kill, kill!' attacked his house, stormed his stables, wounded two grooms and killed a horse. That night the crowd attacked other houses. The blame, said the commissioner, lay with the city authorities, who connived at tax frauds. The troubles continued at least to the following January, when the duke of Uceda went to Santiago on the same mission but faced the same riotous mobs of students and people. 'These people', he reported, 'went through the streets in broad daylight, armed and celebrating.'[106]

Few malcontents entered into sedition without very careful planning. When the viceroy of Valencia in 1668 heard from his spies that a rising in the city was imminent, he explored the situation carefully and found that members of the clothiers guild planned a revolt to show their opposition to trade with France. He also got an outline of their plans:

. . . that two hours before dawn they would meet with their weapons in the plaza near the monastery of San Agustin; that they would ring the bell loudly; many people would as usual rush to see; that they would tell them the French in the city had rioted, in the view that telling them this would win them all the people; that being then of sufficient number they would occupy the armoury, and being masters of that would be masters of the city . . . that to secure the revolt they would make use of the peasants, so that when the bell rang they would enter in armed groups of a hundred through each of the four main gates of the city . . . and they would likewise rally the students and the clothiers.[107]

Six of the conspirators paid with their lives for this plan: their heads were set up over the Llotja and the armoury.

Severity was normal in the major cities. Granada, which had been at the heart of the mid-century revolts, was no exception. On 5 January 1669 letters were found pinned up on all the major public buildings, threatening the chief public officials. Their significance will be touched on later.[108] A correspondent blamed 'the common people; every day among them there are seditious voices'. The council of Castile was concerned that 'the city of Granada is composed of over

45,000 vecinos, most of them desperate and propertyless, for which reason this town is more susceptible than others to troubles, and particularly when there is a shortage of bread'.[109] It was the bread shortage, following poor harvests in 1697 and 1698, that caused problems throughout the peninsula in 1699. In the spring, riots in Madrid toppled the ministry of the count of Oropesa. On 28 April early in the morning a huge crowd in Madrid went to the royal palace demanding bread, and the appointment of Don Francisco Ronquillo as corregidor: the noise of the tumult reached the ears of the terrified councillors, who immediately appointed Ronquillo. The mob then went to Oropesa's palace and besieged it, stoning and breaking the windows; the Count's men fired back and killed three or four. Oropesa could not get out and had to be rescued by Ronquillo.[110] Other Castilian towns suffered disturbances, but the greatest alarm was felt by the government over events in Toledo.

A petition from 'the guild of silkworkers and other guilds of this city of Toledo', dated 14 July 1699, complained that 'since July last year, 1698, the people have borne and suffered scarcity and lack of bread, without being able in all this time to obtain the slightest relief'. The petition went on to complain of unemployment, with 3,000 people out of work in the silk industry alone. If this situation of no food or work were to continue, they threatened, 'it would not be surprising if, in order to obtain bread, they were to resort to all the means permitted by natural law and even to those not so permitted. The people have no wish to be angered or to cause riots or a scandal; all they desire is that since God has brought better weather their lot should also be bettered.'[111] A plot to sack the houses of the regidores was discovered in time. 'The main complaint', reported the council of Castile, 'is that the administrators of bread supplies are alleged to make a profit of twenty reales on every fanega.'

Who were the urban rebels? It was claimed that those in Catalonia in 1687–90 were 'people of low degree'.[112] In Calahorra in 1665 an official said of the rebels that 'all these people are the poorest in these parts and most of them are from outside and have nothing to lose'.[113] This was the standard view, that rebels were always shiftless poor with nothing to lose by revolt. In a big city like Granada, most of the rebels were associated with urban industry. Here, as in Toledo and Valencia, textile workers were a key factor. But in numbers the rural labourers were certainly a more important force. In Córdoba, the city's corregidor explained in 1683, 'most of the population are day labourers and spend the whole week working out in the fields and on the mountains'.[114]

The numbers involved in riots were usually large: in Córdoba in 1652, for instance, the rebels were estimated at over 6,000 by an eyewitness.[115] The most significant aspect, however, is not the size of revolts but the reason why so many people held together. This brings us back again to the communal character of urban risings. In Granada in 1648 all the poorer quarters of the city teamed together and set up their own militia, which they trained in the streets.[116] The sense of community which has been an enduring aspect of Spanish history, made some townships – obviously in areas where ties of kinship and regional loyalty were strong – identify themselves wholly with rebellion. In November 1689, for example, when the viceroy of Catalonia sent a large force against the town of Sant

Feliu de Llobregat, the entire population withdrew to the hills.[117] In 1647 in the town of Albuñuelas near Granada, the customary solidarity of the people was illustrated in a dramatic way: a correspondent wrote to the duke of Béjar, seigneur of the town, that 'here the alcaldes and regidores are imprisoned [for rebellion], but they call themselves Fuenteovejuna, and the judges don't know what to do about it'.[118] This is a remarkable instance of the theme of Lope de Vega's play, which was very well known at the time, being translated into historic reality.

Who led the revolts? In some riots the participants were held together and driven by a common feeling of social outrage. In others, as we can see from the conspiracies in Valencia in 1668, Granada in 1669 and Toledo in 1699, careful planning was a necessary prerequisite. Leadership in these circumstances tended to come from skilled labourers or from sections of the privileged classes; the professions of twenty-one of the leading rebels in Córdoba in 1652 are known: they included hatters, dyers, tailors, a barber, a shopkeeper, a schoolmaster and so on.[119] People of this grade might be well-off in their community: the dyer Alonso Fernández, a leader of the events in Granada in 1650, was described as a 'rich man'. Barbers had status, since their skill with the knife made them often double as surgeons in their communities: the Valencian rising of 1693 was led by a barber-surgeon from Muro. In Calahorra in 1665 one of the leaders was a tailor and one an *hidalgo*, Don Rodrigo de Fuenmayor. The two main leaders of the 1687–90 risings in Catalonia were prominent in their own regions: Antoni Soler de la Torre, a wealthy farmer of Sant Boy de Llobregat, and Enric Torras, an official and councillor of Sant Quirce de Centelles; though such men were respected on their home ground they had no influence beyond it. Rioters and rebels felt themselves vulnerable here. The point is well illustrated in the exchange of conversation between one of the lesser leaders of the Catalan rising, Pedro Terméns of Penedés, and the captain who arrested him. The latter sneered that the rebels were actually leaderless, since their leader Soler was only 'an ordinary man of low origin'; Terméns retorted that 'not only did they have a leader, but they had many gentlemen and persons of rank in this city of Barcelona, and it was on their orders that they had disarmed the soldiers and officers'.[120] The claim was totally untrue, but it reflects the basic social insecurity of all rebels lacking aristocratic support.

Clergy were prominent in most of the Spanish revolts. In Tarifa in 1652 the disturbances, reported the corregidor, were 'occasioned by a few clergy, who are the moving spirit behind the laypeople'. In Seville the cardinal blamed the clergy of one of the parishes for their activities.[121] In Calahorra a prior, Juan Cordón, was one of the leaders. One of the plotters in the conspiracy in Granada in 1652 was 'a priest of the city of Alhama, who for his part in the rising a few years ago in that city had been imprisoned for three years for the crime'. Clergy were prominent in the Santiago disturbances. In 1699 the duke of Gandía wrote to the vicar-general of the archdiocese of Valencia to thank him for having removed from the town of Oliva a certain priest 'who keeps my vassals in a state of discontent, and in whose shadow there is no atrocious crime that has not been committed'.[122] In Madrid the anti-Oropesa riots that year were led by a priest. Sympathy with the just claims of rioters sometimes found support in high ecclesiastical quarters: the bishop of Córdoba in 1652, and the bishop of Vic in Catalonia in 1689, were anxious to plead for compromise.[123] There is no evidence however that clergy in general tended to side with the disaffected. Their most usual stance was to stay neutral. A few, particularly at episcopal level, were outrightly hostile.

The role of students in urban riots could be crucial. Students were prominent in the riots in San Lucar in November 1651.[124] The plotters of 1668 in Valencia planned to team up with the students in the city; students were the principal agitators in the disturbances in Santiago in 1683; in 1691 the viceroy of Valencia reported that 'for many years past this city has experienced various disturbances caused by the university students'.[125] Students tended to be an alien and disharmonious element in their host communities; they came from strange parts, showed little patience with indigenous patterns of obedience, and provoked conflict in situations where it might not have arisen. It was the arrest of a student from Vigo that precipitated the riots in Santiago in 1683. When the viceroy of Valencia in 1691 tried to take judicial action against some students, he found it impracticable mainly because the culprits were 'outsiders' (forasteros), for the most part Catalans, who were arguably outside his jurisdiction.

We know little about the nature and purpose of revolts, given our poor state of knowledge about patterns of obedience and social control in Habsburg Spain. Society was firmly and indubitably traditionalist; loyalties were heavily localised. In none of the riots was there any identifiable class hatred or anticlericalism. Respect for the nobility was shown unmistakably by the adoption of nobles as leaders; respect for the Church was shown by a universal refusal to attack churches or the buildings of the Inquisition. The authorities exploited respect for religion to a degree that in some cases can only be described as sacrilegious. When a riot or uprising began, the clergy would go on to the streets in procession with the Blessed Sacrament: the method was almost infallible. When riots occurred in Valencia in 1691, we are informed by a contemporary diarist that 'they took out the Blessed Sacrament from the Jesuit church and other places, and by midnight everything was quiet'.[126] When the 1648 revolt began in Granada, a crowd of 5,000 assembled on the Campo del Príncipe. Immediately, reports a Jesuit present at the time, 'the archbishop and senior clergy took out the Blessed Sacrament and took it to the Campo del Príncipe; the people adored it and said they were Catholics but that they desired bread'.[127] Perhaps the most startling case of this misuse of the Sacrament occurred in 1688 in Villamayor in Catalonia. The populace attacked the house of the captain of cavalry lodged there, whereupon some clergy displayed the Sacrament inside the captain's house.[128] Rebels attacked clergy only exceptionally, as in the tithe revolt in Manresa in 1688. But fear of betrayal by the clergy might also lead to violence. In Seville in 1652 an alleged royal pardon was published through the streets by a procession of clergy chanting 'Peace, peace, peace'; the people's militia in the Plaza de la Feria mocked at them and cried out, 'Hang the friars and Christians!'[129]

There was inevitably some hostility to nobles, not as a class but only where they could be identified with oppression. In Córdoba a local doctor blamed the 1652 rising on 'the tyranny of the nobles, who treated the people as though they were slaves',[130] and in the revolt there were indeed threats against aristocrats. Attitudes to the nobility depended on such a multiplicity of factors that it is impossible to give simple explanations. Undoubtedly in regions of gentry predominance as in New Castile, Andalucia and Valencia, tensions between tenant and seigneur were greater. Otherwise regional differences were perhaps less significant than the perennial quarrel between the privileged and the deprived. Whether in areas of strong aristocratic control or not, conflicts between nobles and other sectors tended to be communal by nature rather than to have any broader 'class' basis. We would expect an unusual degree of deference to nobles in a society as aristocratically orientated as Spain. But, in default of a substantial urban middle class to act as a social buffer, tensions between the two extremes of noble and plebeian were also more starkly polarised. Noble violence in the cities was a particular object of popular resentment. In Calahorra in 1665 extensive damage was wreaked 'against the houses of the well-to-do; there is not one which does not have doors and windows smashed'. Civic antagonisms, of the type we have already seen, emerged in the conflict in the town of Cardadeu (near Valls, Catalonia) in 1688 'between the nobility and the common people, the latter intending to attack the privileges of the former, who have the chief hand in the administration'.[131]

Popular revolt in pre-industrial times could be both visionary and revolutionary. This was not the case with urban insurrections in late Habsburg Spain. The demands of the rioters were invariably limited and moderate. Participants in risings cannot strictly be called 'rebels', since they were not opposed to the values or nature of the existing order. As their viewpoint was often accepted not only by local worthies but even by members of the councils at Madrid, it is possible to argue that the riots, far from disrupting moral order, were aimed at restoring (and were generally seen to be restoring) equilibrium to a moral order that had already been disrupted by such factors as maldistribution of food supplies and illegal imposition of taxes.

Apart from demands arising out of economic distress, there were three main categories of protest in the urban riots of this period. Firstly there were demands for changes in the civic administration, as in Calahorra, Ubeda, Sitges and Caspe. It was by far the most common type of riot, and in none of the disturbances did persons or causes extraneous to the community have any significant part to play.[132] The second category of protest, instanced by the Valencian rising of 1693, involved demands for the abrogation of seigneurial taxes. Thirdly, there were direct political demands, made in this period only in the Catalan revolts of 1687–90. The Valencian and Catalan revolts are considered in the next chapter.

Both insurgents and authorities were aware of a pattern of continuity with past revolts. On the rebel side it was important to obtain some historical sanction by identifying with movements of the past. The dissidents of 1693 in Valencia even adopted the same name – els Agermanats – used by the rebels of 1521. Certain regions, certain towns, and certain quarters of towns, earned notoriety as regular founts of insurrection: Játiva in Valencia was one such place. But there is some evidence that such towns were unquiet primarily because of their own internal social tensions.[133]

It is vital to stress the almost complete bloodlessness of urban revolt. In the mid-century risings in Granada, Córdoba and Seville, not a single death was caused directly by the populace. In a disturbance in the Catalan town of Valls (near Tarragona) in 1694, the rebels, who styled themselves 'the Poor' (*los Pobres*), rioted for two whole days and 'in all the disturbance there was no shot fired, nobody killed, no house burnt'.[134] The great risings of 1687–90 in Catalonia were astonishingly bloodless. Peasants descended on the troops but did not harm them: 'the cavalry were disarmed and the saddles taken from the horses'.[135] This very strange way of attacking troops[136] was adopted throughout the principality. In no recorded instance were troops attacked or killed without provocation. In the riots in Madrid in 1699 there were four deaths, caused as we have seen not by rioters but by Oropesa's retainers firing on the crowd. The victims of mob violence were few and far between; popular riots almost never became jacqueries, despite the fears of the upper classes.

Violence of course occurred, sometimes on a frightening scale. The selective burning of houses was common. In Manresa in 1688 'they burnt five or six houses and the furnishings of others'; in Villamayor that year 'the people gathered in order to burn the house of Dr Derrocada and others exempt from the military tax'.[137] Terror was a regular weapon and extreme threats, including that of death, were frequent but seldom carried out. Property rather than life was the target for communal hatred. The crucial point is that property was singled out for destruction in a ritualistic manner common to all popular uprisings of the period.[138] Theft was never the motive force of rioters. Reporting on the Valencian rising of 1693, an administrator wrote to the duke of Gandía that 'as for scandalous robberies and other sins that happen during such events, nothing has occurred'.[139] The possessions of profiteers and exploiters were marked down not for seizure but for annihilation. When the house-burning occurred in Manresa in 1688 'they burnt the house of canon Gelabert then went to the houses of the other canons, entered them, threw out of the windows the furniture and whatever they could find and lit a bonfire in the street and burnt everything there was'.[140] Ritual destruction was part of the popular mystique of revolt.

Unlike rebels, the authorities were not sparing of life. Bloody retaliation was commonplace. Punishment was invariably selective, as at Ubeda in 1677, when only the commoners were imprisoned and the nobles were left at liberty.[141] Leniency was sometimes practised in smaller communities. In big risings no risks were taken. In 1689 some 1,300 troops and two pieces of artillery descended upon the little Catalan town of Sant Feliu de Llobregat.[142] The turmoil of these years is sufficient proof that Spain was no freer of rebellion than other societies in western Europe.[143]

## THE FRENCH COMMUNITY IN SPAIN

Some of the disturbances in seventeenth-century towns were directed against foreigners. Racial unrest had always been a feature of peninsular history. With the expulsion of the Moriscos in the early century the last nonconforming minority had disappeared. But large numbers of foreigners were now settled in Spain, and their presence created new tensions. Religion was no longer a cause for conflict: the settlers were almost without exception Catholic. Disagreement arose instead out of economic and social rivalry.

Little is known of foreigners in Spain apart from those active in the American trade.[144] They played in any case only a minor role in Spanish society. The French, on the other hand, were a large and powerful minority with a decisive interest in Spain's economy. It is difficult to understand the significance of some aspects of seventeenth-century Spain without considering their role.

We may approach the problem through the two anti-French riots in Valencia city in 1678 and 1691. On 7 June 1678 there was serious rioting against the French in Valencia city.[145]

The cause was that the evening post from Catalonia brought news that the French had taken the fortress of Puigcerdà . . . A great crowd went through the city burning the houses of the *gavachos* . . . All the mounted guard and alguaciles blocked the streets but did not dare act, for the people all carried pistols and cried 'Long live the King of Spain and death to the *gavachos*' and they forced the officers of justice to do the same. In three or four places in the market, clergy and friars tried to pacify the people, and in the rest of the city where there were no officers (they were all on horse in the market, where they were most needed) riotous mobs roamed, crying 'Long live the King of Spain'. They went through the monasteries and shops and flooded into the houses of Spaniards and Valencians, robbing all that they could and doing thirty thousand ills.

On 17 June a large number of those deemed responsible for the riots were arrested and transported to Ibiza. To prove that its measures were in no way pro-French, the city on 23 June sent a petition to the king recommending that nobody of foreign origin should hold office in the city.[146]

The riots of 1691 were far more serious. In July 1691 the French fleet appeared off Barcelona and heavily bombarded the city. It then moved south and threatened Alicante. In Valencia city, anti-French feeling was at a high pitch and on the night of 22 July a major disturbance broke out in the market square, to shouts of 'Long live the king and death to the bad government'. The riot continued the following night, despite efforts of town officials to pacify the market area and patrol the streets. On the 23rd the Jurats were forcibly locked up in the Llotja and the Jurat en cap was wounded in the arm. The rioters demanded the expulsion from the kingdom of all French, four of whom were murdered during the disturbances. Powerless to refuse, the authorities responded by decreeing that all unmarried Frenchmen should leave within three days. Not until September 1691 was the viceroy in a position to send to penal servitude some sixty people involved in the riots. Meanwhile on 25 July the French fleet began a murderous bombardment of Alicante, with disastrous consequences for the French still resident in the area.[147]

These incidents were not exceptional. There was, for instance, a major anti-French riot in Saragossa in June 1694, when French houses were sacked.[148] What lay behind this communal hatred? The constant state of war with France may seem to offer an explanation. It was common practice for the Madrid government to decree reprisals against resident French whenever war broke out. There were reprisals in 1625 and 1635, and again in 1667, 1673, 1683 and 1689.[149] In 1667 embargoes were made against at least 611 Frenchmen in Valencia, realising a sum of 85,253 lliures.[150] All French who had been resident for over ten years, and all who had married Spaniards, were normally excepted from such embargoes. Traders were sometimes allowed to buy exemption; in 1667 ten of the Valencian traders paid about 2,500 silver reales each and were left unmolested.[151] It was in the interest of the authorities that commerce should not be seriously disrupted by reprisals. The existence of a state of war, however, was basically irrelevant to the origins of Francophobia. In some cases, as with the bombardment of Alicante and Barcelona in 1691, popular fury was clearly stirred by hostilities. The disorders in Alicante were unrestrained.

The people felt that they had a right to compensate themselves from the goods of the French. . . . Eight thousand men had gone from other parts of the realm to help Alicante, and there were also four hundred soldiers from the levy for Milan, together with the citizens of Alicante: and all this great number of people were those who committed the robberies. . . . The soldiers sacked the house of Diego Mirasol.[152] . . . Friars and clergy did not refrain from this infamous conduct.[153]

But there were other interests, notably those of textile manufacturers, that welcomed hostilities. In July 1668 in Valencia the authorities frustrated a plot by silk workers to rise and massacre the French population; the fear of the plotters was that peace was about to be declared with France: this would have given back to the French their control, interrupted by war, of the textile trade.[154]

The unpopularity of the French arose not from the international situation but from their very presence in Spain. They were the largest foreign minority and their influence was felt in every aspect of daily life in the large towns. There are no reliable estimates of their numbers. The only comprehensive account, that made by the French ambassador Villars in 1680, may be quoted here at length.[155]

There are about 65,000 French scattered through the following provinces. *The kingdom of Navarre*: there are held to be about a thousand, namely 250 traders, the rest shepherds, agricultural workers, water carriers, servants and other services. Traders have business there worth about 1,500,000 livres of French merchandise, inclusive of the wools they purchase from the country. In addition the French in Castile send a great deal of bullion from France through this kingdom, either through the agency of Frenchmen or that of the Navarrese themselves. In return a large quantity of French cattle and fish is sent there. *Kingdom of Aragon*: There are about 20,000 French, namely 2,000 traders, the rest labourers. The former do over three millions worth of trade, including about a million of wool purchased in the country. . . . The labourers carry off a lot of bullion to their countries, such as Béarn, Gascony, Languedoc and Auvergne. . . . *In Catalonia* there are about 1,000 French, namely 100 traders, who buy some oil for France and who trade a bit in the seaports; the rest are labourers. It is quite a large province and the inhabitants are very hardworking, which is why there are few Frenchmen. *In Valencia and Murcia* there are about 12,000 Frenchmen, namely 600 traders, the rest labourers. The former do about three millions of business every year, inclusive of about 1,500,000 livres spent on wool. The latter carry off a great deal of money. These realms are populated with all types of foreigners and have a big trade. . . . *The two Castiles*: There are about 16,000 French, inclusive of those in Madrid: 3,500 are merchants, dealers and retailers, the rest are labourers. The former carry on about six millions worth of business in all kinds of French goods, including purchases of wool from Segovia and other places. The others also take out a lot of money. There are in Madrid some traders who do about a million livres of business a year. *Extremadura, Galicia, Asturias and Cantabria*: There are about 1,000 French; most are in Extremadura as being the best area, and nearly all are domestics. In Galicia and Asturias there are a few traders because of the sea-ports. In Cantabria the biggest trade of the French, who are in Bilbao and San Sebastian, is in cod from Newfoundland, French produce and some manufactures. *Andalucia*: There are about 16,000 French, namely 500 traders, the rest labourers. The traders do about nine millions worth of business a year, including both the Indies and Spain. The natives are not very hardworking, which is what attracts a lot of French there.

Villars's figures were never intended to be exact, and the figures for each region add up to 67,000 rather than the 65,000 first stated. Moreover in his memoirs the ambassador claimed, with a complete lack of concern for the figures in his own report, that the French in Spain 'have been estimated at up to 70,000'.[156] Our confidence in these various figures must be further undermined by the specific example of Valencia. A figure of 12,000 (there were few French in Murcia) is certainly too high. The only detailed census available in this period is one of 1674, carried out principally with the aim of sequestrating the goods of all Frenchmen in the province. Its findings were summarised in a report made by the viceroy of Valencia, the count of Paredes, in February 1674: 'The declaration of all the French that there are in this kingdom, and the embargo of their goods, has been made; and it has been found that there are 2,239, though many of them have no goods.'[157] If this appears a low reckoning we may compare it with the comments of viceroy Castelrodrigo in 1691. He then denied allegations made in the Valencian Estates that 'there were 30,000 French in the realm, when by the surveys made under the governorship of the count of Altamira [his predecessor as viceroy] there were only about 2,000'.[158] These estimates make it improbable that there were more than 2,500 French in Valencia at any one time during the late century. The figures given by Villars therefore need to be treated with great scepticism.

The same may be said for his figures on Andalucia, though we must note that his estimates are exceeded by those of other contemporaries.[159] What cannot be doubted is that there were tens of thousands of French in Spain, particularly in the large cities. Their function may be gauged from the observations made by Père Labat at the end of the century:

During my stay in Cadiz I was assured that in Andalucia alone there were over 20,000 French from the provinces of Auvergne, la Marche, Limousin, and around the Garonne. Their employment was carrying water to the houses, selling coal, oil and vinegar in the street, serving in hostels, ploughing the soil, harvesting and tending vines. These people seldom fail to return home after three years, taking three or four hundred piastres or more.[160]

The places of origin of French immigrants as stated by Labat had been the same for over a century. In Madrid over the period 1617–73 a sample of over 2,600

French shows that some 52 per cent came from Auvergne, 14.5 per cent from Gascony, and others from Limousin, Béarn and other regions.[161]

The great majority of French concentrated in the large cities. Few were permanent residents. A later French ambassador reported that 'if some French marry and settle down in Spain, they are usually only simple workers such as cobblers or tailors, or if they are people with some capital in commerce; very rarely do they cut all links with the part of their family in France'.[162] What professions did the urban French pursue? An analysis of a random 850 from the period 1617–73 in Madrid, shows that 22 per cent were bakers, 11 per cent domestic servants, 11 per cent cobblers, 10.1 per cent street vendors, 8 per cent tailors, 7 per cent water-carriers, and so on.[163] These professions are similar to those given for the French of Andalucia, of whom a survey for reprisal purposes was made in 1674. At this date there were said to be 87 French in Seville, 161 in San Lucar and 95 in Cadiz.[164] Among the Cadiz number were twenty-four bakers, four hostellers, four inn-keepers and several other professions. Our clearest picture of any French community in Spain at this period comes, however, from Valencia.

The information available for the French in Valencia in 1674 is unique. In November 1673 the Crown had ordered the expulsion of all French. This was a standard gesture, the prelude to a royal decree issued by the viceroy of Valencia on 9 February 1674, requiring a cash payment from all those wishing to stay rather than be expelled.[165] The registers contain details of some 1,500 French in Valencia city and its environs who paid the required contribution.[166] The list permits us to analyse the professions of these French and also their place of residence in Valencia city. The main professions are listed in Table 6.5, with a rough estimate of the percentage out of 1,500 cases:

Table 6.5

| | | |
|---|---|---|
| Traders (*mercader*) | 48 | 3.2% |
| Agricultural labourers | 243 | 16.2 |
| Innkeepers | 33 | 2.2 |
| Bakers | 13 | 0.9 |
| Coach-drivers | 141 | 9.4 |
| Shepherds | 40 | 2.7 |
| Cobblers | 26 | 1.7 |
| Millers | 64 | 4.3 |
| Fishmongers | 53 | 3.5 |
| Domestics | 101 | 6.7 |
| Carters | 32 | 2.1 |
| Ice-vendors | 24 | 1.6 |
| Textile workers | 27 | 1.8 |
| Oil vendors | 20 | 1.3 |
| Tailors | 18 | 1.2 |
| Shopkeepers | 28 | 1.9 |
| Cooks and pastrycooks | 24 | 1.6 |
| | | |
| Profession not specified | 200 | 13.3 |
| Others | 365 | 24.3 |

186

Only 200 of the French in the survey, or 13.3 per cent, lacked a specific profession, which suggests that they represented floating labour. Apart from agriculture, which occupied a good proportion, the French were clearly concentrated in petty commerce and the service industries. A Moroccan visitor to Spain in 1690 confirmed this when he reported that 'the greater number of those who follow those employments which are despised in Spain are Frenchmen, and they have become very numerous in Spain for the sake of service and acquiring and heaping up property'.[167] In his satirical *El no importa de España* (1667) Francisco Santos presented two portraits that would have been a good reflection of Spanish opinion, one of a cobbler and the other of a comb-maker, both raised in poverty in Paris but acquiring great wealth in Spain.[168] Such swift acquisition of riches at the expense of the Spanish people aroused continuous resentment. The contemporary Valencian priest and annalist Miñana was later to refer to 'traders and the numberless other hosts of French, who carried on contemptible and disgraceful profiteering in several provinces of Spain, with no other aim than to get hold of all the gold and silver and transport it to France'.[169]

Apart from traders enjoying favour under commercial treaties, the French in Spain enjoyed no special privileges. They were subject to Spanish law and punished accordingly: cases in Valencia present us with Antoine Gastau who was tortured in December 1669 and confessed to the murder of a lady; Joseph Jacob, a labourer of Novelda, who was in 1693 sentenced to five years in the galleys for a theft; and François Estop who was in July 1696 hanged for robbing and murdering his uncle.[170] Since they lived in Spain on equal terms with the natives, fully subject to laws and taxation, the small French minority should not have attracted hostility. That they did so throughout the century can be attributed to two main causes: their refusal to settle and be integrated into the local Spanish community, and their control of crucial sectors of the economy.

In the Cortes of Saragossa in 1684 the third of the four Aragonese Estates, that of the Caballeros, set out for discussion a memorandum against the import of French goods. In the course of their argument the Caballeros gave some cogent reasons for the ill-feeling then current against the French:[171]

You will find no legacies or pious foundations made by Frenchmen or by their descendants. . . . Recently when one died he showed how little he, like all of them, was attached to our land, since even the memorial masses were arranged to be said in France. They do not buy property nor do they apply themselves to the laborious and fruitful growth of agriculture, but only to that of trade, whereby they get rich in a short time and transfer the wealth to their homelands. They have no fixed domicile, nor do they nourish love for our country, as shown by the fact that in these six years since the Cortes of 1678 some have left with their assets and others have married off in France and richly endowed their daughters who were born in this realm. The young men trade, but marry in France, coming and going with complete liberty, living in this city in tiny rented houses with furniture not worth thirty reales. They live humbly while they are here, but put on fine and sumptuous clothes on returning to their own country. In every way they show how little they love, and how passing is their commitment to stay in, our land.

Successive governments in Spain tried to encourage the French to show more dedication to the country of their career, and in particular to marry Spanish women. But the *gavachos*, as they were rudely termed, failed to comply. Their refusal to integrate is amply illustrated in the will of Jean Vidal, sworn before a Madrid notary in 1670.[172] A gardener by trade, Vidal came from Verdun. 'I declare', runs his testament, 'that in the said town of Verdun in France I have a vineyard which is my own, and a house which is mine and my sister's. . . . Also in the said town of Verdun and its area I have a tract of wheatland which is mine and my sister's. I declare that I have no goods in these realms of Spain, and I neither owe nor am owed anything.' The words reflect a sturdy independence, behind which lay the need to acquire a little capital in Spain to take home and invest in the family smallholding. The commitment to settle in Spain was clearly non-existent. Those few French who became naturalised and integrated themselves into the Spanish population, remained tainted by the attitude of the majority.

French immigrants played a key role in the country's economy. In Catalonia they constituted the agrarian proletariat of the principality. In Mataró they helped fishing and navigation.[173] In 1626 the French ambassador in Madrid reported home that his countrymen in Spain were so necessary to the country's welfare that it would suffer grave prejudice if they all left.[174] A Valencian diarist, commenting in April 1693 on the aftermath of the expulsion of the French a year previously, observed that 'the gavachos multiplied and came back in twice the numbers they left the year before. But what would have happened to the quantities of wine got this year, if they had not returned?'[175]

The fact was, as the Aragonese found to their dismay when they attempted to exclude Frenchmen from trade, that commerce would collapse were any effective ban introduced. Spaniards made outraged noises about French control, but their threats were all empty. Here, for instance, are the Jurats of Valencia in 1684 claiming that 'in order to ruin Spain the French have managed with cunning to induce laziness of spirit into Spaniards, to deaden their hands for laborious tasks, and to take from them their money and substance by sending all their wool to France'.[176] The French presence was crucial in all spheres, and had long been so recognised. Martínez de Mata claimed in 1650 that the French had taken over the menial professions: 'Over 120,000 Frenchmen, with their pretence of poor clothing and slovenliness, have introduced themselves into servile and other posts and have taken them from the Spaniards who used to have them: professions such as water-carriers, grinders, porters, cobblers, vendors of old clothes, carriers, bakery boys, ostlers, inn-keepers, chair-makers, food suppliers, tavern keepers and many others'.[177]

In the larger towns the French dominated those professions on which society depended. Willughby's impression in 1664 was that 'if there be any employment that you would set them about which they think themselves too good for, they presently say send for a Frenchman. Indeed the French do almost all the work in Spain. All the best shops are kept by Frenchmen, the best workmen in every kind are French.'[178] It is also significant that the French were alleged to form a high proportion of the urban beggars. Contemporaries therefore resented them not only for their numbers but also for simple reasons of social status. The French were small-traders (professions of the Jew) and water-carriers (professions of the

Moor). They had slipped into the despised social niche vacated by the ethnic minorities expelled in 1492 and 1609. In the very century that Spain is supposed to have rid itself of all dissonant minorities, it in fact acquired a large urban minority that invited social prejudice on all points save religion.

The result was that urban patriciates defended themselves vigorously against any invasion by successful members of this new minority. In both Saragossa and Valencia, where French were particularly numerous, steps were taken to prevent French merchants obtaining civic dignities. This was not easy to do, since racial origin alone could not by law incapacitate a Spanish citizen. When in 1678 the Valencian authorities deliberately omitted from the ballot for Jurats the name of Vicent Prats, the son of a Frenchman, he appealed to the Audiencia and won judgment in his favour; but though his name was now entered he failed to get elected.[179]

## NOTES

1. Domínguez Ortiz, A., *Golden Age of Spain* (London 1971), pp. 132, 136.
2. My main sources are González, T., *Censo de población* (Madrid 1929); Domínguez Ortiz, *Sociedad española*, I, 463–91; and Vincent, B., 'Récents travaux', *Annales de Démographie Historique* (1977) pp. 480–1. A few data come from other sources. In general I have adopted a multiplier of 4.5 persons per vecino.
3. Among the great number of books on Madrid, see in particular the study by Deleito y Piñuela, J., *Sólo Madrid es Corte* (Madrid 1968).
4. 'In ye late fire in ye Plaza Mayor thirty persons were destroyed, inhabitants of that part which was burnt': PRO:SP 101/91/299, newsletter of 14 Sept. 1672.
5. This invaluable list is in AHN Consejos 12.470.
6. Willughby, *A Relation*, p. 489. He contrasts this to Catalonia, where 'the people are generally poor. They use neither glass nor paper in their windows, but only shuts of wood': *ibid.* p. 473.
7. Maiso González, J., 'Peste de Zaragoza', *Estud. Dep. Hist. Mod.* (Saragossa 1973), p. 42.
8. This discussion of Barcelona is based on Nadal, J. and Giralt, E., 'Barcelona en 1717–1718' in *Homenaje a D. Ramón Carande* (Madrid 1963).
9. Census in ADZ 628: 'Vecindario de Zaragoza echo por el Señor Intendente D. Juan Antonio Diaz de Arze en el año de 1723'.
10. There is no seventeenth-century survey of Valencia. But see the interesting study by García Cárcel, R., 'Notas sobre Valencia', *Saitabi*, 25 (1975), 133–53.
11. Recaséns Comas, J. M., 'Tarragona', *Bol. Arqu.*, 77–84 (1962–63), 81–94.
12. González Muñoz, *Talavera,* pp. 253–4.
13. AGS:CJH 1960.
14. Memorandum of 30 June 1683, in *ibid.*
15. Consulta of 21 Feb. 1682, *ibid.* 1052.
16. Based on report of D. Pedro Veluti, 19 May 1683: *ibid.* 1063.
17. D. Pedro de Oreytia to the Council, 3 Mar. 1683: *ibid.* 1066.
18. The figures are for 1717, cited in Llovet, *Mataró,* p. 43 n. 69.
19. Domínguez Ortiz, *Golden Age of Spain*, p. 136.

20. *Idem*, 'Concesiones de votos', in *Crisis y Decadencia*, pp. 97–111.
21. Calonge, M. Pilar, *et al.*, *Castilla la Vieja*, p. 46, in **Artola, M.**, ed., *España del Antiguo Régimen* (Salamanca 1967).
22. *Ibid.* pp. 38–9.
23. Mateos, M. Dolores, *Salamanca*, p. 14; in Artola, *ibid.* (Salamanca 1966).
24. Report to French foreign secretary Torcy, 22 Apr. 1710, AE:CP (Esp.) 203/141.
25. Cited in Ortiz, *Sociedad española XVIII*, p. 299.
26. Royal towns, however, were invariably the biggest: Kamen, *War of Succession*, pp. 269, 246.
27. **Domínguez Ortiz, A.**, 'Ventas de lugares', *Anuario Hist. Der. Esp.*, 1964, 163–207.
28. A sale in 1605 is noted in AGS:DGT Inv. 24 leg. 304.
29. Consulta of council of Finance, 7 July 1682, AGS:CJH 1047.
30. See the figures for 1626–68 in **Gentil da Silva, J.**, *En Espagne* (Paris 1965), p. 182. His figures are incomplete: in 1667, for instance, where he lists two towns sold I have details of at least six.
31. All cases cited in this paragraph are from AGS:DGT Inv. 24 leg. 304.
32. Domínguez Ortiz, *Sociedad española*, I, 258.
33. *Ibid.* pp. 262–3.
34. Kamen, *War of Succession* p. 246.
35. Report of marquis del Castillo, 14 Aug. 1683, AGS:CJH 1056.
36. Report by Miguel Gerónimo Ximénez in 1693, *ibid.* 1988.
37. All details on Elche come from reports and letters dated 1682 in ACA:CA 669. For a balanced assessment of the finance of other Valencian towns at this time, see Casey, *Kingdom of Valencia*, pp. 154–66.
38. 'Memoria de les cantitats en que la ciutat de Alacant te arrendats sos drets y rentes', 1664, in ACA:CA 919.
39. Printed memorial from Tarragona in ACA:CA 534.
40. Full details in BCB Follets Bonsoms 8436 and 2593.
41. Redondo **Veintemillas, G.**, 'El siglo XVII zaragozano', *Estudios* (Saragossa 1977), 119–35.
42. Memorial of May 1695 from Jijona, ACA:CA 933. There is a similar detailed statement dated 1693 in *ibid.* 932. The biggest single *censalista* was D. Nicolás Escorsia of Alicante.
43. **Bennassar, B.**, *Valladolid* (Paris 1967), p. 254.
44. Consulta of 26 Feb. 1667, AGS:CJH 886.
45. Printed memorial of 1681 in *ibid.* 1038.
46. 'Memoria Valenciana' of Onofre Esquerdo, RCPV MS. 32/4.
47. Phillips, *Ciudad Real*, p. 70.
48. AGS:CJH 1031.
49. Information on Guadix and adjacent towns is from the report by Miguel Gerónimo Ximénez in *ibid.* 1988.
50. **Ringrose, D.**, *Transportation* (Durham, N.C. 1970).
51. Lantéry, *Memorias*, p. 59.
52. *Relation d'un voyage* (Paris 1664), p. 119.
53. Osorio y Redín, *Extensión Política*, p. 20.
54. Swinburne, *Travels*, I, 327.
55. **Eiras Roel, A.** and **Villares Paz, R.**, 'Inventarios post mortem', in *Las Fuentes y los Métodos* (Santiago 1977), pp. 93–112.
56. Cited in **Sureda Carrión**, *La Hacienda castellana* (Madrid 1949), p. 209, where the

total is short by ½ maravedi, thus slightly distorting my percentages.

57. Memorial by Borruel, p. 25, in ACA:CA 1370. Estimates in Aragonese money.
58. Osorio, *Extensión Política*, p. 20.
59. Osorio, *Discurso Universal* (1686) in Campomanes, *Apéndice*, I, 334.
60. Details in AHN Consejos 7217. The same source gives estimates for the diocese of Cadiz, with some variations, e.g. 2.7 oz soap and 6 oz meat daily.
61. Domínguez Ortiz, 'Aspectos del vivir madrileño', *Anales Inst. Estud. Mad.*, 7 (1951), 232.
62. Sánchez Rivero, *Viaje de Cosme de Medicis*, I, 84; Willughby, *Relation*, p. 489.
63. See Bennassar, *Recherches*, p. 72.
64. Consulta of 18 Apr. 1671, AGS Estado 4128.
65. Cited in Deleito y Piñuela, *Sólo Madrid es Corte*, pp. 136–7. For Juanini, see below, p. 323.
66. See Deleito y Piñuela, *op. cit.*, pp. 142–4.
67. *Idem. La mala vida* (Madrid 1948), ch. 17.
68. Source: AHN Sala de Alcaldes, Inventarios de causas criminales, libros 2786–2788 (years 1665–1717). My classification follows these lines: 'assault' includes all offences of *heridas* as well as those involving weapons of any sort (*cuchilladas, aprehension de pistolas*); 'brawls' are all *desafíos* and *alborotos*; 'sex' offences are normally prostitution (*trato ilícito*) but also cohabitation (*amancebamiento*); 'swindles' covers *guimera* and *estafas*; 'marital' offences are usually one spouse beating the other; and 'other' includes insults, resistance, usury, etc.
69. In Table 6.3 columns a, c and e are used for violence; columns b, f and h for sex; and d and g for theft.
70. Source: ARV Maestre Racional, Justicia criminal legs. 266–267, expedientes 6403–6430. 'Arms' means illegal carrying of weapons. 'Sex' was either, most commonly, illicit relationships or prostitution.
71. Report by council of Castile, 19 Mar. 1665, AHN Consejos 7175/16, with lists of all vagabonds at fo. 59.
72. Report of 10 Oct. 1665, *ibid.* 7255.
73. Consulta of 22 Sept. 1665, *ibid.*
74. Consulta of 4 Nov. 1669, cited in Maura, *Vida y reinado*, I, p. 162.
75. Consulta of 9 Nov. 1671, AHN Consejos 7181/96.
76. Consulta of 30 May 1672, *ibid.* 7182/14.
77. The cases of Castellar and Ontecilla occur in *ibid.* 7255.
78. Consulta of State, 16 Mar. 1684, AGS Estado 4146.
79. Governor of Castile to king, 22 May 1683, AHN Consejos 7194/158.
80. D. Fernando Ramírez to bishop of Jaén, governor of Castile, 21 June 1682, *ibid.* 7194/200.
81. Letter of 23 July 1668 in *ibid.* 7255.
82. Ortiz, *Sociedad española*, I, 269.
83. On penalties and indeed on the whole context of criminal legislation at this time, see the excellent study by **Tomás y Valiente, F.**, *El derecho penal* (Madrid 1969).
84. 'Papel de D. Pedro Borja', undated but about 1650, ACA:CA 929.
85. Consulta by governor of Castile, 8 Jan. 1694, AHN Consejos 12499.
86. For vagabondage in the eighteenth century, see the useful study by **Pérez Estevez, M. R.**, *El problema de los vagos* (Madrid 1976).
87. Report by Real Hospicio de Pobres de Ave Maria y San Fernando, AHN Sala de Alcaldes, libros de gobierno, 1675/59.
88. Letter from D. Manuel Arias, 16 Nov. 1694, *ibid.* 1694/462.

89. Viceroy to king, 8 Nov. 1689, ARV:RC 593/92.

90. Vargas to council of Castile, 18 Apr. 1692, AHN Consejos 7205/33.

91. All details for 1672 and 1673 are from AHN Sala de Alcaldes, libros de gobierno, 1673/76, 294, 370, 421.

92. Copy of consulta of 19 Aug. 1690, in AGS Estado 4138.

93. Order of 7 June 1691, AHN Sala de Alcaldes, libros de gobierno 1691/53.

94. See Tomás y Valiente, *op. cit.*, ch. III.

95. ARV:RC 546, Electos de los tres estamentos, fo. 116. This volume contains an interesting record of tortures executed in Orihuela, on fos. 94–115.

96. Viceroy Castelrodrigo to king, 23 Jan. 1691, in ARV:RC libros registros 593/261–5.

97. The text is the 'Noticias de la Sala' in AHN Sala de Alcaldes, libro 1420, discussed and dated by Domínguez Ortiz in 'Aspectos del vivir', cited above.

98. From AHN Sala de Alcaldes, libro de acuerdos, libro 1039, year 1751.

99. 'Noticias de la Sala', chap. 59 on 'alborotos del pueblo', in AHN Sala de Alcaldes, libro 1420.

100. **Domínguez Ortiz**, *Alteraciones andaluzas* (Madrid 1973).

101. AHN Consejos 7175/53.

102. In addition to the letter from the cathedral chapter, letters from various persons in *ibid.* 7175/93 give a good perspective of events.

103. Petition of Sept. 1677 from Mariana Ruiz and Catalina Martínez, *ibid.* 7187.

104. Consultas of council of Aragon, 3 Aug. 1678 and 16 Jan. 1679, in ACA:CA 331.

105. Report from Feloaga, 14 May 1683, AGS:CJH 1064.

106. Uceda to council, 9 Jan. 1684, *ibid.* 1072.

107. Count of Paredes, viceroy of Valencia, to D. Pedro Fernández del Campo, 7 Aug. 1668, AGS Estado 2687.

108. In Chapter Thirteen below, in connection with Don Juan of Austria.

109. Consulta of Castile, 19 Jan. 1669, with correspondence, AHN Consejos 7179/11.

110. 'Relacion Historica del Tumulto de Madrid', copy in BL Eg. MS. 899. There is a further treatment of the riots of 1699 in Chap. XVI.

111. The memorial of the discontented is enclosed with correspondence of 14 July 1699 from the corregidor of Toledo, D. Alonso Pacheco, in AHN Consejos 7225.

112. From a declaration with a consulta of the council of Aragon of 5 Apr. 1690, ACA: CA 338. The Catalan revolts are discussed below, p. 213.

113. Corregidor of Calahorra, 18 Feb. 1665, AHN Consejos 7175.

114. D. Francisco de Ronquillo, 24 Feb. 1683, AGS:CJH 1059.

115. 'Relacion de la alteracion de Cordoba de 6 de Mayo de 652', BN MS. 9198/128.

116. 'Granada. Lo suzedido en sus inquietudes . . .', BN MS. 11017/106–119.

117. Viceroy to king, 26 Nov. 1689, ACA:CA 211/2.

118. Miguel Gerónimo Ferrer to duke, 16 Apr. 1647, AHN Osuna 247/1/16. In Lope de Vega's play *Fuenteovejuna* the whole village assumed joint responsibility for a killing and was subsequently pardoned.

119. Domínguez Ortiz, *Alteraciones*, appendix xvi, pp. 195–7.

120. Marquis of Rupit to viceroy of Catalonia, 2 Jan. 1690. AGS Estado 4142.

121. Domínguez Ortiz, *Alteraciones*, pp. 146–7.

122. Duke to D. Joseph de la Torre, 5 Aug. 1699, AHN Osuna 1021/99.

123. For the bishop of Vic, see the viceroy's letter of 4 Dec. 1689, AGS Estado 4137.

124. AHN Consejos 7261.

125. Viceroy to council of Aragon, 11 Dec. 1691, ACA:CA 586/21.

126. Diary of Ignacio Benavent, RCPV, MS. 41/17.

127. Domínguez Ortiz, *Alteraciones*, p. 59–60.
128. Consulta of Audiencia of Barcelona, 8 Apr. 1688, ACA:CA 240/43.
129. 'Tumultos de la ciudad de Sevilla', BN MS. 2383/147–55.
130. Domínguez Ortiz, *Alteraciones*, p. 149.
131. Council of Aragon to king, 5 Oct. 1688, ACA:CA 457.
132. See, e.g. the case of the uprising in Puzol in 1680: Viceroy of Valencia to king, 25 Feb. 1681, ACA:CA 921.
133. Játiva at this period was split into two factions, the *maulets* and the *botiflers*, whose struggle affected the whole region. Cf. the role of the *nyerros* and *cadells* in Catalonia: Elliott, *Catalans*, p. 75.
134. Letter to D. Manuel de Lupián, 14 Sept. 1694, ACA:CA 233/54.
135. Letter from city of Lérida, 27 Nov. 1689, *ibid.* 458.
136. Cf. the Austrian peasants in 1595 in my *Iron Century*, p. 339.
137. Letter to D. Joseph de Haro, 19 June 1688, ACA:CA 458; viceroy to king, 17 July 1688, *ibid.* 240.
138. Cf. my *Iron Century*, pp. 378–80.
139. Dean of Gandía to duke, 10 Aug. 1693, AHN Osuna 1030/5/1.
140. 'Relazion del tumulto', ACA:CA 458.
141. Petition of 1678, AHN Consejos 7188.
142. Viceroy to king, 26 Nov. 1689, ACA:CA 211/2.
143. Elliott, J. H., refers to 'Castile's immunity from rebellion after 1521', in his 'Revolution and continuity', *Past and Present*, 42 (1969), 46; and Laura Rodríguez in 'The Spanish riots of 1766', *ibid.*, 59 (1973), 145, refers to a lack of agitation as 'Spain's peculiarity'.
144. See the studies by Domínguez Ortiz, A., and Sánchez de Sopranis in *Estud. Hist. Soc. Esp.* 4 no. 2 (1960), pp. 293–426, 643–877.
145. The report that follows is from Ayerdi, 'Noticies de Valencia', BUV MS. 59, under June 1678.
146. Perales, J., *Décadas* (Valencia 1880), III, 800.
147. The riots of 1691 are detailed in the viceroy's report, ARV: RC 593/342–5; and in Benavent's diary at fo. 16 vo.
148. ACA:CA 148; AGS Gracia y Justicia 329.
149. Girard, *Commerce français*, pp. 254–5.
150. 'Relazion del estado', ACA:CA 22/1.
151. Consulta of council of Aragon, 11 Dec. 1683, ACA:CA 595/5.
152. A leading French merchant. The property looted from his house was valued at 30,000 ducats.
153. Official report to the viceroy by Pedro Borrull, 1692, in ACA:CA 844.
154. Viceroy Paredes to Queen Regent, 15 July 1668, *ibid.* 580/34/2, 4.
155. 'Memoire des françois qui sont en toutte l'éttendue d'Espagne, occupés en differents employs, suivant les advis des consuls françois establys dans le Royaume et autres gens qui peuvent en avoir la connoissance', in AE:CP (Esp) 64/273.
156. Villars, *Mémoires* (Paris 1893), p. 253. This figure has been reproduced by Girard, *Commerce*, p. 560.
157. Viceroy to D. Agustín Benedis, secretary of council of Aragon, 1674, ACA:CA 592/10.
158. 'Consulta a S.M. sobre los tumultos', 25 July 1691, ARV:RC libros registros 593/342.
159. Cf. the inflated figures cited in Girard, *op. cit.*, p. 567.
160. Labat, J. B., *Voyages* (Paris 1730), I, 286.

161. **Alcouffe, D.**, 'Emigrés français de Madrid', *Mél. Casa Velaz.* 2 (1966), 179–98.
162. Amelot in 1712, cited in Kamen, *War of Succession*, p. 121.
163. Alcouffe, *op. cit.*
164. See Girard, *op. cit.*, pp. 553–4.
165. ARV Maestre Racional leg. 486 exp. 9938.
166. *Ibid.*, exp. 9939: 'Memories de les francessos que havien de pagar'. The list has also been analysed by A Poitrineau, 'La inmigracion francesa', *Moneda y Crédito*, 137 (June 1976), 103–33.
167. Stanley ed., *Account of an embassy*.
168. **Santos, F.**, *El no importa de España* (Madrid 1667), pp. 140–4.
169. **Miñana**, *De bello rustico valentino*, cited in Kamen, *War of Succession*, p. 274.
170. For Gastau, ARV: RC, Estaments 546/108–11; for Jacob, *ibid.*, Maestre Racional, Tesoreria, 365/8733; for Estop, Benavent's diary, fo. 26 vo.
171. *Motivos que justifican la prohibicion de texidos*, ADZ 577/186.
172. AHPM, notary Antonio Bonilla, year 1670, 9767/165.
173. For Mataró, **Nadal, J.** and **Giralt, E.**, *La immigració francesa a Mataró* (Mataró 1966). See also the same authors' classic *La population catalane de 1553 à 1717* (Paris 1960). There is a short recent study on French in Barbastro by **Salas Ausens, J. A.**, 'Inmigración francesa', *Estudios* (Saragossa), 1977, 41–92. For Andalucia in 1689 see **Ponsot, P.**, 'Immigrants français', *Mél. Casa Velaz.*, 5 (1969), 331–41.
174. Girard, *Commerce*, p. 559.
175. Benavent, fo. 20.
176. ARV:RC libros registros 592/119–22.
177. *Memorial en razon de la despoblación* (1650), cap. 51, in Anés, *Memoriales*, p. 309.
178. Willughby, *Travels*, p. 497.
179. Ayerdi, 'Noticies', under June 1678.

# CHAPTER SEVEN

# The Rural Population

The rural history of *ancien régime* Spain has never been attempted. We know nothing about the life of the communities that represented most of the people in the peninsula. The sources agree, however, on the fragile existence of the primary social unit, the *pueblo*. It was constantly under threat from external authorities, from the tax system, and from the limits of its own resources. Its greatest strength – perhaps its only strength – was its community spirit, demonstrated particularly in Castile and León by the still surviving medieval practice of the *concejo general* (general assembly). In medieval Spain the concejo general or *cabildo abierto* (open council) was a system of direct democracy practised in smaller towns, whereby a public meeting of all the citizens was empowered to make decisions on important matters relating to the life of the community. The system was common even in the late seventeenth century. The town of Haro (near Miranda del Ebro) in 1666 held concejos 'according to the use and custom we have of meeting together at the sound of the bell'.[1] In practice the concejos survived only in areas where towns retained their independence or where the system of office-holding did not conflict with it. A public assembly, normally summoned after mass on a Sunday, tended to be called only in exceptional circumstances, as in Estepa in 1666,[2] when the reason was a proposal to relieve the municipal debt. Such meetings were invaluable mechanisms of social stability, and kept alive in smaller communities the democratic process that had all but disappeared at city and state level. The practice underscores both the ancient democratic traditions of Spain and the populism of the pueblo in modern times. Despite their internal tensions, towns often held together, particularly under external pressure.

One crucial question for a rural community was whether there were enough producers to help in the development of resources. Northern Spain fortunately had a high proportion of independent peasants. In the province of Burgos proprietors made up a good 36 per cent of the agricultural population. A survey of 1704 among the lands of eighty-four towns in Vizcaya showed that nearly 51 per cent of families working the land were proprietors.[3] Holdings were not always adequate. Galician smallholders, as we have seen, had to supplement their income by going south to help with the harvest. The independent peasants of Vizcaya and Catalonia seem to have managed quite well compared to the majority of small proprietors, whose condition was described by a Castilian writer in 1629 as 'the most wretched and downtrodden to be met with'.[4] Such peasants were, none the less, the producers. The threat to resources came from the presence everywhere of two groups – the privileged and tax-exempt on one hand, the rural unemployed on the other – that created unhealthy trends in the life of the community.

The first group, consisting of nobles, clergy and widows, was essentially parasitic, and has been so considered by all commentators. Even when nobles and widows contributed to the wealth of the town by their agricultural output, they escaped the most serious obligations by usually being exempt from taxes. Were they the principal liability? Take the example of Melgar (Valladolid), with seventy-eight households in 1686. Only thirteen, exactly one-sixth, were peasant farmers; thirty were clergy, widows and paupers, all unproductive and tax-exempt; and thirty-five, or some 45 per cent, were landless labourers (jornaleros).[5] By the standards of the time, only the thirteen farmer households were considered productive; their output would help to feed the town and also to pay its taxes. The labourers, in contrast, would have no resources of their own and were consequently held to be the principal liability on the town. In Santa Olalla (near Talavera de la Reina) in 1683, some 121 out of 169 households, or 71.6 per cent, were deemed unproductive in a complaint made by the town.[6] The figure for 'poor jornaleros' was ninety households, over half the town. These cases suggest that some 50 per cent at least of the rural population, equivalent to the greater part of the work force, contributed little if at all to local wealth.

Because historians do not normally take a pessimistic view of rural labourers, my argument needs to be put with some emphasis. Jornaleros were considered unproductive by contemporaries because they frequently had to migrate from the village in order to earn a living, and their efforts were seldom a contribution to the resources of the local community. They laboured on the estates of neighbouring landlords, or with the herds, or on the mountains cutting wood; they came home with provision for their families, but having made no addition to the wealth of their own pueblo. In all accounts of the time, the existence of this landless proletariat is taken to be an unfavourable factor. Yet if we add their numbers to those of the clergy, nobles and widows, we find that together these 'non-producers' constituted the bulk of the rural population. In seasons of low employment jornaleros were a severe burden on resources. In the whole province of Avila in 1693, nearly two-thirds of all households, both urban and rural, consisted of labourers of this type.[7] In the city of Ciudad Real in 1681 jornaleros ('who have nothing to sell but their labour') accounted for 500 of the 800 households.[8] Presumably most of them normally worked in the fields. In the principality of Asturias, where the total population in 1683 was put at 82,000 households, the number of 'pobres jornaleros' was put at 30,000 (36.6 per cent) households, 'and of these 10,369 are tax-paying, almost all tenants, and most of their produce goes in paying tithes, rents and dues'.[9]

The predominance of labourers in rural communities was balanced at the other end by a core of independent farmers whose cattle guaranteed the survival of agriculture. Take the 127 households that made up the village of Villamesias, near Trujillo, in 1690.[10] The base of the pyramid consisted of forty-seven households of poor jornaleros; the substance of the community consisted of sixty farmers owning between one and three plough teams; the remainder consisted of three ecclesiastical households, twelve widows and five minors, all exempt from taxes. Further profiles of rural population are given in Figure 7.1, first, of the

Fig. 7.1  Profile of two Castilian towns.

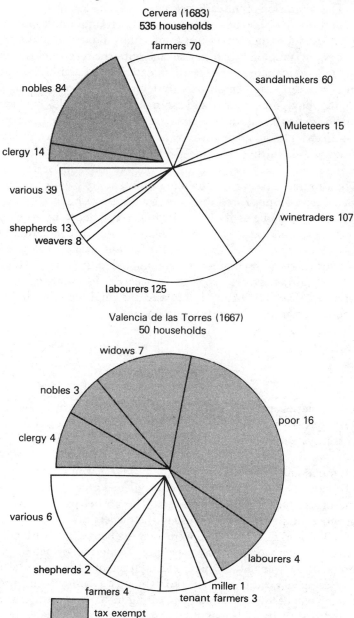

Cervera (1683)
535 households

farmers 70
sandalmakers 60
nobles 84
Muleteers 15
clergy 14
various 39
winetraders 107
shepherds 13
weavers 8
labourers 125

Valencia de las Torres (1667)
50 households

widows 7
nobles 3
poor 16
clergy 4
various 6
labourers 4
shepherds 2
miller 1
farmers 4
tenant farmers 3

tax exempt

197

thriving town of Cervera del Río Alhama (near Logroño) in 1683,[11] second, of the decaying town of Valencia de las Torres (Llerena) in 1667.[12]

The worst problems of the Spanish peasant had been associated with the depopulation and inflation of the early seventeenth century. From mid-century, as we have seen, agrarian output increased. In the countryside this was reflected in a greater demand for land and a corresponding rise in rents. The phenomenon has been illustrated by Angel García Sanz from the lands of the chapter of Segovia cathedral. The depression of the early century led to a fall in rent levels, between the 1590s and 1650s, of some 30 per cent. Other landlords complained of a decline of 50 per cent or more in returns from rentals. From the 1650s population levels in the Segovia region began to rise, and with them the yields from rented land.[13] Demographic increase generated an extension of arable throughout the area.[14] From the early eighteenth century legislation supported this trend by permitting the conversion of waste and common lands to arable. Evidence for the late seventeenth century is difficult to come by. There are however several examples of licences being granted to towns, allowing them to convert common lands to tillage or viticulture. The one given to Arjonilla (near Córdoba) in April 1663 allowed it to till and sow 400 fanegas of common land for a period of two years.[15] The aim was to enable the town to raise money to pay its tax debts. Most licences that I have found shared this concern to raise cash. In 1666 Estepa was allowed to lease out some of its lands for fourteen years.[16] In 1667 Corral de Almaguer (near Aranjuez), whose population had fallen by one-third in the early century, was allowed to lease out some of its communal lands (*propios*), to sell another portion, and to use common mountain land for pasture.[17] The village of La Alameda (Madrid) was in 1674 granted a licence to lease out commons.[18] The population rise of the late century stimulated the rural economy and helped to develop the resources of vulnerable communities.

## THE TAX BURDEN

Many contemporaries argued that the income of villages was quite sufficient, and that the real fault lay with excessive taxation. A modern authority has suggested that 'the fiscal system accelerated the rural depopulation of Castile'.[19] How true was this?

There is no doubt that too many people were exempt from taxes. They included those who were too poor to pay, privileged groups such as nobles and clergy, and others such as military officers. The greater part of a town's assets might therefore escape taxation because of the owners' status. In the village of Plasenzuela (Trujillo) in 1690, there were forty-six households with noble status and only fourteen that were *pecheros* (taxpayers). The former owned 67 per cent of capital assets, the latter only 33 per cent; so that most of the wealth in this community escaped taxation.[20] The problem was a familiar one throughout Spain. The town of Sarriá (Barcelona), appealing in 1679 against an assessment, demonstrated that of its 111 households only fourteen were liable to taxation.

The remainder were exempt in the following way: forty-four houses, although inhabited by peasant farmers, were owned by gentry and so enjoyed noble status; forty-four others belonged to the very poor; three belonged to familiars of the Inquisition and six to the jurats, exempt by their office.[21] Sarriá was an extreme example, but judging by the evidence it would not be very wrong to suggest that about half the population in an average small town might be exempt.

The obvious consequence of exemptions was that the most productive class, the peasant smallholder, had to shoulder a burden that ought to have been shared by the whole village. Peasant debt in such circumstances can readily be blamed on taxation. It does not follow, however, that the community always suffered because of exemptions. A village such as Plasenzuela might on the whole benefit as more and more of its assets eluded the grasp of the tax-gatherer. Provided the exempt fed their assets back into the village, the community would benefit substantially, regardless of the tenor of complaints they might make to the government.

Taxpayers in Spain were liable to the same obligations as in other countries: dues were payable to the Church, the king, the seigneur and the landlord. The Church tithe was traditionally given precedence over all other taxes. In most cases it was levied as a strict tenth of produce, though in some areas it was drawn from a tenth portion of arable specially set apart. The burden of the tithe was heavier than at first sight appears. Theoretically about a tenth of the initial harvest, it could represent as much as 50 per cent of net income after a taxpayer deducted other costs and taxes.[22] Opposition to tithes was frequent in the sixteenth century,[23] but feeling in the seventeenth was more subdued. Income from tithes did not go only to the local clergy but had to be shared with the bishop. In general the Church took about two-thirds, the Crown about one-third. Parish clergy received the *primicias*, which was normally the first portion of the tithe. Peasants avoided the full burden of the tithe by separating the most inferior tenth for the clergy. In Belmonte (Aragon) in 1691 the archbishop criticised local tithe methods, whereby 'many do not pay all but only the half and that which is the worst part, bringing the harvest to their homes and not wanting to pay on the threshing floor'.[24] Clergy wanting a fair share would insist on being present at the harvest before the division of grain.

Land rents, where applicable, may have been the biggest single financial burden. Salomon has argued that in sixteenth-century New Castile rents might be as much as four times the amount of the tithe.[25] Cellorigo in 1600 stated clearly that rent normally exceeded the tithe, and the situation was the same in the early nineteenth century.[26] The balance between rents and tithes may be considered from the example of the town of San Asensio, near Logroño. Its principal land rents were an annual 600 fanegas wheat to a nobleman, 700 to a monastery and various other dues amounting to a total of 1,936 fanegas annually. In the good year 1680 San Asensio's harvest in wheat came to 13,500 fanegas; tithes were 10 per cent, and rents would absorb a further 14.3 per cent. In the bad year 1681, however, when the harvest amounted to only 2,500 fanegas, the rents if enforced would have taken up as much as 77.4 per cent of the total, whereas tithes would be only 250 fanegas.[27] These figures apply only to the town's grain and not to its vineyards, which were also heavily burdened by dues. Tithes, in short, were a variable imposition, whereas rents continued at the same level regardless of output and could rapidly become a millstone round the necks of the rural community.

Seigneurial taxes varied so widely that it is impossible to generalise. Salomon suggests that in New Castile feudal impositions accounted for some 5 per cent of the total paid, in contrast to tithes and government dues, which each came to over 47 per cent of the tax total.[28] This conclusion need not be true for other regions, or for the seventeenth century. Thanks to the alienation of tax rights by an indebted exchequer, and the transfer of villages to lay control, it became possible for taxes paid to a seigneur to exceed government taxes. In numerous towns the most productive of all Castilian taxes, the alcabala, passed into noble hands. In 1681 the village of Almenar (near Soria) owed to the Crown for all its state taxes the sum of 55,685 maravedis annually; but to Don Pedro de Salcedo of Soria, its seigneur, its annual dues (including the alcabala) came to 174,216 maravedis, over three times as much.[29] The annual tax rate per household was 1,114 maravedis to the state and 3,484 to the seigneur.

Government taxes always provoked the strongest criticism. Many were new and consequently did not enjoy the sanction of tradition. In monetary terms, moreover, the burden had greatly increased. At the end of the sixteenth century a rural household in New Castile might have paid some 472 maravedis annually to the government.[30] A hundred years later this sum had increased by a probable average of 400 per cent. In a dozen villages near the city of Zamora in the year 1683, each household was required to pay annually for the three principal taxes (the alcabala, millones and unos por ciento) a sum varying from 1,082 to 2,428 maravedis.[31] This level was common to most cases in the records. The whole truth is not, however, reflected in the figures. The real burden could be much higher. Cabrejas del Pinar (Soria) was in royal jurisdiction and in 1683 its annual tax liability to the government was 108,338 maravedis, of which alcabalas made up 59.3 per cent and millones 29.2. There were 103 households in the town, creating an apparent liability of about 1,052 maravedis per household. But forty-seven of these were exempt, leaving only fifty-six to bear the whole burden, which therefore stood at 1,934 maravedis a household.[32] Other examples show quite incredible divergences. In Aldeanueva de Figueroa (Salamanca) the total payable per household was as much as 5,600 maravedis. The government was quick to recognise that this level of taxation was intolerable and threatened the very existence of the rural community.

It is difficult to believe that the tax system in Spain was any more inequitable than elsewhere in contemporary Europe. Martínez de Mata argued in mid-century not that the taxes were excessive but that the economic power of taxpayers had deteriorated.[33] Even if it were accepted that tax levels in Castile between 1580 and 1680 had risen by a nominal 400 per cent, we must remember that wheat prices over the same period had risen by some 300 per cent.[34] Tax increases can be shown to be not much greater than the rise in the cost of living. Within the same century scores of commissioners had visited towns and villages and systematically tried to reduce tax levels to the capacity of taxpayers. The

*Relaciones topográficas* of New Castile drawn up for Philip II in 1575–80[35] are a sample of the government's efforts. A similar programme was planned by Don Juan in 1678 but not brought to fruition. After dispensations had been granted for reasons of war, plague and natural disaster, the exchequer was probably left with a decline in its tax income. Why then did complaints continue to proliferate?

Consider the case of Yepes (Toledo): in 1678 it had 211 households, of which 67 per cent were liable to taxation; by 1689 the population had increased to 225 households, but the number of paupers had also risen, so that the proportion of taxpayers actually fell, to 45.8 per cent.[36] In a town that appeared to be growing there was in reality a decrease in taxpaying capacity. It is easy to see how onerous the tax burden could be in towns where there was not a rise but a drastic decline in population. One such case was Aldeanueva de Figueroa, mentioned above. The vanishing resources of this decaying town led the royal commissioner to advise that the tax burden be reduced by half in order to save the town from depopulation.[37] The case of Leganiel, near Huete, was similar. An official reported in November 1677:[38]

I went to the said town and received information, and from the testimony of six witnesses I examined it emerges that between 1636 and 1640 the town had about 300 households with 80 mule teams, and at present it has 147 households and 25 mule teams, and there are 150 fallen or ruined houses . . . and since they have to pay for their taxes the same as when they had 300 households, they were unable to pay.

In El Toboso (Toledo), 284 households in 1685 were likewise having to pay a tax figure originally levied on 1,247 households in 1627.[39] The conclusion is that changes in wealth and population within the towns were primarily responsible for the seemingly excessive weight of taxation. It is important to recognise, as historians seldom do, that the Spanish government made regular efforts to reduce the tax burden. In 1683, for instance, the alcabalas in the district of Llerena were reduced by 32 per cent, the millones by 33 per cent.[40] But factors beyond official control continued to affect the ability of Spaniards to pay taxes.

## THE BURDEN OF CENSOS

Production could improve, taxes could be remitted. No such relief was forthcoming for the largest nail in the coffin of the rural economy: debt. Debts could be either communal (contracted by the concejo) or private, but the effect was the same. Both damaged the wealth and resources of the town. The Spanish rural community was extremely vulnerable and could seldom count on a good surplus from produce. Profits were often diverted to the support of absentee landowners, and it was rare to find money for reinvestment. We do not know under what circumstances the villages of the sixteenth century drifted into debt. By the late sixteenth century much of the Castilian countryside had fallen into the hands of urban moneylenders.[41] A century later the cumulative effect of difficulties, disaster and debt could be seen throughout the countryside.

Censos (called censals in the Crown of Aragon) were loans made to municipalities, nobles or the peasantry, under varying conditions but at a moderate interest rate. In principle the extension of credit through censos might give peasants the capital they sorely needed for improvement. In practice many were unable to repay their debts in the time agreed. The burden of debt consequently mounted up in the countryside, and rural property had to be surrendered to urban moneylenders. As Bennassar has demonstrated for Valladolid in the sixteenth century, censos became less an aid to the peasantry than a means to dispossess them.[42]

Among the numerous cases of rural debt, let us take the official report on the twenty-five towns in the *partido* of Trujillo in 1690.[43] In 1680, twelve years after the end of the Portuguese wars, this area had a population of over 25,000 people, in itself a steep decline from previous years. By 1690 the population had fallen by a further 40 per cent. At the same time the wealth of the region, measured principally by its livestock, fell in value by 40 per cent. About one-fourth of the value of all peasant property in the area was mortgaged in censos, though in some villages the proportion was higher. In the town of Navalvillar, for example, whose population of 334 households in 1635 had declined to 150 by 1690, the censos of the townspeople added to the communal debt equalled in value the entire non-landed wealth and capital assets of the town. Navalvillar would have had to sell all its possessions to pay its debts. What was a community to do in such circumstances? The town of La Yesa in Valencia illustrates one desperate attempt to solve the problem.[44] In 1651 it had made an agreement to pay off its censals at sixpence in the pound for a period of twenty years. In 1671 it entered into another agreement to pay at fourpence in the pound for a duration of ten years. By 1681 the creditors were clamouring for final repayment. Predictably the town had by this time shrunk in size, from 200 to only eighty households, of whom thirty were in receipt of poor relief. The full debt on the town by 1681 was 24,800 lliures. To pay this off at the agreed annual rate was estimated to cost 1,030 lliures a year, whereas the available income from the town's resources was only 450 lliures. In the event La Yesa could only plead for a further twenty-year agreement.

It is easy to imagine the consequences of debt. An object lesson was the village of Rivaroja in Valencia, whose lord the marquis of Benavites complained in 1680 that because of debts totalling over 3,000 lliures the village had been entirely deserted. 'It is a town with over fifty households but now there is not one; as a result the fields lie untilled since the owners dare not work them.'[45] This was a state to which peasants were seldom if ever driven by government taxation alone. Though taxes and dues might well be heavy it was the burden of censos – that is, of money borrowed to meet bad years, to improve the soil, or simply to pay other debts – that was primarily responsible for the annihilation of the villages. Consider the plight of Uceda (near Alcalá de Henares), reduced from 227 households in 1639 to eighty-five in 1683.[46] The capital sum of censos on these inhibitants amounted to 138,137 maravedis per household. At the current payment rate of 5 per cent, this meant an annual debt obligation per household of 6,906 maravedis, about four times the level of government taxation.

The ruin of the countryside should not be laid at the door of the government, which always showed great concern for potential taxpayers. It only required a few unfavourable harvest years for a village to fall irreversibly into the hands of its creditors. Puente de Duero, a village which lies just outside Valladolid, was in 1688 reduced in population to 'only six poor jornaleros with no trade or crop and no harvest of either grain or wine, because the lands that most of its inhabitants used to have, have been seized by the public officials of Valladolid to pay for the several censos upon the village and its households'.[47] The censos contracted by the rural classes were placed almost without exception with moneyed men from the city. It was to those same interests that the peasants had to sell their land if they defaulted. As in other parts of Europe, the Spanish smallholder was economically destroyed by urban capitalists.

Who were the owners of censos? Over most of Spain the principal source of money for rural investment was the Church, but in many towns the nobles and professional classes filled this role and in commercial centres the merchants were the chief moneylenders. When peasants could not pay back loans their property was taken instead. What the townspeople did not purchase directly was seized by default. Arroyo, a little village outside Valladolid, was already dominated by the Church in the sixteenth century. A report drawn up in 1688, when Arroyo was wholly depopulated, estimated that apart from a few small tracts still owned by relatives, 'all the other lands and holdings belong to various citizens of this city, to the convent of Our Lady of Prado, to the Order of St Jerome and other entails, and most of all to the Order of St John'.[48] The process of alienation and of the extension of ecclesiastical control through censos, is strikingly illustrated by La Guardia, a town in Jaén province which in 1683 had 240 households.[49] The major industry of La Guardia was market gardening, with some culture of flax. In the period 1638–83 over 83 per cent of the town's holdings were alienated to citizens of Jaén, four-fifths to Church bodies; and their remaining property was heavily burdened with censos.

Pressure caused by the burden of debt destroyed rural communities from both without and within. A regular source of strife in pueblos and towns was the unequal weight of impositions. Inequality was tolerated only within certain parameters of status and tradition. A breaking point occurred in 1680 for the inhabitants of the village of Puzol in Valencia, who

realising the many debts and obligations on the town, and their limited means, managed for a while to make the landowners contribute jointly with themselves. After that they began to disagree, some saying that the landowners should pay in full like the inhabitants, others that they pay only half; which the landowners did not accept. The result in June 1680 was a riot involving most of the inhabitants.[50]

The breakdown described by the viceroy arose not from unequal taxation but from the failure of the rich to contribute to the communal debt. In different circumstances discontent could, as in the Valencian revolt of 1693, take the form of social rebellion.

The most common consequence of debt was depopulation, a theme on which I have already touched. Temporary depopulation was a tactic regularly employed by peasants who wished to escape accumulated debts and taxes. It was reported in 1682 of Murviedro (modern Sagunto) that 'it now has only a third of the inhabitants it used to have; to avoid continual tax demands they have changed their domicile, and so the town finds it impossible to pay its debts.'[51] When Castrobol (Valladolid) was depopulated in the 1680s, its parish priest kept a watchful eye on his village from the neighbouring town of Mayorga. Gómez Narro, also in Valladolid, was deserted by its people 'because of the fear of extortion by the tax-collectors'.[52] The rarity of complete desertion is seen in the case of Rubiales del Páramo (near Castrogeriz, in Burgos), which in 1681 was reduced to only one household, that of a lawyer called Don José de Palacio, who lived there with a servant. 'This depopulation has been caused', according to the official report, 'by the failure of crops over several years, and because the soil is very poor; also by the steep royal taxation; so that having nothing with which to pay they left their homes and went with their poor families to other villages.'[53]

## LAW AND ORDER

A distinguished historian has described the people of old regime France as essentially 'a rooted, sedentary, stable population', he goes on to say that 'old France is characterised not by unrest, social mobility and popular migration, but by sedentariness'.[54] The great sheet-anchor of stability, in Spain as in France, was the land. No labourer dependent on it for his living would leave it willingly for an uncertain future elsewhere. Although Spain as it emerged from the crisis of the early seventeenth century was still subject to rural population movements and seasonal migration, it is possible to overstate the degree of mobility among Spaniards. Only further enquiry, however, can tell us whether society was as sedentary as that of France.

The problem may simply be one of perspective. In Spain the relationship of larger social units to each other showed every sign of stability: provinces, cities, social classes tolerated a certain harmony. But in the comarcas and pueblos there was a level of disorder and violence that belies the accepted picture of a quiescent Spain. Much of this social tension was a necessary feature of the local community, generated within that community because there was no other universe wherein Spaniards existed.

For a brief look at rural tensions we shall consider the question of law and order in Valencia and Toledo. In the area around Valencia city judicial officials collaborated with village policemen in maintaining order. The city court of the magistrate for petty crimes (the so-called *Justicia de 300 sueldos*) in the years 1683 and 1684 seems to have dealt with little more than petty rural offences. Among these were theft of hay, unauthorised conversion of vines to pasture, letting cattle stray, plucking fruit from another's garden, and similar misdemeanours. The interesting aspect of the majority of cases before this court, is that offences were motivated by malice, not by poverty. The largest group of offences in 1684, for instance, were provocations committed by the family of Macia Bochons, a tailor of the village of Benetuser, against the land of the farmer Joseph Ballester.[55] Antagonisms on this level were part of everyday life. We need to go to the criminal court to discover the next level of conflict in the rural communities. The records of the criminal justice reveal regular violence in the pueblos. In 1684, to take one year at random, the justices had to deal with six murders and about ten major acts of violence in the villages of Vinalesa, Alboraya and Aldaya.[56] The general impression gained from the Valencian countryside at this epoch is that it was infested with apparently gratuitous violence. This was made all the more possible by the widespread — and illegal — possession of firearms. In 1668 the viceroy himself admitted, possibly with some exaggeration, that 'in the huerta there are 5,000 homes with nearly 15,000 arquebuses'.[57]

Violence was also typical of the *tierra* of Toledo. As in Valencia, the city of Toledo appointed and controlled the law officers in the rural areas.[58] Officials appointed in each village held their posts for a year and their activities were examined annually by a regidor of Toledo. The types of offence general in six of the villages of the tierra (Yebenes, Ventas, Pulgar, San Pablo, Nava and Navalpino) show a marked conformity with crime in the region of Valencia. Dr Weisser has analysed some 1,988 cases for the period 1550–1700. They cover too broad a period to offer an exact parallel, but a summary can be made as follows:[59]

| | | |
|---|---|---|
| Violence | 42.3 | (assault 21.2, disorderly conduct 8.8, insults 6.5, armed assault 3, brawling 2.8) |
| Lawbreaking | 19.6 | (breaking injunctions 11.3, dereliction of duty 4.7, price violations 3.6) |
| Rural offences | 10.6 | (theft of wood 6, illegal grazing 4.6) |
| Sexual offences | 5.6 | |
| Other | 21.9 | |

Weisser suggests that 'rape, homicide, mugging, armed robbery . . . were largely unknown' in the criminal behaviour of the Toledo region.[60] His evidence also shows that theft in the village communities was negligible.

Simple violence (such as brawls, insults and assaults) was provoked in both town and country by identical factors. Gaming houses were a regular source of abuse. In 1679 the authorities in Valencia enjoined the law officer of Alcira 'to take particular care in inspecting gaming houses and punishing those who play prohibited games'.[61] Drunkenness was the major precipitant of all the quarrels, challenges, woundings and occasional killings that seemed to be accepted as part of public behaviour. Prostitution and adultery also led to acts of violence. Beyond these categories of individual conflict there were cases of group conflict: feuds within and between families, between professional confraternities and even between parishes.

The tensions I have noted were part of the traditional environment. At certain stages there were intrusions into this fixed environment. The most decisive of such outside influences was the army. Thousands of young Spaniards from sheltered homes must in this imperial age have been thrust unwillingly into the open world of which they knew nothing. Take the case of Francisco Millán, born in 1639 in Alcázar de San Juan (Toledo).[62] Abandoned by his parents at eighteen months and brought up by relatives, at the age of thirteen he went off to Murcia to work for four years as a groom. He then went to Alicante, enlisted as a soldier and served in Tortosa for two years. After this he went to Valencia, entered the Franciscan Order for a year's novitiate, then returned to Alcázar where he married and had four children. It was in the same town of Alcázar that young Juan de Molina in 1651, at the age of sixteen, teamed up with a group of friends and enlisted for military service in Catalonia. He returned after the war and got married in Alcázar at the age of twenty.[63]

We know of these cases because both men were later in their lives denounced to the Inquisition for swearing and blasphemy, bad habits which they may well have picked up in the army. It is possible that they also brought new habits of violence with them. The degree of movement from Spanish rural communities, much of it engendered by military service and the search for employment, was modified by the eventual return of emigrants to their home *país*. But in the process there took place a significant broadening of the mentality of towns and villages which otherwise would have had limited contact with the world outside.

Disorder in rural society was not exclusively internal. Outside influences continually modified the character of existence. Soldiers passed through, itinerant beggars lingered. Outsiders might be responsible for theft and similar offences not normal in the community. But on balance it appears that violence and disorder were usually generated from within the pueblo. Clashes and squabbles were commonplace throughout the countryside. The duke of Bournonville, viceroy of Catalonia, informed the Crown in 1678 that 'with reference to the robberies, homicides and other crimes that are being committed in this principality, I have asked the Audiencia why they have not been punished and have been told that the scarcity of funds makes it impossible for them to appoint officials'.[64] Lack of a police force was a serious drawback in the Spanish countryside, not merely in Catalonia. The duke's comments referred primarily to areas under royal jurisdiction. An even more serious problem was constantly posed by the numerous seigneurial territories where royal officials had no authority. In Catalonia a remarkable case was that of the barony of Peralada.

The barony belonged to the count of Peralada, and lay in the mountainous north of Catalonia towards the French frontier, around the towns of Figueres, Navata and Massanet de Cabrenys.[65] Enquiries by the Audiencia of Barcelona into the breakdown of law and order in the area indicated that repeated French invasions had played some part in creating a problem, but a detailed enquiry by a special royal judge, Dr Buenaventura de Tristany, who visited the barony in November 1680, revealed that the subjects of the count were living in terror of the seigneurial officials and were unwilling to testify against them. His final report blamed the 'evil treatment of their vassals by the count and the countess his mother'; and concluded that 'in the county of Peralada from 1670 to 1680 there have been thirty-four crimes committed, among them twenty-two homicides'. The facts were undisputed, but nobody seems to have been brought to justice as a result.

The fact is that old regime Spain had neither the money nor the machinery to secure a peaceful countryside. In Catalonia in 1678, as the Sala Criminal of the Audiencia admitted, justice was enforced mainly through heavy fines, which at least helped to defray expenses; but the consequence was that criminals knew they could escape simply through payment.[66] Peacekeeping was therefore at all times a haphazard business. In every town law and order was normally the joint duty of the elected officials and one police officer, the alguacil or justicia. In Alcira (Valencia) the justicia was a deputy of the justicia of the city of Valencia; his single biggest expense was 50 lliures for the upkeep of his horse on which he patrolled the neighbourhood. There was throughout Spain a rudimentary police force of this type, but it could be a risky profession and murders of law officers were common.

The most famous of rural police forces was the Castilian *hermandad* or brotherhood, to which Queen Isabella had given formal organisation. In nature a voluntary mounted police force drawn from different localities, it was still active in New Castile at this time, though both its functions and its reputation had severely diminished. Some reports complain of it being little more than a gangster organisation. However, a petition to the Crown from the Santa Hermandad Vieja of New Castile in July 1687, described itself as divided into three sections based on Talavera, Toledo and Ciudad Real,[67] with considerable duties. Styling itself a 'shield to wayfarers, succour to property in the countryside', it described its various achievements in recent years: the break-up and punishment in 1677 of a large gang of counterfeiters, the pursuit and capture of bandits. Distance was no object: they had chased and captured near the border with Portugal a bandit calling himself Pedro Andrés, who led a band active in Extremadura under the name of 'The Gipsies'.


## BANDITRY IN SPAIN

The part of Spain best known for banditry is Catalonia, thanks to contemporary works such as *Don Quijote* and to the researches of modern scholars.[68] The reputation survived in the late seventeenth century. A writer of 1678 wrote that

> Los montes de Cataluña
> Son pueblos de salteadores.[69]

(The mountains of Catalonia are the homes of highwaymen). The opinion is confirmed by the terms of a proclamation issued by the viceroy of Catalonia, the marquis of Cerralbo, in 1676, against 'the many great and enormous crimes committed and perpetrated in the principality of Catalonia and county of Cerdaña by robbers, highwaymen and bandits, armed with arquebuses and blunderbusses and other weapons, as well as by other persons, both in the mountains, woods and deserted places as well as in the cities, towns and centres of dense population'.[70] The period in fact experienced a relative decline in Catalan banditry. Violence continued in the countryside. The viceroy, duke of Bournonville, complained again in 1679 of 'the liberty and daring with which many criminals and men of evil life commit atrocious murders and other horrifying crimes, without fear of justice'.[71] But no bandit leaders of importance emerged in the late century. The national struggles of the 1640s seem to have brought about their eclipse and they never again played a significant role in Catalan history.[72]

Banditry continued, on the other hand, to be important in the rest of Spain. Little is known of its incidence in the north, in the Basque lands or in upper Aragon. In the rest of the country it was regular and widespread. All the documents deal with it as a regular phenomenon rather than as a sudden breakdown in order.

It has been suggested that though aristocratic banditry was common in earlier times, popular banditry was unknown before the 1630s and was brought about by the crisis of a Spain in decline.[73] This view cannot be substantiated. Even in the sixteenth century, the social problem in southern Spain, aggravated by Morisco discontent, gave rise to popular banditry. A decree of 1562 referring to 'bandits, robbers and delinquents from Aragon, Catalonia and Castile' taking refuge in Valencia,[74] emphasises the broad popular basis of the phenomenon.

There are few references to bandits in the north and centre of Spain. The council of Castile in January 1681 reported that 'the roads from Madrid to San Sebastián are infested with highwaymen. . . . It is understood that these persons are cavalry soldiers from the companies quartered in Old Castile.'[75] A complaint of the following year, 1682, refers to bandits in Aragon robbing 'the ordinary mail taking letters from Lérida to Saragossa'. On this occasion the viceroy of Catalonia stated that theft of the mail was a common occurrence in Aragon.[76] The larger bands operating in the Crown of Aragon tended to take refuge behind the fueros by committing crimes in one realm and then hiding in another. One case reported in 1689 was that of the Aragonese bandit calling himself Don Juan de Borja, who 'with a band of thieves had made several incursions from Valencia and Aragon into the whole of Old Castile as far as Navarre'.[77]

Bandits were most active in the southern half of Spain. We can find their bases over the entire sweep from Valencia to Extremadura. A proportion were gipsy or Morisco by origin, but most were undoubtedly Old Christian. Our Cadiz merchant Raymond Lantéry, when he travelled from Ecija to Córdoba in 1687, took care to have with him eight companions and 'eleven shot-guns, all of which were necessary since this road to Madrid was where most robberies had occurred. It is said that the robbers come from Ecija and are gentlemen of the town.'[78]

The kingdom of Murcia was heavily infested by bandits in this period. In 1685 the president of the council of Castile commented that 'the kingdom of Murcia and its region is the area where this misfortune has been longest known, and their numbers have increased either through the proximity of the kingdom of Valencia or because of the local inhabitants' giving support.'[79]

The mountainous terrain provided ideal cover. The biggest and most notorious bandit centre was the town of Yecla, which lay close enough to the frontiers of Castile and Valencia for criminals from those realms to seek refuge. In 1669 a lengthy report from the corregidor of nearby Chinchilla (Albacete) outlined the extent of the problem.[80] This was resolved in spring 1671 when sixty of the Yecla bandits accepted an amnesty by which they went overseas for a period of service in Orán.[81] But the problem continued. In 1678 a large band under the Menarques brothers Miguel and Ginés were active locally, and were strong enough for the council to suggest that two companies of cavalry be sent against them.[82]

The most serious threat came from the bandits Martín Muñoz and Pedro Ponce. Muñoz, the principal bandit in Yecla territory, teamed up in April 1671 with others from Cieza, entered Yecla one night, killed two peace officers and 'escaped into the harsh mountain-side'.[83] In 1679, according to a local citizen, Muñoz appeared to have the active support of several rich men and clergy in Yecla.[84] In November 1683 he besieged the town with eighty armed men, freed a bandit from the jail, and stole 300 of the town's sheep and cattle.[85] By this time Muñoz was collaborating with Pedro Ponce and his gang. In August 1684 they murdered the alcalde mayor of Albacete,[86] and were terrorising the whole region as far north as Cuenca. In October Pedro Ponce and his followers entered Iniesta (Cuenca) in broad daylight, hanged the alcalde from the king's public gibbet, and murdered several others. In the same month they burned the houses of their enemies and abducted a married woman. The other officials of Iniesta proved so weak-kneed that the council of Castile immediately sequestrated the town's independent jurisdiction and vested it in the king by appointing a royal corregidor. One unfortunate alcalde of Iniesta complained to the government in February 1685 that Pedro Ponce and his bandits had wounded him, burnt down his house and that of his mother, stolen all his valuables and grain, destroyed his vines, slaughtered his draught animals and cut the throats of all his sheep.[87] Ponce then moved into Castile and the sierra de Guadarrama. In the first week of April 1685 he murdered the alguacil mayor of Arévalo and the alcalde of Torrelodones; in the second week he was reported in Alcalá, the week after in Cuenca.[88] For some twenty years, apparently, Muñoz and Ponce terrorised the law officers of Castile.

In New Castile and Andalucia the symptoms were the same. A report of 1679 states that 'in the cities of Baza and Huéscar and other surrounding towns there are more than seventy bandits of evil life and ways who commit various crimes and excesses and some murders, but are protected and sheltered by citizens of those places'.[89] The official sent to examine matters, Don Alonso de Herrera, a judge from the Chancery of Granada, doubted whether the bandits could be brought to justice, in view of 'the protection they get from those in power in that region'. Beyond the primary issue of crime, then, lay the insuperable issue of local jurisdictions over which the crown had limited control.

Some of the persistent banditry in Jaén was aristocratic in leadership, to judge by the negotiations conducted by the bishop of Jaén in 1684 with two of their leaders.[90] One was Don Pedro de Escobedo, a knight of Calatrava, who had outlawed himself with seven companions and a slave for over two years, on the excuse that he had been unjustly accused of various crimes; the other was Don

Juan de Frias, who had built up a band of ten followers, most of humble origin. Both leaders agreed to purge their crimes by military service on one of the war fronts. Escobedo and Frias virtually controlled the countryside around Jaén; they acted together to smuggle wine and defraud the exchequer, and entered the city openly by day or night to kill enemies or hold people to ransom. 'Here everybody fears them', reported a treasury official. 'They are so much masters of life and property that they can do whatever they dare. . . . They destroy the rich by sending them papers demanding money, and if they refuse they break into their homes. And the poor groan and keep quiet for fear of their lives.'[91]

By the last decade of the reign the level of banditry was apparently as high as ever. In 1695 the Council sent out a special official, Don Manuel Ventura, to act against bandits and highwaymen in Castile in the area of Mondéjar, Huete, Cuenca and beyond.[92] The council in the same period, commenting on 'the infestation of the Sierra Morena, La Mancha and the kingdom of Jaén and other parts by different individuals and bands of criminals who continually threaten the villages and roads with murders, robberies, rapes and other crimes', commissioned a noble from the town of Torrenueva to pursue two specific bands, and pardoned him for any excesses committed during his highly successful work.[93]

Valencian banditry at this time was primarily 'popular' in character.[94] Morisco participation disappeared with the expulsion of their community in the early century, and the new aristocratic landholders were concerned to maintain stability. In the countryside of Valencia, however, there was a high level of rural violence. Over two-thirds of all the criminal cases coming before the justiciar for crime in 1692, involved use of prohibited firearms.[95] The contemporary diary of Joachim Ayerdi noted an average of about two murders a month in the region around Valencia city. The record for the month of March 1678 was a dismal catalogue of violence: on the fourth a watchman in Rovella was murdered; on the sixteenth a woman was slashed by a man, another was publicly flogged for prostitution, and a farmer in Cuart murdered his wife; on the twentieth a notary was murdered, and another man was stabbed in the face; on the twenty-second a woman was found dead; on the twenty-sixth the seven-year-old son of a leading nobleman stabbed another boy.[96] The bandits came from a violent background where a variety of causes contributed to social tensions and aggression.

In Valencia the viceroys were obstructed in their campaign against bandits both by a lack of funds and by the *furs* of the realm, which forbade any extraordinary measures such as raising troops or money or pursuing fugitives into seigneurial jurisdictions. When the duke of Veraguas exercised rough justice on a friar-bandit in September 1680 by hanging him from the walls of the prison, he was excommunicated, made to do public penance in bare feet, and summarily recalled to Madrid.[97] Viceroys had no soldiers. 'In this kingdom', a committee reported in 1693, 'the viceroys have no forces to repress popular riots; the only resource they have is the provincial militia, the mounted coastguard, and the fifty horse of the viceregal guard.'[98] The extensive number of independent feudal jurisdictions in the kingdom impeded the authority of the justices. Banditry, claimed the viceroy marquis of Castelrodrigo in 1692, 'is like grass which springs from the soil and is watered by the judicial administration'. He summed up his views in an observation that eventually proved to be true: 'It goes without saying that there will be bandits so long as there are fueros.'[99]

The intensity of banditry in Valencia remained constant throughout the late century. In the 1660s the most enterprising bandit was Joseph Artus, who on one occasion attempted to kidnap the viceroy. In the 1670s it was Juan Berenguer, who operated in the *marina* of Valencia. 'Bandit movements in this part of Valencia', runs a report sent to the king in 1681, referring to the marina, 'are ancient and well-known; although they are made up of different bands, each with its own head, for active operations they join together to form only two.'[100] The most successful method of curbing their activities was to induce their leaders to accept a free pardon and go overseas for an agreed period of military service. Artus, for example, went to Naples in 1668 with thirty-five members of his band; Berenguer went to Milan in 1680 with 118 others under his command. This way of dealing with bandits was common in other Mediterranean countries. It did not, however, guarantee a cure to the problem. The most prominent bandit of the 1680s was Mathias Oltra, who twice made agreements, to go to Milan and then to Orán, and broke them. He eventually went with fifty of his men to Naples in 1685, for a period of three years. On his return he resumed his career. It was not until 1696, as we are told by the diarist Benavent, that 'the soldiers of the guard caught the famous bandit Mathias Oltra in the village of Torres Torres, and after he had killed a soldier they took him, gravely wounded, to the prison. He died there repentant and was buried in San Bartolomé.'[101]

Extremely harsh measures under the marquis of Castelrodrigo in the 1690s, including an unprecedented frequency in the use of the death penalty, failed to curb the bandits. When the new viceroy, Don Alonso de Guzmán, took up office in 1696, he commented on 'the innumerable bandits who in their gangs dominate both the countryside and the towns'.[102] The authorities inevitably considered banditry to be a temporary form of crime. In reality it was deeply rooted in the environment. Bandits were heavily regionalised in certain comarcas where they drew strength from family links and local loyalties. In Valencia bandits were always in the prime of life. The age distribution of 113 members of Berenguer's band is set out in Figure 7.2.[103] The youngest was aged twelve, the oldest forty-six.

With the exception of a few university students and an occasional noble, bandits were recruited from the villages. Most of the accused appearing before the courts on charges of banditry were described in depositions as peasants or labourers (*llavrador*). Their popular origins contributed to the esteem in which even the most notorious killers were held. Clergy were often friends of the bandits and gave them shelter. Some clergy, like the Franciscan friar Francisco Sánchez, noted as responsible in 1693 for several robberies and killings, were themselves bandits.[104] The admiration with which men like this were regarded – Benavent in 1671 referred to two executed bandits as 'great friends of Valencia'[105] – can in part be explained by the fact that their crimes were not normally directed against the community but rather against personal enemies and law officers.

The principal cause driving Valencians into crime was poverty. Men who had

Fig. 7.2   Age distribution of 113 members of a bandit group in Valencia, 1680.

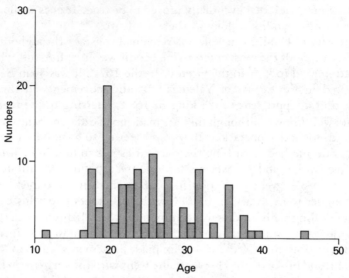

spent some time struggling for a meagre living, gave up the struggle and went out on to the highways. In the trial of the bandit Vicent Ferrer of Torrent, it was stated that 'in order to meet the obligations of his household he had to apply himself to earn a daily wage (*jornal*)', a situation that was considered unacceptable by the peasant who was giving testimony. The work ethic in rural Valencia held that it demeaned a free man if he had to labour each and every day in order to survive. A fellow-villager testifying for Christófol Montesinos, sandal-maker from Vall de Uxó, said that 'in order to maintain and feed his family he had to be working at his job for the most part, or making journeys as a sandal-vendor, going through the towns and villages of this kingdom'. A witness for Pere Cortés, labourer of Benisanó, said that he was totally poor and 'had to be working continuously with his hands to earn a daily wage, and after he changed this way of living he went about in the dress and costume of a bandit'. There was, finally, Joseph Vicent, who had a mill in the village of Paterna. A labourer from Cuart testified of him:[106] 'He was a poor man, so impoverished that in order to maintain his family it was necessary for him to work continuously, and since he was unable to meet the obligations of the mill he had to sell it as well as the goods he possessed, and to break up his household, and then he went to serve His Majesty in Naples.' According to another witness, 'in Lent 1693 he returned from Naples and was arrested for killing his wife'. After that he fled and became a bandit.

## PEASANT REVOLTS

The high level of violence in the Spanish countryside acted as a form of safety valve. Passions that in another country might have led to public protest, were in

Spain diffused into at least three major directions: the widespread and illegal holding of firearms; general collusion with bandits; and frequent attacks on tax officials. In Castile the most hated tax was the millones, first introduced under Philip II to offset the cost of the Armada, and levied principally on food. Its unpopularity was recognised by the government. In 1686 the archbishop of Saragossa, then president of the council of Castile, put all his authority behind a move to abolish the tax which was, in his opinion, 'the one that most harms and prejudices the body of the kingdom'.[107] Revolts against the millones were rendered unnecessary by the way in which Castilians either subverted the tax by fraud or attacked officials operating the tax. In this reign the death rate among millones officials was unacceptably high. Evidence for the year 1682 in Andalucia refers to the murder of two tax-men by smugglers in Jérez, and the murder of three others in Seville.[108] A correspondent from Motril, reporting general hostility to the millones, wrote of 'continual riots every day and armed men in the streets'. The council of Finance admitted that attacks on the tax were common not only in Andalucia 'but throughout the realm, where the same thing can be seen: in Segovia the inspector of millones was killed for wishing to stop a quantity of smuggled wine, and the same has happened in Cuenca and in Jérez'.[109]

In addition to rural violence the late seventeenth century experienced rural uprisings. There appears to have been one in Galicia in 1673.[110] Towards the end of the reign there occurred the two largest peasant revolts of the entire Habsburg period.

The so-called revolt of the *barretines* in Catalonia in 1688–89 was indubitably the biggest rural uprising of seventeenth-century Spain.[111] Unlike the uprising of the *segadors* (reapers) in 1640, which was aggravated by a general political and military crisis in Spain, that of 1688 had humbler origins. The immediate cause was the failure of the harvest in 1687, brought about by the locust swarms. The breeding of the locusts stopped during the bitter cold of March 1688, leaving the peasantry in a state of ruin. War broke out with France in 1689, but thanks to the grain crisis the villages refused to accept billeting of troops. A crisis similar to that which had faced Olivares in 1640 was therefore likely. On 20 May, 1687, three leading members of the Diputació – Don Antoni Sayol and his brother Don Daniel Sayol, both canons of Barcelona, and Don Joseph Ciges, the *oidor militar* – addressed a letter to the king, drawing attention to the grievances provoked by the billeting. Their letter raised a storm in Barcelona. The other Diputats (the Diputació consisted of six) were furious that a letter should have been sent claiming to speak on behalf of the whole body. The viceroy, the marquis of Leganés, accused them of stirring up rebellion. The three were arrested, removed from their posts, and replaced by three others.

On Tuesday, 7 October, Leganés ordered a cavalry detachment to move into the town of Centellas, which was refusing to pay the contribution for the troops. One soldier fell into a dispute with a woman over a chicken, and struck her. She took up the traditional cry, '*Via fora!*', the tocsin was rung, and the whole village and its neighbourhood seized arms.[112] The cavalry withdrew, and the viceroy used the good offices of Enric Torras, jurat of the village of Sant Quirce de Centellas, to try and win the townspeople over. 'The blaze in Centellas has been put out', Feliu de la Peña observed to Don Pedro de Aragon, president of the council, 'but the ashes are scattered throughout Catalonia, and we are in a state of great disquiet.'[113] Opposition to billeting was rooted in the most densely populated part of Catalonia: 'the environs of Barcelona up to Penedés in the region of Tarragona, Vallès, Llusanes, the plain of Vic, and the sea coast', to quote a contemporary.[114] There was widespread anxiety that the authorities should not overreact. 'Experience has taught', Feliu pointed out to Don Pedro, 'that in Catalonia sweet medicine cures, sharp medicine aggravates.' There was a clear understanding of the lot of the peasant. In October Dr Olaguer Monserrat, the chancellor of the Audiencia, had written to Don Pedro that

the poverty of the peasants who pay the contribution is such that the sad tale would cause the hardest heart to weep. The rich, such as the clergy, gentry, lawyers and doctors, and there are an infinite number of these, are exempt, and they extend this exemption to houses they do not live in. They claim that payment is the king's responsibility. The officials of the Holy Office also fall into this category. Thus the burden of the poor peasant increases, and the poor soldier who is lodged also suffers, since many of them have to beg in order to eat, and this burden has lasted for the last thirty-seven years.[115]

The quarrel did not die down, and broke out with renewed vigour in the spring of 1688. On 4 April a dispute between a cavalry soldier in the village of Villamayor and the woman in whose house he was billeted, led to a riot and the ringing of tocsins. Armed peasants poured in 'from Centellas, Garriga, and from other places as far as Tona, all shouting together that they wanted to get rid of the tax on the principality, and other highly seditious demands'.[116] The insurgents decided to march on the town of Mataró, which they entered in force on 6 April. The next day at 8 a.m. they began a demonstration, shouting 'Visca la terra!' (Long live the land!) and rang the bells, demanding that Mataró should join their cause. The common people of Mataró rallied to them, and four of the town's leading citizens[117] were forced (under the threat of having their houses burned) to accompany the malcontents and to act as their spokesmen. The entire host then decided to march in force on Barcelona and to present their demands there. By 8 April they were in sight of the city walls. On Friday, 9 April, as the astonished secretary of the Consell de Cent reported in the minutes, 'from the walls of the city could be seen a great number of armed people from the province, covering the entire plain before the city, from Sant Andreu to Hospitalet'. By Saturday, he noted, 'according to information the numbers exceed 18,000 people'.[118]

The demands of the rebels were five in number: a general pardon for all rebels, an adjustment in the military contribution, a pardon for the three imprisoned Diputats, an official recording of all the foregoing, and the release of an imprisoned notary. The Audiencia met in immediate session and advised the viceroy not to concede anything. But the massed hordes of segadors camped outside the walls forced it to change its attitude. Most of the peasants were armed, and amply supplied with food, so that a siege of the city might have been successful. Mataró alone sent a daily 750 individual rations for its people encamped before Barcelona. From their positions, reported the Audiencia, the peasants 'called on the city's inhabitants who were looking at them to rise up and take to arms, telling them not to miss this opportunity, that there would be no other, claiming that it was now time for the students to take up arms, and crying out "Long live the king, death to the bad government", and many other insults to public order and the government'.

On Saturday, 10 April, the Audiencia agreed with the viceroy that a pardon should be granted. On Sunday the peasants started drifting back to their homes; by Monday they had all gone. The Audiencia lamented its surrender, but explained to the king[119] that

the present state of this province is the unhappiest that can be imagined, for the law has no authority because of the lack of funds in the treasury, and now with these disorders justice has totally perished. Officials cannot leave the city in safety to draw up prosecutions or to receive testimony about crimes, nor even to arrest wrongdoers; and though we pass sentences they cannot be carried out. This is aggravated by excesses in use of firearms, since all the roads are full of people who openly carry them. Soldiers cannot cross the province in safety . . .

The statements of the Audiencia show that the ruling classes of Barcelona had received a quite unprecedented shock. This was the first uprising to have taken place in Catalonia for some thirty-five years. Both the Consell de Cent and the viceroy capitulated to all the rebel demands. The peasants then made it known that they required not merely the pardon of the Diputats but their return to their posts in the Diputació; if this were not done by 20 May they would return to besiege Barcelona. The council of Aragon reported on 1 May that everyone in Barcelona was absolutely terrified by the threat and that the authorities unanimously advised concession.

For the rest of 1688 Catalonia passed effectively into the hands of the rebels. Clashes took place in a number of places. In June in Sabadell a group of fifty or sixty segadors entered the town and issued a declaration in the main square 'prohibiting', said the viceroy, 'the inhabitants from using any other segadors but themselves, under the threat of killing those who did otherwise, and burning their houses'. In the same month after a major riot in Manresa the populace took over the city and forced the council to abolish the tithes. 'There is a constellation of risings', a correspondent wrote to the secretary of the council of Aragon.

In Sant Boy de Llobregat some segadors tried to burn a house; in Solivella the lord of the place was besieged, they tried to burn his villa because he had made no effort to kill the locusts, the rioters set fire to his woods and fields and vineyards and virtually the whole area was reduced to ashes. In Castelbó the governor had to withdraw. . . . In Martorell, a riot. . . . Also in Cardona. . . . And in all these tumults there have been cries of *Visca la terra!*[120]

Agitation died down in the autumn. There was a plentiful harvest in 1688, the first good one for four years. War was declared in April 1689, and the authorities were concerned to avoid provocations. But the conflict was about to enter into a second stage. In spring 1689 the new viceroy, the duke of Villahermosa, was obliged to levy a *donativo* on the province in order to finance the troops. He obtained the approval of the Consell de Cent, of some of the Diputats, and 'of representatives of each estament. When he attempted to collect the tax, however, he encountered a solid refusal to pay. In April leaflets began circulating through Catalonia, calling for opposition to the donativo and to any other taxes not agreed upon in a full assembly of the Corts. The situation was discussed anxiously in Madrid. Feeling was unanimous in the councils that the situation was too close to that of 1640, and that no Corts should be summoned.[121]

The attitude of Madrid was supported fully by all the higher authorities in Barcelona. The leaders of the rural opposition found themselves abandoned by their own upper classes. Indeed the major significance of the revolts of 1688–89 was the divergence of interest between urban and rural Catalonia, and the clear realisation that Barcelona was not necessarily Catalonia. In October 1689 a native of Centellas, Joan Castelló, known as the Roig of Centellas, was arrested for having persuaded peasants not to pay the donativo. He was tortured and executed. Under torture he implicated Enric Torras and others in the movement against the donativo. Torras had since March 1689 been seeking French help against what he regarded as illegal taxation.[122] He was joined in his campaign against taxes and billeting, by Joseph Rocafort and by Antoni Soler, a wealthy landowner from Sant Boy de Llobregat. Their plans were for an insurrection in the late autumn.

On Sunday, 20 November, at 10 a.m., five cavalry soldiers and officers were on their way to the village of Arbos, south of Vilafranca, when they were surrounded by about fifty armed men led by Pedro Terméns and forced to give up their arms. On Monday in the village of Gavá a cavalry company was set upon and its arms and horses taken by the peasants.[123] The movement spread rapidly from village to village. By 23 November, troops were being disarmed as far afield as Santa Coloma and Moncada. Masses of peasants moved from village to village, and the tocsin was sounded throughout the countryside. The peasants aimed solely to disarm, not to attack, the soldiers. The cavalry were ordered to withdraw to Barcelona. On Thursday, 24 November, the viceroy decided on punitive reprisals. A force of 500 men and 800 horse, with two pieces of artillery, was sent out to punish the village of Sant Feliu de Llobregat. The troops razed the village, killed thirty villagers, and took another thirty-four prisoner. The survivors retreated to the hills. On Friday the villagers from Moncada cut off the water supplies to Barcelona. The viceroy sent out 400 men and 200 horse to drive them away. By Saturday the segadors had risen.

Angered by the sacking of Sant Feliu, the entire peasantry from Vilafranca in the south to the plain of Vic in the north marched on the capital. 'They have occupied all the roads', reported a correspondent from Lérida, 'so that nobody can pass, and they are sending papers through all the villages up to the plain of Urgell, ordering under pain of death that all men aged over fourteen should go to Barcelona where the Army of the Land is. The papers are signed in the name of The Land.'[124] 'At two o'clock on the 27th', writes Feliu in his Anales, 'we could see from Barcelona a large number of peasants.'[125] Their numbers were in the region of 8,000. Villahermosa refused to repeat the inaction shown by Leganés in the previous year and sent out four companies to engage the peasants. The soldiers were forced back, but the viceroy's tough policy eventually proved successful.[126] In three subsequent incidents in Mataró, Sarriá and La Roca, the peasants were driven back with casualties. On 30 November, dismayed, they lifted the siege of Barcelona and started drifting back home. On 2 December Antoni Soler was treacherously murdered and his head taken to Barcelona and exposed in a cage on the wall of the Generalitat. Deprived of its most notable leader, the rebel movement collapsed.

The rebel movement of 1688–89 failed to win support from any prominent person, clerical or lay, in Catalonia. The only significant sympathy came from the bishop of Vic, who was sharply criticised in both Barcelona and Madrid. In the public pardon issued by the viceroy on 14 March 1690 it was claimed that 'only a minority of the principality, and people of low degree, took part in the sedition'.[127] Figure 7.3, which locates the main areas of agitation in 1688–89, shows that on the contrary a very large part of Catalonia was affected.

Fig. 7.3   The revolt of 1688–89 in Catalonia.

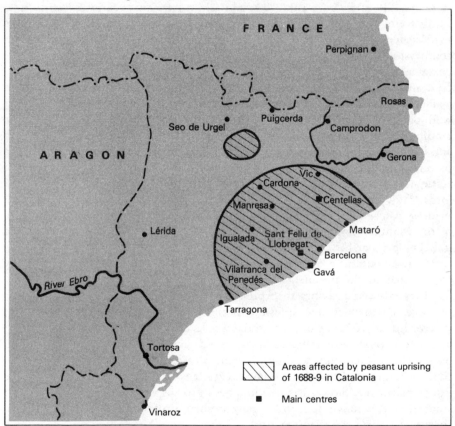

Nor were the rebels exclusively of low degree. All their leaders were mature, respected and wealthy men, holders of public office with authority over other men. Torras was in a position in 1689 to offer to raise 15,000 men for the viceroy in exchange for concessions.[128] Some of the leaders, like Soler and Terméns, both of advanced years in 1689, were undoubtedly veterans of the struggles of the 1640s. They all shared a marked hostility to Castilians. Torras and Rocafort, in conversations with French agents in 1689, 'denounced the Spaniards, and said that they only worked to destroy the Catalans, as they had done at the siege of Salces'.[129]

Because of the extent of the rising, punishment had to be selective. Antoni Soler was foully betrayed and murdered by his own adopted grandson, who cut off his head and took it to the viceroy to claim the reward of 500 lliures. Soler's house was razed to the ground and a tablet erected on the spot to perpetuate his infamy. 'This was the end of Antoni Soler, a man of seventy-four years, who lived peacefully and beloved by his neighbours.'[130] Only seven people were excepted from the general pardon issued by the viceroy. Most of them fled to French Catalonia, where they joined other insurgents fighting under the French flag against Spain.

Four years after Soler's murder, and while remnants of the *barretines* were vainly trying to ignite another revolt in Catalonia, a major insurrection took place in Valencia.[131] There had been no major insurrection in the Valencian countryside since the Germanías of 1521. Since then the whole structure of peasant landholding had changed. The lands vacated by the Moriscos were repopulated by Old Christians, the overwhelming majority from elsewhere in Valencia itself. Many of the new settlers benefited. But an even greater number were obliged to settle the land on harsh and onerous terms laid down by the landlords. The Cistercian monastery at Valldigna gave its settlers a house each and land, but required in return a huge proportion of peasant produce.[132] In the barony of Alberique, a property of the duke of Infantado, the conditions of settlement put most of the settlers into a state of permanent debt towards their lords.[133] By mid-century in Alberique, many of the peasants were overwhelmed by debts whose value exceeded that of their assets. In the town of Muro, property of the count of Cocentaina, the burdens on the peasants were unusually and unbelievably harsh.[134]

The unfavourable economic situation of the Valencian peasantry undoubtedly contributed to the prevalence of banditry in that region. At the same time, banditry allowed peasants to express their grievances in a way that released pressures and avoided any explosion or confrontation. Only one attempt at a riot is recorded, in 1672, against the hated monks of the monastery at Valldigna.[135] This uneasy peace was disrupted by two men, a lawyer (Dr Leonardo Pintor) and a notary (Felix Vilanova), who on different occasions advised groups of peasants that the seigneurial taxes were completely illegal and against their own and the king's privileges. Slowly the peasants began to suspect that right was on their side. It was this conviction, and not any harshening of their economic conditions, that precipitated the events of 1693.

Vilanova, a notary of Albalat de Cegart, began his agitation in 1689 but nothing came of it then. In February 1693 he was again active, this time in the village of Petrés. The orderly way in which peasant grievances were formulated leaves no doubt that the whole movement was initiated by the privileged sectors of the rural community, by lawyers, clergy and officials (*síndics*). Representatives of thirty-five seigneurial towns in central Valencia elected three of their number to present their case. The three were Felix Rubio, Francisco García and Bartolomé Pelegrín, all síndics of their towns. The viceroy, Castelrodrigo, accepted their right to a legal examination of their claims and convoked a special session of lawyers and members of the Audiencia. On 12 February these legal officials ruled that there was no basis for the claims. Undismayed, the síndics went personally in March to Madrid, taking with them a concise memorial which they presented to the council of Aragon. The viceroy, however, had meanwhile reported unfavourably on their pretensions, and on 'the villages of the marina, which have been accustomed to afflict this realm with bandits, and are naturally inclined to violence and disturbance'. The council of Aragon felt that there was no case to answer, and that all such questions were not in its jurisdiction but only in the Audiencia's. An attempt was made to arrest García, who fled from Madrid.

The rejected memorial[136] claimed that the rulers of Aragon had, since the thirteenth century, granted their Christian vassals in the realm freedom from taxes. Notwithstanding this, the present lords 'have levied on their poor vassals such extraordinary and heavy tribute that they have reduced them to utter poverty and misery'. They gave specific examples: in his villages the Admiral of Aragon took one-fifth of all grain and one-third of all oil; the duke of Gandía took one-sixth of all grain and one-fourth of all wine and oil; the count of Villafranqueza in Benimeli took one-fourth of all produce. The monastery of Valldigna, seigneur of the towns of Tabernes, Benifairó and Simat, took

from every household two hens and four sous, one-third of carob-beans, one-third of oil, one-fourth of wheat, two sous from every fanega of land, four reales on every fanega of alfalfa land, one pig of every six born, two chickens from every farm; and vassals are not allowed to sell meat themselves, and the monastery arranges a high price for them to pay and a low one for itself; and when the flour-mill broke down the monastery forced its vassals to mend it at their expense.

The Audiencia of Valencia, seigneur of the village of Benilloba, took a sixth of all grain and a third of all oil.

With the Audiencia as a party to the dispute, it seemed unlikely that the claims of the villages would be heard at all. In May and June several communities refused to pay their dues. The first protest was in Carlet, whose síndic Felix Rubio was then in Madrid. A troop of cavalry was despatched to the village. By early May, García was back in Valencia, going through the countryside and coordinating resistance to payment of the seigneurial dues from the forthcoming harvest. In June the viceroy ordered the arrest of Dr Leonardo Pintor for encouraging Petrés not to pay. On 26 June twelve farmers from Ráfol de Almunia, García's village, made a statement before a notary that they would pay their dues if their lords could present written proof of their privileges.[137] On 8 July the archbishop of Valencia, Juan Thomás de Rocaberti, published a pastoral letter in which he argued against the claims of the peasants, and announced the sending of some clergy to the villages to explain the real position.[138] His letter was strongly criticised by the council of Aragon, which felt it was not firm enough. On 9 July a riot broke out in Villalonga, a town of the duke of Gandía.

The cause of the riot was the arrest by the duke's bailiff, Don Miguel Pérez Pastor, of four peasants who refused to pay their dues. As soon as the news broke, the inhabitants of nearby villages made immediately for Villalonga. It is clear that the peasants, with the help of the bandits, had long been preparing their defences. In the villages of the duke, in Potríes, Almoynas and other places, the officials encouraged the people to join; in Villalonga the law officers did nothing to stop the riot.[139] On 10 July Pastor wrote that in Villalonga 'this morning I am assured that there are three thousand people, with drums and banners, shouting "Long live the poor!" and "Death to the bad government!" ' The peasants held a general assembly in Fuente de Encarrós, where they put themselves on a military footing, elected José Navarro, a surgeon-barber of Muro, as their General del *Eixercit dels Agermanats* (evoking by this name the cause of the Germanías of 1521); and chose Francisco García as their síndic. They then sent an ultimatum to the bailiff, demanding the release of the prisoners. On 11 July they arrived at El Real de Gandía, where the four prisoners were handed over. Pastor reported of the rebels that they were 'men with no military experience, over a third of them unarmed. . . . The leader is Francisco García of Ráfol, and only he is on horse.'[140]

The marquis of Castelrodrigo reacted speedily to the news of the uprising. He put the campaign in the hands of his lieutenant Don Ventura Ferrer. By 13 July Ferrer had mobilised in Gandía 400 horse, 400 infantry and two artillery pieces. The viceregal guard, the coast guard and the provincial militia were the main body of this force. Meanwhile steps were taken to secure the main cities of the marina, particularly Játiva. On the 14th Ferrer spent the night in Albaida and was reinforced by local militia. The army of the Agermanats was variously estimated at between 1,500 and 4,000, but there was never any doubt about the outcome of a clash between the forces. On the 15th the rebels set out from their base at Muro to confront the royal troops. At dusk there was a two-hour engagement near the village of Cela de Núñez, in which the peasants were completely routed. Ventura Ferrer reported that 'a dozen of them were killed, the same number wounded, forty-three taken, and no casualty suffered by us except a slight wound to one of Your Excellency's guard'.

The victory was not complete, for the two principal leaders of the uprising, Navarro and García, managed to escape. At the end of July the chief administrator of the estates of Gandía informed the duke that 'there is no certainty that there will not be another disturbance, since García is going around stirring people up and claiming to have found the papers proving the freedom they claim'.[141] It was impossible to find men willing to take on administration of taxes. Rumours of another rising were rife: in July a friar reported a plan to rise at the end of the year, with the help of the students in the university of Valencia; in August an anonymous paper circulating through the villages announced a general rendezvous for 8 September. Throughout the summer and autumn the troops remained in a state of alert. On 29 September, Castelrodrigo reported to Madrid that 'García is going around the villages with a number of men, in the hope of raising 400 men to persuade other towns to join him. . . . He can be seen by day in Ráfol, Tormos and Sagra, but at night withdraws to the hills.'

Navarro remained at liberty until December 1693. He lived mainly in Villena, where he had many relatives. Finally on 14 December he was arrested. In the course of 1694 sentence was pronounced against those involved in the rebellion. All the prisoners were put into the Serranos tower in Valencia; some (those captured in July 1693) were there for sixteen months. Most were condemned to the galleys. José Navarro was the only one condemned to death, a sentence carried out on 1 March 1694. This tall, slim, fair-eyed man was a person of property and position in his home town of Muro.[142] The nominal rather than real leader of the rebels, he was an unfortunate victim of repression. García, who gave leadership to the whole movement, was aged forty in 1693, of medium height, a dark man with a swarthy complexion and slow of speech. He managed to escape all attempts to capture him, and kept alive among the peasantry the flame of insurrection. In 1698 a petition to be pardoned and allowed home with his wife and four children, was firmly rejected by the council of Aragon. The refusal was certainly a major error. When the War of Succession moved into Valencia, García played a primary part in arousing the peasants of the marina against their seigneurial oppressors.[143]

The uprising of 1693, restricted in its extent to the marina and to the seigneurial holdings centred on the duchy of Gandía, was as much a reflection of the economic tensions in the region as banditry was. Like all popular movements in Spain, it was heavily supported by the rural clergy.[144] The viceroy singled out the parish priest of Ráfol de Almunia for 'preaching publicly that the peasants were not obliged to make payments to the seigneurs, that the dues were unjust and that they should not be afraid to steal from their lords: Francisco García was one of his flock and learnt from his teaching'. Carmelite and Franciscan friars helped actively in the rebellion: by August many of them were languishing in the cells. The upper clergy and the secular lords combined to crush the pretensions of the people.

## NOTES

1. AGS:CJH 892.
2. Consulta of Finance, 23 June 1667, *ibid*. 894.
3. Fernández de Pinedo, *Crecimiento económico*, pp. 258, 262–3.
4. Benito de Peñalosa, cited in Ortiz, *Golden Age*, p. 153.
5. AGS:CJH 1963.
6. Petition of 16 Oct. 1683, *ibid*. 1055.
7. The figure is about 11,000 out of 17,734 vecinos: report of 30 June 1683 by D. Pedro Núñez de Prado in AGS:CJH 1960.
8. Printed memorial of 1681 in *ibid*. 1038.
9. Report by marquis of Castillo, 14 Aug. 1683, from Oviedo, in *ibid*. 1056.
10. Notarial statement of 26 Oct. 1690 in *ibid*. 1158.
11. Report of Don Pedro Veluti, from Cervera, 14 May 1683, *ibid*. 1062.
12. Report by council of Finance, *ibid*. 890.
13. García Sanz, *Segovia*, pp. 300–3.
14. *Ibid*., p. 153.
15. AGS:CJH 890.

16. *Ibid.* 894.
17. *Ibid.* 892.
18. *Ibid.* 978.
19. Lynch, *Spain*, II, 141–2.
20. Deposition of 26 Oct. 1690 on towns around Trujillo, *ibid.* 1158.
21. ACA:CA 531.
22. See the nineteenth-century estimate in Anés, *Las crisis agrarias*, p. 294.
23. See e.g. **Garzón Pareja, M.**, *Diezmos y Tributos* (Granada 1974), pp. 93–4.
24. Tolosana, *Belmonte*, p. 270.
25. Salomon, *La campagne*, p. 243.
26. Cf. Anés, *op. cit.* p. 294.
27. Report of 21 Oct. 1681 by D. Pedro de Veluti, AGS:CJH 1030.
28. Salomon, *op. cit.* p. 234.
29. Report by D. Pedro de Veluti, 10 Apr. 1683, AGS:CJH 1067.
30. Salomon, *op. cit.* p. 234.
31. Calculated from a statement in AGS: CJH 1055.
32. Don Pedro de Veluti to council, 22 July 1683, *ibid.* 1060.
33. *Discurso Cuarto en el cual se prueba como los demasiados tributos no han despoblado a España*, in Anés, ed., *Memoriales*, p. 133–6.
34. Cf. Hamilton, *American Treasure*, p. 241.
35. They are the basis for Salomon's study, *La campagne*.
36. Statement dated 1690 in *ibid.* 1169. Paupers had increased from under a third to over half the population.
37. Don Joseph de Aguirre, 7 Dec. 1686, *ibid.* 1963.
38. Report of 2 Nov. 1677, *ibid.* 1941.
39. Petition from the town, 1684, in *ibid.* 1086.
40. Statement by Don Luis Pacheco in *ibid.* 1057.
41. Cf. Salomon, *op. cit.*, pp. 247–50; and Bennassar, *Valladolid*, pp. 326–8.
42. Bennassar, *op. cit.*, pp. 258–64.
43. Details that follow are based on the report of 26 Oct. 1690 in AGS:CJH 1158.
44. Petition of Dec. 1681 in ACA:CA 923.
45. Report from marquis, in *ibid.* 921.
46. Report of 19 Nov. 1683 by D. Miguel Crespo, AGS:CJH 1078.
47. 'Minuta de la planta de las villas y lugares de la provincia de Valladolid mas adeudados': AGS:CJH 1029.
48. *Ibid.*
49. Don Leonardo de la Cueba to council of Finance, 14 Apr. 1683, *ibid.*, 1063.
50. Viceroy of Valencia to king, 25 Feb. 1681, ACA:CA 921.
51. *Ibid.* 923.
52. Both towns in 'Minuta de la planta', AGS:CJH 1029.
53. *Ibid.* 1033.
54. **Goubert, P.**, *The Ancien Régime* (London 1973) p. 42.
55. All details from ARV Maestre Racional, Justicia de 300 sueldos, leg. 274 expedientes 6844, 6848, 6849.
56. ARV Maestre Racional, Justicia criminal, leg. 266 expediente 6421.
57. Count of Paredes to Queen Regent, 15 July 1668, ACA:CA 580/34/2.
58. What follows is drawn from **Weisser, M.**, 'Crime and subsistence', unpublished Ph.D. Thesis (Northwestern University, 1972).
59. I have modified a couple of Weisser's categories.
60. 'Crime and subsistence', p. 119.

61. Order to the justicia of Alcira, 27 July 1679, in ARV Maestre Racional: Justicia, leg. 275 expediente 6900.
62. Statement in AHN Inq. 41/21.
63. *Ibid.* 41/26.
64. Bournonville to king, 3 Dec. 1678, ACA:CA 439.
65. What follows is taken from the folder of documents on the case in *ibid.* 443.
66. Report from Sala Criminal, 12 Nov. 1678, *ibid.* 439.
67. Printed petition, in AHN Consejos 7199/25.
68. In particular **Reglà, J.**, *El bandolerisme* (Barcelona 1966).
69. Quoted in García, *Ideas de los españoles*, p. 300.
70. *Edictes e cridas fetas* (Barcelona 1676), in BCB Follets Bonsoms 2850.
71. Bournonville to king, 10 June 1679, ACA:CA 437.
72. There are scattered references to bandits in the late seventeenth century in Reglà, *op. cit.*, pp. 183–5.
73. Tomás y Valiente, *Derecho penal*, pp. 265–6. For bandits in the earlier period see also Deleito y Piñuela, *La mala vida*, pp. 98–105.
74. Cited in **García Martínez, S.**, *Bandolerismo, piratería* (Valencia 1977), p. 16.
75. Consulta of 3 Jan. 1681, AHN Consejos 7191.
76. Bournonville to Don Francisco Izquierdo, secretary of the council of Aragon, 31 Oct. 1682, ACA:CA 446.
77. Count of Oropesa to duke of Villahermosa, viceroy of Catalonia, 27 Aug. 1689, BN MS. 2400/310.
78. Lantéry, *Memorias*, p. 212.
79. Report of 28 Mar. 1685, AHN Consejos 7197/19.
80. Report from corregidor, 14 Mar. 1669, *ibid.* 7179/87.
81. *Ibid.* 7181/31.
82. Consulta of council, 4 Nov. 1678, *ibid.* 7188.
83. Report by council, 21 Apr. 1671, *ibid.* 7181/69.
84. Letter of June 1679 in *ibid.* 7189.
85. Corregidor of Yecla, 30 Nov. 1683, *ibid.* 7152/5.
86. Corregidor of Hellín, 30 Aug. 1684, *ibid.* 7152/18.
87. Memorial in *ibid.* 7152.
88. Council reports of April 1685 in *ibid.*
89. Consulta of council, 8 March 1679, *ibid.* 7189.
90. Bishop of Jaén to council, 8 Nov. 1684, *ibid.* 7152/14.
91. D. León de la Cueba to council of Finance, 17 Dec. 1683, AGS:CJH 1063.
92. Report by Ventura, 30 Oct. 1695, AHN Consejos 7208/32.
93. Consulta of 24 Jan. 1696, *ibid.* 7209/4.
94. What follows is derived from **Kamen, H.**, 'Banditry in Valencia', *Jl. Eur. Econ. Hist.* 3 (1974), 654–87, where fuller details and references are given.
95. ARV Maestre Racional, criminal, leg. 267 expediente 6429.
96. Ayerdi, 'Noticies', BUV MS. 59.
97. Benavent, 'Cosas mas notables', RCPV MKS. 41/8; and ARV:RC Estamentos 546/323 ff.
98. Report of 21 July 1693, ACA:CA 581/17.
99. Viceroy to king, 25 Mar. 1692. *ibid.* 930.
100. 'Informe que se embió a Su Magestad', 1681, ARV:RC libros registros 591/196–8. On bandits at this period see also **García Martínez, S.**, 'Josep Cases', *I Cong. Hist. País Val.* (Valencia 1976), III, 460–72.
101. Benavent, f. 26.

102. Viceroy to king, 11 Dec. 1696, ACA:CA 935.

103. Details from 'Lista de los bandidos', ARV:RC libros registros 591/48–152.

104. Consulta of Aragon, 16 Oct. 1693, ACA:CA 844.

105. Benavent, f. 4 vo.

106. This and preceding testimonies come from ARV Maestre Racional, Tesorería, Informaciones de Pobreza, leg. 365 expediente 8733, year 1693: 'Primer quadern de miserabilitat'.

107. The archbishop, D. Antonio Ibáñez de la Riba Herrera, was president of the Committee of Means which suggested abolition. The proposal to abolish was made in a council consulta of 5 Dec. 1686. See the archbishop's memorial in BL Add. MS. 21536/185–201. He put the proposal forward again in 1701. For other memoranda by him, see **Gan Giménez, P.**, 'Las Consultas del Presidente Ibáñez', *Miscelenea Antonio Marín Ocete* (Granada 1974), I, pp. 295–322.

108. For Jérez, the letter from D. Pedro de Legaso to D. Gabriel Pacheco, 13 Dec. 1682, in AGS:CJH 1054; for Seville, the consulta of the Sala de Millones of 3 June 1682, in *ibid*. 1049.

109. Consulta of Sala de Millones, of 16 Feb. and 24 Sept. 1682, in *ibid*. 1049.

110. **Durán, J. A.**, *Historia de caciques* (Madrid 1972), p. 103.

111. The barretina was the cap worn by Catalan peasants. The account that follows is drawn mainly from **Kamen, H.**, 'Catalan peasant rising of 1688', *J M H*, 49 (June 1977), 210–30, which gives fuller details and references.

112. Account in letter of Dr Olaguer Monserrat to D. Pedro de Aragon, 11 Oct. 1687, ACA:CA 240/43.

113. Feliu to D. Pedro, 17 Oct. 1687, *ibid*.

114. 'Sucesos de Cataluña', BCB MS. 504/19.

115. Letter cited in n. 112 above.

116. Report from the Audiencia, 8 Apr. 1688, ACA:CA 240/43.

117. The four were Miguel Pou y Partella, Juan Pablo Gassia, Melchor de Palau, and Joseph Feu y Feliu.

118. *Dietari de l'Antich Consell* (Barcelona 1965), XX, 311.

119. This and the previous quotation are from their letter of 14 Apr. 1688, ACA:CA 240/43.

120. Letter to D. Joseph de Haro y Lara, 19 June 1688, *ibid*. 458.

121. Consultas of the council of State, 26 Apr. and 7 May 1689, AGS Estado 4137. Villahermosa suspended the donativo in May.

122. For the links with France, see Kamen, 'Catalan Peasant Rising', pp. 221–4.

123. The best summary of the events of these days is the letter of Villahermosa to the king of 26 Nov. 1689 in ACA:CA 211/2.

124. Copy of letter dated 27 Nov. 1689, *ibid*. 458.

125. *Anales*, III p. 402.

126. Villahermosa to council, 4 Dec. 1689, AGS Estado 4137.

127. Decree with consulta of 5 April 1690, ACA:CA 388.

128. Testimony of Coq, Guerre A[1] 899/52.

129. Guerre A[1] 899/39. José Rocafort y Portell was a *ciutadà honrat* and since 1681 *veguer* of the city of Balaguer.

130. A transcription of the tablet is in AGS Estado 4137, my quotation and other details on Soler are from 'Sucesos de Cataluña', fo. 68. Soler's son was allowed back to the property in 1690 after paying a composition. The adopted grandson, Pau Petit, had to flee with his accomplice to Madrid in January 1690 because of threats to his life. Despite its distaste for him, the government found him employment.

131. The summary that follows is based on **Salvá Ballester, A.**, *Sedicion del año 1693* (Valencia 1941); **Momblanch y Gonzálbez, F.**, *La Segunda Germanía* (Alicante 1957); **García Martínez, S.**, 'Problemas del campo', *VIII Cong. Hist. Cor. Aragon*, **3** no. 3 (Valencia 1973), 215–34; and **Kamen, H.**, 'Nueva luz sobre la segunda Germanía', *Homenaje Reglà* (Valencia 1975) I, 647–59. See also Casey, *Kingdom of Valencia*, pp. 118–20.

132. See **Domínguez Ortiz, A.**, and **Vincent B.**, *Historia de los Moriscos* (Madrid 1978), p. 220.

133. **Ciscar Pallares, E.**, 'El endeudamiento del campesinado valenciano', *Estudis*, 4 (1975), 147–62.

134. Momblanch, *op. cit.* There is a good summary of peasant grievances and of the subsequent rebellion in Lynch, *Spain*, II, 258–60.

135. García Martínez, 'Problemas', p. 216.

136. Printed in Kamen, 'Nueva luz', pp. 649–50.

137. García Martínez, *op. cit.* p. 220.

138. The pastoral is printed in Momblanch, *op. cit.* p. 113.

139. See the report on events in the duke's estates, in Kamen, 'Nueva luz', pp. 657–9.

140. Letters of Pérez Pastor to viceroy, 10 and 11 July 1693, ACA:CA 581/2/14–15.

141. Dr Francisco Pí to duke, 27 July 1693, AHN Osuna 1030/5/9.

142. Details of his property in Kamen, 'Nueva luz', p. 655.

143. See Kamen, *War of Succession*, pp. 275–9.

144. Martínez, *op. cit.* p. 225; Casey, *Kingdom of Valencia*, p. 119.

# CHAPTER EIGHT

# The Aristocracy

'Though this be a great monarchy', the English ambassador Stanhope wrote from Madrid in 1691, 'yet it has at present much aristocracy in it, where every grandee is a sort of prince.'[1] By the late seventeenth century Spain was probably the only west European country to be completely and unquestionably under the control of its titled aristocracy. Other nations, notably the France of Louis XIV, had found leisurely pursuits for the higher nobility; and had extended the powers of the state at the expense of the traditional ruling class. The Spanish Habsburgs, on the other hand, had fostered their nobles and upheld their authority. It is unlikely that any significant change in the status or function of the aristocracy occurred during the seventeenth century. They remained unmolested in their privileges until the War of Succession in the early eighteenth century.

Spain was unique in having a huge proportion of its population classified as noble. The picture varied from the Basque provinces of Guipúzcoa and Vizcaya, where virtually the whole population claimed noble status, to the south of Spain where less than one per cent could claim this privilege.[2] With so many 'nobles', considerable effort was spent on clarifying distinct status levels within the class. The humblest level was the hidalgo, heavily satirised in contemporary literature as impoverished but proud; and indeed pride or *honor* was the basic ethic of the class. There were some obvious privileges that an hidalgo might claim, such as exemption from taxes, but the rank was desired less for such material gain than for the honour it bestowed. An hidalgo who was such by race (like the Basques) or by common fame, was more to be esteemed than one who bought his position or had to prove it in court by obtaining a certificate (*ejecutoria*). In any case, an hidalgo was required to live in a style befitting his status, and invited contempt when he fell into poverty or put on pretences of wealth. Foreign travellers were amused by the attempts of humble Spaniards to maintain their pretensions to status. Muret in 1666, commenting on the right of hidalgos to bear arms, reported that 'the cobbler wears a sword when he is mending shoes, the barber when he is shaving, the apothecary when he is dispensing'.[3]

The level of nobility above these unnumbered hidalgos was that of *caballero*. These were recognisably noble, with adequate wealth, some sort of title, and other distinctions such as a coat of arms. Many hidalgos called themselves caballeros with impunity, for the distinctions between grades were usually so fine as to be indistinguishable. More generally, caballeros were the largest recognisable class of noble and tended to live in the towns, where their ranks were infiltrated by the rising middle class. In the towns they held public offices and much of the commercial business. Though most owned country properties their authority in the countryside was limited, 'few of them having any priviledges for Hunting or Hawking'.[4] Among the caballeros we may also place the numerous holders of estates or encomiendas owned by the great military Orders of Santiago, Calatrava and Alcántara in Castile, and Montesa and St John in the Crown of Aragon.[5] The last of these was the only Order to cover the whole peninsula. It was divided into four priories, one in Navarre, two in Aragon and one in Castile — León.

The higher aristocracy in Castile was divided into two status levels. Charles V had set at the top of the noble pyramid a fixed number of twenty-five great lords who were termed grandees (grandes) and whose main privilege was to be addressed by the king as 'cousin' and to be able to keep their hats on in his presence. Below this elite stood the other great nobles, known generally as the titled aristocracy (títulos). In the course of the seventeenth century both grandees and títulos increased in number. Thanks to intermarriage between the various great families, the Castilian nobles soon found themselves mixed with non-Castilian houses. But there remained quite distinctive features in the aristocracy of the Crown of Aragon.

There were far fewer titled nobles in the realms of Aragon. In the 1660s Aragon had two dukes, seventeen marquises, twenty-one counts and four viscounts; by 1709 there were still two dukes, but over twenty-eight marquises. Valencia in 1709 had four dukes, over twenty-three marquises, and twenty-one counts.[6] Catalonia had by far the fewest titled nobles. In Aragon[7] a small core of families claimed descent from the ricos hombres or great lords of medieval times. They made up the Estamento de Nobles or second chamber of the four-chamber Cortes. Below them came the very much larger class of lower nobility or Caballeros, known also in Aragon as infanzones, who were privileged to have a separate chamber in the Cortes and formed the most active section of the Aragonese nobility. Rivalry between the higher and lower aristocracy of Aragon broke out into open conflict in the public assemblies held during the reign of Charles II.

In Valencia both higher and lower aristocracy sat together in the Estament Militar, where decisions could be made only on a unanimous vote.[8] In Catalonia the rarity of titled nobles[9] meant that the Estament (or Braç) Militar was dominated by nobles who were caballeros rather than great nobles. In both Catalonia and Valencia a significant part in political life was played by the gentry group known as ciutadans honrats (distinguished citizens). Madramany defines the ciutadans as 'a sort of middle class between the common people and the nobility', and says that they rose 'through political office and through letters'.[10] Many of them, as we shall see, also rose through commerce. In Saragossa likewise there was a body of ciudadanos honrados. Juridically these men were nobles, but because of their peculiar position in the social hierarchy I shall be discussing them in the context of the middle class.

The privileges of the noble class were wideranging. When the government opposed granting noble status to a petitioner, it often did so because of the noble right to tax exemption. There were however a great many other privileges, as we learn from a report made by the viceroy of Valencia in 1689:[11]

The principal privileges of caballeros and nobles are: not to be arrested for debt save in cases of debt to the king; not to be distrained in their arms, horse, bed or goods; not to be summoned to seigneurial courts save where they have estates in that jurisdiction; not to be compelled to enlist in the army, save their duty to pursue rebels against the king in the town where they live but not beyond; to enjoy the dowry of their wife on her death; in criminal cases not to be imprisoned in the public gaols; they may not be banished unheard; they may sit when making confession; they may not be tortured for any cause, or condemned to any degrading punishment; they may not be sentenced to death by this Audiencia without a special report by the council to Your Majesty.

The most obvious sign of noble power was their extensive jurisdiction. I have already noted above, in considering the towns, that the aristocracy controlled most of the centres of population, which in turn consolidated their authority in the countryside.

An outstanding example of noble jurisdictions may be found in Don Juan Tomás Enríquez de Cabrera (1646–1705), duke of Rioseco and count of Melgar, known simply as the Admiral of Castile, a grandee of the first class and one of the most eminent in lineage of all the nobles.[12] At the end of the century he owned the jurisdiction of ninety-seven towns and villages, not counting twelve deserted villages. We have already seen that ownership implied 'jurisdiction, lordship and vassalage'. In practice the seigneur controlled most taxation, justice and public administration. The vast area under the Admiral's jurisdiction was focused on the city of Medina de Rioseco. In Medina he had the right to nominate the corregidor, six councillors (regidores), three justices (one *procurador general* and two *procuradores de causas*), one municipal notary (*escribanía de ayuntamiento*) and fourteen public notaries. In every town under his jurisdiction he had the right to nominate the chief judicial officials, for justice was an essential privilege of lordship. In addition to control over secular matters he had extensive privileges over local churches. In Medina, for example, he was the 'patron' or lord of two monasteries and two nunneries, presumably founded by his predecessors. In the other towns the Admiral was either patron of a church or had the right to appoint members of the local clergy.

In Aragon and Catalonia jurisdictions were on a more limited scale. Among the exceptions was the duchy of Cardona in Catalonia. Travelling through it in 1664, Willughby commented that 'Cardona is a Dukedom containing three or four villages besides the town. The Duke thereof is one of the richest Grandees of Spain. . . . He lives for the most part at Madrid, but sends every three years a Governour. The King of Spain hath nothing at all to do with this city.'[13] Willughby's estimate of Cardona's size was inaccurate: a statement of 1682 shows 157 towns in the duke's jurisdiction, but the nominal total was certainly higher.[14] The wealth of the duchy made it the object of one of the biggest cases of litigation in this century.

In the kingdom of Aragon there were few great estates. The nobles, on the other hand, held a theory that great lords had 'absolute' powers over their subjects, a theory that was seldom put into practice but which provoked constant opposition from the lesser nobility and the urban classes.[15] In the Cortes of 1677 the Aragonese towns presented a discussion paper in which they stated that 'the secular lords of the kingdom of Aragon claim to have absolute power over their vassals, and to be able to take their property and lives without them having any appeal to His Majesty or to the royal officials'. After a debate it was accordingly agreed by the third chamber (Caballeros) of the Cortes to pass a law removing any such absolute right of lords over vassals.[16]

Though there was a theoretical right of appeal from the judgment of a great lord, in practice his privileges were difficult to contest. The lord was the final authority in an average seigneurial town: Willughby grasped the right spirit when asserting that the king had no power in Cardona. Take as an example the rights exercised in the Valencian town of Denia by the marquis of Denia, better known under his Castilian title of duke of Medinaceli.[17] By a royal privilege of 1431 the marquis was granted full ownership of the towns of Denia, Ayora and Javea, the only restriction being that he could not coin money. Further extensions of privilege at the beginning of the seventeenth century made his rights only just short of absolute. He exercised full and supreme legal jurisdiction; nominated the corregidor, mayor and councillors; elected the notaries; filled the posts of officers of the peace; and appointed the harbour officials. He exercised full property rights over all cultivated and uncultivated land, and all waters; exceptions were made of certain lands that the town was permitted to use freely for pasture. He could claim all income from vacant posts and could change municipal laws at will. He was patron of the parish church and of all foundations within the town walls; he also owned all mills and bakeries in the area. He could levy any taxes he wished, a right removed in 1707 when the furs of Valencia were abolished. The fifth payable on the sale of slaves was his, as were certain taxes on dwellings, and three-tenths of the tithe of all produce in the area, including fruit, grain, wool and fish. He nominated all judges and similar officials and got the income from fines. The most important port duty at Denia, the *peaje*, was surrendered to the Crown in 1668 in return for an annual payment of 2,500 lliures, but the marquis could still levy certain duties, for example, three sous on every full pipe of wine or oil, one sou on every cahiz of grain.

In practice it is unlikely that such rights were ever fully exercised by a noble. Evidence suggests that seigneurial justice was sparingly used. Where we find baronial courts at work, as on the estates of the duke of Gandía, the crimes were minor and the sentences light. Major crime was always the responsibility of the royal officials appointed by the Chanceries and Audiencias.

In the sixteenth century many towns anxious to preserve their independence had appealed against the growing power of the nobles.[18] In most towns there was a wide range of types of government: some did not allow hidalgos to stand for office, others limited noble participation to only half. The growth of venality helped to undermine these safeguards, and the seventeenth century in Catalonia, for example, experienced a gradual takeover of municipalities by moneyed men of noble status.[19] The struggle between bourgeois and hidalgos for civic control had many incongruities; Medina de Rioseco, for instance, belonged to the Admiral of Castile, but it continued to keep nobles out of its government until the middle of the seventeenth century.[20] In the principal Castilian cities, most of them under royal jurisdiction, the greater nobility held undisputed sway.

## INCOME AND ESTATE ADMINISTRATION

The wealth of Spanish nobles was legendary. Indeed, by definition a noble was required to be wealthy, and the ancient laws of Castile stipulated that one who fell into poverty thereby lost his noble status. At the same time, wealth alone did not qualify one for nobility and there were various traditional barriers to the social ascent of those who relied solely on it.[21] Ostentation was common but also widely disapproved. The marquis of Varinas in 1689 denounced the president of the Casa de la Contratación, the count de la Calzada, for maintaining a level of expenditure well above his station and income. 'He is scandalising everybody', wrote the marquis, 'with twenty-four mules in his stables, and four horses and three coaches, thirty-six people in his household, with six children and a madwoman of a wife who spends everything on vanities. Calzada cannot afford the pomp he displays, for which he needs 20,000 whereas his salary is 4,000.'[22] Beyond the pomp, however, the reality was still impressive. Anyone who doubts the pleasures of living in a noble household, should read slowly the delicious menus laid out for the duke of Gandía in 1665.[23] The duke ate well, and presumably therefore lived well.

Noble families were never able to enjoy all their assets, because it was the rule for these to be in entail. The document setting up an entail or *mayorazgo* would list all the properties included in the transaction, name the beneficiaries, and lay down restrictions on the use of the property. The purpose was to prohibit sale or alienation. Entails required royal assent and were common practice in the early century as a method of preserving inheritances from dissolution. But by prohibiting alienation of an estate while allowing families to live off the effective income, entails caused a serious problem, for they left many nobles inadequately protected against inflation.

A nobleman might be extremely wealthy because he possessed several mayorazgos, but in real terms he might be poor. On what income could he rely? The question is crucial to an understanding of the seventeenth-century nobility, who habitually claimed to be overwhelmed by debt. A Spanish noble's income came from four main sources: estate production, seigneurial rights, rents and leases (including censos), and government annuities (juros).

The third marquis of Leganés, Don Diego Felipez de Guzmán, was a grandee of Castile, viceroy of Catalonia in 1684 and governor of Milan in 1691. His estates were partly in the area south-east of Madrid, and partly in Italy. In 1681 his effective annual income, as calculated by his treasurer and accountant Don Juan Morales de Gamarra, was 29,368 ducats.[24] Some 41.5 per cent of the income came from juros, about one-fourth from seignoriage rights on the Seville mint, and half from the alcabalas and millones of Madrid. The figure confirms the claim of the marquis in 1670 that juros were his main source of income.[25] The full breakdown of Leganés's income in 1681 was as shown in Table 8.1.

Table 8.1

| | | | (%) | (%) |
|---|---|---|---|---|
| Annuities | : | Juros | 41.5 } | 45.5 |
| | | Censos on towns of Arganda and Perales | 4 } | |
| Rents | : | Houses, let to count of Monterey | 12.8 | 12.8 |
| Seigneurial | : | Alcabalas in Cifuentes | 11.8 | |
| | | *Ibid.* and taxes in Leganés | 3 | |
| | | *Ibid.* and taxes in Morata | 5.6 | |
| | | *Ibid.* in Poza | 3.4 | 27 |
| | | Offices in Leganés | 0.5 | |
| | | Alcabalas in Perales | 2.7 | |
| Estate | : | Grain dues in Leganés | 2.2 | |
| | | Rents in kind, etc. | 3.5 | 14.7 |
| | | Estates in Italy, contract | 9 | |
| | | | 29,368 | ducats |

With his heavy investment in juros the marquis relied on the royal treasury for support, and would have suffered from the various discounts which the administration was making on payment of annuities. The whole estate was tied up in entail, and unusual efforts were required in order to raise extra cash. The need occurred in mid-century when the Guzmán family entered into a lawsuit over the duchy of San Lucar, which had been willed to them by the count duke of Olivares. The case was tried before the Chancery of Granada and heavy loans had to be raised in 1658 and particularly in 1680 in order to pay the costs. The action was won in 1696. By 1684 the total debt burden created by the lawsuit was well over 60,000 ducats.[26]

Loans were paid off slowly and did not necessarily consume all income. As a consequence the statement of the marquis's outgoings in 1681 looks fairly promising:

Table 8.2

| | (%) |
|---|---|
| Annual payment for various censos | 35.2 |
| Salaries of officials | 1.2 |
| To churches, for masses, etc. | 1.5 |
| Costs of lawsuits | 1.5 |
| Building repairs | 1.8 |
| To various financiers | 38 |
| To Juan de Morales, for costs, etc. | 20.8 |
| | 19,198 ducats |

231

The statement shows the low running costs of the estate, assuming that the payments to Morales also fall under this head. This would seem to have left the marquis with a net income of some 10,000 ducats in the year 1681.

By the seventeenth century a great number of the higher aristocracy had committed themselves to living near the court and hence in the capital. The consequences were similar to what happened in the Versailles of Louis XIV. Although estate management was not neglected, quantities of cash that could have been reinvested were diverted to meet the high cost of living in Madrid. The richer aristocrats built large new palaces for themselves, others rented residences from their peers.

The house of Infantado[27] was one of the greatest in Spain. The Mendoza family had immense possessions throughout the peninsula. Its principal representative during this reign was Don Gregorio de Silva y Mendoza, fifth duke of Pastrana and ninth of Infantado, marquis of Cenete (d. 1693). His authority extended in whole or in part over nearly 800 towns and villages,[28] including the Mendoza seat at Guadalajara; at a rough estimate, over 500 public officials throughout Spain were nominated by the duke. The income derived from his holdings was in theory enormous: 'From two towns as small as Alberique and Alcocer (in Valencia)', reported Macanaz, 'the duke of Infantado gets 31,000 pesos a year.'[29]

I have been unable to arrive at a computation of the duke's complete income. At the beginning of the century his annual income is supposed to have been in excess of 120,000 ducats, but we need to know exactly what this figure represents. A statement for 1637 puts his annual revenue at 81,044 ducats,[30] but with obvious omissions. The sum was made up 91 per cent from seigneurial rights in cash and grain, 9 per cent from juros on various taxes. At the same date his expenses were put at 73,263 ducats, with administration taking up 17.5 per cent, censos 61.3 per cent, grants to the Crown 3.5, and repairs 8.4 per cent. These details are by no means complete. Infantado had so many different sources of revenue that conflicting and incompatible statements are quite common. Domínguez Ortiz has commented on the apparent contradiction of the report in 1656 that the duke of Pastrana was about to found a new mayorazgo, with the fact that the estates of Pastrana had been in debt administration since 1640.[31] The house of Infantado was likewise in debt. In July 1661 the government took over general administration of the Infantado estates in order to 'give satisfaction to the creditors in proper order, and grant adequate supplies to the duke and duchess'. A *concurso* or arrangement to pay creditors was set up. The arrangement was renewed in 1690.[32]

Not all parts of an aristocrat's resources were equally lucrative. Seigneurial rents were a particular casualty of inflation. We can see their evolution in the cluster of estates around the town of Jadraque (Guadalajara), which had belonged to the predecessors of the duke since the year 1439. Jadraque and its partido or region was located near the river Henares north of Guadalajara. It consisted of six towns (Jadraque, Carrascosa, Huermeces, La Toba, Cendejas de la Torre and Casas de San Galindo) and nearly forty villages, the whole forming part of the marquisate of Cenete, one of the titles of the duke. The main seigneurial functions[33] in the partido were appointment of all military officials, mayors, notaries, police officials and regidores. From taxes the duke enjoyed the alcabalas, tercias and several other duties, as well as income from local fairs. The cash dues paid by the region to their lord were virtually unchanged over one hundred years:[34]

Table 8.3

|      | ducats |
|------|--------|
| 1581 | 6,379  |
| 1584 | 6,617  |
| 1586 | 6,248  |
| 1593 | 5,876  |
| 1597 | 5,786  |
| 1636 | 6,204  |
| 1688 | 5,553  |

In addition to these sums, all towns had to give at least one cow (Jadraque gave twelve a year), so that in 1636 for instance the whole partido, in addition to its dues, had given a total of 58 cows and 18 chickens. A tithe was also levied on the harvest, for the duke. Over a century, the amounts given to this duty (known as the *tercias*) were as shown in Table 8.4.

Table 8.4

| Year | Wheat | Barley (fanegas) | Rye | % (1580–2 = 100) |
|------|-------|------------------|-----|------------------|
| 1580 | 862   | 128 | 103 |     |
| 1581 | 617   | 129 | 52  |     |
| 1582 | 656   | 72  | 83  |     |
| 1588 | 1,023 | 99  | 142 | 140 |
| 1590 | 726   | 80  | 180 | 110 |
| 1591 | 1,060 | 81  | 204 | 149 |
| 1592 | 853   | 94  | 138 | 121 |
| 1669 | 365   | 72  | 379 | 91  |
| 1674 | 301   | 36  | 164 | 56  |

The figures for both cash and grain are revealing. The slight fall in cash income between 1581 and 1688 was due to depopulation in the villages of the *partido*, which was only partially offset by a corresponding increase in the population of Jadraque. The tax figures (in ducats) for Jadraque and four other towns at random bear testimony to how Jadraque grew and the villages declined (Table 8.5):

Table 8.5

|          | 1581 | 1597 | 1636 | 1665 | 1688 | 1688/1581% |
|----------|------|------|------|------|------|------------|
| Jadraque | 695  | 773  | 806  | 1,297 | 1,088 | + 56 |
| Robledo  | 159  | 80   | 92   | 113  | 95   | − 40 |
| Viana    | 43   | 11   | 13   | 11   | 3    | − 93 |
| Riofrio  | 147  | 109  | 94   | 67   | 62   | − 58 |
| Jirueque | 160  | 128  | 125  | 130  | 73   | − 54 |

Though the nominal cash income remained much the same, the fixed seigneurial dues obviously made no allowance for inflation, so that in real terms the dukes suffered a serious fall in revenue from the partido. Normally a lord might expect to recoup these losses from the payments in kind. The figures for grain, however, were poor. This is particularly surprising, since in Jadraque the area of arable remained constant between 1490 and 1730.[35]

Our next glance is at a great lord of the Crown of Aragon. Don Pascual de Borja, duke of Gandía, was the most prominent aristocrat of the kingdom of Valencia. His estates, centred on the town of Gandía, formed the largest single concentration of seigneurial land in the realm. The principal estates making up the duchy formed a great arc around Gandía and towards the sea. Because the duke was an almost permanent absentee in Madrid, like all the principal peers of Valencia, he appointed administrators for his estates; each estate was contracted out to a financier for an agreed sum and period. This meant that the formal income of the duchy could be found simply by adding up the price of the leases. In the 1690s the total came to about 41,000 ducats a year for the Valencian estates alone.[36]

Leases were for collection of seigneurial rents and other dues. Returns were uncertain, particularly from tithes, and administrators often found themselves in debt. The estate of Gandía was normally leased in this period for 7,000 lliures (about 9,500 ducats) a year. Accounts for this and the other Valencian estates show that little if any effective income was expected by the duke. This happened for two main reasons: firstly, all estates were expected to cover their own costs; secondly, specific ducal obligations were unloaded on to each of the estates, wiping out any likely surplus. Returns for the year 1670 show how it was managed.[37] In Gandía 56.2 per cent of costs that year went to cover debts and 24.3 to expenses of the ducal household; salaries and wages by contrast, took up only 5.4 per cent. In Oliva as much as 56.9 went towards ducal expenses. In Llombay the proportion for ducal expenses was only 7.5, but as much as 58.6 went towards administrative debt. In Villalonga the very substantial proportion of 49 per cent went to cover a wholly external item: debts contracted in Valencia city.

All the evidence suggests that the duke was a conscientious landowner, and that although an absentee he paid close and minute attention to events in Valencia. A surviving letter-book of the duke's letters from Madrid to his estates in Llombay unfortunately covers only the years 1699–1700 but it reveals his active part in all decisions.

In May 1699 we find him directing that no licences be granted to fell trees on the estate, and that no alterations in rents be made without asking his permission: 'keeping in mind my intention that nothing be done without notifying me'.[38] On 27 May he protested that his administrators, out of mistaken zeal, had omitted to inform him of a riot in Llombay: 'this conduct of yours disturbs me, and is not to my service. . . . Nothing could disturb me more than the fact that in business affairs the hatred or enmity of those who serve me, is being hidden from me.'[39] On 3 June the failure to inform him of a rise in meat prices in the estate 'has astonished me'.[40] The current famine in Madrid prompted him to write the same day 'for my vassals to aid me with 50 cahices (about 900 bushels) of wheat for the upkeep of my family'.[41] He took a close interest in the arrest and punishment in August of those responsible for disturbances in Llombay, Catadau and Alfarbe: 'I have no doubt', he wrote in September, 'that you will manage the imprisonment of the rioters with all secrecy.'[42] In December 1700 the duke wrote complaining of 'the great anguish caused me by the unavoidable expenses that I have had since coming to Madrid', and asked his subjects for a donativo.[43] Every conceivable detail of life and administration in the marquisate of Llombay came under the duke's scrutiny. It is quite likely that he was not a typical seigneur. But his example is a distinct refutation of claims that all absentee landlords neglected their estates.

It is difficult to arrive at a rounded estimate of the duke of Gandía's income, since each estate had a separate treasury, and the finances of the duke in Madrid are unknown. The area of Gandía was not simply a collection of feudal estates, it was a complete society, in which towns and countryside together lived under the fiscal and criminal laws of the Borja family. To the duke Gandía was his patrimony, and he was the loving father of his vassals.[44] The official regulations drawn up in 1700 for the government of Llombay, laid down rules for every aspect of public life.[45] There was strict control over all commercial activity. Basic items such as wine, rice, oil, soap, tobacco, cheese were sold only under licence, and only in the public market, and only after payment of seigneurial taxes. Flour and bread were likewise controlled; the only available mills to be used were those of the duke. No outsiders or strangers were allowed to stay overnight in the marquisate without notice being given to the authorities. All offences of trespass, use of arms, and gambling at cards were liable to prosecution. All distribution of water came under ducal control. It is clear from these typical regulations that the subjects of the duke of Gandía were directly dependent on him, and not on the government of Valencia or even of the king of Spain. Repression of popular disturbances, as we have seen from the events of both 1693 and 1699, was entirely in the hands of the duke's officials. All crime was rigorously punished within the limits of capacity, though major offences such as banditry and murder were normally referred to the royal jurisdiction of the Audiencia in Valencia city. Income received from criminal fines on the Gandía estates totalled 1,030 ducats in 1671 and 972 ducats in 1672.[46] Many buildings on the estates were let out by the duchy, but the system of accounting makes it difficult to determine how far rentals were a significant source of income. The duchy had a special relationship with the Church, thanks to the work of the great duke, St Francis, who had given the Jesuits a privileged position in Gandía. The result was that donations to local religious foundations were a large item in expenditure.

The volume of debt to religious communities is shown by the finances of the city of Gandía itself. Using data for a slightly later period, the years 1719–24, we find that the annual municipal income of 2,083 lliures came 29 per cent from sales licences, 24 from the municipal granary, 24 from the taxes on meat, 10 from the general consumer tax, and the rest from various sources. In that same period, however, the annual debt on censals alone was 2,332 lliures. Of this sum, a percentage of 27.7 was payable to the cathedral in Gandía, 25 to the hospital,

11.3 to the College of the Patriarch in Valencia, and smaller sums due to other ecclesiastical foundations, leaving only 26 per cent of the censals payable to laymen.[47]

Sources of ducal income are illustrated by returns for the five towns in the estate of Cofrentes. In this area between 1718 and 1721, seigneurial rights (including the obligation to grind corn at the lord's mill) came to about 32 per cent of income, money rents came to about 11 per cent, and rents in kind made up the remaining 57 per cent.[48]

Apart from his estates, the duke's principal source of income appears to have been juros. In 1670 the nominal annual revenue from this source, which was inalienable because all the juros were in entail, was 27,930 ducats.[49] Unfortunately half of this was taken to pay the media anata tax, the juros themselves cost about 2.5 per cent to collect, and after further discounts only about a third of the original sum was actually received. All the juros were from Castilian sources, 23 per cent from Salamanca, 21 per cent from Madrid, and the balance from other cities such as León and Guadalajara.

The dukes of Gandía were fortunate in managing to keep their estates out of the hands of creditors. But like everybody else they suffered economic problems. In 1653, for example, the then duke refused to contribute to the costs of fighting the French in Catalonia, on the grounds of his difficulties.[50] Only careful management of the estates made it possible to cover the heavy costs of living as well as administration: there can be no doubt that the upkeep of the ducal household, whether in Gandía or in Madrid, was the biggest single item of expenditure, as we have already seen from the partial breakdown of costs for 1670. The costs of the duke in Madrid were not directly put on the estates, and only when he made occasional visits to Gandía (as in 1678, when his visit quintupled the food bill and increased household costs by 50 per cent)[51] was he a serious burden on the Valencian administrators.

Like other nobles, the dukes remained out of debt by borrowing and then repaying over the long term. By the early seventeenth century this had created a massive long-term debt, but by careful administration the dukes managed to survive. In 1622 the duke agreed to spread the burden of repayment over each of his estates.[52] By this agreement or *concordia* a sum of between ten and twelve thousand lliures (about 15,000 ducats) was to be set aside annually to pay censalistas. Subsequently in 1664 duke Don Francisco Carlos sold the towns of Turis, Albalat and Chella to the count of Sallent in order to meet expenses. The debt by the end of the century was however still very large. Between 1692 and 1697, for reasons that are not very clear, borrowing on an unprecedented scale was undertaken by the duke and his administrators. The result was that by 1701 the principal of the censals owed by the duchy came to 215,139 lliures (293,370 ducats) and the annual repayments totalled 10,696 lliures (14,585 ducats).[53]

We turn now to a great lord of Andalucia, Don Gaspar Téllez Girón, marquis of Peñafiel and count of Ureña, fifth duke of Osuna (1656–94).[54] Don Gaspar had a singularly colourful career. When he succeeded to the title in 1656 at the age of thirty-one, he became lord of twenty-six towns in Andalucia and fifty-four in Castile. All these, together with his estates, he lost in a famous dispute with the chief minister Medinaceli in 1680. Dan Gaspar was disgraced for four years but had his fortune returned in July 1684.[55] He was a great builder: in 1673 he bought a group of houses in Madrid for 11,000 ducats, demolished them and constructed in their place a great palace costing 300,000 ducats.

Like the duke of Gandía, Osuna was an absentee landowner but a conscientious one. Dr Gladstone suggests that he 'was in constant touch with his administrators. Not only was he fully cognisant of the state of his properties, but he even took the time to make routine appointments'.[56] His total annual income as duke was in the region of 150,000 ducats. Only a fraction of this, varying from four per cent in 1670 to 21 per cent in 1690, came from his Andalucian estates. Osuna was, in brief, unable to live off his patrimony: 'The extensive tracts of land and numerous townships held by Don Gaspar . . . provided revenues which covered little more than administrative costs and the bare living essentials of the ducal household.'[57] The bulk of his income came instead from juros, from his wife's property holdings, and other sources.

The duke's known and estimated expenditure at two distinct epochs is summarised in Table 8.6 as percentages of his total outlay.[58]

Table 8.6

|  | 1664–76 | 1677–94 |
| --- | --- | --- |
| Administration | 1.5 | 2.8 |
| Lawsuits | 0.2 | 0.8 |
| Royal obligations | 16.8 | 2 |
| Institutions (university of Osuna) | 10.2 | 9.3 |
| Personal and household | 14.8 | 30.7 |
| Palace in Madrid | 32.4 | |
| Gifts and donations | 16 | 8.6 |
| Dowries | | 13 |
| Censos | 3.8 | 28.9 |
| Payments and loans | 5.2 | 3.9 |

## ECONOMIC PROBLEMS OF THE NOBILITY

The seventeenth century in Spain, it has been agreed by all historians, was one of an economic decline among the aristocracy. Nobles at the time seem to have been in no doubt about this. In 1667, when the Crown asked the higher nobility for a donativo, they excused themselves with a wide range of explanations. Among them were the count of Benavente, the marquis of Mondéjar and others.[59] Refusal of grants was commonplace; in the 1640s and 1650s (the refusal by the duke of Gandía, noted above, was typical) most nobles proved uncooperative. They continued to protest poverty in the reign of Charles II, and we should look closely at their claims.

In 1671, when the government asked for a servicio from the kingdom of Aragon, the marquis of Aytona explained that 'the marquis his father left so many debts, that to pay them he had assigned the income of his property in Aragon, so that for the present he could not offer anything'. The count of Sobradiel claimed that 'his obligations and recent heavy costs make him beg His Majesty to excuse him on this occasion'. The count of Castelflorit excused himself 'because of hail on his estates'; and the count of Fuenclara said he could not pay because 'he was heavily committed in taking up the viceroyalty of Mallorca'.[60]

There is no doubt that the aristocracy was going through serious economic difficulties. It is more doubtful whether we can talk of a 'decline'. Like the marquis of Aytona, most nobles could justifiably blame their predecessors for the straits in which they found themselves. The duke of Medina Sidonia pointed out in 1678 that when he succeeded to the title there were censos on it whose annual burden came to 50,000 ducats.[61] The count of Barajas stated in 1684 that 'long before he or his father entered into the estate of Barajas, their predecessors took out various censos on the goods and income of the estate'; which had led now to a seizure of their property to pay for these past debts.[62] Every noble family had a similar story to tell. The main problem with which they were faced was not current costs so much as the debt inherited from past members of the family. It is true that had they made drastic economies they might have reduced their debts. But in many cases the burden was too heavy to shake off even within one generation.

We have seen that the duke of Infantado and Pastrana was in difficulties by the reign of Charles II. In 1638 Pastrana had been put into concurso, and Infantado followed in 1661. The Infantado estates were already by 1637 burdened with an annual censo debt of 44,886 ducats, an enormous sum by any standards. The unredeemed capital debt at this date was 897,731 ducats of censos, which had been contracted within the preceding fifty years as shown in Table 8.7.[63]

Table 8.7

|  | *ducats* |
|---|---|
| Dowry for daughter Ana's marriage to Admiral | 60,000 |
| Dowry for daughter Mencia's marriage to duke of Alba | 60,000 |
| Dowry for daughter Juana's marriage to duke of Béjar | 60,000 |
| Dowry for daughter Isabel's marriage to duke of Feria | 60,000 |
| Other dowries | 132,085 |
| Journey to Valencia for marriage of Philip III | 174,986 |
| Gifts to Philip III, and supply of soldiers 1589–91 | 88,332 |
| Change of capital from Valladolid to Madrid | 110,753 |
| Repair of houses in Madrid 1622 | 14,000 |
| Festivities for prince of Wales 1623 | 20,000 |
| Other censos | 126,565 |

Further large loans were contracted after 1637. In 1642, for example, a sum of 40,000 ducats was raised to cover the costs of active service in Catalonia. But they were few in number. When the concurso occurred in 1661 no further loans were permitted until the reign of Philip V. In the duchy of Pastrana, likewise, no loans were permitted after the concurso of 1638.[64] These details on the debts of the house allow us to put into perspective the story recounted in 1693 by Stanhope. According to the English ambassador, writing in September, 'the duke of Pastrana and Infantado, first duke of Spain, died last week of a violent fever, with this extraordinary circumstance, that when ready to expire he called to the bystanders and bid them take notice he died not a maravedi in debt to any person living – which is the only instance of a Spanish grandee in this age!'[65] The duke's claim, if it applied to the censo debt, was untrue: in 1721 his house was still paying off some of its obligations. On the other hand, it must be admitted that the majority of the loans had been redeemed by the end of the reign of Charles II. In this respect the duke may well have been unique.

How had the aristocracy fallen into debt in the first place? From the fifteenth century onwards the Crown had encouraged nobles to consolidate their holdings through the entail (mayorazgo). The advantage of the mayorazgo was that it saved estates from being split up or alienated: the country was thereby assured of an effective, propertied ruling class. The disadvantage to nobles was that if, in an age of inflation, they wished to raise a large sum of money, they had little to sell. Some sold property not protected by entail: a town, perhaps; or a tax, a house, or even furniture. In 1681 the French ambassador Villars reported from Madrid, with the exaggeration that distorted all his reports, that 'you would think this town is being pillaged, to see the rich furniture sent abroad by people of quality who are being forced to sell it cheaply in order to live.'[66] For those with huge estates, the surest way was to obtain credit on the security of the mayorazgo. This could only be done through royal licences (facultades) which were issued with frequency from the late sixteenth century onwards. The loans or censos thus raised were repayable in the last resort from the income of the mayorazgos, which could never themselves be alienated.

Licences provided an excellent solution to the economic problems of the aristocracy. Censos contracted in this way, however, became a major burden during the critical years of the early seventeenth century. The situation arrived, as it did for Infantado by mid-century, when even large seigneurial incomes could not hope to meet the annual repayments on censos. In these circumstances it became necessary to call in the creditors.[67] The indebted nobleman had several alternatives. He could put his estates 'into administration', whereby he agreed through the courts to take on an administrator who would supervise the long-term repayment of debts, while guaranteeing him an adequate minimum income. Alternatively he could come to an agreement through the courts with his creditors, in a concurso de acreedores, known also in the Crown of Aragon as a concordia. The concurso gave guarantees about the repayment of specific debts from specific sources; allowed the noble a basic income; and was normally supervised by an official of the council. Occasionally a concurso might be formed not on entailed estates but on property which was free (this happened to the marquis of Los Vélez and to the duke of Villena). The problems that arose from having an official supervise private concursos led in 1706 to the suspension of this practice.[68] The government continued, however, to lend its good offices to the nobility through the appointment of a representative (called a juez conservador) who supervised the payment of debts while still leaving the actual administration of the estate in the hands of the debtor nobleman. This third way of solving the problem of repayment proved to be more popular than the concurso because it imposed fewer restraints. The dukes of Alba, Arcos and Medina Sidonia were the most prominent users of this facility.

The attempt of the house of Alvarez de Toledo, dukes of Alba, to become solvent, began in 1616.[69] In that year, with the help of a juez conservador, the duke set aside 60,000 ducats a year to pay his creditors. Seven-twelfths of this was for censos on the entails, one-sixth for censos on the non-entailed properties, and the rest for other debts. By 1668 duke Antonio was paying off the debts with only small arrears. However there had meanwhile been serious shortfalls in estate income from lands in Extremadura near the Portuguese war front, and by the end of the century the house had accumulated arrears of over 98,000 ducats.[70]

I shall now look briefly at the economic position of three prominent nobles: the Admiral of Castile, the count of Cifuentes and the count of Oropesa. For most of the reign of Charles II the relevant Admiral was not Don Juan Tomás, whom we have encountered above, but his father Don Juan Gaspar Enríquez de Cabrera (d. 1691). His house was unfortunately burdened with heavy debts from the late sixteenth century. In 1610 his father Don Juan Alfonso had been given a unique permission by the Crown: to devote all the revenues of his estates to paying off not the interest but the principal of his censos, and thereafter to paying off outstanding annuities. This permission, which was intended to help the Admiral through a concurso initiated in 1597, set aside the sum of 6,000 ducats for his personal needs. So huge were the debts, however – 764,226 ducats in 1610 – that even this radical measure of depriving the Admiral of virtually all his income, and allowing him to redeem the principal before the interest, had limited success: by 1655 only 261,775 ducats had been paid off; in 1677 the debt stood at 199,670 ducats. At this date the Chancery of Valladolid estimated that the average annual income of the Admiral's estates was over 37,000 ducats, and that the various costs on it (including the 6,000 assigned to the Admiral) came to over 26,000, leaving about 11,000 a year to pay off creditors on the terms laid down in 1610. With this sum in hand the debts would have been paid off long since, according to the Chancery, had it not been for the Crown allowing Don Juan Alfonso to suspend some payments in order to draw extraordinary cash expenses: between 1633 and 1640 the Admiral had obtained about 148,000 ducats in this way.

Despite great efforts, by the late century the Admiral was still far from solvent. Special expenses, like that of 20,000 ducats in 1663 on the marriage of his son the count of Melgar, added to the debt. The rebellion and French intervention in Messina in 1674–78 cut off income from his Sicilian estates of Modica, and created major problems.[71] In 1691 the last Admiral, Don Juan Tomás, was obliged to ask the council for a further 30,000 ducats to cover his expenses.[72] There is little doubt that the house had been through difficult times. One effect of the concurso of 1597 had been that all the non-entailed property of the family was put 'into administration'. Careful checks were made of all household goods, paintings and books.[73] Exceptionally, paintings were sold to pay off debts. Not until 1685 were the Admiral's goods released from administration.

Don Juan Tomás, when he succeeded to the title in 1691, was still an extremely wealthy man.[74] In September 1702, when he left Madrid to take up his ambassadorship in Paris, he took with him a retinue of 300 persons in 150 carriages, and luggage including a great number of jewels and paintings. At that date he also owned three of the largest mansions in the capital. Royal protection of the family through measures such as the concession of 1610, had guaranteed that their property would not be alienated. But the debts remained massive. All the Madrid mansions had censos on them. By 1703 the unpaid debts of the Admiral, *excluding* the principal of his censos, exceeded 275,658 ducats.[75] The man who turned traitor to the Bourbons in 1702 was fleeing as much from his creditors as from the regime.

Don Fernando de Silva Meneses y Zapata, count of Cifuentes, was a mortal enemy of the Admiral,[76] but like him was deep in debt. His holdings were scattered throughout Spain. They included the title estate of Cifuentes in Guadalajara (2.8 per cent of total income), extensive holdings around the towns of Torviscón and Albuñol in the Alpujarra mountains of Granada (51.8), pasture around Talavera de la Reina (20.6), pasture on the estate of Velilla in Toledo province (15.3), taxes and rents in Llerena (4.2), seigneurial income from Villarejo de Fuentes in Cuenca (4.6), and juros in Madrid and Seville (0.7).[77] The total annual revenue from his estates in 1706 was 14,980 ducats. In the course of the century, however, the property had been put 'into administration'. By 1683 the administrator of the consurso complained that the net income was barely enough to pay the 2,000 ducats assigned for the count's expenses.[78]

Don Manuel Joaquín García Alvarez de Toledo, count of Oropesa, was not only a great seigneur but also one of the chief ministers in the government. The marriage in mid-century of his father Don Duarte Fernández to Doña Ana de Córdoba, countess of Alcaudete and marquesa del Villar, brought a substantial addition to the family estates but little real financial relief since both Alcaudete and El Villar were heavily burdened with censos.[79] In 1706 the effective estate income of the counts of Oropesa was in excess of 50,000 ducats.[80] But numerous debts had been contracted by the count's predecessors. Between 1635 and 1665 over 100,000 ducats of principal were raised for various needs.[81] This sum, contracted on his entailed estates, formed only one part of the count's debt. On his possessions in Madrid, which included the large Oropesa palace in the square of Santo Domingo, the censos and debts by 1713 totalled over 71,500 ducats.[82] It is not clear what his total debts were, but as late as 1685 he was complaining of being unable to redeem some of his censos 'because of the great straits in which the count his father had left him, and because of the expenses occasioned by serving Your Majesty in Madrid, and in accompanying Your Majesty'.[83]

The Admiral, Cifuentes and Oropesa were men in considerable debt; all three rebelled against the new Bourbon regime after 1700. Was there a connection between these facts? The Habsburg regime had certainly made it possible for the aristocracy to survive indefinitely despite a mountain of accumulating economic difficulties. Protected by the privileges of their rank, which precluded imprisonment for debt; and secure in the knowledge that their mayorazgo assets could never be alienated; the nobles lived content. Nobles protested genuinely about poverty, but were never absolutely poor.

Consider a further example. In 1670 Don Gaspar Silvestre Vigil de Quiñones Benavides y Pimentel, count of Luna and marquis of Jabalquinto, died in Valladolid. His widow immediately claimed her dowry out of her husband's assets. It was soon found that all his unentailed assets, mainly household goods in Valladolid, came to only 16,242 ducats. Were her claim (for 52,000 ducats) to be paid in full, not enough would be available to pay the other certified debts of the late count, which apart from the dowry claim amounted to over 22,350 ducats. The count had left a long string of debts to the tradespeople of Valladolid. He owed 7,996 ducats to a silk merchant for clothes, 155 to his tailor, 106 to the postman, 343 to the chemist and 1,958 to the butcher.[84] He thus died wholly bankrupt. His heir was his father the count of Benavente, of an ancient family with extensive possessions in Old Castile. The estates of Luna and Jabalquinto were both covered by censos on the entail: since 1597 Luna had accumulated over 40,000 ducats of censos and Jabalquinto since 1611 had accumulated 25,700 ducats. Benavente could hardly come to the relief of his deceased son, since his own estates had already by 1580 contracted over 400,000 ducats principal of censos.[85] Between 1580 and 1612 the house took on further censos exceeding 242,000 ducats in value. Despite these enormous burdens the family continued to maintain its position.

From the various documents dealing with aristocratic debt it is clear that the Crown and its courts made exceptional efforts to relieve the financial burden. One common relief was to grant exemptions from the tax on juros. An official document granting relief in 1680 includes the following names:[86]

Count of Humanes, 'because of the many debts caused by his employment in the royal service, and in particular as ambassador to Portugal'[87]

Marquis of Villavenazar, 'because of having to support his mother, wife and three brothers, with no other income to help them'

Count of Cantillana, 'who has not the means to support his five brothers according to their rank'

Countess of Orgaz, lady-in-waiting, 'because of her lack of means'

Count of Orgaz, 'because of his censos, and not having enough on which to live or meet his many obligations'

Count of Palma, 'who has many debts'

Marquis of Castro and Torres, 'because of the services of his house, and since he has a very large family of brothers and children'

Duchess of Nájera, 'who has a very small income'

Viscount of Ambite, 'whose whole income is in these juros, and who has to maintain a house and family'

Marquis of Santillán, 'in view of his debts caused by the two journeys he made to France as ambassador extraordinary'

Count of Villamanrique, 'since his father left many debts and obliged him to live in great discomfort'

Marquis of Los Balbases, 'because of his many debts caused by heavy costs incurred as ambassador to Germany and to France'[88]

Marquis of Santofloro, 'because of his exiguous means, and to let him live with the decency befitting his duties'

Viscount of La Frontera, 'who has no other income to support him'

Countess of Gondomar, 'for her exiguous means and large family'

Marquis of Ayamonte, 'because of his lack of means and great debts'

Countess of Chinchón, widow, 'who has no other means to help her maintain her large family'

Viscount of Mendinueta, 'who is obliged to maintain his brothers without any income for it other than these juros'

Marquis of Navamorquende, 'who has eight children unplaced, and no other income to do it with'[89]

Marquis of La Torre, 'who has many obligations to his children and family, and very few means since his property is in concurso'

Count of Galbe, majordomo of the king, 'who has lost a large income with the death of his wife, and has to support a very large family'[90]

Count of Torrepalma, who 'has many debts'

Count of Toreno, 'because of the discomfort he suffers since his main income is from these juros'

Marquis of La Conquista, 'since his estate is in concurso and he enjoys no income other than these juros'[91]

Marquis del Fresno, 'because of the small income of his house and since he is in economic straits'

Countess of Villalba, 'whose estate is in concurso'

Count of Montalvo, 'whose many great debts have forced him to retire to a village'

Marquis of La Vega, 'since the juros are the main income he has with which to maintain himself and his children and pay his many debts'

Marquis of Valenzuela (Don Antonio Fernández de Córdoba), 'because of his lack of means'

Marquis of Santa Cruz and Don Alvaro Bazán his brother, 'since they have no income to maintain themselves and support two sisters'

Marquis of Villaflores, 'because of his dire straits'

Marquis of Villahermosa, 'because of his great necessity'

Duke of Uceda, 'because his many debts prevent him living with the decency befitting his rank'[92]

Count of Cifuentes, 'greatly in debt because of his expenses in the royal service'.

What then were the general causes of these undoubted problems facing the richest Spaniards? Like everyone else, they had suffered from the general price rise of the time. Inflation by itself was however not seen as the major cause for complaint. Even in difficult times, as has recently been plausibly argued for the house of Mondéjar in the sixteenth century,[93] a nobleman had enough resources to live comfortably. Simple debt was normally no problem, since like the count of Luna most rich men felt it part of their privilege and honour to live off extended credit. The major problem was without any doubt the formal debt known as the *censo*, and in particular those censos which nobles were licensed to raise on their entailed properties. Although licences normally specified a fixed term for redemption, seldom more than ten years and usually much less, it is clear from the cases cited above that most nobles were unable to pay off their debts in time. A censo of 16,000 ducats granted to the duke of Infantado in 1589, for instance, was still largely unredeemed by 1721.

Conspicuous consumption, which features prominently in charges against the English aristocracy, cannot be accounted a primary cause of Spanish noble debt. A popular failing of grandees was to spend large sums on embellishing their coaches,[94] but several sumptuary laws attempted to restrain this extravagance. The greater nobles also had high household costs, but these were a necessary aspect of their feudal obligations. The duke of Gandía, for example, held an open table for meals in Gandía, as was right and proper for a good father of his vassals. In October 1663 the cost of his table was 414 lliures: over twelve months this would make a huge sum of 6,700 ducats.[95] The duty of a lord to support convents and churches of which he was patron could also be extraordinarily high. Various other seigneurial obligations took their toll. The count of Luna, for example, promised in writing to pay the dowry of one of his dependent vassals, and this sum of 1,275 ducats was the fifth largest sum he owed at the time of his death. In short, though the general costs of a Spanish aristocrat may seem high, they were the result not of extravagance so much as of trying to maintain the due level of social obligations.

The real extravagances were caused almost exclusively by the demands of Court etiquette. With the final and permanent transfer of the capital back to Madrid in 1606, most of the higher aristocracy began to establish themselves there. A few bought houses, most rented them. The burden this represented to the nobility is shown clearly in the expenses, noted above, contracted by Infantado. Throughout the century we find numerous complaints by nobles of the high costs of living in Madrid. Even these charges may well have been tolerable but for the demands made by the Crown. The most notorious example is the year 1623, when the king expected his lords to outdo each other in the festivities arranged for the prince of Wales's visit to Madrid. In general, any movement of the Court involved extra costs for those in attendance. These progresses or *jornadas* occurred regularly every year, whether to Aranjuez or Segovia or the Escorial; but fortunately they were short journeys. A lengthy jornada, such as that made by Philip III to Valencia in 1599 to meet his new bride, obliged Infantado to raise 174,986 ducats to cover his costs. Charles II was not a great traveller, and jornadas in his reign were therefore not what they used to be. But the festivities for his marriage, and the attendant jornada, were considered by the Aragonese grandee the duke of Hijar in 1681 to be the chief reason for his financial difficulties.[96]

The duke of Hijar also complained in 1683 that his salary as viceroy of Aragon (6,000 ducats a year) had not been paid for over two years. Even when salaries were paid, the extra expenses falling on nobles in government service were notoriously high. Ambassadorships and viceroyalties produced many casualties in this respect, but lesser appointments such as governorships were equally vulnerable. Among those with recognised claims were the count of Castañeda, granted a licence for censos for 20,000 ducats in 1605 to cover his costs as ambassador in England, and the count's son in 1631 for his costs as governor of Orán;[97] the count of Fuensalida in 1684 'because of the great expenses and debts he has contracted when serving in the posts of viceroy of Navarre, Galicia and Sardinia';[98] Don Baltasar de Fuenmayor, marquis of Castelmoncayo, in 1698 for 'the great expenses he contracted in different posts in the royal service', principally as ambassador in Venice;[99] and numerous others. The duke of Osuna claimed that troops he equipped for the royal service in Andalucia in the 1660s cost him 200,000 ducats, and that tenure of viceroyalties in Catalonia and Milan cost him 160,000 ducats.[100]

Direct demands for money were a regular feature of royal policy in the seventeenth century. It was an accepted obligation of the nobles to contribute with men or money when their sovereign required aid.[101] By mid-century many were unable to serve with money, and incompetent to serve with men. We have seen above that the normal response of nobles to a request for a donativo, was to plead poverty. When the Admiral of Castile offered in 1679 to give the Crown 100,000 ducats, the government was forced to turn down the offer, since the sum could only have been raised by imposing more censos on an estate already incapable of repaying its existing debts.[102] Although donativos and other financial demands cannot essentially be considered a cause of debt, they appear frequently as the reason for censos, and must therefore be seen as a long-term burden. Among the debts taken on by Infantado in the seventeenth century were 20,000 ducats for a donativo in 1625 and 54,000 ducats for serving in person and with soldiers: fortunately, all these were redeemed by 1664. Of the 30,000 ducats of censos contracted by the count of Aguilar between 1589 and 1591, 14,000 were for military contributions to the king.[103] A large proportion of Oropesa's debts had the same origin: between 1635 and 1638 his family contracted 80,000 ducats of censos to cover the costs of a company of 2,000 men raised for the king's service.[104]

Dowries were certainly the most common single cause of indebtedness among the higher aristocracy. The details for Infantado given above show that dowries accounted for over 41 per cent of the debt total in 1637. Since a good marriage helped to secure a family's fortunes, dowries could be considered an investment rather than expenditure. A dowry was not a transfer of assets but a strict settlement on the bride and her heirs. It had to be matched by a contribution or endowment (arras) made by the groom to his bride; by law the arras was not to exceed one-tenth of the groom's goods. The sums involved in aristocratic dowries were so large that raising loans on the mayorazgo proved to be an easier solution than the earlier method of borrowing at interest. The count of Barajas, Don Diego Zapata, stated in 1684 that all the censos on his house had been raised for two purposes only: to supply dowries, and to make grants to the king.[105] The size of dowries raised through censos varied from the large to the very large. The count of Benavente at the beginning of the century was giving his daughters dowries of 20,000 and 30,000 ducats; the duke of Arcos in 1659 settled one of 50,000 on his daughter Catalina Ponce de León for her marriage to the marquis of Fromista and Caracena.[106] The duke of Béjar in 1600 arranged to raise 120,000 ducats of censos for the dowries of his three daughters.[107] By the mid and late seventeenth century dowries of 100,000 ducats were fairly standard among the higher aristocracy.[108]

Of the many and varied reasons for long-term debt in the Spanish aristocracy, the one which has so far received least attention is litigation. For England, Lawrence Stone has pointed out how old habits of noble violence were superseded by a new and growing resort to the law courts. In Spain, intermarriage between lineages was bound to lead to an eventual harvest of lawsuits over the succession to estates and titles. High mortality rates would likewise have robbed families of their rightful heirs and led to disputes. The delays and expense involved in litigation were foreseeably immense. A dispute over the estates of the Catalan count of Eril, in which the title was disputed between members of the male and the female line, was said in 1679 to have been going on for fifty years.[109] Among the most prolonged lawsuits of the century was that of the dukes of Hijar against the dukes of Alba over three baronies in Catalonia. The case had begun in 1527 before the Audiencia of Barcelona; in 1665, or 138 years later, Hijar was still pleading with the court to deliver judgment so that his costs could be terminated.[110]

It is difficult to estimate the long-term impact of lawsuits on the economic fortunes of the Spanish noble class. Since the sixteenth century Spain had been a highly litigious society, and continued to be so, to the great profit of the lawyers, whom Melchor de Macanaz later referred to as 'the plague of the monarchy'.[111] Money was lost not only in court expenses but also in terms of seigneurial income. In 1695 a long-standing lawsuit between the duke of Gandía and Don Otger Català, prince of Cariati, over the estate of Nules in Valencia, was decided in favour of Català, to whom the council of Aragon granted also the revenues that Nules had paid to the duke during the disputed period. There was however no way the council could enforce payment of old dues, and Català, in addition to his other costs, was left with an unsatisfied claim for 50,000 ducats.[112]

We have an authoritative opinion of the effect that decades of this type of conflict had on the Aragonese aristocracy, in the form of a report from the archbishop of Saragossa in 1705:[113]

I must inform you that all the ancient noble houses of Aragon are at present undergoing litigation, for example the estate of Villahermosa, the *condado* of Aranda, that of Luna, that of Fuentes, that of Castelflorit, that of San Clemente, and others. In that of Sástago, only a few days ago a Castilian came in to live on the estates; and the count of Belchite has a lawsuit with the duke of Hijar. And all the other nobles and gentry have such low incomes and salaries that they can barely maintain themselves.

The truth is that despite considerable problems at no time were the nobles ever under serious threat. The mayorazgo protected all their major holdings from alienation, and licences to contract censos proved to be an indispensable aid, in spite of the consequent huge increase in debt. When the need arose the Crown also allowed parts of a mayorazgo to be sold in order to raise cash, which however always had to be used to redeem other entail debts. In 1670, for example, the count of Puñonrostro, Don Arias Gonzalo de Avila, was given leave to sell land from a mayorazgo in Segovia in order to raise 6,000 ducats.[114] The Crown also eased the debt burden by regulating the interest rate, which in this reign was generally 5 per cent.

In view of the very heavy reliance many nobles placed on their income from government annuities, the Crown found it helpful, as we have seen from the lists for 1680, to give relief from the tax on this revenue. Sometimes the relief was very substantial. In 1669, total tax relief of 100,000 ducats was granted to needy aristocrats.[115] In 1670 the marquis of Leganés, who had a total juro income of 13,784 ducats a year, was given tax exemption on just under a third of it, 'in view of his difficulties and since these juros are his main income'; the duke of Abrantes, Don Agustín de Alencastre, was given full exemption on his juro income of 9,675 ducats; the count of Monterey, Don Juan Domingo Méndez de Haro, likewise received exemption on most of his 22,000 ducats of juros. Among the most needy were the marquis of Aguilafuente who, 'since his main income consists in 8,296 ducats of juros to support his wife and ten children, has retired to a village'; the count of Montalvo, whose 'great straits have forced him to retire to live in a village'; and the count of Toreno, who was 'so in need that he is forced to live in Asturias'. All were granted concessions.[116]

## HABITS OF VIOLENCE

Despite the great frequency of litigation, personal violence remained a common method of resolving quarrels. Not all these cases, or even the majority of them, involved the supposed Spanish zeal for questions of honour. As the one class entitled to bear arms, the aristocracy exploited its privilege freely. Unfortunately they were happier drawing their weapons in the streets of Madrid than where the state wanted them to, on foreign battlefields. Commentators in mid-century were unanimous that the younger nobility of blood – as against aspiring hidalgos, who were always anxious to win their spurs and so establish their status – were no longer going to the wars as their fathers had done.[117] By 1700 the marquis of Villena was urging the new king's grandfather, Louis XIV, 'to re-create the army, and to make the nobles appreciate it',[118] a phrase that emphasises the decay of a great military tradition.

In 1672 six grandee members of the council of State suggested that one inducement to military service would be to raise the salaries of officers:[119]

We have discussed the very little effort that has been made by the higher nobility to serve in the war, though this employment most befits their duties and is of the most service to Your Majesty. Those who are at present serving in Flanders, Milan and Catalonia are so outstanding that we can mention it without embarrassing Your Majesty; we do so not without sorrow (for they are very few) at the great decay among those who are the true basis of the armed forces, and the most suited to be leaders and generals, with the experience and discipline required by those who have to command armies. Realising how infinitely useful it would be to discover the reason for this unwillingness to serve, the council has arrived at the conclusion that the most important cause is the lack of means of those who have a natural wish to serve but who bear in mind the great expenses incurred on campaigns.

Whatever the reason for their reluctance to go to war, nobles were not slow to provoke violence in their own country. Challenges (*desafíos*) were so frequent that, as we have seen, the council of Castile in 1684 proposed introducing the death penalty for fatal incidents. The council of State lamented in 1688 that[120] 'we see the nobles at variance with one another, wholly occupied in frivolous and senseless pursuits that can seriously endanger the public peace and the service of Your Majesty unless a prompt and effective remedy is found'.

The problem of retainers was a crucial one. It is difficult to tell whether retainers were simply household personnel or rather attached to a lord like French *fidélités*.[121] The constant danger was that a quarrel affecting only one member of the group, not necessarily the lord himself, was taken up by all the other members. The propensity of aristocrats to maintain large followings (Oropesa in this reign was said to have 74 retainers[122]) opened the doors to continued street violence. A variation from the type of street violence known in the cities, is the case of the count of Fuensalida, viceroy of Navarre in 1677. After failing to obtain the favours of a girl, a commoner and poor, who would not accede even for money, he sent six armed men to kidnap her. The mother created a scene, neighbours joined in, and soon a crowd was besieging the viceroy's palace.[123] Fuensalida was subsequently removed from his post.

In seventeenth-century society violence born of individual frustrations was infrequent. Most violence was related to the place of the individual in the community. *Honor* was not a personal but a communal concept. Two examples illustrate how feudal loyalties created violence.

In November 1678 officials of the royal treasury in Valencia went to Gandía to make some arrests, but the inhabitants disarmed and imprisoned them and sent off to inform the duke. The officials were kept in cells for two nights. On the third night the duke's bailiff released them and told them to leave at once, though it was dark and pouring with rain. Afraid of worse to come, the officials avoided the main road back to Valencia and took another route. They were however followed by six men who set upon them. The next morning one of them was found dead by the river. The viceroy of Valencia protested to the king, who in December ordered the duke of Gandía to be arrested, and confined in the castle at Morella in Valencia. In fact he was kept under house arrest in Ocaña, and allowed to return to Madrid in April 1679.[124] His bailiff was condemned to serve in Orán for ten years; two other ducal officials were sent to the galleys for two years, and a third was banished for ten.[125]

The second example is that of the quarrel between the Admiral of Castile and the count of Cifuentes. Enmity between them was based on an incident in August 1697, when the Admiral was chief minister of the Crown and Cifuentes challenged and lampooned him publicly.[126] The English ambassador, referring to the frequent challenges they interchanged in 1697, observed that 'Cervantes has not wholly reformed this nation; there are still Quixoterias left among them'.[127] In 1699 when the Admiral was passing through Granada a local nobleman, the marquis of Los Trujillos, went up to his room uninvited, forced his way through the retainers and handed the Admiral a written *desafío* from Cifuentes, at that time prowling around the vicinity with a gang of forty horsemen.[128] In both these cases violence was related to the system of loyalties that bound men to their feudal lord.

## INFLATION OF HONOURS

The reign of Charles II was the last age of preponderance of the blood nobility. In such a period it would be unusual to see the aristocratic élite allow any great addition to its numbers. Yet this is what happened. In both Castile and Aragon the number of nobles created reached a new peak.

Sale of honours was a sensible way for the state to reward services or recognise social success. Certificates of *hidalguía* (noble status) were sold by both Charles V and Philip II, against strong opposition from the Cortes, and continued into the next century. Philip IV sold 102 during his reign.[129] There was usually great hostility to these grants, which were obtained to gain exemption from taxes and played a minimal role in the process of social mobility.

Granting of titles of nobility was a more important matter. The earlier Habsburgs had allowed a considerable increase in the number of titled nobles (*títulos*) and grandees. In 1520 Castile had twenty grandees and thirty-five títulos; by the end of the reign of Philip III the total of both was over 140. Philip IV, like other monarchs who needed money, took the increase further: he created sixty-seven new marquises and twenty-five new counts.[130] Charles II outdid all his predecessors. He approximately doubled the size of the Castilian titled aristocracy. In the thirty-five years of his reign the Crown created twelve new viscounts, eighty new counts, and 236 new marquises. The dates of their creation are set out in Figure 8.1.[131] In addition to these, some twenty-six nobles were raised to the rank of grandee during the reign.[132]

Fig. 8.1  Creation of Castilian nobles under Charles II.

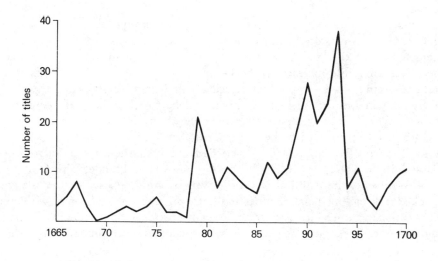

The increase in títulos had little unsettling effect on Spanish society. Most if not all newcomers were already well established in their local communities, and a title merely confirmed their social ascent. Pedro Fernández del Campo y Angulo had been alcalde of Bilbao; his father was alcalde and regidor in 1625–26. The fortunes of both were based on trade and agriculture.[133] Pedro moved to Madrid, served in the administration, and was created marquis of Mejorada in 1673. Ascent from the ranks of the wealthy merchant class into the titled nobility of Castile was a common phenomenon. When the Savoyard trader Lantéry first came to Cadiz in 1673 the city had only two títulos – one was the merchant Don Antonio Fernández de Castro, created marquis of Villacampo in 1666 – and six holders of *hábitos* of military orders. By 1705 there were 'at least a hundred gentry with various hábitos, and thirty títulos of Castile'.[134] The numbers are a clear indication of the inflation of honours under Charles II.

The fact that most new titles were purchased rather than bestowed, may have diminished their status. This had already happened with the wholesale creation for money under Philip IV of knighthoods (hábitos) of the historic military Orders.[135] 'In my childhood', a writer of 1617 declared, 'a whole village would stand in awe to see a hábito. The villagers would almost beat on their chests to see the Señor Comendador pass by.'[136] This no longer happened, because of the multitude and the lower economic status of hábitos. By the late century hábitos, once the preserve of the warrior élite, were being granted for minor services to the Crown. In the same way, the open sale of noble titles could only have evoked contempt from the older aristocracy.

The needs of the treasury, however, came first. Sales of titles multiplied as the war debt soared, particularly after the peaces of 1678 and 1689. The government consistently raised its prices. Finally in 1692 it decided that all those to whom titles had been sold since 1680 (the year of the great deflation) for less than 30,000 ducats, should make up the cost to this amount: unless they did so, their titles would be regarded as for life and not hereditary.[137] A quick estimate shows that if all the titles granted between 1680 and 1692 were finally priced at about this level, the treasury in those years probably benefited by about 5,300,000 ducats.

Ministers of the Crown were more discriminating about the sale of grandeeships. This exalted rank, with its singular privileges, was a highly prized characteristic of the Spanish and particularly the Castilian nobility. Here too there was a notable increase, from 41 in 1627 to 113 by 1707.[138] Existing grandees seem to have accepted the creation of new grandees so long as their own privileges remained untouched. A revealing debate took place in the council of State in 1690.[139] It was proposed to raise money by various means including the sale of a grandeeship to a member of the Grillo family, prominent Italian bankers of the Crown. Domingo Grillo, who had obtained the title of marquis of Clarafuente in 1682, now offered 300,000 pesos for a grandeeship. Only one grandee present, the Admiral of Castile, was strongly opposed to the sale and attacked it as 'bad medicine that destroys rather than cures the Crown'. He chose the occasion to launch into a bitter tirade against useless talk in councils. 'There is no other ruler in Europe', he claimed, 'who spends so much money on councils, on superfluous officials, and on collecting his own revenue.' By contrast, the other grandees saw no objection in principle to the sale, and only queried the price. The duke of Osuna claimed that 'not so long ago, 20 to 40,000 pesos was paid for a title of Castile, and now there are persons who receive this favour for 40,000 reales [less than 3,000 pesos]. . . . If we follow this practice with grandeeships, we shall find ourselves with more grandees than títulos, and more títulos than commoners.' There were demands that the price be raised to 400,000 or even 600,000. Grillo obtained his grandeeship in 1691, apparently at the price he offered.[140]

Nearly half the new grandees were non-Spaniards. This helps to explain why no imbalance or resentment was created in the ranks of the peninsular aristocracy. In Italy the new grandees could display their status without offending the time-honoured rules of precedence accepted in Spain.

Because proportionately few of the titled aristocracy came from the non-Castilian provinces of Spain, little attention has been paid by historians to inflation of honours in those realms. The biggest single block of *mercedes* or honours granted in this reign was at the Cortes of Aragon in 1677–78. The occasion was used by Don Juan of Austria to reward those who had helped him to power. The relatively small number of honours bestowed gives the lie to contemporary critics who accused him of lavishly dispensing favours. Only two títulos were created; ten *caballeratos* and twenty-three hábitos were granted. Various other concessions brought the total to under 200 mercedes.[141]

In the Crown of Aragon there were traditionally three grades of lesser nobility below the titled lords. In ascending order, these were the rank of distinguished citizen (*ciudadano honrado*) followed by that of knight (*caballero*) and then by the rank of noble (*noble*). In the Cortes of Monzón in 1510, Ferdinand the Catholic granted to the *ciutadans honrats* of Barcelona the same privileges as those of the upper gentry (*cavallers* and *nobles*). This brought them into line with the *ciutadans* of Valencia, who had enjoyed this equality since 1420.[142] The ciutadans were thus recognised as being of noble rank, with corresponding privileges such as tax exemption. In what follows I shall deal exclusively with Catalonia. Ciutadans in the principality were economically privileged but politically underprivileged. They did not as a group have a right to sit in the Corts, as cavallers and nobles had; they could not be insaculated for office in the Diputació except as representatives of towns; and they could not be registered or take part in the elitist committee of ciutadans, which met annually on 1 May in Barcelona, except by invitation.[143] The chief problem posed by the creation of new ciutadans, in a province where the tax for billeting troops had always been contentious, was that of their tax exemption. The fact that ciutadans were politically less privileged than cavallers made the government reason that logically their economic privilege should also be removed.[144] After 1671, accordingly, a compromise was evolved whereby pretendants to the honour of ciutadà had to agree to a special clause removing their exemption from the tax for billeting.[145] This left the government free to grant further mercedes without the worry that it was reducing its military income in Catalonia.

The problem was inevitably serious in the principality. On one hand there was the pressing need to finance the wars against France. On the other, there was a deliberate policy of rewarding loyalty and service, and attempting to retain the goodwill of Catalans. Honours in Catalonia were given – and sold – with an open hand. In 1669 the minimum number of honours granted through the council of Aragon, which had the duty of debating the merits of each application, was twenty ciutadans, six cavallers and two nobles; in 1670 and 1671 together it was twenty-two, six and four respectively.[146] This seems to have been the approximate quantity in which privileges were issued. In 1675, for example, at least thirteen ciutadans, four cavallers and three nobles were created, in 1684 at least seven cavallers and five nobles.[147]

The hundreds of new gentry created by this process, were cause for serious alarm in Catalonia. In February 1678 the viceroy observed that

. . . the liberality with which Your Majesty honours your vassals who are citizens of this principality, in granting privileges and titles of distinguished citizens, knights and nobles, has become in my view deserving of criticism, both because of their great number as also because of the bad consequences for Your Majesty's service. These honours mostly fall on those who have done little to merit them. In addition, the exemptions make billeting impossible, and all the tax burden is borne by those who are unable to bear them.

Responding to the letter from the viceroy, the council of Aragon agreed that

the number of privileges, particularly citizenships, granted since the recovery of Catalonia has been very high. . . . So numerous are the exempt – clergy, knights, citizens, lawyers, doctors and familiars of the Inquisition – that the burdens and obligations of the towns are borne by the meanest and the poorest.[148]

After years of this type of criticism, the Crown on 7 December 1684 restricted the further sale of privileges. A report in 1685 from the Chancellor of the Audiencia to the viceroy, Leganés, emphasised the continuing problem.[149]

I feel it my obligation to represent to Your Excellency [he wrote] the many disturbances caused by the multitude of new cavallers, both in the towns where they live and have their property, as well as in the Braç Militar, where they are resented by those who see them as acting to the detriment of the noble estate. The complaints are above all over their exemption from billeting. It is true that there can be no complaint over the cavallers who live in cities, where there is no billeting. But others, who are the wealthiest, have one, two or more houses in the country, where they keep tenants who till their land; and it is these, with the support of the owners, who refuse billeting, or to pay communal taxes, and thereby provoke disputes.

Only two or three honours were granted in 1685; then in 1686 the number began to grow.[150] In 1687 the viceroy, protesting in principle at a request for a citizenship, claimed that 'these grants are contrary to the king's service, and cause the burden of the principality to fall only on the poorest'. His protest was supported by Don Pedro de Aragon, president of the council of Aragon, against all the other members of the council: the king supported Don Pedro and quashed the grant.[151] Thereafter and for the rest of the reign a very firm hand was kept on the granting of privileges in Catalonia. Most applicants, particularly for the rank of ciutadà, were kept waiting.[152] There was by no means a complete stop, which would have been impolitic; in 1690, for instance, at least one ciutadà, one cavaller and three nobles were created. The rule adopted was that privileges creating an exemption would not be granted, whereas candidates already exempt were usually permitted to proceed.

This deflation of honours bred no discontent in Catalonia. In fact the generosity of grants made since the recovery of Barcelona from the French, was without equal in the history both of the principality and of Aragon. The unshakeable loyalty of the Catalan ruling classes in the events of 1688–89, described above, proves this amply. It must also be remembered that Charles II began the systematic creation of a titled Catalan aristocracy, which benefited the leading gentry of a province hitherto lacking in titles, and counterbalanced the drift of the older titled aristocracy to Madrid. Among the new titles conceded in this reign were those to Don Juan de Carriera, count of Solterra (1671); Don Miguel Zalva, marquis of Vilanat (1680); Don Francisco Bournonville, marquis of Rupit (1680); Don Francisco de Monserrat, marquis of Tamarit (1681); a marquisate to the heir of the count of Eril (1689); Don Félix de Marimón, marquis of Cerdanyola (1689); Don Manuel de Sentmenat, a marquisate (1690); Don Francisco de Llar y Pasqual, count of Llar (1691); Don Ramón de Zagarriga, count of Creixell (1691); Don Miguel Juan de Taverner, count of Darnius (1691); Don Juan de Sentmenat, marquis of Sentmenat (1691);[153] Don Narcis Descallar,[154] marquis of Bessora (1698); Don Miguel de Clariana, count of San Esteban de Munter (1698).[155]

## CROWN, COURT AND ARISTOCRACY

An inescapable mood of pessimism hung over the magnates of the late seventeenth century. Foreign commentators portrayed them in the most unfavourable colours. The Venetian envoy Federico Cornaro reported in 1681:

There is hardly a noble who does not live off the king's treasury or who, in the absence of royal pensions, could keep himself on his own income. Because of this, the principal lords, attracted by offices in Madrid, have abandoned their estates from which they draw empty titles rather than material benefit.[156]

The French ambassador Rébenac reported in 1689 that

the king of Spain gives immense sums to the lords of his court. Pensions of thirty to fifty thousand pesos for idlers are common. It would seem natural to save this expense, but those who receive this money have nothing else to live on. They maintain a large number of servants in Madrid, and the consumption of Madrid is by itself the most substantial source of income for the king. Duties are about 300 to 400 per cent, so that what enters for one peso sells at four in the town. If the benefits of these people are cut back they will have to go to their estates, where it is impossible for them to live, since the countryside doesn't return one tenth of what it did forty years ago.[157]

The reports suggest that the grandees of Spain had become an impoverished and effete court aristocracy, living as parasites off estate revenue or juros and indulging in conspicuous consumption in Madrid. Despite all their distortions and exaggerations, there is no reason to believe that the foreign commentators were utterly wrong. Spaniards were themselves aware of the shortcomings of their élite. Writing in about 1680, a contemporary recorded

. . . that in these times the produce of their estates in Spain has diminished because of depopulation, and the lords have spent excessive sums at court on vanity and appearances, as well as on their own excesses. Matters have reached such a state that most of them have lawsuits with creditors and limited allowances assigned to them by the royal council. They realise that they cannot exist without making use of employment in the army or the government or the royal household.[158]

The picture of a ruling class that had ceased to perform its normal functions and obligations effectively was a commonly held one. The new French rulers of Spain in 1700 were gratified to find how widely the aristocracy were hated. As we have seen, they were informed in 1703 by cardinal Portocarrero that 'the nobility were brought up and educated without any application, in pure idleness, accustomed to the fact that they could obtain the principal employments in military and political government without knowledge or experience or any merit of their own'.[159]

It is impossible not to agree with the picture. In a world where much was changing, the aristocracy remained firm and immovable, a barrier to change. Indebtedness compromised but did not destroy them. In the last resort it was always the Crown that stepped in to save them from their creditors. Most important of all, they remained totally in control of the machinery of government. No chief minister, not even a prince of the blood like Don Juan, was capable of withstanding their power. Because they invariably split into interest groups, identified mainly by family and lineage, it was sometimes possible to overcome them. But when they combined together, as they did to destroy Valenzuela, they were invulnerable.

It required a great crisis like the War of Succession to annihilate grandee power in Spain.[160] When that happened, the state was fortunately able to make use of the services of the great host of lesser nobles who had benefited from the inflation of honours under Charles II and now found the way open to their advancement.

## NOTES

1. Stanhope to Nottingham, 22 May 1691, in Stanhope, *Spain under Charles*, p. 18.
2. See the map, based on the census of 1797, in Domínguez Ortiz, *Sociedad española XVIII*, p. 80.
3. Muret, *Lettres*, p. 30.
4. Bertaut, *Journey into Spain*, p. 29.
5. The discussion on encomiendas in Domínguez Ortiz, *Sociedad*, I, 198–201, is particularly useful.
6. *Ibid.* pp. 301, 357–60.
7. The most useful work on the Aragonese nobility remains **Montemayor de Cuenca, J. F.**, *Summaria Investigación* (Mexico 1664).

8. For Valencia the authority is **Madramany, M.**, *Tratado de la nobleza* (Valencia 1788).
9. See **Elliott, J. H.**, 'A provincial aristocracy', *Homenaje Vicens Vives* (Barcelona 1967), II, 125–41.
10. Madramany, *op. cit.* pp. 237, 271.
11. 'Informe a Su Magestad sobre la pretension del Collegio del Arte de Notaria desta Ciudad del goze del Privilegio Militar', Viceroy to king, 26 April 1689, ARV:RC libros registros 593/172–7. The privileges mentioned are those granted by Alfonso III to the notables of Valencia.
12. See **Fernández Duro, C.**, *El último Almirante* (Madrid 1902). The details that follow are from the 1716 confiscation lists in AHN Consejos 7335.
13. Willughby, *Relation*, p. 471.
14. 1682 statement of censales on Cardona, in ACA:CA 205. Elliott, *Catalans*, p. 98, estimates the Cardona jurisdictions at 238.
15. See Domínguez Ortiz, *op. cit.* pp. 301–3.
16. Full printed paper, and conclusion of debate, in ADZ 734/2114–18.
17. 'Denia: derechos que poseia el Marques de Medinaccli 1669–1720', ARV Real Patrimonio, Bailia B: leg. 32 exped. 399.
18. Domínguez Ortiz, *op. cit.* pp. 254–6
19. *Ibid.* pp. 263–4.
20. *Ibid.* p. 263.
21. Discussion in *ibid.* pp. 224–7.
22. Letter from Cadiz, 31 April 1689, BN MS. 1001/141.
23. AHN Osuna 1030/4.
24. Accounts of *asiento* between Leganés and D. Juan Morales, contador mayor de la casa y estados de Su. Excelencia, AHPM 8817/564, notary Juan de Medina.
25. Report of Junta de Reservas, 12 Oct. 1670, AHN Consejos 7259.
26. The raising of the loans through censos is detailed in the report of the Cámara of Castile, 14 April 1684, AGS Cámara de Castilla 1490, and in a petition of 1699 from Leganés in *ibid.* 2098.
27. **Arteaga, C.**, *La Casa del Infantado* (Madrid 1944), covers the sixteenth century, as does **Serrano, L.**, *Guadalajara y sus Mendozas* (Madrid 1942).
28. A list of these towns is in AHN Osuna 3350/2, in a survey of 1797.
29. Cited in Kamen, *War of Succession*, p. 271.
30. 'Razon de lo que montan los estados de la casa del ymfantado', 1637, AHN Osuna 3009.
31. *Sociedad*, I, 249 n. 75.
32. Orders for concursos of 18 July 1661 and 15 Sept. 1690 in AHN Osuna 1724/11.
33. *Ibid.* 3329/27.
34. Returns in *ibid.* 1703[2]/26.
35. See *ibid.* 3329/7 ff.
36. Average from figures in *ibid.* 806/46 and 1021/16. Cf. Casey, *Kingdom of Valencia*, p. 262.
37. AHN Osuna 4083.
38. *Ibid.* 1201/57 fos. 35–7.
39. *Ibid.* fo. 54 vo, duke to Don Hipólito de Villanueva.
40. *Ibid.* fo. 58–9, duke to Dr Domingo Ruiz.
41. Duke to canon Felipe Pi, 3 June, *ibid.* fo. 62.
42. To Dr Ruiz, *ibid.* fo. 108 vo.
43. To Dr Ruiz, *ibid.* fo. 338.
44. Duke to Don Thomas Ros, 30 Sept. 1699, *ibid.* fo. 121.

45. 'Capitols pera el bon govern y regiment de les regalies del Marquesat de Llombay', Madrid 18 Aug. 1700, *ibid.* fo. 227–8.
46. AHN Osuna 4083. The actual sums were 755 and 713 libras.
47. *Ibid.* 811/9, 'Planta forma de las pensiones, salarios y otros gastos que la Ciudad de Gandia paga'.
48. *Ibid.* 1015/8$^{1-7}$.
49. *Ibid.* 4083/8.
50. *Ibid.* 745$^2$/125. For Borja debts in the early century see Casey, *op. cit.* pp. 129, 136.
51. *Ibid.* 4083/180. The year 1678 was that of the celebrated clash between the duke and the council.
52. Agreement of 23 Jan. 1622, in *ibid.* 1031/100.
53. Full details of all censals are in *ibid.* 4082. The baronies of Turis, Albalat and Chella were sold for 106,000 lliures: see Casey, *Kingdom of Valencia,* p. 133.
54. What follows is drawn exclusively from the study by Dr Lorna Jury Gladstone, 'Aristocratic Landholding' (unpublished Ph.D. thesis University of Virginia, 1977). I am extremely grateful to her for letting me quote from her findings.
55. Details in Gladstone, *op. cit.* p. 54 ff.
56. *Ibid.* p. 40.
57. *Ibid.* pp. 313–14.
58. *Ibid.* p. 282.
59. Domínguez Ortiz, *Sociedad*, I, 231 n. 21.
60. AGS Gracia y Justicia 887 antiguo.
61. Memorial of April 1678, AHN Consejos 7188.
62. Memorial of Jan. 1684 from Don Diego Zapata, count of Barajas, AGS Cámara de Castilla 1489.
63. Details from 1637 statements in AHN Osuna 3009 and from the 'Libro bezerro universal de todas las facultades concedidas a los Exmos Señores Duques del Infantado', in *ibid.* 344. Other debts had also been contracted within this half century, but they were redeemed by 1637.
64. The one exception was a *censo* of just over 32,000 ducats raised by the duke in 1679 to finance a mission to Paris, to carry a gift from the king to his French bride: 'Libro becerro . . . Duques de Pastrana', *ibid.* 3414.
65. Stanhope to Nottingham, 16 Sept. 1693, *Spain under Charles*, p. 54.
66. Villars to Louis XIV, 3 Oct. 1681, AE:CP (Esp) 66/229.
67. See Jago, C., 'The influence of debt', *Econ. H.R.,* 16 (May 1973), 218–36.
68. Decree of 16 Sept. 1706, AHN Consejos 7214. The decree lists the following noble concursos: Medellín, Osuna, Priego, Baena, Fuensalida, Castelrodrigo, Palma, Abrantes, Feria, Castellar, Infantado, Montijo, Alcañizas, Lerma, Villena (on non-entailed part), Rivas, Cerralbo (on non-entailed part), Pastrana, Canete, La Conquista, Los Vélez (on non-entailed part), Carpio, Astorga, Salvatierra, Miranda.
69. Documentation of 1668 in *ibid.* 7228/26.
70. Consulta of council of Castile, 8 June 1705, *ibid.* 7268. The largest arrears on censos were to other nobles: the count of Oropesa was owed about 35,600 ducats by 1705.
71. For the preceding details, report of the Chancery of Valladolid, 20 Oct. 1677, AHN Consejos 7187; and Domínguez Ortiz, *Sociedad*, I, 237–9.
72. AHN Consejos 7204/79.
73. Lists in *ibid.* 7020.
74. For an excellent account, see Fernández Duro, *El último Almirante.*
75. Consulta of council of Castile, 17 Sept. 1703, AHN Consejos 7019.
76. 'Autos fechos contra el Conde de Zifuentes', 1699: *ibid.* 7242/1.

77. This estimate of income is based on the confiscation lists in AGS Secretaria de Hacienda 972; and AHN Consejos 50481–3.
78. Memorial by Don Juan de Astudillo, Dec. 1683, AGS Cámara de Castilla 1488.
79. Memorial by countess, March 1684, *ibid.* 1489. The payment of Alcaudete censos had been suspended by royal permission since 1623.
80. Estimate based on figures in AGS Secretaría de Hacienda 972.
81. Report of Cámara de Castilla, 17 May 1683, AGS Cámara 1486.
82. Statement of 17 July 1721 in AHN Consejos 7021.
83. Petition of May 1685, AGS Cámara de Castilla 1494.
84. Detailed report by Don Antonio de Salinas to council of Castile, 29 July 1671, in AHN Consejos 7181/49.
85. Report by Cámara, 8 Oct. 1684, AGS Cámara de Castilla 1492.
86. 'Relacion de Grandes y titulos', 1680, AGS:CJH 1051.
87. Don Balthasar de Herasco, count of Humanes, was in 1669 permitted to contract 6,000 ducats censos to cover expenses in the royal service. His father contracted 7,000 ducats in 1618 and 1623. See report of 28 Feb. 1684, AGS Cámara de Castilla 1489.
88. On the Spinola family who had this title, see below, p. 371.
89. Don Juan de Vergara, marquis of Navamorquende, in a statement of 19 April 1684, asking for a licence for a censo of 10,000 ducats to help pay for a dowry, stated that his estate had only one small censo of 295 ducats on it: AGS Cámara de Castilla 1489.
90. Galbe was a member of the Infantado family. In 1711 the title had jurisdiction over eight villages (total 146 households) and three despoblados. The annual income of the mayorazgo was only 2,792 ducats. See 'Raçon de la jurisdicion y rentas del Condado de Galbe', AHN Osuna 3128.
91. His main estate was in Trujillo: see Kamen, *War of Succession*, pp. 104–5.
92. In April 1684 the duke, whose estates of Montalbán were in concurso, complained of 'the debts on his house', AGS Cámara de Castilla 1490.
93. **Nader, H.**, 'Marquises of Mondéjar', *Econ. H. R.*, **30** (Aug. 1977), 411–28.
94. At the ceremony of Charles II's birthday in 1666, Muret reports seeing over 600 coaches before the royal palace, the Alcázar: *Lettres*, p. 35.
95. Accounts for the duke's meals from 1570 onwards are in AHN Osuna 806.
96. Consulta of council of Aragon, 23 July 1681, and memorial from Hijar, 1 April 1683, in ACA:CA 31/128, 131. Likewise the count of Altamira in 1679 raised 50,000 ducats in censos to cover his costs in assisting at the king's marriage: AGS Cámara de Castilla 1491. The count of Benavente contracted over 72,000 ducats in 1580 for the *jornada de Portugal* and 20,000 in 1599 for the *jornada de Valencia: ibid.* 1492.
97. Report of 3 Mar. 1684, AGS Cámara de Castilla 1489.
98. Report of 12 April 1684, *ibid.* 1490.
99. *Ibid.* 2098.
100. Gladstone, 'Aristocratic Landholding', p. 246.
101. Cf. Domínguez Ortiz, *Sociedad*, I, 229–30.
102. *Ibid.* p. 239.
103. Report of 6 July 1684, AGS Cámara de Castilla 1491.
104. Report of 17 May 1683, *ibid.* 1486.
105. Report of Jan. 1684, *ibid.* 1489.
106. For Arcos, report of 11 Dec. 1686, *ibid.* 1493.
107. Report of 9 June 1683, *ibid.* 1486.
108. Several are mentioned by Maura, *Carlos II y su Corte*; the dukes of Gandía had

100,000 ducats as standard, see Casey, *op. cit.* p. 139.

109. Consulta of council of Aragon, 6 Feb. 1679, ACA: CA 330.

110. Petition from Hijar, 1 Sept. 1665, ACA:CA 521.

111. Cited by Kagan, R., 'Lawyers and litigation', a seminar paper prepared for the Shelby Cullom Davis Center for Historical Studies, Princeton 1978, p. 17.

112. Report from viceroy of Valencia, 26 May 1699, ACA:CA 855.

113. Archbishop (Don Antonio Ibáñez de la Riba Herrera) to Don José Grimaldo, secretary of the Despacho, 26 Sept. 1705, AHN Estado 264/4.

114. Provision of 23 March 1670, in report of 1 Sept. 1684, AGS Camara de Castilla 1491.

115. Decree of 14 Feb. 1669, AHN Consejos 7259.

116. All these cases are in *ibid.*, discussed by the Junta de Reservas.

117. Cf. Domínguez Ortiz, *Sociedad*, I, 273–4.

118. Danvila, *Poder civil*, III, 370.

119. Consulta of State, 17 Sept. 1672, AGS Estado 4128. The councillors were Peñaranda, Alburquerque, Lafuente, Constable, Admiral, and Don Lope de Ayala.

120. Consulta of State, 10 July 1688, *ibid.* 4136.

121. For *fidélités*, see e.g. **Mousnier, R.**, *Les Institutions de la France*, I (Paris 1974), ch. 3.

122. Domínguez Ortiz, *Sociedad*, I, 278.

123. Marquis of Villars to Louis XIV, 18 Sept. 1677, AE:CP (Esp) 62/391.

124. ACA:CA 645/84/1, 16, 25.

125. ARV Audiencia, conclusiones criminales, 1837/57–9, judgments in Sept. 1679.

126. Maura, *Vida y reinado*, II, 159–63.

127. Stanhope to Vernon, 18 Dec. 1697, *Spain under Charles*, p. 122.

128. AHN Consejos 7242/1.

129. Domínguez Ortiz, *op. cit.* pp. 182–4. See the important article by Thompson, I. A. A., 'The purchase of nobility in Castile, 1552–1700', *Jl. Eur. Econ. Hist.*, 8 ii (1979), 313–60.

130. Domínguez Ortiz, *Sociedad*, I, 210.

131. My figures, which are virtually complete, are derived from the authoritative *Títulos del Reino* (Madrid 1951). Cf. the total of 5 viscounts, 78 counts and 209 marquises in Domínguez Ortiz, *op. cit.* p. 210, which he derives from AHN Consejos 5250.

132. The new grandees were Aguilar (1666), Torrecuso (1666), Altamira (1674), D. Pedro de Aragon (1677), Linares (1678), San Pedro (1679), prince of Albano (1683), Mancera (1687), Castrillo (1690), Mansfeld (1690), Domingo Grillo, marquis of Clarafuente (1691), Paredes (1692), Burgomayne (1693), Cesare Visconti, count of Galarate (1694), Don Alonso de Guzmán (1695), Santisteban del Puerto (1696), Montealegre (1697), Montijo (1697), Palma (1697), Los Arcos (1698), Castromonte (1698), prince of Castiglione (1699), prince of Cariati (1699), prince of Castellón and Ferolito (1699), prince of Otayano (1700), Don Pirro Borromeo, count of La Pleve de Brevia (1700).

133. Fernández de Pinedo, *Crecimiento económico*, p. 59. Pedro Fernández del Campo succeeded a fellow Basque, Blasco de Loyola, as secretary to the Junta de Gobierno. He died on 3 March 1680.

134. Lantéry, *Memorias*, p. 6.

135. **Wright, L. P.**, 'Military orders', *Past and Present*, 43 (1969), 34–70.

136. Quoted in Domínguez Ortiz, *Sociedad*, I, 202.

137. Cf. Domínguez Ortiz, *op. cit.* p. 213. The decree also applied to the Crown of Aragon. There is a copy in BL Eg. MS. 329/7.

138. Cf. Domínguez Ortiz, *op. cit.* p. 220.

139. Consulta of 20 Dec. 1690, AGS Estado 4138.

140. See Stanhope to Nottingham, 21 Mar. 1691: 'The poor envoy of Savoy is in desperation to see the supineness and impotence of the Spaniards, who to save their Duchy of Milan, have with great difficulty consented to make one Grillo, a Genoese banker, a Grandee of Spain, for which he pays 300,000 pieces of eight', *Spain under Charles*, p. 13.

141. 'Relacion de las mercedes que el Rey ha hecho', ACA:CA 1368.

142. Valdeavellano, *Instituciones españolas*, p. 338.

143. Consulta of council of Aragon, 20 July 1657, ACA:CA 241/2, outlines the privileges of ciutadans.

144. In the consulta of 1657, just cited; and in a letter of the viceroy, duke of Sessa, on 12 Sept. 1671, in *ibid.*

145. Documentation in ACA:CA 326 and 328.

146. ACA:CA 322, 324. One of the cavallers of 1671 was Dr Gerónimo Campmany (ancestor of Antonio de Capmany), who asked that his name be thenceforth spelt Capmany; see ACA Cancillería Real, Diversorum 5930/144–9.

147. It is difficult to establish complete figures. Mine are based in part on ACA Cancillería Real, Registros de Privilegios 6002–3, and Diversorum 5925–30.

148. Viceroy to king, 26 Feb. 1678, with consulta, ACA:CA 330.

149. Dr Olaguer Monserrat to viceroy, 20 Sept. 1685, *ibid.* 242/42.

150. I have traced three ciutadans, one cavaller and four nobles in 1686.

151. Consulta of council, 29 Jan. 1687, ACA:CA 242/35.

152. 'Relacion de los pretendientes de ciudadanatos, cavalleratos y noblezas que se hallan detenidos haviendo acordado el Consejo se guardasen para quando se havriese la puerta a este genero de gracias', ACA:CA 242/17.

153. For the income of the Sentmenat family, see **Serra i Puig, E.**, 'Evolució d'un Patrimoni', *Recerques*, 5 (1975), 34–71.

154. In 1671 the annual income of Don Narcis was put at 3,680 lliures, his censal debts at 983, ACA:CA 524.

155. Sources for this list are: 'Memoria de los titulos que Su Magestad ha concedido en el Principado de Cataluña desde 1680 hasta 1692', *ibid.* 340; and ACA Cancillería Real, Diversorum 5937/189–97, 227–31.

156. Barozzi and Berchet, *op. cit.* p. 455.

157. Rébenac to Louis XIV, 13 Jan. 1689, AE:CP (Esp) 75/342.

158. *Menor edad de Carlos II*, CODOIN, 67, p. 61.

159. Cited in Kamen, *War of Succession*, p. 83.

160. *Ibid.* ch. 5.

# CHAPTER NINE

# The Bourgeoisie

As in western Europe generally, Spanish society was divided into status groups rather than economic classes of the post-industrial type. The 'middle class' did not exist juridically, and it is consequently impossible to define it. Status, defined primarily by law but also to some extent by practice, was what distinguished some members of the élite from others. Since the highest status to which one could aspire was that of a 'noble', a successful career usually ended in acquisition of noble rank.

For a historian to accept the schema of a society divided into estates and orders, however, is to take the official mythology of the time at its face value. In reality there was already in existence a large middle sector, to which I shall refer for convenience as the bourgeoisie. González de Cellorigo in 1600 had observed that 'the middling sort . . . have attained a particular status, that of a self-made group; and since they belong neither to the rich nor to the poor nor to the middle, they have thrown the state into the confusion we now see it in'. The bourgeoisie had no recognisable position in society, and were spread over several status groups. In the Basque country, where all the upper class were technically noble, many would by their calling and style of life be better defined as bourgeois. In Catalonia many of the *ciutadans honrats*, formally noble, may usefully be classified as bourgeois. In Andalucia, on the other hand, there were rich bourgeois who, by privileges of late medieval origin, classified themselves as *caballeros cuantiosos* (moneyed gentry), which meant a claim to nobility almost solely on the basis of wealth and of services rendered.[1] The desire for noble status was a dominant social aspiration shared by virtually all successful bourgeois. It is consequently essential to realise that the noble ethic in Spain coexisted with and did not exclude the bourgeois ethic. By function and calling one might be a bourgeois, but for status one had to be a noble.

The middling sort of people, noble or otherwise, were principally those who lived in and administered the towns. At the upper level they included the patriciate of merchants, officials and lawyers; at the lower level they were members of the guilds, or traders. Looking at them in terms of function makes it possible to estimate their numbers in a town. In Barcelona in 1717, for example, those employed in commerce, the liberal professions and public office, made up

11.8 per cent of heads of households.[2] In Tarragona in 1669 some 10.9 per cent of those paying civic taxes were employed in liberal professions and in commerce. This Catalan city, in which the nobility exercised no influence, supplies an interesting profile of the bourgeoisie as an élite. The highest level of the body politic consisted of the ciutadans honrats, mainly qualified in the liberal professions of medicine and laws; the middle level consisted of doctors, lawyers, notaries, merchants and shipowners; the lowest level was made up of artisans and wealthy farmers.[3] Cities that drew part of their living from the sea, as these two did, had an active middle sector engaged in trade, fishing, finance, shipbuilding and related work. By contrast, many inland cities drawing their living from the soil had no scope for the functions we might associate with a bourgeoisie. A good example, cited above,[4] is that of Calahorra in 1683, with an active agrarian sector of 16 per cent; clergy, widows and the poor at 30 per cent; and casual labourers at 41 per cent. This structure gave no opening to the emergence of a qualified middle sector, and was typical of heavily rural areas.

The view transmitted by distinguished students of Spain's past is that the bourgeoisie were so weak that they compromised Spain's ability to develop into a capitalist power. The argument has been put at its most concise in Fernand Braudel's concept of a 'betrayal' by the bourgeoisie of Mediterranean Europe.[5] Many Spanish writers have gone farther than this in attempting to explain their country's deviation from the capitalist path of western Europe. They have spoken of a national character, no less, that 'scorned wealth' and preferred spiritual values.[6] How applicable are these views to the Spain of Charles II?

## THE CAPITALIST ETHIC IN SPAIN

It is no coincidence that the scholars who have elaborated the accepted view of Spaniards as being hostile to work, have all been specialists in medieval history or literature. From their knowledge of the warrior ethic in medieval and early modern times, they have concluded that Spaniards in later ages continued to be influenced by a hostility to earned wealth. One influential study of 1917, for example, deduced Spanish social ideals from the concepts in the *Poema del Cid*.[7] Yet it is certain that by the time of the Habsburgs Spaniards were no longer thinking as some of their medieval forebears may have done. In Renaissance Spain it was not enough to be noble and proud: you also had to be rich. 'The rich are the backbone of the state', claimed a seventeenth-century writer. Another argued that 'those who become nobles through wealth do so because of the wealth and irrelevant of the means by which they have gained it.' Working for wealth was not ignoble. Profit-making was acceptable so long as it was carried out with due concern for status. *Honor* — the noble ideal — was not incompatible with work. 'Working and sweating in order to acquire property in order to maintain honour',[8] was perfectly reconcilable with traditional values. By the same token nobles could take part in trade and finance. The arbitrista Luis Ortiz, in a memorial he presented to the Crown in 1558, demanded that the sons of gentry and nobility be made to follow a trade or profession in order to serve the state.[9]

Social developments in the post-Renaissance world created confusion in received ideas about wealth and honour. Old-style aristocrats tried to defend their status against new nobles by formulating an official idea of what it was to be noble,[10] but in reality there were as many different concepts of nobility as there were types of noble. Many apparent prejudices against manual labour and capitalism were suspiciously like attempts to eliminate economic competitors. The old prejudice against Jews, expressed in the cult of *limpieza de sangre*, became extended eventually into the idea of *limpieza de oficios*, purity from manual labour. Prejudices worked at all levels and in different ways. In Segovia in 1648, for example, the flock-owning nobles who controlled the municipality passed a law 'that no cloth manufacturer, merchant or trader, notary or attorney, or their sons, can be regidores'.[11] In 1781 in the town of Horche (Guadalajara) the farmers who monopolised municipal posts refused to allow local manufacturers to participate and treated their profession as dishonourable.[12] Both cases illustrate a clash not so much of work ethic as of politics. The problem arose repeatedly with all established élites. The guilds, as we shall see, attempted continuously to exclude newcomers by passing restrictive regulations. The struggle to remain exclusive and to hold on to a monopoly explains why, as Richard Kagan has shown, it was in the reign of Charles II that the college of advocates of Madrid 'in 1684 in an unprecedented action required that new entrants had first to meet rigorous tests of lineage and blood purity'.[13] One member of the college, Melchor de Cabrera Núñez, published in 1683 his *Idea of a Perfect Advocate*, which suggested that advocates were nobles and that entry to the profession should be limited to those who were not 'descendants of a tainted race, and had not followed any low or mechanical trade'. The reiteration of 'honour', 'race', 'mechanical trade' and other concepts, were ritual invocations used to cover up status struggles, and by no means signified that the country was in the grip of a reactionary ethic.

On the contrary, by the reign of Charles II most of the old prejudices were on the defensive. Osorio y Redín wrote in 1687:

Some people say that the crafts and trade are a barrier to nobility, because they are mechanical. But all man's actions are mechanical: it is mechanical to eat, to walk, to write: all exercise is mechanical. . . . The worst callings are those that consume the blood of the poor. They are the vilest, but today are held to be the most noble, because the most lucrative.[14]

In 1677 and in the 1680s the Aragonese declared formally that there was no incompatibility between manufacturing and nobility. The most decisive official move against old prejudices came about as a result of a representation from the corregidor of Segovia to the council of Castile on 11 November 1682. The letter, clearly written on behalf of Segovia manufacturers, asked that the court wear Segovia textiles, that textile manufacturing be not considered a bar to nobility, and that manufacturers be exempt from having to take the guild examinations.[15] All these proposals were accepted and put into immediate effect. On 13 December the Crown issued a famous *pragmática* that 'destroyed whatever legal obstacles had existed against the participation of the nobility in economic enterprises of a certain level'.[16]

The pragmatic[17] declared that 'to maintain or have maintained manufactures has not been nor is contrary to the quality, immunities and prerogatives of nobility . . . so long as those who have maintained or do maintain manufactures do not labour with their own persons but through their servants and officials'. The restrictive clause was not a serious one, since no substantial manufacturer worked with his own hands. The pragmatic, like most government legislation, did not break new ground: it merely put into law what was already commonly recognised. Its importance in helping an entrepreneurial class to emerge was, however, considerable. After 1682 the capitalist bourgeois was no longer faced by legal obstacles to higher status, nor was the enterprising nobleman debarred from industry.

The crumbling of such barriers was admittedly only a small part of the problem facing economic growth in Spain. The major obstacles to advance were basically two: a lack of resources, and the subjection of both industry and trade to foreign interests. Any discussion of a capitalist ethic fades into virtual irrelevance before these two problems. The crisis of the early seventeenth century left the country weak and vulnerable. No matter how dedicated he was, a native entrepreneur in seventeenth-century Spain would have found it difficult to maintain his investment and profit margins over a long period. Those who did so – we have touched on some in connection with the Committee for Trade – had to compete against superior foreign capital. The well intentioned efforts of the government were never radical enough; and the only extreme policy decision of this reign, that of the Aragonese to prohibit all imports, was an outright failure. The issue then was not one of uncapitalist Spaniards without the capacity for enterprise, but of a country which had slipped into a pattern of underdevelopment from which it could not escape, and within which it could offer few opportunities to its own bourgeoisie.

Lack of economic incentive was crucial to the Spanish predicament. It was possible to work and become rich, but of what use was this if inflation wiped out the profits? With wealth uncertain, status seemed the only worthwhile pursuit. Security could be found in things that both endured and brought status, such as land, or a large house. Annuities from the government seemed the safest of all investments. 'No sooner has a trader, artisan or farmer got himself five hundred ducats income in juros', wrote Fernández de Navarrete in the early century, 'than he sets up an entail with them for his eldest son, whereupon the latter and all his brothers feel too ashamed to follow the humble callings in which the money was obtained.'[18] Spanish commentators were all critical of this retreat from enterprise. A writer of the time of Charles II attacked 'the lack of application of Spaniards, for we see that if a tailor or cobbler leaves his son a hundred ducats annual income, the son thinks he does not need to work and begins to strut around like a caballero, and if he wishes to take up a profession to get a good restful life he becomes a priest or a friar'.[19] A distinguished writer in Saragossa in 1684 commented that 'in Aragon, with a natural longing to improve their estate, few sons follow the profession of their fathers, and they thereby lose the fortune that their fathers gained. . . . How many we have seen leave their trading for the honourable ambition of becoming a ciudadano!'[20]

Until more work is done on the private papers of the bourgeoisie, it is difficult to make reliable generalisations about their motives and aspirations. The brevity of their commitment to capital enterprise was, I have suggested, largely dictated by the insecurity of the business world. It is likely that they themselves would have liked to see their business flourish from one generation to the next. Some did not have this opportunity. Narciso Feliu de la Peña, one of the symbols of the capitalist spirit in Catalonia at this time, had no heir. Half the text of his will was, as befitted a pious Catholic, devoted to religious matters.[21] However, he took care that his property should not be alienated into non-business use but should pass into the hands of other male members of his family who were still actively engaged in trade. Felipe de Moscoso, likewise a symbol of the enterprising capitalist trader, was also unmarried. His property was willed to his brother in Madrid. The last bachelor to whom I shall refer is the Madrid cloth merchant Manuel González Montesinos. His will, drawn up in 1680,[22] confirms the worst presuppositions about a lack of dedication to business. By its terms he left 1,000 ducats to his brother, a priest; and 500 each to his two sisters. The rest of his property was left to 'my only and universal heir, my soul', to be spent on charities, prayers and masses. There was no concern about preserving the business. The lack of a direct heir is sufficient explanation.

For a full portrait of a bourgeois committed to his calling, consider the naturalised Spaniard Felipe Peris, whose career is also a fascinating case study in social mobility. A native of Marseille, Peris came to Valencia as a boy and worked in the city market as a porter.[23] He became assistant to a fishmonger and eventually set up his own stall. One day he bought a barrel of fish in Alicante and took it back to Valencia, only to find (so we are told) that half the contents were gold doubloons, obviously hidden by smugglers. The windfall enabled him to diversify his goods and set up more shops: he left shopkeeping and became a merchant, trading on his own account. His son-in-law in Alicante acted as an agent. By the 1670s he had become a wealthy merchant, bought and furnished a fashionable house, and was reputedly worth over 150,000 ducats. He married twice, firstly Vicenta Algarra by whom he had three sons and four daughters; and secondly Jusepa Cuiper, sister of the leading merchant Felipe Cuiper: she married Peris in 1669 and bore him one son and two daughters.

Peris died in December 1679 but had drawn up his will in 1674. By its terms[24] he left 450 lliures for funeral expenses and masses, a further 100 as principal to pay for requiem masses, 100 to charity, and a token five sous to each of his grandchildren. His wife Jusepa received back her dowry, numerous valuables (including a string of pearls bought for 278 lliures in 1673 and a gold brooch set with 175 diamonds bought for 399 lliures in 1672), and a life annuity of 150 lliures conditional on her not remarrying. His unmarried children (there were five of them in 1674) were each willed the enormous sum of 4,000 lliures, to be had when they married or, in the case of the boys, reached a suitable age. The crucial aspect of these sums was that they were not to be in cash, but only in the form of rents or other income from the estate. Peris, in short, stipulated that no part of his property should be alienated, and that an entail should assure the continuation of his capital. Jusepa Peris died in Alicante in 1684, survived by her two daughters.[25]

In his instructions to his sole heir, his eldest son Crisóstomo,[26] Peris ordered him to invest 16,000 lliures or more, from available cash or other moneys owing to him, in censals, property and other assets: 'so that my inheritance may be enriched, and so that my heir and his successors may live in ease and prosperity on the income from the houses, lands and censals acquired by me and on that produced by the investment of the said 16,000 lliures'. No alienation from the entail was to be permitted. Peris went on:

And since Our Lord in his infinite goodness and mercy has seen fit to advance and add to my house with temporal goods acquired by me through trading and negotiating in merchandise and commissions by land and by sea, and in many other legal and honest dealings that I have had with persons of import and estimation . . . it is my firm wish that my son and heir Crisóstomo Peris continue in the same trade with merchants and particularly with Anthony Basset and Josiah Cranforth, English merchants in Alicante,[27] with whom we at present have the most business.

And he went on to emphasise the very great need for his son to continue in commerce:

It is important that he do so, so that by God's favour he and his children may prosper, for otherwise through idleness and without the said occupation and business he might consume the income of his inheritance, which would vanish and come to an end in a short time if he had to rely on it alone for the upkeep of his house and family and the maintenance of his children.

This remarkable capitalist credo cannot be dismissed as the philosophy of a non-Spaniard. All Peris's adult life was spent in Spain, all his property was in Spain, his second son was a canon of the cathedral in Valencia. In its form there is nothing to distinguish the will from those of other Spanish merchants. The only difference is the unusual expression of the testator's personal outlook on business.

For the philosophy of a born Spaniard, there is the minor financier Andrés Núñez Boceta, a resident of Madrid who drew up his will in 1680.[28] Núñez had two daughters as his only heirs. A native of Villagarcía de Arosa in Galicia, he had married one daughter off to José López Fajardo of Villagarcía, and had then moved to work in Madrid. In 1658–59 he helped to farm some taxes in Galicia and made a large profit from it. While there he also acted as agent for the banker Francisco Grillo. In 1662 he farmed the alcabalas of Málaga. By the 1670s he was well placed, with substantial investments such as a censo of 40,000 reales principal against the municipality of Madrid, at 8 per cent annual interest; and one of 200,000 reales principal against the Jesuits of Madrid. What were the social priorities of this successful small-town financier?

He was a good Catholic; his will asked for 200 masses for his soul, and in earlier days he contracted for a chapel to Our Lady of the Rosary to be built in the parish church of Villagarcía for 50,000 reales. In one form or another he settled most of his goods on his son-in-law, so ensuring the survival of his fortune.[29] There was no undue dissipation of property to the Church or to his family. Núñez's only unusual bequest was 500 reales 'to the poor blind man who lives by the convent of Mercy'. His principal boast was that he had never squandered a penny but had spent his time in accumulation: 'I have no silver plate or jewels or furniture. All I possess is the bed in which I sleep, and some linen.' The precious bed, the only asset of this austere capitalist, was left to his maid, who was also willed 300 ducats. Finally, a word on his wife: 'Ana de Moure Marino brought no dowry nor any money at the time that she married me, nor did I receive any later. The money and capital which was then mine came to 100,000 reales more or less. All the other money that I now have, I acquired by the favour of God our Lord, and while I was away from the said Ana de Moure Marino my wife.'

Possibly not all middle-class Spaniards were like Peris or Núñez, but a great many were. Their aspirations appear, in the context of other documentation, to have been perfectly normal for Spaniards. God's blessing on their enterprise, their austerity and dedication to their chosen calling, together constituted an ineradicably Catholic capitalist ethic. Peris and Núñez reflect that sector of the bourgeoisie which was still rising in the social scale, and was firmly conscious of the need to keep on working in order to maintain family fortunes. The momentum was not always maintained. After the death of his parents, Crisóstomo seems to have ignored his father's precepts. In 1690 he obtained a *caballerato* for 2,000 lliures, and in 1700 acquired the title of marquis of Castellfort.[30]

Crisóstomo's success story was not necessarily a 'betrayal'. All great capitalists in modern times have found status irresistible. Crisóstomo may have continued trading through agents, as other nobles did. In Mallorca during this reign the greater part of foreign trade was controlled by nobility and gentry, who collaborated with merchants and *conversos* in the formation of trading companies. The outstanding nobleman was Don Joan-Miquel Sureda, who in the 1680s invested his money in several companies dedicated to imports and exports, and conducted retail trade through agents.[31] Throughout the Crown of Aragon, the alleged incompatibility of trade and status was taken less seriously than in the Crown of Castile. In the third or Caballero estate at the Cortes of Aragon in 1677, we find a petition from the 'mercaderes infanzones (noble merchants) resident in Saragossa', claiming that their participation in commerce was acceptable to law and custom, but asking that public honours be granted to traders in their own right.[32] In 1689 the Diputados of Aragon asserted that trade and manufacture did not derogate from nobility.[33]

Declarations like that of 1689 in Aragon and 1682 in Castile were in a sense superfluous. Many sections of the élite were now firmly committed to business activity. The Basque and Catalan gentry had long been occupied in it, and the whole policy of the Committees for Trade was based on the assumption that capitalist activity was much to be desired in Spain. Greater social mobility blurred the frontiers between bourgeois and noble, and made old prejudices more difficult to apply. The entrepreneurial spirit of the time was epitomised by a bourgeois with noble status, Narciso Feliu de la Peña. There was, in short, little reason to doubt that Spaniards were engaging freely and seriously in capitalist activity, and that their aims were not limited to social advancement. The alleged anticapitalist ethic of Spaniards was visibly on the retreat in the Spain of Charles II.

## MOBILITY AND SOCIAL STATUS

The means whereby men rose through society were the same as elsewhere in Europe: profits from the soil, investments, tenure of office. The prerequisites for advancement in Spain, however, were only three: a good income, a respectable position in society, and freedom from semitic blood. Without all three it was virtually impossible to move to the top of Spanish society. Fortunately the aristocracy in Spain was not a closed caste, despite the attempts of some of its members to pretend that it was. One consequence of the easy access to nobility, was that few successful men tarried long in the middle sector, or what we would call the bourgeoisie. Indeed most of the men we are about to discuss would have denied that they were anything but noble in status.

As mentioned above, in Catalonia the rank of ciutadà honrat was the first step into the grades of nobility. How then did one become a ciutadà? A typical bourgeois who made the step was Francisco Argemir. His important financial services to the royal army in Catalonia, and purchase of the lordship of the village of Papiol, together helped him to obtain a ciutadanat in 1664. He followed this up quickly with the rank of cavaller in 1675 and noble in 1677. In 1670 his younger brother Onofre, a merchant whom we have met already as a correspondent of Felipe de Moscoso of Alicante, also became a ciutadà.[34] In Catalonia the practical difference between cavaller and noble was negligible. Ascent to the one was usually followed by the other. The crucial step was to become a ciutadà.

Wealth by itself was not the way. In 1671 the rich merchant Jaime Falguera, with an annual income of 2,000 escudos, was not granted a citizenship. Jaime Guell, on the other hand, a modest farmer of Alcover (Tarragona), worth 600 escudos a year, was in 1675 made a ciutadà without difficulty. He was said to be 'the son of well known parents, and with property sufficient to keep himself decently'.[35] In his case, as in that of many other Catalans granted mercedes at this period, the overriding criterion was loyalty of the family to the Crown during the secession of 1640–53. Domingo de Abenía was a soldier who had served the Crown long but had little income of his own: he was granted a citizenship not for himself but for his daughter, to be bestowed upon the man who married her, thus rewarding Abenía and giving his family dowry and status at the same time.[36] Apart from such war honours, pretendants to nobility needed above all to prove their acceptance by the community. Jaime Guitart was reported by the viceroy to be 'of ancient extraction and his family have always been considered caballeros and been treated with great distinction, and his income consists of rents and lands worth over 1,000 ducats income a year'. The viceroy claimed of Dr Isidro Pallares that 'his forefathers have been held in great esteem and distinction'. Juan Fel was said to be 'of ancient farming stock, and well considered'.[37]

A diarist in the early century in Catalonia sneered at merchants 'who the day before yesterday were peasants, yesterday merchants and today cavallers engaged in commerce – and all in the space of thirty years'.[38] His comments, which are applicable to the late century, confirm that noble aspirations were not seen to conflict with business. The former bourgeois and new noble would continue to seek a role in politics; to extend his holdings, most of which he would let through controlled leases; and to invest his money in municipal censos or in trade. The ciutadans honrats of Valencia were apparently of the same quality. A writer in the 1680s claimed their qualifications to be that 'neither they nor their parents exercised a mechanical calling in the state, that they have lived for ten years in the city and have an income of 300 ducats'.[39] Many of the ciutadans, in spite of their aristocratic way of life, took part actively in the commerce of Valencia and Alicante.

The inflation of honours under Charles II was not seen as a threat by the established bourgeoisie and patriciate, so long as their hold on power remained unchallenged. The old ciutadans of Barcelona protected their position by resolving themselves into a committee (junta), into which new citizens had to be matriculated in order to be accepted as genuine members with full civic rights. The practice, initiated in 1519, was confirmed by Philip II in 1599; it meant that non-matriculated ciutadans could not take part in civic elections in Barcelona. The privilege also allowed the committee to matriculate people into its own ranks, and in effect create ciutadans independently of the king; this right lapsed in 1698, after which only the Crown could create ciutadans.[40]

The foreign community in Spain's ports had in the course of the century drifted into and consolidated the ranks of the urban élites: the outstanding example was Cadiz.[41] Elsewhere in Spain there were regular cases of naturalised merchants joining the local bourgeoisie. Traditional hostility to the French, however, precipitated conflict in Valencia in 1696. The case is interesting for the light it sheds on the social outlook of some of the Valencian patriciate.

In 1695 the Valencian merchants Benito Bertet, a Franche-Comtois by origin, and Ignacio Vicent, a Frenchman by origin, were allowed by the council of Aragon to enter the ballot for the elections for Jurats of the city. Precedents for this had been created in the past by other domiciled foreign merchants. The city council nevertheless refused to allow their names to enter the ballot, and proceeded to election without them. The arguments of the city are worth noting.[42]

Those who are to enter the ballot for higher office in this city, must have had not only their own hands but also their father's, free of any taint of manual labout. . . . It would be a great dishonour for this magistracy to see this subject, Bertet, elevated to the preeminence of being one of themselves, when the very clothes his colleagues wear might have been produced by his hands.

Bertet's father had come to Valencia and begun his career as a stallholder in the market; his own son had produced cloth with his own hands. Vicent's father likewise had been a humble trader, selling directly from his own shop; Vicent however became a merchant.

Although it is true that dealing in merchandise is not mechanical, and therefore does not tarnish the lustre of nobility; to trade in small goods and sell publicly with one's own hands, dims it so as to demean a noble's own being and cause his nobility to fall asleep; while he who is not noble is confirmed as plebeian and mechanical.

The council of Aragon refused to accept the validity of the protest and annulled the results of the elections in which Bertet and Vicent should have been entered.[43] There was little doubt that much of the city's case was based on prejudice rather than principle. Vicent's position as a big merchant and as familiar of the Inquisition was vouched for by two leading nobles and two patricians of the city. The dispute was nevertheless settled in May 1697 in favour of the city of Valencia.[44]

Though merchants of French extraction found obstacles in their way, other nations such as the Savoyards (the Solicofres in Alicante, Lantéry in Cadiz) and the English (Basset in Alicante) encountered few problems. Among the most prominent domiciled bourgeois of Valencia was Felipe Cuiper. He was born in Antwerp, where in 1611 he married a Flemish girl. In 1630 we find him settled in Valencia: in that year he was married again, to Angela Serrut. He prospered as a merchant, becoming in the 1630s resident consul for the Flemish, English, Dutch and Hanse traders in Valencia. He acquired an army commission as captain of cavalry, obtained the rank of ciutadà of Valencia, and was entered in the ballot for office in the city. He died in 1668, after an unfortunate period of banishment from the city for having shot a man.[45] His sister married Anthony Basset; one son entered the Church; one daughter married the Valencia merchant and ciutadà Jaume Vinch, and another married Felipe Peris. All Cuiper's possessions, after appropriate deductions (gifts to his four servants, jewellery and pearls to his wife), were willed to his son Juan Bauptista Salvador, under the guardianship of Felipe's brother-in-law Basset.[46]

Cuiper was highly respected in Valencia (one of the witnesses at his defence in 1668 was the celebrated ciutadà, Jurat and annalist Onofre Esquerdo), and we may presume that his wealth was fairly typical of that of the Valencian upper bourgeoisie. Unfortunately his will shows no concern for the continued participation of his son in commerce. Juan Bauptista's interests – military service and landed rents – were exclusively aristocratic, culminating in a successful petition for the rank of cavaller in 1690. By this date the total Cuiper fortune was estimated to be worth over 26,000 silver pesos (or lliures) in capital.[47] The family home, in Valeriola street in Valencia, facing the home of the marquis of Benavites, was worth over 2,000 lliures and was filled with oil paintings.[48] In addition, Juan Bauptista owned three other houses, one inn, a large landed estate in Foyos and several other lands around Valencia; a carriage with four mules; and sundry other property and valuables. The distribution by value of his property was:

| | |
|---|---|
| Own house | 7.7% |
| Houses to rent | 12 |
| Land to rent | 51.1 |
| Censals | 6.5 |
| Furniture, carriage, etc. | 22.7 |

In the words of a witness supporting his application for nobility, Juan Bauptista 'lived in the large house and leased out the other houses, estate and lands; drawing on the rents from these houses and lands as well as the annuities, and performing all the other seigneurial activities that such lords of houses, estates, lands and censals usually do'. The wording is a precise description of the noble way of life, albeit exaggerated in order to support the claim. Absence of public office from the total holdings was no doubt due to the fact that Juan Bauptista inherited his father's commission, and had been a serving officer for four years. Military service completed his qualification for nobility. In 1683 he confirmed his position in the Valencian patriciate by contracting marriage with Cecilia, daughter of Josep Martínez, ciutadà. The dowry was a substantial 5,000 lliures, settled in the form of land and rents.[49].

Despite his position as trader and consul, Felipe Cuiper seems never to have had large sums involved in commerce. What we have seen of Felipe de Moscoso's activity shows clearly that foreign interests dominated all aspects of the Valencian and Alicante trade. In these circumstances there was limited room for investment in trade. A breakdown of the merchants trading in Alicante in 1686, when both Basset and Moscoso were resident, shows that out of ninety-six individuals and firms barely twenty were Spanish, and they were not the largest.[50] It is not surprising that many bourgeois merchants chose to invest in land in their own communities rather than attempt to compete with foreign capital.

Historians have yet to study the various ways in which the rising bourgeoisie of the reign of Charles II became the progressive élite of the early eighteenth century. One group of considerable importance were the *indianos*, entrepreneurs (mainly Basques) who went out to the Indies, became rich, and returned as a new nobility. One such was Domingo Martín de Gortázar of Bilbao.[51] His father Alejo (d. 1679) was a gentleman with property worth nearly 6,000 ducats; some two-thirds of this was in land, and 5 per cent consisted of a share in an ironworks. Alejo was a regidor of Bilbao in 1676 and 1679. Domingo Martín was born in 1670, obtained a hábito of the Order of Calatrava in 1702, and went out to Peru in 1706. He returned rich in 1721, consolidated his property for his children (only three out of twelve survived into adulthood), and in 1724 was elected as a diputado for Vizcaya. At the time of his death in 1743 about half his income came from house rents in Bilbao and one-third from coal and ironworks.

The lesser nobility of the Basque and Navarrese lands also produced the most outstanding industrialist of the late seventeenth and early eighteenth century. This was Juan de Goyeneche, who left his village of Arizcun in the valley of Baztán in Navarre and came to Madrid in the 1680s. His career, which has been studied by William Callahan,[52] developed profitably in the last two decades of the reign of Charles II, and blossomed out under Philip V into the accumulation of real estate and the establishment of industries. Goyeneche was a traditionalist: although an entrepreneur, he did not care to take great risks with his money. When he died, he tied his property up securely in an entail. Nevertheless, as Callahan admits, 'there can be no doubt that he sincerely accepted the point of view advanced by many Spanish economists of his time that more than any other class the nobility was obliged to contribute to the economic progress of the nation'.[53]

The life style of the upper bourgeoisie and urban patriciate included aspects of both the commercial and noble interest without being exclusively committed to either. This could hardly be otherwise in those parts of Spain, particularly the great ports, that relied heavily on trade for communal wealth. Capitalists wished on one hand to continue existing commitments, on the other to pursue social status which could be obtained through their profits. The labours of the mercaderes infanzones in Saragossa, of Feliu de la Peña and Aparici in Barcelona, of Peris in Valencia and Moscoso in Alicante, would be incomprehensible if we did not recognise this duality of purpose. In Catalonia we have the example of Joan Serrals of Igualada, who saw no contradiction in becoming a feudal landowner while continuing his trade as a wool dresser. In 1677 Serrals bought the lordship of Orpí, a little village with fifteen houses, in which he exercised civil jurisdiction, took half the Church tithe and received various annual payments in grain, chickens and cash. His holdings passed through marriage into the Padró family and began the rise of the Padrós of Igualada.[54]

All investments of the bourgeoisie were carefully considered, none more so than marriage. The most striking phenomenon to be found in the documents is endogamy within status groups. This certainly occurred because families did not wish to risk their property too far afield. Bourgeois marriages were therefore, as a rule, investments. In Valencia in the 1670s the patriciate made dowries of around 2,000 lliures. The level can be contrasted with the dowries of 300 lliures normal for a fisherman and a farmer at the same period.

Occasionally, as with Andrés Núñez of Madrid, merchants must have been reluctant to commit any money to the life style required for social mobility. Lantéry was one case:

On 11 September (1698) I sent my youngest son Bernardo to Madrid so that he could be settled in the capital as page to some great lord, since he had a splendid appearance for it, being as everybody knows very charming and having all the right skills, such as dancing, playing a guitar with great skill, carrying a sword well, well written, very well spoken and very courteous. In short, all my friends advised me to do it. But he did nothing more than spend money and bear himself like the son of a great lord, whereupon I decided to bring him back.[55]

## THE GROWTH OF THE BOURGEOISIE

The travails and disasters of the reign of Charles II have tended to obscure the move to recovery. Emphasis on hidalgo mentality and a feeble bourgeoisie has likewise created a misleading picture of entrepreneurial decadence. The active élite, whose outlook has been sketched above, can be encountered in trade, in urban expansion, and in the guilds.

All available evidence points to a substantial increase in Spain's external trade in the late century. At Seville, figures for the export duty called the *blanca al millar*, amounting to a rate of 0.1 per cent, have been used to show an increase in trade from an index of 100 in 1657–61 to one of 150 in 1690–95.[56] In Bilbao, as we have seen, the annual income of the Consulado from port duties increased by 250 per cent between 1650 and 1700.[57] The increase was not necessarily a sign of health, and for the most part may have represented an expansion of commerce by foreigners. There is no doubt, however, that particularly after greater price stability in the 1680s a number of Spaniards felt able to commit themselves to long-term investment. The best known example is Mataró, where support for commercial enterprise came from 'the chief tax-payers in the population, many of whom enjoyed aristocratic privileges but were not strangers to mercantile business'.[58] These investors in trade included Jaume Baró, ciutadà honrat of Barcelona; Miquel Pou i Partella, ciutadà honrat; Bru Sanroma, ciutadà honrat; Felix Tarau, *pagès*;[59] Josep Tarau, later a ciutadà; various members of the nobility, such as Melcior de Palau, and of the pagesia; and above all the *magnífic* Francisco Feliu de la Peña, ciutadà honrat. Other shareholders in the shipping enterprises included surgeons, silversmiths, apothecaries, shopkeepers and wax merchants.[60]

The participation of all sectors of the bourgeoisie and of some of the nobility, can be seen in the activities of the textile trading associations that originated in Barcelona in 1676 around the trader Pau Feu, later ennobled as a cavaller, and the retailer Salvador Feliu, who was matriculated into the merchant élite in 1682. The trading company Feu-Feliu specialised in the 1680s in the import of textiles, working with a capital of over 40,000 lliures; but Salvador Feliu also exported abroad, principally through Mataró, and advanced money at interest. We have seen above that a ship chartered by him was captured by the French in 1684. Despite the active commitment of Feliu's capital to commerce, he became compromised in the next reign by his support of the Archduke Charles and of the New Gibraltar Company. His sons withdrew from civic life and lived on their estates, a measure perhaps of caution rather than of defection from the bourgeois ethic.[61]

The part of the bourgeoisie in urban expansion was certainly important in some towns, but has never been adequately studied. In western Europe the urban middle class came to monopolise civic office, urban finance and eventually the land around the towns. This happened rarely in Spain. More usually the urban nobility dominated officeholding and urban ecclesiastical bodies came to possess the land through censos.

A major development of this period was the growth of a new system to replace the medieval trade corporations.[62] 'From the beginning of the seventeenth century', we are told, 'clear signs began to appear of a decline in the guild system.'[63] The old guilds enjoyed legally protected privileges over the number of masters and apprentices in a trade, the type and quality of work, working conditions and so on. In the early century, traders and producers had looked to the guilds to protect them against the flood of foreign goods. The big merchant bodies, however, like the Arte Mayor de la Seda (for silk) in Seville, or the Consulado of Burgos, were by now unrepresentative and ineffective. Expanding population in the late century created more varied demand for consumer goods, and independent artisans conspired to escape the controls laid down by the guilds. The demand for industrial freedom, made particularly in the Cortes of Aragon, was one of the problems considered by Don Juan of Austria when he set up the Committee for Trade in 1679. In its various enterprises the Committee did more than any other single body to destroy the old guild system, by changing regulations and creating exceptions to established rules. The 1682 decree declaring nobility compatible with industry was part of this programme of innovation.

Inevitably, however, the Committee supported the big merchants rather than the smaller professions. In Madrid this policy took fruit in discussions between the Committee and the Five Great Guilds in 1679.[64] The guilds — representing jewellers, mercers, drapers, linen merchants, and the powerful silk merchants of the Puerta de Guadalajara — were called 'great' because they were the biggest corporate taxpayers in Madrid. The Committee encouraged them to combine into a union, which was formalised by ordinances issued in March 1686. The purpose was to strengthen the economic power of the traders and therefore indirectly to help the state. In their new form, the Guilds represented the combined resources of the trading bourgeoisie of Madrid.

Guild reorganisation occurred at the same period in Barcelona, where in 1680 the fine arts guild was founded, and in 1699 the merchant drapers' guild. All the new guilds had reformed statutes. Their growth was a sign of the resurgence of industry in Catalonia. The spirit of exclusivism operated in the new guilds as in the old, thanks to bitter competition for status, especially in Barcelona where members of some guilds were eligible for municipal office. In Madrid the Five Great Guilds demanded qualifications such as freedom from manual labour, and limpieza de sangre. The new bodies were not a complete break from the attitudes of the past, nor were they accompanied by any major changes in the organisation of industry. They reflected nevertheless the determination of producers, traders and the upper reaches of the urban élite, to claim for themselves an identity that the old system had not allowed them.

## NOTES

1. The *caballeros cuantiosos* were extinct by the end of the century: Domínguez Ortiz, *Sociedad*, I, 192–4.
2. Nadal and Giralt, 'Barcelona en 1717–18', see p. 155 above.
3. Recaséns Comas, J. M., 'Tarragona', p. 89.
4. See p. 158 above.
5. Braudel, F., *The Mediterranean* (London 1973), II, 725.
6. For example, Castro, A., *La realidad histórica* (Mexico 1973), pp. 308–9.
7. Corominas, P., *El Sentimiento de la Riqueza* (Madrid 1917).
8. The foregoing quotations are from Maravall, J. A., *Estado moderno*, II, 119, 126–7; his ch. 4 is an excellent summary of the commercial ethic in Renaissance Spain.
9. See Grice-Hutchinson, M., *Early Economic Thought* (London 1978), p. 129.
10. Studies like García Valdecasas, A., *El Hidalgo y El Honor* (Madrid 1948), use literary quotations to arrive at a single definition of nobility.
11. García Sanz, *Segovia*, p. 220.

12. **Callahan, W.**, 'La estimación del trabajo manual', *Rev. Chileña de Hist. y Geog.*, 132 (1964), 59–72.
13. Kagan, 'Lawyers and litigation', p. 15.
14. Osorio, *El Zelador General*, in Campomanes, *Apéndice*, I, p. 277.
15. Consulta of Castile, 24 Nov. 1682, with letter of 11 Nov. from corregidor to Medinaceli, AHN Consejos 7223.
16. **Callahan, W.**, 'Crown, nobility and industry', *Intern. Rev. Soc. Hist.*, 11 (1966), 444–64.
17. Novis. Recop. lib. VIII, tit. xxiv, leg 1, in **Martínez Alcubilla, M.**, *Códigos Antiguos* (Madrid 1885).
18. Cited in Castro, *La realidad histórica*, p. 268.
19. 'Discurso politico sobre el estado presente de la Monarchia', BN MS. 1442/138.
20. **Dormer, Diego Josef,** *Discursos Históricos-Políticos* (Saragossa 1684), p. 41.
21. Text of will in my introduction to his *Fénix* (1975), pp. 7–12.
22. Will in AHPM 9491/24, notary Juan de Siles.
23. The details that follow are largely from Joachim Ayerdi, 'Noticies de Valencia', BUV MS. 59, under January 1679.
24. Testament dated 28 Sept. 1674 in APV, notary Antonio Morón 1674.
25. ARV Manaments y Empares, 1689, libro 2, mano 22 fo. 42.
26. Though the whole inheritance was to be perpetually under entail, Crisóstomo was given a personal gift of lands and property in the town of Torrent.
27. Basset at this date was the biggest merchant in Alicante, according to the Alicante port returns: ARV Maestre Racional 516, aduana de Alicante, exped. 10396. Cranforth was possibly his partner since he does not appear as an independent trader.
28. Testament in AHPM 9490/132, notary Juan de Siles.
29. López was married to one heiress and was made guardian to the other: he therefore controlled the whole inheritance.
30. The *caballerato* is detailed in ACA:CA 147.
31. I owe this information to a paper by P. de Montaner and Aina Le-Senne, of the History Department at Palma de Mallorca, on 'Nobleza, comercio y corso en Mallorca: Los *negocis per mar* de Sureda (ca. 1650–1730)'.
32. ADZ 734/412. There is another copy in ACA:CA 1370.
33. Cited in Carrera Pujal, *Economía Española*, II, 381.
34. Consultas of council of Aragon in ACA:CA 241/9, 12, 17.
35. *Ibid.* 241/7, 14.
36. *Ibid.* 241/46.
37. The three men are in *ibid.* 241/4, 27, 67.
38. Dr Pujades, quoted in Elliott, 'A provincial aristocracy', p. 129.
39. Mares, *Fénix Troyana*, p. 105.
40. **Cabestany Fort, J. F.**, 'Nomina de "Ciutadans" ', *Documentos y Estudios*, 10 (1962), 11–61.
41. See in particular **Domínguez Ortiz, A.**, 'La Burguesia Gaditana', in *La Burguesia Mercantil Gaditana (1650–1868)* (Cadiz 1976).
42. Memorial by Jurats of Valencia to king, Jan. 1696, ACA:CA 933.
43. Letters of June 1696 from city of Valencia to king, in AMV Lletres Misives, libro 62.
44. Details in ACA:CA 934.
45. The shooting is detailed in the printed *Memorial de Felipe Quiper, ciudadano* in BMV Pragmaticas, Ch. 1647–105 no. 3; and in a memorial of 1668 in ACA:CA 933.
46. Cuiper's will is in APV, notary Vicent Corts 1668.
47. Memorial of 1690 in ACA:CA 932, with a sworn inventory drawn up by the notary Fortunato Añón.

48. A complete inventory of house goods in 1668, accompanies the will.
49. ARV Manaments y Empares, 1683 libro 3, mano 22, fo. 39.
50. ARV Maestre Racional, aduana de Alicante, 516 exped. 10,398. The biggest Spanish merchant was Francisco Mora y Moxica.
51. **Basas Fernández, M.**, 'Los Gortázar', *Anuar. Hist. Econ. y Soc.*, 1 (1968), 403–59.
52. **Callahan, W.**, 'Don Juan de Goyeneche', *The Business History Review*, 43, ii (1969), 152–70. See also **Caro Baroja**, *Hora navarra* (Pamplona 1969), p. 85 ff.
53. Callahan, *op. cit.* p. 168.
54. **Torras i Ribé, J. M.**, *Els Padró d'Igualada* (Barcelona 1976), pp. 31, 219.
55. Lantéry, *Memorias*, p. 331.
56. Smith, *Guild Merchant*, appendix VI B.
57. *Ibid.* p. 89.
58. Llovet, *Mataró*, p. 37. See also **Molas, P.**, *Mataró 1718–1808* (Mataró 1973).
59. The *pagesia* in Catalonia were the rural gentry.
60. Llovet, *op. cit.*, appendices I–V.
61. Molas, 'La Companiya Feu-Feliu', p. 116, accuses them of 'abandó dels valors burgesos'.
62. What follows is based on Domínguez Ortiz, *Golden Age*, pp. 142–3; **Capella, M.** and **Matilla Tascón, A.**, *Cinco Gremios Mayores* (Madrid 1957); and the important surveys by **Molas, P.**, *Los Gremios barceloneses* (Madrid 1970), and *Comerç i Estructura Social* (Barcelona 1977). See also **Molas, P.**, 'Cuerpos Generales de Comercio', *Cuad. Hist. Econ. Cat.*, 19 (Nov. 1978), 213–46.
63. Domínguez Ortiz, *Golden Age*, p. 143.
64. Capella and Matilla Tascón, *op. cit.* p. 74.

# CHAPTER TEN

# The Underprivileged

At least one-fifth of an average Spanish town would consist of the wholly poor or paupers. If we add to these the poor labourers, who had no regular employment and no reliable income, the lower-class poor might total, as in Valencia de las Torres (page 197 above), as much as 40 per cent of the population. In Saragossa, if we add to the registered poor all menials and servants, the total is 42 per cent. We would not be far wrong to take these figures as indications of the social problem in seventeenth-century Spain. Foreign travellers saw beggars everywhere. As late as the 1780s Joseph Townsend said beggars 'abounded in every street' in León, and in Alicante the streets 'swarmed all day with beggars'.[1]

Attitudes to poverty in Spain were basically what they had been in the sixteenth century, when Luis Vives had pioneered poor relief, and when influential writers such as Cristóbal Pérez de Herrera had (in 1598) proposed a ban on begging, and the succour of the genuinely poor in special hospitals.[2] Begging was never in fact prohibited. The greater bulk of Catholic opinion favoured tolerating it, since it both relieved the destitute and allowed the faithful to win grace by acts of charity. The real difference of opinion was over how to control begging. The most significant study of the subject written in the reign of Charles II was the *Triumphant Monument of Catholic Piety*, published by Pedro Joseph Ordóñez at Saragossa in 1672, to justify the hospital for the poor recently built in the city. A priest and doctor in theology, Ordóñez followed the thinking of those writers, notably the Jesuit Juan de Mariana whose views he closely reflects, who encouraged voluntary institutionalisation. He held that 'states have a duty to see that everyone works', and that they 'have an obligation to house and maintain beggars'.[3] Not, of course, all beggars. It was a common conviction (often justified, as we shall see, in Spain) that most urban beggars were vagrants from elsewhere. It was also common knowledge that defrauders, tricksters and *pícaros* made up a good proportion of so-called beggars. Eliminate these two categories and, it was felt, the problem of giving relief to the genuine, disabled poor would be reduced to manageable proportions. The policy of taking the real poor off the streets into an institution arose not, Ordóñez insisted, from a wish to remove a nuisance, 'but from a desire to succour them'.

The Spanish poor relief system was exclusively local. Each town made its own regulations and arrangements for controlling begging and distributing alms. Constant emphasis in urban laws on expelling vagrants, was motivated by concern to help only local poor. Since the sixteenth century, licences for begging within defined parishes were granted to a limited number of the poor. The practice was generally discredited by the late seventeenth century, when hospitalisation was more favoured by the authorities. A major weakness of the Spanish system was that it relied wholly on voluntary Christian charity. England by this period had secularised its poor relief by paying for it out of local rates. In Spain most of the burden still fell on the Church and on ecclesiastical bodies. Charitable institutions of all kinds, mostly financed by the Church but often also by pious donations, therefore littered the landscape. Seville in the 1670s had over seventy foundations devoted to the poor. It was in Seville also that one of the most notable pious donations by a layman was made. Don Miguel de Mañara (1626–79), a Sevillan nobleman, was converted to godliness and devoted his money to building the Hospital de la Santa Caridad, which was completed in 1674 from plans by Bernardo Simón de Pineda. When he died he left virtually all his wealth to the hospital, which remains famous for its paintings by Murillo and Valdés Leal.[4]

Since beggary and vagrancy threatened law and order in the towns, some municipalities were eager to subsidise hospitals. A very early example was the Hospital General of Valencia, created in 1512 by merging a number of smaller institutions. The city acted as patron and gave it an annual grant of 350 lliures, until such time as the Hospital might find other sources of income. In addition various tax exemptions were granted. By the seventeenth century inflation had hit the Hospital's income and few landed assets. The Valencian Corts of 1645 directed 2,000 lliures to be paid to the Hospital out of the revenue of the archbishop, who refused. Many people had over the years invested money in it, but this had created by 1686 a censal debt principal of 80,000 lliures, with annual payments of 4,000.[5]

In explaining why he could not contribute more to the Hospital out of his diocesan revenues, the archbishop in 1686 gave a valuable summary of the contribution of his own see to poor relief:[6]

Of the revenues received by this see (he explained), one-third is set aside to pay the sums granted by Your Majesty to the pope. Another third goes towards the distribution of alms and is still insufficient, for distribution is made daily to 600 poor at the gates of the palace, and to as many students on Sundays to help them with their studies, and to the Casa de Misericordia to help 600 poor every day; besides other alms. . . . According to the accounts these charities come to about 12,000 ducats a year. The final third has to meet the expenses of the archbishopric, and any surplus is for the upkeep of my household. The Hospital has no reason to complain of this see, since in the past twenty years it has enjoyed 40,000 ducats from it, six thousand of these in my time. . . . The 1,800 aforementioned poor to whom alms are given every day, constitute a Hospital General in my own house.

This picture of ecclesiastical generosity pouring out charity at the palace gates, while an institution built for the same poor decayed into debt, was a common one but not always recognised as incongruous. In his study of Saragossa, Ordóñez shared the view of those who felt that outdoor relief aggravated a problem that was better solved by institutionalisation. 'In 1668', he wrote, 'a count was ordered of the beggars who turned up at the gates of the archbishop's palace to receive alms every morning, and it was found that they exceeded one thousand. When the Hospital was opened, they fell to 400.'[7] This was because disabled poor now had to be registered. The conclusion he drew was that the missing 600 were vagrants, foreigners and feigned poor who responded to indiscriminate charity but did not dare come forward when genuine poor were being helped.

Saragossa already had a Hospital General (of Our Lady of Grace) which, like that in Valencia, was primarily a hospital for the sick poor. It was subsidised annually by the kingdom of Aragon to the extent of over 5,500 libras,[8] and from other sources; but in the 1660s it was so overcrowded that its death rate was reported to be over 800 persons a year.[9] For reasons both of health and social control, a new building was required. A group called the Congregation of Piety therefore obtained public support for a new non-medical hospital or House of Mercy (Casa de Misericordia), on which construction was begun in July 1668 and which opened on Sunday 8 September 1669.[10] On that day 'there were voluntarily housed in the new hospital 400 beggars of all sexes, ages and conditions; and all the men ate in one refectory, and the women in another'.[11] The hospital was to be financed by organised almsgiving from each parish of Saragossa, and on this basis the Congregation hoped to raise an annual income of 11,000 escudos.[12]

The excellent conditions in the Saragossa hospital, carefully described by Ordóñez, seem to have guaranteed it some success. Indeed from about this period the municipal and archiepiscopal authorities in Spain's cities began to ensure a firmer footing for public charity. There were no doubt exceptions. In Segovia the Hospital General of Our Lady of Mercy complained in 1666 that, with a capacity for 2,000 invalid poor, its annual expenditure was currently 12,000 ducats whereas its reliable income came to only 1,500, barely enough, so it said, for fifty invalids.[13] Valencia, on the other hand, founded in 1670 one of the most successful hospitals of the time.

Established by a decision of the city council in 1670, the project was controlled by the archbishop, who laid the first stone of the new building in the Moorish quarter in February 1671. The building was completed in four years and in March 1675 the first beggars were housed, while public begging was forbidden.[14] The numbers in the hospital varied between two and three hundred, and soldiers were housed as well as civilians. The single and widowed of either sex were kept separate, but married couples were allowed together in a special section. In numerous memorials the hospital claimed to be keeping unsociable people off the streets and thus lessening crime and the danger of popular agitation.[15] Insecure funding was its major problem, and in 1699 both the Misericordia and the Hospital General threatened to close for lack of means.[16] They survived.

The decisive change to an emphasis on institutionalisation, with a corresponding ban on begging, 'appears to have begun at the end of the seventeenth century',[17] according to one authority. In the eighteenth century Casas de Misericordia became common all over Spain, consonant with the liberal view that the poor must be taken off the streets and trained to work. By 1797 there were 101 such poorhouses in the country, with nearly 12,000 inmates.[18]

Madrid had a very special problem with poverty and vagrancy. As the capital, it attracted vagabonds from every side. In 1664 an order directed to the council of Castile spoke of 'the great numbers of people who come from all parts and live here in idleness and without employment'; in 1665 it was said that 'each day we see greater excesses in the number of idle and shiftless people who fill Madrid'.[19] In March 1665 a complete sweep of the town, parish by parish, was made by the alcaldes in order to establish the number of outsiders who had moved into residence.[20] In an attempt to control begging the council fell back on the old system of licences. On 18 August 1671 all disabled beggars were ordered to present themselves for examination in order to receive a licence. Those who continued to beg without a licence would suffer expulsion from the town for two years for a first offence, four years for a second, and six years labour for a third. Women would be sent to a house of correction (galera). Another decree of 22 September ordered all beggars arriving in Madrid to register with an alcalde within two days.

In 1684 and 1685 further orders were passed to expel non-resident beggars and to enforce the licensing and registration of mendicants.[21] The problem was never brought under control, and grew worse towards the end of the reign. In 1675, as we have seen above, it was claimed that many of the vagrants then in Madrid were Galicians fleeing from the levies being made in their country.[22] In 1694 the council made a radical decision: to send all vagrants to labour in the African garrisons, and to round up all idlers until there were enough to be sent to the army.[23] By 1699, however, the government was still complaining of 'great numbers' of vagrants in Madrid and other parts of Castile;[24] that spring the number of outsiders in Madrid alone, thanks to the famine conditions, was put at 20,000.[25]

Writers in the early seventeenth century were convinced that most vagrants in Spain were from abroad. Fernández de Navarrete in a famous passage claimed that 'all the scum of Europe have come to Spain'. 'Since Spaniards give so many alms', Ordóñez wrote in 1672, 'the poor of all nations come here.'[26] It is likely, however, that French and foreign beggars were numerous only in Madrid. The major problem for towns was rather the influx from rural areas. A small sample for Seville in 1675 shows that of 231 beggars issued with licences, 137 came from outside the province.[27] Improvements in charity were likely to attract more outsiders to the big towns. In 1666 when the Congregation of the Sweet Name of Mary asked permission to set up two new hospices to cater for disabled beggars, the alcaldes of Madrid successfully opposed the proposal, on the grounds that beggars who by current regulations should be expelled from the town, would instead be retained and housed.[28]

The poor of Madrid were in any case fortunate to have the help of a number of voluntary organisations, known as brotherhoods (hermandades). Each brotherhood, consisting of a few priests and several prominent laymen, was dedicated to good works for spiritual motives. Among those founded in the reign of Charles II, the Brotherhood of San Fernando (1673) gathered beggars from the streets 'to be fed, clothed and served'; the Congregation of St Philip Neri (1694) worked in the Hospital General on Sundays and feast days throughout the year; and the Congregation of Consolation (1681) provided burial to paupers who died in the city's hospitals.[29] The most active of all the organisations was the Brotherhood of Refuge, which was founded in 1618 and went through its most flourishing period in the 1670s. It 'provided Madrid with its first ambulance service for the transport of the sick poor to hospitals, paid the cost of moving insane paupers to asylums, took infants abandoned at its door to the foundling hospital, gathered the most destitute of the poor from the streets each night and established a college for the education of orphan girls'.[30]

The first Misericordia or poorhouse established in Madrid, was constructed in 1673 in the Fuencarral and administered by the Brotherhood of San Fernando; it held up to 1,000 inmates.[31] The disabled poor were cared for by several large hospitals. The Hospital General in the Atocha, described by the contemporary Francisco Santos as 'one of the finest buildings in Spain',[32] was run in 1676 by a staff of 205 and during that year took in 9,807 patients, of whom less than 10 per cent died.[33] The Desamparados, or Hospital of Our Lady of the Forsaken, took in orphans and strays collected by the Brotherhood of Refuge. In 1676 it had 330 children, and twelve administrative and eleven teaching staff. It had in addition a wing with twenty beds for expectant mothers: 417 women gave birth there in 1676. The so-called Hospital of Antón Martín, in the square of that name, treated the poor for venereal and other skin diseases. In 1676 it had a permanent staff of nine, and took in 757 patients.

The Hospital General, the Desamparados and the Antón Martín derived their only reliable income from the municipality of Madrid. Investment income (juros and censos) provided another source of money. They all, however, relied heavily on charity for survival, and consequently had to work under very unsatisfactory conditions. In 1676 the contribution from Madrid covered only one-third of the General's expenses. The difficulties of the Desamparados in 1680 were described by an official visitor who discovered '257 boys, all naked and barefooted, without enough beds so that they had to sleep five together and covered with mange'.[34] Other sections of the hospital, for women and pregnant girls, were equally overcrowded and underfinanced. In February 1681, according to the same witness, the Desamparados housed 218 boys, of whom 160 were aged between four and eight years. Bearing in mind the high proportion of young people in the population, it follows that the vagrancy problem primarily concerned children. The work of the Brotherhood of Refuge[35] unfortunately suffered from a shortage of money, and from the lack of any place to house the large number of vagrant girls on the streets. The large Hospital of the Passion was meant for disabled female poor. The three institutions for women subsidised by the municipality – the Magdalena, the Penitencia and the galera[36] – were meant principally for prostitutes and could together accommodate less than 150 women. Boys were well catered for: in 1694, when the Desamparados had 350 boys in residence, several were about to be put out to trades, or sent to sea to train as cabin boys; the oldest, eleven boys aged from sixteen to twenty-three years, were sent to serve in the army.[37]

## ABANDONED INFANTS

Abandoned infants in Madrid were taken into the Hospital of Our Lady of Charity, known as the Inclusa. In 1676 the Inclusa had a staff of thirty-three, of whom twenty-five were wet-nurses. In that year 926 babies were accepted.[38] Infants depended for survival on the availability of wet-nurses; hospital practice was to put out those babies it could not accommodate, to be nursed by paid helpers. In 1698 something like 1,400 infants were being cared for under the auspices of the Inclusa, by wet-nurses scattered through 160 towns and villages.[39] This ambitious exercise in charity had its unfortunate side: a great many of the babies died. The wet-nurses, family women who undertook the job only for the money, were certainly guilty of negligence; many failed to report the death of their charges and continued to draw their payments. An administrator in 1700 estimated that in that year wages were still being paid for some 1,200 babies that had been dead for four or five years but were being falsely reported alive by their wet-nurses.[40]

The records of the Hospital of St John of God in Murcia, which was dedicated to the care of abandoned infants, suggests that the entire exercise was an unmitigated disaster.[41] Generalising from the hundreds of cases listed, we can say that in Murcia in the 1690s most abandoned children were left, newly born and wrapped in a cloth, between the hours of 7 p.m. and midnight on the steps of the hospital. If a note was left with the child it usually gave his name and stated that he was baptised. There can be little doubt that most infants were being disowned and were therefore presumably illegitimate. It was rare to have a mother who, as in 1695, came forward to say that the baby belonged to her and a married man, and that she would like him back. Some infants were exposed because of poverty: a new-born girl was left in 1696 with a note explaining that the mother 'has no means to care for her'; an eighteen-month old boy was abandoned in 1697 by parents who 'because of their great poverty are forced to put him out of their home and have recourse to Christian charity'. The hospital committed itself to baptising a child and caring for it for one year. As with the Inclusa if there was no room in the hospital the child was put out to a paid nurse. At the end of the year, if not before, the child was offered for adoption.

Leaving an infant with the hospital in Murcia was equivalent to a death sentence. In an average year some sixty babies might be abandoned with the hospital: this was in a city of about 20,000 people. Infant mortality could be expected to carry half of these away, but the death rate was in fact higher than this. Of the sixty-two infants left with the hospital in 1697, only five survived: this was a mortality rate of 92 per cent. The babies who died in 1697 survived for an average of 2.7 months after entering the hospital; most of them perished not in the hospital but when in the charge of their wet-nurses.

Teófanes Egido has shown that in Valladolid in the late century abandoned infants accounted for about one-fifth of all children baptised.[42] This roughly confirms the figures for Murcia, and emphasises the depressing prospect for illegitimate babies among the urban poor.

## GIPSIES

The gipsy question in Spain was older than the Habsburg monarchy, and had always been approached through punitive legislation.[43] Gipsy communities first penetrated Spain in the early fifteenth century, and from 1499 began to suffer from official repression. They were sometimes termed 'Bohemians' and occasionally in Castile were known as 'New Castilians'. Their economic and moral life offended the sensibility of a government that was consistently intolerant of minorities. The most brutal legislation was passed under Philip III, who in 1619 decreed their expulsion from Castile. In 1624 the viceroy, marquis of Povar, also decreed their expulsion from Valencia. Since the gipsies were not a settled community, it was impossible to put these decrees into effect. A pragmatic of Philip IV issued in 1633 forbade them wearing gipsy dress or using gipsy customs on the ground that they were not really gipsies at all.

Under Charles II the whole weight of official persecution continued to press on the gipsies. They were accused of every imaginable crime, from incest and murder to espionage. Many were certainly organised in groups as thieves and bandits. When caught, they suffered disproportionately severe penalties. In 1672 the alcaldes of Madrid sentenced two young men and a boy of thirteen, all gipsies, to six years each in the galleys for theft; two others, aged twenty-one, were sent to Almadén for four years for the same offence.[44]

Navarre experienced incursions of gipsies from France and reacted accordingly. In 1602 a viceregal order specified that all vagrants and gipsies be sent to the galleys. In 1662 the Cortes of Navarre asked for firm action and eventually in 1678 the Cortes passed a Perpetual Law on Gipsies, which in effect excluded them permanently from the kingdom.

In Castile the principal measures were passed in 1692 and 1695. The pragmatic of 20 November 1692 repeated the pretence adopted by the pragmatic of 1633, proclaiming that it 'wished to extinguish totally the name of "gipsy" that many men and women of evil life adopt as a cover for their excesses, teaching themselves to speak romany; when the truth is that there have never been real gipsies in these realms . . .'. The pragmatic repeated previous laws prohibiting all the customs, dress and language of the gipsies, ordered them to live in towns of over a thousand inhabitants, and forbade them being called gipsies: 'since they are not of that race, let the name be forgotten'. The pragmatic of 12 July 1695 announced a census of the gipsy population, and ordered them all to declare themselves within thirty days. There is no surviving evidence of this census.

In Valencia the furs did not recognise gipsies, who could live in the realm only if they were naturalised. In 1690 viceroy Castelrodrigo confessed himself unable to expel a number of them 'because they were born in Valencia and have been declared naturalised'. In 1694 he referred to 'these worst sort of people who have spread through the kingdoms, while the complaints of the trouble they cause grow every day'.[45] In these years an important test-case arose about a group of gipsies who had settled in the areas of Játiva and Castellón de la Plana. It is worthy of mention since it was, for fifteen years, favourable to the gipsies.[46]

In 1680 a royal order signed by the king himself had allowed the family of

Maria de Montoya, with her husband, seven children and two brothers, to settle in Valencia. In 1690 the viceroy count of Altamira revoked the privilege after constant pressure from the estaments of Valencia, which maintained that it was in breach of the furs. On appeal the privilege was restored to Montoya in 1692. Castelrodrigo thereupon protested strongly that 'the gipsies live as idle vagabonds, from trickery and barter of goods which are mostly stolen, from pilfering, lying, casting spells, procuring and other mischief'. Moreover, royal letters of naturalisation to gipsies were forbidden by the furs, and the Corts in 1564, 1585 and 1604 had prohibited their residence in Valencia. Finally, the various viceroys in 1576, 1581, 1586, 1623, 1628, 1647 and 1648 had all passed orders expelling gipsies from the realm. Despite this, the Crown ordered Castelrodrigo 'to confirm to these people what was conceded, so long as they live in peace'. The respite was a short one. On 25 January 1695 a royal order gave Castelrodrigo authority to proceed against the gipsies, and included the family of Montoya in its terms, regardless of the privileges of 1680.

## SLAVERY IN SPAIN

The Mediterranean states had the longest experience of slavery in Europe. In medieval Spain slavery had arisen out of the military clash between Christians and Muslims, making Moorish slavery common in the peninsula. The development of black slavery in America stimulated the limited demand for it in the mother country. Brunel observed in 1655 that 'the Commerce of the Indies hath restored rights of servitude in these Countries, and in Andalusia there are few other Servants. The greatest part of these are either Moors or Blacks'.[47] Moors were sometimes confusingly called 'white slaves' to distinguish them from blacks.

The biggest centre of Spanish slavery in the seventeenth century was Andalucia. Seville at the end of the reign of Philip II was estimated to have one in thirteen of its population a slave.[48] Because Cadiz and Seville had the easiest access to supplies, whether of Moorish captives or African slaves, they tended to have a disproportionate number. Outside Andalucia the most active centres were the ports and towns of the eastern seaboard. There were few slaves in the north of Spain. In Madrid a law of 1601 forbade their employment, but many households continued to employ them. In Aragon an early eighteenth-century writer testified that 'there is much slavery in the coastal lands, but hardly any in this realm',[49] a claim borne out by the relative lack of documentation for Aragon. In Murcia in 1690 a survey showed that in the whole city there were only twenty-one Moorish slaves, and twenty-three free Moors, mostly ex-slaves.[50]

Slavery as penal labour was practised in only one place in Spain: the mercury mines at Almadén. Conditions there were so terrible that the authorities generally considered it suitable only for the worst convicts. Gipsies, Moriscos and blacks were also singled out for penal servitude in Almadén, whereas whites were sent to the galleys. When labour was scarce in the mine those condemned to galleys were sent there, but with a remission of part of their sentence.[51] In 1686 the prime minister, Oropesa, objected to convicts being sent to Almadén since this was to send them to death. His advice was that slaves be purchased to do the work. The superintendent of the mine, however, objected that unlike convicts with a short sentence, slaves remained till they were old and useless.[52] Slaves were never bought unless there was a shortage of convicts: in 1686 about one-sixth of the work-force were slaves.

Slaves were also in demand for galley-service. They constituted only a small part of the labour force on ships, which normally relied on *forzados*, those condemned to galleys by the courts. But whenever a shortage of forzados occurred, the quickest solution was to press slaves into service. Government attempts to seize domestic slaves were strongly resisted. A decree to enlist slaves in Málaga in 1670 was successfully resisted by householders, and only three were obtained over a period of eight months.[53] The need arose again in 1691, when 'because of the very great shortage of slaves in the galleys of Spain', as a royal directive to the council of Aragon put it, orders were sent out for Moorish slaves on the coasts of Valencia and Andalucia to be purchased by the state and registered for galley service.[54]

In Madrid slaves were a luxury commodity, owned principally by the great lords, among them the count of Oropesa.[55] A sample from three parishes in the town in the late century shows that they were overwhelmingly Moorish, with a small percentage of blacks; and that nearly nine-tenths were owned by nobles. Their function was invariably domestic, but it is likely that most were decorative rather than menial servants. Small black page boys, here as in the papal court in Rome, added to the character of a household. Among prices paid at this period was the sum of 25 doblones for a black man in 1684, and 42 doblones (over 200 ducats) for a black girl in 1683.[56]

The biggest centre of slavery outside Andalucia was the kingdom of Valencia.[57] In both Italy and the south-east coast of Spain, slavery drew its victims from the Christian–Muslim conflict. Habsburg victories over the Turks in eastern Europe in the 1680s led to the export of thousands of prisoners, many of whom were sold in the Cadiz market. In 1690 the Moroccan government sent a special embassy to Madrid to negotiate over the exchange of large numbers captured by either side in recent conflicts in Africa. Both in Valencia and in Catalonia there were religious confraternities actively devoted to the redemption of Christian captives from the Moorish powers.

Slavery through naval engagements was sometimes numerically significant, but not the most typical way in which Moors were brought into Valencia. The notable action in 1693, when the armed frigate specially built and equipped by the fishermen of Valencia city, captured an Algerian pirate vessel and sold twenty-six prisoners into slavery, was exceptional.[58] Spaniards on the Levant coast no longer had the means to carry out an active war at sea against the Barbary corsairs, and if they obtained slaves in this sphere it was almost exclusively due to the naval power of the Dutch and the English. In August 1661, for instance, the English captured four Algerian vessels and 170 of the prisoners were sold in Alicante as slaves.[59]

Slaves in Valencia in the late century were overwhelmingly Moorish. Between

1661 and 1665, no more than half a dozen Negro slaves seem to have entered Valencia. Between 1666 and 1686, on only three occasions were Negro slaves registered with the authorities. A sample of 137 slaves found in Valencian documentation[60] over the period 1661–86 yields some interesting conclusions. The biggest category of slaves entering Valencia consisted of those captured in Africa. The chief source was Orán, the most accessible of the African forts under Spanish control. Our most valuable commentary on the Orán trade comes from Felipe de Moscoso. His letter-book for July 1661 has the entry: 'I have received two slaves from Orán in the galleys.' In November 1663, after a visit to Orán, he informed a correspondent in Genoa that 'I made a purchase of twenty-six slave girls, and a load of wax, lead and other commodities, which have left me with a reasonable profit'. The following summer he wrote to a correspondent in Livorno:

As to the slave girls you find yourself with, there is little outlet for them here. I am continually being brought them from Orán, and they market very poorly, since people don't pay what they're worth. At present I find myself with seven, and I am trying to sell them as best I can in different places. So I do not think it advisable for you to send them unless they are very cheap over there, because here the best price I get is not more than two hundred pieces of eight.[61]

In addition to this active slave trade, there were two other significant categories in Valencia: slaves who came in from the sea, and those who fled from masters elsewhere in the peninsula. Among the former was Saen, aged thirty-five and captured in Valencia in 1672 on suspicion of being a runaway. He stated that 'he is a Turk, and a year ago he fled from the galleys of Spain in Cartagena and thence came to the town of Elche, where he has been eight or nine months, serving in the house of the duchess of Gandía'.[62] The latter category, runaway slaves, were an interesting group that I shall examine presently.

An analysis by age of 132 slaves registered in Valencia in 1661–86 yields the following result:

Table 10.1

| Age | Male | Female | Total |
|-----|------|--------|-------|
| 1–9 | 7 | 14 | 21 |
| 10–19 | 20 | 12 | 32 |
| 20–29 | 31 | 17 | 48 |
| 30–39 | 17 | 1 | 18 |
| 40–49 | 8 | 2 | 10 |
| 50–59 | 2 | 0 | 2 |
| 60–69 | 1 | 0 | 1 |

The figures show that two-thirds of the slaves were aged under thirty. Almost without exception, those listed as being over thirty had not been acquired voluntarily by Valencians but were forced on to the market by accident, as shipwrecked Moors or runaways. Demand in Valencia was exclusively for children or young people.

Prices depended on many factors. There was naturally a high premium on youth. Figure 10.1 shows the general trend of prices for slaves in Valencia.[63]

Fig. 10.1   Valencian slaves by age, sex and price, 1661–86.

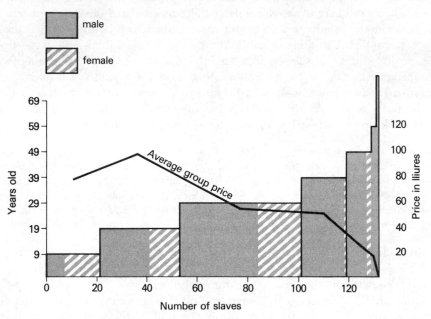

A typical price in the youngest age group was 80 lliures for the boy Luis Joan, exported from Orán at the age of six, and sent to a priest in Valencia. Some of the highest prices occurred in the ten to nineteen cohort, such as 80 lliures for a boy aged twelve. The highest price for a male was 110 lliures, paid for Mohamet, aged nineteen, captured on the high seas in 1668. The peak prices were for two teenage girls, one aged seventeen and valued at 146 lliures in 1663, one aged fifteen and bought for 150 lliures in 1678.

Slaves in Valencia had an exclusively domestic function and were never used for onerous physical labour. It is not clear whether any of them were *cortados*. This was a system widely practised in Andalucia[64] and also known in Madrid. Slaves were purchased purely for investment, contracted to pay their master a fixed regular sum, and were then allowed to earn their living in any way they wished. I have traced the professions of seventy slaveowners in the years 1661–86. Merchants were by far the largest group (twenty-one), followed by nobles, ciutadans and members of the professional élite.

The life of a slave was not necessarily as miserable as we imagine. Some north Africans went so far as to choose a career of servitude because of its variety and interest. In coming to Christian territory they may have wished to escape their own depressed circumstances. It was in any case well known that some 'slaves', such as those in Málaga in the late century, were very free in their movements and could even become rich.[65] There was perhaps one major reason for north Africans crossing over into Spain at the risk of their freedom: the search for adventure.

They were driven by an unmistakable spirit of vagabondage, ranging across the peninsula and through the Mediterranean, from city to city, from one master to another, content to suffer some adversity but careful always to avoid the total servitude of the galleys.

Among these Islamic vagabonds was Miguel de la Cruz, who left Algiers in 1649 at the age of sixteen and came to the peninsula:[66]

Fourteen years ago, more or less, he left the city of Algiers and went wandering through the world, and for most of the time he has been resident in the town of Sella and afterwards he lived in the city of Granada, from where he has come to the present city of Valencia . . . and was baptised in the city of Cartagena.

Another such traveller was Amet, aged thirty-five in 1671:[67]

He said he is from Sale in Morocco, from where he went to Melilla, which is a fortress of the King of Spain, and thence he went in a French ship to Cadiz, where he stayed for a fortnight working for his living and after that he came to the present city in search of a master.

This remarkable testimony of a man who, if we can believe him, left his own country where he was free in order to come to Spain, where his freedom was at risk, is paralleled by the account of Ali, aged twenty-five, seized by the Valencian authorities in 1671:[68]

He said that he is a native of Algeria from near Tlemcen and that he left there about ten or twelve years ago and together with other Moors came to Spain freely, where he has lived ever since . . . serving different masters freely and for a wage.

The movements of eight Moorish slaves whose careers were recounted to the authorities in Valencia, are traced in Figure 10.2. The eight include Christófol

Fig. 10.2   The travels of eight Moorish slaves captured in Valencia, 1669–86.

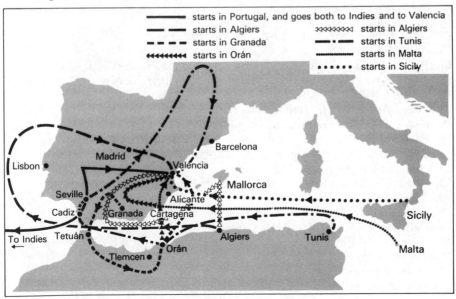

287

Velázquez, aged forty in 1683, who served his master for seventeen years and 'after his master's death went wandering through the world, mostly working as a fisherman, and has served as a sailor and has made two voyages to the Indies serving as a cabin-boy'.[69]

The later years of a slave were never easy. In early life slaves were usually well cared for, but they were seldom manumitted until old. The merchant Felipe Peris, for example, in his testament in 1674 granted his black slave her freedom, but only twenty years after his death. Manuel de San Francisco, freed by his master on his deathbed after twenty-two years service, was by then over sixty-five years old. The travails of their declining years were, nevertheless, perhaps no worse than those of the other poor in Spain.

## NOTES

1. Cited by **Callahan, W.**, 'Corporate Charity', *Histoire Sociale* (Ottawa), 9 (1976), p. 160.
2. For a general survey see Kamen, *Iron Century*, ch. 11 and sources there cited; for Spain, **Jiménez Salas, M.**, *Asistencia social* (Madrid 1958); **Rumeu de Armas, A.**, *Previsión social* (Madrid 1944); **Deleito y Piñuela, J.**, *La mala vida* (Madrid 1951).
3. *Monumento triunfal* (Saragossa 1672), pp. 9, 32.
4. Some of Mañara's valuable documentation on the poor of Seville has been used by **Mary E. Perry**, 'Fantastic Fandango', unpublished Ph.D. thesis, (UCLA 1977).
5. D. Gerónimo Frigola to king, 7 May 1686, ACA:CA 925.
6. Archbishop of Valencia to king, 18 June 1686, *ibid.*
7. *Monumento triunfal*, p. 120.
8. The figure is for 1689: ADZ 595.
9. AMZ Actos Comunes, libro 62, año 1668 fo. 2–3.
10. *Monumento triunfal*, p. 114.
11. *Ibid.* p. 118.
12. AMZ Actos Comunes, libro 62, año 1668 fo. 2–3.
13. AGS:CJH 883.
14. Perales, *Décadas*, III, p. 801; Benavent, 'Cosas mas notables', fo. 4–5.
15. ACA:CA 613/55/5; also viceroy Castelrodrigo to king, 12 May 1693, *ibid.* 841.
16. ACA:CA 857.
17. **Canga Arguelles, J.**, *Diccionario de Hacienda* (Madrid 1833), I, 537.
18. *Ibid.* I, 537; Jiménez Salas, *op. cit.* pp. 198–9.
19. Orders of 31 Dec. 1664 and 4 June 1665, AHN Consejos 7175/5.
20. Report of council, 19 March 1665, *ibid.* 7175/16.
21. Jiménez Salas, *op. cit.* p. 130.
22. Report by Hermandad del Real Hospicio de Pobres de Ave Maria y San Fernando, AHN Consejos, Alcaldes 1675/59.
23. Letter from D. Manuel Arias, 16 Nov. 1694, *ibid.* 1694/462.
24. Decree of 31 Aug. 1699, AHN Consejos 7212.
25. Consulta of 14 May 1699, AGS Estado 4149.
26. *Monumento triunfal*, p. 24.
27. Perry, 'Fantastic Fandango', p. 263.
28. Consulta of council, 17 Apr. 1666, AHN Consejos 7176.

29. Callahan, 'Corporate Charity', p. 170.
30. Callahan, W., 'Paupers and nobles: the Santa y Real Hermandad del Refugio' (unpublished dissertation), p. 179. I am extremely grateful to Professor Callahan for letting me consult this work.
31. Callahan, 'Corporate Charity', p. 177 and n. 78.
32. Santos, F., *Día y Noche* (Madrid 1674), p. 193.
33. This and subsequent information on the Madrid hospitals comes from the invaluable summary by Galdiano y Croy, L., *Breve Tratado de los Hospitales* (Madrid 1677). For the location of these and other hospitals in old Madrid, see Deleito y Piñuela, *Sólo Madrid es Corte*, pp. 93–6.
34. Licenciado Antonio de Gonsalves to bishop of Avila, Feb. 1681, AHN Consejos 7194/82.
35. Apart from Callahan, 'Paupers and nobles', see the memorial of 1685 in AHN Consejos 7197/4.
36. For these three, see Galdiano y Croy, *op. cit.* pp. 35–41.
37. Consulta of governor of council, 16 Jan. 1694, AHN Consejos 12,499.
38. Galdiano y Croy, *op. cit.* pp. 16–19.
39. Memorial of 1700 by D. Francisco Ruiz, ACA:CA 940.
40. *Ibid.*
41. Biblioteca de la Diputación de Murcia, papers of the Hospital de Nuestra Señora de Gracia, Libro de niños expósitos, 1695–1711.
42. Teófanes Egido, 'La Cofradía de San Jose', *Estudios josefinos* (1973), cited in Bennassar, *L'homme espagnole*, p. 150.
43. The most useful studies for my purpose are Sánchez, M. H., *Los gitanos españoles* (Madrid 1977); and García Martínez, S., 'Los gitanos en Valencia', *I. Cong. Hist. País Val.* (Valencia 1976), III, 251–69.
44. AHN Consejos, Alcaldes 1673/370–2.
45. Letters of viceroy, 6 June 1690 and 30 Nov. 1694, ACA:CA 934.
46. Details in ARV:RC libros registros 594/178–80; also García Martínez, 'Los gitanos', pp. 262–5.
47. *A Journey into Spain*, p. 90.
48. For slavery in Spain, see Verlinden, C., *L'Esclavage* (Bruges 1955); Domínguez Ortiz, 'La esclavitud', *Estud. Hist. Soc. Esp.*, 2 (1952). There are short discussions in Bennassar, *L'homme espagnole*, pp. 86–95; and Pike, R., *Aristocrats and Traders* (Ithaca 1972), pp. 170–92.
49. Cited in Domínguez Ortiz, 'La esclavitud', p. 382.
50. AMM 3082.
51. As in 1691: AHN Consejos, Sala de Alcaldes, libros de gobierno 1691/53.
52. D. Antonio Muñoz to D. Ignacio Baptista de Ribas, 14 Nov. 1686, AGS:CJH 1100.
53. Consulta of Castile, Mar. 1671, AHN Consejos 7181/25.
54. Consulta of Aragon, 27 Nov. 1691, ACA:CA 930.
55. Details on Madrid come from Larquié, C., 'Les esclaves de Madrid', *Rev. Hist.*, 244 (1970), 41–74.
56. AHPM 8820/306, 8819/620.
57. What follows is derived from Kamen, H., 'Mediterranean slavery', *Anuar. Hist. Econ. y Soc.* (1975), 211–34. Slavery for the earlier period is discussed by Cortes, V., *La esclavitud en Valencia* (Valencia 1964).
58. Benavent, fo. 21.
59. Letter of Felipe de Moscoso, 5 Sept. 1661, in ARV, Varia, MS. 74.

60. Sources used are the register book of the Bailia General for 1609–66, and that of the Royal Chancery for 1666–86, both in ARV.
61. The references are to Moscoso's letters of 21 July 1661 to Genoa, 28 Nov. 1663 to Genoa, and 12 Aug. 1664 to Livorno.
62. ARV:RC, Vendes de Esclaus, libros registros 629/68.
63. The number of prices represented in each age-group is as follows: 1–9, three; 10–19, seven; 20–29, twenty-five; 30–39, thirteen; 40–49, seven; 50–59, two; 60–69, one.
64. For cases in 1672 in Málaga, see Domínguez Ortiz, 'La esclavitud', pp. 427–8.
65. *Ibid.* pp. 427–8.
66. Statement of 14 Dec. 1663, ARV Bailía libros de cautivos 210/440.
67. Statement of 6 Oct. 1671, ARV:RC Vendes de Esclaus, 629/51.
68. Statement of 26 Aug. 1671, *ibid.* 629/48.
69. Statement of 7 July 1683, *ibid.* 629/111.

# CHAPTER ELEVEN

# Religion

No force bound the peoples of Spain more closely together than their common faith. Foreign commentators, coming from countries both Catholic and Protestant where a robust scepticism was now fashionable, looked aghast at religious practice in the peninsula. 'In the midst of all these bowings, genuflexions, breast-beatings and innumerable other superstitious externals', commented a Catholic envoy in 1688, the real conduct of Spaniards consisted of lies, thieving, murder and concubinage.[1] French visitors like Madame d'Aulnoy and the marquis de Villars corroborated the image of a people sunk in superstition. Few descriptions are as evocative as that by d'Aulnoy of Spanish flagellants in procession whipping themselves so that the blood splashed on bystanders. By discussing the reign of Charles II primarily in terms of the alleged 'bewitchings' of the king, a consistent historical tradition has succeeded in dismissing the late seventeenth century as a period of spiritual decadence and religious torpidity.

There is no evidence that under the last Habsburg there was any unusual growth of superstition or any decline into ritualism. Spain was, it is true, separated from the mainstream of philosophical thought, and the new tendencies developing in European Catholicism remained unknown to the mass of Spaniards. Peninsular religion did not however become atrophied. Secure in the belief that they alone were true and good Catholics, Spaniards became committed even more fully to their traditional faith. An impressive number of new Spanish saints was added to the Roman calendar in this reign. The measure of Spain's isolation from theological developments elsewhere can be seen in three specific *causes célèbres*: the growth of probabilistic theology, the controversy over the writings of Molinos, and the doctrine of the Immaculate Conception. In all three affairs the growing influence of the Jesuits was unmistakable.

The many saints canonised in the late century included St Peter Alcántara and St Magdalena de Paz in 1669, St Luis Beltrán and St Rose of Lima in 1671, St Pedro Pascual in 1674, St John of God in 1679, St Pascual Baylon and St Juan de Sahagún in 1691.[2] The two most important canonisations of the period were decreed by Clement X in 1671: one was that of St Ferdinand, king of Castile, whose body rested in Seville and whose canonisation led to enormous rejoicing and celebrations in the city.[3] The other was of the great duke of Gandía, the Jesuit St Francis Borja. Benavent reports from Valencia that 'at the news there were great fiestas, a procession with many triumphal carriages, great lights and fireworks, decorations along the streets and two days of bullfights'.[4]

The Spanish court at this time achieved one of the most significant victories in the history of Church dogma. There had in Spain been a long tradition of support for belief in the Immaculate Conception of the Virgin. What was still disputed elsewhere in the Catholic world, was in Spain a virtual dogma. The vast number of Conceptions painted in this century, from the sublime study by Velázquez to the prolific output of Antolínez (d. 1675), who specialised in the subject, is eloquent testimony to the devotion of the people. The Jesuits made the cause their own. In 1615 a deputation from the see of Seville asked the Crown for support: thereafter Madrid was a leading proponent of the doctrine in discussions with Rome. The Cortes of Castile added its pleas in the early century. Philip IV, encouraged by his adviser, the nun Sor Maria de Agreda, made fruitless attempts to have the belief declared a dogma. Rome remained stubbornly cautious, and the controversy began to cause serious dissension among theologians in Spain. The riots at the university of Barcelona in 1665 between followers of the Suarist (Jesuit) professors who favoured the doctrine, and followers of the Thomists who opposed it,[5] were typical. Disruption was common at other universities. In Valencia in 1691 riots among the students led to the smashing of statues of the Conception and of St Thomas Aquinas. The viceroy deported the ringleaders.[6]

With Nithard (a Jesuit) in power in the early years of Charles II, the immaculist cause took a great step forward. After his retirement to Rome in 1669, Nithard continued to press the cause. Meanwhile one of his principal enemies in Spain, Don Pedro de Aragon, was also an immaculist. As viceroy of Naples in 1668, Don Pedro had ordered an oath to the Immaculate Conception to be among those taken at the start of the university term. The ensuing uproar led to the dismissal of some Dominican professors. Throughout the reign, Spanish envoys to the Holy See were regularly instructed to promote the cause of the dogma.[7] Success for these efforts came in 1696, when a papal brief created the feast of the Immaculate Conception as a second-class rite, with its own octave. One of the clauses in the will of Charles II asked his successor to pursue the cause of the dogma, which was not given universal status until 1854 in the bull *Ineffabilis Deus*.

Probabilistic moral theology arose out of attempts by theologians to resolve what could or could not be permitted by confessors giving advice to penitents. Probabilism, or laxism as it was also called by its opponents, was condemned by Pascal in his *Lettres provinciales* (1656) as an invention of the Jesuits. The issue created a great noise in Europe, but little controversy in Spain, where many of the theologians taught. Among the most influential probabilists in Spain in the late sixteenth century was the Dominican friar Bartholomé de Medina. Another Salamanca friar, Enrique de Villalobos, was widely read in the mid-seventeenth century.[8] Pascal and the Jansenists in France preferred to believe that probabilism was an invention of the Jesuits, and singled out for attack the Valladolid Jesuit Antonio de Escobar (d. 1669), who confessed that he was puzzled by the attention being given abroad to his writings. The most prominent Jesuit probabilist in Spain was in fact the Basque Miguel de Elizalde (d. 1678).

Controversy within Spain and within the religious orders was relatively muted until about 1670, when the Provincial of the Jesuits, Tirso González, published an attack on probabilism which was so spirited that it was condemned by Rome, which had already, between 1665 and 1680, issued several condemnations of laxist propositions. In 1687 Tirso became General of the Jesuits and continued his campaign on a broader scale.[9]

The other great theological controversy of the time, again of far more significance outside Spain, was Molinism. The spiritual tendency known as 'quietism' was associated in the late century with Madame Guyon in France and Miguel de Molinos in Spain. Molinos was born in Muniesa (province of Teruel, Aragon) in 1628, studied and served as a priest in Valencia, then went to Rome at the end of 1665.[10] The circle of friends and adepts in Valencia apparently influenced his subsequent outlook. In Rome he became the admired centre of a group of people who followed his ways of spiritual reflection. In 1675 his *Spiritual Guide . . . to the Interior Route towards Perfect Contemplation* was published in Rome, and was followed swiftly by other editions in various languages. The highest Catholic authorities approved of and recommended his works, particular support coming from the bishop of Iesi, Pier Matteo Petrucci. The Jesuits in Italy kept a close eye on the success of the *Guide*, and in 1680 the Roman Inquisition asked the Spanish Inquisition to look into the racial antecedents of Molinos, but found nothing to suggest that he was Jewish. In May 1685 Molinos was arrested by the Roman Inquisition; he was tried in September 1687 and condemned to perpetual imprisonment, a sentence he served till his death on 28 December 1696.

Since all these events occurred outside Spain they would seem to have no part in our account. Menéndez Pelayo once maintained that 'Molinos never taught in Spain, he had no followers here till the eighteenth century, his heresy left no mark, nobody read his book'.[11] The truth is that Molinos played a part, though a small one, in the religious history of Spain. The first formal denunciation of his work in Spain was made by Fr. Francisco Neila to the Inquisition of Saragossa in September 1685.[12] In October, when the news of Molinos's arrest was already known in Spain, the archbishop of Seville, Don Jaime de Palafox, took the surprising step of ordering a printing of 6,000 copies of the *Guide* in Spanish.[13] He explained that he understood that the arrest of Molinos had nothing to do with any alleged heresy (a conclusion supported by modern commentators).[14] The ideas of Molinos seem to have spread quite far in Spain, a country with a long history of mystical religion, and even the council of the Inquisition was split over whether to treat quietism as a serious threat.

From about 1687 the Inquisition began to prosecute quietists in Spain. The problem with all the cases is to determine whether they really involved Molinism, or were arbitrarily identified as Molinist by the inquisitors. A group of Molinists was to be found in Seville in 1687; another case occurred in Valladolid.[15] In 1689 a number of clergy in the Catalan town of Reus, including the parish priest and the local Carmelite superior, were accused of 'following, practising and teaching the doctrine of Miguel de Molinos'.[16] In 1691 a Carmelite priest in Vic and a farmer in Reus were charged with Molinism.[17] There was a persistent undercurrent of quietist thinking, unearthed by the Inquisition in several parts of the peninsula and denounced by writers of the early eighteenth century.

## THE INQUISITION AND RELIGIOUS CONTROL

The inability of new ideas, heretical or otherwise, to penetrate Spain was certainly due to the apparatus of the Inquisition. Though it was rapidly losing its political influence, its hold over the masses was as strong as ever and its activities give a unique insight into the religious life of the Spanish people. The power of the Inquisition rested not on a conscious tyranny but on a fundamental conviction among Spaniards that it was necessary. They felt that there were certain features of their society of which the Holy Office was the only guarantor. Wrong-doing, wrong belief, contact with foreigners, careless language: all these were matters to be referred to the tribunal. It follows that though the Inquisition was popular it was also widely feared. The priest and doctor Juan López Batanero confessed his fear in 1674 when he admitted having certain papers 'which he will not reveal now for fear of the Inquisition, but which can be published after his death'.[18]

Fear among the people, and inviolable secrecy on the part of the tribunal, created a bizarre image of the Inquisition in the common mind. This is shown most remarkably by folk memory of the Inquisition in modern Galicia, as investigated by Carmelo Lisón Tolosana.[19] For the older Galician peasants, the Inquisition as experienced by their fathers was still a living and frightening memory. The inquisitors came in the night in carriages specially fitted with rubber wheels that would make no noise; they listened at doors and windows to hear what people were saying; they took away beautiful girls; their favourite torture – there was widespread unanimity on this – was to sit their victim down and drip boiling oil on his head until he died. Every one of these images was completely false. That people were able to believe it is evidence of the great chasm that had opened up by the nineteenth century between the Inquisition and the society it purported to defend. Since the same degree of secrecy about its methods and acts existed in the seventeenth century, there is every possibility that similar incomprehension, misconception and possible hostility existed at that time.

The Inquisition acted as a universal judge over all aspects of religion. It protected the faith but in no sense imposed it. We can best understand its function by remembering that it seldom initiated cases. The real prosecutors were those ordinary people who brought their fears or prejudices before it and used it against their neighbours. Its evil lay in its availability. So few of the prosecutions were undertaken at the instance of familiars that it would be correct to say that the Inquisition did not operate as a religious secret police. Hostility to the tribunal arose for two main reasons: its claim to certain legal and financial privileges, and its function as a defender of private or public prejudices. Of the latter the most important was the institutionalised prejudice about purity of blood (*limpieza de sangre*), which took root in Spain in the fifteenth century and is discussed below. The Inquisition was the body that most helped to perpetuate limpieza doctrines. It consistently maintained that 'all its own officials are not only free of all bad race but of any suspicion thereof';[20] it believed that all heresy tended to be Jewish in origin; any condemnation by it tended to bring infamy on the accused and a suspicion of impure blood; and its employees were often kept busy investigating the racial antecedents of people under suspicion. In 1681 Jaime Casas, parish priest of Aiguaviva, near Barcelona, abused officials of the Inquisition who were visiting the village in search of proofs of limpieza from the baptismal records. In front of his parishioners, he told them 'not to write lies, and that it was not the first time they had done so, by altering signatures and other things'.[21] He was reprimanded and fined for his temerity.

Denunciations to the Holy Office were concerned above all with religion, and a high proportion of cases dealt with blasphemy and disrespect. When a fifty-year-old goatherd was accused in 1680 of declaring that 'the Blessed Sacrament is a whore of the Inquisition', the tribunal of Saragossa accepted his excuse that he had been drunk.[22] Mildness was customary in all such prosecutions. It was enough that the Inquisition was being accepted as a control over religious behaviour. Difficulties arose when the denunciations happened to be, as the majority possibly were, actuated by malice. A great deal depended on the inquisitors being men of common sense. A typical case was that of the corregidor of the Cuatro Villas, denounced to the tribunal at Logroño in 1669 for blasphemous swearing.[23] He effectively proved that all his accusers were mortal enemies, and had his case dismissed. Contrary to a common assumption, the Inquisition was quite aware of the part played in denunciations by malice. When Pascuala Gil, aged twenty-eight and wife of a shepherd, came before the inquisitors in Saragossa in 1679 on a charge of witchcraft, they 'recognised her great truth and innocence'. When María Pérez, aged forty-five, came before them in 1680 on the same charge, the inquisitors agreed unanimously that all twenty-nine of her accusers (including the local priest) were actuated by malice, and 'recognised her innocence'.[24]

A good proportion of denunciations was spontaneous, inspired neither by fear nor by malice. An excellent example of 1680 illustrates the problem. Pedro Palacios was a young man from a prominent family in the town of Lerín, within the jurisdiction of the Inquisition at Logroño. While he was playing at cards one day, his naked sword scratched his knee. He joked to his fellow players that 'it would be a shame to lose such noble blood, which is good enough to redeem the entire human race'. 'Señor Palacios', one of the others joked back, 'I'm sure the world is worried about it.' After the game, when Palacios had left, the players discussed what had been said and decided that they must give an account of it to the Holy Office.[25] Palacios was eventually summoned for this and other matters, but thanks to his family connections got off with a light fine. Basic to the denunciation which the players made of themselves and of Palacios, was a strong sense of moral obligation of a type still familiar in some societies. The function and success of the Inquisition in Spain cannot be understood without being aware of the strength of this obligation.

In a country of such rich religious traditions, there were inevitably excesses that the Inquisition tried to control. Popular superstition was the biggest single problem, in the form of witchcraft. Extreme mariolatry was among the most common theological excesses. In 1677 the Toledo tribunal investigated the beliefs of a group of young nobles, followers of a certain Agustín Sarmiento who taught that the body of Mary was contained together with that of Christ in the Sacrament.[26] The same tribunal in 1683 had to deal with a Cistercian friar who seemed to be preaching that the glories of Mary were greater than those of the Sacrament.[27]

In addition to religion the Inquisition watched over the morality of Spaniards. Lea's analysis of offences in the Toledo Inquisition in the late sixteenth century[28] shows that wrong attitudes to sex accounted for more cases than any other type of offence. The Holy Office was less worried by sin than by the intention behind the sin. When it punished, it was less severe than others. In 1668 the tribunal of Toledo denounced the civil authorities for having arrested Juan de Ocaña for bigamy and having sentenced him to 200 lashes and ten years in the galleys; the inquisitors successfully had the case brought under their jurisdiction, and sentenced Ocaña instead to five years in the galleys.[29]

The papers of the Inquisition make it possible to examine the sexual attitudes of seventeenth-century Spaniards. In 1663 Esteban Núñez, a travelling actor of Portuguese origin, was denounced to the Inquisition of Toledo by his wife, who was jealous of his mistress. A witness claimed Núñez had said that 'to live thus with a woman was to live in the grace of God'. Forty years old, Núñez had been thrice married; he was banished for four years from the Toledo region.[30] In 1674 the priest Juan López Batanero was accused of 'maintaining that fornication by itself was not a sin, and that he has papers where the reasons for this opinion are explained'.[31] A priest and doctor of Alcázar de San Juan, Batanero was also accused of 'giving prescriptions to bring about abortions'. From the many confessions of ordinary Spaniards, as well as of clergy accused of soliciting women in the confessional, there seems to have been a considerable body of opinion that held sex outside the rules to be natural and permissible. Prenuptial intercourse was, as we have seen, common in some communities. It was widely held that parish priests should have concubines, for a number of pragmatic reasons. The prevalence of prostitution everywhere, allowed scope to male appetites and kept marriages safe.[32] Willughby in 1664 shared an impression common to most foreign travellers when he observed of Spaniards that 'for fornication and impurity they are the worst of all Nations, at least in Europe'.[33] The permanence of marriage itself was brought into question by some. In 1694 Don Francisco Cossió was arrested by the tribunal of Toledo on a charge of bigamy. The prosecution quoted against him a letter he had written ten years before to his parish priest in Valladolid: 'It is true that, according to the opinion of those with whom I have discussed it, marriage is valid; but in my case it was necessary to revalidate it in order to continue it.'[34]

A certain liberality of sexual practice in the Spain of Charles II is suggested by the manual for confessors published at Seville in 1673 by Fr. Joseph Gavarri. The following propositions, on abortion, may surprise the modern reader:[35]

Bringing about an abortion before the child has life, is permissible when there is no other way to avoid a danger to the life of, or great infamy for, the mother, particularly if she is a girl of honour.

If a man is in doubt whether or not he has killed a child by giving the mother a drink with which to abort, and has made all the necessary enquiries and nevertheless remains in a state of doubt, the child must be held to have been without life, and thus he who gave the drink has not acted wrongly.

If a priest is asked by a woman for methods of aborting, and the priest gives her some advice in good faith, and the woman later uses the methods on herself and aborts, the priest incurs no penalties.

The broad range of questions over which the Inquisition claimed to exercise control, may seem to have made it a perfect instrument for religious tyranny and social repression. In practice the Holy Office never developed into a system of terror imposed on all Spaniards: in the late seventeenth century its activities were surprisingly limited. The evidence from the tribunal of Barcelona is perfectly clear.[36] Between 1665 and 1692 the annual number of prosecutions of Spaniards varied from a low of ten in 1677 to a high of thirty-seven in 1675. In 1675 as many as fourteen of the cases were for minor superstitious practices, and throughout the period these were the biggest category involved. There were times when the tribunal seemed to have little to do but prosecute foreigners: in 1676 it persuaded sixty-four foreign soldiers and sailors to recant their heresies, under what circumstances is not clear; on the other hand, only fourteen Spaniards were prosecuted that year. Documentation for other tribunals supports the general picture of a moderate Inquisition under Charles II.

## HOW CATHOLIC WAS SPAIN?

Throughout the seventeenth century and for most of the eighteenth, Spain remained a society massively devoted to the Catholic faith. Total participation in religious festivals, and mass attendance at *autos de fe*, show the popularity of religion's public face. Italian ambassadors in their reports sneered at all this and put it down to Spanish hypocrisy. But foreigners who were naive enough to believe they could speak offensively in public about the Catholic faith, ended in the cells of the Inquisition and sometimes, like the 23-year old Englishman in Barcelona in 1689,[37] died there. This apparently wholesale dedication to the faith was accompanied by a deep-rooted and officially encouraged distrust of all things foreign. The phrase *tierra de herejes* (a heretical country) keeps recurring in the papers of the Inquisition. A notary of Barcelona was accused in 1689 of visiting such a tierra, but the country to which the term was applied was France! For the average Spaniard only Spain was a truly Christian country; all others were tainted by heresy, France by 'Lutheranism', Italy by Judaism. An actress was accused in 1665 of eating meat in Lent and of saying that 'Italy is a better country than Spain'; an actor was charged with blasphemy and with saying that 'he wanted to go to Livorno because there he could live as he wished'.[38] Both were acquitted, but their statements survive as examples of the type of sentiment disapproved by the Inquisition. Xenophobia remained an integral part of the public face of Spanish Catholicism, on a par with their feelings that Spain was 'a world apart, and· that other nations existed only to serve them'.[39]

Innumerable denunciations to the Inquisition demonstrate the readiness of Spaniards to defend their religion. In Toledo one day in 1686 three men were dicing in a gaming-house when a stranger seated near a window began to blaspheme, 'that he had broken a priest's head, and that he would knock off Christ's crown and his horns'.[40] The players got up immediately and went straight to the Inquisition. In a different category is the case of Joseph Plá, wool-dresser of Solsona. In 1667 he stood watching a religious procession when a pretty girl in the procession asked if he wanted to kiss the crucifix she was carrying. 'I would prefer to kiss you,' he said. He was taken before the Inquisition of Barcelona, but acquitted.[41]

Catholic belief and practice had its extremes in Spain. In a culture wholly dominated by expectations of another existence, it is not surprising to find evidence of mystical experiences as well as narratives of physical contact with demons.[42] Religious practice embraced the totality of life, and inevitably declined easily into its coarser aspects. Francisco de Santos in the late century denounced the immorality and frauds committed under guise of celebrating Holy Week.[43] The crudity of popular attitudes was balanced by a few lives of heroic sanctity. The bishop of Guadix and later of Plasencia, Fray Juan de Montalván (d. 1720), was a pious and zealous prelate, devoted to the poor and dedicated to poverty: 'He had no coach', reports his biographer, 'but walked on foot, like all the sons of Adam.'[44] In Barcelona the learned José Oriol (d. 1702), despite his doctoral degrees, lived and served among the poor of the city on a restricted diet which earned him the name of Dr Bread and Water. He was canonised in 1909.

Since neither vulgarity nor sanctity was typical of the state of popular religion, it is difficult to assess the quality of everyday belief. Masses were thronged, and most people took communion. In his *Day and Night in Madrid*, Santos makes one character ask another 'If so many people went to communion all the time?' To which he answered, 'Yes, and for as long as the masses go on, which is until two o'clock in the day.'[45] Was this evidence of merely passive belief? Certainly the Jesuits were not satisfied. Among the most impressive religious achievements of the period is the amazing series of missions carried out between 1665 and 1676 by the Jesuits Tirso González (d. 1705) and Gabriel Guillén (d. 1675). Their efforts took them to Navarre and Galicia in the north, Seville and Málaga in the south. Everywhere they aroused the mass emotion familiar in modern evangelical rallies. In Cáceres, to take a city at random, Tirso reported that

the mission in the cathedral lasted eighteen days, from the second Sunday in Lent to the Wednesday after the fourth Sunday. On the last Sunday there was a general communion and a sermon and so many people came that Cáceres had never seen such a gathering. Three thousand people communicated. The Sacrament was exposed until five in the afternoon and then the sermon followed. Before the sermon they said the rosary.[46]

The records of the mission show clearly that Spanish Catholicism had not lost its dynamism.

A major exception to the rule of general observance was represented by the urban poor. They made up well over one-fifth of the towns. In addition to these, the unsettled and itinerant population were unreliable Catholics. Writing of the foundation of the Misericordia in Saragossa in 1669, Ordóñez expressed his astonishment at 'one woman who was received into it; aged sixty, she had lived for forty years in Saragossa but did not know the Our Father or how to cross herself'.[47] Ordóñez was not, on the other hand, surprised at the lack of religion among wandering beggars. 'In Madrid a beggar was asked how many persons there were in the Holy Trinity, and he said four.'[48] His judgment on the vagabonds was a sweeping one: 'They live like barbarians, for they are never known or seen to go to mass, confession or communion, nor are they instructed in Christian doctrine.'[49]

If the wandering poor in Spain were in any way typical of the poor in western Europe,[50] we must accept that a proportion of Spaniards had ceased to have any real contact with the faith. The gipsies formed part of this area of unbelief. Many of them must have been practising Catholics. But the common attitude towards them is reflected in a report on their religion discussed in the diocesan synod at Solsona in 1684:[51]

They do not comply with their obligations as good and true Catholics. They live scandalously in groups, sometimes within sight of towns, often in woods and deserted places, sleeping all together with men, women, boys and girls cramped in a small space, exposed to the weather and lacking clothing so that they seek shelter by huddling together so closely as to verge on immorality. They live as married persons without us being able to check whether they have first taken the sacrament of matrimony. They do not baptise their children, or at least it is difficult to find out if anyone has been baptised. On occasion when we have succeeded it has been found that they have been baptised several times in different parishes, thereby using the sacrament sacrilegiously for their own purposes. . . . It is almost unknown for any of them to comply with the precept of hearing mass on feast days, and what is most to be lamented is that they go neither to confession nor to communion at Easter.

Apart from marginal groups — the urban poor, vagabonds, gipsies — the majority of Spaniards practised their religion and, which is crucial, were adequately informed about it. We can adopt no better test for their knowledge of the faith than that which the Inquisition itself adopted. Take Francisco Millán, aged thirty-four in 1673, a saltpetre trader from Alcázar de San Juan.[52] Though illiterate, he had had a varied career. 'He hears mass on holidays of obligation and many other holidays, confesses and communicates at Easter and many other times in the year. . . . He crossed himself, said the Our Father, Ave, Credo, Salve Regina and commandments, all well said, but knew nothing more of Christian doctrine.' Juan de Ocaña in 1668 'crossed and blessed himself, said the Paternoster, Ave Maria, Credo, Salve Regina, commandments of the law of God and of Holy Mother Church, the Sacraments and the general confession, all well spoken in Castilian, and knew no more of Christian doctrine'. He was a soldier, aged twenty-seven, and illiterate.[53] Isabel Maeso, of Daimiel (Ciudad Real), was a twenty-three-year-old illiterate washerwoman in 1670: 'She crossed and blessed herself, said the Paternoster and Ave Maria, Credo and Salve Regina in Castilian, well said, and moderately well the articles of Christian doctrine.'[54] Inés Martín of Peñalsordo (near Almadén), a seamstress, was illiterate and aged over fifty in 1668: 'She hears mass on feast days as well as working days. She said the Paternoster, Ave Maria, Salve and Credo, but did not know the commandments well nor the mysteries of our Holy Faith.'[55] Virtually all persons examined by the Inquisition were like these. The case of Inés López, a fifty-year-old hospital nurse in 1664, and illiterate, was exceptional: 'She crossed herself, said the Our Father and Ave very well in Spanish, but did not know the Credo, Salve, the Confiteor, the commandments of God and the Church, the articles of faith or the sacraments. The inquisitor warned and ordered her to learn them, for she has an obligation to do so as a Christian.'[56]

This evidence suggests that most Spaniards had a basic knowledge of the prayers and ceremonial of the Church, and all knew the Our Father and Ave by heart. As might be expected, knowledge beyond the formalities was very limited. Esteban Núñez in 1663 knew his Paternoster, Ave, Credo, Confiteor and commandments in Castilian, but 'did not know which person of the Trinity had become incarnate, said that the Blessed Sacrament was three persons, and that Christ was all three persons of the Holy Trinity'.[57]

It is certain that religious observance in Spain was not wholly voluntary.

The obligation of annual confession and communion at Easter was attended to very strictly. For this purpose every parish priest had a list of his parishioners, and as they fulfilled their obligation he would hand them a certificate to the effect and make a corresponding entry in his list. Later he would send the bishop a note of those who had not fulfilled their duty.[58]

A minority may well have found these controls irksome. A pharmacist arrested by the Inquisition at Laguna (Tenerife) in 1707 was accused of saying 'that one could live in France because there there did not exist the poverty and subjection that today exists in Spain and Portugal, since in France they do not try to find out nor do they make a point of knowing who everyone is and what religion he has and professes. And so he who lives properly and is of good character may become what he wishes.' In 1741 another native of the Canaries contrasted Spain unfavourably with Paris, where life was free and unrestricted, 'and no one asks where you are going, or questions who you are, nor at Easter does the priest ask if you have been to confession'.[59]

What are we to make of the frequent expressions of hostility to religion in Spain? The records for the tribunal of Toledo alone give a surviving total of 644 prosecutions for blasphemy in the sixteenth century. The problem is to determine whether blasphemy implied a falling away from faith. In practice the Inquisition tended to excuse blasphemous swearing as arising from ignorance, bad habit and heavy drinking. In 1678 Andrés González, a twenty-year-old carpenter's assistant, was accused in Toledo of swearing 'that he renounced God, and knew neither God nor the Virgin', that 'he didn't believe in God' but 'believed in Mahomet'.[60] The Inquisition realised that González's swearing arose out of drinking and despair at unhappy domestic conditions. The same was true of Rafael Roca, a priest of Viure (Catalonia), aged thirty-four in 1665, who wrote in a letter that was taken to the Holy Office: 'For some time now I have renounced God and his saints and the mother and father who bore me, because of the state that I am in, and now I would willingly give myself to the devil if he would have me.'[61]

A different view was taken in 1677 of Isidro Más, a twenty-year-old cobbler of La Bisbal (Catalonia). He quarrelled violently one day with his mother and refused to go to mass; witnesses testified that 'when asked why he did not, he replied that he believed neither in God nor the devil. . . . Moreover he ate meat on Fridays and Saturdays and when reprimanded said that for him those days were like any others.'[62] He was sent to serve in the garrison at Rosas for two years. In 1697 we have the case of Manuel Noves, a forty-one-year-old farmhand of Manzanares. His mother-in-law claimed that he swore foul oaths all the time; for example, that 'the lower parts of the woman with whom he was living were better than those of the Virgin'. 'About two weeks ago', his mother-in-law testified, 'when some Jesuits were preaching a mission in this town I told him off in front of his wife for not going to confession and to hear the word of God, and Manuel Noves answered "that he did not want to go, and if he did it would be to f--- them"; and as far as she knows it is over two years since her son-in-law went to confession or to church, and when she reprimanded him he said "that he does not want to go to confession or communion because he is already damned".'[63] Noves was condemned to five years in the galleys.

It is likely that there was little formal unbelief in seventeenth-century Spain. A friar in 1655 claimed that 'atheism has never been known in Spain, and is not congenial to the Spanish mind. Atheists have only been found in fickle nations, like the Hebrews; and in our own times, the English and French.'[64] This absurd statement nevertheless contains a grain of truth. Judging only from cases documented by the Inquisition, it would seem that many Spaniards *deviated* in detail from orthodoxy but did not consciously *defect* from the faith. The extent and significance of deviation of course remains to be studied. Some of those accused by the Inquisition were making thoughtless utterances. Others, like Juan Sicart, a priest in the diocese of Urgell, are to be taken more seriously. He was accused in 1667 of questioning indulgences and of maintaining 'that the Supreme Pontiff has no power to bring souls out of purgatory, and that only God has the absolute power'.[65] Alvaro Romero, an army captain in the *tercio* of the province of Toledo, appeared in 1677 before the Inquisition of Barcelona. In earnest discussion with a priest, a doctor in theology, he had stated that sacramental confession was instituted not by Christ but by the apostles. The priest asked him to watch what he was saying or he would report him to the Holy Office. The captain 'answered that he had no time for the inquisitors, they were a lot of drunkards, and there had been lawsuits in a certain city once when they had been dealt with like dogs'.[66] Doubts over indulgences and confession do not amount to unbelief. Even assertions such as that by Francisco Grajal, tobacco dealer of Valdemoro in 1707, that 'there is no hell, it was invented only to frighten children',[67] may be seen not as heresy but as deviations within an orthodox structure.

Anticlericalism was far more subversive of religion, and disrespect towards the clergy a surer guide to latent defection from Christianity. The solidarity of small communities with their priest, was balanced on the other side by a disrespect for which the clergy were most to blame. In an age when bishops still mounted steeds and rode to war,[68] clerics continued to be involved in violence of all sorts, from crime to banditry, which compromised their sacred function. It is arguable that a decline in respect for the sacred, was the single most powerful sign of an erosion of the authority of religion.

In 1665 Francisco Dalmau, a farmer in the archdiocese of Tarragona, was accused of entering the pulpit before mass and preaching ridicule and absurdities for fifteen minutes before the priest entered. Witnesses said that he would habitually leave the church when a sermon began and return only when it was over. On another occasion he ridiculed the ceremony of the descent of Christ from the cross on Good Friday.[69] In 1676 Manuel Sánchez, police officer of the town of Pastrana, went out for the day with his friends the town butcher and tailor, their wives and other friends. After lunch they came to a chapel one league outside the town, where Sánchez and his two friends dressed up in the church vestments and celebrated a mockery of the mass, 'laughing and joking while the women there also laughed at it'. After saying mass the three left the altar, 'laughing a great deal, and threw the vestments down on the cases with great contempt'.[70]

The most disturbing aspect of popular attitudes in an apparently Catholic society was the frequency of sacrilege. There are no known cases of church-burning in *ancien régime* Spain, but the theft of sacred objects from churches occurred with some regularity. The criminal records of Madrid[71] mention numerous thefts from churches and monasteries of silver, jewels and lamps. Two notable cases were the taking of jewels and a ciborium with hosts from the church in Camarma de Esteruelas in 1674, and that of two chalices and patens and ciboria with hosts from churches in Baza and Castril in 1680.

Sacrilegious thefts were not restricted to the great metropolis of Madrid. In 1672 a chalice with hosts was stolen from the Jesuit church in Orense;[72] in 1698 a similar theft occurred at the Dominican friary in Valencia. We can appreciate the gravity of such a crime in a Catholic society by looking at the reaction in Valencia.[73] The viceroy offered a reward of 1,000 ducats, all the gates of the city were shut, and orders were given for a search to be made throughout the realm. The city offered another reward of 1,000 ducats for the apprehension of the culprits, and the Diputació added 600 escudos. Public mourning was to be observed in all churches and public buildings, and no music was to be played at masses. Eventually the chalice and hosts were found buried at the foot of a tree in the Capuchin friary. There were processions of thanks, and universal public rejoicing. The shocking aspect of these crimes was the theft of consecrated hosts rather than of the chalices, but the evidence is that the thieves did not intend sacrilege. In the theft from Camarma de Esteruelas in 1674, one of the thieves consumed all the wafers so that they should not be defiled; and in Valencia all the wafers were recovered intact.

As in other Catholic societies, anticlericalism was often based on opposition to tithes. In 1669 Lorenzo Sánchez, a notary of the Inquisition in Fuensalida, was accused of saying that 'tithes belong to us, and the priests are our servants, which is why we give them tithes'.[74] Pedro Palacios, of Lerín, was even more forthright in 1680. While helping to gather in the harvest he remarked to others that 'of ten handfuls one goes to the priests, and to think of it makes him wish his arms would fall off'. A confirmed anticlerical, he said that 'so as not to be buried by the priests he would ask in his will to be buried out in the fields'.[75] The Moroccan ambassador who visited Spain in 1690 had a revealing encounter. 'A handsome woman at Seville came to see him with her mother and two sisters, and many Christians were present, and they began to talk of the friars and clergy. And the young woman said, He who trusts to the friars is accursed. And he asked her why she said this, and she answered, I know them all, and have no need to give more explanations.'[76] Anticlericalism in a sacral society is a well-known phenomenon; the problem is whether it can to any extent be equated with unbelief.

## CONVERSOS AND JEWS IN SPAIN

The late seventeenth century was the last great period of converso activity in Spain. The most active and successful conversos were of Portuguese origin. They had fled from intense persecution in their own country and settled down in Spain, only to be uprooted by the vigilance of the Spanish Inquisition. Under Philip IV they had been granted considerable freedom at court and extensive privileges in finance and trade. At that period they had claimed that 'the New Christians are today in Portugal and Castile those who maintain commerce, the farming of the revenues to Your Majesty, and the contracts to supply money outside the realm'.[77] This was still true to some extent under Charles II.

The 1650s saw the beginning of wholesale arrests and trials which constituted nothing less than a reign of terror for the Portuguese conversos in Spain. The repression lasted into the early 1680s. In the Granada *auto de fe* of 30 May 1672 there were seventy-five judaizers out of ninety accused; fifty-seven of them were Portuguese. The great Madrid *auto* of 30 June 1680 included 104 judaizers, nearly all of Portuguese origin. The Córdoba *auto* of 29 September 1684 included thirty-four judaizers among the forty-eight penitents.[78]

The intensity of persecution was not exclusively a measure of concern for the faith. Since the fifteenth century racial discrimination against Spaniards of Jewish origin had become an established feature of public life. The cult of purity of blood (limpieza de sangre) became written into the law.[79] All those who could not produce a certificate proving that they were free of Jewish blood, and that they had never been punished by the Inquisition, were excluded from public office. Employment and preferment were denied to thousands of Spaniards on the grounds of their racial antecedents. Like most forms of discrimination, limpieza caused problems. By the time of Philip IV it was being recognised that the laws tended to cause injustice and social strife. No steps were taken to abolish them, but ways were sometimes found round them.

The Moroccan ambassador in 1690 was interested to find that hatred of Jews was often accompanied by respect for Moorish blood. In Madrid he met a man of

303

rank who told him that 'we are of the race of Muslims of the lineage of the sons of Al-Serraj; and the ambassador inquired about him afterwards and learned that he was one of the Secretaries of the Council'.[80] He found also that there was still criticism of the expulsion of the Moriscos in 1609, and that the duke of Lerma was denounced as a Jew for his action in driving them out of Spain.[81] Though persecution of secret Muslims still continued, with for instance a sensational case in Granada in 1728,[82] the main burden fell on judaizers.

The biggest single outbreak of persecution was directed against the so-called Chuetas, the converso minority of Mallorca. Since the fifteenth century the Inquisition had been busy uprooting judaizers. After a lull in the late sixteenth and early seventeenth centuries, the storm burst over the Chuetas in 1675, when a young man aged nineteen was burnt in the *auto de fe* of 13 January held in Palma.[83] Repercussions from the case led in 1677 to a general arrest of conversos and by 1678 the Inquisition had arrested 237. Now followed two great waves of devastation in 1679 and 1691. In the spring of 1679 no less than five *autos* were held in Mallorca, with a total of 221 reconciliations. The confiscations reached a record total of over 2,500,000 ducats.[84] Crushed by events, the conversos waited ten years before they could stir again. In 1688 some of them attempted to recoup all in a plot which failed and led directly to the four *autos* held in 1691, at which thirty-seven accused were burnt alive.

The most famous *auto* in the history of the Inquisition was held in Madrid on 30 June 1680. A lengthy written account of it, published that year by an official;[85] and an enormous painting of the event by Francisco Rizi, currently in the Prado; are responsible for its reputation. It was probably the most grandiose ceremony ever conducted by the Holy Office. The procession that instituted the *auto* was led by twenty-five grandees, thirty-seven títulos and twenty-three illustrious persons. The king himself presided over proceedings, which lasted from 7 a.m., when he appeared, to 9 p.m., when he withdrew. The *auto* was otherwise unremarkable. At best, it was a presentation of the Church militant to Spaniards who in that very month were threatened by the onset of plague and famine in Andalucia.

The French ambassador, the marquis de Villars, was present at the *auto*. He observed that:

These punishments do not significantly diminish the number of Jews in Spain and above all in Madrid where, while some are punished with great severity, one sees several others employed in finance, esteemed and respected although known to be of Jewish origin. Shortly after this *auto*, a certain Don Ventura Donis obtained a title of marquis from the king for 50,000 crowns. His father had given even more to obtain the Order of Santiago, and it was known that his uncle was one of the chief men in the synagogue at Amsterdam. There are a great number of them in the tax farms and revenues of the king, where they are usually left in peace for a while, until they are rich enough to be investigated. They are then had for large sums if they wish to escape the ultimate punishment. It makes one think that this great machinery for punishing a few beggars is rather a wish for display by the inquisitors than true zeal for religion.[86]

The fate of the converso financiers was the most significant aspect of persecution in this reign. Under Philip IV many of the leading Portuguese financiers had been eliminated, ranging from Juan Núñez Saravía in 1630 to

Fernando de Montesinos in 1656. Despite the immense fines which the Inquisition managed to extort from men like these, it was not to the government's interest to destroy pillars of the financial community. Their disappearance threatened the fiscal system. On 7 September 1654 the council of Finance came to an agreement with the Inquisition that the latter could confiscate only the personal property of accused, and that money involved in official contracts would be dealt with by the former. The agreement had the virtue of distinguishing between a financier and his firm, so that the imprisonment of principals such as Montesinos did not automatically lead to dissolution of their business.

Among the most prominent conversos in mid-century was the financier Manuel Cortizos de Villasante, born in Valladolid of Portuguese parents.[87] His astuteness and financial dealings raised him to the highest ranks in the kingdom, and he had become by the end of his life a knight of the Order of Calatrava, lord of Arrifana, a member of the council of Finance and secretary of the Contaduría Mayor de Cuentas, the principal department of the treasury. All this occurred at a time when the statutes of limpieza were in full force. Suddenly, after his death in 1650, it was discovered that he had been a secret judaizer and been buried according to Jewish rites. The discovery would normally have led to the ruin of his family. But their rank and influence saved them from disaster. Indeed, notwithstanding the strong suspicion that other members of the family were secret Jews, Manuel's son Don Sebastián was in 1657 appointed Spanish ambassador to Genoa; while another son, Don Manuel José Cortizos, continued his father's work as a financier of the Crown, obtained the title of viscount of Valdefuentes in 1668 and shortly afterwards that of marquis of Villaflores. Throughout the reign of Charles II, Cortizos was second to none in the financial services he rendered the Crown. In 1679, thanks to defaulting by his creditors, he was obliged to ask for a moratorium on his transactions, even though his assets were worth several million ducats.[88]

Another fortunate example was Simón de Fonseca Piña, who was denounced in 1661 as a judaizer,[89] but who continued to serve as one of the Crown's biggest financiers for payments in Flanders. The number of those who did not escape was, however, considerable.[90] Among them was Diego Gómez de Salazar, administrator general of the tobacco monopoly in Castile, whose trial lasted from 1659 to 1664, and who eventually succeeded in escaping with most of his family in 1671 to Bayonne in France.[91] Another tobacco administrator in a high social position, Luis Márquez Cardoso, was reconciled together with his wife at an *auto* in Toledo in November 1669.[92] In August 1691 Simón Ruiz Pessoa, a leading Portuguese financier who had managed the customs duties of Andalucia from 1683 to 1685, was arrested by the Inquisition in Madrid.[93] In 1694 Don Francisco del Castillo, a member of the Contaduría Mayor de Cuentas, born in Osuna and resident in Ecija, was arrested in Seville by the tribunal.[94]

The most eminent Portuguese financier to suffer in this reign was Francisco Báez Eminente. He took no part in international exchange but restricted his considerable fortune to the administration of the customs duties of Andalucia, Seville and the Indies (the *almojarifazgos*), as well as provisioning the royal army and navy in Andalucia. During his term of administration in 1686 such severe measures were taken against smugglers that, according to Lantéry, 'we came to experience what was held to be impossible in Cadiz, namely that there should be no smuggling'.[95] Eminente was a member of the Contaduría Mayor, and in view of the fact that most of Castile's trade passed through Andalucia his work was of the highest importance to the Crown, which he served, as the government later admitted, 'for over forty years with credit, industry and zeal that were well known'.[96] Despite this long service and his advanced years, on 26 December 1689 he was suddenly arrested by the Inquisition in Madrid.[97] His colleague Don Bernardo de Paz y Castañeda was arrested at about the same time. The arrests made no difference to the firm of Eminente, which had been handed over to his son Juan Francisco in April 1689, and continued successfully under him well into the next century.[98]

Conversos seem to have been resigned to the hardships of life in Spain. Very few emigrated, and then only when the alternative was ruin or death. After centuries of repression, they had come to terms with their existence. In order to circumvent the limpieza statutes they possessed, as the Márquez Cardoso family did,[99] paid agents of Old Christian origin and noble rank to swear that they too were Old Christians. Their ranks continued to be fortified by refugees from Portugal. In 1671, for example, the council of State reported in alarm that an estimated 60,000 New Christians were being expelled from Portugal and that most would inevitably come to Spain.[100] There was no effective way to stop this movement of population within the peninsula. Meanwhile, the Spanish government itself had eliminated the last officially tolerated enclave of Jews in Spanish territory: the community of Orán in North Africa.

The Jews had been tolerated in Orán since the days of Ferdinand the Catholic.[101] They acted usefully as intermediaries with the Moors, and their best known representative in the seventeenth century was Jacob Cansino, who was official Arabic interpreter to the Spanish government and to Olivares. On Cansino's death in 1666, the Queen Regent asked why the post of interpreter should not now be filled by a Christian. This led to further queries as to why the Jews were permitted at all in Orán. Good reasons were soon found for proposing their expulsion, a move suggested to Madrid in 1667 by the marquis of Los Vélez, governor of Orán. Jacob Saportas, *xeque* or secular head of the Orán Jewish community from 1655, who had been banished to Italy for an unspecified cause in 1657,[102] was now asked by the Orán Jews to mediate on their behalf. He came over from Genoa to Cartagena, intending to go to Madrid, but he died in Cartagena in 1668. His brother Samuel was appointed the next xeque.

The Regent's order for the expulsion was issued in Madrid on 31 October 1668 in secret, so that no appeal or measures against it could be initiated. It was not until 31 March 1669 that Los Vélez had it publicly proclaimed in the town square in Orán, giving the Jews eight days to leave. He wrote to the Regent with congratulations 'that under your wise government the monarchy is free of a race so at variance with its Catholicity'. The blow caught the Jews unprepared. Los Vélez reported that 'most of them realised there was no escape, and on the very day the edict was proclaimed they prepared to dispose of their property. They agreed to be taken to Nice, where they could stay if it were convenient, but if not they would go to Livorno. . . . On 16 April all the clothing was put on board in the morning, and in the afternoon the expulsion was effected of 476 persons, who are those who by God's judgment were tolerated in this little town.'[103] This tragic little episode, carried through in the very same decade that Jews were permitted back into England, undermined Orán's limited trade, rid all Spanish soil of Jews, and exposed the outdated views of Spain's policymakers.

In 1681 the town and fortress of Orán were captured by the Moors, and its garrison slaughtered.

Among the most significant conversos of the late century, and a man whose career aptly illustrates the strange mixture of tolerance and intolerance of those days, was Dr Diego Mateo Zapata.[104] Born of Portuguese parents in Murcia in 1664, Zapata was brought up by his mother as a secret Jew. In 1678 she was arrested, tortured and emerged in an *auto de fe* in 1681. His father was arrested on suspicion, but set free. Zapata went to the university of Valencia to study medicine, and then to Alcalá, where he was befriended by Francisco Enríquez de Villacorta, a doctor with Jewish origins. He moved to Madrid and thanks to his connections managed to prosper. In 1692 he was arrested in Madrid by the Inquisition on charges of Judaism, and spent a year in the cells of the tribunal at Cuenca; the prosecution was suspended, and he was released in 1693. In 1702 he was elected president of the Royal Society of Medicine in Seville. The early eighteenth century found him rich and successful in Madrid, in possession of a large library that included the works of Bacon, Gassendi, Bayle, Paracelsus, Pascal and other philosophers. In 1721 he was suddenly arrested, again on charges of Judaism, and appeared in an *auto de fe* in Cuenca in 1725, condemned to ten years banishment and the loss of half his goods. He returned to active work in Madrid, helped to found the Royal Academy of Medicine in 1734, and died in 1745.

## NOTES

1. Giovanni Andrea Spinola, in Ciasca, ed., *Ambiasciatori Genovesi*, p. 170.
2. The names are compiled from Benavent's diary in Valencia, and Labayru, *Señorío de Bizcaya*, V, p. 558.
3. Ortiz de Zúñiga, D., *Anales* (Seville 1677), p. 801.
4. Benavent, fo. 4 vo.
5. Consulta of council of Aragon, 9 May 1665, ACA:CA 319.
6. Viceroy Castelrodrigo to king, 11 Dec. 1691, *ibid*. 586/21.
7. Vazquez, I., *Las negociaciones inmaculistas* (Madrid 1957).
8. See Caro Baroja, *Las formas complejas* (Madrid 1978), pp. 529–44.
9. Astraín, A., *Compañía de Jesús* (Madrid 1920), VI, 119–372.
10. I have been unable to obtain recent Spanish scholarship on Molinos, notably the edition of the *Guía espiritual* by Fr Tellechea (1976). My account therefore follows that in Caro Baroja, *op. cit.* pp. 481–6.
11. Menéndez Pelayo, M., *Heterodoxos* (Madrid 1964), IV, p. 280.

12. **Ellacuria Beascoechea, J.**, *Reacción Española* (Madrid 1956), p. 59.
13. *Ibid.* pp. 63–6.
14. Tellechea, *op. cit.* apparently emphasises the political context of the denunciations, and concludes that the condemned views are not precisely found in the *Guía*.
15. Cited in Caro Baroja, *op. cit.* p. 483 n. 108–9.
16. AHN Inq. lib. 735/385.
17. *Ibid.* lib. 735/392. For several cases in Toledo, see those cited by Caro Baroja, *op. cit.*, pp. 484–5.
18. AHN Inq. 218/20.
19. Lisón, 'Breve Historial Brujesco Gallego', esp. pp. 193–7, in *Ensayos* (Madrid 1973).
20. Quoted from a case in 1696: AHN Inq. 127/6.
21. *Ibid.* lib. 735/349.
22. *Ibid.* lib. 998/207.
23. *Ibid.* 1679/3.
24. Both cases in *ibid.* lib. 998/189, 212.
25. 'Diciendo entre ellos que aquello era caso de Inquisicion y que no podian dexar de dar quenta': *ibid.* 1679/7.
26. *Ibid.* 221/16.
27. *Ibid.* 217/12.
28. Lea, *Inquisition*, III, 552–4.
29. AHN. 27/17/2, 109.
30. *Ibid.* 73/17.
31. *Ibid.* 218/20.
32. Cf. Bennassar, *L'Homme espagnol*, pp. 151–4.
33. *A Relation*, p. 496.
34. AHN Inq. 24/7.
35. **Gavarri, P.**, *Instrucciones Predicables* (Seville 1673), p. 198.
36. AHN Inq. lib. 735, 'Relaciones de Causas de fe desde el año de 1665 hasta el de 1692'.
37. *Ibid.* lib. 735/385.
38. Both cases in Barcelona in 1665: *ibid.* lib. 735.
39. Muret, *Lettres*, p. 75.
40. AHN Inq. 36/10.
41. *Ibid.* lib. 735/156.
42. On demons see e.g. Caro Baroja, *op. cit.* pp. 64–5, 72–3.
43. Cf. Deleito, *La vida religiosa*, pp. 174–50.
44. Quoted in Caro Baroja, *op. cit.*, p. 450.
45. **Santos**, *Día y Noche* (1974), p. 25.
46. Astraín, *Compañía de Jesus*, VI, 76.
47. *Monumento triunfal*, p. 119.
48. *Ibid.* p. 24.
49. *Ibid.* p. 22.
50. Cf. Kamen, *Iron Century*, ch. 11.
51. Report enclosed with letter from bishop of Solsona to secretary of council of Aragon, 7 Oct. 1684, ACA:CA 451.
52. AHN Inq. 41/21.
53. *Ibid.* 27/17.
54. *Ibid.* 90/3.
55. *Ibid.* 90/14.

56. *Ibid.* 79/24/38.
57. *Ibid.* 73/17/52.
58. Domínguez Ortiz, *Golden Age*, p. 208.
59. Both cited in Kamen, *Inquisition*, ch. 16.
60. AHN Inq. 37/1.
61. *Ibid.* lib. 735.
62. *Ibid.* lib. 735/330.
63. *Ibid.* 36/1.
64. Quoted in Caro Baroja, *op. cit.* p. 200 n. 38.
65. AHN Inq. lib. 735/155 v.
66. *Ibid.* lib. 735/334.
67. *Ibid.* 221/13.
68. Kamen, *War of Succession*, p. 249, referring to the bishops of Calahorra and Murcia.
69. AHN Inq. lib. 735/26.
70. *Ibid.* 226/10.
71. AHN Consejos, Sala de Alcaldes, Imbentario de causas criminales, 2786–8.
72. Royal decree of 13 Aug. 1672, AHN Consejos 7182/18.
73. Benavent, fo. 31–2.
74. AHN Inq. 209/25.
75. *Ibid.* 1679/7.
76. *Account of an embassy*, p. 18.
77. **Adler, E.**, 'Marranes d'Espagne', *Rev. Etud. Juives*, 49 (1904), 63–5.
78. BN MS. 9475; **del Olmo, J.**, *Relación* (Madrid 1680); **Matute y Luquín, G.**, *Colección de los Autos* (Córdoba 1840), p. 210.
79. **Sicroff, A.**, *Les controverses* (Paris 1960); **Domínguez Ortiz, A.**, *Los conversos de orígen judío* (Madrid 1957); Kamen, *Inquisition*, ch. 7.
80. *Account of an embassy*, pp. 2–3, 5.
81. *Ibid.* p. 10. The expulsion, denounced before it happened by Cellorigo, and after it happened by Navarrete, was widely condemned in seventeenth-century Spain.
82. AHN Inq. 4755–58.
83. The whole persecution is considered by **Braunstein, B.**, *The Chuetas* (Philadelphia 1936, new edn New York 1972).
84. AHN Inq. 4776–9.
85. José del Olmo, *Relación*, cited above.
86. **Villars**, *Mémoires* (Paris 1893), pp. 188–9. The text of the memoirs is in AE Mem. et Doc. (Esp) 75/117–349.
87. **Caro Baroja, J.**, *Los Judíos* (Madrid 1961), II, ch. 5.
88. Memorial from Cortizos in 1679, in AHN Consejos 7189.
89. Caro Baroja, *Los Judíos*, II, 138. Fonseca was married to the daughter of the sentenced financier Pasarino.
90. *Ibid.* II, chs 4 and 5.
91. *Ibid.* II, pp. 84–9.
92. *Ibid.* III, p. 51; AHN Inq. 5019[5], memoir of Hacienda, 13 Dec. 1679.
93. AHN Inq. 5047[1].
94. *Ibid.* 5047[1].
95. *Memorias*, p. 187.
96. *Cédula* of 19 Aug. 1712, AGS Contadurías Generales 190.
97. Consulta of council of Finance, Oct. 1691, AGS:CJH 1150.
98. Juan Francisco died on 23 Feb. 1711, after which the firm was administered by D. Joseph Franco. The firm was transferred to Juan Francisco on 15 Apr. 1689, AHN Inq. 3666/4.

99. Caro Baroja, *Los Judíos*, III, 51.

100. Consulta of State, 24 July 1671, AHN Estado 2693.

101. What follows is derived from the *Breve relación . . . de la general expulsion de los hebreos de la Juderia de la Ciudad de Orán*, of D. Luis de Sotomayor y Valenzuela, as summarised in Caro Baroja, *Los Judíos*, I, 215–20.

102. Jacob Saportas lived in Genoa. One of his sons was our Alicante merchant Felipe de Moscoso. In 1660 Felipe went to Madrid to plead his father's case but without success. I am greatly indebted to Dr. Jonathan Israel for giving me valuable information on the Saportas family.

103. Los Vélez to Regent, Orán 5 May 1669, AGS Estado 4128.

104. **Vilar Ramírez, J. B.**, *Zapata* (Murcia 1970).

# CHAPTER TWELVE

# Towards a Spirit of Criticism

Illiteracy in Spain was high: as late as 1860 some 75 per cent of Spaniards were unable to read and write. Since the Renaissance the authorities in Church and State had made efforts to teach young children the three Rs – reading, writing and arithmetic; but with limited success.[1] By the seventeenth century a child's chance to be educated depended on whether his village could afford a teacher, or whether indeed there were enough qualified teachers.

Many historians adopt as a sign of minimal literacy the ability to sign one's name. This is not always reliable evidence. Some people, such as soldiers, learned to sign in order to pick up their wages; but were otherwise illiterate. Esteban Núñez, a travelling actor, in 1663 signed his name perfectly but also said that 'he can sign but cannot write'.[2] With poor educational attainments, the average Spaniard was unlikely to broaden his cultural outlook.

Rudimentary education in village classes was followed by the grammar school, where the grammar was of course Latin. By the seventeenth century 'almost every town of substantial size, that is those with 500 vecinos or more, possessed a Latin school of its own'.[3] Ambitious parents from areas with no such school would send children away. Andrés González, a humble carpenter's assistant whose father was a small farmer in Madrid, was sent out of town to the village of San Sebastián de los Reyes to live and learn grammar there for five years in the late 1660s.[4] His motive was clearly that denounced by the writer Pedro de Valencia in the early century: 'nowadays every farmer, trader, cobbler, blacksmith and plasterer, each of whom loves his sons with indiscreet affection, wishes to remove them from work and seek for them a more glamorous career. Toward this end, they put them to study.'[5]

Rising costs for both colleges and parents were a source of difficulty. Our witness is Raymond Lantéry, who in 1686 sent his second son José to college in Córdoba.[6]

The fees for a year in the college are 50 ducats vellón and a *cahiz* of wheat for his food, because although Sr. Anton López its founder left enough revenues for maintenance, with time they have declined in value and this solution has been arrived at. . . . On top of this I supplied chocolate for José and his friends, and every month I sent him a doblon for pocket money. Despite this he always asked for something. The truth is that he was better

311

off than anyone else in the college, and there were four others from Cadiz. I was looked upon as the richest parent, because the softest, since I sent him whatever I could. Besides, I had in Córdoba a French colleague, Charles Delarue, and whenever José fancied something he went to him and got it from him and I like a good fellow repaid Delarue. So this son has cost me more than all the others together.

The colleges were the highest level of formal instruction for most Spaniards. After this secondary education, pupils went out equipped for most walks of life. José Lantéry, for example, was sent directly to America after his stay at Córdoba, in order to learn the Indies trade at first hand.[7] The popularity of the colleges, which trained boys up to the age of about fifteen, owed a great deal to the Jesuits, who by 1600 had nearly 100 of them in Castile alone. In Pamplona at the end of the century the Jesuit college was taking in up to 400 students a year.[8] By the eighteenth century if not before, the Jesuits were the single most powerful force in Spanish education.

The next stage of education above college was the university. By mid-century the Crown of Castile had nineteen universities and the Crown of Aragon fourteen (six in Catalonia, three in Aragon, four in Valencia and one in Mallorca).[9] In practice they had long ceased to contribute seriously to the cultural life of Spain, and were little more than a training ground for the bureaucracy of state. University professors and other distinguished graduates received preference for appointment to posts in the Castilian bureaucracy. Academic standards decayed as intellectual talent was creamed off into the professions, and the appeal of a university education consequently evaporated. Between 1630 and 1680 the number of entrants to the Castilian universities fell by approximately half, and the decline went on. The crisis was part of Spain's early seventeenth-century recession. It was caused by three main factors: the population decline of the early century, economic and inflationary problems, and the growing appeal of alternative centres of higher education.

Within the universities an élite came into existence in the course of the sixteenth century. These were the students attending the Colegios Mayores, the prestige university colleges at Salamanca (where there were four), Valladolid and Alcalá. Their status increased until by 1670 their membership was roughly two and a half times bigger than in 1570.[10] Even more than the universities, the Colegios Mayores virtually monopolised senior appointments in the state bureaucracy. At the same time the expanding Jesuit colleges attracted away students who might otherwise have attended the traditional institutions. The decline of the university at Saragossa was explained as follows in the Cortes of Aragon in 1677:

The lack of students is caused by the calamity of the times, for they either go to other universities that are closer and cheaper, or else they can go to Estudios Generales that are increasing every day; and the same lack of students is being suffered by Salamanca and Alcalá. If some go from Aragon to Salamanca they are very few, and they go not for the teaching so much as to broaden their minds and learn good manners.[11]

Higher education in Spain seemed to be directed to administration rather than letters. In this it was not substantially different from the practice of other

European universities.[12] The difference was that in Catholic Spain the study of canon law was preferred over all other disciplines. In 1675 in Salamanca canon law attracted 59 per cent of all matriculations, in Valladolid 65 per cent.[13] The ecclesiastical emphasis in education, the decline in numbers, the bias of the system towards career professions: all meant that academic subjects were given low priority and eventually ceased even to recruit professors to teach them. A major consequence of this abdication of traditional seats of learning from their early functions, was that the religious orders, led by the Dominicans, began to take over the teaching of arts subjects and of theology in the leading universities. While other European universities in the late century were becoming more secularised, those of Spain were falling more under the influence of orders with a dogmatic interest in traditional Catholic philosophy.[14]

The decay under Charles II was unquestionable, whether we consider subjects taught or teachers or the number of students. Foreign visitors were without exception unfavourably impressed. One witness is Lorenzo Magalotti, who accompanied Cosmo I of Tuscany to Spain in 1668–69. Passing through Lérida, he was horrified to find that the governor of the city was illiterate, 'with no polish of manners or experience or letters, not knowing how to read or to sign his own name'. In Saragossa he found that 'the ignorance is immense and the sciences are held in horror'. Writing to Cosmo's uncle, prince Leopold, in November 1668, Magalotti observed that 'the whole of literature in Spain at present boils down to scholastic theology and outdated medicine as found in the works of Galen. . . . To prove this it is sufficient to tell you that in Alcalá – I beg you, Your Excellency, to mark this – in that celebrated and renowned institution, they have not taught anatomy for the last eight or ten years.' In all their travels in Spain, Magalotti went on, they found nobody with whom they could converse in Latin (a patent exaggeration), and very few who knew any Greek.[15]

Although the governor of Lérida can in no way be taken as representative of his class, there is no doubt that a problem existed. In November 1713 Melchor de Macanaz, as fiscal of the council of Castile, undertook a nationwide enquiry into the possibility of setting up special colleges for the children of the aristocracy. 'One of the biggest problems the monarchy suffers', he wrote, 'is that the greater and lesser nobility do not pursue civil or canon law or theology, nor do they have colleges where they can study rhetoric, mathematics and other arts. If a nobleman wishes to educate his sons, which is reasonable, he has to send them to colleges in Bologna, Rome, France and other places.'[16] Salamanca welcomed the proposal and suggested that annual fees for each student would come to 200 ducats.

The comments of Francis Willughby on the state of learning in Valencia in 1664 are valuable. 'In this city is an University. I heard a Professor read Logic. The scholars are sufficiently insolent and very disputacious. One of them asked me, Quis est Ens universale? and whether I was of Thomas Aquinas his opinion: another, Quid est Genus? None of them understood anything of the new Philosophy, or had so much as heard of it. None of the new books to be found in any of their Booksellers shops. In a word the University of Valence is just where our Universities were 100 years ago.'[17]

The foreign observers were correct to note that Spain had lost touch with world scholarship. This happened because of the rarity of creative contact with foreigners, and because of the policy of censorship. Restriction of contacts can be dated back to the policies of Philip II. The siege mentality which typified the 'closed society' of Habsburg Spain, induced the authorities to treat all non-Spanish influences as suspect. There was a peculiar irony in this, since as members of the world's greatest empire Spaniards of all social levels travelled more than other Europeans. There is no evidence that by the late seventeenth century they had absorbed anything of cultural value from outside. Conversely, travellers to Spain were rare. Spanish inns were notoriously the worst in western Europe. The west European gentry who did the Grand Tour never considered Spain worth visiting, and Protestants tended to avoid the country because of the Inquisition.

Censorship was an important impediment to freer contacts, though its significance for most Spaniards can easily be exaggerated. Few would have been likely to come into contact with disapproved works. The reign of Charles II laboured under the weight of the Index of Prohibited Books issued by the Inquisition in 1640. Though this edition was an exhaustive compilation of the errors of the Reformation period, it was clearly out of date a generation later. Inquisitor General Diego Sarmiento de Valladares began drawing up a new one but it was not completed until after his death, when it was published in 1707 by Inquisitor General Vidal Marín. The new Index differed very little from its predecessors, and the inquisitors were obliged to issue a supplement in 1739.

The persons best placed to bring in books from abroad were merchants. Moscoso in 1661, for example, asked a correspondent in Livorno to send him two works 'for a doctor friend'.[18] The ports became in this way the most vulnerable flank of the Inquisition, and new ideas were to be found more readily there than in any other part of the peninsula. The literature of ideas from across the frontiers began to trickle into Spain: wherever a foreign ship touched Spanish soil, in Bilbao, Barcelona, Alicante, Valencia or Seville, a book could get through. By the end of the reign of Charles II the works of the philosophers of Europe could be obtained in Spain. When in 1691 the Inquisition of Seville arrested a cleric in minor orders, Juan Cruzado de la Cruz, they found in his possession a library of 1,125 books.[19] In addition to well-known works by Góngora, Luis de Granada, Navarrete, Porreño, Garcilaso and so on, there were others in English, French, Italian and Dutch. These included a volume of Francis Bacon; the letters, *Colloquies* and *Enchiridion* of Erasmus; two works by Descartes; six volumes of Gassendi; Grotius's *Mare liberum*; Hobbes's *Elements of Philosophy* in French; and numerous other volumes showing a clear interest in the kind of literature prohibited by the Inquisition and available freely only outside Spain.

Censorship under Charles II was largely an inactive and blunt instrument. It was seldom used against native scholars, who all worked within an orthodox framework. It threatened few, and hurt fewer. It remained as the formal protection against heresy, but did not seriously impede the quiet and inconspicuous entry of new ways of thought. Apart from the travails of the conversos, there was less repression in this reign than in that of any previous Habsburg. The ground was prepared for ideas that marked a new phase in the intellectual history of Spain.

# THE ARTS UNDER CHARLES II

The great artists of Spain's great era worked under the patronage of the Crown. Philip II and his son and grandson employed outstanding men without trying to impose any official style. The result was a great flowering of diversity, but primarily within the sphere of influence of the court. The late seventeenth century by contrast is usually seen as a period of decline. It may be more helpful to look at the changes of the period in terms of a loss of initiative by a court bereft of moral influence thanks to the incapacity of the king. The result was a return of creativity to the provinces.

Among the factors that determined the level of artistic output under Charles II were a relative decline in court commissions, and a near saturation point for building development in the Church, made more emphatic by official opposition to new foundations. Despite the lull of the late century, there was no lack of originality. At court, continuity of the high standards of Velázquez (d. 1660) was maintained by the leading official painters. The most notable was Juan Carreño de Miranda (d. 1685), an Asturian who was appointed court painter late in life and who turned out, in addition to his striking portraits of the rickety king, riches of splendour in creations such as *Belshazzar's Feast* and *The Founding of the Trinitarian Order* (1666). His friend Francisco Rizi (d. 1685) was also a court painter at the same period, and is perhaps best known for his large canvas of *The Auto de Fe* of 1680. The other significant contemporary of the Madrid school was the Sevillan Herrera el Mozo (d. 1685). Rizi's best known pupil, who succeeded Carreño as chief court painter, was Claudio Coello (d. 1693), whose varied work for the Crown culminated in his masterpiece *The Sacred Form* (1685–90), at the Escorial. A huge canvas of vision and depth, the painting is also notable as the only one we have depicting the members of the court of Charles II. Because these painters and their associates fall historically in the shadow of Velázquez, it has been common to belittle their achievement. Recent commentators have conceded that they did not fall below the highest standards of their art.

Some of the most memorable work of the reign was accomplished not in the capital but in the provinces. Juan Valdés Leal (d. 1690) spent most of his working life in Seville. A vivid and original painter, in the 1660s he was appointed president of the Seville Academy of Painting. He is perhaps best known for his striking and telling *Triumph of Death* and his *Finis Gloriae Mundi* (both 1672), in the chapel of the Hospital de la Caridad in Seville. Few paintings have been more misrepresented by historians. Scholars have suggested that they are typical of the consciousness of decay and decline that permeated the Spain of Charles II. In fact they are an unexceptional *memento mori*, representing little more than the brooding thoughts of the man who commissioned them, Don Miguel Mañara, founder of the Hospital.

The paintings of the greatest artist of the reign, Bartolomé Esteban Murillo (d. 1682), show how far from decay and introspection the creativity of this period could be. Murillo lived all his life in Seville, and in 1660 was founder-president of the Seville Academy of Painting. Neglected by foreign critics because of the cloying tenderness of some of his work, particularly his portrayals of the

Immaculate Conception, Murillo in fact has a broad awareness of life that falls very little short of the achievement of Velázquez. Some of his most convincing treatment of lower class life can be seen in canvasses such as *St Diego of Alcalá feeding the Poor* and *St Thomas of Villanueva*. Few painters of the seventeenth century succeed in conveying as Murillo does the sincerity and brightness of the Spanish temperament.

Because of the decline in building for religious purposes, some of the most outstanding artistic work of the period is in decoration, both in painting and in sculpture. Here again the Andalucians triumphed. The great genius of mid-century was Alonso Cano (d. 1667), whose tormented life produced some outstanding paintings and, particularly in his last years which he spent in Granada, some memorable statues. His pupil Pedro de Mena (d. 1688), who worked in Granada and Málaga, created sculptures of a dazzling intensity. His figures represent ordinary people caught up into religious contemplation: Mena succeeds in communicating the experience in a way that rivets the imagination. The flavour of Andalucian creativity at this time is perhaps best embodied in Mañara's foundation of the Caridad, partly through its rich paintings by Murillo and Valdés Leal but conspicuously through the triumphant late Baroque altar created by Bernardo Simón de Pineda, with sculptures by Pedro Roldán and painting by Valdés Leal.

Because of the restriction on new religious buildings, old ones were redesigned or decorated. A typical case is Valencia city, where many old churches were remodelled by Juan Bautista Pérez in this period, notably the cathedral sanctuary in 1682, San Nicolás in 1693, and San Andrés. The most imaginative renovation carried through was on the façades and towers of the cathedral at Santiago de Compostela, a move that was intended to enhance the prestige of the famous shrine. The only major church constructed in the late century was the vast cathedral housing the Virgin of the Pilar at Saragossa. The scheme, decreed by the pope in 1675, was intended to discontinue the long-standing rivalry between the existing cathedral and the shrine of the Pilar by merging them into one church. The plans were drawn up mainly by Francisco de Herrera the younger (d. 1685), who was appointed master of the royal works by Charles II in 1677. Today the most striking aspect of the Seo at Saragossa is not so much Herrera's vast building beside the river, as the unusual Baroque tower erected in 1683 by the Italian architect Contini, a pupil of Bernini.

Native extravagance in building is best known through the work of the Churrigueras, who came to Madrid from Barcelona in the 1670s. José Benito Churriguera (d. 1725) was the family's chief representative in the reign of Charles II. The style associated with their name was similar to that of other decorators, such as Pérez in Valencia, but became more established early in the following century.

## WRITING AND JOURNALISM

The reign of Charles II features in no histories of Spanish thought, yet it is precisely in this period that the beginnings of a critical spirit can be located. The great scholar and bibliophile Nicolás Antonio (1617–84), whose library in Rome apparently contained 30,000 volumes, was an outstanding product of the generation of Charles II. His *Bibliotheca Hispana Nova*, published in Rome in 1672, listed the works of several thousand Iberians writing between 1500 and 1670. Of some 10,000 authors listed for this period, less than 400 had written on mathematics and the sciences, less than 500 on medicine and medical science; in contrast, over 500 had written on mariology alone.[20] The predominant interest in religious matters during Spain's great literary age is thus beyond dispute. In the very years that Nicolás Antonio was making his analysis of literary production, however, a new trend of scholarship, above all in the historical sciences, was emerging.

The outstanding sixteenth-century histories of Juan de Mariana, Jerónimo de Zurita and the Americanists, were followed in the early seventeenth century by occasional chronicles, notably those of Pellicer, and by a resurgence of pseudo-historical if not wholly fictitious narratives dealing with the past.[21] These fictions were attacked firmly by Nicolás Antonio. Their most effective antagonist was the ninth marquis of Mondéjar, Don Gaspar Ibáñez de Segovia (d. 1708), a distinguished scholar and bibliophile whose library was reputedly second only to that of the Escorial. His *Dissertations . . . against modern fictions* (1671) was followed by other studies in which he critically examined the writings of historians such as Mariana, whose work was usually accepted without question by contemporaries.

An analysis by Sebastián García Martínez of 330 historical books issued in the late century shows that Church history continued to be the largest category, with ninety-six titles, followed by studies of America, with seventy-four titles. The relatively few titles devoted to Spanish history nevertheless included major contributions to the nation's historiography. Among the most successful official authors were Alonso Núñez de Castro, the chronicler of Madrid; and Antonio de Solís, author of a popular *History of the Conquest of Mexico* (1685). Their efforts, representing traditionalist narrative, were outclassed by those of the provincial historians.

In Seville Diego Ortiz de Zúñiga published his *Annals* (1677) of the city, a serious attempt to break away from the mythological style. In Navarre Father José de Moret published his pioneering *Historical Investigations* (1665), and his *Annals of Navarre* (1684–1704), which traced the kingdom's history down to the fourteenth century. In Aragon the undoubted erudition of Dr Diego José Dormer produced several commentaries on history, and an invaluable discourse on trade, but failed to come up with any significant history of the realm. A luminary of the University of Huesca, where he read Philosophy and Jurisprudence and obtained his doctorate,[22] Dormer was appointed to the coveted post of Chronicler of Aragon in September 1674, and held it for nearly thirty years. In 1681 he made an official visit, which lasted twenty-four days and cost the Diputación 500 libras in expenses, to the archive of Simancas. 'I have', he wrote in November to the Justiciar of Aragon, 'been to the archive twice, and been amazed at the building and the documents and the infinite number of papers relating to our realm.'[23] He also made a visit to the archive in Barcelona to search for papers relating to his proposed life of Charles V. Despite all this activity he never managed to fulfil the principal duty of his office, which was to continue the Chronicles of Aragon begun by Zurita. After various squabbles the frustrated Diputados finally removed him from the post in August 1703 and appointed Don José Lupercio Panzano in his place.[24] The most important historical work produced in the Crown of Aragon at this time was the massive *Annals of Catalonia* of Narciso Feliu de la Peña, published in 1709. In concept and presentation the most modern of all the historical works written under Charles II, the *Annals* are a milestone in Spanish historiography.

The collapse of the court of Madrid as an active patron was, in literature as in art, probably the single most important reason for the miserable level of literary output under Charles II. On the other hand, technical and juridical works continued to come out, reflecting as they did the interests of the professions. The appearance in 1672 of Veitia y Linaje's *Norte de Contración*, and in 1681 of the four-volume *Recopilación de Indias*, which I have noted above, were part of this development. A recent survey has managed to unearth some 145 juridical authors published between 1665 and 1700, of whom seventy were contemporaries.[25]

The reign is important for the first systematic appearance of Spanish journalism. In mid-century a few printers began to issue newsletters in imitation of those now common in Germany and the Netherlands.[26] The newsletters appeared infrequently, and were often unreliable. The major impetus to journalism in Spain came from Don Juan of Austria. In 1659, at the end of his three years as governor of Flanders, he returned to Spain bringing with him his Franche Comtois secretary Francisco Fabro Bremundan. In 1660 Philip IV approved proposals to issue a gazette and the first number of the *Relación o Gazeta* appeared in January 1661 under Bremundan as editor. From February it was called simply the *Gazeta*; it appeared twelve times in 1661 and eight in 1662. Some of the issues were devoted to the successes of Bremundan's patron Don Juan in the campaigns against rebel Portugal. The *Gazeta* was temporarily suspended from 1663, possibly because of Don Juan's failures on the Portuguese front. Its success, however, had encouraged the emergence of local gazettes in Seville, Saragossa, Valencia and Mexico, all modelling themselves directly on Bremundan's paper.

The years of Don Juan's conflicts with Nithard mark him out as 'the first Spaniard of high estate to use the printing press as an instrument of policy'.[27] The flood of propaganda unleashed on his behalf from 1665 to 1669 may have been masterminded by Bremundan, but there is no direct evidence of this. In 1676, when Don Juan was based in Saragossa, Bremundan was entrusted with editing a new periodical, *Regular Notices of the Affairs of the North*, which continued publishing for nine months and expressed Don Juan's policy for peace in northern Europe.

In the two years, 1677 to 1679, that his patron was chief minister of Spain, Bremundan exercised a monopoly right over gazettes. The *Gazeta Ordinaria de Madrid*, issued as a weekly from July 1677, had official status and was scrutinised by the king's council before publication. The demise of Don Juan in September

318

1679 led to a reaction against the relative freedom of the press that he had encouraged. The final issue of the *Gazeta Ordinaria* on 8 April 1680 stated that 'it is ordered that no more gazettes be distributed or printed, which puts an end to this one'. A decree of 11 November prohibited all other similar papers.

*Relaciones* continued to appear, albeit illegally. Then, on 16 November 1683, papers were again authorised. Bremundan's *Gazeta Ordinaria* reappeared on the same day as the decree. This time there were competitors: the *Singular News* of Sebastián de Armendáriz and the *Gazeta General* of Lucas Antonio de Bedmar, both of which appeared in 1684. In May 1684 Armendáriz and Bremundan merged their papers, which appeared in this form until the latter's death on 12 September 1690. The *Gazeta* thereafter fell under the control of the Hospital General of Madrid but was mismanaged and fell into debt; it was eventually acquired by Juan de Goyeneche in 1697 and its title was changed to *Gazeta de Madrid*, in which form it continued as a weekly. The first official and regular newspaper of modern Spain, it was open to subscribers from the time that Goyeneche took over, and thereby secured a dependable income.[28]

## THE EARLY SCIENTIFIC REVOLUTION IN SPAIN

In 1664 Willughby had observed that 'in all kinds of good learning the Spaniards are behind the rest of Europe, understanding nothing at all but a little of the old wrangling Philosophy and School-divinity'.[29] Within a generation there took place one of the most momentous changes to have occurred in Spain since the Renaissance. Without departing fundamentally from the accepted tenets of philosophy, innovators began to propose major changes in scientific method. The new trends occurred mainly in medicine but extended their view over all aspects of science.

Early seventeenth-century science in Spain was based exclusively on what had been known in the Renaissance.[30] The regime of Philip II had cut off the country from its links with European culture. By the middle decades of the century some knowledge of foreign achievement was seeping in. The first known mention of Descartes was in a work by a Jesuit professor in Oviedo in 1655.[31] Leading scientists of 'moderate' inclination accepted many of these achievements, but grafted them on to the existing orthodoxy. In medicine Gaspar Bravo de Sobremonte (d. 1683), professor of Valladolid and physician to both Philip IV and Charles II, strongly defended (in 1662) the theories of William Harvey and other foreign scholars, but rejected any basic modification to the general doctrines of Galen, who was still accepted as the standard authority. Harvey's theory of the circulation of blood was at the time unacceptable to most Spanish physicians.[32] In physics the outlook of Luis Rodríguez de Pedrosa (d. 1673), professor of medicine and natural philosophy at Salamanca, was likewise poised between the old orthodoxy and new perspectives.[33] He rejected many of the premises of traditional Aristotelianism, and in one discourse cited Copernicus and Tycho Brahe as authorities. The most remarkable quasi-departure from tradition was that of Isaac Cardoso (d. 1680), a professor of Madrid and Valladolid who left Spain in 1648 to live as a Jew in Venice, where he published his *Philosophia libera* (1673), an exposition of atomist philosophy based principally on the theories of Gassendi.[34]

The ground was already prepared for the advances of the late century. What occurred was not a surreptitious growth: it was open, and well publicised. Nor was it linked to the experience of isolated individuals such as Feijoo, long regarded as a solitary harbinger of new ideas. The prerequisites for the transformation under Charles II were, firstly, the change of direction initiated in all aspects of public policy by the regime of Don Juan of Austria; secondly, the formation of salons or discussion groups under distinguished patronage, and the evolution of these circles into formal scientific Societies; and finally and most important, intellectual and cultural links with Italy.

The freedom of discussion provoked by the short and turbulent period of Don Juan's tenure of power, stirred the nation in a way that had not occurred since the days of Charles V. His appeal to the reformers, to the cities and to the provinces was the principal stimulus to debates in Barcelona, Saragossa, Madrid and across the country. A well-travelled prince, Don Juan was interested in all aspects of modern science. He was familiar with the techniques of astronomical observation, observed experiments in chemistry and physiology, was present at anatomical dissections, and interested enough in mechanics to construct models himself. His patronage of Juan Bautista Juanini was of great significance. Among books dedicated to the prince at this time were Juanini's own *Political and Physical Discourse* (1679), and the mathematical treatise *Civil architecture* (1678) of Juan Caramuel y Lobkowitz.

Much of the energy released during the period of Don Juan's government would have been dissipated but for active patronage. There was no precedent for the salons which grew up under Charles II. The universities had long ceased to be centres of intellectual renewal, and the distinguished Imperial College (1625) in Madrid was under Jesuit control. Don Juan and other members of the nobility therefore played host to the private 'academies', which had hitherto been literary in character rather than scientific. For Madrid we have the testimony of the illustrious converso physician Diego Mateo Zapata: 'I can assure you that from 1687, when I went to Madrid, there were in the capital well-known and public salons on which lustre and renown were shed by men of the highest distinction, bearing and culture, such as the Marquis of Mondéjar; Don Juan Lucas Cortés of the Council of Castile; Don Nicolás Antonio, whose knowledge, erudition and intelligence seemed to exceed the bounds of possibility, as evidenced by his *Bibliotheca Hispana*; Dr Don Antonio de Ron; the abbé Don Francisco Barbara; the learned Don Francisco Ansaldo, a Sardinian nobleman; who used to discuss modern philosophy and all the Sciences.'[35]

In Valencia there were also active groups.[36] The two leading literary salons in the city in the 1670s were the Parnassus and the Alcázar, which took an interest in poetry. Another 'academy' met from 1685 in Bisbe street under the presidency and patronage of the Count of Alcudia, and discussed both literature and the sciences. At the same epoch a group met in the private library of the Marquis of

Villatorcas, Don José de Castellvi (d. 1722): it included the historian Fr Manuel Miñana, and scientists such as Fr Tomás Vicent Tosca, Juan Bautista Corachán and Baltasar Iñígo. For its meetings Villatorcas himself translated the proceedings of French academies. The most significant of these academies was the exclusively scientific one which included Tosca and Corachán, and began to meet from 1687 in the house of the mathematician Iñígo.

Historically the most important of the Spanish academies was that which met from 1697 in Seville in the house of the physician Juan Muñoz y Peralta, whose influence at court enabled him to win royal patronage for his group. In 1700 Charles II granted the academy official status as the Royal Society of Medicine and other Sciences, the first institution in Spanish history to be devoted exclusively to the new tendencies in science. It was denounced in 1702 by the Rector of Seville University as 'a society which aims to introduce modern Cartesian doctrines . . . to overthrow that of Aristotle, and to reject those of Hippocrates and Galen, accepted in all universites'.[37] The foundation of the Society was an achievement of the scientific movement in Spain rather than a cause of it, and owed a great deal to Dr Diego Zapata. Despite his Judaism, Zapata was a passionately conservative Galenist, and in 1690 at the age of twenty-four he published a virulent attack on the Genoese doctor Gazola and other innovators. His success took him to court, where he was physician to the cardinals Portocarrero and Borja, and several other men of distinction. By the end of the century, however, Zapata had firmly rejected both Galen and Aristotle. His *Crisis médica* of 1701 (in which he cites Francis Bacon) was a warm defence of the Royal Society and the new learning. His posthumous *Sunset of the Aristotelian forms* (1745) became his best-known work.[38]

The crucial part played by academies in the scientific movement, would have been meaningless but for the intervention of foreign ideas. We have seen that despite the menacing role of the Inquisition as the sentinel of orthodoxy, new books and therefore new ideas could infiltrate the country. Even had the process continued, it would have been inadequate. For the vital drawback to the movement was that virtually all its contacts with outside knowledge were *indirect*. Unlike the late eighteenth century (when the Inquisition also existed), Spanish *savants* under Charles II could not correspond freely with scientists elsewhere, did not have the requisite knowledge of foreign languages, and could not travel freely to foreign parts. Possibly the only scientist with international links at this time was Juan Caramuel. Crisóstomo Martínez went to Paris at the end of his life. A few progressive links existed with, for example, the University of Montpellier. But the majority had to imbibe their knowledge circuitously. When Feijoo read English philosophy, it was in French translation. In 1684 the professor of Astronomy at Salamanca, José Pérez, complained to a French Jesuit correspondent in Madrid that 'these wars with France are extremely irksome to us, since they impede the passage of books from there'.[39] Ideas were spread by discussion rather than direct study. All the more valuable then was the presence in Spain of men such as Juanini and Gazola, who came from a country – Italy – where there was no effective restraint on science. Thanks to the great freedom of movement between Spain and Italy, a scientific revolution in Spain became possible.

Given the serious obstacles to change in Spain, we may well wonder at the tenacity of the innovators. Juan de Cabriada in 1687 exclaimed: 'How sad and shameful it is that, like savages, we have to be the last to receive the innovations and knowledge that the rest of Europe already has. And when we bring this to the attention of Spaniards who should know it, they get offended and are irritated by the truth. How true it is that to try and shift people from an established opinion is the most difficult thing to attempt!'[40] The most serious obstacle, by its mere existence rather than by any active pressure, remained the Inquisition. The fate of astronomy is a case in point.[41] Though Copernicus and Galileo were never formally condemned in Spain – the former's work was taught publicly in the 1590s, and the latter made three attempts to come to Spain – the Roman condemnations of 1616 and 1633 made their mark on Spanish orthodoxy, and the heliocentric theory was thereafter rigidly suppressed by the Inquisition. Its fate may be measured by that of the sixteenth-century scholar Diego de Zúñiga, who had supported Copernicus and whose work therefore appeared in all the Indices of the Inquisition down to 1747. The Copernican system was not openly professed by any astronomer of this period. Those who accepted it, like Father Zaragoza (d. 1679), were obliged to say that as a working hypothesis it was permissible, but untenable in that it was heretical and disagreed with Scripture. Scientists were forced into an unnecessary conflict with the Church.

The progress made in scientific disciplines under Charles II was very uneven. Natural sciences, in which Spain had been prominent during the Renaissance and was again to be during the Englightenment, were at a low ebb.[42] On the other hand, there was minimal interest in the magic and superstition that many have wrongly associated with the time of Charles II. Analysing some 356 titles of science-related books published in the reign, Lopez Pinero shows that 42 were on mathematics, 44 on astronomy and astrology, 32 on geography, 10 on nautical sciences, 6 on physics, 6 on natural philosophy, 4 on minerology, 6 on natural history, 21 on pharmacy, 3 on veterinary science, 3 on civil engineering, 15 on military engineering, and 164 on medicine and related subjects. This, in sum, is the known output of the early Scientific Revolution in Spain.[43] It represents the most significant change to have occurred in Spanish thought since the Renaissance.

The enormous resurgence in medical science was no accident. It was connected with the role of Valencia, 'one of the first centres of the revolution in Spanish medicine and science'.[44] A leading centre of medical studies in the sixteenth century, Valencia had decayed since Philip II cut off all its links with foreign scholarship. But under Charles II it produced a new breed of men. The date 1687 was the turning point: it was the year when Baltasar de Iñigo's scientific 'academy' began, the year also when the anatomist Crisóstomo Martínez arrived in Paris from Valencia, the year finally of the appearance of Cabriada's challenging *Philosophical Letter*.

For the stages, impulses and personalities that made up the early Scientific Revolution in Spain, we have to go back to the influence of Don Juan José of Austria, whose interest in the sciences has been noted above. He gathered round him men who favoured experiment and enquiry. Among them were two of his early physicians, the Catalan Jacinto Andreu and the Aragonese Matías de Llera, both Galenists but also active practitioners of anatomy. In mid-century Don Juan had also brought to Madrid the Flemish mathematician Jean de la Faille to teach at the Jesuit College in Madrid. The most important of his appointments was Juan Bautista Juanini (1636–91),[45] a Milanese who studied at Pavia and in 1667 became private physician to Don Juan until the latter's death in 1679. Juanini worked first in Saragossa, where among his friends we find the university professor of medicine José Lucas Casalete. At the same period he was friendly with Juan d'Alós, the professor of Medicine at Barcelona university. His later years were spent in Madrid, where he died in 1691. The first and best known of his works was the *Political and Physical Discourse* (Madrid 1679), dedicated to Don Juan, which studied the chemical composition of air pollution in Madrid and went on to discuss other medical questions on the basis of iatrochemical principles. His second work, the *New Natural Physical Idea* (Saragossa 1685), was an attempt to explain the physical world as being based on two basic chemical substances, acid and alkaline salts. The third and last work, his *Letters* (Madrid 1691), pursued the same argument. The iatrochemistry of Juanini was only a primitive phase in the history of European medicine, but for him and Spain it represented a radical break with scholastic method. His *Political Discourse* was the first public statement of a basic change in outlook; 'our method', he wrote in his *New Idea*, 'will be completely different from that hitherto used, for we shall avoid any kind of scholastic reasoning'. More than being a proposer of new systems, Juanini was also an active experimenter and anatomist. He performed at least five major autopsies in Madrid, Salamanca and Saragossa, one of them being on Don Juan himself in 1679 before the latter's embalming and transfer to El Escorial.

Though Juanini's writings were the first public statement of new ideas, he showed due caution in expressing them, and formally professed Galenic principles; he is more significant as a precursor, and a communicator of foreign influences, showing due recognition of the ideas of Harvey, Descartes, Bacon and the iatrochemical scientists. The circle he knew at Saragossa was likewise progressive. Casalete wrote a preface to the *New Idea*, but himself came under attack in 1684, when a committee of professors from seven national universities condemned his views as 'false, erroneous, rash, absurd . . . opposed to the doctrine of Galen', and recommended that they be prohibited. He remained free, however, to publish another work in 1687; and other writings of the time show a steady advance of non-traditional medicine in Aragon.

The new tendencies in Barcelona are represented by the work of Joan d'Alós (d. 1695), who had also written a prologue to Juanini's *New Idea*. A professor at the university and holder of several high public posts, Alós was a moderate Galenist who firmly supported many new theories (the circulation of the blood was a 'solid and obvious truth') but integrated them into the old system. In Valencia, the experimental work of Crisóstomo Martínez (d. 1694) was exceptional in being based on the use of the microscope for anatomical research. Thanks to his being also a brilliant engraver (the visit abroad from 1687 until his death, was to help him find better facilities for engraving), his work became popular abroad.

The revolutionary manifesto for scientific advance in Spain was the

*Philosophical Letter* of Juan de Cabriada, which he published in Madrid in 1687 when just over twenty years old. There were three prefaces to the book: one by Fr Antonio de Ron, one by José Casalete, and one by Dionisio de Cardona, physician to the Queen Mother. Cabriada was a young doctor from Valencia, son of one of the professors of medicine at the University. His book was completely modern and innovatory. It lamented the backwardness of Spain in all scientific and medical matters so that (as quoted above) 'like savages we have to be the last to receive the innovations and knowledge that the rest of Europe already has'. He hailed Harvey's doctrine as 'the new sun of medicine', and emphasised the primacy of experiment and experience in all medical knowledge. He called for the creation in Spain of academies and laboratories, to which foreign scientists could be invited: 'Why not found at court a Royal Academy, as there is at the French Court, and the English, and the Imperial?'

The provocative nature of Cabriada's book unleashed a bitter controversy. The most interesting stage of this dispute was the publication in 1690 in Madrid of *Medical enthusiasms*, by the Veronese doctor José Gazola, in which he praised Cabriada for supporting 'liberty of philosophy'. This was immediately attacked by the young Diego Zapata, then a fierce Galenist, in his *True apology in defence of rational medicine* (1691). Cabriada's work now became the basic reference point for the innovators. In 1698 Tomás Fernández repeated his call for free research: 'this freedom of enquiry is what has made the medicine of northern Europe so advanced'.[46]

Cabriada's suggestion of a Royal Academy in Madrid came to nothing. However, in May 1700 there came into existence in Seville the Royal Society of Medicine and other Sciences, the first and most famous society of the Scientific Revolution in Spain. Of its ten foundation members, among them Muñoz y Peralta and Zapata, both members of the academy of 1697, one name in particular stands out: that of Juan de Cabriada.

The uneven development of Spanish science was caused in part, as we have seen, by apparent conflicts with Scripture in the realm of physics. Despite this, significant advances were made in the mathematical field. Juan Caramuel y Lobkowitz (d. 1682), born in Madrid of Bohemian and Flemish stock, studied in Spain but spent most of his life outside the country, principally in Bohemia, Flanders and Italy. A Cartesian by outlook, Caramuel had little influence in Spain but is an excellent example of the new links being opened up with the world of science outside. More significant as a mathematician in the Spanish context was José de Zaragoza (d. 1679), a Valencian who studied at the university of Valencia and subsequently entered the Society of Jesus. His last years were spent as a professor of mathematics at the College of San Isidro in Madrid. He was also the most distinguished Spanish astronomer of his time, and a study of his published in 1675 shows direct knowledge of the major European authorities, including Galileo. A convinced Copernican, he never committed himself in writing to the heliocentric theory.

The resurrection of learning in Spain owed little to the scholars of Castile. The pessimistic observations of Feijoo in this respect show little awareness on his part of the work being done in Spain as a whole, particularly in centres such as Seville and Valéncia which were open to international ideas. The fate of mathematics at San Isidro in Madrid was symptomatic of the Spanish situation: the first holder of the chair, a protégé of Don Juan, was the Fleming De La Faille, to be followed in turn by another Fleming and a Frenchman. Father Zaragoza in 1670 was the first Spanish holder, but he was Valencian. The rebirth of science in Spain was in a real sense the rebirth also of the non-Castilian provinces.

Many of the scientific generation of Charles II lived on to do their best work under the first Bourbon, Philip V. They remain, however, more closely identifiable with the new spirit of enquiry of the previous reign. Typical of them are the Valencians Juan Bautista Corachán and Fr Tomás Vicente Tosca, who were both principally mathematicians. Corachán (d. 1741) was professor of mathematics in Valencia from 1696 to 1724. Around 1690 he wrote a dialogue (not published until 1747, by Gregorio Mayáns) defending experiment against authority, as the true basis of science; and proposing the Cartesian method as an ideal. Tosca (d. 1723), a priest of the Oratory, prepared in the 1690s a *Mathematical Compendium* which was not published till 1707–15. This work[47] was an encyclopedia of the physical sciences, in nine volumes. A monument of synthesis, the *Compendium* covered all major branches of mathematics, physics, engineering, optics, and astronomy. Its unique importance for the historian is that it summarises the major achievements not only of Spanish but of all European knowledge until a terminal date somewhere in the 1680s. The work reveals the astonishing amount of information about European science that was being sought and obtained by progressives in Spain. Among the few names absent from his work, since the knowledge had not yet been diffused, was Newton. For the rest, Tosca's volumes, written at the end of the reign of Charles II, reflect clearly both the achievements and the limitations of the scientific movement in Spain.

The literature of the Scientific Revolution unfortunately helped contribute to the myth of Spanish decadence. In looking abroad for inspiration, the leaders of the revolution ignored what had been done in their own country. Studies on navigation written at this time remained unaware of Spain's brilliant achievements in the science. The iatrochemists, like the Cartesians, felt that what was best must be foreign. Men like Feijoo belittled Spanish capabilities. Yet the new curiosity of Spaniards extended to all areas of the scientific imagination. The scheme of the Capuchin Antonio de Fuentelapeña for a flying machine (1676)[48] is one of the first printed texts on the subject. In looking at the generation of Charles II, it is just to consider not only the decay but the new and eventually triumphant spirit of experimental science.

# NOTES

1. An excellent and pioneering study of Spanish education is **Kagan, R. L.**, *Students and Society* (Baltimore 1974).
2. AHN Inq. 73/17/56.

3. Kagan, *op. cit.* p. 42.
4. AHN Inq. 37/1.
5. Quoted in Kagan, *op. cit.* p. 43.
6. *Memorias*, p. 200.
7. *Ibid.* p. 331. By 1698 José had been twice to America.
8. Kagan, *op. cit.* p. 55.
9. *Ibid.* p. 64.
10. *Ibid.* pp. 144–5.
11. ACA:CA 1370.
12. Cf. Kamen, *Iron Century*, ch. 8.
13. Kagan, *op. cit.* pp. 250, 252.
14. *Ibid.* pp. 213, 188–9.
15. Sánchez Rivero, ed., *Viaje*, I, 47, 65, xxi.
16. Memorandum of 29 Nov. 1713, AHN Consejos 7294/6.
17. *A Relation*, p. 474.
18. Moscoso to the Borges, 28 Sept. 1661, ARV: Varia libro 74.
19. AHN Inq. 4695[2].
20. See the analysis in Caro Baroja, *Las formas*, pp. 603–15.
21. **García Martínez**, 'Las ciencias históricas', *Actas II Cong. Esp. Hist. Med.*, I, 295–7.
22. *Servicios y Títulos del Doctor Dormer*, 1673, in ACA:CA 1370/1.
23. Dormer to Justiciar, Simancas 30 Nov. 1681, ADZ 755/6.
24. 'Auto de respuesta a la renunciacion hecha por procurador legitimo del Arcediano Dr Diego Joseph Dormer del Oficio de Coronista', ADZ 754/11.
25. **Peset Reig, M.**, 'Historia de la Ciencia jurídica', *Actas II Cong. Esp. Hist. Med.*, I, 303–8.
26. Most of what follows is derived from **Schulte, H. F.**, *The Spanish Press* (Chicago 1968), pp. 73–86, which gives a bibliography of Spanish studies.
27. *Ibid.* p. 75.
28. On Goyeneche and the gazette, Caro Baroja, *La hora navarra*, pp. 101–2. For a Moroccan view of the *Gazeta*, see *Account of an embassy*, pp. 13–14.
29. *A Relation*, p. 497.
30. The general presentation of this section is based on the pioneering studies of **José María López Piñero**, summarised in his *La Introducción de la Ciencia* (Barcelona 1969). There is a fine collection of scientific texts in **López Piñero** *et al.*, *Materiales* (Valencia 1976).
31. **Ceñal, R., S. J.**, 'Cartesianismo en España', *Rev. Univ. Oviedo*, 1945, pp. 5–97.
32. **López Piñero** 'Harvey's Doctrine of the Circulation', *Jl. Hist. Med.*, **28** iii (July 1973), 230–42.
33. **García Ballester, L.**, 'El Galenismo de transición', *Actas II Cong. Esp. Hist. Med.*, I, 385–92.
34. **Yerushalmi, Y. H.**, *Isaac Cardoso* (Columbia 1971), pp. 221–51.
35. Cited in López Piñero, *La Introducción*, p. 44.
36. **García Martínez, S.**, *Els Fonaments* (Valencia 1968), pp. 152–69.
37. Ceñal, 'Cartesianismo', p. 34.
38. For Zapata see above, p. 307; also Caro Baroja, *Los Judios*, III, pp. 71–7.
39. Ceñal, *op. cit.* p. 30.
40. Cited in López Piñero, *La Introducción*, pp. 105–6.
41. **López Piñero**, 'Galileo en España', *Rev. Occ.*, 40 (July 1966); **Peset Llorca, V.**, 'Sistema copernicano', *Actas II Cong. Esp. Hist. Med.*, I, pp. 309–24.
42. The main spur to natural sciences in the earlier and later periods was American

travel. Very few expeditions took place in the seventeenth century.

43. The emphasis is on 'early'. Since most of the savants associated with the Revolution continued their work well into the next reign, the dates 1687–1727 (see **Peset Llorca**, 'La Universidad de Valencia', *Asclepio*, 16 (1964), 214–31) for the full cycle of the Revolution are the most appropriate.

44. **López Piñero**, 'Valencia y la medicina', *Actas III Cong. Nac. Hist. Med* (Valencia 1969), II, 95–108.

45. More correctly, Giovanni Battista Giovannini. See the studies by **López Piñero**, 'La contribución de Juanini', *Actas II Cong. Esp. Hist. Med.*, I, 403–22; and **Morales Meseguer, J. M.**, 'Las *Cartas* de Juanini', *ibid.* pp. 423–30.

46. Cited in López Piñero, *La Introducción*, p. 113.

47. **Marco Cuéllar, R.**, 'El *Compendio Mathemático* del Padre Tosca', *Actas II Cong. Esp. Hist. Med.*, I, 325–57.

48. López Piñero *et al.*, *Materiales*, pp. 279–80.

# CHAPTER THIRTEEN

# The Regency and Don Juan

Philip IV, called The Great, died on 17 September 1665 in Madrid, at the age of sixty-two. On Monday the 14th he took the Sacrament and drew up his secret testament. On Tuesday he received his ministers and advisers, some of them individually. He took leave of his wife Doña Mariana, and ordered that the Golden Fleece be granted to his infant son. When the prince, Carlos José, then aged four, was brought to him he embraced him and sighed, 'My son, may God in his mercy make you happier than I have been.' At the end of the day he made his confession. Wednesday he spent alone, in meditation, after taking the Sacrament at dawn. Early in the morning a messenger came to request an audience for Don Juan José. Later a second came, then a third. 'Who asked him to come?' protested the king. 'Let him go back to Consuegra. This is a time only for dying.' Shortly after 4 a.m. on Thursday the 17th he passed away.[1]

Philip IV left the Spanish monarchy in grave crisis. An infant now sat on the throne; the previous year the currency had been devalued; that very summer the Portuguese rebels routed an army of Spain at Villaviciosa. There was peace abroad, with the 1659 Peace of the Pyrenees, but it accorded ill with the king's popular epithet 'The Great'. 'The king our lord', Francisco de Quevedo had bitingly observed, 'is great as holes are: the more soil you remove, the greater they become.' The loss in 1659 of the soil of all Catalonia north of the Pyrenees, and the current threat of the loss of Portugal, were major disasters for the unity of Spain.

The succession of a child, the first to occur in national history, posed problems. Ministers had to send to the archive at Simancas to find out what precedents existed for the new situation. The king's will had nominated a Committee (Junta) of Government to be formed after his death. It was distinguished by the absence from it of the duke of Medina de las Torres, who had helped to govern the state since the death of Philip IV's last valido, Don Luis de Haro, in November 1661. The five members of the new Committee were men of the highest experience and distinction.[2] They were the count of Castrillo,[3] the count of Peñaranda,[4] the vice-chancellor of Aragon Don Cristobal Crespi de Valldaura,[5] the marquis of Aytona,[6] and the Cardinal of Aragon.[7] The secretary of the Despacho Universal, Don Blasco de Loyola, was to serve as secretary to the Committee. By some coincidence not intended by the late king, the five members represented a broad range of experience: they were, in the order I have named them, respectively a bureaucrat, a diplomat, a lawyer, a soldier and a churchman. If we include the secretary, they also represented the major nationalities of Spain: one Andalucian, one Castilian, one Valencian, two Catalans and one Basque. A sixth member of the Committee was to have been the archbishop of Toledo, who died a few hours after the king.

The function of the Committee was basically to administer the government. Executive authority was placed in the hands of the Queen Mother, Doña Mariana, who was to be Regent and guardian of the boy king till he reached the age of fourteen. The will of Philip IV stated that 'the ministers must meet every day in the room of the palace chosen by the Queen', who must act 'always with the advice of the Committee and in no other way'. A balance of powers and personality was thus created. But there were factors capable of undermining the coalition. Two were immediately relevant: the character of the Queen, and the figure of Don Juan of Austria.

Mariana, Archduchess of Austria (1634–96), was daughter of the Emperor Ferdinand III and betrothed to Philip IV's son Baltasar Carlos. When the prince died prematurely, Philip in 1649 married Mariana even though she was his niece and thirty years his junior. The unfortunate Habsburg practice of near incestuous intermarriage bred its unhappy fruit of infant mortality. Eventually, on 6 November 1661 she gave birth to Carlos. In April 1666 her only other surviving child, twelve-year-old Margarita, left Spain for the Empire to marry her uncle the Emperor Leopold. Mariana was left alone in Madrid with a sickly son and an entire monarchy in her care. She had never wanted the task and was clearly 'unfitted to rule a vast and complex empire'; but it is less than just to describe her as 'unstable, ignorant and obstinate'.[8] She had days of depression, when she retreated into the palace; and when she emerged she dressed habitually as a widow or as a nun – her portraits, obviously at her own wish, present her always in this attire. Strongly attached to her son, she fought to stay by his side, and many of the conflicts of the next few years centred on control of his person.

Don Juan José was the most powerful personality in the kingdom and one of the most significant figures in the history of Habsburg Spain. He was born on 7 April 1629 in Madrid to the actress María Calderón, then mistress of Philip IV; and brought up quietly in the country at Ocaña by distinguished guardians and expert tutors, to whom he owed his lasting interest in culture. In May 1642 he was officially recognised as a natural son of the king: he shared his father's blue eyes with his mother's dark hair and gipsy looks. By 1643 he was established as a prince, with the title of Serenity and a household of several gentlemen, retainers and servants. He was made a knight of the ecclesiastical Order of St John, with the title of Grand Prior of the Order in Castile and León and his seat at Consuegra, south of Toledo.[9] The income settled on him was in excess of 100,000 escudos a year. In 1647 he was given the title of Prince of the Sea, and set out from Cadiz in April with six galleys on an expedition to Barcelona in the course of which he captured a French ship. Later that year he was nominated Vicar of the Crown in Italy, and commanded the fleet that sailed to Naples to suppress the

Masaniello rebellion. He remained in Sicily as viceroy from 1648 to 1651.

In 1650 he was appointed to the council of State. On returning from Sicily he was made commander-in-chief of the armies in Catalonia, where he brought the campaign to a successful conclusion. On 10 October 1652 the Conseller en cap of Barcelona came to offer the city's submission and prostrated himself at the general's feet. Don Juan refused to let him kneel and raised him up.[10] It was a symbol of the generosity that was to win him the constant support of the Catalans. On 13 October he entered and occupied Barcelona. In February he was appointed viceroy of Catalonia. His next major responsibility was the Spanish Netherlands, where he served as viceroy from 1656 to 1659. Here he clashed with the Spanish commander, the marquis of Caracena, and with the Prince of Condé, who was now serving Spain after his defeat in the Fronde. The loss of Dunkirk to the French (who were aided by Cromwell's Roundheads) did credit neither to Don Juan nor to Condé. France and Spain were moving towards peace and in March 1659, eight months before the Peace of the Pyrenees, he was recalled to Spain and given a safe-conduct through France. In Paris he had a brief interview with his brother-in-law the young Louis XIV. Mademoiselle de Montpensier, who met Don Juan, describes him as a 'very short man, quite good looking but a bit stout. . . . A rather attractive head, dark hair, a very noble and agreeable face.'[11]

In Spain he was made commander-in-chief, from 1661 to 1664, of the armies fighting Portugal. His inability to reverse the unfavourable situation cooled his father's enthusiasm. With military decay on every side, Philip IV was looking to his son, namesake of the great hero of Lepanto, for victories. Now he kept him at arm's length, away from court, and toyed with the idea of giving him a senior Church post suitable to his ecclesiastical status as a Prior of St John, such as the see of Toledo. By the end of his father's reign, Don Juan was in the curious position of being his country's most distinguished general, yet denied any political honours suited to his status. Philip IV's refusal to legitimise him effectively blocked his way to any higher dignities. The most obvious candidate as acting head of state, he was nevertheless excluded from the Committee of Government. The Queen regarded him with suspicion as a threat both to her and to her son. With good reason, Don Juan believed that his talent and services should be called upon. The Queen and government felt, with equally good reason, that this was not the proper time. Small wonder that Don Juan, who had no lack of friends and admirers, should become a focus of opposition to the regime.

Ill at ease in high politics, Mariana relied increasingly on the advice of her confessor Juan Everardo Nithard (to give the Spanish version of his name) (1607–81), an Austrian Jesuit who had accompanied her to Spain in 1649 on her marriage to Philip IV. Knowing Nithard's key position, several notables, including Don Juan himself, at various times approached him for help and advice. Early in 1666 the Queen wrote to her confessor intimating that she intended to put all her confidence in him and bring him into office. She could not, however, vary the terms of her husband's will and so had to find another way of making him a member of the ruling Committee. The last archbishop of Toledo had died twelve hours after Philip IV. Application was made to Rome for the post to go to Don Pascual of Aragon, who was asked to step down from his recent appointment as Inquisitor General since both posts provided *ex officio* membership of the Committee. The Cardinal of Aragon, who was then in Naples serving as viceroy, received his pallium as archbishop in March 1666, handed the viceroyalty over to his brother Don Pedro in April, and by early June was in Madrid.

A major obstacle was clause 33 of the late king's will, which specified that no foreigners should serve in the councils of state. Only a Cortes could issue the decree of naturalisation: Mariana therefore applied individually to all the cities with a vote in Cortes and received thirteen affirmatives, which enabled her to issue a decree naturalising Nithard on 20 September. In October she obtained from pope Alexander VII a bull allowing Nithard, who as a Jesuit could not hold superior office without papal approval, to take up his new post as Inquisitor General, already held by him since 22 September. The appointment of an obscure foreigner to the highest offices in the state was the direct cause of the constitutional crises of the next two years. But the spark that ignited the flame was the chafing impatience of Don Juan, waiting at Consuegra for the call that did not come.

Foreign policy and the crisis in the Netherlands brought the prince back into politics. In June 1667 he was authorised to come to Madrid and attend discussions in the council of state. On 11 June he was received in audience by the king who, nurtured in his fears by his mother, refused to let Don Juan kiss his hand and turned his back on him. The situation in Belgium offered Nithard and the Queen a chance to get rid of the prince. With the support of the councils, on 14 September the Queen Regent directed him to prepare to serve as commander in Flanders. In reply, the prince claimed that two major problems needed to be dealt with first: these were the war with Portugal, currently the chief internal burden on the exchequer; and the 'monstrous nature of the present government'. In November 1667 the Infante Don Pedro took control of the government in Portugal and began to make soundings for peace with Spain. The first of Don Juan's conditions was soon to be met; it was the second that remained insoluble.

As Governor of the Netherlands Don Juan was offered virtually sovereign powers of war and peace, the right to grant honours, and a guarantee of large sums of money as well as troops. He asked for further powers, mainly to raise money for what he knew from experience to be the high cost of the military effort in the north. The council of State agreed, and so did Nithard, but when a committee of theologians heard that this would involve dealing with the heretical English and Dutch they ruled against acceptance. Don Juan thereupon declined the Governorship. The government accepted his resignation, ordered him back to Consuegra, and appointed the Constable of Castile to Flanders. The duke of Pastrana and Infantado, a friend of the prince, was banished from Madrid. In March 1668 the count of Castrillo, now an octogenarian, retired from politics after receiving a grandeeship that had been promised him four years before by Philip IV.[12]

Don Juan meanwhile had been persuaded to withdraw his resignation. In a meeting of the council of State, with Nithard present, he sarcastically proposed

331

sending the confessor to Flanders to save the situation: 'he is so holy a man that Heaven could not fail to grant him whatever he asked, the very post that he now holds being proof of the miracles he can work.'[13] On Palm Sunday 25 March Don Juan left Madrid for La Coruña in order to take ship for Flanders. He reached La Coruña four weeks later and waited for his convoy to arrive from Cadiz. There were further delays. The eventual date fixed for departure was 25 July, the feast of St James, patron of Spain.

At the end of May 1668 a supposed plan to assassinate Nithard by an Aragonese gentleman, Don José Mallada, was discovered in Madrid. Don Juan was said to be behind the plot, but there was no proof. On the authority of Nithard, Mallada was executed by garroting in his cell on 2 June. When the prince heard the news he wrote an angry letter to Peñaranda, Aragon and Crespi on 25 June, promising that Nithard 'will account for this evil action and for the others he has done to destroy the monarchy and the lustre of Spain'. He refused to go to Flanders, on some specious excuse of ill health (the Constable went in his place), and by a decree of 3 August was banished to Consuegra and forbidden to come within twenty leagues of Madrid.

On Saturday 13 October, as the Regent and king were about to set out on a visit, a gentleman came asking to deliver an urgent message personally to the Queen. He reported a plot by Don Mateo Patiño, secretary of Don Juan, to kidnap Nithard. When the story was found to be true the Committee of Government (with the exception of Peñaranda, who absented himself) voted on 19 October to arrest the prince. The vote was in secret, as were the preparations to send a small force with sealed orders on Sunday the 21st to arrest Don Juan. When the orders were opened, however, most of the officers refused to carry them out. Forewarned, the prince had in any case fled from Consuegra with sixty attendants the morning after the secret vote. He left behind a letter denouncing Nithard, *el padre Everardo* as he was termed throughout the controversy, and justifying his attempt to remove him forcibly from power.

Don Juan's letter, soon replied to by the Inquisitor General, initiated a major battle of pamphlets that was certainly the first of its kind in Spanish history. Frustrated by Nithard and the Queen in his attempts to assume leadership of the country, he resorted now to the pen and to public opinion. Since the odium in the dispute was personal rather than political, details of the controversy have no lasting importance. The practical consequences of the battle were, however, very important. The two chief councils, of State and of Castile, refused to take any active measures against the fugitive, and resorted to delay. Don Juan fled to Aragon, where he found a hostile viceroy (the Count of Aranda, a recent nominee of Nithard), and moved on towards Catalonia, where he hoped for a better reception from the viceroy, the duke of Osuna, a former colleague in the war against Portugal. At his first stop in the principality, the town of Bot, he slept under a roof, having camped out in the open ever since his escape from Consuegra.[14] It was a measure of the security he felt at having reached Catalonia.

Thanks to his policies in Catalonia in the 1650s, the prince was greatly loved and respected in the province. Osuna was aware of this, and also had his own differences with the government. On 9 November the viceroy and the prince had a lengthy and secret meeting of over five hours in Sant Feliu de Llobregat. It was agreed that he should take up residence in the Torre de Lledó, next to the monastery of Santa Eulalia on the hill of Tibidabo, overlooking Barcelona. There he was treated as a royal personage and the people thronged to see him. He was visited by official delegations from the City, the Diputació, the cathedral and the noble Estate. On 17 November 1668 a representative of the prince was allowed to address the Consell de Cent and present Don Juan's case against Nithard.[15] From Barcelona the prince unleashed a flood of letters throughout Spain: to the Queen, the ministers, the councillors, the kingdoms of Aragon and Valencia, their Estates and their viceroys, to every archbishop and cathedral chapter, and every Castilian city with a vote in the Cortes, not to mention the main public bodies and cities of Catalonia.

It was an unprecedented attempt to remove the Crown's chief minister. The demands he made were three: withdrawal of any threat to himself, the release from arrest of Patiño, and 'the departure of Father Everard from Spanish territory'. Whatever they thought of the demands, the manner of his appeal appeared unacceptable to many public bodies, who saw in it an invitation to revolution against the throne in support perhaps of Don Juan's own ambitions. The reactions of a few are worth considering in detail. The city of Barcelona was never in any doubt. After they had heard the prince's case on 17 November, the Consell de Cent wrote a letter to the Regent interceding on his behalf. Don Juan capitalised on this by sending letters to the other Catalan cities on 20 November, informing them of Barcelona's action and asking for their support as well. The cities of Urgell and Vic opened their letters, read them, and sent a copy to the Regent.[16] This was, in effect, a gesture in favour of the prince.

The various letters to public authorities in Valencia were taken there personally by Don Balthasar de Borja Lanzol, the son of the recent viceroy of Mallorca.[17] The viceroy, the count of Paredes, sent his letter unopened to Madrid. This was a neutral gesture, but unfavourable to Don Juan. The representatives of the ecclesiastical Estate, under pressure from the archbishop of Valencia, resolved not to open their letter, and sent it unopened to Madrid. In the Estate of the Nobles an agent of the archbishop persuaded them to send the letter to Madrid unopened, and since all their decisions had to be unanimous those present agreed. In the Consell General of the city of Valencia, which began its sessions on 11 December, a different mood prevailed. The viceroy reported that 'the populace and other more responsible persons believe that the attempt to get rid of the Father confessor is helpful to Your Majesty's service'.[18] 'What happened in the Consell General', reported the archbishop, 'is that apart from two persons whom I had influenced, all agreed to do what Don Juan asks.'[19] They commissioned a letter of support to be sent to the prince. The decision was attributed by the viceroy to 'the unrestrained passion of a people poisoned by those who have advised and influenced them'.[20]

In Castile the reception of Don Juan's letter was universally cautious. So far as is known, all the recipients sent their copies on to Madrid unopened. This formal action, however, gives us a deceptive idea of the real impact of the letter. The prince's intervention in affairs of state had touched off a chord among the people of Spain. Weary of defeat abroad and crisis at home, Spaniards of all conditions – and not simply those in the Crown of Aragon – looked for a strong ruler in Madrid. The advent of Don Juan promised them one such. At the same time his appeal, as we have seen from Valencia, found a ready response in the middle and lower orders of society. In Granada on 5 January 1669 a letter was found nailed to the door of the cathedral sacristy. It said:[21]

Let all the residents of this city know that Don Juan of Austria, moved by holy concern, has written to all the cities of these realms about his just claims, moved at seeing the oppression of these poor subjects. In this city there is one who will rise to his defence, cutting off the heads of these tyrannical presidents and judges and sticking them on the battlements as a warning to others. The same will happen to the city council if they do not act justly and support his cause. These and other matters will be remedied from the start, and it will not be as in other times when we began and then left off at the best time. . . . With God's will all shall be remedied.

Similar letters were pinned to the doors of other public buildings in the city. The council of Castile did not take the threat lightly. Rumours had been flying through the country of the degree of popular and military support Don Juan might have. An uprising in Spain's biggest industrial city – Granada was the biggest Spanish city after Madrid – would have been a disaster. The military commanders in Andalucia were consequently put on the alert, and the corregidor of Granada was replaced.[22]

To add to the literature disseminated by Don Juan, a great number of popular refrains and pasquins now spread through Spain. Under Charles II, pasquins became a form of political commentary that continued in vogue throughout the reign. We have no idea of the authorship of these verses: many may well have been written by order and not been of popular origin. Some were against Don Juan. But early in 1669 most were decidedly threatening to the government. A verse pinned to the doors of the palace in Madrid read:

> Para la Reina hay Descalzas
> y para el Rey hay Tutor,
> si no se muda el Gobierno,
> desterrando al Confessor.[23]

Perhaps more threatening was the long pasquin which claimed to speak for Andalucia and ended with the verse:

> Abrid Señora los ojos
> buelva Don Juan buelva luego
> que en fin es hijo de casa
> y es el cariño mas cierto.[24]

Ministers in Madrid were in a quandary, since they agreed with Don Juan in disliking the Inquisitor General, but opposed any direct pressure on the Crown. They asked Osuna to mediate with the prince. Mariana, finding herself isolated, compromised to the extent of informing Osuna on 1 December 1668 that if Don

Juan returned to Consuegra she would discuss differences with him. The prince refused the offer, protesting that to accept it would place his life in the confessor's hands. Sensing that events were unfavourable to the government, and not wishing to compromise the peace in defence of the confessor, the councils in Madrid began one by one to recede from their support of Mariana's position. On 19 December the council of Castile supported further approaches to Don Juan and a limitation on Nithard's authority; a minority vote from five councillors suggested that the confessor would be better accommodated in Rome. The council of Aragon the following day suggested that 'it would be worthy of the calling and dignity of the Father confessor to ask for permission to leave Spain' for Rome. On 21 December the council of State voted that he be sent even farther, as ambassador extraordinary to Vienna. By a majority of one the Committee of Government approved the tenor of the resolutions taken by the councils, and carried the unwelcome news to the Regent.

Don Juan's return was a continuous triumph. He left Barcelona on 31 January 1669 with a troop of 400 horse, which he claimed to need as a bodyguard. Lérida on 5 February gave him a triumphal welcome. He spent the night in the bishop's palace and at dawn took the road to Fraga in Aragon. From Fraga to Saragossa, as he went through the towns, 'you heard and saw nothing but hats in the air and shouts of "Life and victory to Don Juan, restorer of the honour of Spain!" '[25] Since the authorities in the Aragonese capital, from the viceroy downwards, had been ordered by the Regent not to give any public honours to Don Juan, the prince stopped instead at La Puebla, just outside Saragossa. Mariana's orders, though scrupulously observed by the viceroy Aranda and by several others, were largely ignored in principle. The entire higher aristocracy of Aragon came out to La Puebla to pay their respects, as did the Justiciar, the cathedral chapter and all the Diputados of the realm. Don Juan was eventually persuaded to enter Saragossa. So as not to compromise the authorities, he informed the viceroy that he was entering incognito and as a private person. The crowd that greeted him in the city was the biggest within memory. Excited students burnt a straw figure of a Jesuit in front of the buildings of the Society.

News of all this caused dismay in Madrid. Don Juan's march on the capital, even with his small escort, threatened civil war. On Sunday 17 February certain ministers were seen depositing their valuables in the safety of the religious houses. The Admiral of Castile, Don Juan Gaspar Enríquez de Cabrera, attempted to persuade ministers to make a military stand, but they refused such a step. The prince's representative in Madrid, Don Diego de Velasco, was sent out to talk to Don Juan, who met him at Junquera, six leagues outside the capital, and sent him back on 23 February with an ultimatum to the government. That very night, a Saturday, the troops which the Admiral had helped raise for the defence of Madrid, deserted to Don Juan.

On Sunday the Committee of Government accepted the mediation of the papal nuncio. But when the prelate visited Don Juan the latter angrily told him that 'if by Monday the Father had not left, he would go in person on Tuesday and throw him out of the window'. On Monday the 25th a hurried meeting of the Committee decided at first not to surrender to the threat of force; but then seeing the danger in inviting force they agreed to the expulsion. The decree was taken in to the Queen who signed it weeping. That afternoon Nithard was taken by coach out of Madrid, to the catcalls of street urchins and the tears of his well wishers.

In Torrejón de Ardoz, where he now was, Don Juan bided his time. He had carried out what may perhaps be called the first *pronunciamiento* in modern Spanish history: a military coup against Madrid with the aid of the provinces. It was completely bloodless. The prince also declared that 'I have never entertained the ambition of elevating myself to the control of government'. He did, however, issue a manifesto: reduction of taxes, fiscal equality, cleansing of the finances and administration, strengthening of the army, justice for all. These were empty words, and Don Juan must have known it. The manifesto, in the form of a letter to the Regent dated 1 March and despatched from Torrejón on the 4th, was published and duplicated. On 5 March he withdrew to Guadalajara and stayed in the ducal palace of his friend Infantado. He remained there for three months.

The military danger still persisted, so on 11 March the Committee of Government granted all: Patiño was freed, and Nithard was appointed ambassador extraordinary to the Empire or to Rome, whichever he preferred, and told to leave immediately. He chose Rome, and went. The government had even further concessions, such as the setting up of a (shortlived) Committee for Reform (*Junta de Alivios*), the suspension of Aytona and Valladares from the ruling Committee, and the erasure from the records of all the recent decrees against Don Juan. By these steps they disarmed any possible rebellion. To make sure, all available troops were recalled from the Portuguese front and quartered in Madrid, Segovia and Toledo. Unable to proceed further, Don Juan on 4 June accepted appointment as Vicar General of the Crown of Aragon, with his seat in Saragossa. On the last day of the month he was received with full solemnity and festivities in the city which so recently shunned him.[26]

Those in Saragossa who had opposed the prince now had good cause to regret their stance. Don Juan moved into the palace of the archbishop, Fray Francisco de Gamboa, and made the prelate find other quarters. Early in 1670 the prince received information that there was a plot to poison him, involving Aranda in Saragossa and Valladares and Aytona in Madrid. One night in March the Vicar's men arrested the viceroy and his household, and Aranda subsequently fled the city. The plot, however, was found to be false. Don Juan now had the firm support of the entire Crown of Aragon. The Consell General of Valencia in August 1669 sent a special ambassador, Don Pedro Boïl de Arenós, to congratulate the prince, who received him with head uncovered in the presence of the civic dignitaries of Saragossa.[27] In Madrid his position was strengthened by the death of Aytona on 17 March 1670,[28] though the subsequent death of Crespi de Valldaura in 1672 and his replacement by Don Melchor de Navarra y Rocafull gave the prince cause for alarm.[29] There was further cause for concern at the new advisers whom Doña Mariana was consulting.

Her principal support for the next few years was Don Fernando Valenzuela, who was born in Naples in 1636 of Andalucian parents. At sixteen he became a page of the duke of Infantado, then viceroy of Sicily; at twenty-three he was back in Madrid, seeking to advance himself. In 1661 he made a fortunate marriage with a lady-in-waiting of the Queen and thereby obtained the favour of the Regent, who gave him a post in the palace and in 1671 a hábito of the Order of Santiago. By 1673 he and his wife were being consulted by the Regent on matters of policy; and Valenzuela, who fed her information about various matters, became known as 'the palace ghost' (*Duende de Palacio*).[30] In 1674 he was given a post on the council of the Indies, though he did not attend its sessions. He was then created marquis of Villasierra in November 1675.

Valenzuela's rise was not exclusively personal. It was associated with a general expansion of her retainers by the Queen, so that the royal household was soon as large as it had been under Philip IV. This meant that several aristocrats took up posts which made them active supporters of the Regent and Valenzuela, among them the new duke of Medinaceli.[31] The regime became in effect one of a ready distribution of honours and an attempt to win popularity on all sides. Price controls, public entertainments, plays and artistic performances, were among the hallmarks of Valenzuela's style. Perhaps the most lasting of his achievements was his rebuilding of Madrid: he ordered the Plaza Mayor rebuilt (it had been partly destroyed in a big fire in 1672); constructed two bridges over the Manzanares, including the Puente de Toledo; and added to the royal palace, the Alcázar.

On 6 November 1675 Charles attained his fourteenth year and came officially of age. By the terms of Philip IV's will the powers of the Committee of Government therefore automatically ended. But nobody was prepared to let the boy king, still an obvious invalid, assume sole power; and the cause of Don Juan was again taken up. At the end of July the council of Italy proposed that in view of the deteriorating military position in southern Italy Don Juan be sent to Sicily as viceroy. Early in October the Queen, following a unanimous decision of the council of State, ordered the prince to take ship for Italy. Unknown to Mariana, the boy king had also written to his half-brother in Saragossa. As the prince reported to the Justiciar of Aragon: 'My journey is not to Italy, but to Madrid, where the king has summoned me to be of service to his royal person, since he has resolved to assume power on the sixth, and I am to be there on that day.' A message to Don Juan from Charles II went: 'On the sixth I enter into the government of my kingdoms. I need your person at my side to help me, and to rid me of the Queen my mother. On Wednesday the 6th at 10.45 you will be in my antechamber.'

On 4 November the secretary of the Committee, Mejorada, presented to the king a decree extending the existing regime for two years on the grounds of the King's incapacity: Charles refused to sign. On the 5th there was a corrida in the Plaza Mayor. Returning from the spectacle, the king informed his mother that he had summoned Don Juan. Early on the 6th, every state councillor and grandee resident in Madrid received a copy of a letter from Don Juan informing them that he had been called to the side of His Majesty. That morning the prince drove through the cheering crowds to the royal Alcázar; he was greeted as an Infante of Spain, and ushered into the king's presence at the appointed hour; the brothers embraced each other and Charles assured Don Juan of his protection. After mass and a Te Deum, the prince went to the Buen Retiro and the king went to visit his mother.

Charles was closeted with Mariana for two hours, and emerged with tears in his eyes. The English ambassador Sir William Godolphin was in court trying to discover what was happening. He reported that 'Don Fernando Valenzuela whispered me in the Ear and said all this Stir will come to nothing. I found the Queen much afflicted, her Eyes swol'n and tears dropping while I was speaking to her.'[32] It took several hours to put pressure successfully on the king. Shortly after six the duke of Medinaceli came to Don Juan at the Buen Retiro, with a handwritten order from the king to leave for Italy at once. Next morning, 7 November, the councils of State and Castile advised that the king should in future sign decrees, but that the Committee of Government should continue to act in its present form and under the presidency of the Queen for two more years, that Don Juan should leave for Italy and Valenzuela should leave Madrid.

Don Juan left Madrid that evening. In a letter of 8 November to the Diputación and city of Saragossa, accounting for the sudden change of events, and published openly as all the prince's letters were, Don Juan explained that he had withdrawn in order to avoid a confrontation. To rescue 'His Majesty from the situation he is in' he would have needed the help of the aristocracy, but a minority of them had been hostile. The common people of Madrid, on the other hand, had supported him fully: 'It seems that the honourable blood which has disappeared from the veins of some of the most elevated, has been transfused into them.' The balance of parties was also analysed by Godolphin as follows: 'Those of the great men who seem to favour Don John are reckoned the Cardinal of Aragon, his brother Don Pedro, the Condes de Medellín, Monterey, Ayala, Talhara, Duke of Alba, Marquis of Castelrodrigo, Prince of Stigliano etc. But beyond the great men (what he most relyeth upon) he has on his side that great Monster the People.'

The sixth of November – the Day of Dupes of the Spanish monarchy – had in fact been a defeat for everyone, not just for Don Juan. Banished from Madrid, Valenzuela was appointed Captain General of the kingdom of Granada and installed himself in the Alhambra. By April 1676, thanks to the Queen, he was back in Madrid and at court. In June he was made Master of the Horse. In July he was made chief gentleman of the chamber to Charles II, with rights of precedence over all other nobles. There were secret meetings of discontented aristocrats in the houses of Don Pedro de Aragon and the duke of Alba. On 22 September the meeting of the Committee of Government was suspended indefinitely, on the legitimate ground that most of its members no longer attended. On 2 November the marquis of Villasierra was created a grandee of the first class and given control of the government as 'prime minister'; he was also lodged in the Alcázar in the apartments of the Infante.[33]

The aristocracy revolted. Grandees would not attend functions, such as mass in the royal chapel, at which Valenzuela had precedence. Their complaint, though founded on resentment at the favourite's origins, went further than social and personal hostility. They objected to the order that in future the presidents of all councils save that of Castile should consult the 'prime minister', and to the exercise by Valenzuela of the royal prerogative of attending council meetings. On 8 December 1676 only one grandee attended the royal mass. On the 15th a public manifesto against Valenzuela was issued and signed by twenty-four leading grandees.

This unprecedented document began by protesting the total devotion of the signatories to His Majesty. It then denounced 'the bad influence' of the Queen Mother on the king, and made three demands: the permanent separation of the Queen from her son; the imprisonment of Valenzuela; and the establishment at the king's side of Don Juan of Austria. The document was a bold step, and clearly reflected the fury of all the noble class, but it was also a political move, for the signatories were all adherents of Don Juan — who himself appeared somewhat modestly as the eleventh signatory on the list — and many uncommitted nobles refused to sign. Those who did included Medina Sidonia, Alba, Osuna, Uceda, Pastrana, Arcos, Benavente, Gandía, Lemos and Veraguas; those who refused, included Medinaceli, Oropesa and the Admiral of Castile. On Thursday 17 December the councils of State and of Castile unanimously called for the imprisonment of Valenzuela in the Alcázar of Segovia. At the same time, however, they warned Don Juan not to take up arms against Madrid. Since Valenzuela had begun to assemble troops in the capital, a military conflict appeared possible.

Once again a fever of crisis gripped the court. The fall of the favourite appeared inevitable, but there was little agreement in the Queen's circle on how to proceed. Finally on 23 December the cardinal archbishop of Toledo, Don Pascual de Aragon, accepted a post that he had been pressed by Mariana since the 18th to accept: that of president of a new Junta, consisting this time of the Admiral, the Constable and Medinaceli. On the 24th this Junta decreed the arrest of Valenzuela. The same night the Admiral reluctantly advised the king that there was no alternative to summoning Don Juan. On Christmas Day 1676 Valenzuela fled to the Escorial where, at the king's command, he was lodged in the royal apartments. A letter to Don Juan was despatched on the 27th and reached Saragossa on New Year's Eve.

## DON JUAN OF AUSTRIA 1677–79

The collapse in Madrid had been occasioned quite simply by the very real military threat from Don Juan. In December, responding to a request from the prince, Lieut. Gen. Don Gaspar Sarmiento brought over from Catalonia to Aragon a force of 600 cavalry, without the knowledge or permission of the viceroy of Catalonia. On 1 January 1677 Don Juan sent the following instructions to the duke of Alba and other adherents:

Make known to people of every sort that what has recently been done at court by the grandees and other subjects has been with the knowledge, influence and approval of the lord Don Juan; and that His Highness is now on the march to uphold it against any Spaniard, good or bad, who, failing God, our king and the good of the country, tries to undo it. Stir up all honourable and faithful men to oppose such people and devote themselves to their destruction.

The prince marched out from Saragossa on 2 January with a small number of troops. Profiting from his experience in the Day of Dupes, he knew that he could not rely exclusively on the king's summons: a more powerful guarantee was needed. As Don Juan progressed, his troops increased in number. Volunteers came from Valencia, Catalonia and Aragon. On Sunday 10th at Ariza, where he stayed in the palace of the marquis, Don Francisco de Palafox y Cardona, he reviewed his men: they now totalled 7,000 infantry and cavalry. He crossed over into Castile and by incredibly rapid marches reached Hita the next day. His army now numbered 15,000, including eighteen grandees of Castile, the flower of the Aragonese aristocracy, and several other nobles: it was possibly the biggest force ever collected in Spain in peacetime. On 13 January the president of Castile, Villaumbrosa, advised Charles II to give way: he should transfer Valenzuela to Segovia, separate himself from the Queen Mother and move his residence to the palace of Buen Retiro, and disband the troops in Madrid. On the night of the 14th the king moved secretly to Buen Retiro. On Sunday the 17th a force of 500 cavalry under the command of the duke of Medina Sidonia and the marquis of Villanueva del Río[34] arrived at the Escorial from Hita and demanded the person of Valenzuela. After several days of negotiation with the prior of the monastery, who threatened excommunication of anyone violating Valenzuela's sanctuary, the soldiers broke in on the 22nd and seized their prey.[35] Meanwhile an agreement had been reached at Hita that the garrison in Madrid would be sent to Catalonia, a move that began on the 22nd. Early on Saturday 23rd, at 6 a.m., Don Juan entered the Buen Retiro, had the king awoken, and offered him his services.

The events of January were more than a pronunciamiento: they were also a *coup d'état*, the first to occur in modern Spanish history. But unlike many later coups, this one had the overwhelming support of both the ruling classes and the people of Spain. In contrast to Valenzuela, who was a petty favourite of no historical importance, Don Juan was supremely significant as the first real national leader in Spain's history. From every side he was looked up to as the saviour of Spain. Congratulations poured in from the Crown of Aragon. In Barcelona, where the news of the prince's accession to power arrived on Friday 29th January, there was wild rejoicing and shooting of firearms. On the Saturday and for the next two weeks there was a constant succession of Te Deums, processions, festivities and celebrations.[36] In Valencia the viceroy published the news on Sunday 31st and there was general rejoicing and celebration.[37] His popularity was not limited to the Crown of Aragon, nor would it be correct to see his role exclusively as a symbol of Aragonese resurgence. For at least one Aragonese noble, the march was an attempt to save all Spain from disaster: 'Everyone knows', he claimed, 'that the empire is in decay and heading rapidly towards ruin.' After denouncing corruption in Madrid and military disasters abroad, he went on, 'What more glorious role could be offered us than to be the solution to so many ills? What greater loyalty can there be, than to join the lord Don Juan in freeing our king from oppression and saving from ruin so many realms that look to our zeal for their salvation?'[38] Despite their many reservations, the grandees of Castile rallied to him and helped to finance the march from Saragossa.[39] Don Juan was never, for all that, a puppet of the grandees. He had a keen eye to his popular support and took pains to satisfy his critics. When on 11 February the first pasquin against him appeared in Madrid, to the effect that he had so far done nothing, he ordered a copy brought to him and wrote beneath it in verse, 'The harvest has not yet been gathered in'.[40]

He began by removing his enemies. Doña Mariana was sent off to live in the Alcázar at Toledo; the threat of the mother meeting her son was thereby removed. The Admiral was banished to his estates, Don Melchor de Navarra was removed as vice-chancellor of Aragon, and several other changes were made. For someone who had been the centre of political tensions for well over a decade, the number of alterations he made was small: they hardly justify the criticism, made both at the time and later, that his was a regime of vengeance. The administration could never have functioned well with enemies within it.

Don Juan was concerned to make his brother truly king. Where Mariana had continued to treat Charles as a boy, Don Juan reshaped court etiquette so that full respect was paid to the person of the king. Foreign dress, notably the use of wigs, was introduced. One day when Don Juan showed the king a letter from duke Victor Amadeus II of Savoy, Charles remarked on the beautiful handwriting. Don Juan said, 'The duke is younger than Your Majesty, and Your Majesty will need to reply in your own hand.' The king said, 'But I don't know how to.' 'Jesus,' Don Juan exclaimed, 'that a king of Spain should say such a thing!' Thereafter every morning the prince personally gave his brother a lesson in handwriting and style.

Don Juan's primary political commitment was to reward the three realms of the Crown of Aragon for their loyalty to his cause. He intended to have Charles visit each realm in turn and take his oath as king in a full meeting of the Cortes. The principal obstacle was Charles' health. Though the king was eager to travel – in all his life he had never been farther than Aranjuez or the Escorial – the season and his own condition were alike unfavourable. Don Juan nevertheless fixed the beginning of spring as the time for a royal visit to Saragossa, the closest of the three capitals and also fortuitously the one which had most sheltered and aided him. The king's absence would also helpfully keep him away from his mother in Toledo.

The royal party set out for Saragossa early on Wednesday 21 April 1677. It was the first and longest of the only three great journeys that Charles ever made. The distance both ways was carefully split into ten short excursions. At each stop the king stayed in a palace: at Alcalá, for instance, with the Cardinal archbishop; at Guadalajara with the Infantado family. On the first of May, the solemn feast day of Saints Philip and James, the king knelt in the great cathedral at Saragossa and swore to respect the fueros of Aragon. On Monday 2 June the party left the Aragonese capital for Madrid. We shall consider shortly the proceedings of the Cortes of Aragon.

Spaniards who expected miracles from Don Juan's government were quick to complain. In early April a Madrid diarist was already noting that 'the new government is very ill spoken of '.[41] In July he made a similar observation. Another contemporary claimed that all Don Juan's actions were partisan and petty, and that this was the main cause of the growth of satires against him in Madrid. He condemned the prince's 'incapacity, inexperience, pride, ambition, and vengeful spirit'.[42] These hostile sources fail completely to do justice to one of the most conscientious ministers Spain ever had. The English minister in Madrid reported by contrast in July that 'Don Juan of Austria applieth himself with indefatigable zeal to remove the corruptions which have for many years past crept in by degrees into the Springs of this government as well by purging the very constitutions of the Councils as by dismissing the suspected members thereof'.[43] Sir William Godolphin reported in October that Don Juan spent most of his day at the king's side in royal diversions such as hunting and visiting. Not to cultivate Charles would clearly have opened a dangerous gap between the brothers and driven the king back to his mother for emotional support; the prince made up for this 'by a constant application to Business at Night, appearing indefatigable in both Attentions, towards the King's Person and Government, whereof the Marks are daily more legible in his Countenance, somewhat broken of late'.[44] The important point, forgotten by all critics of the prince but remarked by Godolphin, is that he was forced to waste valuable time in the company of the invalid king. From 30 September to 3 November, for example, was spent on the regular annual outing to El Escorial. Time was a commodity of which Don Juan had very little to spare.

It was in fact the worst possible time for a minister to have come to power with the hopes of the people to support him. In 1677, as we have seen, the harvest in most of Spain failed. The French ambassador reported in May that 'bread is extraordinarily dear in this town and in both Castiles . . . officials have been sent everywhere to inventory the grain in private hands, and two hundred bakers have been forced to sell their bread daily at twelve *cuartos* a piece',[45] instead of the market price of eighteen cuartos. Early in August Don Juan had to borrow money to purchase 400,000 fanegas of wheat for the needs of Madrid.[46] The acute food crisis became even worse in 1678, which was the year of highest grain prices in the whole reign. In the hot July of 1678, there were murmurings among the people of Madrid against the government of His Highness.[47]

Don Juan was as powerless against this natural disaster as he was against the other that was likewise affecting the most populated areas of Spain: the plague epidemic. Fortunately the capital was not affected, but the obligatory suspension of trade with infected cities added to the discomforts of the people of Madrid. Even worse than the internal crisis was the accelerating disaster abroad. By autumn 1678 Spain had been pushed into the humiliating Peace of Nijmegen; despite his aim to consolidate his brother's empire, Don Juan was forced into further surrenders.

The famine, the epidemic, the war, all required money; but, as the prince found, there was none available. It was unlikely, despite all his promises to cut taxes, that he would solve within a few months a treasury debt problem that was over a century old. Inflation had reached its highest point ever in Spanish history. Don Juan made preparations to reform the currency, as we have seen, but his proposals did not take effect until after his death. He now tried to raise a donativo. Most of the grandees protested, perhaps justly, that they could not afford to pay. Once again the great nobles became a focus of discontent. In mid-July 1678 it was reported that 'the people place their hopes in the duke of Osuna to free them from Don Juan of Austria'.[48]

In these months Don Juan also had to resolve the most important issue of the reign: the marriage of Charles II. Since 1673 the candidate favoured by Mariana and by the new Imperial ambassador, Count Harrach, was the Emperor's infant daughter and Charles's own niece, the Archduchess Maria Antonia. Many advisers, including Don Juan, were opposed to such a marriage since there was a difference of five years in the respective ages and this would delay the birth of an heir. The only other serious candidate proposed in Madrid was Marie Louise, daughter of the duke of Orleans and almost the same age as Charles.[49] Though Don Juan in principle also opposed the marriage with the Archduchess because it would strengthen the position of Doña Mariana, the final decision for Marie Louise was in fact made not by him but by the unanimous vote of the council of State in August 1677. The vicissitudes of war intervened and delayed the proposal, but a further unanimous vote of the same council on 11 January 1679 confirmed the choice. Negotiations took up further time. As late as June 1679 Villars was warning the French foreign minister (in cipher) that Charles was physically repulsive[50] and might not appeal to the princess, but in July the French agreed to the marriage.

The year 1679 had also been planned by Don Juan as the time for royal visits to Catalonia, Valencia and Navarre. Preparations were made early in January to go to the Crown of Aragon, and it was thought that a single joint Cortes for both Catalonia and Valencia might be preferable because of the king's inability to travel.[51] Another possibility suggested was that the king might swear to the fueros in Barcelona and Valencia without summoning any Cortes. In the event, most of the councillors in Madrid advised strongly against holding any assembly in Catalonia. On 18 January 1679 the council of Aragon drew up a list of thirteen points arguing against a Cortes.[52] They concluded that the Catalans would be bound to demand the privileges they had lost after 1640, and that this would cause grave difficulties; the council of State on 30 January agreed with this view.[53] No final decision, however, was made against a Cortes. The question of the marriage, and the possibility that Charles might have to travel to the frontier to meet Marie Louise, obliged Don Juan to postpone the matter.[54]

In Madrid the prince was finding it increasingly difficult to please the aristocracy. Although he stayed close by the king at all times and controlled all access to him, the flow of letters from Doña Mariana to her son grew. Discontented nobles began to visit the Queen Mother in the Alcázar at Toledo. In the second week of July 1679 Don Juan was taken ill with a fever, but he continued to direct important business, such as the plan to devalue the currency, from his sick bed. After over two months illness he died, at the age of fifty, at midday on Sunday 17 September. It was the fourteenth anniversary of the death of his father. 'In his gall-bladder', goes the autopsy by his physician Juan Bautista Juanini, 'there were found two round, white stones, like pumice stone; one was the size of a walnut, the other the size of a hazel-nut; the latter obstructed the duct through which the bile issued, and because of this the liver was swollen, red and engorged with the quantity of blood.'

'The demonstrations of sorrow in Madrid have not been great', reported a correspondent. 'The theatres stay open and the corrida has not been cancelled.'[55] On the 20th Don Juan's mortal remains were laid to rest in the Escorial; his heart was deposited in Saragossa, at the shrine of the Pilar. On the 21st Charles II arrived at Toledo and was reunited amid tears with his mother. 'It was a day of great joy for those of us who were there, to see the demonstrations of affection between their Majesties,' Medinaceli wrote later.[56]

Don Juan José of Austria was, according to a contemporary,

of average height, and of a good and agreeable aspect; in music and mathematics, painting, languages, history, in discreet use of his natural eloquence, in the individual and smooth style of his pen, unique and admirable. He wrote some verse and wrote it well: a devotee of pelota, shooting and hunting. . . . . He was a great prince, and would have been greater if to this collection of gifts he had added liberality of giving, generosity to complainants, and candour and sincerity in his dealings.[57]

Six years after his death his private physician for twelve years, Juanini, wrote in his *New Physical Idea* that:[58]

I have never known a prince of such universal and outstanding talents. . . . He did not give his leisure time to rest but to the honest and learned exercise of his mind. . . . He was perfectly versed in all aspects of mathematics; could handle instruments expertly; distinguish between the teachings of Aristotle, Ptolemy, Tycho Brahe, Copernicus, Galileo and others; and converse excellently on geometry, geography and cosmography. . . . The sea was the first command to which his father appointed him, and his knowledge of navigation was perfect. In music he had also reached the peak of perfection: there was no instrument he could not play with dexterity. . . . In painting his application was equally masterly, in water, oils and in porcelain. He engraved in gold and silver like an experienced master, as can be seen by the lamp he sent to be hung in the shrine at Compostela.

With the talent and experience at his command, Don Juan was among the best qualified of Spain's leaders in the seventeenth century. A notable general and an astute politician, he helped to bring scientific learning into Spain and encouraged journalism. Unlike Olivares, he favoured neither imperialism abroad nor the imposition of Castilian policy on the Crown of Aragon. He was the only statesman of his day to come to power with universal acclaim, and the most promising measures of the reign, such as the establishment of the Committee for Trade, are identified with his rule.

Why then did Don Juan fail? In 1679 a satire asked: 'Are there less taxes? Fewer donativos? Has the price of food come down? Have the fleets been repaired? Have we lost fewer and smaller towns? Are the prospects better that the people will be relieved, the kingdom saved and our fortunes improved?' The prince had seemingly achieved nothing. The reason was twofold: he came to power at the wrong time, and under the wrong king. The years 1677 to 1679 were among the most disastrous in national history, with famine, plague and inflation at home and military defeat abroad. Don Juan was not given sufficient time to begin any programme of recovery. Perhaps more crucial was the person of the king.

Learning from his Day of Dupes, Don Juan made extraordinary and daily efforts to keep the king away from his mother. His tenure of power depended on the fragile thread of royal approval, which he tried to cultivate. But Charles never ceased to be emotionally dependent on his mother. As soon as Don Juan lost control of the king by being confined to his sickbed, the tide of events flowed against him.

The prince was ill-judged both by contemporaries and by later historians. 'We Catalans owe little to the lord Don Juan', wrote Feliu de la Peña at the end of the century.[59] This was not because of the failure to hold a Cortes. Feliu recognised that 'the poor health of the king did not allow him to carry out his wish to come and swear the fueros in Barcelona. Catalonia accepted this, trusting in the king's word, so often given.'[60] Charles continued to make attempts, even after Don Juan's death, to go to Catalonia. Villars reported in 1680 that 'the Catholic king has an uncontrolled desire to go to Barcelona and Valencia this summer. The duke of Medinaceli wants to dissuade him because of the impossibility of financing such a journey.'[61]

The Cadiz merchant Raymond Lantéry, writing in 1696, came to the conclusion that Don Juan and other ministers had done less for Spain than Valenzuela, 'in whose time the monarchy was better governed than it has been since, and I write this now thirty years later, in which time the greatest lords of Spain have entered the government'.[62] Valenzuela had been removed at the height of his power, there had long been hopes that he might return (in 1690 papers in his favour were circulating in Andalucia[63]): it was possible then to consider his promise unfulfilled, largely because so little had been expected of him. In the case of the prince everything had been hoped for, and nothing obtained. 'In this year 1679', a Valencian annalist recorded succinctly, 'died the lord Don Juan of Austria, which was no small blow to Spain for the king to lose so good a support.'[64]

## THE CORTES OF ARAGON 1677–87

The most notable event of Don Juan's ministry was the holding of a Cortes in Aragon. The last Aragonese Cortes had been held in 1646. By 1676 the Diputación of Saragossa was making serious protests to Madrid that the king must come to Aragon to swear to the fueros. On 18 September 1676, on the eve of setting out for his autumn stay in El Escorial, the king promised the emissaries from Aragon that he would visit Saragossa 'very soon, when the affairs of the monarchy permit'. Sensing the influence of Don Juan behind the Aragonese demands, Valenzuela kept the king at El Escorial until 2 November.

With the king's promise and his own obligations in mind, Don Juan when he attained power gave priority to the Cortes. Deputies from the four Estates were summoned to Saragossa where in their presence on 1 May the king swore to the fueros in the temple of the Pilar. The formal meeting of the Cortes was due to commence at Calatayud on 10 May, but orders were now given for it to take place instead in Saragossa. The plenary session opened on 14 May under the presidency of Don Pedro of Aragon, in the presence of Charles II.

Aragon was the only Spanish realm to retain four Estates in its Cortes. The ecclesiastical *brazo* consisted of prelates and representatives of cathedrals and colleges: thirty-three deputies had registered by the opening session. The noble estate, consisting of feudal and titled nobility ('they have either blood, or ink, or gold' in their veins, commented an observer referring to their several origins[65]), was represented by fifty-seven persons in the first session though in the session of 1684 nearly 100 registered. The gentry estate, *caballeros hijosdalgo* ('the third in order, but the first in disorder, through the excessive number in it', claimed the same commentator), was represented by 259 registered deputies. Thirty-six towns (*universidades*) were registered.[66] Though the right to register as a deputy was highly prized, attendance was seldom complete. Early in June 1677, when the Caballeros began their separate sessions as an Estate, attendance was only just over 100, but reached 180 by the end of the month.

The business of the Cortes was governed by a programme which the president controlled. Articles for discussion were debated by each Estate individually. However, discussion papers could also be presented to each and every Estate by anyone in the kingdom, and this tended to complicate matters. At a later stage a small committee of two from each brazo, called the *concordadores* or 'coordinators', was set up to pilot through any agreements made between the Estates. The Cortes was one of the most interesting ever to convene in Habsburg Spain. It was inundated by proposals and complaints from all over Aragon, and itself discussed a broad range of subjects. In the nine months it sat its sessions were disrupted by repeated uproars which always originated in the brazo of Caballeros. In August 1677 disputes were provoked in the brazo by a representative of the guilds of Saragossa, the elderly and wealthy José Tudela, who took the quarrel on to the streets of the city. There were riots, part of the brazo refused to sit in the Diputación and moved to a nearby church for its sessions, and Don Pedro of Aragon considered moving the whole Cortes to another city; finally he succeeded in having Tudela replaced as a deputy.[67] The other major disturbance occurred on Saturday 4 December, when swords were drawn in a debate over granting honours to people of French origin. On Monday 6th the Justiciar of Aragon had to appeal to the members to behave 'as good Aragonese'.[68] The Cortes was brought to an end on 25 January 1678.

The main benefit obtained by Madrid was a grant of 1,500 soldiers to be paid for by the realm, but it proved extremely difficult to raise the money from individual towns. Reporting from the region of Calatayud, one official complained that the only way he might convince 'these idiots' was 'if you send me a troop, and chains to bind the jurados'.[69] By March 1679 only three-quarters of the required money had been raised.

Of the many important issues debated in the Cortes, three were crucial: the regulation of trade, the control of French influence, and the navigation of the Ebro.

Action on trade had commenced in 1673, when the Diputados of Aragon asked the Vicar-General, Don Juan, to investigate the problem of French imports. The committee he set up reported in May 1674 that the production of textiles should be fostered, import of manufactured goods should be prohibited, and customs dues should be abolished, making all trade free.[70] These radical proposals dominated Aragonese thinking for the next fifteen years. One of the first acts of the Cortes in 1677 was to return to the theme. A special committee of thirty-two (eight representatives from each Estate) was set up in June to debate the trade proposals. It met for six weeks in the chapter house of the cathedral and eventually proposed a ban on the import of all textiles of wool, silk, and luxury fabrics, from whatever source (France or Spain), for a trial period of six years. A special standing committee of sixteen deputies (two from each Estate plus the eight Diputados) was to be set up to observe the progress of the ban, and at the end of the six years another full Cortes must be summoned to debate the matter.[71] The aim of the ban was to promote industry with Aragon. The idea of abolishing excise was accepted, but no agreement was reached on the compensation that would have to be paid to the king and to the seigneurs. The proposals of the committee were accepted and made law by the Cortes, but not before the Estate of Caballeros had been thrown into uproar, as we have seen, by Tudela and his associates, who called for a ban on all items of trade.

The problem of the French in Aragon was approached in a spirit of compromise by the committee of sixteen. In the Cortes of 1646 a controversial fuero had banned all Frenchmen or their descendants from holding office or working in Aragon. The committee judged that this law should be revoked as being contrary to natural rights, but agreed that foreigners or their descendants should be domiciled if they wished to trade. The uproar of 4 December in the Estate of Caballeros was provoked by those who opposed the revocation of the 1646 fuero.

In July 1677 the Cortes set up a committee of eight to look into the possibility of making the Ebro navigable to the sea, and obtaining for Aragon a Mediterranean port such as Tortosa, Vinaroz or Los Alfaques.[72] The issue, now largely forgotten by historians, was one that deeply affected the aspirations of Aragonese. As the only landlocked kingdom in the peninsula, Aragon felt that lack of access to the sea deprived it of the riches available to the rest of Spain through commerce. In 1607 there were discussions with Valencia about obtaining use of Vinaroz as a port, and a road from Madrid through Aragon to Vinaroz was suggested.[73] The Cortes of 1677 appointed two engineers, Luis de Liñan y Vera and Felipe Busiñac y Borbón, to examine the problem of communications. They found that the main road from Saragossa to Vinaroz (partly constructed in 1607–39) was no longer used and would need 5,000 escudos to restore. They also tested the navigability of the Ebro by sailing down its entire length from Saragossa in the summer of 1677: their estimate for making it fully navigable was over 400,000 escudos. The dream of finally obtaining a seaport inspired one petitioner to the Cortes to propose the foundation of a trading company called the Company of Aragon,[74] but no further steps were taken at this time to obtain the port.

Important as the proceedings of the Cortes were,[75] the most crucial matter, trade, was in effect left undecided and specifically postponed to a new Cortes. Another meeting of the Estates was accordingly called for 1684. The new assembly opened on 17 March 1684 in the Diputación in Saragossa, under the presidency of the duke of Hijar. The business it discussed was so lengthy and controversial that sessions continued for three years and the Cortes was formally closed only on Saturday 15 February 1687. In September 1685 the Estates of the Church and the towns could not form a quorum (twenty-one people) and had to ask for permission to make resolutions without one. The steering committee (or *Junta Magna*) of the new Cortes, set up in April 1684, consisted of six representatives from each Estate.

The Cortes of 1684–87 is important both in its conclusions and in being the last active Cortes of old regime Aragon. All the unresolved questions from 1678 were aired again with even greater ferocity. The official Chronicler of Aragon, Diego Dormer, wrote his *Discursos Históricos-Políticos* specially for the meeting of the Estates. It provides the simplest guide to the issues.

The protectionist Cortes of 1678 had banned the import of all luxury textiles, and had doubled the customs duty on other imports and exports from 10 to 20 per cent. Dormer called for an end to any restraint on trade. The six-year ban and the 20 per cent duty had, he said, brought Aragon to ruin: 'Transport has ceased, banking has disappeared, we even lack necessities.' He also opposed any ban on the export of raw wool from Aragon, and quoted the opinion of four leading merchants made to the 1674 committee set up by Don Juan, that 'it would be excellent to prohibit the export of wools, but unless it were made general throughout Spain the ban would not only be useless but even very harmful'. Finally, he argued for the complete abolition of all customs duties on goods entering or leaving Aragon, and proposed that the revenue be raised instead by a hearth tax.

Dormer's book was almost certainly commissioned by representatives of the clergy and towns. Its arguments and conclusions were exactly those arrived at in the sessions of these two Estates. A powerful attack was directed against it by Joseph Gracián Serrano y Manero on behalf of the Estate of gentry. In numerous publications presented to each member of the Cortes, both in his own name and under the pseudonym Marcelo Nabacuchi,[76] he emphasised his main argument that 'the source of our ills rises from foreign manufactures'. He proposed that all foreign manufactures be forbidden entry, that all customs duties be suppressed and their value made up by a tax on wheat flour, and that all Frenchmen and their descendants be excluded from employment. Gracián Serrano and Dormer thus agreed only on the ending of duties. On the prohibition of imports, the former argued that it had been beneficial: 'in those days in the first two years after the ban, factories expanded and the number of looms increased';[77] Dormer, however, pointed out that it was wrong to ban goods from other parts of Spain 'since we all form a single body in the service of the king'; that Navarre had in retaliation banned Aragonese goods, leading to debts among textile producers in Teruel and Albarracin; and that there would be no point in pressing for a port if imports were to be forbidden. The failure to enforce the prohibition properly was no doubt also kept in mind by the deputies. Eventually, though the Estates of nobles and gentry had supported continuing the ban, the Cortes decided to revoke the fuero of 1678 and restore liberty of imports. At the same time universal opposition to the heavier taxes of 1678 led all the Estates to combine in attacking customs duties.[78] The *peajes* were feudal excise duties owned principally by the king and administered by his officials in Aragon. Levied at a rate of 5 per cent, they were an irritant to free internal trade. The Crown accepted the demands of the Cortes and agreed in 1686 to suppress them forever, in return for an annual payment of 6,000 libras. Attempts to abolish the principal customs duties, the *generalidades*, were less successful. The Cortes succeeded only in halving the rate from 20 to 10 per cent.[79]

Hatred of the French was the dominant emotion in Saragossa in 1684, and made it difficult to discuss the question of trade in a rational frame of mind. Writing to Don Pedro of Aragon in September, the viceroy duke of Hijar said that 'the universal prejudice that everyone in this realm has conceived against the French is such that I consider it impossible to wean them from believing that they are being ruined by them'.[80] The most violent expression of this hatred came in the document written and presented by Don José Tudela to the Caballeros in 1684,[81] in which he claimed that 'the only way to populate and enrich the kingdom of Aragon is to prohibit all trade with the French'. Like Gracián Serrano, he believed that discrimination against or even expulsion of the French traders in Aragon was a possibility, since there were only a few of them.

Forty-eight French traders live in Saragossa, twenty-eight of them with shops, twelve with large stores; the rest are occupied in the households of the royal family and the bishop, selling textiles; others with lesser capital sell on street-corners and squares. Only about a dozen of them are married. Although there are some French traders in other cities of the realm, they are few and all are dependent on those in Saragossa.

Tudela continued his tract with inflammatory attacks against the French. 'As Indians work to enrich Spaniards, so do these to enrich the French'; 'France has never acted in favour of Spain, nor has Spain ever needed the French'; 'God Our Lord created the Pyrenees as a bastion and protection to free Spaniards, and particularly Aragonese, from the French.'

Anti-French feelings ran so high that when in July 1684 the first Estate voted to discuss the question of customs duties without mentioning the role of the French, members of the third Estate rioted, dashed out of their session and went to attack the clergy with weapons, shouting 'Death to the Estate of the clergy!'[82] In October there were anti-French riots in the streets of Saragossa, and six officials of the guild of taffeta artisans sent a strongly worded letter to the archbishop. The letter began: 'Loyal Aragon says with deep feeling: that it fears dishonour to see so many people of French origin present in the Estate of the Church'; and went on to threaten the spilling of blood if clergy of French extraction were not expelled from the brazo.[83] One official was seized, whipped and banished for ten years; the other five fled and were sentenced to death.

The other major issue under consideration was that of obtaining Vinaroz as a port. No progress had been made since the last Cortes. In 1684 the merchants and financiers of Aragon combined to present a memorial asking for Vinaroz as a port, for a House of Trade to be established in Saragossa, and for a joint-stock company to be founded with the title of Compañía General de Aragón.[84] When the Cortes concluded in 1687, the Diputación of Aragon was instructed to keep pressing for the port. In 1692 the realm published tracts stating their case,[85] but in November that year the kingdom of Valencia petitioned the Crown that the matter should not proceed, and the idea was never again revived.

Despite the fury and confusion of the Aragonese Estates of 1677–87, they were a significant and important event. Set in motion by ideas kindled by Don Juan in 1674, they ended by discussing every aspect of public life in the kingdom.

## WAR AND PEACE 1665–78

One of the most trying problems of the Regency was the inability of the Queen to manage Spain's imperial problems while the man with the experience, Don Juan, was deliberately excluded from power. Regardless of who was in control in Madrid, was the Spanish army able to meet its commitments?

Between 1665 and 1678 peninsular Spain had two active fronts: in Extremadura, against the Portuguese rebellion, and in Catalonia, against French aggression. In May 1666 the military establishment on the Portuguese front was:[86]

Table 13.1

|  | Officers | Men |
|---|---|---|
| *Cavalry* | 600 | 5,248 horse |
|  |  | 1,008 foot |
| *Infantry* |  |  |
| 7 Spanish tercios | 726 | 3,851 |
| 14 foreign regiments | 1,365 | 3,020 |
| 1 Swiss regiment, 4 tercios |  |  |
| militia, and garrisons | 355 | 3,270 |
| Totals | 3,046 | 16,397 |

The war effort against the Portuguese was never in a happy state. In 1664 a French observer claimed, with considerable exaggeration, that the 'Spanish infantry appears in a miserable state, most of them naked, poorly armed and badly disciplined'.[87] The Spanish commander, the marquis of Caracena, suffered a defeat by a much larger Portuguese force at Villaviciosa on 17 June 1665; and the campaign thereafter became a series of raids rather than engagements. The attacks by both sides helped to devastate Extremadura, Galicia and the border. As a consequence the Spanish forces were relying for lodging and supplies on areas of New Castile and Andalucia, a situation that the French ambassador rightly saw as 'a novelty in this country and one that the people will not easily accept'.[88] The indecisive military position continued till the end of the war, confirming less the ineptitude of Spanish generals than the resolve of the Portuguese to keep their independence. In July 1666 an English resident in Badajoz reported that 'the enemy gives us continuall allarmes evry daye to the very gates of this towne. . . . The wether is excessive warme and all is misery. Who desires his purgatory in this world may come hither for to pass it.'[89] In 1668 peace was signed with Portugal.

In November 1667 a report drawn up for the Regent by Don Juan showed that the full military establishment within Spain was as shown in Table 13.2:[90]

Table 13.2

| | Infantry | | Cavalry | | |
|---|---|---|---|---|---|
| | Officers | Men | Officers | On horse | On foot |
| Extremadura | 2,602 | 7,500 | 819 | 4,488 | 1,334 |
| Galicia | 733 | 5,768 | 253 | 1,554 | 563 |
| Old Castile | 106 | 731 | 186 | 462 | 405 |
| Catalonia | 482 | 2,203 | 33 | 401 | – |
| Armada | on ship 2,764 | | | | |
| | on land 600 | | | | |
| Totals | 3,923 | 19,566 | 1,291 | 6,905 | 2,302 |

To these numbers we would need to add figures for a few garrisons and some militia. The total was disconcertingly low. However, the real demand for troops after the peace with Portugal was not in Spain but in the north of Europe, where in February 1668 Louis XIV had seized various Belgian fortresses and the whole of Franche-Comté.

Franche-Comté was returned at the Peace of Aix-la-Chapelle in May 1668 but the fortresses were not. The continuing crisis between the two countries forced Spain into an alliance with the United Provinces and the Empire in the new war against France from 1672 to 1678. At the Peace of Nijmegen (September 1678) Spain lost Franche-Comté permanently but recovered most of the fortresses in the Netherlands.

This war was, as we have seen, disastrous for Don Juan, who was expected to extricate Spain from commitments incurred long before his rise to power. There were three major fronts – the Netherlands, Messina and Catalonia – and all ended in defeat. The losses in Flanders damaged Don Juan's personal prestige, since he still claimed to be life Governor of the Netherlands. Messina had revolted against the Spanish in 1674, and a French fleet under the admiral duke of Vivonne succeeded in inflicting crushing defeats on the Spanish and Dutch naval forces in March, April and June 1676. It was at this juncture, in November 1676, that Don Juan received orders to join the Dutch in Sicily but preferred to retire to Aragon.

The Catalan situation seemed the most disturbing of all, and indeed continued to be the chief military preoccupation of the government throughout the reign. Spanish troops in Catalonia in 1669 numbered 2,567 cavalry with 167 officers and 2,967 infantry with 780 officers.[91] The garrisons were small and undermanned; the frontier had been a theatre of war for so long that ironically both French and Spaniards made little more than token defences. Puigcerdà in

1669 had shrunk to being a town of only 300 houses, of which one-fifth were used by the army; the garrison of 300 men was entirely non-Spanish and usually Italian.[92] In autumn 1673, when the duke of Sessa and Baena ended his term of office and was succeeded by the duke of San Germán, there were in Catalonia 4,295 infantry with 893 officers and 2,627 cavalry with 173 officers;[93] at this date the garrison of Barcelona consisted of only 400 infantry.[94]

These figures explain the fate of the Catalan front in the war of 1672–78. The situation got worse after May 1675, when the French crossed into Spain with some 12,000 infantry and 3,000 horse.[95] In October unpaid troops were deserting to the French, and in March 1676 the council of Aragon observed that the viceroy, marquis of Cerralbo, seemed to have only 2,500 infantry at his disposal and that the garrison of Barcelona was reduced to 200 men.[96] The figures were rapidly increased, but military results were poor. The worst incident of the Catalan war occurred in July 1677, when the Spanish troops in a moment of confidence attacked a smaller French force at the town of Espollà and were routed with extremely heavy losses. The dead included the duke of Monteleón and the count of Fuentes.[97] Then in May 1678 the French under Noailles captured Puigcerdà. The unfortunate viceroy, the count of Monterey, was blamed for both disasters. Don Juan had him recalled and replaced.[98] All Spanish territory was returned at the peace, but the power of France had been amply demonstrated.

# NOTES

1. Unattributed detail in this and later chapters is usually drawn from the fundamental studies by the duke of Maura: his *Vida y Reinado* (Madrid 1954, 2nd edn), and *Carlos II y su Corte* (Madrid 1911, 1915).
2. The king's will in 1658 had stipulated that the Committee must consist of the heads of the councils of Castile and Aragon, together with the archbishop of Toledo, the Inquisitor General, a councillor of State and one other grandee. The actual names were not specified until the special testament in 1665.
3. D. García de Haro Sotomayor y Guzmán, an Andalucian, was younger brother of the marquis del Carpio and uncle of Don Luis de Haro. Professor and rector at Salamanca, he went on to the councils of Castile and State, presidency of the council of Indies, viceroy of Naples and, on Haro's death, president of Castile. He derived his title from his marriage in 1630 to Doña Maria de Avellaneda Enríquez de Portocarrero, countess del Castrillo.
4. Don Gaspar de Bracamonte y Guzmán, of minor Salamanca gentry, read theology at Salamanca; entered the councils of Orders and Castile; married his cousin María, countess of Peñaranda; councillor of State 1648; viceroy of Naples and twice president of Indies; plenipotentiary at Westphalia 1645. An expert on European affairs, he spoke Latin, Tuscan, German and French; d. 13 Dec. 1676.
5. Don Cristóbal was Valencian, b. 1599 in San Mateo, studied civil law at Salamanca and Valencia; 1632, judge (*oidor*) of the Audiencia of Valencia; 1642, regent (i.e. councillor) of the council of Aragon in Madrid; 1652, vice-chancellor of council of Aragon; d. 22 Feb. 1671.

6. D. Guillén Ramón de Moncada, a Catalan, grandee of Spain in 1640, served in Flanders with his father, whom he succeeded 1635; instrumental in fall of Olivares 1643; marr. Ana, daughter of marquis of Orani, 1644; 1645, viceroy of Galicia; 1647, of Catalonia; councillor of State. One of the few active soldiers at court; d. 17 March 1670.

7. D. Pascual Folch de Cardona y Aragón, a Catalan, fifth son of the duke of Cardona who was viceroy of Catalonia after the murder of Santa Coloma in 1640, and brother to D. Pedro of Aragon; cardinal *in pectore* 1660; doctor of laws at Salamanca, professor at Toledo, regent of council of Aragon, ambassador to Rome at age of 35; viceroy of Naples 1664; councillor of State and Inquisitor General, Sept. 1665; d. 28 Sept. 1677.

8. Lynch, *Spain*, II, 236. Cf. Maura, *Vida y reinado*, I, 54–5.

9. According to Magalotti, *Viaje de Cosme de Medici*, p. 160, the Priorate included 13 towns, of which the chief was Alcázar de San Juan, and its income, mostly tithes, amounted in 1668 to 60,000 escudos a year. He estimated the whole income of Don Juan at 300,000 escudos.

10. **Fabro Bremundan, F.**, *Hechos del Seteníssimo* (Saragossa 1673), p. 431.

11. Cited by A. Morel-Fatio in Villars, *Mémoires*, p. 309.

12. He was succeeded as president of Castile and therefore member of the Committee, first by the bishop of Plasencia, D. Diego de Quirós, who died in May 1668; then by a nominee of Nithard, the inquisitor D. Diego Sarmiento de Valladares, who was at the same time created bishop of Oviedo.

13. *Memorias Históricas*, in **Valladares de Sotomayor**, *Semanario Erudito*, (Madrid 1788), XIV, 15.

14. Feliu de la Peña, *Anales*, III, p. 351. Osuna was D. Gaspar Téllez Girón, viceroy since 1667; he became governor of Milan 1670–74.

15. *Dietari*, XVIII, 64.

16. ACA:CA 322.

17. For events in Valencia, see the detailed account by **García Martínez, S.**, 'La actitud valenciana', *I Cong. Hist. País. Val.* (Valencia 1976), III, 421–57. He erroneously identifies D. Juan's messenger as Rodrigo de Borja (pp. 423, 433). Don Rodrigo was from 1663 to 1667 viceroy of Mallorca.

18. Paredes to Queen Regent, 12 Dec. 1668, ACA:CA 646/54/5.

19. Archbishop to Queen Regent, 15 Jan. 1669, *ibid*. 932.

20. Paredes to Regent, 15 Jan. 1669, *ibid*.

21. AHN Consejos 7179/11.

22. Consulta of council of Castile, 19 Jan. 1660, *ibid*.

23. 'If the government is not changed and the confessor banished, the Queen will be put into a convent and the king put under charge.'

24. 'Lady, open your eyes and let Don Juan return at once, for he is a son of the family and certainly the best beloved': 'Memorial que dio a la Reyna Nuestra Señora la Probincia de Andalucia a 23 de henero de 1669', BN MS. 2582/124.

25. 'Relacion del Festejo y Aplauso con que fue recivido el señor Don Juan de Austria en Çaragoca y transitos', *ibid*. 2582/134.

26. AMZ Actos Comunes libro 62, año 1669, fo. 95.

27. García Martínez, 'Actitud valenciana', p. 447.

28. Aytona was succeeded by the Constable of Castile, D. Iñigo de Valasco (d. 1696). The secretary of the Committee, Loyola, had died on 14 Oct. 1669 and was succeeded by D. Pedro Fernández del Campo, created marquis of Mejorada 1673, d. March 1680. In Sept. 1669 Valladares was created Inquisitor General and remained

on the Committee in that capacity. His post as president of Castile was taken over by the count of Villaumbrosa, D. Pedro Núñez de Guzmán.

29. Crespí, d. 22 Feb. 1672. Don Melchor, an enemy of Don Juan, was duke of La Palata through his wife. He was sacked by Don Juan in Feb. 1677 but reinstated in June 1678. Created viceroy of Peru 1680; d. April 1691 in Portobelo.

30. *Memorias Históricas*, in *Semanario Erudito*, XIV, 24–5.

31. D. Juan Tomás de la Cerda, 8th duke, succeeded to the title on the death of his father D. Antonio in 1671. He was later prime minister: see below.

32. Godolphin to Mr Secretary Coventry, 10 Nov. 1675, *Hispania Illustrata*, p. 248. Godolphin was England's ambassador from 1671 to 1679, despite his conversion to Catholicism shortly after his appointment. He died in Madrid in 1696.

33. *Menor Edad de Carlos II*, CODOIN, LXVII, 17. Valenzuela had been unofficially recognised as grandee since 31 Oct., when he had been accidentally wounded by the king during a hunt at El Escorial and in recompense had been ordered to 'cover himself'.

34. D. Antonio de Toledo, eldest son of the duke of Alba.

35. Valenzuela was deprived of his grandeeship and honours and confined at Consuegra. A decree of 9 Feb. 1678 exiled him to prison for ten years in the Philippines. On 14 July he sailed from Cadiz and arrived at his prison in the Philippines on 29 Nov. He served his sentence in full, was freed in 1689, went to Mexico and waited for permission to return to Spain. He received this at the end of 1691, but within two months died of a horse-kick, on 7 Jan. 1692.

36. 'Relacion breve . . . de las demostraciones de gozo', BCB Follets Bonsoms 225.

37. ACA:CA 613/53; BUV MS. 700/66.

38. CODOIN, LXVII, 63.

39. 'Les grands qui suivent son party luy ont envoyé 30,000 pistoles pour les dépences de son voyage': *Nouvelles d'Espagne*, 7 Jan. 1677, AE:CP (Esp) 62/368.

40. 'Vino su Alteza, / Saco la espada / Y no ha hecho nada', to which the prince replied in rhyme 'Villano: / Aun no se ha cogido el grano': *Diario de Noticias de 1677 a 1678*, CODOIN LXVII, 84.

41. *Ibid*. p. 107.

42. *Memorias Históricas*, pp. 33–6.

43. From ambassador Jenkins, 18 July 1677, PRO:SP 101/92/149.

44. From Godolphin, 21 Oct. 1677, *ibid*. 101/92/59.

45. Villars to Louis XIV, 29 May 1677, AE:CP (Esp) 62/382.

46. *Diario de Noticias*, p. 124.

47. *Ibid*. p. 132.

48. *Ibid*.

49. She was born on 27 March 1662.

50. 'Le Roy Catholique est laid, a faire peur, et de mauvaise grace': Villars to Pomponne, 22 June 1679, AE:CP (Esp) 64/62.

51. Consultas of council of Aragon, 18 and 22 Jan. 1679, ACA:CA 1351/241–2. The documents for summoning a Cortes in Valencia in 1679 were actually prepared: see the blank forms in ACA:CA 1372/27.

52. ACA:CA 1351/240.

53. AGS Estado 4129.

54. The decision to postpone a visit to Barcelona is written on the consulta of State of 9 March 1679 in *ibid*.

55. Letter of 19 Sept. 1679, BL Sloane MS. 1087/109.

56. Medinaceli to Constable of Naples, 23 Sept. 1679, in 'Lettere Spagnuole all' Eccmo.

Contestabile D. Lorenzo Colonna', BL Add. MS. 16539/66.

57. *Menor Edad*, p. 51.

58. Juanini, *Nueva Idea Physica* (Saragossa 1685), pp. 2–6.

59. *Anales de Cataluña*, III, p. 373.

60. *Ibid.* p. 458.

61. Villars to Louis XIV, 3 April 1680, AE:CP (Esp) 64/320 v.

62. *Memorias*, p. 44.

63. Marquis of Varinas to king, 14 Sept. 1690, *Cartas del Marqués de Varinas*, *CODOIN Ultramar*, XII (Madrid 1899), p. 111.

64. Benavent, f. 7 vo.

65. BN MS. 8454.

66. These figures are from the official 'Primera Parte del Registro de Cortes celebradas en Zaragoza en los años 1677 y 1678', ADZ 732. The gentry Estate included all who were hidalgos and *infanzones* (gentry with jurisdiction over vassals). Some towns, such as the Cinco Villas, had privileges of hidalguía and were represented in this Estate rather than in the universidades.

67. Don Pedro to D. Joseph de Molina, 8 Aug. 1677, ACA:CA 1366/31/2. Tudela was reputedly the richest merchant in Saragossa, with an income in 1668 of 10,000 escudos: see *Viaje de Cosme de Medicis*, I, 66.

68. Don Pedro to the council, 6 Dec. 1677, ACA:CA 1366/54/2; ADZ 734/1897.

69. D. Juan de Altaniba to D. Pedro, 10 and 20 Sept. 1677, ACA:CA 1366/37/53 and 1366/38/4.

70. 'Registro de libro de actos de la Diputación', by D. Thomás Fermín de Lezaún, BN MS. 9825/17–25.

71. The detailed recommendations included the following: that the export of raw materials other than wool be prohibited; that the restrictive examinations for entry into guilds be abolished; that industry should not be a bar to noble honours; and that since the ban on imports would hit income, the tax on textiles be increased. The full printed report is in ACA:CA 1370.

72. ACA:CA 1369/23/2.

73. The whole question of a port for Aragon was discussed by Dormer in his *Discursos* of 1684. There had been discussions over Vinaroz in 1614: see ADZ 576/473–88.

74. *Repítense tantos Memoriales de Arbitrios*, clause 28; included in ACA:CA 1369.

75. There is a fair summary in Danvila, *El poder civil*, III 220–31.

76. His publications, all issued in the summer of 1684, include the *Manifiesto convencimiento de los daños que padece el Reyno de Aragón, y arbitrios para su remedio* (in ADZ 580/124–31); and the *Exortación a los Aragoneses al remedio de sus calamidades* (in *ibid.* at f. 548). His 'Estado infeliz de Aragón, su causa y su remedio', written like the *Exortación* under the name Nabacuchi, repeats the same arguments (BN MS. 11262/16).

77. *Manifiesto*, f. 128 vo. The *brazo de Caballeros* declared that 'in silk, when the ban was observed in the first two years, there was an increase from 85 artisans to 158, and 170 looms to 790'. After giving other examples, it concluded: 'Today, with non-observance of the ban, all these have returned to their previous decay': ADZ 577/175 vo.

78. Examples were given in the Cortes of how the existing system raised prices. Timber brought down the Ebro from upper Navarre would pay 9 per cent on leaving Navarre, then 15.5 per cent when passing briefly through Castile near Alfaro, then 20 on reaching Aragon: a cost increase in duty alone of nearly 50 per cent: ACA:CA 1368/47/2. Sugar from Catalonia paid 10 per cent exit duty, then 5 per cent *peaje* at

Saragossa and 20 per cent *general*, a total cost increase of 35 per cent before adding carriage costs: *Manifiesto*, ADZ 580/125.

79. At the lower rate the generalidades were farmed out over the next few years to D. José Tudela: see Asso, *Economía política de Aragón*, pp. 248–52.

80. Hijar to D. Pedro, 26 Sept. 1684, ACA:CA 1367/6/1.

81. *Un zeloso y apasionado de la mayor utilidad y beneficio del Reyno*, a document of forty pages, without name of author, included in ADZ 580/2339–59.

82. Consulta of council of Aragon, 13 July 1684, ACA:CA 1368/36/2 and 1368/37/5.

83. Duke of Hijar to council of Aragon, 26 Oct. 1684, ACA:CA 1367/9/2, 14.

84. *Los Comerciantes, Hombres de Negocios y Mercaderes* . . ., in ADZ 580/244–9.

85. *Diligencias del Reyno de Aragón para establezer su principal comercio por el puerto de Vinaroz del Reyno de Valencia,* quoted in BMV Pragmáticas Ch. 1636 – 105/39. See also the pamphlet *El Fidelíssimo Reyno de Valencia . . . en orden al intento que ha expressado el Reyno de Aragón*, in BUV MS. 700/23 bis.

86. Statements dated 7 June 1666, based on a general muster of 25 May, in AGS Estado 2684. In 1664 the foreign regiments were: five Italian, four German, two Walloon, one French, one Irish.

87. Memoir of 30 Nov. 1664 in AE:CP (Esp) 50/162.

88. Archbishop of Embrun to Louis XIV, 10 Sept. 1665, *ibid.* 51/203.

89. Letter of 10 July 1666, PRO:SP 101/91/68.

90. 'Copia de consulta que hizo el Sr D. Juan a la Reyna Nra Sra, Madrid 18 de nov. 1667', BL Eg. MS. 347/536 vo: 'Mapa del numero de gente que ay en los exercitos de España y armada del mar Oceano'.

91. Report of 8 Dec. 1669 from duke of Osuna, BL Add. MS. 28445/5–11. The same report is also in ACA:CA 323 and AGS Estado 2690.

92. Report in ACA:CA 211.

93. Report of 15 July 1673 from duke of Sessa, in BL Add. MS. 28445/30–45 and in ACA:CA 328.

94. Report of 5 Oct. 1673 from duke of San Germán, ACA:CA 328.

95. Feliu de la Peña, *Anales*, III, 371.

96. Consulta of Aragon, 9 March 1676, ACA:CA 232/1.

97. Feliu de la Peña, *Anales*, III, 374.

98. For the long list of complaints against Monterey, see the many consultas of Jan. 1679 in ACA:CA 331.

# CHAPTER FOURTEEN

# The Years of Crisis

In July 1668 the president of the council of Finance, Don Lope de los Ríos, wrote to the Queen Regent: 'On various occasions I have represented to Your Majesty how impossible it is to meet the many growing costs involved in Your Majesty's service. . . . In particular I represented to Your Majesty in May this year that when you were pleased to honour me with the presidency of Finance [in 1667], I found entirely spent all the income for 1667 and 1668.' The shortfall for the rest of 1668 had to be found from extraordinary taxes and from American bullion; but even these sources left an urgent debt for 1668 of 3,578,053 escudos vellon, not to mention another million required for ordinary costs.[1]

Debt was a problem of long standing. The famous bankruptcies of Philip II had been repeated into the reign of Philip IV. The last formal suspension of payments under the late king was in August 1662. Insecure finance was a problem of all states at this period, but the case of Spain was aggravated by the unusual level of imperial expenditure.

Taxes in the Crown of Castile were supervised by the council of Finance (Hacienda) in Madrid, which employed the money to finance all the needs of empire: the cost of imperial policy thus fell on Castile alone.[2] Taxes from overseas territories such as Italy and the Netherlands were used to pay for administration in those realms and did not go to Spain. The council was divided into several departments, including the Sala de Millones (which controlled the millones tax) and the Contaduría Mayor de Cuentas (the accounting section), as well as various subcommittees (juntas). Taxes in Castile were raised in three ways: by *arrendamiento* or tax-farming, where the contractor advanced the value of the tax to the state and then collected the revenue himself, hopefully at a profit, with the help of tax officials; by *encabezamiento*, where towns or regions agreed on a lump sum and raised it themselves; and by *administración*, where the council both levied and collected the tax with its own officials. In 1667 just over 7 per cent of the council's revenue was in administration: all the rest was raised by the first two methods, which had the advantage of requiring fewer government personnel.

Administrative problems facing the Hacienda were immense, and many people, including the Venetian ambassadors of this period, saw them as the chief obstacle to solvency. In 1666 Francisco Centani, a leading financier and member of the Contaduría Mayor, presented to the council a detailed paper[3] in which he attacked the system of indirect collection of taxes. He estimated that the actual income of the Crown from taxes was about 112.4 million ducats, but that frauds in the system of arrendamientos reduced this figure to about 20 million only. The solution he proposed was that all existing taxes be abolished and replaced by a single direct 'capitation' tax, to be levied on households according to their means. In reply, the council said 'it recognises that the main reason the realm is in such poverty is the excess of taxes with which it is burdened',[4] but saw various difficulties in implementing change.

The biggest single liability on state finance was the juro debt. Since no such thing as a national debt existed at this time, the Spanish state relied principally on its system of juros.[5] Though similar in form to the *rentes* of France and to public debts in other countries, juros in Spain had various forms and functions. A juro was an annuity paid by the state at agreed rates of interest on capital advanced to the Crown, and was normally assigned out of specified tax revenue. Kings had found it a useful instrument for raising loans to be repaid out of future taxes. The so-called state bankruptcies from the time of Philip II onwards, were in effect massive grants of long-term juros on Castile's taxes as a substitute for cash repayments to the state's bankers. By the end of the seventeenth century the juro liability was crippling. Table 14.1, based on the revenue position of the Crown in 1702, shows in percentages the sources of tax income and the juro debt on each tax:[6]

Table 14.1

| Taxes | Percentage of total | Total juro debt as percentage of year's income | Percent annual income to juros |
|---|---|---|---|
| Alcabalas | 20.8 | 158.8 | 53.7 |
| Cientos | 10.1 | 112 | 33 |
| Salt | 9.7 | 97 | 36 |
| Wool | 4.1 | 120 | 82.1 |
| Servicios | 4.4 | 96.2 | 37.5 |
| Stamped paper | 2 | 114.5 | 24.5 |
| Media anata | 1.9 | 124.3 | 38.3 |
| Customs, etc. | 13.8 | 158.4 | 48.4 |
| Tobacco | 7.1 | 8.5 | 6.2 |
| Servicios de Millones | 22.4 | 58.5 | 30.5 |
| Other millones | 3.7 | 34.3 | 22 |
| | 100 | 104.4 | 37.1 |

By the end of the reign it would have required more than the total ordinary revenue of the Crown to extinguish the juro debt. In practice no attempts were made to do this even had it been possible, since juristas relied on the system for income.

The table shows the main Castilian taxes in the seventeenth century.[7] The alcabala, which originated in the fourteenth century, was a tax of about 10 per cent on sales. The *cientos*, created in 1639, were originally levied at a rate of 4 per cent on top of the alcabala, but reduced by half under Charles II in 1686 to a rate of 2 per cent. The salt tax, a duty of 21 reales on every fanega of salt, had been a state monopoly since the time of Philip II. The taxes on wool included duties on trade, and the *servicio y montazgo* on each sheep at pasture. The *servicio ordinario y extraordinario* was a fixed sum apportioned among the households of Castile: Granada was exempt from it and paid other dues. Stamped paper (*papel sellado*), or tax on paper, had been a royal monopoly since 1636. The media anata, instituted in 1631, took half the first year's salary on any public office, but the tax was also extended to cover other sources of income, notably juros. The main customs duties were the important almojarifazgos or customs of Andalucia (the duty at Seville was known as the almojarifazgo mayor), which accounted for over 6 per cent of the Crown's ordinary revenue; and the various duties, known most commonly as *puertos secos*, payable at Castile's land frontiers. Tobacco was a royal monopoly in Castile since 1636, in Aragon since 1686. The millones were a major group of taxes created in 1590, and fell on consumer goods, principally food. Extra servicios (that is, grants made by the Cortes) in later years increased the total burden of the tax: in 1638 the *servicio de 8,000 soldados* increased taxes on meat and wine in order to pay for the war; in 1650 the *servicio de 24 millones*, renewable every six years by the Cortes, aimed to raise 24 million ducats in six years, or four million a year.

The foregoing made up ordinary revenue, the *rentas reales*. To find the total revenue of the Crown we need to add Church revenue, bullion from America, and money from other parts of Spain. Donativos or free gifts were also raised, but their income was irregular and difficult to assess.

The other realms of Spain produced no significant income for the Hacienda. The point is made simply by looking at royal revenue in Aragon and Valencia (Table 14.2).[8] The accounts in both realms balance comfortably, but in practice royal administration in the Crown of Aragon normally operated with a debt, leaving nothing for the royal Hacienda.

The Church in Spain paid three global taxes to the Crown. The Cruzada, originally granted by the pope to finance the wars against the Moors, was raised by the sale of bulls of indulgence. The *subsidio*, first granted in 1561, was apportioned among bishoprics, colleges, parishes and religious orders. The *excusado*, granted in 1567, came from a tithe in Aragon but in Castile the Church elected to pay a lump sum. Together they were known as the Three Graces. The Spanish Church also contributed a proportion of its tithe and several other grants. Altogether it paid to the treasury annual sums in excess of two million ducats. Like other revenues, those from the Church were heavily mortgaged to juros. In 1665, when the Cruzada of Castile was being farmed by Andrea Piquinotti, most of its yield had been pledged up to 1679; in Aragon the Cruzada was pledged up to 1680.[9]

Because so much tax revenue was mortgaged, the government found it impossible to rely on ordinary sources of money. Soaring inflation, a decreased population, the relentless rise in war costs, all forced statesmen to realise that an expensive foreign policy was no longer possible and that the Castilian taxpayer

Table 14.2

| Receipts | | Expenditure | |
|---|---|---|---|
| *Aragon 1678/9* | | | |
| Customs (generalidades) | 66.7 | Salaries, customs officers | 8.2 |
| Other duties (peajes) | 17 | Other salaries, incl. council | 49 |
| Farming of offices, etc. | 15.7 | Army: 2 tercios | 22.2 |
| Rents | 0.5 | Cost of Cortes | 7.3 |
| Other | 0.1 | Debt to customs farmer | 11 |
| | | Other | 2.3 |
| | 154,206 libras | | 151,448 libras |
| *Valencia 1685* | | | |
| Customs (*peaje y quema*) | 33.2 | Salaries of council | 36.6 |
| Land rents | 47.6 | Salaries of viceroy, Audiencia, etc. | 35.3 |
| Salt | 11.3 | Annuities | 25.2 |
| Other | 7.9 | Other (military) | 2.9 |
| | 67,901 lliures | | 66,589 lliures |

was contributing more than his fair share. The demand for equity in the fiscal structure of the peninsula, voiced by Macanaz early in the next reign, grew out of his experience of the reign of Charles II. When considering the dismal state of the Hacienda at this time, however, it is worth remembering three major achievements which set the regime apart from any other in seventeenth-century Spain. This was the only period when no new taxation was imposed on the people, the only one when thorough changes were attempted in the system and level of tax collection, and the only one when inflation was decisively checked by government policy. On all three counts it was fiscally the most progressive reign of the Habsburg epoch.

The Regency began with a bankruptcy. In May 1666 payments from the treasury were suspended and commitments reviewed.[10] The move was an attempt to start afresh but its practical effect was to increase the juro debt. In 1667 when the realisable annual income of the Hacienda was put at 12,769,326 ducats the juro obligations against this sum were put at 9,147,341 ducats, or nearly three-fourths.[11] Table 14.3 presents a rounded picture of the state budget for the year 1680.[12]

Gloomy budget statements like this had been common in Spain for over a century and were part of the normal pattern of finance. It would be wrong to look at the account in terms simply of a shortfall of over 10 million. In fact the money

Table 14.3   Budget requirements and finance available, 1680.

## REQUIREMENTS

| Silver (foreign) | Escudos | Percentage |
|---|---|---|
| Netherlands | 1,500,000 | 26.4 |
| Germany (against France) | 400,000 | 7.1 |
| Milan (supplied from Naples) | – | – |
| Embassies abroad | 107,000 | 1.9 |
| Extraordinary for embassies | 200,000 | 3.5 |
| Navy (in foreign ports) | 500,000 | 8.8 |
| Frontier garrisons (Ceuta, | | |
| Pamplons, Orán) | 120,400 | 2.1 |
| Catalonia | 600,000 | 10.6 |
| | 3,427,400 | |

| Vellón (Spain) | | |
|---|---|---|
| Navy (supplies and wages) | 1,500,000 | 7.6 |
| Frontier garrisons | 679,085 | 3.4 |
| Extremadura | 144,460 | 0.7 |
| Castilian frontier garrisons | 40,000 | 0.2 |
| Galician garrisons | 35,000 | 0.2 |
| Gunpowder (part cost[13]) | 250,000 | 1.3 |
| Troop levies | 500,000 | 2.5 |
| Aid to Portuguese exiles | 60,000 | 0.3 |
| Extraordinary expenses | 1,500,000 | 7.6 |
| Royal outings to Aranjuez, etc., | | |
| per annum | 160,000 | 0.8 |
| Household of King | 669,835 | 3.4 |
| Household of Queen Mother | 510,400 | 2.6 |
| | 6,048,780 | |

| Total costs (converting the silver | | |
|---|---|---|
| to vellón) | 18,044,680 | |

| Add 10 per cent for costs of | | |
|---|---|---|
| administration | 1,804,468 | 9.0 |
| TOTAL REQUIREMENTS | 19,849,148 escudos vellón[14] | |

## AVAILABLE FOR REQUIREMENTS

| Silver | Escudos | Percentage |
|---|---|---|
| From fleet from Mexico | 296,797 | 10.7 |
| From galleons from Peru | 80,000 | 2.9 |
| | 376,797 | |

| Vellón | | |
|---|---|---|
| Media anata of juros for 1680 and 1681 | 3,296,000 | 34.7 |
| Discounts on annuities | 500,000 | 5.3 |

Table 14.3   Budget requirements and finance available, 1680.

**AVAILABLE**

|  | Escudos | Percentage |
|---|---|---|
| From council of Indies | 400,000 | 4.2 |
| Anticipated from tax-farms of 1680 |  |  |
| and 1681 | 1,600,000 | 16.8 |
| Anticipated from tax-farmers | 1,000,000 | 10.5 |
| Taxes on grants | 120,000 | 1.3 |
| Media anata on grants | 200,000 | 2.1 |
| Tax on titles and honours | 300,000 | 3.2 |
| Voted by inn-keepers' guild of Madrid | 300,000 | 3.2 |
| Voted for king's marriage[15] | 292,000 | 3.0 |
| Voted for militia (lanzas) | 200,000 | 2.1 |
|  | 8,208,000 |  |
| TOTAL AVAILABLE |  |  |
| (silver converted to vellón) | 9,499,471 escudos vellón[16] |  |

available in vellon was more than adequate for the immediate internal needs of the government. The real deficit arose in imperial costs, where there was a huge gap of over 3 million in silver. Ministers were able to muddle along through the chaos in state finance but were at their most vulnerable when it came to finding silver for foreign needs.

There were only two sources of silver: America and the financiers of Europe. In Chapter Five above I have outlined the probable quantity of bullion coming to the Hacienda from the New World. The sums noted did not necessarily reach the treasury; in 1667, for example, out of 366,355 pesos coming for the king a total of 283,906 was paid out immediately in Seville to financiers; in 1670 even before the fleets arrived the government had pledged to pay out 443,117 pesos of its share to financiers. On the other hand the Crown sometimes obtained additional bullion that did not feature in the accounts. This was the case in 1691 when a massive *indulto* was levied on those trading in the galleons of that year. According to Lantéry this ruined a great many traders and the money vanished into thin air after reaching Madrid.[17]

American silver was an essential complement to the supply of silver in Europe by Spanish financiers through the contracts known as asientos. A financier (asentista) would agree to supply a sum of money through his agents abroad, under stated conditions of place and time, and would be promised repayment from the galleons or from tax income. The crucial part played by silver asientos in making up budgetary deficits may be seen from the summary of asientos for the years 1674–76 and 1680–83 presented in Table 14.4.[18]

There is no doubt that the devaluation of February 1680 caused confusion among financiers and contributed to the low level of advances in the 1680s. In that year the Crown was unable to obtain any asientos between February and November, save for a solitary agreement by Simón Ruiz Pessoa in May.

Table 14.4    Summary of asientos 1674–76 and 1680–83

|  | Places | | Asentistas | |
|---|---|---|---|---|
| *1674* | | | | |
| 1,619,000 escudos | Milan | 50,000 | Alonso de Aguilar | 300,000 |
| | Vienna | 64,500 | Benito and Francisco Piquinotti | 239,000 |
| | Flanders | 1,505,000 | | |
| | | | Antonia Fonseca Piña | 200,000 |
| | | | Marquis of Hacialcázar | 200,000 |
| | | | Juan Thomas Bianco | 200,000 |
| | | | Manuel Cortizos | 160,000 |
| | | | Francisco del Castillo | 120,000 |
| | | | Domingo Grillo | 100,000 |
| | | | Gil Ribero de Olivares | 100,000 |
| *1675* | | | | |
| 1,860,333 | Amsterdam | 100,000 | Benito and Francisco Piquinotti | 554,333 |
| | Vienna | 102,500 | | |
| | | | Domingo and Francisco Grillo | 309,000 |
| | Sicily & Naples | 319,000 | | |
| | | | Diego de Castro | 225,000 |
| | Flanders | 1,338,833 | | |
| | | | Manuel Cortizos | 200,000 |
| | | | Francisco del Castillo | 150,000 |
| | | | Luis de Castro (Fonseca Piña) | 100,000 |
| | | | Cardoso and Ruiz Pessoa | 88,000 |
| | | | Juan Bautista Crotta | 80,000 |
| | | | Juan Thomas Bianco | 60,000 |
| | | | Francisco Solerana | 94,000 |
| *1676* | | | | |
| 1,401,833 | Sicily | 22,500 | Manuel Coritzos | 400,000 |
| | Vienna | 80,000 | Francisco del Castillo | 300,000 |
| | Amsterdam | 100,000 | Pedro de Pomar | 300,000 |
| | Flanders | 1,199,333 | Cardoso and Ruiz Pessoa | 104,333 |
| | | | Juan Andrea Spinola | 100,000 |
| | | | Juan Bautista Crotta | 80,000 |
| | | | Luis de Castro | 60,000 |
| | | | Benito Piquinotti | 35,000 |
| | | | Francisco Grillo | 22,500 |

Table 14.4    Summary of asientos 1674–76 and 1680–83

| | Places | | Asentistas | |
|---|---|---|---|---|
| **1680** | | | | |
| 851,998 | Milan | 200,000 | Francisco Piquinotti | 278,666 |
| | Flanders | 651,998 | Mateo Fonseca Piña | 100,000 |
| | | | Luis Márquez Cardoso | 100,000 |
| | | | Simon Ruiz Pessoa | 100,000 |
| | | | Francisco de Lemus | 100,000 |
| | | | Juan Thomas Bianco | 66,666 |
| | | | Juan Bautista Crotta | 66,666 |
| | | | Pedro de Pomar | 40,000 |
| **1681** | | | | |
| 900,470 escudos | Pamplona | 36,000 | Benito and Francisco Piquinotti | 271,600 |
| | Madrid | 117,000 | Alonso de Aguilar | 120,000 |
| | Flanders | 747,470 | Pedro de Pomar | 143,200 |
| | | | Francisco del Castillo | 112,670 |
| | | | Alberto Martini | 100,000 |
| | | | Francisco Argemir | 50,000 |
| | | | José de Aguerri | 36,000 |
| | | | José de Morales | 37,000 |
| | | | Juan Bautista Crotta | 30,000 |
| **1682** | | | | |
| 1,114,000 | Madrid | 12,000 | Andrés Squarzafigo | 240,000 |
| | Milan | 220,000 | | |
| | Flanders | 882,000 | Marquis of Villaflores | 200,000 |
| | | | Antonio de Padilla | 150,000 |
| | | | Francisco Centani | 120,000 |
| | | | Pedro de Pomar | 132,000 |
| | | | Juan Bautista Crotta | 85,000 |
| | | | José de Aguerri | 90,000 |
| | | | Alberto Martini | 62,000 |
| | | | Francisco Piquinotti | 45,000 |
| **1683** | | | | |
| 566,650 | Pamplona | 79,140 | José de Aguerri | 315,140 |
| | Madrid | 159,870 | Francisco Bermudez | 109,870 |
| | Flanders | 327,640 | Pedro Cavaleri | 61,000 |
| | | | Juan Bautista Crotta | 48,000 |
| | | | Andrés Squarzafigo | 32,640 |

Though the devaluation was an effective reform it brought few immediate benefits. The historian Antonio de Solís wrote to a colleague that the measure 'has totally destroyed trade and private fortunes. No one uses money. The bankers conveniently say they are in straits, and poverty has become fashionable. . . . Everywhere there is poverty and bankruptcy. . . . I, my friend, am in no state to take a coach into the streets, for I have many creditors who would pick on me if they saw me in new shoes.'[19] The marquis of Villars explained that 'the effect of the change was that everything kept its price in vellon but doubled it in terms of gold and silver': in parts of Castile, he said, barter was being practised because of the flight of good money. In April 1680 Villars reported that 'within three months most people will have left the court; many have already begun'. Public order collapsed. 'You cannot go out at night because of the thieves. . . . The King has stopped going out: the last time he did a crowd of children gathered and hooted at him.'[20] Solís commented sardonically that 'theft will be legalised, since it makes men prudent and perspicacious, as Thomas More suggests in *Utopia*'.[21]

Traders were the chief victims of devaluation. In Medina de Rioseco the bankers lost over half their capital by the devaluation, and by 1683 some twenty-two of them had gone out of business.[22] The city of Granada complained that its silks had fallen in price by 30 to 50 per cent, and that thousands had been thrown out of work.[23] In 1683 Don Pedro de la Puente Guevara, recently ennobled as marquis del Castillo, reported from León that commerce was depressed and prices were a fifth of what they had been before February 1680.[24]

The government was resigned to large losses in taxation. The devaluation decree had allowed a term of three (later extended to six) months during which debts to the state could be repaid at the old rates of exchange. Tax concessions had to be made to towns which suffered economic distress because of the devaluation. Was the chaos justified? An answer is provided by the cash receipts of the salt factory at Badajoz in 1680: of the coins it received as income, 80 per cent were false or clipped.[25] The February decree aimed to drive this bad money out of circulation, and succeeded.

In March 1680 two ministers of the council of Finance, Don Luis Moreno Ponce de León and Don Juan de la Hoz Mota, presented a memorandum suggesting that the system of tax-farming was wasteful, and that introduction of encabezamientos would be fairer and also more productive.[26] They proposed that a minister should be sent to each of the provinces of Castile to examine what had been paid in taxes in the previous five years. He should agree with the region on a new rate to be collected by local officials. Only monopolies such as salt, tobacco and customs would be farmed out. Although the full council voted by nine to three against the proposals,[27] the king's decision, which reflected that of the duke of Medinaceli, was that ministers be sent out to prepare the encabezamientos.[28]

While a Committee of Means (Junta de Medios) tried to find new ways of raising money for the Hacienda, plans went ahead for reform of the tax system in 1683. A special committee (Junta de Encabezamientos) of six members of the councils of Castile and Finance, under the presidency of Medinaceli, supervised the work, against the protests of leading tax officials. Twenty-one leading ministers and experts were sent out to the provinces,[29] with detailed instructions to arrive at a just rate of taxation and with full powers to remit debts where necessary. Although encabezamientos had been common since the sixteenth century and were an established method of taxation, the operation of 1683 was a major change since it both extinguished the general system of tax farming and reassessed the population's capacity to pay. It is very likely that the whole proposal arose out of the two nationwide surveys ordered by Don Juan in 1678, for which unfortunately no documentation survives.

The energy and courage involved were formidable. For most of 1683 the appointed ministers, many of them of mature years, wandered in person around the cities and villages of Castile, often facing fierce hostility and days of argument with local officials, 'travelling by day and by night, which at my age no one else would do', as Don Julián de Cañas complained from Seville. In Jaén Don Leonardo de la Cueva had to ask for an armed guard; in Santiago Don Juan de Feloaga precipitated the riots we have described above; from Granada Don Juan de la Hoz reported at the end of the year that

I have finished the encabezamientos for this whole province and have settled 340 cities, towns and villages with new agreements. Only by God's favour has it been possible to carry out such a difficult task in the present miserable state of this realm, regulating the taxes to the present condition and capability of these poor villages which were utterly crushed by the fantastic levels to which the tax-farmers had unjustly raised them.[30]

Don Leonardo de la Cueva expressed a different view from Jaén:

I have had long talks in all the towns of this province. . . . Many oppose the encabezamiento in principle, saying it is more of a burden than a relief to the poor, since the powerful and rich are those who govern the state and are looked after in these tax adjustments, while the poor carry the burden.[31]

The taxes mainly affected by the change were the alcabalas, cientos and millones. By March 1684 agreements for seventeen provinces had been completed, each agreement to run for three years. The average reduction in taxes for the provinces was about 15 per cent. In some areas the reduction was much higher: in Cuenca the millones were reduced by 22 per cent, in Llerena the alcabalas were reduced by 32 per cent; similar figures can be found across the country.[32] Not everybody was satisfied: the marquis of Ugena found towns near Alcalá which refused to cooperate until they were granted a reduction of one-third. The concessions achieved something quite unprecedented in the history of Habsburg Spain: a real reduction in taxation, at the very time that the government was looking for more revenue.

Ministers were alarmed at the scale of reductions. In February 1684 Medinaceli accused the officials who had negotiated the changes of neglecting their instructions. 'The only result,' he complained, 'has been a considerable drop in revenue, and the people have been shown that they can let their debts increase in the hope of new remissions.' A full meeting of the council of Finance and the Sala de Millones was called for 10 March 1684. Since a majority of the council had always been opposed to the changes, the result was a foregone conclusion. Don Francisco de Guadalfajara (who had carried out the reassessment in Guadalajara) confessed that he had opposed the encabezamiento in 1681 but now saw its justice: 'this monarchy has declined through tax-farming'. Don Ignacio Baptista Ribas pointed out that it was too early to judge the new system, and that factors beyond human control had been principally responsible for recent difficulties in raising taxes; the winter had experienced 'three months and more of continual rain which has caused floods and enormous losses . . .; the encabezamiento cannot be blamed for such reverses . . . the epidemics have not been caused by the encabezamiento'. The council nevertheless decided by thirteen votes to five that the system had failed; it should continue where it had been agreed, but the remaining provinces should be farmed out.[33] By 1691 only two provinces were still wholly under encabezamiento.

The first casualty of a search for income was the funded debt. Payment of juros was always deemed a most sacred duty by the treasury, for any defection brought a collapse of confidence and therefore of credit. However, since the sum set aside to pay the debt was considerable it was an obvious target. From the 1630s, discounts on juros became a regular and fruitful source of income.[34] Throughout the reign of Charles II the deductions made from juros every year ranged from 50 per cent (the media anata) to 75 per cent. The importance of these discounts for the budget can be seen in the table given above for 1680, where they account for over one-third of state income. It followed that thousands of juristas who looked to their annuities for an income were disappointed. The government therefore from 1637 onwards set up a special committee (junta de reservas) to decide who should be exempted from the discounts. Preference was given to sections of the Church and nobility.

The other major solution to financial problems was a general suspension of payments. In its classic form under Philip II this was the so-called medio general or bankruptcy, when large debts were converted into long-term annuities. Total or partial suspensions occurred regularly in the century. In the disastrous summer of 1678 the council of Finance reported to the Crown that 'all the revenue has been applied to juros and other payments, leaving nothing with which to meet the many pressing expenses that arise daily'.[35] In November the government consequently suspended paying any debts contracted before the end of 1677, with the exception of asientos and military expenditure.[36] It was an emergency measure dictated by the war. On 3 February 1686 a similar order suspended all grants, honorific salaries and juro exemptions, and diverted all money to public needs.[37]

The fat and cheerful marquis of Los Vélez, Don Fernando Fajardo, who was appointed president of the Hacienda by the count of Oropesa, failed to find any easy solutions to the financial crisis. According to his estimates in May 1687, the available revenue of the Crown was only 8,409,779 escudos vellón, while the projected commitments for the coming year amounted to 12,297,155 escudos.[38] Since 1686 the usual jornadas of the court had been discontinued for lack of money. The council of Castile went into lengthy sessions on the crisis, with the result that Oropesa suffered a breakdown in health because of the late meetings. Finally a special committee was set up and began its sessions in January 1688. As a result of its deliberations[39] a firm plan was conceived. A special decree on 6 February 1688 remitted all tax debts up to 1686, then continued:

Table 14.5   Budget for 1690

|  | escudos vellón | Percentage |
|---|---|---|
| **King's household** | | |
| Household, chamber, wardrobe | 206,087 | |
| Chapel | 44,000 | |
| Lighting and medicine | 37,612 | |
| Alms | 13,200 | |
| Gentlemen and pages | 69,543 | |
| Guards | 66,126 | |
| Servants | 60,881 | |
| Stables: provisions | 30,500 | |
| : personnel | 53,930 | |
|  | 586,841 | 13 |
| **Queen's household** | | |
| Ordinary expenses | 185,995 | |
| Lighting | 15,882 | |
| Chamber | 90,617 | |
| Servants | 54,480 | |
| Stables | 53,805 | |
|  | 400,779 | 8.8 |
| Royal palaces | 137,508 | 3.0 |
| Queen Mother's household | 441,176 | 9.7 |
| Councils and Chanceries: salaries | 412,334 | 9.1 |
| **Military and administrative:** | | |
| Invalid soldiers | 120,000 | |
| Mail to Italy and Flanders | 38,880 | |
| Garrisons in Spain | 188,265 | |
| Other | 342,304 | |
|  | 689,449 | 15.2 |
| **Financiers, for asientos** | | |
| Don Francisco Eminente | 422,391 | |
| Others | 526,042 | |
|  | 948,433 | 20.9 |
| **Extraordinary payments** | | |
| Juristas, pensions, widows | 149,585 | |
| Officers: salaries, etc. | 61,707 | |
| Alms, etc. | 39,934 | |
| Other | 377,006 | |
|  | 628,232 | 13.9 |
| **Special payments, all military** | 286,814 | 6.4 |
| Total | 4,531,566 escudos | 100 |

Since the royal finances have been completely absorbed by the juros on them, for many years now no other income has been available for the commitments of the Crown other than discounts on the same juros, and with the fall in revenues it has been necessary to hold back some of the juros in their entirety, giving juristas payment from other sources; and this had led to great confusion.

In future, therefore, from what remained after paying preferential juros a sum of four million escudos was to be set apart exclusively for state needs; a further 500,000 was to go to pay asentistas; and 200,000 was to be set aside for grants, pensions and salaries.[40] Other expenses could be met only from what was left.

This arrangement remained in force for over a quarter of a century, until superseded by the Bourbon reforms. Though it did not solve the basic problem of inadequate revenue, which continued to become graver, it gave the government the security of a minimum income. The budget projection for 1689, for example, showed that taxes would produce 8,504,761 escudos, of which juros would consume 3,632,959 (42.7 per cent), making it just possible to realise 4,700,000 for the Crown.

In 1690 the sum of 4,700,000 was divided up rather differently from original intentions. Nearly one million was set aside for asentistas. Table 14.5 gives details of the budget for this year,[41] which totalled 4,531,566.

## THE ROLE OF FINANCIERS

Without the active support of financiers and bankers, the Crown's credit would have collapsed. Under Philip, the great financiers were either conversos or Italians. Their contacts with bankers in Milan and Flanders enabled Spain to keep its armed forces abroad supplied. Under Charles II the level of spending on foreign wars was sharply decreased. Greater attention to domestic finance made it possible for native Spaniards, who had never been strong in international finance, to emerge to prominence. Though Italian names continued to appear in the late century, they were overtaken in number and later in wealth by Spaniards.

The biggest financier of the reign was Francisco Báez Eminente, who has been discussed above (Chapter Eleven). He contracted for the Andalucian customs from 1663 to 1680 at a total cost of 12,254,034 ducats vellon. In this period complaints against him poured in to the Hacienda, and the contract was subsequently given to Simón Ruiz Pessoa and then to Martín de Vera, but returned to Eminente in 1686. He held the contract for the armada without interruption: in 1679 alone its value was 464,654 ducats silver.[42] Despite the many financial crises of the reign the house of Eminente survived with its assets unimpaired; in 1690 the council of Finance described it as 'the only house at present to have credit in business'.[43] It was unaffected by the disaster of 1689, when the aged Francisco had been arrested by the Inquisition, in whose prisons he presumably perished. The Hacienda calculated in August 1690 that the total current value of contracts in the hands of the firm (now run by Juan Francisco Eminente) was 22 million ducats.[44] These immense sums obviously meant that the state was falling in debt to the Eminentes. By 1697 the government owed the firm 2,044,488 ducats.[45]

Another great financier of the reign was Don Francisco Centani, administrator in the 1680s of the vast tobacco monopoly, active international financier, member of the Contaduría Mayor and the council of Finance, founder member of the 1679 Committee for Trade and an indefatigable proponent of tax reform. He was apparently Genoese by origin. From the 1660s we find him taking part in international transactions for the Crown: in 1668 he advanced 300,000 escudos in Antwerp, in 1671 a smaller sum of 33,300. His several plans for fiscal reform, put forward in 1666, 1671, 1674 and 1675,[46] were deemed impracticable by the council. He lived in Madrid in a large house in the calle de Atocha, and died on 4 July 1684. An English correspondent reported: 'Here dyed one Don Francisco Centani, a poore, meane man that came up to vast riches and dealings with the King. . . . The prompt effects of this man are valued at an hundred thousand pounds sterling.'[47]

The most significant financiers were the conversos, most of them (like Eminente) Portuguese by origin. I have touched briefly above on some. Ventura Donis, mentioned by Villars in 1680 as a known converso, continued to function despite his origins.[48] His surname was transmuted to De Onis, and he obtained for his eldest son and successor Ambrosio an hábito of Santiago, a place in the Contaduría Mayor and, in 1680, the title of marquis of Olivares. Francisco del Castillo, who has also been mentioned above, was arrested by the Inquisition in 1694; the asiento lists show that besides being active in peninsular finance he advanced very large sums abroad, but little information about him is available.

Simón de Fonseca Piña, despite his brush with the Inquisition in 1661, went on to advance huge sums to the government: in 1664 he advanced one million escudos as well as 300,000 in Flanders; in 1665 he supplied 350,000 escudos in Flanders, and in 1667 the sum of 400,000 escudos. On all these the rate of interest he received was 8 per cent. Further supplies he made in Flanders were 15,000 in 1668–69, 270,000 in 1670, 400,000 in 1672, 200,000 in 1674, 100,000 in 1675 and 60,000 in 1676.[49] The total sums advanced in Flanders between 1664 and 1676 were 3,095,000 escudos in silver.

Manuel José Cortizos, marquis of Villaflores, whom I have discussed above, was possibly the Crown's biggest asentista in the 1670s. The advances he made between 1665 and 1678, at an interest rate of 8 per cent, were as follows: in 1665, 500,000 escudos, of which 300,000 were for Flanders; in 1667, 75,000; in 1668, 1,216,000 escudos; in 1673, 360,300 in Flanders; in 1674, 177,500 escudos; in 1675, 100,000 in Sicily and another 100,000 in Flanders; in 1676, 400,000 in Flanders; in 1677, 80,000 in Italy, another 188,300 in Spain and 300,000 more in silver; in 1678, 480,000 for Flanders. These asientos totalled 3,977,100 escudos,[50] mostly silver. Because the Crown was slow to repay, Cortizos in 1679 petitioned for a concurso to pay off his creditors. In that year he estimated his assets, in terms of what was owed by the state in juros and by others in cash, as 1.3 million ducats vellon and over 130,000 ducats silver; he put his debts at nearly 306,000 ducats silver and over 351,000 ducats vellón.[51]

Since the Crown had greater difficulty repaying silver advances, the asentistas who suffered most were those specialising in payments outside Spain. From the days of Charles V the most prominent of these had been Italians. The asientos listed above show the continuing importance of Italians, notably the houses of Piquinotti, Grillo, Crotta, Spinola and Squarzafigo. Other famous names — Strata, Centurión, Imbrea — were still active but had for the most part retired into the titled aristocracy and were trying to liquidate their debts. The Centurión family possessed the titles of marquis of Estepa (since 1560) and marquis del Monasterio (since 1632).[52] In 1679 the marquis of Estepa, whose estates had been in concurso since 1642, petitioned for the arrangement to be ended since most of the debts were being paid.[53] The Monasterio side, whose fortune was based on Philip IV's financier Octavio Centurión, was in 1672 hard pressed by creditors who were claiming 660,000 ducats in silver and 32,000 in vellón. The problems of the house, which was also under concurso, were aggravated by litigation within the Centurión family and by huge debts owed by the Hacienda, amounting in 1671 to 2,100,000 escudos silver.[54] The Strata family represented in this reign by Don José Strata, marquis of Robledo (a title of 1649), was likewise in severe financial difficulties: the Hacienda by 1652 owed it over 380,000 ducats silver and in 1668 and 1682 special payments had to be made to members of the family.[55] The Imbreas went the same way. In 1667 the Hacienda calculated that it owed Juan Esteban Imbrea, count of Yebes (a title of 1648), the sum of 2,697,053 ducats silver and 12,118 ducats vellón.[56] The count was assigned 12,000 escudos vellón a year towards the debt, but his heirs failed to receive full satisfaction.

In view of these sombre examples it is astonishing to see that Italians continued to advance money. The three most notable bankers were the Grillos, who managed the slave trade in the early part of the reign,[57] the Spinolas and the Piquinottis. The immense services of Bartolomé Spinola to Philip IV were rewarded with the title of count of Pezuela, but he died in 1644 with his loans unrepaid. He was succeeded by his nephew Juan Andrea Spinola, who came over from Genoa and carried on the business up to his death in 1678. In 1679 the house ceased to trade, thanks to various deficiencies in income, particularly the non-payment of juros. Some 235,000 ducats in principal of juros had been granted by the Hacienda in part payment of debts, but the annuities were always in arrears. Among other services to Charles II, Juan Andrea in 1676–77 advanced 300,000 escudos in Flanders, and between 1674 and 1679 had lent the Crown within Spain 161,104 ducats silver and 27,932 ducats vellón: in 1684 his son Francisco claimed that the house was 'without the means to maintain itself as it should'.[58] The Piquinottis, of whom we know little, seem to have fared better. Philip IV's banker Andrea Piquinotti functioned actively until his death in 1670, when his house was taken over by his nephews Ansaldo and Benito, who together with Francisco María Piquinotti continued to act as asentistas into the 1680s; in 1675 José Piquinotti, brother of Benito, obtained the title of count of Villaleal.

The importance of foreign bankers decreased as the Crown cut back its overseas commitments. By the 1680s the bulk of the government's transactions was in the hands of native financiers, as the asiento lists above show. In the budget estimates of 1690 only Spanish names occur: the principal asentistas were Eminente; the Barcelona financiers Pau Feu and Juan Navarro; Don José de Aguerri (ennobled in 1689 as marquis of Valdeolmos); Gabriel de Campos; and Martín de Vera. Of these, Eminente and Vera certainly were conversos. The rise of Aguerri, and his early association with Juan de Goyeneche, symbolises the emergence of Basque entrepreneurship in Spain's affairs.[59] As yet we know nothing of the background of other big Spanish financiers such as Alonso de Aguilar, Pedro de Pomar,[60] and Antonio de Padilla. Throughout the country native capitalists dominated state finance. In Aragon in the 1670s and 1680s the biggest state financiers were Don Francisco Sanz de Cortes, marquis of Villaverde, and Miguel Iñiquez, who farmed the customs together.[61] In Catalonia in the 1680s the biggest financiers were Villaverde, Don Francisco Argemir and Don Francisco Monserrat, later marquis of Tamarit.[62] Their activity was a clear sign of the revival of Spanish financial acumen.

## 1679–89: NEW FACES, NEW POLICIES

The proposed marriage of Charles II to Marie Louise of Orleans, originally negotiated by Don Juan, was a matter of the greatest importance since it both extended the influence of France and created a possible rival to the Queen Mother for the king's affections. The letters written by Charles to Louis XIV on the marriage are extraordinary items; scrawled in large shaky words, they look more like the efforts of a child of six than a king of eighteen.[63] The engagement was celebrated by proxy in Paris on 30 August. The duke of Pastrana at the end of August took the king's engagement gift (a portrait by Carreño, surrounded with diamonds) to Paris, and attended a sumptuous celebration in honour of the event at Fontainebleau on 14 September. On the 20th Marie Louise set out for Spain.

The king likewise set out from Madrid on 21 October on the second long journey of his life, northwards through Aranda to Burgos. It was a slow progress, interrupted by continual poor health. Marie Louise crossed the frontier on 3 November and travelled through Vitoria and Miranda towards Burgos. The couple met in the little town of Quintanapalla and were able to converse through the good offices of the French ambassador Villars. Marie Louise was seventeen, a lively girl with long dark hair and flashing eyes, wholly confused by a country whose customs she did not understand and whose language she did not speak. They were married quietly in Quintanapalla[64] and went to Burgos on Sunday the 19th, where they spent their first night together. The court buzzed with gossip as to whether the marriage had been consummated. All we know is that Charles seemed enchanted and the queen had no complaint. The royal couple retired to the palaces just outside the capital and made a formal entry into Madrid only on Saturday 13 January. Fears that Mariana would resent Marie Louise were quickly dissipated, and attention turned back to the problems of government.

Villars reported in December 1679 that 'the king seems determined to have no prime minister'.[65] Shortly after the great devaluation early in the new year, however, the king on 21 February declared that 'I now recognise that the form of government appropriate to my monarchy and the exigencies of the moment both call for a prime minister', and appointed the duke of Medinaceli. Aged forty-five in 1680, Don Juan Tomás de la Cerda, eighth duke of Medinaceli, was possibly the wealthiest and now certainly the most powerful man in Spain after the king. His antagonism to the party of Don Juan was resolved by the marriage in July of his sixteen-year-old daughter Catalina Ana to her seventy-year-old uncle Don Pedro of Aragon.[66]

The duke had no pretensions to be an active statesman, and limited his efforts to the major problem of regulating the financial chaos in Castile. The biggest event of the year in Madrid was the gigantic *auto de fe* of 30 June in the Plaza Mayor. In general the duke's policies, as for example with the Committee for Trade, were little more than a continuation of those begun by Don Juan of Austria. He was ably helped by José Veitia y Linaje, secretary of the Indies, who became secretary of the Despacho in April 1682. Relations between Medinaceli and the queen were poor, and prompted the prime minister's resignation in April 1685. He left Madrid in disgrace in July. Poor in health, he died paralysed in February 1691.

The chief ministers of this period were not expressly chosen by the king, but emerged rather out of a sort of consensus among the grandees. In June 1684 the count of Oropesa, Don Manuel Joaquín Alvarez de Toledo, became president of the council of Castile. Handsome, gracious and above all young – he was only thirty-four in 1684 – he quickly took over power from Medinaceli. When Veitia y Linaje resigned with his patron in April 1685, Oropesa replaced him in the Despacho with Don Manuel de Lira, former ambassador in Holland, secretary for Italy and one of the most fascinating men active in politics under Charles II.[67] Both Oropesa and Lira were widely praised by contemporaries. The duke of Montalto, writing to Don Pedro Ronquillo, ambassador in England, was more sceptical: 'No one is more in the good graces of the king than the count of Oropesa, but this will not be enough to solve anything.'[68] A contemporary numbered among his chief enemies the Constable, the Admiral, the cardinal archbishop of Toledo and the dukes of Arcos and Infantado. The same source also suggested that Oropesa's very devotion to efficiency was self-defeating. He would take state papers home in order to work on them, but keep them there 'days, months and years'.[69] A general lack of confidence among the nobles led inevitably to 'total contempt and vilification of the government, as shown by the abundance of satires that come out against it every day'.[70] The major achievements of Oropesa's ministry were the regulation of the finances, with the aid of his protégé Los Vélez; the monetary reform of 1686 and the budget reform of 1688; and the attempt to reduce administrative personnel in 1691.

By 1686 Marie Louise had lost most of the public goodwill of her early years. Leading grandees found her an obstacle when they tried to approach the king. The aggressions of Louis XIV did not endear her to Spaniards. The most painful aspect of her lonely existence at court was the absence of an heir. Along the streets of Madrid urchins sang the song whose principal refrain was:

> Parid, bella flor de lis,
> En fortuna tan extraña,
> Si parís, parís a España,
> Si no parís, a París.[71]

The birth of an heir would have ensured a Habsburg succession and wrecked the ambitions of France. In 1685 the queen seems to have been accused of aborting a possible birth. Marie Louise became more hostile to those around her and hinted at attempts to poison her. In August 1687 she suffered serious gastric troubles and even lost consciousness; her condition was excellent in the spring of 1688 but in the autumn she was taken ill again for several months. At this time she had conversations with the French ambassador Rébenac, to whose despatches we owe the first mention of alleged bewitchings. In his despatch of 23 December 1688, written in cipher,[72] Rébenac stated that Marie Louise had told him 'that she was not really a virgin any longer, but that as far as she could figure things she believed she would never have children'. Rébenac also gave details of a proposed exorcism ceremony meant to cure the king's apparent impotence.

In February 1689 an unfortunate turn of events stunned the court. On Tuesday the 8th Marie Louise hurt herself slightly when out riding near El Pardo. The next day she kept to her bed but became ill during the night and kept saying that she had been poisoned; she remained close to death, with fever and incessant vomiting, for two more days, and died shortly before 9 a.m. on 12 February.

Pressure of international events and the need for an heir made advisers look around immediately for another queen. After various deliberations the council of State met on 8 May and examined the candidates in a lengthy consulta. The king studied the advice and a week later on 15 May made his decision to seek the hand of Mariana of Neuburg, daughter of the Elector Palatine, duke of Neuburg, a Wittelsbach. The Imperial ambassador in Spain, the count of Mansfeld, acted as go-between for the marriage, which was celebrated by proxy in Neuburg, on the banks of the Danube, on 28 August 1689.

The new queen left Neuburg on 3 September on a journey that was to take seven months. She reached Dusseldorf on the 18th and remained there until 13 November because of a delayed schedule; she then went down the Rhine to Dordrecht. There were further delays. Not until 29 December, in Flushing, did the whole party transfer to the English escort under Admiral Russell. Bad weather meant that they reached Portsmouth only on 4 February. Safe in an English warship, *The Duke*, and escorted by twenty men of war, the queen eventually entered the harbour of El Ferrol on 27 March. She set foot on Spanish soil on 6 April. Charles, making the third long journey of his life, came out to meet his spouse in Valladolid on 4 May. They went through a second marriage ceremony and stayed in the city until the 11th. Their formal entry to the royal Alcázar of Madrid took place on Saturday 20 May.

Mariana of Neuburg, unlike her predecessor as queen, had a long and active part to play in Spanish politics. In September 1690 her father the Elector Palatine died and Charles II decreed official mourning for him at the Escorial, to which the whole court proceeded at great cost. The occasion is notable for the dedication of a chapel to the Sacred Form, immortalised in the painting by Claudio Coello. The act was in expiation of the sacrilege committed by those who had seized Valenzuela from his refuge in the Escorial.

One of the queen's first achievements was the fall of Oropesa and Lira. Domestic opposition to the minister was general and easily harnessed; in addition

Mariana was receiving confidential instructions from the Empire to bring about changes in the government. The queen was a tall, singleminded blonde German who spoke Spanish and had an excellent mastery of politics. She did not get on well with her mother-in-law, though they were both Germans.

In April 1691 Manuel de Lira resigned his post, pleading weak eyesight, though the real reason was a difference over policy in the Netherlands. He was succeeded as secretary of the Despacho by Don Juan de Angulo. On 24 June Oropesa received a note in the king's own hand, inviting him to resign. The next day he went to the palace and asked for an explanation. 'They desire it,' confessed the unhappy king, 'and I must conform.' The count then went to see the queen. He resigned that day, and on the evening of Tuesday the 26th withdrew quietly to Puebla de Montalbán, the seat of his brother-in-law the duke of Uceda.

The queen was not solely responsible for these events. The explanation obtained by the English ambassador, Stanhope, who had the year before described Oropesa as 'the ablest man I have met with in Spain', was that 'about a month before, the duke of Arcos in the name of most of the grandees represented to the king the calamitous estate of the monarchy in a long memorial, insinuating that all was occasioned by the maladministration of the count of Oropesa'.[73] The new councillors of State announced on 27 June suggest a change of personnel not exclusively in accordance with the queen's wishes.[74]

The most interesting consequence of Oropesa's dismissal was that the king refused to appoint anyone else as prime minister, and decided to govern for himself. 'In those first days he dedicated himself with unbelievable application to the management of affairs; but early enthusiasm was followed by the weariness occasioned by ill health, and he referred matters to many and different ministers.'[75] It was the only attempt Charles made to be truly king, and should not be forgotten. The reiterated attacks of historians on a young man burdened by insuperable infirmities, do less than justice to his constant efforts to care for his monarchy.

## NOTES

1. D. Lope de los Rios to Queen, 28 July 1668; and consulta of 2 Aug. 1668; both in AGS:CJH 900.
2. For the Hacienda before Charles II see **Domínguez Ortiz, A.**, *Política y Hacienda* (Madrid 1960); for the subsequent period see Kamen, *War of Succession*, ch. 9. For a summary of some aspects of Charles II see **Garzón Pareja, M.**, 'Hacienda del reinado de Carlos II', *Miscelanea Antonio Marín Ocete* (Granada 1974), I, pp. 325–47.
3. 'Un vasallo celoso del servicio de Dios', BL Add. MS. 21536/62–92.
4. Consulta of 27 July 1666, AGS:CJH 885. The council spent many hours discussing Centani's projects.
5. Among other studies of juros, see Domínguez Ortiz, *op. cit.*, ch. 8; and **Torres López, M.**, and **Pérez Prendes, J. M.**, *Los Juros* (Madrid 1967).
6. Calculated from my *War of Succession*, p. 209–11.
7. The best modern survey of the Castilian taxes is **Ulloa, Modesto**, *La Hacienda Real*

(Madrid 1977). The best contemporary survey is **Ripia, J. de la**, *Práctica de la Administración* (Barcelona 1694).

8. 'Cuenta del Reyno de Aragon desde 20 de Henero 1678 hasta 19 de Henero 1679', ACA:CA 170; 'Recepta de la Baylia General de Valencia, 1685', *ibid*. 647/26/4. Further figures for Valencia in the early century are in Casey, *Kingdom of Valencia*, pp. 179–80.
9. Statement of 10 Oct. 1665, AGS:CJH 900.
10. Domínguez Ortiz, *op. cit.*, pp. 106–7.
11. Consulta of 14 March 1667, AGS:CJH 885.
12. 'Provisiones generales para el año de 1680', 12 Jan. 1680, *ibid*. 1951. Totals have been left in escudos in order to keep the rounded figures.
13. The normal annual cost of gunpowder was 400,000 escudos, but the factory at Plasencia was paid off partly in juros (on tobacco and millones).
14. The total in the official document is incorrect.
15. This source was the *servicio del chapín de la reina*.
16. This is also a corrected total. It should be noted that the document here converts silver at a premium of 242.75 per cent, whereas in the first part of the budget it is converted at 250 per cent.
17. *Memorias*, pp. 276–7.
18. Sources are principally AGS Contadurías Generales 167–9, 173–6.
19. 'Cartas de Don Antonio de Solís', in **Mayáns i Siscar, G.**, *Cartas morales* (Madrid 1734), pp. 175, 184, 188.
20. Villars to Louis XIV, April 1680, AE:CP (Esp) 64/322, 339.
21. Mayáns, *Cartas*, p. 184.
22. D. Pedro de Oreytia to council of Finance, 7 April 1683, AGS:CJH 1066.
23. Granada to council, 19 Sept. 1681, *ibid*. 1039.
24. Marquis del Castillo to council, 28 Jan. 1683, *ibid*. 1960.
25. Account of 20 Jan. 1681 in AGS Contadurías Generales 2698.
26. Memorandum of 25 March 1680, AGS:CJH 1023.
27. Consulta of council, 7 April 1680, *ibid*. 1028.
28. Decision written on consulta of 9 Nov. 1680, *ibid*. The final decision was agreed by the council on 12 Oct. 1681.
29. Among the officials were: D. Julián de Cañas for Seville, D. Pedro de Oreytia for Valladolid, D. Francisco Ronquillo for Córdoba, D. Pedro Núñez de Prado for Avila, D. Pedro Veluti de Haro for Soria, D. José Francisco de Aguirre for Salamanca, D. Pedro de la Puente for León. The printed *Instruccion de lo que han de observar los Ministros que han de salir a los Encabeçamientos*, in 29 articles, is in AGS:CJH 1966.
30. AGS:CJH 1060.
31. D. Leonardo to council, 23 June 1683, *ibid*. 1960.
32. In 1688 the council of Castile claimed that taxes were reduced by 'nearly one-third' (consulta of 10 Jan. 1688, BL Add. MS. 21,536/125), but the figures I have seen do not bear this out.
33. All documentation in *ibid*. 1079.
34. Details of juro discounts are listed in Ripia, *Práctica*, pp. 205–7, 287–8; and for the whole period 1621 to 1727 in 'Origen de Rentas Reales', BRAH Est. 24 gr. 5a B. no. 128 fos. 39–50.
35. Consulta of 27 Aug. 1678, AGS:CJH 1007.
36. Order of 5 Nov. in consulta of Hacienda of 30 Nov. 1678, *ibid*. 1009.
37. *Ibid*. 1137.

38. **Canga Argüelles, J.**, *Diccionario* (Madrid 1833–34), II, 99.
39. 'Cartas del Duque de Montalto', CODOIN, 79 (Madrid 1882), pp. 420, 424, 426. Its proposals were the result of a long process of deliberation. In 1686 a Committee of Means, powerfully supported by the president of Castile (archbishop Ibáñez), twice advised the suppression of the millones (see consulta by him in BL Add. MS. 21,536/190). The plan was crushed by the full council in its consulta of 10 Jan. 1688 (*ibid.* f. 111), which outlined the measures that the special committee eventually proposed.
40. Decree in AGS:CJH 1112.
41. 'Relaciones de las quatro millones de la causa publica', AGS Estado 4138. Totals have been corrected.
42. All figures and details from AGS:CJH 1956.
43. Consulta of 18 Feb. 1690 on house of Eminente in *ibid.* 1132.
44. Account of 18 Aug. 1690, *ibid.* 1131.
45. Report by count of Adanero, 6 July 1697, *ibid.* 1249. For the later history of the Eminentes see Kamen, *War of Succession*, p. 71.
46. His 1666 plan has been discussed above; that in 1671 was published as *Tierras: Medios Universales* (Madrid 1671); those of 1674 and 1675 are in copy in BL Eg. MS. 2084/321, 342.
47. Letter of 6 July 1684, PRO:SP 101/92/162. A list of all his household goods, and full summary accounts of the tobacco farm, are in AHN Consejos 7028.
48. See **Domínguez Ortiz, A.**, 'Banqueros y asentistas', *Hacienda pública española*, 55 (1978), 172–4.
49. AGS:CJH 887 and 1947.
50. Accounts in *ibid.* 1947.
51. Memorial of 1679 in AHN Consejos 7189.
52. Cf. Domínguez Ortiz, *Política y Hacienda*, pp. 111–12.
53. Memorial of Aug. 1579, AHN Consejos 7189.
54. Report of council of Castile, 26 April 1672, *ibid.* 7182.
55. AGS:CJH 1947.
56. Account of 23 April 1667, *ibid.*
57. **Scelle, G.**, *Traite négrière* (Paris 1906), I, 505–632.
58. Memorial of 1684 in AGS Cámara de Castilla 1489.
59. Though a Basque, Aguerri's career is associated principally with Saragossa: see Caro Baroja, *Hora navarra*, p. 57. He worked in Madrid from 1644 to 1685.
60. There are papers on Pomar in AGS:CJH 1956.
61. Consulta of council of Aragon, 28 March 1679, ACA:CA 1366/60/1.
62. ACA:CA 146.
63. Originals in AE:CP (Esp) 63/15, 19.
64. The marriage originally planned for Burgos cathedral could not take place because of the sudden illness of the archbishop, who died on 20 Nov.
65. Villars to Louis XIV, 15 Dec. 1679, AE:CP (Esp) 64/212.
66. Medinaceli, an Andalucian, had an income of 50,000 ducats when he held his first title of duke of Alcalá. In 1653 he married Doña Catalina de Aragón, only daughter of the duchess of Lerma, who was first wife of Don Luis de Aragón, 6th duke of Segorbe and 7th of Cardona; the dowry was 100,000 ducats. In 1659 her unmarried brother died, and she inherited from him the Valencian titles of Lerma and Denia, with an income of 60,000 ducats. In 1671 Don Juan Tomás's father duke Antonio died, leaving his son the riches of the Medinaceli title. Then in 1675, after a lawsuit lasting five years, Doña Catalina was granted the estates and titles of Segorbe and

Cardona, against the pretensions of Don Pedro de Aragón, brother to the late duke. Don Juan Tomás died in 1691. His wife had two sons and nine daughters. He was succeeded by Don Luis Francisco, marquis of Cogolludo, who perished miserably during the War of Succession.

Don Pedro of Aragon, b. 1610, was brother to the duke of Cardona and to Don Pascual, cardinal of Aragon. He was marquis of Pobar by his first wife (d. 1641), and duke of Feria by his second (d. 1679). His marriage to Doña Catalina Ana in 1680 was within the forbidden degrees. D. Sept 1690 without heir; his widow in 1697 married Don Juan Tomás, the last Admiral of Castile.

67. I have not consulted the collection of his letters, dated 1677 to 1679, in BN MS. 10695/61.
68. Letter of 25 Nov. 1685, CODOIN 79 334.
69. *Memorias Históricas*, in *Semanario Erudito*, XIV, 53–4.
70. Montalto to Ronquillo, 9 May 1686, CODOIN, 79 349.
71. 'Give birth, lovely fleur de lys; in this strange situation, if you give birth you benefit Spain, if you do not you benefit Paris.'
72. AE:CP (Esp) 75/274. Extracts are given in English in **Nada, J.**, *Carlos the Bewitched* (London 1692), pp. 125–6.
73. Stanhope to Nottingham, 27 June 1691, *Spain under Charles*, pp. 19–20.
74. They were Infantado, Montalto, Villafranca, Melgar, Frigiliana, Burgomayne (Don Carlo d'Este, then ambassador to the Empire), and Pedro Ronquillo, ambassador to England. Ronquillo died shortly after, aged 74. Melgar was Don Juan Tomás Enríquez de Cabrera, holder since the death of his father in Sept. 1691 of the title of Admiral of Castile.
75. *Memorias Historicas*, p. 86.

# CHAPTER FIFTEEN

# The Succession

## THE WAR IN CATALONIA (1690–1697)

For some time before 1688 rumours of war had been brewing in Madrid. In Catalonia the peasants were too preoccupied with their harvest crisis to be concerned about the French presence nearby. In May 1689 the Grand Alliance was formed against France, and joined by Spain in June 1690. In that month the total number of Spanish troops in Catalonia, where hostilities had already begun, was officially put at 10,356 infantry and some 4,000 cavalry.[1] Circumstances conspired to make the war in the principality the most disastrous since the reverses suffered fifty years previously under Olivares. As in 1640 there was inadequate money and troops; worst of all, there was the revolt of the *barretines*.

The French invasion of Catalonia was the gravest threat to Spain since the accession of Charles II, and the country's biggest military commitment since the ending of the war with Portugal. Across the frontier, the intendant of Roussillon, Raymond de Trobat, envisaged a rapid conquest, 'because of the few troops in the country, the bad condition of the fortresses and frontiers, and the poverty of all their troops'.[2] The organisation of the Spanish war machine in Catalonia had not materially improved since the days of Olivares. The duke of Villahermosa,[3] who was appointed viceroy in December 1688, made it his first duty to tour the military posts and sent back dismayed letters to Madrid. In mid-February he stopped three days in Gerona, the principality's most important barrier against invasion, and discovered it to be 'in the most miserable state conceivable since, like the other fortresses in the principality, it lacks everything'. His reports from other cities were the same: 'the artillery everywhere is out of action. . . . The lack of men is notorious . . . total unpreparedness and defencelessness . . . soldiers begging for alms in the streets, and no hay for the horses . . .'[4] The picture is confirmed from the French side. After the capture of Camprodon in mid-May 1689, Trobat wrote to Louvois that 'it is almost unbelievable to see the state in which the Spaniards kept this fortress. We have been working for two days to clear out the filth, and have barely managed. . . . The barracks are like pig-sties.'[5]

Part of the problem in Catalonia was manpower. The Catalan contribution was limited to a tercio of 500 infantry maintained by the city of Barcelona, and another of 400 maintained by the Diputació. In emergencies these numbers were increased: by 1693, for example, the city was maintaining two tercios totalling 1,400 men, and the Diputació had increased its tercio to 600 men. In addition the government could count on the tercio raised and financed by Aragon, in accordance with the recent Cortes; and the city of Valencia contributed a force of at least 500 men. All the other soldiers active in the principality were Castilian, or under Castilian command: the latter included a regiment each of Germans, Walloons and Neapolitans. Campaigns in Catalonia seldom took the form of field encounters: the nature of the country made sieges the only decisive form of warfare, and the militia raised by the cities were consequently an important help to defences.

Money was a perpetual problem since Catalonia had a different currency and most cash payments therefore had to be in silver.[6] Part of the heavy cost of maintaining cavalry was traditionally met by billeting groups of men among the cities and towns. In these circumstances the peasant disaffection of 1688 was a major obstacle, for the leaders of the rebellion opposed both billeting and the donativo for the war. The towns refused to pay any money, and both Torras and Rocafort had by April 1689 become paid agents of France. There is little doubt that the French could have captured Barcelona that season, as Torras was pressing them to, but Louis XIV's real effort was being concentrated in the Rhineland, and Louvois preferred Catalonia to collapse from within rather than through an expensive conquest. At the end of June the duke of Noailles, commander on the Catalan front, pulled his troops back into Roussillon. In August the Spaniards moved up, besieged and razed Camprodon, and turned round to root out the peasant agitation.

The events of 1689 could have meant the loss of Catalonia. Early in April Villahermosa sent leading Catalan gentry out to the districts to collect a *donativo universal*, to be paid over three years. No sooner did they start than Barcelona and the districts were flooded by leaflets threatening death to those who paid. At the end of April the gentry returned empty-handed. On Palm Sunday, 3 April, Torras, Rocafort and Rocabruna, who were jointly responsible for the leaflets, murdered an official who had helped to burn Torras's house. That summer the Roig of Centellas and other agitators went about dissuading villagers from any payment. Villahermosa, on his way back from the front, made a special point of passing through Centellas, where he arrested a jurat and sent him to the galleys. In early November he was complaining of the 'needs and miseries of this army'. At this point the tensions in the principality exploded into the events of 21–22 November, when the troops throughout lower Catalonia were disarmed by the population.

The viceroy's swift and bloody counterattack, and the treacherous murder of Soler, saved the day. Villahermosa admitted that his actions had made the Catalans look on him with 'horror and hate'.[7] More important, he was at last able to raise the donativo. From 23 December onwards, members of the Diputació went out personally to ask for the money: the Count of Plasencia, Diputat Militar, took the region of Tarragona and Barcelona; others went to Mataró,

Lérida and the other cities. The French immediately sent out agents 'with orders to go through the countryside that the Diputats visit and work themselves into the confidence of the leaders in order to persuade them not to trust their word'.[8] But the opportunity had passed, and the efforts of the rebels became more and more ineffective. 'The greatest harm to have come out of this and preceding disturbances, has been the realisation that the spirits of the people of Catalonia, and of most of the citizens of Barcelona, are wholly hostile to the soldiers, officials and government', concluded the nineteen judges of the Audiencia of Barcelona in a report dated December 1689.[9] It was a sombre judgment, with little cause for satisfaction.

The duke of Noailles and intendant Trobat had a difficult programme when the new campaign began in May 1690. On the one hand they had to be scrupulously careful of the feelings of Catalans; on the other they had to occupy Catalonia. Their practical policy reduced itself to 'letting the army live off enemy territory comprising numerous towns and villages, who promised in March search out support for France. In the event, though various plots were set afoot in Barcelona, the main support won was from the officials of the duchy of Cardona, a territory comprising some ninety towns and villages, who promised in March 1691 to rise for France if the army reached their area.[11] In fact, by 1691 the French had largely given up hope of a successful rising. Their hopes in Cardona were dashed when the plot was discovered and the new viceroy, the duke of Medina Sidonia, hanged the plotters in December 1691 in Barcelona.

The biggest French military successes of the war were achieved not with men — their forces were often much smaller than those of Spain — but with firepower. In 1691 the French navy carried out two actions which earned them the lasting hatred of the Levant peoples. On 7 July about thirty-six vessels appeared off Barcelona and on 10 July began a bombardment of the city that lasted from 6 a.m. to the evening, and continued the next day from 6 a.m. to midday.[12] On 13 July the fleet sailed southwards. About 800 bombs had been used, over 300 houses were levelled. To the Spaniards it was a barbarous and gratuitous attack on the civilian population, and a thrill of horror ran through the country. Worse was to come. In Alicante there were riots against the resident French on the nights of 22 and 23 July, when the news from Barcelona arrived; on the 25th the French navy appeared off Alicante and turned its guns against the city. In the space of four days, as the city council reported to Madrid, the French fired over 3,500 bombs into Alicante, causing immense devastation and leaving only one-tenth of the buildings untouched. Their 'barbarous inhumanity' (the words of the municipality) also led to fires that burnt out the town hall and the city archive.[13] After nine days before Alicante the French passed on. They left behind a city in total disorder, with fires and destruction on every side, their own French nationals totally ruined by the sacking and looting that was perpetrated by the populace.[14]

The savagery of the attacks on Barcelona and Alicante united Spaniards. The Catalan leadership in particular was now resolutely on the side of Spain. In gratitude for the loyalty of the ruling classes during the popular revolt, the Crown in February 1690 granted back to the Consellers of Barcelona the privilege of keeping their heads covered in the royal presence, which had been denied them since 1632 in the Corts presided over by the Cardinal Infante. The Diputació was granted the titles of Most Illustrious and Most Faithful, and the Braç Militar that of Most Faithful.[15] These highly significant concessions sealed the reconciliation between Barcelona and Madrid.[16] They also emphasised the split between Barcelona and Catalonia. The rural classes continued the agitation. In July 1691 though most towns in the vicinity of Barcelona had paid the donativo, in the area of Tarragona about one-third and in Cervera nearly half still refused.[17]

On 28 May 1693 the fortress of Rosas, Catalonia's chief naval base, was invested at sea by over fifty French vessels and on land by the main invading army under Noailles; on 9 June it capitulated, and its gallant governor[18] died of his wounds. Medina Sidonia, viceroy since December 1690, made no attempt to excuse its fall on the grounds of inadequate men or supplies; on the contrary, he admitted, there were more than enough of both: the problem was that 'there is no fortification in Catalonia that can resist such heavy artillery and bombing'.[19] The campaign of 1694 was equally disastrous. On 27 May the Spanish troops were beaten in a bloody encounter at the river Ter, near Gerona. The following week the fortress of Palamos was occupied by the French. On 29 June the fortress city of Gerona capitulated after a week's siege.[20] The marquis of Villena, viceroy since December 1693, proved unable to reverse the tide of losses and was replaced the following November by the marquis of Gastañaga.

On seeing the situation in Catalonia the new viceroy lamented that 'no one man (even one more able than I) could work miracles on this scale'.[21] The struggle now was to save Barcelona. The Anglo-Dutch fleet under Russell gave some token help by sea, and in June 1695 German forces under prince George of Hesse-Darmstadt reinforced the garrison. The most successful Spanish actions of the period were carried out less by the main troops than by the peasant irregulars or *miguelets*, under their commander Blas Trinxería.[22] In February 1696 the Diputació addressed to the king an exaggerated lament of their defencelessness.[23] In fact the relative strengths of either side by land were in favour of Spain: official French figures state that in summer 1696 the French had in Catalonia 8,862 infantry, 2,177 cavalry and 1,154 dragoons, a total of 12,193 of which some had to be used as garrison troops, whereas the Spaniards early in 1697 had garrisoned Barcelona with 12,380 troops, with a further 8,640 outside the city, and a separate force of 2,140 under the viceroy, giving a defence force of over 23,000.[24] Superior artillery and a naval presence, however, gave the French under the duke of Vendôme a clear advantage. In the first week of June 1697 the enemy invested Barcelona with 18,000 infantry and 7,000 cavalry, according to Feliu de la Peña.[25] By sea the investing force consisted of fourteen warships, thirty galleys, three bomb-ships and eighty small vessels. The Chancellor of the Audiencia, Dr Miguel Taverner, reported:[26]

The enemy laid siege to Barcelona on 12 June. All the nobility remained in the city and the besieged defended themselves for two whole months with great valour among the soldiers and indescribable endurance among the citizens. This siege has witnessed more blood and fire than any seen in our time. The bombs ruined a great part of the city, both private houses and public buildings and churches . . . The persistence of the enemy and the impossibility of relief were cause for responding to the demand to capitulate which the enemy made.

The city capitulated on 10 August and on the 15th Vendôme entered. Feliu de la Peña and other members of the élite left the city rather than live under French rule.

As soon as the news of the surrender reached Madrid there was anger and dismay. Despite his recurrent illness, on 20 August the king issued a decree expressing his intention to go to Saragossa, as his father had done in similar circumstances in 1642, and thence to the Catalan front.[27] The plan was overtaken by events. On 20 September peace was signed at Rijswijk. The news reached Madrid the next day, to the great joy of the king and the entire people.

## THE QUESTION OF THE SUCCESSION

The problem of the succession dominated European politics throughout the lifetime of Charles II. Public interest in the person of the queen and in the health of the king was invariably involved with the hope for an heir to the throne. The sad death of Marie Louise, and the malicious rumours that arose from it, impugning in particular the count of Oropesa,[28] were unfortunate complications in the way of a solution to the succession. The king's rapid remarriage, to Mariana of Neuburg, brought no heir. Indeed by this time it was universally recognised that short of a miracle the king would be unable to sire an heir. Only in this limited context does the matter of a bewitching assume any importance. The case of Fray Froilán Díaz, which will be discussed below, is relevant for its political undertones rather than for its nominal connection with witchcraft.

Louis XIV's interest in the Spanish throne went back to his marriage, formalised by the treaty of 9 June 1660, to María Teresa, daughter of Philip IV.[29] Both the treaty and Philip IV's later will made it clear that María Teresa and her issue were excluded from succession to the throne of Spain. At no time did Louis or his advisers ever take the renunciations seriously; from the first they looked on the marriage as a means of unifying the two crowns. The ambassador to Madrid, the archbishop of Embrun, was instructed in 1661 to sound the opinions of Spaniards, and in August that year he reported back to Louis that the secretary of Don Luis de Haro had confided to him that he considered the renunciations invalid. Louis was not surprised. Don Luis himself, he wrote to the archbishop, had said much the same to the late Cardinal Mazarin.[30]

The subsequent policy of France towards the Spanish succession became the primary issue in Euopean war and diplomacy.[31] Bribery in Madrid, diplomatic pressure in foreign courts, and military aggression against the Spanish empire, made up Louis's three-pronged attack on the succession question. The initial — and correct — excuse was that the dowry of Maria Teresa had never been paid, and that this automatically made the renunciations invalid. Yet the marriage treaties had never made payment of the dowry an explicit condition of renunciation. Moreover, Louis himself betrayed what importance he attached to the money by ordering the archbishop of Embrun in November 1661 to suspend all demands for payment, since the recent death of the Spanish heir, Baltasar Carlos, left the succession momentarily vacant. Only when a new heir, Charles, was born on 6 November did he decide to resume his demands.

Failing complete possession of the monarchy, Louis had to provide for partial possession. A partition treaty, signed secretly at Vienna on 19 January 1668 with the Emperor Leopold I, who firmly maintained his own direct claim to the throne as the grandson of Philip III, agreed on a division of the monarchy if the sickly Charles II died without an heir. The Emperor would get Spain, the Indies and the north Italian territories including Milan. France would get the Netherlands, Franche Comté, the Philippines, Navarre, Naples and other dependencies. The treaty had followed Louis's first substantial aggressions into the Netherlands in 1667, when Turenne's forces seized Charleroi, Douai and other fortresses. It was in turn followed immediately by Condé's invasion in February 1668 of Franche Comté. Louis was skilfully using war to support his diplomacy, and the subsequent peace negotiated at Aix-la-Chapelle (May 1668) gave him an initiative which he never thereafter lost.

All Spaniards had good reason to consider Louis XIV their principal enemy. But the enmity was only formal, and it would be impossible to understand the eventual outcome of the succession if we did not appreciate the immense reserves of reluctant admiration for France that existed in Madrid. As early as May 1666 there is the following report from the English ambassador Godolphin:[32]

There is nothing which the people of this country (and I believe of all the other kingdoms of Spain) . . . abhorre more than a warre with France. . . . I have heard some say that a war between them and France would bee very unnatural, the French king being next in succession to this Crowne, and by all the notices I have of the present temper of this people I am persuaded, if it should happen that the young king dye as things now stand, they would tamely goe into the obedience of France.

The mood changed somewhat in later years, particularly in the Crown of Aragon where hostility to France, founded it is true on social reasons rather than foreign policy alone, became an overriding passion that readily explains the events of the War of Succession under Philip V. Attitudes to a possible French succession became strongly politicised with the growth of German influence at Madrid. In 1689 the Emperor Leopold obtained two great advantages: he was given a guarantee by England and the United Provinces, both now under the command of William III of Orange, of possession of Spain at the death of Charles II; and he obtained powerful influence at court through the marriage of Mariana of Neuburg.

The maritime powers – England and the Dutch – consequently became arbiters between the conflicting interests of France and Austria. Since the succession of either would create a major change in the European balance of power, there were good grounds for finding an alternative. By the end of 1693 Louis XIV was tending to concede the succession to the infant son (born 1692) of the Elector of Bavaria. There was also a strong movement in this direction at the Spanish court. The Queen Mother, Mariana of Austria, was a strong supporter of

Fig. 15.1 Claimants to the Spanish Succession.

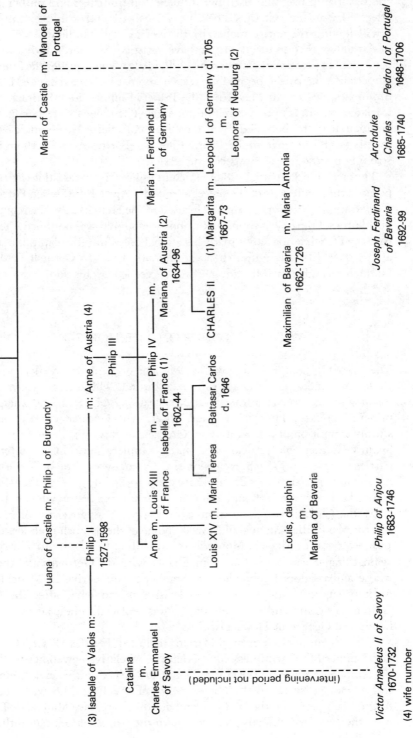

the Bavarian cause, and used her influence on ministers and on her son to this effect. That autumn Charles II became seriously ill, and on 14 September drew up a will leaving the entire monarchy to the Bavarian candidate.

Although this solution might have satisfied Spaniards, who were wholly concerned to preserve the monarchy undivided, it kept neither the French nor the Imperialists happy. So began four years of intense manoeuvring at Madrid and in diplomatic circles. In May 1697 the Imperial ambassador Harrach arrived, to initiate a strenuous pro-German campaign. The omens were not in his favour; German help to besieged Barcelona was considered inadequate, and many members of the government with Cardinal Portocarrero at their head were strongly opposed to an Imperial succession.

The arrival in January 1698 of Harcourt as French ambassador was the turning point in the whole saga of the succession. From April 1698, when Portocarrero in conversation with him committed himself to the French cause, Harcourt began to build up a solid party of support. Curiously enough it was not until 15 September that the French ambassador made his official entry into the capital: a sumptuous affair, more like a triumph than a diplomatic visit. In October Ferdinand von Harrach retired from Madrid. He was succeeded by his son.


## DARK CLOUDS ON THE HORIZON

The fall of Oropesa in June 1691 left Mariana of Neuburg in effective control of the court, since there was no valido appointed. The queen's German advisers insinuated themselves into the administration. Chief among them was her private secretary, Heinrich Xavier Wiser. The German connection was not simply a question of court intrigue. On the contrary, it reflected the realities of Spain's international position and made complete sense in the interests of all parties opposed to French expansionism. Germany was the only great Catholic nation in a position to offer military help to Spain. The councillors of State realised this very well, though reluctantly. It was the reason why on 4 December 1691 the Council voted unanimously to appoint as governor of Flanders the Elector Maximilian Manuel of Bavaria. None of the Spanish grandees offered the post – Montalto, Melgar, Monterey – was willing to take it on. The current war against France was being fought in alliance with the Germans and the English, whose ambassadors Lobkowitz and Stanhope were active in Madrid. German military support, finally, was the decisive reason why, after the failures of Gastañaga's command in Catalonia, he was replaced, albeit far too late, by the Landgrave George of Hesse-Darmstadt.

The influential circle around Mariana included, besides Wiser, the lady of the bedchamber Maria, countess von Berlepsch. A relative newcomer to politics was the temporary Master of the Horse, Don Pedro de la Cerda y Leiva, count of Baños and a grandee since 1691. The secretary of the Despacho was Don Juan de Angulo, appointed to the post in October 1691 to replace Manuel de Lira. These were the principal officials identified with the period of German influence, and their names were repeated endlessly in the satires scattered through Madrid.

Throughout the 1690s the Spanish government existed in a state of what can suitably be called permanent bankruptcy. The principal cause of the undoubted breakdown in command at this time was the lack of funds. When introducing his budget figures for 1690 the president of the council of Finance, Los Vélez, had stressed the seriousness of the situation, but looking forward to 1691 he saw virtually no hope of sufficient income. All the standard methods of raising income were also not helpful: stopping salaries was bad, stopping payment to bankers ruined both them and the state, and 'asking for donativos is a waste of time'.[33]

The Hacienda reform of 1688, although assuring ·the Crown a minimum income, had never attempted to solve its financial problems, and in August 1692 a special committee was accordingly set up to try to find money for the war. This Committee of Means consisted of various members of the councils headed by Don Antonio Ibáñez de la Riba Herrera, president of Castile and archbishop of Saragossa, and by Don Pedro Núñez de Prado, count of Adanero since 1691, president of the Hacienda. The principal effective measure taken, and decreed in November 1692, was the suspension of all payment of state debts contracted up to the year 1690, other than those affecting the royal household or the war.[34] This decree affected pensions, salaries and similar payments. It inevitably brought the Committee into disrepute, as did the other measures — such as a donativo — decreed by the government. Few ministers with financial expertise were available; Los Vélez died on 2 November 1693.

In January 1693 Stanhope reported that

the present exigencies of the monarchy are inconceivable, most of the bills they have sent for Flanders lately being sent back protested. . . . I am assured by a person allowed to understand the public revenue as well as any man, that upon no branch of it can be found a credit for 100,000 crowns, be the occasion ever so urgent.[35]

In one form or another, all government payments from 1693 to 1699 were suspended.[36] The suspensions were not always the same; in 1694, for example, the pay of all officials of the councils was cut by one third;[37] in 1694 and 1695 asentistas were repaid only for current contracts but not for preceding ones. It is not surprising to find, as Stanhope informed a correspondent in 1694, that 'all the funds are already anticipated for so many years that he [the president of the Hacienda Adanero] can find nobody will advance'. In 1698 Adanero was reported as saying that 'he is not able to find money for his Majesty's subsistence, all branches of the revenue being anticipated for many years'.[38]

In July 1699 the council of Finance produced a balance sheet for the current financial year showing that taxes would produce just over 9 million escudos vellon. Over one-third of this would go to pay juristas, and under a third towards the 4 million set aside by the 1688 decree; lesser sums were reserved for pensions and asentistas.[39] This left about 2 million available for the war. The sum was unfortunately of limited value, particularly since half the payments in Catalonia had to be made in silver.

Concern over the war, the succession, finance and general policy, was intensified by the lack of adequate central direction in Madrid; there was no coordination of policy between 1689 and 1694. It was impractical to approach the king. Foreign envoys were perplexed and impatient at the chaos. Stanhope wrote at the end of 1692: 'Here is a hot rumour of a Valido to be suddenly declared. . . . I heartily wish it were done, for then I should know whom to apply to, whereas nobody pretends to do anything and so nothing is done.'[40]

To this period of indecision belongs one of the most curious experiments in Spanish history, the brainchild of the Imperial ambassador Lobkowitz.[41] In October 1693 the king sent a letter to all the councils, all cities with a vote in Cortes, and all the provincial capitals of Spain, informing them of the appointment of four lieutenant-generals to govern Spain. The nominees were all grandees with military experience. Montalto was appointed to New Castile, the Constable to Old Castile, the Admiral to Andalucia and the Canaries, Monterey to the Crown of Aragon. Each was given 'authority over all captains general and governors . . ., and since matters of civil policy and finance are not therein included they may intervene only in expenditure relating to military matters'.[42] Their duties were in effect exclusively military. The grandiose plan quickly collapsed. First Monterrey withdrew because of his rivalry with Montalto, then the Constable decided to pull out early in 1694. For a brief while they had taken a major part in government: for example, the special meeting of the council of State on 21 January 1694 to discuss Louis XIV's peace terms consisted only of three lieutenant-generals with Portocarrero and Mancera.

By the spring of 1694, as Stanhope observed, 'the chief minister here in effect is the duke of Montalto'.[43] The duke was an industrious minister who refused to entrust any of his administrative work to a secretary; he kept letter-books of his official correspondence, and wrote out all his consultas in his own hand.[44] His period of influence was short. By 1695 the crisis in war and finance had stirred the councillors to protest.

Any observer of political life in Madrid in the 1690s would have been familiar with the scores of satires and pasquins written up on walls or distributed in sheets.[45] Many were clearly influenced by factions among the nobility; others were an expression of public opinion that ministers could seldom afford to ignore. In December 1694 the council of Castile took the startling step of presenting itself as the voice of the people arraigning the government. Ire was directed principally against the queen's German advisers and, as Stanhope reported, 'the assembling of the Cortes was proposed by some in the Council, as the only remedy to save the monarchy'.[46] When the consulta of the council of Castile was debated in the council of State, Cardinal Portocarrero criticised its failure to name names and supplied them: Berlepsch, Wiser, and the rest. Montalto called for their expulsion from Spain, and was supported by Monterrey, who felt it to be as necessary as the expulsion of the Moriscos had been. The Admiral was one of the few to defend the Germans. The conflict went from bad to worse. The king refused to follow the feeling of his councillors. Wiser condemned the whole move as a plot against the king,

with the intention of summoning a Cortes, no less; when what they secretly intend is to declare the king incapable of governing, confine him, send the queen to a convent and bring the son of the Elector of Bavaria and set him on the throne under the Regency of the Queen Mother . . . When the king told Montalto that the queen had had three miscarriages within fourteen months, he replied that nobody believed it . . .[47]

The ludicrous allegations of a plot were merely a sign of the tense political situation. It was also clear to everybody that the queen was trying to control Charles II through spurious hopes of a son and heir. On 4 January 1695 Portocarrero presented to the king a strongly worded representation demanding that 'these people (*esa gente*) leave Your Majesty's dominions'. The queen's response was to obtain from the king, on 9 January, the appointment of the Admiral to the coveted post of Master of the Horse; a few days later she also obtained the dismissal of Don Alonso Carnero, secretary since the death of Angulo in 1693, from the Despacho. The grandees combined to put pressure on the king and obtain some satisfaction. At the end of January Wiser was accordingly notified that he must leave Madrid. On 28 February he left with orders to proceed to Italy.

Though Wiser was dropped the German party continued in power, and the grandee most identified with their cause was the Admiral, who in these days exercised great influence but without the position of chief minister. In September 1695 a serious diplomatic incident took place, when the Dutch ambassador, Schoenberg, a Jew, was expelled from Madrid for giving protection to converso merchants persecuted by the Inquisition.

On Wednesday 16 May 1696 Mariana of Austria died after a painful illness caused by breast cancer. Her body was entombed the following Sunday in the Escorial. The king and queen were also both intermittently ill during most of this year. Stanhope reported of the king's sickness in early September that 'they cut his hair off, which the decay of nature had almost done before, all his crown being bald. He has a ravenous stomach and swallows all he eats whole, for his nether jaw stands so much out that his two rows of teeth cannot meet.'[48] Important state business was neglected because of preoccupation with the health of the thirty-five-year-old king.

Barcelona fell, as we have seen, in August 1697. The victorious French took great care to preserve untouched all the privileges of the Catalans, but gave themselves the luxury of suppressing the Inquisition. Prince George of Hesse-Darmstadt returned to Madrid in November and was rewarded for his services with the Golden Fleece and a grandeeship; he was also made a gentleman of the bedchamber and appointed next viceroy of Catalonia, where he returned to take the oath, after the French withdrawal, in February 1698.[49]

The most significant changes at court early in 1698 were the appointment in March of a new royal confessor, Fray Froilán Díaz, and the recall to power that month of Oropesa, who assumed the presidency of Castile. From January there was also a new secretary of the Despacho, Don Antonio de Ubilla. Throughout the year political attention was concentrated on the king's health and the succession. It was agreed that the king would not long survive. Stanhope in June described Charles's fainting fits, and in July believed that 'there is not the least hope of the king's recovery';[50] Charles, he wrote to his son, 'looks like a ghost and moves like an image of clock work. They talk of a diet of hens and capons, fed with vipers' flesh.'[51]

Towards the end of 1698 the mood in Castile and Madrid was overwhelmingly in favour of a French succession. No less a person than the Admiral, who had always been the leader of the German faction, let it be known in September than an accommodation should be made with Louis. At this juncture Madrid was shaken by news of the First Partition Treaty, signed by Louis with Holland on 11 October. According to this, the Electoral Prince would receive Spain and its empire outside Europe, leaving Milan to the archduke Charles of Austria, and the Sicilies, some Italian possessions and Guipúzcoa to the Dauphin. The Spanish reaction was firm and unanimous. On Friday 14 November the council of State, presided over by the king, met in secret session for three hours. Three days before, on 11 November, Charles had drawn up and signed a new will, nominating the Electoral Prince as sole heir to the whole monarchy, 'in all my kingdoms, states and dominions'. He now read this out in full to his councillors. Like the Partition Treaty, Charles's decision was never made public, though it became common knowledge; he continued to deny the will's existence even in closed sessions with foreign ambassadors, notably Harrach and Harcourt.

The death of the Electoral Prince in February 1699 threw Madrid into confusion. Hard on the heels of this disappointment came the popular disturbances occasioned by food shortages. The riots of 28 April in the capital were directed against Oropesa, but in fact threatened all parties. Councillors and grandees took refuge in the royal palace; different mobs shouted their support for France or for the Empire, resulting in differing reports home from Harcourt and Harrach. Stanhope said the riots were 'such as the like never before happened in Madrid in the memory of the oldest men here'.[52]

The riots caused confusion in the government. The councils of State and Castile refused to accept the resignation of Oropesa, which had so clearly been the result of mob terror. Commonsense prevailed, and on 9 May Charles issued instructions for the exile of the valido. The power vacuum led to hurried negotiations between factions: the principal casualty was the Admiral, exiled by a decree of 23 May. The group now in control was that led by Cardinal Portocarrero.[53] Popular feeling blamed the queen's party for mistakes of government policy. The capital remained tense throughout the summer. On 5 June a diplomat reported that 'trade is dead, there are 40,000 artisans out of work, beggars are dying of hunger and crimes are committed daily in the streets for want of bread'.[54]

The succession was resolved for Louis XIV by an agreement with William III at the Hague, signed by the parties on 11 June. According to this proposal the archduke was to receive the bulk of the Spanish empire, leaving the Dauphin with what had been assigned by the First Partition, together with Lorraine, and the duke of Lorraine was to receive Milan or Savoy. The agreement was not formalised because it was hoped to gain the support of the Emperor. Charles II was meanwhile undergoing some unusual treatment.

Early in 1698 a Dominican friar in the Asturias had revealed to Fray Froilán Díaz that a recently exorcised nun was claiming that the king had been bewitched since the age of fourteen through the agency of a drug that made him impotent. The Inquisitor General, Rocaberti, was sceptical; but after his death in June 1699 Froilán Díaz felt free to extend his enquiries.[55] Using his influence over the royal couple, Díaz persuaded the king to see a wandering exorcist of Savoyard origin, Fray Mauro Tenda. The interview with the exorcist took place in June, and a detailed report of the bizarre proceedings was sent to Vienna by the Imperial ambassador, Harrach.[56] The part played by the affair in the king's long illness was minimal, and has usually been exaggerated. In January 1700 Tenda was arrested and interrogated, and Froilán Díaz was subsequently disgraced.

For the moment the exorcisms had their desired psychological effect. The king felt better, well enough indeed to make a jornada that autumn to the Escorial. For Charles and his queen it was like a second honeymoon, and the hope of a succession was renewed. At the end of November several new councillors of State were named, including the new duke of Medinaceli, Medina Sidonia, Veraguas, Santisteban; all were partisans of the queen.

The following spring, on 1 April 1700 the court went again to the Escorial, largely because the air outside Madrid seemed to make the king healthier. The party returned in May because of inclement weather and went instead to Aranjuez. News then came through of the signature on 25 March of the last stage of the Second Partition Treaty, between France and the maritime powers, with the provisions agreed upon the previous June; the Emperor was not a party to it, but other powers were invited to sign. The papal nuncio handed a copy of the text to Cardinal Portocarrero. Ministers of state advised a broad range of urgent steps: separate approaches to each of the powers, an appeal to the pope, summoning the Cortes and so on. In June 1700 the Emperor's reaction to the treaty reached Madrid: without in any way rejecting it, he described it as 'unjust' and asked to learn what Charles II's intentions were. This ambiguous message confirmed the growing opposition to the Imperial candidate, who was supported in the council of State by only one grandee, Aguilar.

The feelings of the council, which met on 6 June, were quite clear.[57] Uppermost in the minds of all ministers was the need to preserve the integrity of the monarchy, and to put it in hands powerful enough to guarantee that integrity. Their view was crystallised in the vote of the marquis del Fresno, 'that Your Majesty cede the whole monarchy to a grandson of the king of France, on the assurance that there will be no unification of the two Crowns'. The decisive influence on the king's decision was the pope's opinion, dated 6 July 1700, agreeing with 'the view of Your Majesty's royal council, based on the primordial need to assure preservation of the unity of the monarchy'. The French ambassador, who closely observed Charles II during a corrida on 21 June, felt that 'since the meeting of the council the king is more relaxed than usual'.

All through the summer there were delays, because Charles was unwilling to make a will that the French king might reject. On 13 August the Spanish ambassador, Castelldosrius, was received in audience by Louis but failed to receive a clear answer about French intentions. Louis's dilemma was obvious. As he put it to his envoy Blécourt on 30 August, if he accepted the Crown for his grandson he stood condemned for breach of faith with the Partition Treaty, and if he said no the Crown would go to the Emperor's son.

That month Charles became seriously ill again. As his sickness grew worse, the alarm in Madrid grew greater; the king refused to make a will regulating the succession. On 28 September he was administered Extreme Unction. From day to day the diplomats awaited news of his death. Finally on 7 October Blécourt sent this report to the Sun King: 'On Sunday the 3rd, between six and seven in the evening, the king signed a will drawn up by Cardinal Portocarrero. The duke of Medina Sidonia, who was present, sent me a message to say that it is in favour of one of Your Majesty's grandsons.' Clause thirteen of the will named Philip, duke of Anjou, second son of the Dauphin of France, 'to the succession of all my kingdoms and dominions, without exception of any'.

His health failing, Charles on 29 October appointed Portocarrero as Regent of the monarchy. The same afternoon he received the last sacraments. Just before 3 p.m. on 1 November 1700, All Saints' Day, the last Habsburg king of Spain died. On 6 November after the customary exposition his body was taken to the Escorial and interred the next day.[58] Within the month the new French king was proclaimed in Madrid.

## NOTES

1. BN MS. 2401/270–1, 294.
2. Trobat to Louvois, 6 Jan. 1689, Guerre A[1] 899/2.
3. Don Carlos de Gurrea, count of Luna and Sástago, an Aragonese nobleman; governor of Flanders 1675–80; d. Aug. 1692.
4. Letters of Feb. 1689 in ACA:CA 230/46.
5. Letter of 25 May 1689, Guerre A[1] 899/125.
6. The accounts of the war chest from 1689 to 1690 are summarised in BL Eg. MS. 328/18–31.
7. Viceroy to Don Manuel de Lira, 17 Dec. 1689, BN MS. 2400/187.
8. Du Bruelli, governor of Bellegarde, to Louvois, 25 Jan 1690, Guerre A[1] 1013/51.
9. Their consulta of 10 Dec. 1689, in BN MS. 2402/296–305 in copy, is the single best survey of the rebellions of 1687–89.
10. Trobat to Louvois, 6 May 1690, Guerre A[1] 1015/22.
11. Full names and details of plotters in *ibid.* 1106/88.
12. Details in the printed accounts in BL Eg. MS. 328/35–7; and Guerre A[1] 1104/103.
13. Letter of Valencia to council of Aragon, 2 Aug. 1691, ACA:CA 672.
14. A detailed report in *ibid.* 844.
15. Cf. Kamen, 'Catalan Peasant Rising of 1688', pp. 228–9.
16. Feliu in his *Anales* (III, 404) claimed that the privilege of covering was the same as grandeeship, and the Consellers also claimed this, but the Madrid authorities resolutely refused to admit this; see correspondence of Sept. 1690 by the council of State in AGS Estado 4163.
17. Duke of Medina Sidonia to council, 27 July 1691, ACA:CA 461.
18. D. Pedro Rubi y de Sabater: his correspondence is in BL Eg. MS. 328/50–3.
19. Medina Sidonia to council, 12 June 1693, ACA:CA 465.
20. This was the third siege of Gerona in this reign: the others were in 1675 and 1684.

21. Gastañaga to Medina Sidonia, 11 Jan. 1695, ACA:CA 232/30.
22. Feliu, *Anales*, III, 419.
23. Diputació to Charles II, 25 Feb. 1696, ACA:CA 230/52.
24. 'Estat des troupes qui composent l'armee du Roy', Guerre A[1] 1418/2; 'Estat des troupes d'Espagne', *ibid.* 1418/25.
25. Feliu, *Anales*, III, 431–50, gives the best available survey of the siege.
26. Taverner and Audiencia to the council, from Tarragona, 29 Aug. 1679, ACA:CA 470.
27. Diputación of Aragon to king, 2 Sept. 1697, BL Eg. MS. 328/110.
28. It was alleged that Oropesa, who was related to the Braganzas, wanted the queen dead so that he could marry Charles II to Maria, the only child of Pedro II of Portugal: he could then assume the throne of Portugal. The story is refuted by Maura, *Vida y reinado*, II, 237–8.
29. The definitive study of France and the succession is **Legrelle, A.**, *La Diplomatie française* (Paris 1888–92). See also **Mignet, M.**, *Négociations* (Paris 1835–42).
30. Mignet, *op. cit.* I, 74; Legrelle, *op. cit.* I, 31.
31. See Kamen, *War of Succession*, pp. 1–5.
32. Letter of 6 May 1666, PRO:SP 94/50/199.
33. Report by Los Vélez, 4 Dec. 1690, AGS Estado 4138.
34. Decree of 28 Nov. 1692, AGS:CJH 1190.
35. Stanhope to Nottingham, 1 Jan. 1693, *Spain under Charles*, p. 42.
36. Consulta of Finance, 9 Mar. 1697, AGS:CJH 1225; consulta of 12 June 1699, *ibid.* 1240.
37. Decree of 22 Dec. 1693 in consulta of 10 Feb. 1695, *ibid.* 1204. See also Stanhope, *op. cit.* p. 56.
38. Stanhope to Godolphin, 8 Oct. 1694; to Mr Yard, 28 May 1698; *op. cit.* pp. 68–9, 131–2.
39. Consulta of council, July 1699, AGS:CJH 1249.
40. Stanhope to Nottingham, 17 Dec. 1692, *op. cit.* p. 40.
41. Thus according to Maura, *Vida y reinado*, II, 45; but attributed to Montalto by the author of the 1694 *Memorias Históricas*, p. 138.
42. Instructions to viceroy of Valencia, 26 Oct. 1693, ARV:RC 594/257.
43. Stanhope to Halifax, 31 May 1694, *op. cit.* p. 62.
44. *Memorias Históricas*, p. 146.
45. For examples see the selection by **Egido, T.**, *Sátiras políticas* (Madrid 1973), pp. 180–203.
46. Stanhope to Galway, 16 Dec. 1694, *op. cit.* p. 71.
47. Maura, *Vida y reinado*, II, 74.
48. Stanhope to Shrewsbury, 19 Sept. 1696, *op. cit.* p. 99.
49. His predecessor, the count of la Corzana, viceroy since July 1697, was not recognised as such by the Catalans since he took his oath not in besieged Barcelona but in Vilafranca.
50. Stanhope to Methuen, 9 July 1698, *oip. cit.* p. 137.
51. *Idem* to son James, 9 July, *op. cit.* p. 138.
52. *Idem* 29 April 1699, *op. cit.* p. 167. The political aspect of the riots is discussed in Maura, *Vida y reinado*, II, 258–64.
53. Don Luis de Portocarrero, brother of the count of Palma, Cardinal 1669, councillor of State and archbishop of Toledo 1677, later Regent of Spain under Philip V, d. 1709 aged 74.
54. Maura, *op. cit.* II, 270.

55. For the relation of the Froilán Díaz affair to the internal politics of the Inquisition see Lea, *Inquisition*, III, 168–78.
56. See Maura, *Vida y reinado*, II, 301–3.
57. Text of their votes in *ibid*. II, 356–7.
58. 'He was', wrote Feliu de la Peña, 'the best king Spain ever had. . . . Of all the kings he was the only one who gave his life for his people': *Anales*, III, 458.

# Bibliography

This bibliography is restricted primarily to items cited in the notes and is meant to serve as a guide to the growing amount of material available on Spain during the period of its alleged decadence.

ADLER, ELKAN, 'Documents sur les Marranes d'Espagne et de Portugal sous Philippe IV', *Revue des Etudes Juives*, 48–51 (1904–6).

ALCALA-ZAMORA Y QUEIPO DE LLANO, JOSÉ, *Historia de una empresa siderúrgica española: los altos hornos de Liérganes y La Cavada, 1622–1834*, Santander 1974.

ALCOUFFE, DANIEL, 'Contribution à la connaissance des émigrés français de Madrid au XVIIe siècle', *Mélanges de la Casa de Vélázquez*, 2 (1966), 179–98.

ALDEA VAQUERO, Q., et al., *Diccionario de Historia Eclesiástica de España*. 4 vols, Madrid 1972–73.

ALONSO, SANTIAGO, *El pensamiento regalista de Francisco Salgado de Somoza (1595–1665)*, Salamanca 1973.

ANÉS, GONZALO, *Las crisis agrarias en la España moderna*, Madrid 1970.

ANÉS, GONZALO, ed., *Memoriales y Discursos de Francisco Martínez de Mata*, Madrid 1971.

ARNOLDSSON, SVERKER, *La Leyenda Negra: estudios sobre sus orígenes*, Göteborg 1960.

ASSO, IGNACIO DE, *Historia de la Economía Política de Aragón*, Saragossa 1798.

ASTRAÍN, ANTONIO, S. J., *Historia de la Compañía de Jesús en la Asistencia de España*, VI *(1652–1705)*, Madrid 1920.

BACALLAR Y SANNA, VICENTE, marquis of San Felipe, *Comentarios de la guerra de España e historia de su rey Felipe V el Animoso*, Madrid 1957 edn.

BAKEWELL, P. J., *Silver Mining and Society in Colonial Mexico: Zacatecas, 1546–1700*, Cambridge 1971.

BAROZZI, NICOLO and BERCHET, GUGLIELMO, *Relazioni degli Stati Europei lette al Senato dagli Ambasciatori Veneti nel secolo decimosettimo*. Serie I, Spagna. Vol. II, Venice 1860.

BARREIRO, BAUDILIO, *La Jurisdicción de Xallas en el Siglo XVIII. Población, Sociedad y Economía*. Santiago 1973.

BASAS FERNÁNDEZ, MANUEL, 'Vida y Fortuna de los Gortázar, caballeros ilustrados de Bilbao en el siglo XVIII', *Anuario de Historia Económica y Social*, 1 (1968), 403–59.

BENEYTO PÉREZ, JUAN, *Historia de la Administración Española y Hispano-Americana*, Madrid 1958.

BENNASSAR, BARTOLOMÉ, *Valladolid au siècle d'or. Une ville de Castille et sa campagne au XVIe siècle*, Paris 1967.

BENNASSAR, BARTOLOMÉ, *Recherches sur les grandes épidémies dans le nord de l'Espagne à la fin du XVIe siècle*, Paris 1969.

BENNASSAR, BARTOLOMÉ, *L'homme espagnol. Attitudes et mentalités du XVIe au XIXe siècle*, Paris 1975.

BERTAUT, FRANÇOIS, *Relation d'un voyage d'Espagne*, Paris 1664.

BILBAO, LUIS MARÍA, 'Crisis y reconstrucción de la Economía Vascongada en el siglo XVII', *Saioak. Revista de Estudios Vascos* (San Sebastián), 1 (1977), 157–80.

BRANDES, STANLEY H., *Migration, Kinship and Community: Tradition and Transition in a Spanish village*, London 1975.

BRAUDEL, FERNAND, *The Mediterranean and the Mediterranean World in the Age of Philip II*, 2 vols, London 1973.

BRAUNSTEIN, BARUCH, *The Chuetas of Majorca. Conversos and the Inquisition of Majorca*, Philadelphia 1936; new edn, New York 1972.

BREMUNDAN, FRANCISCO FABRO, *Historia de los hechos del Sereníssimo Señor Don Juan de Austria en el Principado de Cataluña*, Saragossa 1673.

BRINES BLASCO, JUAN, 'Aportación al estudio de la demografía del país valenciano. La comarca de Valldigna durante los siglos XVI al XIX', *III Congreso Nacional de Historia de la Medicina*, 3 vols, Valencia 1969. II, 219–34.

BRUNEL, ANTOINE DE, *A Journey into Spain*, London 1670.

*Burguesía Mercantil Gaditana (1650–1868)*, Cadiz 1976. **Papers of the XXXI** Congreso Luso-Español, Cadiz.

CABESTANY FORT, JUAN F., 'Nomina de la "Matricula de Mercaders" de Barcelona (1479–1696)', *Documentos y Estudios. Aportaciones a la Historia Económica y Social de la Ciudad*, 13 (1964), 167–83.

CABESTANY FORT, JUAN F., 'Aportación a la nomina de los "Ciutadans Honrats" de Barcelona', *ibid.* 10 (1962), 11–61.

CABO ALONSO, ANGEL, 'La Armuña y su evolución económica', *Estudios Geográficos*, 58 (Feb. 1955), 73–136.

CALLAHAN, WILLIAM J., 'Paupers and Nobles: the Santa y Real Hermandad del Refugio y Piedad of Madrid, 1618–1832' (unpubl. dissertation).

CALLAHAN, WILLIAM J., 'La estimación del trabajo manual en la España del siglo XVIII', *Revista Chilena de Historia y Geografía*, 132 (1964), 59–72.

CALLAHAN, WILLIAM J., 'Crown, nobility and industry in eighteenth-century Spain'. *International Review of Social History*, 11 (1966), 444–64.

CALLAHAN, WILLIAM J., 'A note on the Real y General Junta de Comercio, 1679–1814', *Economic History Review*, 21, iii (1968), 519–28.

CALLAHAN, WILLIAM J., 'Don Juan de Goyeneche: Industrialist of Eighteenth-Century Spain', *The Business History Review*, 43, ii (1969), 152–70.

CALLAHAN, WILLIAM J., *Honor, Commerce and Industry in Eighteenth-Century Spain*, Boston 1972.

CALLAHAN, WILLIAM J., 'Corporate Charity in Spain: the Hermandad del Refugio of Madrid 1618–1814', *Histoire Sociale* (Ottawa), 9 (1976), 159–86.

CALONGE, M. P., *et al.*, *Castilla la Vieja*. Vol. III of *La España del Antiguo Regimen*, ed. M. Artola, Salamanca 1967.

CAMPOMANES, PEDRO RODRÍGUEZ DE, count of, *Apéndice a la Educación Popular*, 4 vols, Madrid 1775–77.

CANGA ARGÜELLES, JOSÉ, *Diccionario de Hacienda*, 2 vols, Madrid 1833–34.

CAPELLA, M. and MATILLA TASCÓN, A., *Los Cinco Gremios Mayores de Madrid*, Madrid 1957.

CARANDE, RAMON, *Carlos V y sus banqueros*, 3 vols, Madrid 1943–67.

CARO BAROJA, JULIO, *Los Pueblos de España*, Barcelona 1946.

CARO BAROJA, JULIO, *Razas, pueblos y linajes*, Madrid 1957.

CARO BAROJA, JULIO, *Los Judios en la España moderna y contemporanea*, 3 vols, Madrid 1962.

CARO BAROJA, JULIO, *La hora navarra del XVIII*, Pamplona 1969.

CARO BAROJA, JULIO, *Las formas complejas de la vida religiosa (Religión, sociedad y caracter en la España de los siglos XVI y XVII)*, Madrid 1978.

CARRERA PUJAL, JAIME, *Historia de la Economía Española*, 5 vols, Barcelona 1943–47.

CARRERA PUJAL, JAIME, *Historia política y económica de Cataluña, siglos XVI al XVIII*, 4 vols, Barcelona 1947.

CASEY, JAMES, *The Kingdom of Valencia in the Seventeenth Century*, Cambridge 1979.

CAXA DE LERUELA, MIGUEL, *Restauración de la Antigua Abundancia de España*, Naples 1631.

CEÑAL, RAMÓN, S. J., 'Cartesianismo en España. Notas para su historia (1650–1750)', *Revista de la Universidad de Oviedo*, 1945, special number.

CHAUNU, HUGUETTE and PIERRE, *Séville et l'Atlantique (1504–1650)*, 8 vols, Paris 1955–60.

CIASCA, RAFFAELE, *Istruzioni e relazioni degli Ambasciatori Genovesi*, vols. IV–V, Spagna 1655–1721, Rome 1957.

CISCAR PALLARES, E., 'El endeudamiento del campesinado valenciano', *Estudis*, 4 (1975), 147–62.

CLAVERO, BARTOLOMÉ, *Mayorazgo. Propiedad feudal en Castilla 1369–1836*, Madrid 1974.

CODOIN, *Coleccion de Documentos inéditos para la Historia de España*, vol. LXVII, Madrid 1877; vol. LXXIX, Madrid 1882.

*Colección de Documentos Inéditos para las Provincias de Ultramar*. Vol. XII: *Cartas, Informes y Memoriales de Don Gabriel Fernández de Villalobos, Marqués de Varinas*, Madrid 1899.

COLMEIRO, MANUEL, *Biblioteca de los Economistas españoles de los siglos XVI, XVII y XVIII*, Madrid 1900.

CONEJO RAMILO, RICARDO, 'La sanidad y sus problemas en Archidona durante el siglo XVII', *Actas II Congreso Español de Historia de la Medicina*, 3 vols, Salamanca 1965. II, 113–23.

COSTA, JOAQUÍN, *Colectivismo agrario en España*, Madrid 1898.

DAHLGREN, E. W., *Les relations commerciales et maritimes entre la France et les côtes de l'Océan Pacifique*. Vol. I: *Le commerce de la Mer du Sud jusqu'à la paix d'Utrecht*, Paris 1909.

DANVILA Y COLLADO, MANUEL, *El Poder Civil en España*, 6 vols, Madrid 1885.

DAVIS, RALPH, 'English foreign trade, 1660–1700', *Economic History Review*, 7 (1954).

DELEITO Y PIÑUELA, JOSÉ, *Sólo Madrid es Corte. (La capital de dos mundos bajo Felipe IV)*, Madrid 1943, 3rd edn, 1968.

DELEITO Y PIÑUELA, JOSÉ, *La mala vida en la España de Felipe IV*, Madrid 1948.

DELEITO Y PIÑUELA, JOSÉ, *La vida religiosa española bajo el cuarto Felipe*, Madrid 1952.

DESDEVISES DU DÉZERT, G., *L'Espagne de l'Ancien Régime*, 3 vols, Paris 1897–1904.

DÍAZ DE ESCOVAR, NARCISO, *Las epidemias de Málaga*, Málaga 1903.

*Dietari de l'Antich Consell Barceloni*, vols. XVII–XXII. Barcelona 1922–68.

DILLON, JOHN TALBOT, *Travels through Spain, with a view to illustrate the natural history and physical geography of that kingdom*, Dublin 1781.

DOMÍNGUEZ ORTIZ, ANTONIO, 'La esclavitud en Castilla durante la edad moderna', *Estudios de Historia Social de España*, 2 (1952).

DOMÍNGUEZ ORTIZ, ANTONIO, 'Los extranjeros en la vida española durante el siglo XVII', *ibid.* 4, ii (1960), 293–426.

DOMÍNGUEZ ORTIZ, ANTONIO, *Los conversos de orígen judío después de la expulsión*, Madrid 1955.

DOMÍNGUEZ ORTIZ, ANTONIO, *Política y Hacienda de Felipe IV*, Madrid 1960.

DOMÍNGUEZ ORTIZ, ANTONIO, 'Ventas y exenciones de lugares durante el reinado de Felipe IV', *Anuario de Historia del Derecho Español*, 1964, 163–207.

DOMÍNGUEZ ORTIZ, ANTONIO, *Crisis y Decadencia de la España de los Austrias*, Barcelona 1969.

DOMÍNGUEZ ORTIZ, ANTONIO, *La Sociedad Española en el Siglo XVII*, 2 vols, Madrid 1964, 1970.

DOMÍNGUEZ ORTIZ, ANTONIO, 'La venta de cargos y oficios públicos en Castilla y sus consecuencias económicas y sociales', *Anuario de Historia Económica y Social*, 3 (1970), 105–37.

DOMÍNGUEZ ORTIZ, ANTONIO, *The Golden Age of Spain*, London 1971.

DOMÍNGUEZ ORTIZ, ANTONIO, *Alteraciones andaluzas*, Madrid 1973.

DOMÍNGUEZ ORTIZ, ANTONIO, 'Algunas notas sobre banqueros y asentistas de Carlos II', *Hacienda Pública Española*, 55 (1978), 167–76.

DOMÍNGUEZ ORTIZ, ANTONIO, 'Aspectos del vivir madrileño', *Anales Inst. Estud. Mad.*, 7 (1951), 232.

DORMER, DR DIEGO JOSEF, *Discursos Históricos-Políticos sobre lo que se ofrece tratar en la Junta . . . que el Rey ha mandado congregar*, Saragossa 1684.

DRIESCH, W. VON DEN, *Die ausländischen Kaufleute während des 18. Jahrhunderts in Spanien und ihre Beteiligung am Kolonialhandel*, Cologne 1972.

DUNLOP, JOHN, *Memoirs of Spain during the reigns of Philip IV and Charles II*, 2 vols, London 1834.

EGIDO, TEÓFANES, *Sátiras políticas en la España Moderna*, Madrid 1973.

ELLACURIA BEASCOECHEA, J., *Reacción española contra las ideas de Miguel de Molinos*, Madrid 1956.

ELLIOTT, J. H., *Imperial Spain 1469–1716*, London 1963.

ELLIOTT, J. H., *The Revolt of the Catalans. A Study in the Decline of Spain (1598–1640)*, Cambridge 1963.

ELLIOTT, J. H., 'A provincial aristocracy: the Catalan ruling class', *Homenaje a Jaime Vicens Vives*, 2 vols, Madrid 1967. II, 125–41.

ELLIOTT, J. H., 'Revolution and continuity in early modern Europe', *Past and Present*, 42 (1969), 35–56.

ESCUDERO, JOSÉ ANTONIO, *Los Secretarios de Estado y del Despacho*, 4 vols, Madrid 1969.

EVERAERT, J., *De internationale en koloniale Handel der Vlaamse Firma's te Cadiz 1670–1700*, Bruges 1973.

EZQUERRA, RAMÓN, *La Conspiración del Duque de Hijar*, Madrid 1934.

FANSHAWE, *The Memoirs of Ann Lady Fanshawe*, London 1907.

FELIU DE LA PEÑA, NARCISO, *Político Discurso*, Barcelona 1681.

FELIU DE LA PEÑA, NARCISO, *Fénix de Cataluña*, repr. with introduction by H. Kamen, Barcelona 1975.

FELIU DE LA PEÑA, NARCISO, *Anales de Cataluña*, 3 vols, Barcelona 1709.

FERNÁNDEZ ALBADALEJO, PABLO, *La crisis del Antiguo Régimen en Guipúzcoa 1766–1833: cambio económico e historia*, Madrid 1975.

FERNÁNDEZ DURO, CESAREO, *El último Almirante de Castilla*, Madrid 1902.

FERNÁNDEZ DE PINEDO, EMILIANO, *Crecimiento económico y transformaciones sociales del país vasco (1100–1850)*, Madrid 1974.

FLORES, XAVIER, *Estructura socioeconómica de la agricultura española*, Madrid 1969.

FONTANA LAZARO, JOSÉ, 'Sobre el comercio exterior de Barcelona en la segunda mitad del siglo XVII', *Estudios de Historia Moderna*, 5 (1955), 199–219.

FORBONNAIS, VÉRON DE, *Mémoires et Considérations sur le Commerce et les Finances d'Espagne*, 2 vols, Amsterdam 1761.

FORTEA PEREZ, JOSÉ, 'La evolución demográfica de Córdoba en los siglos XVI y XVII', *Actas I Congreso de la Historia de Andalucia, vol. I, Andalucia Moderna*, Córdoba 1978, p. 371–96.

FREEMAN, SUSAN TAX, *Neighbors. The Social Contract in a Castilian Hamlet*, Chicago 1970.

*(Las) Fuentes y los Méthodos. 15 Trabajos de Historia Cuantitativa serial de Galicia*, Santiago 1977.

FUGIER, A., *La Junte Supérieure des Asturies et l'invasion française*, Paris 1930.

GALDIANO Y CROY, LEONARDO, *Breve Tratado de los Hospitales y Casas de Recogimiento desta Corte*, Madrid 1677.

GAN GIMÉNEZ, P., 'Las Consultas del Presidente Ibáñez', *Miscelenea Antonio Marín Ocete*, Granada 1974. I, 295–322.

GARCIA ARGÜELLES, RAMON, 'Vida y figura de Carlos II el Hechizado', *Actas II Congreso Español de Historia de la Medicina*, 3 vols, Salamanca 1965. II, 199–232.

GARCÍA BALLESTER, LUIS and MAYER BENÍTEZ, J. M., 'Aproximación a la historia social de la peste de Orihuela de 1648', *Medicina Española*, 65 (1971), 317–31.

GARCÍA BALLESTER, LUIS, 'El Galenismo de transición en la España del siglo XVII: Luis Rodríguez de Pedrosa', *Actas II Congreso Español de Historia de la Medicina*, 3 vols, Salamanca 1965, I, 385–92.

GARCÍA-BAQUERO GONZÁLEZ, ANTONIO, *Cádiz y el Atlántico (1717–1778)*, 2 vols, Seville 1976.

GARCÍA CÁRCEL, RICARDO, 'Notas sobre población y urbanismo en la Valencia del siglo XVI', *Saitabi*, 25 (1975), 135–53.

GARCÍA FERNÁNDEZ, JESÚS, 'Champs ouverts et champs clôturés en Vieille Castille', *Annales* (1965) 692–718.

GARCÍA FERNÁNDEZ, JESÚS, *Organización del Espacio y Economía Rural en la España atlántica*, Madrid 1975.

GARCÍA MARTÍNEZ, SEBASTIÁN, *Els fonaments del país valencià modern*, Valencia 1968.

GARCÍA MARTÍNEZ, SEBASTIÁN, 'Las ciencias históricas y literarias en la España de Carlos II (1665–1700)', *Actas II Congreso Español de Historia de la Medicina*, 3 vols, Salamanca. I, 293–301.

GARCÍA MARTÍNEZ, SEBASTIÁN, 'En torno a los problemas del campo en el sur del reino de Valencia', *VIII Congreso de Historia de la Corona de Aragón*, Valencia 1973, III, ii, 215–34.

GARCIA MARTÍNEZ, SEBASTIÁN, 'Otra minoría marginada: los gitanos en Valencia bajo los Austrias', *I Congreso de Historia del País Valenciano*, Valencia 1976, III, 251–69.

GARCÍA MARTÍNEZ, SEBASTIÁN, 'Sobre la actitud valenciana ante el golpe de estado de Don Juan José de Austria (1668–69)', *ibid.* III, 421–57.

GARCÍA MARTÍNEZ, SEBASTIÁN, 'Comisión del virrey duque de Veragua al bandido valenciano Josep Cases (1679–80)', *ibid.* III, 459–72.

GARCÍA MARTÍNEZ, SEBASTIÁN, *Bandolerismo, Piratería y Control de Moriscos en Valencia durante el reinado de Felipe II*, Valencia 1977.

GARCÍA SANZ, ANGEL, *Desarrollo y crisis del Antiguo Régimen en Castilla la Vieja. Economía y Sociedad en tierras de Segovia 1500–1814*, Madrid 1977.

GARZÓN PAREJA, MANUEL, *La Industria Sedera en España. El Arte de la Seda de Granada*, Granada 1972.

GARZÓN PAREJA, MANUEL, *Diezmos y Tributos del Clero de Granada*, Granada 1974.

GARZÓN PAREJA, MANUEL, 'Hacienda del reinado de Carlos II', *Miscelenea Antonio Marín Ocete*, Granada 1974, I, 325–47.

GAVARRI, FR JOSEPH, *Instrucciones Predicables y Morales*, Seville 1673.

GENTIL DA SILVA, JOSÉ, *En Espagne. Développement économique, subsistance, déclin*, Paris 1965.

GIRARD, ALBERT, *Le commerce français à Seville et Cadix au temps des Habsbourg*, Paris 1932; repr. New York 1967.

GLADSTONE, LORNA JURY, 'Aristocratic landholding and finances in seventeenth-century Castile: the case of Gaspar Téllez Girón, Duke of Osuna (1656–1694)', unpublished Ph.D. thesis, University of Virginia 1977.

GODOLPHIN, SIR WILLIAM, *Hispania Illustrata, or, The maxims of the Spanish Court from the year 1667 to the year 1678*, London 1703.

GONZÁLEZ, TOMÁS, *Censo de población de las provincias y partidos de la Corona de Castilla*, Madrid 1829.

GONZÁLEZ MUÑOZ, M. C., *La población de Talavera de la Reina (siglos XVI–XX)*, Toledo 1974.

GOUBERT, PIERRE, *The Ancien Regime*, London 1973.

GRICE-HUTCHINSON, MARJORIE, *Early Economic Thought in Spain 1177–1740*, London 1978.

GUIARD Y LARRAURI, TEÓFILO, *Historia del Consulado y Casa de Contratación de la villa de Bilbao*, 3 vols, Bilbao 1913; repr. 1972.

GUIARD Y LARRAURI, TEÓFILO, *La industria naval vizcaina*, Bilbao 1917.

HAMILTON, EARL J., *American Treasure and the Price Revolution in Spain 1501–1650*, 1934; repr. New York 1965.

HAMILTON, EARL J., 'Spanish mercantilism before 1700', in *Facts and Factors in Economic History*, Cambridge, Mass. 1932, pp. 214–39.

HAMILTON, EARL J., *War and Prices in Spain 1651–1800*, Cambridge, Mass. 1947.

HARING, C. H., *Trade and Navigation between Spain and the Indies in the time of the Habsburgs*, 1918; repr. New York 1964.

HERRERO GARCÍA, MIGUEL, *Ideas de los Españoles del siglo XVII*, Madrid 1928.

HIGHFIELD, ROGER, (ed.), *Spain in the Fifteenth Century*, London 1972.

JIMÉNEZ SALAS, M., *Historia de la asistencia social en España en la edad moderna*, Madrid 1958.

JOUVIN, A., *Le Voyageur d'Europe*, 7 vols, Paris 1672–76. II: *Voyage d'Espagne et de Portugal*.

JOVELLANOS, GASPER MELCHOR DE, *Informe . . . en el expediente de Ley Agraria*, Madrid 1795.

JUANINI, JUAN BAUTISTA, *Nueva Idea Physica Natural Demonstrativa*, Saragossa 1685.

JUDERÍAS, JULIAN, *España en tiempo de Carlos II el Hechizado*, Madrid 1912.

KAGAN, RICHARD, *Students and Society in Early Modern Spain*, Baltimore 1974.

KAMEN, HENRY, *The Spanish Inquisition*, London 1965.

KAMEN, HENRY, *The War of Succession in Spain 1700–1715*, London and Bloomington 1969.

KAMEN, HENRY, *The Iron Century. Social Change in Europe 1550–1660*, London 1972.

KAMEN, HENRY, 'The decline of Castile: the last crisis', *Economic History Review*, 17, i (1964), 63–76.

KAMEN, HENRY, 'Confiscations in the economy of the Spanish Inquisition', *Economic History Review*, 18, iii (1965), 511–25.

KAMEN, HENRY, 'Public authority and popular crime: banditry in Valencia 1660–1714', *The Journal of European Economic History*, 3, iii (1974), 654–87.

KAMEN, HENRY, 'Mediterranean slavery in its last phase: the case of Valencia 1660–1700', *Anuario de Historia Económica y Social*, 3 (1970, publ. 1975), 211–34.

KAMEN, HENRY, 'El Fénix catalán: la obra renovadora de Narciso Feliu de la

Peña', *Estudis*, 1 (1973), 185–203.

KAMEN, HENRY, 'Nueva luz sobre la segunda Germanía de Valencia en 1693', in *Homenaje al Dr D. Juan Reglà Campistol*, 2 vols, Valencia 1975, I, 647–59.

KAMEN, HENRY, 'The decline of Spain: a historical myth?', *Past and Present*, 8 (1978), 24–50.

KENNY, MICHAEL, *A Spanish Tapestry. Town and Country in Castile*, London 1961.

KLEIN, JULIUS, *The Mesta: a Study in Spanish Economic History, 1273–1836*, 1920; repr. New York 1964.

LABAT, J. B., *Voyages du Père Labat en Espagne et en Italie*, 3 vols, Paris 1730.

LABAYRU Y GOICOECHEA, E. J. DE, *Historia General del Señorío de Bizcaya*, 6 vols, Bilbao–Madrid 1895–1901.

LABORDA MARTÍN, JUAN JOSÉ, 'La recuperación comercial de Vizcaya a comienzos del siglo XVIII', *Saioak. Revista de Estudios Vascos*, 2 (1978), 136–79.

LANTÉRY, *Memorias de Raimundo de Lantéry, mercader de Indias en Cadiz 1673–1700*, Cadiz 1949.

LAPEYRE, HENRI, *Géographie de l'Espagne morisque*, Paris 1959.

LAPEYRE, HENRI, 'L'organisation municipale de la ville de Valence (Espagne) aux XVIe et XVIIe siècles', *Annales de la Faculté des Lettres et Sciences Humaines de Nice*, 9–10 (1969), 127–37.

LARQUIÉ, CLAUDE, 'Etude de demographie madrilène: la paroisse de San Ginés de 1650 à 1700', *Mélanges de la Casa de Velázquez*, 2 (1966), 225–58.

LARQUIÉ, CLAUDE, 'Les esclaves de Madrid à l'époque de la décadence (1650–1700)', *Revue Historique*, 244 (1970), 41–74.

LARRAZ, JOSÉ, *La época del mercantilismo en Castilla, 1500–1700*, 2nd edn Madrid 1944.

LARRUGA Y BONETA, EUGENIO, 'Historia de la Real y General Junta de Comercio, Moneda y Minas', 11 vols in MS, Madrid 1789.

LARRUGA Y BONETA, EUGENIO, *Memorias políticas y económicas sobre los frutos, comercio, fábricas y minas de España*, 45 vols in 23, Madrid 1787–1800.

LEA, HENRY CHARLES, *A History of the Inquisition of Spain*, 4 vols, New York 1906–08.

LEGRELLE, ARSÈNE, *La Diplomatie française et la Succession d'Espagne*, 4 vols, Paris 1888–92.

LISÓN TOLOSANA, CARMELO, *Belmonte de los Caballeros. A Sociological Study of a Spanish Town*, Oxford 1966.

LISÓN TOLOSANA, CARMELO, *Ensayos de Antropología Social*, Madrid 1973.

LLOBET, SALVADOR, 'Una descripción geográfica de Cataluña', *Hispania*, 6 (1946), 632–69.

LLORENTE, JUAN ANTONIO, *Memoria Historica sobre qual ha sida la opinion nacional de España acerca del tribunal de la Inquisicion.* Madrid 1812.

LLOVET, JOAQUÍM, *Mataró, 1680–1719: el pas de vila a ciutat i a cap de corregiment*, Mataró 1966.

LÓPEZ PIÑERO, JOSÉ MARÍA, *La Introducción de la Ciencia Moderna en España*, Barcelona 1969.

LÓPEZ PIÑERO, JOSÉ MARÍA, 'La contribución de Juan Bautista Juanini

(1636–1691) y la introducción en España de la medicina y la ciencia modernas', *Actas II Congreso Español de Historia de la Medicina*, 3 vols, Salamanca 1965, I, 403–22.

LÓPEZ PIÑERO, JOSÉ MARÍA, 'Galileo en la España del siglo XVII', *Revista de Occidente*, 40 (July 1966), 99–108.

LÓPEZ PIÑERO, JOSÉ MARÍA, 'Valencia y la Medicina del Renacimiento y del Barroco', *Actas III Congreso Nacional de Historia de la Medicina*, 3 vols, Valencia 1969, II, 95–108.

LÓPEZ PIÑERO, JOSÉ MARÍA, 'Harvey's doctrine of the circulation of the blood in seventeenth-century Spain', *Journal of the History of Medicine and Allied Sciences*, 28, iii (July 1973), 230–42.

LÓPEZ PIÑERO, JOSÉ MARÍA, *et al.* (eds), *Materiales para la Historia de las Ciencias en España: s. XVI–XVII*, Valencia 1976.

LYNCH, JOHN, *Spain under the Habsburgs*, 2 vols, Oxford 1964–69.

MACANAZ, MELCHOR DE, *Regalías de los Señores Reyes de Aragón*, Madrid 1879.

MACLEOD, MURDO, *Spanish Central America: a Socioeconomic History 1520–1720*, Berkeley 1973.

MADRAMANY, MARIANO, *Tratado de la nobleza de la corona de Aragón, especialmente del reyno de Valencia*, Valencia 1788.

MAISO GONZÁLEZ, J., 'La peste de Zaragoza de 1652', *Estudios* (Departamento de Historia Moderna, Zaragoza), 1973, pp. 17–45.

MARAVALL, J. A., *El concepto de España en la Edad Media*, Madrid 1954.

MARAVALL, J. A., *Estado moderno y mentalidad social*, 2 vols, Madrid 1972.

MARCO CUÉLLAR, ROBERTO, 'El "Compendio Mathematico" del Padre Tosca y la introducción de la Ciencia Moderna en España', *Actas II Congreso Español de Historia de la Medicina*, 3 vols, Salamanca 1965, I, 325–57.

MARCOS MARTÍN, A., *Auge y declive de un nucleo mercantil y financiero de Castilla La Vieja. Evolución demográfica de Medina del Campo durante los siglos XVI y XVII*, Valladolid 1978.

MARCILLO, MANUEL, *Crisi de Cataluña, hecha por las naciones estrangeras*, Barcelona 1685.

MARÉS, VICENTE, *La Fénix Troyana*, Valencia 1681.

MARTÍN GALINDO, J. L., 'Arcaismo y modernidad en la explotación agraria de Valdeburón (León)', *Estudios Geográficos*, 22 (1961), 167–222.

MATEOS, M. D., *Salamanca*, Vol. 0 of *La España del Antiguo Régimen*, Salamanca 1966.

MAURA, DUKE OF, *Carlos II y su Corte*, 2 vols, Madrid 1911.

MAURA, DUKE OF, *Vida y reinado de Carlos II*, 2 vols, 2nd edn, Madrid 1954.

(MAURA) PRINCE ADALBERTO OF BAVARIA and GABRIEL MAURA GAMAZO, eds, *Documentos inéditos referentes a las postrimerías de la Casa de Austria*, 3 vols, Madrid 1927–31.

MAYÁNS I SISCAR, GREGORIO, *Cartas morales, militares, civiles i literarias de varios autores españoles*, Madrid 1734.

McLACHLAN, JEAN, 'Documents illustrating Anglo-Spanish trade between the commercial treaty of 1667 and the commercial treaty and the asiento contract of 1713', *Cambridge Historical Journal*, 4, iii (1934), 298–311.

McLACHLAN, JEAN, *Trade and Peace with Old Spain 1667–1750*, Cambridge 1940.

MEIJIDE PARDO, ANTONIO, 'La emigración gallega intrapeninsular en el siglo XVIII', *Estudios de Historia Social de España*, 4, ii (1960), 461–606.

MEIJIDE PARDO, ANTONIO, *Economía maritima de la Galicia cantábrica en el siglo XVIII*, Valladolid 1971.

MENENDEZ Y PELAYO, MARCELINO, *Historia de los Heterodoxos Españoles*, 8 vols, Madrid 1963.

MIGNET, M., *Négociations relatives a la Succession d'Espagne sous Louis XIV*, 4 vols, Paris 1835–42.

MINER OTAMENDI, J. M., *Los Pueblos Malditos*, Madrid 1978.

MOLAS RIBALTA, PEDRO, *Los Gremios barceloneses del siglo XVIII*, Madrid 1970.

MOLAS RIBALTA, PEDRO, 'La Junta de Comercio de Barcelona', *Anuario de Historia Económica y Social*, 3 (1970, publ. 1974), 235–79.

MOLAS RIBALTA, PEDRO, *Societat i poder politic a Mataró 1718–1808*, Mataró 1973.

MOLAS RIBALTA, PEDRO, 'La Companyia Feu-Feliu de la Penya (1676–1708)', *Cuadernos de Historia Económica de Cataluña*, 12 (1974), 77–126.

MOLAS RIBALTA, PEDRO, *Comerç i Estructura Social a Catalunya i Valencia als segles XVII i XVIII*, Barcelona 1977.

MOLAS RIBALTA, PEDRO, 'Los cuerpos generales de comercio. La pequeña burguesía mercantil a fines del antiguo régimen', *Cuadernos de Historia Económica de Cataluña*, 19 (1978), 213–46.

MONCADA, SANCHO DE, *Restauración política de España*, Madrid 1619.

MONTEMAYOR DE CUENCA, JUAN FRANCISCO DE, *Summaria Investigación del orígen y privilegios de los Ricos Hombres . . . de Aragón*, Mexico 1664.

MORANDI, CARLO, ed., *Relazioni di Ambasciatori Sabaudi, Genovesi e Veneti*, Bologna 1935.

MOREL-FATIO, A., and LÉONARDON, H., *Recueil des Instructions données aux Ambassadeurs . . . de France*, vol. XI, *Espagne 1649–1700*, Paris 1894.

MORET Y PRENDESGAST, SEGISMUNDO, *La familia foral y la familia castellana*, Madrid 1863.

MORINEAU, MICHEL, 'D'Amsterdam à Séville: De quelle réalité l'histoire des prix est-elle le miroir?', *Annales*, 23 (1968), 178–205.

MURET, JEAN, *Lettres écrites de Madrid en 1666 et 1667*, ed. A. Morel-Fatio, Paris 1879.

NADAL, JORDI and GIRALT, EMILI, *La population catalane de 1553 à 1717. L'immigration française et les autres facteurs de son développement*, Paris 1960.

NADAL, JORDI and GIRALT, EMILI, *Barcelona en 1717–1718. Un modelo de sociedad preindustrial* (separata of *Homenaje a Don Ramón Carande*), Madrid 1963.

NADAL, JORDI and GIRALT, EMILI, *L'immigració francesa a Mataró durant el segle XVII*, Mataró 1966.

NADAL, JORDI, *La población española, siglos XVI a XX*, 4th edn, Barcelona 1976.

NADER, HELEN, 'Noble income in sixteenth-century Castile: the Case of the Marquises of Mondéjar, 1480–1580', *Economic History Review*, 30 (1977), 411–28.

NÚÑEZ DE CASTRO, ALONSO, *Libro Histórico Político. Sólo Madrid es Corte*, Madrid 1675.

ORDÓÑEZ, PEDRO JOSEPH, *Monumento triunfal de la piedad católica*, Saragossa 1672.

*Original Letters and Negotiations*, London 1724.

OSORIO Y REDÍN, MIGUEL ALVAREZ, all his works are quoted from the edition in Campomanes, *Apéndice*, q.v.

PALACIO ATARD, VICENTE, *El comercio de Castilla y el puerto de Santander en el siglo XVIII*, Madrid 1960.

PARKER, GEOFFREY, *The Army of Flanders and the Spanish Road, 1567–1659*, Cambridge 1972.

PARRY, JOHN, *Sale of Public Office in the Spanish Indies under the Hapsburgs*, Berkeley 1953.

PERALES, JUAN, *Décadas de la Historia de la insigne y coronada ciudad y Reino de Valencia*, 5 vols, Valencia 1880.

PÉREZ, JOSEPH, *La Révolution des "Comunidades" de Castille (1520–1521)*, Bordeaux 1970.

PERRY, MARY E., 'Fantastic fandango: state and underworld in early modern Seville', unpublished Ph.D. thesis, UCLA 1977.

PESET LLORCA, VICENTE, 'La Universidad de Valencia y la renovación científica española (1687–1727)', *Asclepio*, 16 (1964), 214–31.

PESET LLORCA, VICENTE, 'Acerca de la difusión del sistema copernicano en España', *Actas II Congreso Español de Historia de la Medicina*, 3 vols, Salamanca 1965. I, 309–24.

PESET REIG, MARIANO, 'Historia de la Ciencia Jurídica y Económica en la España de Carlos II (1665–1700)', *ibid.* I, 303–8.

PFANDL, LUDWIG, *Carlos II*, Madrid 1947.

PHILLIPS, CARLA RAHN, *Ciudad Real 1500–1750*, Cambridge, Mass. 1979.

PIKE, RUTH, *Aristocrats and Traders: Sevillian society in the sixteenth century*, Ithaca 1972.

PITT-RIVERS, JULIAN, *The People of the Sierra*, 2nd edn, Chicago 1971.

POITRINEAU, A., 'La inmigración francesa en el reino de Valencia (siglos XVI–XIX)', *Moneda y Crédito*, 137 (June 1976), 103–33.

PONSOT, PIERRE, 'En Andalousie occidentale. Les fluctuations de la production du blé sous l'Ancien Régime', *Etudes Rurales*, 34 (1969), 97–112.

PONSOT, PIERRE, 'Des immigrants français en Andalousie: examples de Montilla (1689–96) et d'Osuna (1791)', *Mélanges de la Casa de Velázquez*, 5 (1969), 331–41.

PONSOT, PIERRE, 'Au contact de deux mondes: une chronique gaditane. Les "Mémoires" de Raimundo de Lantéry, "mercader" de Cadiz, 1673–1700', in *Mélanges en l'Honneur de Fernand Braudel*, 2 vols, Paris 1973. I, 471–86.

RAMBERT, GASTON, 'La navigation et le commerce de Marseille avec les ports de la Méditerranée de 1660 à 1789', in Mollat, M., ed., *Le Navire et l'Economie Maritime du Moyen Age au XVIIIe siècle*, Paris 1958.

RANUM, OREST, ed., *National Consciousness, History, and Political Culture in Early Modern Europe*, Baltimore 1975.

RECASÉNS COMAS, J. M., 'La sociedad de la ciudad de Tarragona a mediados del siglo XVII', *Boletin Arqueológico* (Tarragona), 77–84 (1962–63, publ. 1966), 81–94.

REDONDO VEINTEMILLAS, GUILLERMO, 'El siglo XVII zaragozano: crisis en la hacienda municipal', *Estudios* (Departamento de Historia Moderna, Zaragoza), 1977, 109–40.

REGLÀ, JOAN, *Els segles XVI i XVII. Els virreis de Catalunya*, Barcelona 1956.

REGLÀ, JOAN, *El bandolerisme català del barroc*, 2nd edn, Barcelona 1966.

RINGROSE, DAVID, *Transportation and Economic Stagnation in Spain, 1750–1850*. Durham, N.C. 1970.

RIPIA, JUAN DE LA, *Práctica de la Administración y Cobranza de las Rentas Reales*, Barcelona 1675.

RUIZ MARTÍN, FELIPE, 'La empresa capitalista en la industria textil castellana durante los siglos XVI y XVII', in *Third International Conference of Economic History, Munich 1965*, 5 vols, Paris 1968–74, Vol. V.

RUMEU DE ARMAS, A., *Historia de la prevision social en España*, Madrid 1944.

SALAS AUSENS, J. A., 'La inmigración francesa a Barbastro en los siglos XVI y XVII', *Estudios* (Departamento de Historia Moderna, Zaragoza), 1977, 41–92.

SALOMON, NOËL, *La Campagne de Nouvelle Castille à la fin du XVIe siecle*, Paris 1964.

SALOMON, NOËL, *Recherches sur le thème paysan dans la "Comedia" au temps de Lope de Vega*, Bordeaux 1965.

SALVÁ BALLESTER, ADOLFO, *Sedición del año 1693 en el reino de Valencia*, Valencia 1941.

SÁNCHEZ, MARIA HELENA, *Los gitanos españoles. El período borbónico*, Madrid 1977.

SÁNCHEZ, MARIO L., 'The attempts at reform in the Spain of Charles II: a revisionist view of the decline of Castile, 1665–1700', unpublished Ph. D. thesis, Notre Dame 1976.

SÁNCHEZ RIVERO, ANGEL, ed., *Viaje de Cosme de Médicis por España y Portugal (1668–1669)*, 2 vols, Madrid n.d.

SÁNCHEZ DE SOPRANIS, HIPÓLITO, 'Las naciones extranjeras en Cadiz durante el siglo XVII', *Estudios de Historia Social de España*, 4, ii (1960), 639–877.

SANTOS, FRANCISCO, *El no importa de España*, Madrid 1667.

SANTOS, FRANCISCO, *Día y Noche de Madrid*, Madrid 1674.

SCELLE, GEORGES, *Histoire politique de la Traite Négrière aux Indes de Castille*, 2 vols, Paris 1906.

SCHULTE, H. F., *The Spanish Press, 1470–1966*, Chicago 1968.

SÉE, HENRI, *Documents sur le Commerce de Cadiz (1691–1752)*, Paris n.d. [1927].

SERRA I PUIG, EVA, 'Evolució d'un Patrimoni nobiliari català durant els segles XVII i XVIII. El Patrimoni nobiliari dels Sentmenat', *Recerques*, 5 (1975), 34–71.

SERRA I PUIG, EVA, 'Consideracions entorn de la producció i la productivitat agraries de la Catalunya del segle XVII', *Estudis d'Historia Agraria*, 1 (1978), 120–53.

SICROFF, A., *Les controverses des Statuts de Pureté de Sang en Espagne du XVe au XVIIe siècle*, Paris 1960.

SMITH, R. S., *The Spanish Guild Merchant: a history of the Consulado 1250–1700*, Durham, N.C. 1940.

SOLER CANTÓ, J., *Cuatro siglos de epidemias en Cartagena*, Cartagena 1967.

STANHOPE, ALEXANDER, *Spain under Charles the Second: or, extracts from the correspondence of the Hon. Alexander Stanhope, 1690–1699*, London 1844.

STANLEY, H. E. J., *Account of an embassy from Marocco to Spain in 1690 and 1691*, n.d.,n.p.

SUREDA CARRIÓN, J. L., *La Hacienda castellana y los economistas del siglo XVII*, Madrid 1949.

SWINBURNE, HENRY, *Travels through Spain in the years 1775 and 1776*, 2 vols, London 1787.

TAYLOR, HARLAND, 'Trade, neutrality, and the "English Road", 1630–1648', *Economic History Review*, 25 (1972), 236–60.

THOMPSON, I. A. A., 'The purchase of nobility in Castile, 1552–1700', *Journal of European Economic History*, 8, ii (1979), 313–60.

*Títulos del Reino y Grandezas de España*, 3 vols, Madrid 1951.

TOLSADA PICAZO, F., *Bibliografía española de agricultura, 1495–1900*, Madrid 1953.

TOMÁS Y VALIENTE, FRANCISCO, *Los validos en la monarquía española del siglo XVII*, Madrid 1963.

TOMÁS Y VALIENTE, FRANCISCO, *El Derecho Penal de la Monarquía Absoluta (siglos XVI–XVII–XVIII)*, Madrid 1969.

TORRAS I RIBÉ, JOSEP MARIA, *Evolució social i econòmica d'una família catalana de l'antic règim. Els Padro d'Igualada (1642–1862)*, Barcelona 1976.

TOWNSEND, JOSEPH, *A Journey through Spain in the years 1786 and 1787*, 3 vols, London 1791.

ULLOA, MODESTO DE, *La Hacienda Real de Castilla en el Reinado de Felipe II*, 2nd edn, Madrid 1977.

VALDEAVELLANO, LUIS DE, *Curso de Historia de las Instituciones Españolas. De los orígenes al final de la Edad Media*, Madrid 1968.

VALLADARES DE SOTOMAYOR, ANTONIO, *Semanario Erudito*, 34 vols, Madrid 1788: vol XIV.

VÁZQUEZ, ISAAC, OFM, *Las negociaciones inmaculistas en la Curia Romana durante el Reinado de Carlos II de España*, Madrid 1957.

VICENS VIVES, JAIME, 'Gerona después de la paz de Ryswick (1698)', *Anales del Instituto de Estudios Gerundenses*, 1947.

VILAR, PIERRE, *Le 'Manual de la Companya Nova' de Gibraltar, 1709–1723*, Paris 1962.

VILAR, PIERRE, *Catalunya dins l'Espanya moderna*, 4 vols, Barcelona 1964–68.

VILAR BERROGAIN, JEAN, *Literatura y Economía. La figura satírica del arbitrista en el Siglo de Oro*, Madrid 1973.

VILAR RAMIREZ, J. B., *El Dr Diego Mateo Zapata (1664–1745)*, Murcia 1970.

VILLALBA, JOAQUÍN DE, *Epidemiología española*, 2 vols, Madrid 1802.

VILLARS, MARQUIS DE, *Mémoires de la cour d'Espagne de 1679 à 1681*, ed. A. Morel-Fatio, Paris 1893.

VINCENT, BERNARD, 'La peste atlántica de 1596–1602', *Asclepio*, 28 (1976), 5–25.

VINCENT, BERNARD, 'Récents travaux de démographie historique en Espagne

(XIVe–XVIIIe siècles)', *Annales de Démographie Historique* (1977), 463–91.

WEISS, CHARLES, *L'Espagne depuis le règne de Philippe II jusqu'à l'avènement des Bourbons*, 2 vols, Paris 1844.

WEISSER, MICHAEL, 'Crime and subsistence: the peasants of the tierra of Toledo, 1550–1700', unpublished Ph.D. thesis, Northwestern University, 1972.

WEISSER, MICHAEL, *The Peasants of the Montes*, Chicago 1976.

WEST, R. C., *The Mining Community in Northern New Spain: the Parral district*, Berkeley 1949.

WILLUGHBY, FRANCIS, *A Relation of a Voyage made through a great part of Spain*, London 1673.

WRIGHT, L. P., 'The military orders in sixteenth- and seventeenth-century Spanish society', *Past and Present*, 43 (1969), 34–70.

YERUSHALMI, Y. H., *From Spanish Court to Italian Ghetto. Isaac Cardoso: a study in seventeenth-century Marranism and Jewish apologetics*, New York 1971.

# Index